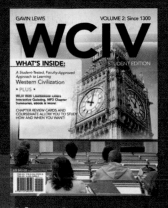

BRIEF CONTENTS

Kasuyoshi Nomachi/Pacific Press Photo; Scala/Art Resource, NY, Kevin Schafter/Corbis

CONTENTS

Image copyright © The Metropolitan Museum of Art/Art Resource, NY

British Museum Photo © Michael Holford

Scala/Art Resource, NY

Qwentes Italia srl/TIPS Images

Bardo Museum Tunis/Gianni Dagli Orti/The Art Archive

The Granger Collection, New York

Scala/Art Resource, NY

De Agostini/SuperStock

{ More for Your Buck }

WCIV has it all, and you can too. Between the text and our online offerings, you have everything at your fingertips. Make sure you check out all that WCIV has to offer:

- Chapter in Review Cards
- Online Quizzing with Feedback
- Robust eBook
- Interactive Maps
- Western Civilization Resource Center

- Flash Cards
- Interactive Games
- BBC Motion Gallery Videos
- Audio Chapter Summaries
- And More!

Visit CourseMate to find the resources you need today!
Login at **www.cengagebrain.com**.

{ Explore It Your Way! }

"**I liked how you could access the eBook online; you could do your reading anywhere.**"
– *Ashlee Whitfield, Student, Grand View College*

"**I liked the questions that were asked (reflection questions, multiple choice) at the end of each of the supplementary documents that were attached to the eBook chapters. They helped me reflect on what I read.**"
– *Ashley Mariscal, Student, University of Texas at Brownsville*

"**I liked the different options that you had: two different books, the eBook and the regular one. There were eBook links you could click on to find further information about that subject in the chapter plus good review questions at the end.**"
– *Rachel Montieth, Student, Grand View College*

We know that no two students read in quite the same way. Some of you do a lot of your reading online.

To help you take your reading **outside the covers** of **WCIV,** each new text comes with access to the exciting learning environment of a robust eBook containing **over 300 tested online links to:**

- **Primary source documents**
- **Interactive maps**
- **Web links for further investigation**
- **Interactive quizzes**
- **Audio resources**
- **Historical simulation activities**
- **Images**
- **Field trips**
- **Video**

THE ANCIENT WORLD,
3000 B.C.–A.D. 500

An essential first step toward understanding the past is to divide it up into periods—longer or shorter stretches of time that mark off important stages in the development of human activities and ideas. Of course, activities and ideas are complex things that change continually, so that the stages of their development are often difficult to recognize. In addition, what makes such stages "important" is to some extent subjective—it depends on what seems important about the past to ourselves, looking backward from the present day. All the same, we have to define historical periods as accurately and objectively as possible, for unless we do so, we cannot arrange facts about the past into any meaningful pattern.

The generally agreed-upon large-scale pattern of Western history is made up of three main periods, each more or less aligned with the lifetime of one or more civilizations that have played a leading part in Western history. The 3,500 years of the early civilizations of Mesopotamia, Egypt, Greece, and Rome make up the ancient period (3000 B.C.–A.D. 500). The thousand years of Christian Europe (500–1500) are the Middle Ages—the "in-between times" separating the ancient from the modern period (1500 to the present). This last period consists of the five hundred years (so far) of the rise of the modern West and the resulting changes in civilization across the world.

The dates that mark off these periods are simply convenient benchmarks, and nothing in particular happened at any of them. At each of them, however, large-scale and fast-moving

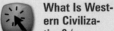 **What Is Western Civilization?** (www.cengagebrain.com) Learn more about the meaning of "the West," "Western," "civilization," and "civilizations" in study material for this book

changes were taking place in many fields of activity and ideas, so that the transition from one era of civilization to the next was well under way. However, the fact that a particular historical period began and ended with spectacular changes does not mean that in between everything stayed the same. On the contrary, massive changes took place within these large-scale periods, so that historians often divide them into smaller-scale ones—"early," "middle," "late," and so on. Except in the case of the modern period, however, such changes within large-scale periods were never quite as far-reaching as those under way at the beginning and ending dates.

In the case of the ancient period, the initial sudden and world-changing development was the rise of the earliest civilizations in Mesopotamia and Egypt, which took place over several centuries around 3000 B.C. Over many centuries, most peoples in the region of southwestern Asia and northeastern Africa took to and adapted these earliest civilized ways. Political structures formed in this region that ranged from city-states (small self-governing communities) to great empires. Technical skills developed that were as varied as ironworking and alphabetic writing. Religious beliefs arose that were as different from each other as the worship of god-kings by the Egyptians and the monotheism of the Israelites (Jews). All these features were taken up by later Western and non-Western civilizations.

Eventually, peoples farther west adopted civilized ways of life and formed them into new patterns as they did so, until the brilliant Mediterranean civilization of Greece and Rome (often called "Greco-Roman") emerged and went through its own lengthy development.

Greco-Roman civilization was the first that today counts as geographically and culturally "Western." Citizen participation in government; the disciplines of science, philosophy, and history; magnificent new styles of archi-
tecture; works of art and literature that conveyed human experiences and perceptions with unprecedented vividness and power—all originated with the Greeks. The Romans then imitated and developed these and other achievements of Greek civilization to the point where they equaled and sometimes surpassed the Greeks. Rome, in turn, became an inspiration and model for civilization's further development—above all in Western Europe, the future heartland of Western civilization.

In two basic respects, however, Greco-Roman civilization had more in common with older civilizations than with later Western ones. First, like nearly all ancient peoples, the Greeks and Romans worshiped not one God but many gods and goddesses. Second, besides adapting the old established government model of city-states, the Greeks and Romans also continued the rival tendency of older civilizations to form vast empires ruled by limitlessly powerful monarchs. The final result was the mighty Roman Empire, which united the Mediterranean lands and Western Europe, as well as Egypt and some of Mesopotamia, under one rule. In these ways, Greco-Roman civilization was both "Western" and "ancient."

Eventually, over about three hundred years around A.D. 500, there came another series of world-changing events. The peoples of the Roman Empire converted to Christianity, with its belief in one almighty God. The empire itself was then broken apart by less advanced European peoples invading from the north, and by Arab conquerors from the south who brought with them another religion that worshiped one God—Islam. Countless traditions of ancient civilization persisted, but the changes were drastic enough for two new patterns of civilization to arise, whose future destinies would be closely linked. One was the non-Western civilization of Islam. The other, and the next in the Western succession, was that of Christian Europe.

CHAPTER 1

FROM PREHISTORY TO CIVILIZATION, 3000–1200 B.C.

LEARNING OBJECTIVES

AFTER READING THIS CHAPTER, YOU SHOULD BE ABLE TO DO THE FOLLOWING:

LO¹ Trace the key developments of prehistory, from the emergence of our human ancestors to the beginnings of village life.

LO² Explain why the society that grew up in Sumer is considered one of the first civilizations, and describe later developments in Mesopotamia.

LO³ Contrast the ancient civilization of the Nile with that of the Tigris-Euphrates, and discuss the defining features of Egyptian life.

"LANGUAGE, RELIGION, ART, TECHNOLOGY, FARMING, FAMILY LIFE, AND VILLAGE COMMUNITIES—ALL THESE BASIC FEATURES OF HUMAN EXISTENCE ORIGINATED IN PREHISTORIC TIMES."

Even the earliest civilizations were a very recent turn in the long road of human evolution and development. Accordingly, this chapter begins long before ancient times, with **prehistory**—the millions of years in which human beings appeared on the earth, spread across the planet, and advanced in organization and skills. Language, religion, art, technology, farming, family life, and village communities—all these basic features of human existence originated in prehistoric times.

 Test your knowledge before you read this chapter.

This earliest development led around 3000 B.C. to the rise of the first civilizations—those of Mesopotamia and Egypt. In these lands, located not far from each other in southwestern Asia and northeastern Africa, there appeared complex social and economic structures, effective and lasting governments, writing systems capable of expressing any thought, compelling religious beliefs, impressive scientific and technical achievements, and sophisticated literary and artistic styles, all of which influenced many later civilizations, both Western and non-Western.

What do you think?

With the development of agriculture and the move away from a hunting and gathering way of life, the quality of human life improved.

Strongly Disagree						Strongly Agree
1	2	3	4	5	6	7

The achievements of these first civilized peoples soon began to spread to their neighbors—a two-way process in which both sides were active. To come into contact with civilization at all, simpler societies had to be at least wealthy enough to be worth trading with or conquering. They took the initiative in learning the skills of civilization, themselves had skills that civilized peoples were glad to learn, and often invaded and conquered civilized neighbors—but that, too, brought them under the influence of civilization. Furthermore, they usually combined their own traditions with the types of civilization that they adopted. Thus, as civilization spread, it was liable also to change.

In these ways, by 1200 B.C., there came into existence an international region of civilization, with many local versions of Mesopotamian and Egyptian traditions.

≪ **The Temple of Amon** This temple, constructed about 1600 B.C. near the Egyptian city of Thebes, remains the world's largest religious building even today. In the Hypostyle Hall (Hall of Columns), a gigantic porchlike structure leading from the temple's outer courtyard to a series of inner shrines where the actual worship took place, priests prepared themselves to perform the holy rituals of the god.

Art Kowalsky/Alamy

5

This region stretched right across the lands where southwestern Asia met northeastern Africa, including the eastern shores of the Mediterranean Sea—and there was no reason for the spread of civilization to stop there.

LO¹ Before Civilization: The Prehistoric Era

Compared with the age of the human race, civilization is a very recent development. If we reduce the time since the first humanlike species appeared (about 2.5 million years ago) to the period of a twenty-four-hour day, the five-thousand-year era of civilization takes up less than the last three minutes! It took thousands of centuries of developing physically and completing a series of successful responses to the environment before human beings were at last able to take the first important steps toward civilization. But humans did not as yet produce written documents, the main material of actual history, so this lengthy time span is called the *prehistoric era*.

The Origins and "Ages" of Human Beings

The beginning of the prehistoric era can be only approximately dated, for prehistory began with the human race itself. The era ended with the rise of civilized societies producing permanent written records, but these societies arose at different times in different regions of the world, so that prehistory has no single worldwide ending date.

Excavations of fossils (remains of organisms) indicate that the earliest humanlike species probably appeared in East Africa. Over hundreds of thousands of years, new species evolved that gradually took on the various physical features and mental capacities that are unique to the human race. Humans began to walk on two legs, thereby releasing their hands to make and use tools and weapons. Their body hair thinned out and their digestions weakened, so that they needed clothing, cooking, and fire. Their brains grew larger, making possible language and abstract thought, as well as complex manual and physical skills.

About 200,000 years ago, probably in southwestern Africa, there appeared a human species that seemingly possessed more of these features than any other, and over tens of thousands of years it replaced all of them. Eventually, this type of human spread beyond Africa into Europe and Asia and then made its way across a "land bridge" that at that time linked the eastern tip of Asia with Alaska to colonize the Americas. By about 14,000 years ago, it had become the worldwide human race of the present day.

As the various human types developed and spread, their tools were mainly chipped from durable stone, so many of them have survived more or less undamaged down to the present. Tools improved over time, and these changes can often be dated by studying the earth layers where tools are found, or by laboratory tests. Accordingly, the stages of prehistory have come to be customarily divided according to the stages of tool development.

The earliest (and longest) prehistoric period is called the **Paleolithic (pay-lee-oh-LITH-ik—Old Stone) Age.** This era began with the earliest human types. With the appearance of present-day humans, the pace of progress in tool development speeded up. Stone tools became stronger, sharper, and more specialized for different tasks. By 8000 B.C., they had advanced

> *"If we reduce the time since the first humanlike species appeared (about 2.5 million years ago) to the period of a twenty-four-hour day, the five-thousand-year era of civilization takes up less than the last three minutes!"*

"The Human Family Tree" (http://channel.nationalgeographic.com/channel/human-family-tree) Learn more about human migration and your deep ancestry.

CHRONOLOGY

2.5 MILLION YEARS BEFORE THE PRESENT (B.P.)	Appearance of first humanlike species
200,000–150,000 B.P.	Scientists have traced our genetic ancestry to a "Scientific Eve" living in Africa at this time
50,000 B.P.	Scientists theorize that humans began migrating out of Africa around this time
8000–4000 B.C.	Agricultural Revolution
3500–3000 B.C.	Rise of first civilizations in Mesopotamia and Egypt
2400 B.C.	Sumer falls to Sargon of Akkad; Sumerian civilization continues under a succession of foreign rulers
1600 B.C.	The Hittites dominate Anatolia
1100 B.C.	End of the New Kingdom in Egypt; Egyptian civilization continues under a succession of foreign rulers

so far in southwestern Asia and northeastern Africa, as well as in neighboring regions including Europe, that archeologists call the subsequent period the **Neolithic (nee-oh-LITH-ik—New Stone) Age**.

When metals replaced stone as the principal tool material in these regions, the Neolithic Age was followed by the Bronze Age (about 3000–1000 B.C.) and then the Iron Age (after 1000 B.C.). Other regions of the world passed through similar stages at later periods, either by imitating and adapting these earliest advances or through independent invention.

The Hunting and Gathering Way of Life

Throughout the Paleolithic Age, all human beings lived as migratory (wandering) hunters, fishers, and gatherers of edible plants, sheltering in caves, in temporary huts, or in the open if the climate was favorable. Most likely their way of life was much like that of hunters and gatherers who have been studied by anthropologists in recent times.

To find food, protect themselves, and rear their children, they would usually have combined into small bands of perhaps twenty to thirty people. Individuals might leave one band to join another, and family groups of men, women, and their children might form within a band, with their own tools and weapons, their own stores of food and supplies, and their own spaces for shelter. Plants and animals, however, did not belong to anyone until they were gathered or killed, nor did the land on which the plants and animals were found—though the band as a whole would try to keep other bands out of the territory that it ranged.

Most likely there was a rough division of labor between men and women. Men would have been mainly responsible for hunting, for making the tools and weapons that were needed for killing and butchering animals, and for whatever violence was needed to protect or expand the band's territory. But most of the food that a band needed to survive would have come from plants, and it was women who were mainly responsible for gathering plants, as well as for the technologies required to store them and prepare them for eating.

Women would also have been mainly responsible for taking care of young children, but there would have been fewer of these than in later times. With no easily digestible cereal or milk foods available, children would have had to be breast-fed until they were old enough to eat normal adult food, and since women are less likely to conceive while breast-feeding, during that period they would produce fewer children. As the main providers of food, and with few children to take care of, women probably enjoyed much the same status and power within the hunting and gathering bands as men did.

As well as struggling to provide food and shelter for themselves and their offspring, early humans seem to have sought to understand and explain the natural world and their own destiny. They made regular rows of markings on pieces of stone or bone, probably to record the passage of time as measured by the movements of the sun, moon, and stars, which they probably saw as living beings with power to help or hurt. On the walls of caverns they painted lifelike images of large animals, as if these beasts, too, had power and could perhaps be influenced by magical rituals (see photo). Sometimes early humans buried their dead, presumably because their fellow humans were still in some way important to them even when no longer alive. The beginnings of what we today call science, art, and religion date back to these early times of the human race.

Cave Paintings These images of wild beasts were painted about 25,000 years ago deep in a cave in southern France. Nearer the entrance, people had their dwellings. To judge from animal bones found in their garbage piles, they did not hunt these beasts; instead, perhaps they worshiped them. Layers of paint suggest that the paintings were continually restored, so they must have been very important objects.

Jean Clottes/AP Photo

The Agricultural Revolution

The Neolithic advances in tool-making were only part of much wider alterations in human ways of life—the shift from the hunter-gatherer pattern to settled agrarian (farming) life. This giant step involved the cultivation of plants, the taming of animals, and the appearance of many new skills and technologies to adapt plants and animals to human needs—a whole series of discoveries that together are called the **Agricultural Revolution**.

Among the consequences of this change were a massive increase in the supply of food and a steep rise in population; the replacement of hunting and gathering bands by families and village communities as the basic human groups; the growth of hereditary differences of wealth, status, and power within communities; and new and less equal relationships between men and women. This new way of life was extraordinarily resilient. It formed the basis of all civilizations and the majority of simpler societies right down to modern times, and it is still to be found in many parts of the world today.

Climate, Skills, and Technologies

The Agricultural Revolution took place not once but several times throughout the world; the first such revolution, however, began in southwestern Asia (see Map 1.1). Along with farming and the domestication of animals, there arose a whole range of new technologies to make the products of the fields and pastures fit for human use. Bread, beer, wine, cheese, edible oils, woven cloth, leather, pottery for cooking and storage (see photo), bricks for house building—all

Map 1.1 **Southwestern Asia**

Humankind's first Agricultural Revolution began in the lands of the Fertile Crescent, where farmers could depend on regular rainfall. To the south of the crescent's curving border, where rainfall was irregular, farmers eventually learned to use river water for irrigation. The resulting abundant crops provided the wealth for the world's first civilization. © Cengage Learning

Interactive Map

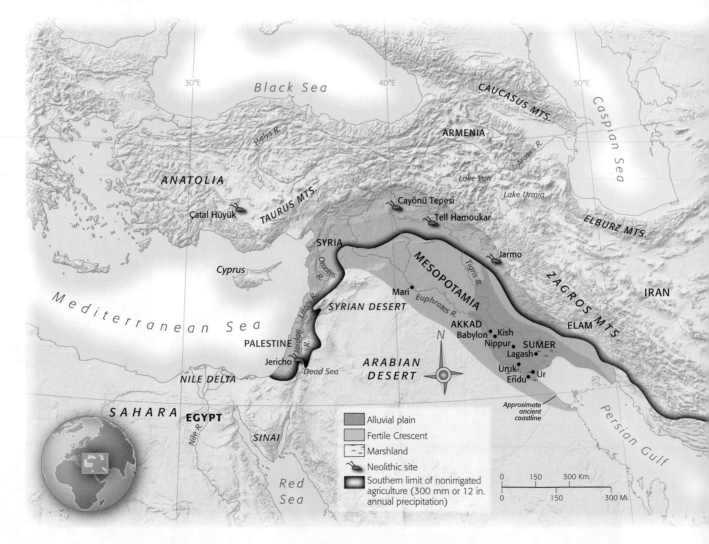

SEVERAL TRENDS CONTRIBUTED TO THE BEGINNING OF AGRICULTURE:

New Environmental Conditions

* Around 10,000 B.C., the planet was warming and the ice sheet that covered much of the Northern Hemisphere began to melt and withdraw northward.

* Southwestern Asia emerged as a region with a mild climate, fertile soil, and a good water supply—key elements for cultivating crops.

* Wild grasses that bore nourishing seeds flourished naturally in the grasslands above the river valleys of the region.

The Development of Techniques for Domesticating Plants

* Women of hunting and gathering bands, who were responsible for plant food, were probably the ones who noticed that the seeds of wild grasses could sprout into plants, and they began tending garden patches.

* By choosing to put back into the soil the seeds of those grasses that grew best and were easiest to harvest, cultivators helped breed (over many generations) wheat and barley.

* Tools were fashioned to make farming possible on a large scale. Stone-bladed hoes loosened the soil for seeding, and flint-edged sickles cut the edible seeds from the stalks.

The Development of Techniques for Domesticating Animals

* Wild dogs were the first animals to be tamed—probably by the men of hunting bands.

* Sheep, goats, pigs, and cattle were domesticated to provide meat, wool, skins, and milk.

* Toward the end of the Neolithic Age, humans began to use oxen for farming, along with a new tool—the plow. The oxen and plow made it possible to cultivate larger fields and feed more people.

* With the invention of the wheel, oxen were also used to pull carts and transport goods and people.

---

of these items of food, clothing, and equipment that we take for granted today were first used by the early farmers of this region. These technological advances, in turn, helped bring about a new way of life for the human race.

Villages and Families

Looking after crops required more or less permanent settlements, and around 6000 B.C. the first agricultural villages appeared in southwestern Asia—clusters of houses made of adobe (sun-dried bricks), where there lived anything up to two or three hundred people. Excavation of the ruins of these settlements, and study of traditional farming communities in recent times, give clues to the way of life that grew up in the villages—one that no longer revolved around migratory bands but around settled families and communities.

Each house, with its living and storage space, would have belonged to a family group of men, women, and children. The equipment and supplies, plants and animals, and also the sections of field that were needed for farming would also have belonged to the family, as well as to

following generations of its offspring. Over the generations, some families might add to their share of these goods, and others might lose them to their neighbors. Within the villages, family relationships, ownership and inheritance of property, hereditary differences of wealth and status, and climbing and slipping on the social ladder became much more important than in earlier times.

But families also needed each other. There were many tasks, such as house building and animal herding, that they could not do on their own. Families could not continue across the generations unless the sons and daughters of different families formed

Neolithic Storage Jar Pottery making, developed at the time of the Agricultural Revolution, made possible the storage of plant and animal products that were now available in much larger quantities than before. In addition, as with this jar, which was made in present-day Iran about 4000 B.C., pottery surfaces gave painters a new medium for artistic creation. Image copyright © The Metropolitan Museum of Art/Art Resource, NY

stable partnerships. They could not prevent or settle disputes with each other, or even among their own members, without agreed-upon rules that all families would obey and uphold, for example, those of inheritance or marriage and divorce. For all these reasons, families in villages could only exist as part of communities. Over many generations, the life of village communities and families came to be regulated by complex systems of tradition, custom, and authority, out of which the law and government of civilized societies would ultimately grow.

Among the most important traditions and customs that governed the life of villages and families would have been those connected with religion. Archeologists excavating larger villages sometimes find buildings bigger than ordinary houses, with a layout much like that of temples of later civilizations. Most likely an ancient belief in powerful beings who could influence the world and humans had already evolved into **polytheism**, the belief in countless humanlike gods and goddesses. Villagers would want to have at least one such being become part of their community. They would build this being a house where he or she could live among them, be served and honored with offerings and sacrifices, and in return watch over and protect them.

Neolithic villages also needed each other. Villagers from smaller settlements would come to pay their respects to the powerful gods and goddesses in larger ones. Resources like clay that was good for making pottery were not to be found in every village, so neighboring villages would negotiate rules for their use and combine to defend them against outsiders. Other necessities and luxuries of village life were even more thinly scattered, and had to travel long distances from producers to consumers. Flint for sickle blades, obsidian (an unusually hard mineral) for knife blades and drill bits, and mother-of-pearl for bracelets and necklaces were traded over hundreds of miles. Out of cooperation among Neolithic villages there grew the organized governments of later times, and far-flung networks of Neolithic trade and travel provided the routes along which civilization would one day spread.

> *"Over many generations, the life of village communities and families came to be regulated by complex systems of tradition, custom, and authority, out of which the law and government of civilized societies would ultimately grow."*

Men, Women, and Farming

Study of traditional farming societies also suggests that the Agricultural Revolution was accompanied by a lasting shift in the pattern of relations between men and women. Probably this was in part the result of a new division of labor between the genders, and partly also of the new importance of families and households.

The Agricultural Revolution made men, for the first time, the main suppliers of food. Domesticated animals—the larger ones mostly herded by men—were a far more important resource than wild ones. In addition, probably because plowing needed large animals, it was done by men, so that they took over the provision of plant products as well. Meanwhile, milk and cereals were providing food that very young children could digest, so that women were weaning babies earlier and becoming pregnant more often. Far more of women's time and effort was taken up with producing and rearing the larger numbers of people that farming could support.

This change, in turn, obliged women to concentrate on tasks that could be accomplished in and around the home and that could be combined with looking after young children. Among these were garden cultivation and the care of small farmyard animals, everything to do with food preparation, from grain grinding to cooking, and the management of the household. Tasks that required distance from the home for any length of time came to be done mainly by men, such as tending to field crops and herd animals, trade and travel, and fighting. As the main providers of basic necessities, and as the ones who were most active outside the household, men were likely to be main decision makers within households, and in the community's affairs.

In addition, now that families had their own wealth and status within communities, they wanted to hand these on to their offspring. That made it important to make sure that children were in fact the offspring of the men and women of the family. Since it was women who ultimately produced the children, it was their behavior that most needed to be surveyed and controlled—both by themselves and also by men.

Male dominance would usually have had its limits, however. Within village communities, women from prominent families could expect deference from men of humbler families. Women's work was just as essential to the wealth of households as men's work, and women and men had demanding expectations of each other. As in all face-to-face relationships, the real decision-making power within households might not in fact lie with those whom the community values said were the masters. And village women would be able to get out and about enough to form their own "public opinion," talk to their men accordingly, and thereby have a say in the decisions of the community.

Still, the distinction between "men's work" and "women's work" persisted, as did the acceptance by men and women of the rightfulness of some kind of male dominance. It was not until the rise of industrial societies and liberal values in modern times that these traditions began to change.

Villages and Civilization

Over many centuries, the Agricultural Revolution spread outward from its region of origin—including to the peoples of Europe, who adapted wheat and barley to the cooler and wetter conditions of their region. In Africa, tropical Asia, and eventually also the Americas, separate agricultural revolutions based on local crops such as yams, rice, corn, and potatoes brought settled village life to the humans of those regions as well. In this way, the small agricultural community, with its farms and families, its customs and traditions, its trusted religious rites, and its inequality between women and men, became the typical way of life of the human race throughout much of the world.

With the emergence of the village way of life, humans were ready for their next social and cultural leap: the rise of the first true civilizations. This was not a simultaneous worldwide development. On the contrary, throughout human history, it has only rarely happened that a prehistoric society of farmers and villagers has evolved on its own into an advanced civilization. The best-known "cradles of civilization" of this kind are the river valleys of the southwestern Asian land of Mesopotamia and the northeastern African land of Egypt about 3500 B.C., where the earliest known civilizations arose; those of northern India and northern China about a thousand years later; and the plains, forests, and mountain valleys of Central America and the Andes toward 500 B.C. All of these played major roles in world history, but the Western civilization of modern times is directly descended from the early civilizations of Mesopotamia and Egypt.

LO² The Earliest Cities: Mesopotamia

The civilizations of Mesopotamia (mes-oh-puh-TAY-mee-uh) and Egypt emerged at about the same time (from roughly 3500 B.C. onward), seemingly independent of each other. They lasted for more than 3,000 years—1,000 years longer than the time span between their disappearance and the present day. Their massive inheritance of cultural achievement, technical and scientific knowledge, and religious belief has been drawn on throughout the subsequent history of Western civilization. For many centuries, all direct knowledge of ancient Mesopotamia and Egypt was lost, but in recent times, archaeologists dug up their cities and scholars deciphered their writing systems and languages. As a result, recorded history now goes back almost to the beginnings of these earliest known civilizations. In the case of Mesopotamia, it is even possible to reconstruct how civilization arose out of the earlier village life of the region.

Sumer

The scene of this development was a vast plain stretching between two great rivers, the Tigris and the Euphrates (see Map 1.1 on page 8). The area bounded by them forms the heartland of the modern states of Syria and Iraq, but in ancient times, the Greeks called it Mesopotamia, "the land between the rivers."

> "*Nurtured by a favorable environment and then toughened by harsher conditions, there grew up in southern Mesopotamia a new kind of society, so much more complex than the older one that today it counts as one of the world's first true civilizations.*"

Landscape, Climate, and Cities

About 3500 B.C., several thousand years after the Agricultural Revolution began, Mesopotamia and the region surrounding it already had many prosperous villages. But the leap to civilization began in a much smaller area: the southernmost portion of Mesopotamia, where the twin rivers ran close to each other before entering the Gulf. In ancient times this district was called Sumer (SOO-mehr).

Sumer was a land of rivers and swamps with little rainfall, and to live there, the local farmers relied on irrigation. Seasonal river flooding deposited water and rich silt (earth materials containing plant nutrients) that had washed down from distant hillsides; the villagers diverted the water onto their fields and palm groves, which were the most productive in all of Mesopotamia. But the sheer size of the rivers made them hard to control, so that villages and patches of cultivation were actually fewer and farther between than elsewhere in the region.

What began the rise to civilization was a change in the local climate, which became slightly colder and drier about 3500 B.C. With less water flowing through them, the twin rivers, especially the Euphrates, became easier to harness for irrigation. The effects were dramatic. Archeological surveys of ancient settlements indicate that between 3100 and 2900 B.C., the population of this area expanded tenfold. Many new villages were founded, and some older ones grew into small towns. Dense clusters of villages and towns sprang up, which came to be grouped around still larger settlements—the first true cities in the history of the world, with populations estimated as high as 40,000 people.

It seems to have been about this time that the Sumerians arrived in southern Mesopotamia as immigrants or conquerors coming from an unknown earlier homeland. Very likely, they were attracted to their new homeland by its growing wealth and fertility, as the environment there began to change. They

dynasty
A line of rulers from the same family.

city-state
An independent state that consists of a city and its surrounding settlements and countryside.

settled in and ruled over the communities of the region, including its growing cities, each of which became the seat of government for a surrounding area of towns, villages, and countryside.

Eventually, as the landscape continued to dry out and water actually became scarce, the wealth and population ceased to grow. But the cities responded to new problems with new solutions. They built large-scale, centrally controlled water conservation and irrigation systems, and fought wars against each other and against foreign raiders and invaders for control of scarcer resources. Governments developed that were powerful enough to plan and organize these undertakings. Nurtured by a favorable environment and then toughened by harsher conditions, there grew up in southern Mesopotamia a new kind of society, so much more complex than the older one that today it counts as one of the world's first true civilizations.

Priests, Kings, and Others

Cities and their satellite towns and villages needed far more direction and control than before, and more productive agriculture provided a surplus that enabled some people to live without personally farming the land. As a result, there developed in Sumer two of the distinguishing features of civilization: many specialized crafts and many ranks of prestige, authority, and power.

Within the various crafts and social ranks, families intermarried and produced offspring so as to continue over generations just as families had always done. But hereditary differences of wealth and status, and distances up and down on the social ladder, were much greater—and the number of families at the top of the ladder, compared to those lower down, was far smaller.

At the top of the system of ranks stood the priesthood. As Sumerian communities became larger and wealthier than ever before, they devoted much of their new resources to the service of the gods and goddesses, and a class of hereditary servants of these mighty beings arose. The servants of the gods directed the building of unprecedentedly large temples to house the gods and goddesses, employed craftsmen to furnish the temples with costly and beautiful works of art, managed vast properties, introduced technological innovations, and were responsible for the invention of writing. In Sumer, the priesthood led the process of social, technical, and cultural innovation out of which civilization emerged.

In time, however, as the waters retreated and resources grew scarcer, there arose another group of leaders—military chieftains and warriors, who fought the cities' wars and thereby rose to wealth and power. By 2500 B.C., each city had a supreme ruler bearing the title of *lugal* or "great man." In effect, the "great men" were kings, with power not only in war but also in peacetime governance. Like everyone else, they did their best to keep their power and position in their families, and they

became founders of **dynasties** (family lines of rulers). Their relationship with the priests seems to have been one of both partnership and competition. Like the priests, the kings claimed that they ruled as servants of the gods. To make sure of divine support, they built temples and took a leading part in temple rituals, and later myths and epics portrayed them as personally beloved of gods and goddesses.

In this way, each city of Sumer acquired its own government and army, independent of—and fiercely competitive with—others of its kind. The city, together with its surrounding towns, villages, and countryside, formed a new kind of community, far larger and more complex than had ever existed before: a **city-state**. From time to time, one of these city-states would gain dominance over the others, but none was able to hold this position for long, and their struggles lasted down to 2400 B.C. Such clusters of competitive city-states would arise in many future times and places—among the Phoenicians on the eastern Mediterranean coastline, in ancient Greece, and in Italy of the Middle Ages and Renaissance (pp. 32–33, 51–59, 195, 263–264).

Below the priests and kings were other people whom the newfound wealth of Sumer had partly or wholly freed from working the land. Excavations have uncovered the remains of specialized workshops that made pottery and metal goods. Early written documents mention skilled artisans employed in temples and palaces to make textiles, weapons, works of art, and many other items for use by priests and rulers. The priests and rulers, and later on professional merchants, also turned to trade on a larger scale than ever before. They set up trading stations hundreds of miles up the twin rivers, where they exchanged the luxuries of civilization for materials that could not be found in the river valleys, such as metals, timber, and stone.

The Generation Gap in Sumer: A Father Lectures His Lazy Son Read a humorous account of a wealthy Sumerian father lecturing his privileged son.

Sumer, however, like every civilized society until recent times, was still overwhelmingly made up of farmers. Ninety percent of the population, including most of the people in the big cities, worked on the land. Most farmers were tenants working for the temple priests, the king, and other wealthy and powerful people who now had ultimate control of the land. Farming families still had enough control of land and other resources to provide for themselves and even to prosper. However, they had to yield large amounts of produce for the upkeep of priests, kings, and artisans, or they had to deliver it to vast temple storehouses from which the community could draw in time of famine or siege. If they failed to prosper or to hand over the expected produce, whole families might be sold (or parents would sell themselves or their children) into slavery as farmhands, artisans, or domestic servants.

In this way, the civilized society of Sumer allowed farmers to go on living their already traditional family and community way of life. However, they could do so only on condition of giving up much of the wealth they produced to those who ranked above them in a newly complex society—and under penalty of having their family and community life destroyed if they failed to do so. Over thousands of years until the rise of modern industrial society, the details of how wealth was extracted from farmers would vary in countless ways, but the basic pattern of a small minority of nonfarmers extracting wealth from a vast majority of farmers would always be the same. Without it, civilization could not have existed.

Men, Women, and Civilization

As the ladder of prestige, authority, and power grew longer, women as well as men were found on the topmost rungs. High-ranking women came to occupy many of the positions of command over lower-ranking men that they would fill in later civilized societies, but the upper ranks had their own forms of inequality that also had a long history ahead of them.

The Sumerian language had a word *nin*, meaning "lady," to distinguish women of high rank from those lower down, and such ladies were important in religion, politics, and government. The temple rituals of male gods were entrusted mainly to unmarried priestesses. Often they were the daughters of kings, who thereby hoped to gain power in the temples (p. 18). Likewise, kings' wives were often daughters of other kings, sent by their fathers who ruled "foreign" city-states to establish family ties between dynasties. Their husbands entrusted large estates to them, with many men and women at their beck and call. Tomb excavations at the city of Ur revealed that when the king's wife Pu-abi died about 2500 B.C., serving women, men from her bodyguard, and other manservants took poison so that they could go on serving their mistress in the world of the dead.

Priestesses, king's wives, and other married ladies, however, were not the equals of their husbands. Unlike the priests of goddesses, priestesses had no power outside their temples. Only one woman is known to have actually ruled a city-state and founded

(above, center) **A Sumerian Banquet** This scene of high life was made by a cylinder seal—an engraved roller used to mark clay jar stoppers while they were soft. Below, hunters bring in a trussed-up animal for a feast. Above left, an upper-class couple drinks beer through straws. By drinking from the same vessel they show togetherness, and the straws enable them to drink from beneath the scum-covered surface of the unfiltered beer. The University Museum, University of Pennsylvania. Image #152079, object #30-12-2

a dynasty, the lady Ur-Bau of Kish—and since the Sumerians had no word for "queen," she had to rule as a "great man."

Lower down the social ladder, written documents give history's first glimpse of what women and men expected of each other in family and household. As part of their training, scribes (writing experts) copied out lists of everyday proverbs, using different versions of the Sumerian language for those supposed to be spoken by women and by men. Sometimes the proverbs express romantic hopes: "A plant sweet as a husband does not grow in the desert." "May Inanna [the goddess of love and fertility] make a hot-limbed wife lie beside you! May she bestow upon you broad-armed sons!" There were also disappointments: "A thriftless woman in a house is worse than all demons," and an idle husband was no better: "A dog moves, a scorpion moves, but my man does not move." The household division of labor, and the contentment and dissatisfaction of both women and men to which it might lead, were already taken for granted.

Business documents and lists of trades and crafts suggest that the newly arisen specialist skills of civilization were practiced mostly by men—even though many of them were carried on around the home, where women could perfectly well have worked at them too. The one type of business that seems to have been carried on mainly by women was innkeeping, perhaps because it fitted into the pattern of women being responsible for everything to do with the preparation of food and drink. Most likely, the belief in the precedence of men over women was already so well established that it seemed natural for men to be the main practitioners of new skills and for women to be their helpers.

In any case, the Sumerians seem to have already followed the principle that the most active and creative roles in trades and crafts, reading and writing, and the fine arts and intellectual life were the province of men. Over the centuries, there would be many exceptions to this rule. Widows would take over family businesses, fathers would train daughters for lack of sons, and gifted and educated women would receive praise and encouragement from at least some of the people around them. But the principle as such survived unchallenged in all civilized societies until recent times.

Wheels, Plows, and Metals

Ancient civilizations had no monopoly on technical inventiveness, and the Sumerians

Bronze Age
The period from around 3000 B.C. to 1000 B.C. in which bronze, a mixture of copper and tin, was widely used for tools and weapons—the first metal to be so used.

cuneiform
A system of writing developed by the Sumerians that consisted of wedge-shaped impressions made by a stylus (a scratching tool made of reed) on clay tablets.

pantheon
The leading gods and goddesses of a people, believed to be a family group.

benefited greatly from a series of innovations, originating in socially and politically less complex societies, that changed the ways of life of many peoples across Asia, Africa, and Europe from about 3500 B.C. onward. Among these were the wheel and the plow (pp. 20, 46), which early written documents indicate were widely used in Sumer by 3000 B.C. Another such innovation, which revolutionized the making of tools and weapons, was the development of metalworking. Over thousands of years, people in the metal-bearing mountains of Anatolia had found out how to mine and work copper. Sometime before 3000 B.C., they had learned to alloy (blend) copper with tin to make bronze, a metal that was hard and strong enough to replace stone as the main material for tools and weapons. By 3000 B.C., the use of the new metal had spread to Sumer. Mesopotamia, as well as many other lands of western Asia, northern Africa, and eastern Europe, had entered the **Bronze Age** . Several other metals besides copper and tin—notably gold, silver, and lead—were also being worked for use or decoration. But bronze remained the king of metals until the development of iron tools and weapons after 1000 B.C. (p. 32).

Accounting and Poetry: The Birth of Writing

In addition, the Sumerians themselves developed one of the world's first systems of writing. The origins of this historic innovation were surprisingly humdrum. Nearly all of the earliest known written documents of Sumer (dating from about 3100 B.C. onward) are accounting records, providing information on supplies delivered to temple storehouses or consumed by temple officials. It seems that writing was developed in response to the increased prosperity of Sumer and the increased need for direction and control—both of which the wealthy and powerful Sumerian priesthood would have been particularly well aware of.

Sumerian writing grew out of a simpler record-keeping system used by Neolithic villagers, based on clay counters with *pictograms* (drawings of objects, such as sheep or bales of cloth) scratched into them. In the Sumerian temples, which had much more property to keep track of and consequently a greater need for detailed records, the pictograms were simplified so that they could be more easily and quickly drawn. Eventually, each symbol became no longer a picture but simply a group of wedge-shaped marks; hence

Cuneiform Learn about how cuneiform was deciphered in this video.

Sumerian writing is known as **cuneiform** (kyoo-NEE-uh-form), from *cuneus*, Latin for "wedge."

Meanwhile, some symbols came to be used as *logograms* (standing for whole words) and *phonograms* (standing for the individual sounds that make up words). Just as important, the new symbols were no longer written singly, each on its own small counter. Instead, any desired combination of symbols was scratched with a sharpened piece of reed, or stylus, into a larger piece of moistened clay, known as a tablet. The tablet was then dried to form a permanent record of complicated transactions involving any number of items.

As a result of all these improvements, the system had outgrown its original purpose. By 2600 B.C., a writer could produce a visual statement not just of business dealings but of anything that was spoken. Writing was a highly skilled task that was practiced only by professional scribes, who had to master hundreds of symbols and many complex rules for using them. "A scribe whose hand can keep up with the mouth, he is indeed a scribe!" said a proverb. But so valuable was the practice of writing that other peoples of Mesopotamia and neighboring lands later borrowed the cuneiform symbols, adapted them to their own languages, and used them for thousands of years, until cuneiform writing was gradually replaced by alphabetic writing after 1200 B.C. (p. 33).

Great Gods and Goddesses

As Sumerian communities grew larger and more complex, some of their deities (gods and goddesses) grew more mighty and splendid than ever before. Countless lesser deities were still worshiped, but at the center of each Sumerian city stood a magnificent temple where one of the great gods or goddesses was believed to make his or her home. There the divine being was honored and served by priests and priestesses as well as by the community in general, and was trusted to protect and preserve it in return. Enki, the god of the life-giving river waters, was worshiped in Eridu at the mouth of the Euphrates. Nanna, the moon god, had his temple up the river at Ur. At Uruk, a short distance beyond Ur, stood the shrine of the goddess Inanna, where solemn ceremonies yearly reenacted her marriage to the god Dumuzi, rising from the ground at harvest time as her fertility-bringing bridegroom. Together, these and other deities formed a **pantheon** (from the Greek words for "all the gods")—a close-knit family group of leading deities wielding power over the whole land.

A Mesopotamian Creation Myth: Earth, Gods, and Humans Read a Sumerian creation story.

The Sumerians had countless traditions, found in myths, temple hymns, and prayers, about their gods and goddesses. These traditions did not amount to a single consistent belief system, and of course, other peoples had different deities and told different stories about them. But the general Sumerian way of thinking about the gods and goddesses was widely shared by ancient civilizations until the rise of the belief in one God, or monotheism (p. 37).

The gods and goddesses were holy, inspiring love and fear in humans because there was nothing that did not depend on them: the fury of storms and war, the abundance of fields and flocks, the survival of great cities, dreams in the night, or sexual desire. They were not necessarily righteous: they might get drunk, have brawling quarrels, or be unfaithful to each other with other deities or with humans. Yet this made no difference to their holiness, for they were above mere human rules and regulations. For example, revered deities were said to practice incest involving all combinations of siblings, parents, and children.

Furthermore, as high and holy as the gods were, there was no fixed boundary between them and humans: gods and humans could interbreed and produce offspring, mighty heroes could achieve immortality and become divine. And traditions about the gods and goddesses changed according to the needs and hopes of their worshipers: rulers and priests in a newly dominant city-state might proclaim their community god or goddess mightier and holier within the pantheon than anyone had suspected before.

In dealing with these mighty beings, there were some basic rules that it was both righteous and prudent to follow. In order of importance, these rules were first, wholeheartedly to serve and honor the god or goddess of one's own community; second, to pay great respect to any other deity, great or small, native or foreign, who might influence one's fate; and third, to observe justice in dealings with other humans.

Immortality after death was a gift that the gods occasionally gave to humans of the highest rank, like the king's wife Pu-Abi. For most people, however, the only true life was life on earth—a life that was brief, hard, uncertain, and utterly dependent on the will of the gods. Creation myths told how the gods and goddesses had fashioned humans out of clay for their service, had sent a flood to destroy them when they grew annoyingly numerous, but had then felt pity and changed their minds. Among the specialists whom Sumerian wealth supported were those who sought clues to the changeable will of the gods: seers who knew the meaning of dreams, priests who studied the shape and size of inner organs of sacrificed animals, and astronomers who observed the movements of the sun, moon, and stars.

This same view of the relationships between mortals and gods is often found in the most famous of Sumer's literary legacies, its **epics**—

The *Epic of Gilgamesh* Describes a Great Flood Read about the Great Flood in the Epic of Gilgamesh.

long poems telling of gods and heroes and their ambitions and struggles. Most of the Sumerian epics concern the career of an early king, Gilgamesh (**GIL-guh-mesh**). Although Gilgamesh was probably a real person, in epic poetry he becomes a half-human, half-divine character who embodies the values and aspirations of the people of Sumer. He fights for his city-state; slays hostile humans and animals; and displays bravery, cunning, and a sense of fairness and mercy. The king's quest for immortality—a principal theme of the epic—ends in failure, as it does for most people. The epic of Gilgamesh, along with many other Sumerian literary works, was preserved, translated, and rewritten throughout the three thousand years of Mesopotamian civilization.

Still, in time, the Sumerians came to a more hopeful belief: that the great gods and goddesses took a personal interest not only in city-states and their rulers but also in ordinary human beings. These "personal gods" watched closely over their devotees, rewarding them with prosperity and punishing them with hardship depending on their deeds. According to a proverb, "A man's personal god is a shepherd who finds pasture for him. Let him lead him like a sheep to the grass where he can eat." This declaration of trust in divine power would echo down to the present day.

Numbers and Measurement

Besides writing, the practical needs of civilized Sumer in cultivation, irrigation, and commerce led to historic innovations in mathematics and science. The Sumerians devised the basic processes of arithmetic: multiplication, division, and the square and cube root. It was they who first divided the hour into sixty minutes, the minute into sixty seconds, and the circle into 360 degrees. They also found out how to calculate the length of the hypotenuse of a right triangle and worked out the method for calculating the area of a rectangle.

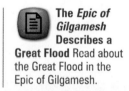

Sumerian Temple Statuettes These miniature statues, the largest of them 30 inches high, date from about 2700–2600 B.C. Each statue represents a worshiper who has donated it to the deity of the temple. By placing these images of themselves in the temple, worshipers proclaimed their loyalty to the deity and hoped to gain his or her protection and support. Courtesy of the Oriental Institute of the University of Chicago

In addition, the well-organized Sumerians, even more than earlier peoples, needed to track the passage of time, as measured by the movements of the sun, moon, and stars. Besides, the sun, moon, and stars were deities whose movements should be carefully watched. Accordingly, Sumerian astronomers devised a calendar—a system for recording days, months, seasons, and years. The calendar's basic unit was a month of twenty-nine days—about the time between two full moons—with the months divided into seven-day weeks.

But the astronomers were also aware of a difficulty with this calendar. They knew that the sun and the stars seem to circle the earth at different speeds, so that it takes about 365 days for the sun to return to the same position relative to the stars. But twelve 29-day months do not add up to this solar (sun) year—and the seasons, so vital to farming, depend on the sun, not the moon. Keeping the months in step with the seasons was a major scientific and practical problem, which the Sumerian astronomers dealt with by adding in an extra month every few years.

Temples and Statues

The raising of huge temples to gain the favor of the gods or palaces to display the power of kings was a challenge that brought forth some spectacular monuments—all of them made of mud brick (adobe), since there was no other building material available in the river valleys of Mesopotamia.

Remains and records show that temples were the most distinguished structures. Typically, a temple consisted of an enclosure placed atop a man-made "mountain," a kind of step-pyramid called a **ziggurat** (see photo). The first level of the ziggurat at Ur was a solid mud-brick mass some 50 feet high and 200 by 300 feet at its base. It supported two ascending set-back levels, the higher one serving as a pedestal for the temple where the deity was thought to live. A structure of this type was probably the model for the Bible's Tower of Babel, with its "top in the heavens."

This general type of mountain-temple has reappeared throughout the world over long stretches of time, notably in Mexico and India, and perhaps, in all cases, it reflects similar beliefs about the relationship of the human and the divine. The hundred-step ramps of the ziggurat suggest a sacrificial climb as the worshiper approaches the deity, or perhaps the descent of the deity from heaven to be present among the people; the sheer mass of the monument symbolizes the power and rank of the god in comparison with ordinary mortals.

Inside Sumerian temples were many statues of both divine and human beings. Like all ancient peoples, the Sumerians thought that depicting persons or objects was a deed of magic

The Chogha Zanbil Ziggurat Ziggurats continued to be built for many centuries after Sumerian times. This one, east of Sumer in present-day Iran, was built about 1250 B.C. It is the best-preserved Mesopotamian ziggurat—about 100 yards on each side, and 170 feet high. Originally it had two more levels on top. © AISA Archivo Iconografico, Barcelona, Spain

that would bring these into actual being. Images of the main god or goddess, as well as of lesser deities that were connected with the main one in myth and ritual, ensured that these would all be present in the temple. Priests and priestesses, kings and their wives and children, as well as humbler worshipers who wished always to be in the presence of the deities, had larger or smaller statues there too (see photo).

Sumerian sculptors displayed extraordinary skill in creating highly stylized humanlike forms. In all the statues, the most prominent feature is the eyes; the pupils are magnified enormously, perhaps reflecting the dominance of eye function in human perception and communication (see photo). Because durable stone was hard to come by in Mesopotamia, sculptors often used sandstone or clay, adding shells, alabaster, and semiprecious stones for dramatic effect. Other artisans crafted exquisite jewelry and metalwork, chiefly for use in the temples and palaces.

Civilization in Mesopotamia

Almost as soon as it arose, the civilization of Sumer began to spread. Through trade and travel, through peaceful immigration and warlike invasion, peoples throughout southwestern Asia encountered, imitated, and adapted the new and more complex way of life that had originated in Sumer. For more than three thousand years, the traditions of Sumer provided a common basic pattern of civilization in a region that eventually stretched from the borders of India westward to the Mediterranean and Black Seas.

Farmers and Nomads

The first peoples to feel the pull of Sumerian civilization were of course those who lived close by, in or near Mesopotamia itself (see Map 1.1 on page 8). Many of these peoples farmed the upstream valleys of the Euphrates and Tigris Rivers. They mostly spoke Semitic languages, which were very different from the Sumerian tongue but closely related to the present-day Arabic and Hebrew languages.

But the up-river farmers were not the only neighbors of Sumer. In the dry plains in and around Mesopotamia where the floodwaters could not reach, there were Semitic-speaking peoples who followed a very different way of life. The Sumerians called them the ones "who know not grain"—wandering **nomads** who lived from their flocks and herds, traded for plant food with farmers, but did little or no farming themselves.

> **"** 218. If a physician performed a major operation on a freeman with a bronze lancet and has caused the freeman's death, or he opened up the eye-socket of a freeman and has destroyed the freeman's eye, they shall cut off his hand. 219. If a physician performed a major operation on a commoner's slave with a bronze lancet and has caused his death, he shall make good slave for slave.**"**
>
> —from The Law Code of Hammurabi, ca. 1800 B.C.

The nomadic way of life was no throwback to the era of hunters and gatherers. It arose in many parts of Asia and Africa in the wake of the Agricultural Revolution, as farmers moved out onto open grasslands that were not good for raising crops but could support large numbers of animals. Nomads lived in family groups that formed part of larger communities not unlike those of farmers, but to find fodder and water for their herds, they had to be continually on the move. In southwestern Asia, they roamed a region that stretched from the plains of Mesopotamia hundreds of miles southward into present-day Arabia.

From time to time, misfortunes such as overpopulation, famine, or war caused the nomads to spill out into the farmlands of Mesopotamia as immigrants or invaders. They constantly threatened the cities of Sumer, but nomads who broke in usually adopted the way of life that they found there. In Mesopotamia and beyond, nomads as well as farmers played a part in the spread of civilization and influenced civilization as it spread.

Mesopotamian Empires: Akkad and Babylon

While the Sumerian city-states struggled with each other, nearby farming peoples northward up the main rivers and eastward on various tributaries were benefiting from the same climate changes that had brought wealth to Sumer, as well as from growing networks of trade and travel. A civilized way of life emerged throughout Mesopotamia and its eastern borderlands that was modeled on that of Sumer. More and more city-states joined in an ever-wider struggle for power across Mesopotamia. From time to time, short-lived Sumerian empires arose that claimed to rule "from the Lower Sea to the Upper Sea"—from the Persian Gulf to the Mediterranean.

 **Art of the First Cities in the Third Millennium B.C.** (http://www.metmuseum.org/toah/hd/trdm/hd_trdm.htm) Learn more about the art of the first cities.

The expanded world of Mesopotamian civilization was too large for any Sumerian city-state to control for long, however. About 2350 B.C., Sargon of Akkad, a Semitic-speaking territory immediately up-river from Sumer, overthrew the last Sumerian empire and replaced it with one of his own. Like later empire builders—the Romans in their relations with the Greeks, for instance (p. 118)—he could not help looking up to the conquered people whose traditions had most influenced his own. He called himself ruler of "Sumer and Akkad," and bound himself by close family ties with the Sumerian city-state of Ur. His daughter Enheduanna—a Sumerian, not a Semitic name—became high priestess in the temple of Nanna, the city's chief god, and was probably the author of several hymns in praise of the goddess Inanna, written in the Sumerian language.

Even so, Sargon's empire fell in its turn, and there followed a new period of struggles for control over Mesopotamia. A Semitic nomad people, the Amorites, moved into the farmlands along the rivers in large numbers, and their chieftains became kings of city-states. The Sumerian language ceased to be spoken in everyday life, though it continued to be used by priests and scholars for the next two thousand years of Mesopotamian civilization. From now on, however, the main language of Mesopotamia, in writing and probably also in speech, was the Semitic tongue of Akkad, whose prestige had outlasted Sargon's empire. Rulers issued orders and merchants transacted business in Akkadian, and the gods and goddesses were usually called by Akkadian names—Inanna was now Ishtar, for instance, and her bridegroom Dumuzi was Tammuz.

About 1900 B.C., the power struggles once again ended in the rise of an empire, which this time lasted for three hundred years. Its rulers were the Amorite kings of the formerly Sumerian city of Babylon—most famously Hammurabi (**ham-moo-RAH-bee**), who reigned about 1700 B.C. So impressive was his authority that under his rule the Creation myth was revised, and Marduk, patron god of the city of Babylon, was portrayed as the Maker of all things. Marduk eventually became the foremost deity of Mesopotamia. Some of his priests even proclaimed that all other deities were no more than different forms of this one and only supreme god.

King Hammurabi's Laws

Among Hammurabi's acts of royal power was the issue of the best-known collection of laws of ancient Mesopotamia. Hammurabi's law code was based on earlier codes issued by Sumerian kings, which themselves were probably written forms of earlier oral customs and traditions. No other law code has been recovered so completely, however, and it gives a vivid picture of a mighty ruler claiming to control the workings of a civilized society (see photo).

The code is engraved in cuneiform writing on a seven-foot-tall black stone pillar; a carving at the top shows the Babylonian god of justice, Shamash, speaking the laws to King Hammurabi. As the chosen servant of Shamash, the king could lay claim to exceptional stature among humans: "The great gods have called me, I am the salvation-bearing shepherd, whose staff is straight . . . to proclaim justice in the land, to settle all disputes, and heal all injuries." Countless future monarchs would claim to rule as doers of justice in the name of divine power.

To settle disputes and heal injuries in the complex society of Mesopotamia took many laws—above all, laws regarding crime and punishment. Death, most often by drowning, was a common penalty. An innkeeper who failed to report customers who used her saloon to plan a crime, for example, or a soldier who hired a substitute for war service and did not pay him, must lose their lives. And for the lesser crime of assault, "If a man puts out the eye of another man, his eye shall be put out. If he breaks another man's bone, his bone shall be broken." Evidently, civilized Mesopotamians were hard even for "salvation-bearing shepherds" to control except by spectacularly brutal punishments.

But fearsome penalties could only work if offenders were found out. To encourage accusers to come forward, they received the proceeds of any fines levied; to discourage false accusations, if a suspect was found innocent, the accuser was executed. Guilt and innocence were decided by "judges" and "elders," who could require witnesses and oaths. Should a matter come down to one man's word against another's, however, the suspect must jump into the Euphrates. If he sank and drowned, he was guilty, "but if the river proves that he is not guilty, and he escapes unhurt, then he who brought the accusation shall be put to death."

Almost fifty of Hammurabi's laws dealt with family life. The main intent here was seemingly the by now traditional one of making sure that families would continue over generations by controlling the behavior of women and keeping property mainly in the hands of men (p. 10). There were careful provisions, for instance, about inheritance by the sons of concubines (female bedfellows) of married men. This was an important matter in well-off families, where husbands often kept concubines—for pleasure, as status symbols, or because they had not fathered sons

The State Regulates Health Care: Hammurabi's Code and Surgeons Read a sample from Hammurabi's law code.

(above, center) **A King and His God** The top of the pillar on which King Hammurabi's laws are inscribed shows the Babylonian god Shamash (seated at right) giving the laws to Hammurabi. It expresses the Mesopotamian concept of kingship, which persisted in Western civilization down to modern times—that kings, though mortal, rule as servants of divine power and must therefore be honored and obeyed. Reunion des musees nationaux/Art Resource, NY

with their wives. But a wife taking a lover was quite a different matter. "If the finger is pointed at a man's wife about another man, but she is not caught with the other man, she shall jump into the river for her husband"—that is, she must let the river prove her guilt or innocence.

Still, in well-off families, women were bearers of family honor and were given in marriage with **dowries**—money and goods that they brought to their new households. It would be a family disgrace and a waste of family wealth if these women were left entirely without rights. If a husband deserted or neglected his wife, "so that she says, 'You are not congenial to me,' . . . she shall take her dowry and go back to her father's house."

In this way, Hammurabi's laws privileged men within family, marriage, and inheritance but gave women enough rights to uphold the status of the families from which they came. Specific provisions of family law would vary immensely in future centuries, but their general intent would be much the same as Hammurabi's for 3,500 years until recent times.

Likewise, the penalties and procedures of Hammurabi's laws, which were probably already ancient in his time, had a long history ahead of them. A thousand years after Hammurabi, the Israelites still punished some offenses on the principle of retaliation, or "eye for eye, tooth for tooth" (p. 42). Three thousand years after the Babylonian code, jumping into water and other types of ordeal or "judgment of God" were routine procedures of English common law (p. 189). Retaliation and ordeal seemed natural and god-given to societies that could not afford prisons and had no knowledge of scientific detection.

> **dowry**
> Money and goods given by a woman's family to her new household when she marries.

The Expansion of Mesopotamian Civilization

The Babylonian empire eventually fell apart in its turn, but other empire builders followed. By 1600 B.C., the Kassites, a farming people from the mountains east of the Tigris, had conquered most of Babylonia. Like earlier invaders, they adopted the Mesopotamian pattern of civilization and dominated the region for four hundred years down to 1200 B.C.

Meanwhile, the civilization that had begun in Sumer flourished and spread not only in Mesopotamia but also far beyond—westward to the Mediterranean coast, northward through Anatolia toward Europe, and eastward toward India (Map 1.2). The spread of civilization through these regions happened partly through normal processes of trade and travel. But

Map 1.2 **Southwestern Asia and Northeastern Africa about 1200 B.C.**

By this date the lands where Africa and Asia meet had become a region of many powerful states, linked together by trade, travel, cultural influences, and warfare. Peoples on the fringes of this region, including the villagers of Europe, were already feeling the effects of its wealth and power. © Cengage Learning

 Interactive Map

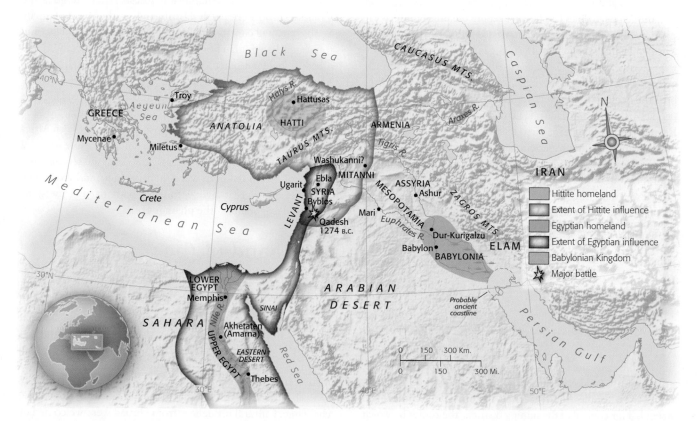

Moo-Cow on Wheels Wagons and chariots were not the only early devices that moved on wheels. When Neolithic farmers in eastern Europe learned of the world-changing device, they used it to make state-of-the-art toys—in this case, a cow that toddlers pulled round a village in present-day Ukraine in the fourth millennium B.C. The Museum of National Cultural Heritage 'PLATAR,' Kiev. Photo: ImagoRomae, Rome

it also resulted from the far-flung migrations of another group of nomadic peoples who lived farther north in the grasslands of what is today southern Russia: the *Indo-Europeans*.

Indo-European Peoples and Languages

Like the nomads of southwestern Asia, those of the **steppes**, as the northern grasslands are called, often settled in farming lands. Again and again, over many centuries between 4000 and 1000 B.C., they moved as immigrants, raiders, and invaders into territories that stretched from western Europe, by way of Mesopotamia, deep into India—hence the name Indo-European. Everywhere they moved, Indo-European peoples gave up their nomadic way of life for farming, while the peoples among whom they settled came to speak the closely related languages of the newcomers. This was a lasting change, though these languages developed away from each other over time. Present-day languages as different as English and Bengali, or Russian and Spanish, are all derived from those spoken by the prehistoric Indo-Europeans.

The Indo-European way of life differed from that of southwestern Asian nomads in one important respect: it revolved around an animal that was native to the steppes, the horse. Around 3800 B.C., the steppe peoples had begun keeping the horse for its meat and hide. By 3500 B.C., they had harnessed it to the earliest known wheeled vehicles, which in time evolved into a formidable new weapon of war, the horse-drawn chariot carrying warriors armed with bows and arrows, spears, and axes. By 1200 B.C.—having bred the horse to be larger and stronger than before—the steppe peoples would learn to ride it. The warriors of Mesopotamia and Egypt would need to learn these skills from the Indo-Europeans, often through painful experiences of defeat in war.

From about 2500 B.C. onward, the pace of Indo-European migration out of the steppes grew faster. Many of the migrants moved westward through Europe, including Greece, where their encounter with Mediterranean peoples influenced by Egypt led to the earliest beginnings of Greek civilization (p. 49). Others raided deep into Mesopotamia, until they settled down and founded kingdoms in the region's northern and western borderlands.

The Hittites

The most powerful and longest-lasting of the Indo-European-ruled kingdoms was that of the Hittites in the land of Hatti in Anatolia (see Map 2.1). In this land of mountains, forests, and high plains, the most valuable resources were metals: copper, gold, and silver were plentiful, though tin was scarce. For centuries, local peoples and then Indo-European newcomers had struggled for control of the mining districts, the routes by which tin was imported to make bronze (p. 14), and the profitable export routes to Mesopotamia, as well as to Syria and Palestine on the eastern shore of the Mediterranean.

By about 1600 B.C., the Hittite kings had won this competition and dominated almost all of Anatolia with the help of powerful nobles living in mountaintop strongholds. They acquired authority as effective as that of any Mesopotamian king and regulated the affairs of their subjects with law codes almost as detailed as Hammurabi's.

With the wealth they acquired from the trade in metals, the Hittites built an army of charioteers and well-trained infantry numbering as many as thirty thousand men, and fought wars with Egypt to control Syria and Palestine. In the heavily fortified cities of the Hittite homeland, priests tended to gods and goddesses who were partly Hittite and partly Mesopotamian. Scribes adapted cuneiform writing to the Hittite language, and translated Babylonian versions of the tales of Gilgamesh and other Mesopotamian heroes. The scribes also composed letters in Akkadian for the kings to send to foreign rulers—for the Semitic tongue of Mesopotamia had become the international language of trade and diplomacy in a region of civilization that by 1200 B.C. stretched across southwestern Asia and northeastern Africa from the Indian Ocean to the Mediterranean Sea (see Map 1.2 on page 19). And among the rulers with whom the Hittite kings corresponded most often were their partners and rivals who ruled the other great civilization that had arisen at the same time as Mesopotamia—the pharaohs of Egypt.

LO³ Land of the Pharaohs: Egypt

During the Neolithic Age, the people of the Nile had moved toward civilization in response to the same influences that gave rise to the cities of Sumer, but Egyptian civilization was more stable than that of Mesopotamia. Political and sectional conflicts did not usually break the country's unity, and for many centuries foreign invasions were few and far between. Occasional times of trouble and change provided an invigorating challenge. Cultural influences from abroad were welcomed or

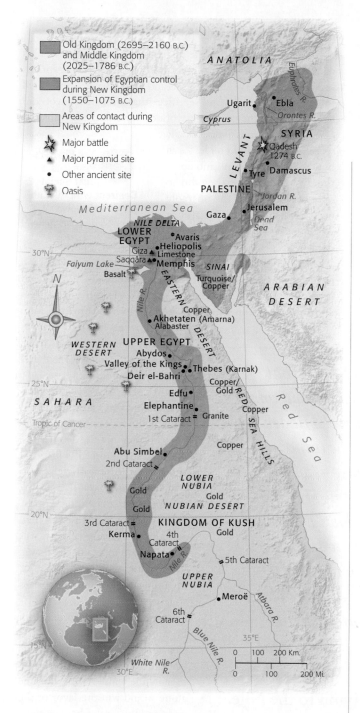

Map 1.3 **Ancient Egypt**

Egyptian civilization grew up in a thin strip of fertile land where the Nile crosses the North African desert, and in the broader region of the river's delta. Beyond these "Two Lands" of Upper and Lower Egypt lived wealthy and powerful African and Asian peoples. In the New Kingdom, Egypt dominated and influenced many of these peoples as well; later on, some of them in turn conquered Egypt.

© Cengage Learning

Interactive Map

The Nile and the "Two Lands"

Egypt stretches along the lower reaches of the Nile's four-thousand-mile course from Central Africa to the Mediterranean Sea (see Map 1.3). The country is divided into two sections, called by the ancient Egyptians the "Two Lands." Upper Egypt is a narrow strip of fertile land, five hundred miles in length and averaging no more than twelve miles in width, that stretches alongside the river as it flows across the North African desert. Lower Egypt is a fan-shaped pattern of waterways, or delta, formed by the Nile in the last hundred miles before it reaches the sea.

The Nile played a role in Egypt similar to that of the Euphrates and Tigris in Mesopotamia. The cycle of labor and of life itself depended on its annual flooding and receding, and the "gift of the Nile" provided the wealth for the earliest Egyptian civilization. About the same time that the Sumerian city-states arose, Egypt witnessed the consolidation of increasingly wealthy communities, scattered along the river, into two kingdoms of Upper and Lower Egypt.

kept at arm's length, as seemed best to the literate elite. The traditions of Egyptian civilization became so strong that they flourished even in its last thousand years, when the country was repeatedly invaded and for long periods under foreign rule.

The Narmer Palette This palette was used for grinding makeup for divine images in an Upper Egyptian temple about 3100 B.C. The intertwined necks of two tethered beasts around the grinding area are believed to symbolize the union of the Two Lands. Above them, a king wears the crown of Upper Egypt; in front of him, some of the earliest known hieroglyphs give his name—Narmer—an army parades, and beheaded corpses are lined up. Evidently unification was not a peaceful process. Werner Forman/Art Resource, NY

pharaohs
The rulers of ancient Egypt.

Then, around 3100 B.C., the Two Lands were unified under a single king, seemingly in brutal warfare (see photo). The country's rulers from then on are usually known as **pharaohs (FAY-roh)**—a name derived from the Egyptian word for "palace," which they used to mean "the king" in the same way that "the White House" is today used to mean "the president." One of the early pharaohs built a new capital at Memphis, south of the delta and close to the boundary between the Two Lands, as the center of government. Thus, unlike Mesopotamia, Egyptian civilization, almost from the start, was linked with a single state under a single ruler.

Government by a God-King

The Egyptians, like other polytheistic peoples, recognized no hard-and-fast boundary between humans and gods, and in the case of the pharaoh, they took this belief much farther than the Mesopotamians. For the Egyptians, the pharaoh was to be obeyed as a man given power by the gods and venerated as a god who dwelt among men.

In his double capacity as god and man, the pharaoh had awesome responsibility and power. The stability and harmony of their state, the Egyptians believed, was part of the stability and harmony of the universe as a whole. The judges dealing out impartial justice in the courts, the tax collectors collecting no more from the peasants than was due, the Nile flooding in exactly the right amount to deliver its riches on schedule, even the sun rising on time in the morning and setting on time in the evening—all were simply different aspects of this same universal stability and harmony, which the Egyptians called *maat* (**muh-AHT**). It was up to the pharaoh to uphold all these aspects of *maat* against the forces of chaos and confusion.

Tending the "Cattle of God"

As a god, every pharaoh was identified in different ways with three of the country's ruling deities. By birth, he was the son of the sun-god Re, the king of all the other gods and goddesses. At his succession, he became the incarnation (living embodiment) of Horus, the falcon-headed ruler of the sky. When he died, he became one with Osiris, who reigned as pharaoh of the underworld. Thus, one or other mighty god was always linked with or actually present in the person of the pharaoh.

Just as important as the pharaoh's divine nature was his nature as a human being. Alone among humans, the Egyptians believed, it was he whom the gods and goddesses had appointed to conduct the rituals and sacrifices that won their favor and made sure that they did their work of upholding the universe. Of course, thousands of priests daily served the gods and goddesses in hundreds of temples up and down the Two Lands. But they did so only as delegates of the pharaoh: not even the most trivial prayer or sacrifice was of any effect unless done in his name.

 **The Pharaoh Promises a Just Social Contract with His Subjects** Read a pharaoh's promise to his people.

Likewise, all of Egypt was deemed to belong to the pharaoh as his personal property. Official monuments usually gave all credit for success in peace and war to his wisdom and prowess and to the favor in which the gods held him. Furthermore, the whole of Egyptian society was organized in such a way as to be under the pharaoh's control and responsive to his will.

At the highest level, the pharaoh maintained a vast household that was also his central administration. Throughout the Two Lands, the pharaoh had at his disposal an army of lesser officials, who qualified for their posts by a lengthy training as scribes (writing experts). Service to the ruler, rather than any kind of private activity, was the main path to wealth and power. Foreign trading expeditions, mining, and other large enterprises were carried on at the pharaoh's orders by groups recruited from his household. Peasants toiled as sharecroppers on the pharaoh's land and were drafted in thousands to build the temples with which he alone would win the favor of the gods, and the tomb where he alone would lie for all eternity.

But pharaohs took seriously the responsibility that came with their power. "Well tended are men, the cattle of god," King Khety III told his son and heir Merikare in a document of advice written about 2200 B.C.; ". . . he made for them rulers in the egg, leaders to raise the backs of the weak." In the opinion of this god-king of Egypt, rulers were made for their subjects, not the other way round. And the Egyptians certainly expected their ruler to deliver benefits for themselves and their families. Throughout the Two Lands, people bought and sold, bequeathed

> "*Hail to thee, O Nile, that issues from the earth and comes to keep Egypt alive! Hidden in his form of appearance, a darkness by day, to whom minstrels have sung. He that waters the meadows which Re created, in order to keep every kid alive. He that makes to drink the desert and the place distant from water: that is his dew coming down (from) heaven.*"
>
> —from The Hymn to the Nile, ca. 1350–1100 B.C.

and inherited land, houses, and goods, treating these as individual and family possessions regardless of the pharaoh's ultimate ownership—and the pharaoh's judges, who ruled on property disputes, evidently agreed. Officials and priests built tombs for themselves and their wives with inscriptions boasting of their virtuous deeds, and handed on their positions to their sons—all with the pharaoh's knowledge and approval.

Men and Women Under the Pharaohs

The women who were closest to the pharaoh, the King's Mother and the King's Principal Wife, also had a touch of divinity, for it was a god who made them pregnant and a god to whom they gave birth. Probably to show the godlike nature of the ruling family—since Egyptian deities, like Sumerian ones, were said to practice incest—the King's Principal Wife was often also his sister or half-sister. In addition, the mother and the principal wife had their own lands and households, and were among the few people besides himself whom the pharaoh sometimes commemorated in monuments for successes achieved under his rule.

The pharaoh had many other wives besides his principal one, most of them daughters of high officials and foreign rulers with whom he condescended to form family ties. Most of these wives lived apart from the pharaoh and were even put to work as weavers, but if one of them caught his eye or he had no sons with his principal wife, the junior wife might in time rise to holiness and power as a King's Mother.

Only very rarely, however, did a woman wield the full authority of a pharaoh. The most successful of these rulers, Hatshepsut **(hat-SHEP-soot)**, reigned as "king" shortly after 1500 B.C., like the Sumerian ruler Ur-Bau five hundred years earlier (p. 13). Even so, Hatshepsut's name was eventually erased from monuments, probably because a female pharaoh was thought to undermine *maat*.

Lower down among the ordinary "cattle of god," women as well as men were entitled to benefit from the pharaoh's rule. Daughters inherited property equally with sons, and wives could divorce their husbands. Daughters could not usually inherit government and temple positions, but priests made sure that their wives were prestigiously employed in their temples as "Great Ones of Musical Troupes," directing the worship of the gods with music and song.

Unlike in Sumer, there are no records of women's expectations of men, but men were certainly expected to respect the women in their families. A book of "wisdom" (advice on the conduct of life) written about 1800 B.C. tells sons and husbands: "Support your mother as she supported you; she had a heavy load in you, but she did not abandon you. When you were born . . . she was yet yoked to you, her breast in your mouth for three years. As you grew and your excrement disgusted, she was not disgusted, saying 'What shall I do!' . . . Do not control your wife in her house, when you know she is efficient; don't say to her, 'Where is it? Get it.' . . . Do not go after a woman, let her not steal your heart."

But this advice still assumed that the wife was responsible to the husband rather than the other way round—and, of course, that there were plenty of bad women who were set on stealing him away from her. In tomb carvings of married couples, the wife is usually depicted smaller compared to her husband than she would naturally be, and is placed at his left—the humbler side.

Gods, Humans, and Everlasting Life

Many Egyptian deities, tracing back to the Stone Age, were originally conceived in the form of animals; during historic times, the divine images often had animal heads or bodies. The sky-god Horus, for example, is usually depicted with the head of a falcon, and the pharaoh himself is sometimes portrayed, as in the Great Sphinx (see photo), with a human head on a lion's body. Other important gods included the sun-god Re and the wind-god Amon, who came to be worshiped as a combined god, "Amon-Re, King of the Gods." Sometimes the two were even joined together with a third, the craftsman-god Ptah, to make a single, overwhelmingly mighty deity.

This custom of worshiping different deities in a single combined form probably arose from the way in which Egypt itself had come into being. The Egyptian deities had originally been local ones, and as the different communities of the Nile

The Great Sphinx This famous monument, carved out of solid rock in the royal burial area at Giza, expresses the Egyptian belief in the pharaoh as god-king. The sphinx's body is that of a lion, symbolic of the god Re, and its face is that of King Khafre (c. 2500 B.C.), who as pharaoh was thought of as the "living image" of the god. The pyramid to the left of the sphinx is Khafre's royal tomb. To the sphinx's right is the pyramid of Khafre's father Khufu.

THE SOUL DECLARES ITS INNOCENCE

By about 2000 B.C., the judgment of the soul after death and eternal life for those judged righteous became widely accepted beliefs. The newly dead were thought to travel by night through tests and ordeals in the underworld before rising to life in the morning with the sun-god Re. Papyrus documents with rites and spells that they would need to help them on their way were placed in their coffins for their guidance. Here, the soul declares its innocence of many forms of wrongdoing before Osiris, king of the dead.

The soul addresses Osiris by different names. The "Two Truths," "Two Daughters," and "Two Eyes" in these names are truth itself and righteousness; *Wennofer* means "eternally righteous." An *arura* is a measure of land area.

THE DECLARATION OF INNOCENCE

To be said on reaching the Hall of the Two Truths so as to purge [name] of any sins committed and to see the face of every god:

Hail to you, great God, Lord of the Two Truths!
I have come to you, my Lord,
I was brought to see your beauty.
I know you, I know the names of the forty-two gods
Who are with you in the Hall of the Two Truths,
Who live by warding off evildoers,
Who drink of their blood,
On that day of judging characters before Wennofer.
Lo, your name is "He-of-Two-Daughters,"
(And) "He-of-Maat's-Two-Eyes."
Lo, I come before you,
Bringing Maat to you,
Having repelled evil for you.
I have not done crimes against people,
I have not mistreated cattle,
I have not sinned in the Place of Truth,
I have not known what should not be known,
I have not done any harm.
I did not begin a day by exacting more than my due,
My name did not reach the bark of the mighty ruler.
I have not blasphemed a god,
I have not robbed the poor.
I have not done what the god abhors,
I have not maligned a servant to his master.
I have not caused pain,
I have not caused tears.
I have not killed,
I have not ordered to kill,
I have not made anyone suffer.

I have not damaged the offerings in the temples,
I have not depleted the loaves of the gods,
I have not stolen the cakes of the dead.
I have not copulated nor defiled myself.
I have not increased nor reduced the measure,
I have not diminished the arura.
I have not cheated in the fields.
I have not added to the weight of the balance,
I have not falsified the plummet of the scales.
I have not taken milk from the mouth of children,
I have not deprived cattle of their pasture.
I have not snared birds in the reeds of the gods,
I have not caught fish in their ponds.
I have not held back water in its season,
I have not dammed a flowing stream,
I have not quenched a needed fire.
I have not neglected the days of meat offerings,
I have not detained cattle belonging to the god,
I have not stopped a god in his procession.
I am pure, I am pure, I am pure, I am pure!

EXPLORING THE SOURCE

1. What sorts of things should a person avoid doing in order to please the divine judges? Which is more important to avoid, transgressions against the gods or against fellow humans?

2. What might be the reason that almost all of the soul's declarations are negative: "I have not . . ."?

Source: Miriam Lichtheim, trans. and ed., *Ancient Egyptian Literature*, pp. 131–133 Copyright © 2006 by the University of California Press. Reprinted with permission of the University of California Press.

combined to form a single state, it made sense to believe that the god or goddess of one community was the same as that of another with which it was now united.

In fact, Egyptian priests and rulers often speculated that, behind all the different deities they worshiped, there lay a single divine power: one god who had created all the others, perhaps, or who ruled, protected, and nourished all the nations of the world. A pharaoh of the New Kingdom, Akhenaten, who identified the supreme god with the Aten, the shining disk of the sun, took this idea so far that he actually tried to abolish the worship of other leading deities. He failed in this "religious revolution," but even so, Egyptian polytheism always had an underlying urge toward the opposite form of belief, monotheism.

Unlike Mesopotamian religion, that of Egypt came to offer a growing hope of immortality. At first, it was believed that only the pharaoh was immortal, though he could confer everlasting life on his close associates. But a time of troubles at the end of the Old Kingdom after 2200 B.C. (p. 27) inspired a creative new idea: local administrators who now held power independently of the pharaoh came to expect that they would also live independently of him after death. Even when the rulers regained their power, this belief in wider access to the afterlife continued to grow. Every person, it was now believed, possessed a supernatural life force or soul (*ka*) that persisted after the body died; and preserving the body (through mummification) and providing it with comforts in the tomb would help it in the life to come.

The hope of immortality strengthened ethical ideas in Egyptian religion—the belief that the gods expected righteous behavior from humans. By 1800 B.C., Egyptians had come to believe that the soul of every deceased person had to stand before Osiris, the ruler of the underworld, for judgment. The soul recited its good deeds and denied doing anything evil. The heart (character) of the person was then weighed in a balance to measure the soul's truthfulness. If the soul passed this test, it was admitted to everlasting life in a garden paradise; otherwise, it was cast into the crocodile jaws of a monster.

The Writing of the Words of God

Writing arose in Egypt, as it did in Sumer, along with civilization itself, but the initial impulse was different. Instead of the record-keeping needs of an expanding economy, what brought about writing was the religious needs of rulers as they rose to become god-kings. The earliest Egyptian writing, the **hieroglyphs** (from the Greek for "sacred carvings"), was devised about 3100 B.C. as part of carvings and paintings intended to honor the pharaohs. By having themselves depicted together with a god who was promising them immortality, for example, the pharaohs believed that they could cause the god to actually make that promise, in a magical world beyond the accidents of time and place. Obviously, the magic would be all the more effective if the god's actual words could be "depicted."

Probably for this reason, the hieroglyphs were actual pictures of real-life or mythical creatures and objects (for examples, see photo on page 27), but most of these pictures also stood for whole words or separate sounds of words. The words they were used to represent were always religious, and they were mostly found in temples and other monuments; in fact, the Egyptian name of the hieroglyphs was "the writing of the words of god."

Soon after the invention of the hieroglyphs, "shorthand" versions of the characters were developed that could be much more easily and quickly written—the *hieratic* (priestly) script. In spite of its name, the hieratic script was used not only by priests but also for general literary and record-keeping purposes. Much later, around 700 B.C., an even faster shorthand, the *demotic* (popular) script, came into use. Like cuneiform writing, all the Egyptian scripts employed hundreds of characters according to complex rules, but they could communicate anything that could be thought or said. Thus, writing became as much part of the everyday life of civilization in Egypt as it was in Mesopotamia.

Most Egyptian writing, especially the hieratic and demotic scripts, was not chiseled into stone but done with ink on papyrus, a paperlike material made from the stems of the water-grown papyrus plant. The convenience of ink and papyrus for everyday writing was soon recognized everywhere, including in Mesopotamia, where it gradually replaced clay tablets and styluses (p. 14). Papyrus scrolls (rolls) became the books of the ancient world.

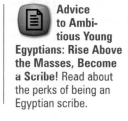

Advice to Ambitious Young Egyptians: Rise Above the Masses, Become a Scribe! Read about the perks of being an Egyptian scribe.

Much of Egypt's literary writing served religious purposes, for example, tales about the gods and books of rituals and spells to aid the passage of the soul to the afterworld. But virtually all forms of literature arose: philosophical essays, books of "wisdom" (p. 23), tales of adventure, romances, texts on medicine and magic, poems, and songs. The Egyptians excelled in the scope and quantity of their literary creations.

Calendars and Sailboats

Egyptian civilization, like that of Sumer, both needed scientific and technical knowledge and had specialists who could provide it. Surviving texts explain how land surveyors and architects computed the areas of fields, the volumes of various shapes, and the properties of pyramids. Likewise, astronomers created a calendar with twelve equal months of thirty days and five "free" days at the end to make up the 365 days of the solar year (p. 16). This was the most successful solution yet devised to the problem of keeping the months in step with the seasons, and its basic principles are still used in the present-day calendar.

The Egyptians were also knowledgeable in practical medicine. They understood nothing of germs or infections and believed that sickness was caused by demons entering the body. But alongside magic formulas and priestly exorcists were some healing drugs and trained physicians and surgeons. The

pyramid
A massive structure with sloping sides that met at an apex, used as a royal tomb in ancient Egypt.

Egyptians also developed systematic procedures for handling cases of illness, wrote books about diseases, and established medical libraries and schools. One reason for the superiority of their medical techniques, no doubt, was the anatomical knowledge (unique in the ancient world) derived from their practice of mummification. Prior to embalming with special preservatives, the body of the deceased was opened and the internal organs (except the heart) were removed.

 **Egyptology Online** (www.egyptologyonline.com/mummification.htm) Learn more about the Egyptian practice of mummification.

The Egyptians were also eager to improve water transportation along their main artery, the Nile. They built larger boats than the traditional dugout canoes by fastening wooden planks together to make the hulls. To propel these heavy craft upstream, by 3100 B.C. they equipped them with masts and sails to catch the wind, which in the Nile Valley usually blows against the current of the river. The Sumerians also used river sailboats, but by 2500 B.C. the Egyptians had adapted these sailboats to travel the open sea to the Mediterranean's eastern shoreline, a source of timber and other valuable products. In this way, the Mediterranean became a highway that would one day stretch from its eastern shores to northern Africa, southern Europe, and the Atlantic Ocean (pp. 32–33).

Pyramids and Temples

The most spectacular Egyptian technical feats, however, were in the field of building. Their inspiration here was mainly religious—above all, the fact that their god-king (and as time went on, many other important personages) must have a stone tomb as a resting place for all time. The best-known tombs are the giant royal **pyramids**—the masterpieces of practical engineering (and social discipline) that come most readily to mind when we think of Egypt.

The great age of pyramid building was in the early centuries of Egyptian civilization, and the largest of them was built by order of King Khufu (often known by his Greek name, Cheops), who ruled about 2650 B.C. Located at Giza (near modern Cairo), the Great Pyramid measures 476 feet in height and 760 feet on each side of its base (see photo on page 23). This mountain of stone consists of some 2.3

million cut blocks, each weighing about 5,000 pounds. The sides of the pyramid were originally coated with polished marble, but that was stripped away by Muslim rulers in the Middle Ages to build the mosques and palaces of Cairo. (The royal tomb within was robbed by thieves in ancient Egyptian times.) Close by is the Great Sphinx, another type of monument, carved soon afterward for another king, Khafre (Chephren). The enormous head of this man-beast, cut from the cliff of the valley wall, rises 66 feet from its base.

 **Building the Great Pyramid** Learn how the Great Pyramid was built in this video.

Later on, the pyramid-building urge faded, but pharaohs still poured resources into gigantic building projects—above all, temples. Temple buildings were usually constructed of horizontal beams held up by columns. The method was very suitable for stone structures, and Egyptian builders had easy access to immense supplies of stone.

The temple of Amon at Karnak (far up the Nile near the city of Thebes) was begun about 1530 B.C. and completed about 1300 B.C. The largest religious building ever constructed, it covered a ground area of about 400 by 110 yards or 10 acres, large enough to contain four of the huge Gothic cathedrals that were built more than 2,500 years later in Europe. The roof of the main hall rests on 134 columns, each made of stone drums carved with hieroglyphs; the central columns are 70 feet high and 12 feet in diameter (see photo on page 4). As the builders intended, the gigantic proportions of Karnak were worthy of one of Egypt's greatest gods, and of the rulers who worshiped him.

Sculptors and painters did much of their work for the interiors of royal and noble tombs. Stone statues of the individuals entombed and of members of their households made them present within the tombs; paintings on tomb walls with scenes of everyday life related to the career of the deceased made those scenes take place in the afterlife. Though

King Menkaure (Mycerinus) and His Queen, 2500 B.C. The queen has her arm protectively around her husband, a typical pose in Egyptian statues of married couples that testifies to the status and power of upper-class women. The king's pose, with arms at his sides, fists clenched, and left foot forward, remained typical of Egyptian male statues for thousands of years and influenced early Greek sculpture (see photo on page 65). King Menkaure (Myerinus) and queen, Egyptian, Old Kingdom, Dynasty 4, reign of Menkaura, 2490-2472 B.C., Greywacke, 142.2 x 57.1 x 55.2 cm, 676.8 kg, Museum of Fine Arts, Boston, Harvard University – Boston Museum of Fine Arts Expedition, 11.1738. Photograph © 2011, Museum of Fine Arts Boston

Isis, Guide of Souls In this tomb painting, Isis leads Nefertari, Principal Wife of the New Kingdom pharaoh Ramses II (about 1250 B.C.), into the land of the dead. The goddess's headdress combines the cow's horns of nurturing fertility and the sun disk of light and power. The picture and the accompanying hieroglyphs remained mostly in darkness, but the Egyptians believed they would bring about what they depicted and described—the continuation of Nefertari's life into eternity. Valley of the Queens, Thebes/Giraudon/The Bridgeman Art Library

lifelike, these representations were seldom naturalistic (the way persons and objects normally look to the eye). Sculptured portraits, for example, had to be made according to set rules. Rather rigid postures were required, and the figures were placed so as to be viewed from the front (this is known as "frontalism"). Usually the left foot was placed forward; wigs and beards were treated in a standard stylized manner. Yet the human quality of these statues comes through all the same (see photo).

This humanistic quality is evident also in tomb paintings, from which we have learned many details about Egyptian civilization. There was no attempt to provide perspective (the illusion of depth) in these pictures; artists were free to arrange their compositions as they thought best within the assigned space. What mattered most was that a painting must reflect established knowledge of the object and must be shown from the angle that best revealed that knowledge. For example, the face is always shown in profile, except for the eye, which is shown as it appears frontally. Shoulders and torso are viewed from the front, legs and feet in profile (see photo).

By depicting the various parts of a human body from the different angles at which each of them was most fully seen, the artist could make a person most fully present on a two-dimensional surface, even if the whole body was not seen, as it would be in real life, from a single viewpoint. In any case, the Egyptian painters, within their rules, developed techniques of line, design, and color that were extraordinarily effective.

The Rhythm of Egypt's History

To hold the Egyptian state together for many centuries on end was no easy matter. From time to time the balance of the Two Lands was upset by weakling pharaohs, boy-pharaohs, and disputes over the succession; by disloyal courtiers and self-seeking officials; and by rivalries among powerful families and unruly communities. Whole dynasties were cut down by failure to produce heirs, or sometimes by violent turnovers. In all, over three thousand years, no fewer than thirty dynasties ruled Egypt. There were even periods of total collapse when the Egyptian state dissolved into fragments, each with its own self-proclaimed pharaoh. But to the Egyptians, such a state of affairs seemed profoundly abnormal and wrong. Sooner or later it must give way to the harmony of *maat*, under a single all-powerful god-king.

As a result, the Egyptian state enjoyed lengthy periods of stability and unity, interrupted by briefer intervals of turmoil. After several hundred years of early state building, the power of the pharaohs first reached its height in the period

 Simulation to Learn About Ancient Cultures (http://college.cengage .com/history/049509286x/ student/assets/simulations/ simulations/wcrc_ simulations_ch01.html) Participate in a simulation of life in ancient Egypt as an Old Kingdom farmer or a New Kingdom warrior.

known to modern scholars as the Old Kingdom, beginning about 2700 B.C. In total command of the country's resources, having few foreign enemies to contend with, and seeking an everlasting resting place, the pharaohs of the Old Kingdom were the builders of the pyramids.

About 2200 B.C., however, a series of weak pharaohs allowed local officials to gain independent hereditary power in the regions that they controlled. Egypt remained in turmoil until about 2050 B.C., when a dynasty from the up-river city of Thebes brought the whole country under its rule, to form the Middle Kingdom.

By this time, the world outside Egypt was changing, with the spread of Semitic tribes and the growth of powerful states in Mesopotamia and Anatolia. Accordingly, the god-kings of Egypt faced a new challenge as part of their general task of upholding *maat*: that of what they called "treading on" foreign nations. The pharaohs of the Middle Kingdom rose to this challenge and poured the spoils of their conquests into building magnificent new temples. Finally, however, internal conflict was renewed about 1800 B.C. Semitic immigrant tribes known as the Hyksos (**HIK-sohs**) were able to move into Lower Egypt, and the Middle Kingdom came to an end. The Hyksos adapted to Egyptian civilization, and for a time their chieftains ruled Lower Egypt as pharaohs.

Native Egyptian pharaohs continued to rule Upper Egypt from Thebes, and in 1600 B.C. they were able to defeat the Hyksos rulers and bring the nation into its imperial era, the New Kingdom. More than ever before, the rulers of Egypt acted as conquerors. Their armies moved south into Nubia and vied with the Hittites of Anatolia (pp. 20) for control of Palestine and Syria. Along with this aggressive warfare and bid for military glory came more open contact with the world beyond the Nile: for example, the pharaohs took to breeding horses and riding—or at least, having themselves depicted riding—chariots, just like their Hittite rivals (see photo).

Yet again, the wealth of the world went to the benefit of the gods and goddesses of the Nile. No longer builders of pyramids, the pharaohs of the New Kingdom instead had their massive tombs hewn out of solid rock in the Valley of the Kings near Thebes, and they constructed vast new temples like that of the

"I Crushed a Million Countries by Myself, on 'Victory-in-Thebes,' 'Mut-Is-Pleased,' My Horses" A scene from the Battle of Qadesh in Syria (1274 B.C.), as described by the New Kingdom pharaoh Ramses II. The Egyptians have fled before a Hittite army—except for the pharaoh, who prays to Amon-Re for help, lashes his horses' reins round his waist, drives against the foe, and scatters them. Ramses' version was carved on temple walls throughout Egypt; meanwhile, however, the Hittites also claimed victory. DEA/G. Dagli Orti/Getty Images

Theban god Amon at Karnak. Partly because of this dedication of wealth to religion, however, the power of the priests eventually came to overshadow that of the pharaohs. This, together with the inability of the then ruling dynasty to produce heirs, led to the end of the New Kingdom about 1100 B.C.

After the New Kingdom, Egypt often became a victim of invaders from elsewhere in Africa, from Mesopotamia, and eventually from Europe. It was dominated at different times—though with intervals of independence—by its western and southern neighbors, the Libyans and the Nubians, and by the Assyrians of Mesopotamia (pp. 34–35). In 525 B.C. Egypt became a province of the empire of Persia (p. 35); from 333 B.C. it was ruled by the Greeks; and finally, in 30 B.C., it was conquered by the Romans (pp. 83, 101).

Even so, Egyptian civilization continued to flourish. Libyan and Nubian rulers were much influenced by Egyptian ways even in their homelands, and they governed as genuine pharaohs, upholding the country's power and independence against Mesopotamian enemies. The Persians and Greeks had their own traditions of civilization, but they still found it wise to rule Egypt in accordance with the country's traditional beliefs and customs. The last great temples of the Nile were built after 250 B.C. by Greek kings acting as Egyptian pharaohs, to uphold the stability and harmony of the universe by tending to the needs of the gods.

Still, Egypt no longer "trod on" foreign peoples but instead was often one of the trodden. The reason had to do with great changes that began in the lands between the Indian Ocean and the eastern Mediterranean around the time that the New Kingdom ended—changes that gave the advantage in skills, wealth, and power to peoples outside Egypt.

 Listen to a synopsis of Chapter 1.

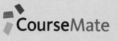 **CourseMate**

Access to the eBook with additional review material and study tools may be found online at CourseMate for WCIV. Sign in at www.cengagebrain.com.

CHAPTER 2

KINGS OF KINGS AND ONE GOD,
1200–300 B.C.

LEARNING OBJECTIVES

AFTER READING THIS CHAPTER, YOU SHOULD BE ABLE TO DO THE FOLLOWING:

LO¹ Describe how the period from 1200 to 900 B.C. was one of both crisis and innovation in the lands between the Indian Ocean and the Mediterranean Sea.

LO² Contrast the Assyrian and Persian methods of conquest and rule, and describe the achievements of these first universal empires.

LO³ Trace the evolution of the Jewish religion as a new kind of faith in one God.

"NEW SKILLS AND INTERNATIONAL CONTACTS HELPED MAKE IT POSSIBLE FOR CONQUERING PEOPLES TO BUILD 'UNIVERSAL' EMPIRES, WHICH RULED LARGER TERRITORIES THAN EVER BEFORE."

Around 1200 B.C., a new era began in the lands between the Indian Ocean and the Mediterranean Sea, when the region underwent a massive crisis. It was weakened by internal conflicts, nomadic peoples attacked it from north and south, and old-established kingdoms were swept away.

Gradually, the region recovered from the crisis, but it was different from before. It possessed new skills that would be basic features of many future civilizations, such as the use of iron and alphabetic writing. It was more closely knit together by trade and travel across networks of flourishing commercial city-states. And these new skills and international contacts helped make it possible for conquering peoples to build "universal" empires, which ruled larger territories than ever before. From time to time, there were spectacular reversals of fortune when one empire fell and another arose to take its place. But the idea took hold that it was normal for the region to have a single mighty ruler.

In this changing environment after 1200 B.C., there also appeared a new religious belief, that of monotheism, which proclaimed a single almighty God as the creator and ruler of the world. Monotheism was mainly the belief of one people, the Jews, and developed among them over many centuries of triumph and disaster in regional power struggles. By 300 B.C., the Jews were wholeheartedly committed to belief in the one God, and their beliefs and practices included many features of later monotheistic religions.

Test your knowledge before you read this chapter.

What do you think?

Monotheism represents an advance over the polytheism of Egypt and Mesopotamia.

Strongly Disagree						Strongly Agree
1	2	3	4	5	6	7

Iconotec/Photolibrary

≪ **"I Am Darius, the Great King, King of Kings"** This scene illustrates a Persian king's account of his deeds, carved into a cliffside at Behistun in present-day western Iran about 500 B.C. The king tramples a defeated rebel while captives representing conquered peoples stand before him, and the winged disk of divine power hovers above. At the time, Darius's empire stretched from Egypt and Anatolia to the borders of India.

Iron Age
The period beginning around 1000 B.C. in which iron became the most widely used metal for tools and weapons.

LO¹ Crisis and Recovery

Civilized societies have often been beset by internal problems and outside invasions, but often these troubles have ended not in collapse but in renewal. This was what now happened to the lands between the Indian Ocean and the Mediterranean Sea, as three hundred years of chaos forced the development of world-changing technical skills as well as empires of unprecedented size.

A Time of Troubles

Around 1200 B.C., the Hittite kingdom in Anatolia (pp. 20) fell to mysterious invaders who arrived by land and sea from the coasts and islands of the eastern Mediterranean. These invaders had perhaps been displaced by overpopulation and war among the peoples of Europe. From Anatolia, they went on to attack Syria, Palestine, and finally Egypt, where they were known as the "Sea Peoples" and where they were eventually repelled or assimilated. At about the same time, the Kassite kings of Mesopotamia were overthrown by invaders from farther east, who, however, were not strong enough to replace them as rulers of that entire region. Of the three great powers of the region, two had been destroyed, and the third, Egypt, was badly weakened.

New groups of Semitic nomads took advantage of the power vacuum to move into Mesopotamia. The northern part fell to the Aramaeans (ar-uh-MEY-ans), from the barren lands between the river valleys, and the south to the Chaldeans (kal-DEE-uhns) from Arabia. In Anatolia, meanwhile, the disruption of the trade in metals that had supplied much of the wealth for civilization led to several centuries of decline and decay, made worse by new invasions of nomadic peoples from farther north.

New Skills and New City-States

Out of the turmoil, however, came more advanced technical skills and a more intensive pattern of trade and travel, than ever before.

The Advent of Iron

In the devastated lands of Anatolia, metalworkers who were short of the imported tin that they needed to alloy with copper to make bronze began to take an interest in another metal: iron. This metal was far more plentiful than copper or tin, but it was difficult to smelt (extract from rock) and work. Forced by necessity, the bronzesmiths started to experiment with improved processes for smelting iron, as well as hardening and toughening it, until they ended with a metal that was superior to bronze and available in far larger quantities. In this way,

> **"In the devastated lands of Anatolia, metalworkers who were short of the imported tin that they needed to alloy with copper to make bronze began to take an interest in another metal: iron."**

Anatolia and neighboring lands moved from the Bronze Age to the **Iron Age**.

Phoenicians, Aramaeans, and the Alphabet

On the Mediterranean coast, another Semitic-speaking people, the Phoenicians (fi-NEE-shuhns), benefited from the absence of great powers. The Phoenicians had traditionally lived by seaborne trade, above all with Egypt, and they seem to have been in some way subject to the pharaohs. Now, however, their seaports became wealthy and independent city-states.

The Phoenicians used the forests in their coastal mountains—the famous "cedars of Lebanon"—to build ships that were no longer the converted riverboats of the Egyptians (p. 26). Instead, they had stout internal timber frameworks to strengthen their hulls against wind and wave. Merchant vessels were escorted by purpose-built seagoing warships propelled not only by sails but also by crews of oarsmen, sitting in two rows one above the other, to provide speed and maneuverability. In battle, they sank enemy vessels with bronze-tipped rams projecting from their bows or hooked up alongside and put soldiers aboard.

In their seaworthy vessels, Phoenician merchants ranged throughout the Mediterranean and out into the Atlantic as far as the British Isles in search of timber, metal, and slaves. They set up trading stations on the coastlines of Africa and Spain that eventually turned into colonies (see Map 3.2 on page 50). Both as traders and as settlers, the Phoenicians linked the peoples of southern Europe with the region of civilization between the Indian Ocean and the Mediterranean Sea.

Meanwhile, in Mesopotamia, the Aramaean and Chaldean nomads adapted, like so many invaders before them, to the civilization that had grown up between the rivers. The Aramaeans in particular established a network of prosperous city-states that dominated the land trade of the region in the same way that the Phoenicians controlled its sea links to the west. And both the Aramaeans and the Phoenicians played a vital role in the transmission of a new and easily learned writing system: the **alphabet**.

Alphabetic writing seems to have developed out of a drastically simplified version of Egyptian hieroglyphs used as early as 1900 B.C. by Semitic immigrants and captives in and around Egypt. Instead of the hundreds of signs and complex rules in hieroglyphic and cuneiform writing, this system had only thirty letters, each representing a single basic sound of speech. Other Semitic peoples, including the Aramaeans and Phoenicians, then started using the alphabet. As the Aramaeans took over inland trade, their tongue, with its alphabetic writing, replaced Akkadian as the international language. Meanwhile, Mediterranean peoples who became advanced enough to feel the need for writing, above all the Greeks, learned the Phoenician version of the alphabet and adapted it to their languages.

LO² Universal Empires: Assyria and Persia

New skills and more intensive trade and travel eventually made it possible for new great powers to arise that would build larger empires than ever before. In an era of limited intercontinental contacts, it was natural for the peoples between the Indian Ocean and the Mediterranean Sea to think of their large and diverse region as "the world," and for the new conquerors to think of themselves as world rulers. Consequently, the empires that they built are often called "universal" (worldwide) **empires**.

Assyria

The Assyrians had lived for centuries in a small homeland along the middle and upper reaches of the Tigris River (Map 2.1 on page 35), more or less successfully holding off powerful neighbors such as Babylonia and the Hittites. But after 1200 B.C., the Assyrians saw an opportunity to fill the regional power vacuum—to begin with, by controlling the profitable trade routes between western Asia and the Mediterranean. As they gradually accomplished this aim, they began to conceive of the larger goal of a universal empire. As one of their rulers would declare, "I am the legitimate king of the world . . . of all four rims of the earth . . . king of kings."

The rise of Assyria began shortly after 900 B.C. with the takeover of Aramaean city-states in northern Mesopotamia. Then the Assyrians struck north and west and took over the southern portion of Asia Minor, as well as Syria, Phoenicia, and part of the Israelite territories in Palestine. By 700 B.C., they had also added the Chaldean-ruled territories of southern Mesopotamia, including Babylon,

alphabet
A writing system in which each letter represents a basic sound of speech.

empire
A territory larger than a kingdom, including many different peoples, and governed by a single ruler (an emperor or empress) or by a single community such as a city-state.

Erich Lessing/Art Resource, NY

≪ **Long-Distance Haulage** Phoenician ships haul cedar logs while sea creatures look on. The logs are beginning a lengthy journey by sea, river, and road from the Mediterranean land of Lebanon to the palace of the Assyrian King Sargon II, far upstream on the River Tigris, where they will end up as roof beams. The king, who reigned about 700 B.C., was proud of importing these large items from a distant land; this depiction comes from his palace.

infantry
Soldiers who fight on foot.

cavalry
Soldiers who fight on horseback.

to their possessions. The empire reached its greatest extent in the seventh century B.C., when the rest of Palestine and most of Egypt fell under its control (Map 2.1 on page 35).

The Assyrians were not a numerous people, but they partly made up for this by innovations in military organization, tactics, and weaponry. All adult males were subject to military service, and war was glorified and pursued as the principal business of the kingdom. The army relied on the combined striking power of chariots, light **infantry** (archers and slingers), and massed heavy infantry clad in bronze helmets and armor and wielding iron swords and spears. Eventually, the Assyrians made use of another innovation, brought by nomadic invaders from the steppes: horse-riding **cavalry**. Their engineers also devised battering rams, undermining, and movable siege towers to break down the defenses of cities (see photo).

As an aid to conquest and to hold down the peoples they conquered, the Assyrians pursued a policy of deliberate terror—skinning and mutilating, impaling, burning alive, and displaying stacks of human skulls. The Assyrians were not the first conquerors lovingly to depict their own bloody deeds (see photo on page 21), and they were certainly not the last to use systematic atrocities to build and maintain their empires. But Assyrian palace art proclaims their acts of violence in exceptionally vivid and explicit images and inscriptions.

Even so, the task of holding such a widespread empire was, in the long run, too much for a small people. The imperial masters relied increasingly on drafted or hired troops drawn from subject peoples, but in the end their strength drained

> *"With battle and assault I stormed the city, I took it. Eight hundred of their fighting men I struck down with the sword, with their corpses I filled the streets of their city, with their blood I dyed their houses. Many men I captured alive with my hand, and I carried off great spoil from them; the city I destroyed, I devastated, I burned with fire."*
>
> —Ashurnasirpal II, ca. 875 B.C.

An Assyrian Emperor's Resume: Ferocious Conquests a Specialty Read an Assyrian ruler's account of how he dealt with a disloyal kingdom.

Ancient Near Eastern Art: New Light on an Assyrian Palace (http://www.metmuseum.org/explore/anesite/html/el_ane_newfirst.htm) Learn more about Assyrian palace art.

 **Simulation to Learn About Ancient Cultures** Participate in a simulation of life as a warrior in Nineveh in 664 B.C.

away. Finally, they were overcome by a rebellion of the Chaldeans of Babylon, aided by invaders from the north and east. In 612 B.C., their high-walled capital at Nineveh, on the Tigris, was broken into and burned. Most of their army and royal family were wiped out, and the Assyrians sank into obscurity, never to rise again.

All the same, the Assyrian kings succeeded in building the largest regional empire so far. This was the first truly imperial government. Conquered lands were usually organized as provinces, with Assyrian nobles appointed as governors by the king. Some local rulers were permitted to keep their lands, in return for regular payments and under the watchful eyes of Assyrian officials. Systematic intelligence and administrative reports flowed to the capital city of Nineveh from all corners of the empire—helped by a well-developed road system, for the Assyrians were forerunners of the Persians and Romans in grasping the importance of good roads for great empires (pp. 36, 115).

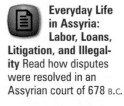 **Everyday Life in Assyria: Labor, Loans, Litigation, and Illegality** Read how disputes were resolved in an Assyrian court of 678 B.C.

The Assyrians continued the traditions of Mesopotamian civilization in literature, culture, and the arts and played a vital role in transmitting them to future generations. The world's first known great library was established by the Assyrian ruler Ashurbanipal (ah-shoor-BAH-nee-pahl) at Nineveh (NIN-uh-vuh) about 650 B.C. It contained some twenty thousand tablets with cuneiform texts in the Sumerian as well as the Akkadian languages, and provided the key to present-day knowledge of ancient Mesopotamia when it was excavated in the nineteenth century A.D.

Persia

The power vacuum left by the fall of Assyria was briefly filled by the Chaldean rulers who had liberated Babylonia and who went on to conquer lands as far away as Palestine. But this Neo-Babylonian Empire, as modern scholars call it, soon fell victim to yet another empire-building people, the Persians.

The Persians, together with their neighbors the Medes, were peoples of Indo-European origin (p. 20) who had moved into the territories to the east of Mesopotamia from about 1000 B.C. onward. Media and Persia formed the western part of a vast plateau, much of it desert and fringed to the north and west by mountain ranges that stretched all the way to India. But

Siege Warfare Assyrian engineers adjust a chain holding a battering ram that they will swing against a city gate, and tunnelers undermine the walls. Defending archers take aim against the besiegers, attacking archers counter them, and defenders fall from their perches. Assyrian methods of attacking fortified positions continued to be used by armies for two thousand years down to the invention of cannon. British Museum Photo © Michael Holford

the region was rich in metals, and farmers there had adopted ingenious methods of exploiting underground water sources. As the wealth and population of the Medes and Persians grew, their rulers began to take an interest in the civilization of Mesopotamia and to intervene in its power politics.

The Persians' rise to empire began when their king Cyrus conquered the Medes in 550 B.C. and took them into partnership for further conquests—on such equal terms that the Greeks used either name, "Persians" or "Medes," to describe the new universal rulers. Thus, in his very first step, Cyrus showed that instead of terrorizing his opponents like the Assyrians, he would seek to win them over by reasonable and decent treatment. Within twenty years after his victory over the Medes, Cyrus was in control of every land from the Indus Valley to the Mediterranean. Four years later (525 B.C.), his son Cambyses added Egypt and Libya to the new empire, making it by far the largest that had ever arisen in the region (see Map 2.1). The Persians were able to hold together this vast empire for two centuries using different methods than the Assyrians.

dualism
The belief in two supremely powerful beings or forces, one good and the other evil, whose conflict shapes the destiny of the world and humans.

 **Simulation to Learn About Ancient Cultures** Participate in a simulation of life in ancient Persia as a government official in Cyrus's empire or a solder for Darius and Xerxes.

Persian Religion: Good, Evil, and Salvation

In religion, the Persians began to break away from traditional polytheism, and their beliefs probably influenced the monotheism of the Jews. The Persian religious thinker Zoroaster (ZAWR-oh-as-ter), who is believed to have lived in the seventh century B.C., preached faith in one God, the author of both good and evil. His followers turned this faith into a **dualism** that

Map 2.1 The Assyrian and Persian Empires

The Assyrians and then the Persians built larger empires than ever before in the lands where Asia and Africa meet. About 660 B.C. the Assyrian Empire included all of Mesopotamia, the Mediterranean's eastern coast, and much of Egypt; in 500 B.C. the Persians ruled most of the region between southeastern Europe, northeastern Africa, and the borders of India, as well as vast lands of nomadic peoples in central Asia. © Cengage Learning

 Interactive Map

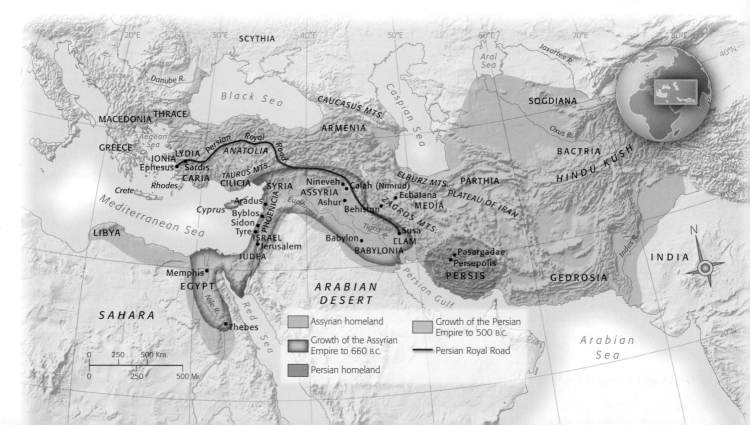

MULTIPLE FACTORS HELD THE PERSIAN EMPIRE TOGETHER FOR TWO CENTURIES:

The Kingship Tradition

- The Persian ruler won the loyalty of his subjects in Mesopotamia by operating within their kingship tradition. He was the "King of Kings," identified with divine will and justice though not himself thought of as a god.

- The "King of Kings" held his subjects in awe: he sat on a gold and blue throne, dressed in purple cloth and laden with jewels, in a huge palace where ordinary mortals were required to lie, face down, before him.

Partnerships with Local Powers

- Positions as King's Friends (leading officials and courtiers), satraps (governors of provinces), and army commanders were generally filled by wealthy landowners and leading warriors. The nobles could look to the king for honors and rewards if they served him well, and the king in turn could make use of their wealth and power in his service.

- The King's Sons and King's Daughters were regularly married off to noble children. The King's Wives played politics behind the scenes, vying to get their sons into positions of power. This pattern of partnership between the ruler and the nobles reinforced by family ties, with the women of the royal court wielding power that buttressed that of the king, was a precedent for many future monarchies, including those of Europe.

Military Might

- Similar in organization and weaponry to the Assyrians, Persian troops constituted the backbone of the heavily armed infantry, which operated together with bow-wielding cavalry and charioteers.

- Large supporting forces, including fleets of warships, were drawn from the conquered populations—Syrians, Phoenicians, Egyptians, and Greeks.

Tolerance of Local Customs

- Taxes and military supplies were rigorously collected, but local customs, languages, and religions were left alone.

As a result, rebellions were unusual, though the Greeks and Egyptians never fully accepted Persian rule.

A Strong Bureaucracy

- The realm was divided into some twenty provinces (satrapies). The satraps ruled with a light hand, under the guiding principles of restraint and tolerance.

- Royal inspectors, the "king's eyes," supervised the work of the satraps and reported directly to the royal palace. They followed existing practice by writing their reports in Aramaic.

- An excellent road system eased the flow of reports and goods between the provinces and the capital (see Map 2.1 on page 35).

- The Persians adopted the use of coins (invented by the Lydians of Asia Minor in the seventh century B.C.) to make payment of taxes easier.

---

taught that the world was the scene of two rival forces: Ahura Mazda, god of goodness and light, and Angra Mainyu, demon of evil and darkness. Righteous humans would go to the heavenly courts of Ahura Mazda upon their death; the wicked would go to hell with Angra Mainyu. At the end of time, however, a savior would appear, miraculously born, to prepare the way for Ahura Mazda's triumph. Angra Mainyu would be made harmless, and all of humanity, including even the captives in hell, would be raised to enjoy eternal bliss. These beliefs were proclaimed in a revered collection of holy writings, the Avesta.

 Virtual Tour of Persepolis (http://www.letsgoiran.com/persepolis/persepolis-travel-guide) Take a tour of Persepolis.

Babylonian astronomers continued, with Persian encouragement, to advance their knowledge of the heavens; one result was their learning how to calculate and predict eclipses of the moon. Persian art and architecture were chiefly adaptations of existing styles and techniques. The most magnificent example, the royal palace at Persepolis, was a successful combination of building and sculptural elements from Assyria, Babylonia, Egypt, and Greece.

The Persian Empire lasted for two hundred years until it was brought down by yet another world conqueror, Alexander the Great, and the Persians gave way to yet another ruling people, the Greeks (pp. 82–83). But in those two centuries, the Persians brought their subject peoples unity, peace, and the freedom of movement and ideas that unity permits, while allowing them to maintain their own identities. United yet diverse, enriched by many different cultural traditions that had grown up over the centuries, the Persian Empire was a high point of three thousand years of civilization in the lands between the Indian Ocean and the Mediterranean Sea.

LO³ The Jews and Monotheism

Of all the changes that took place in the lands between the Indian Ocean and the Aegean Sea after 1200 B.C., one of the most momentous was the appearance of a new kind of religious belief. Alongside traditional polytheism, there appeared the belief in one God, or **monotheism**.

Religion Facts (for Judaism and Zoroastrianism) (http://www.religionfacts.com) Learn more about Judaism and Zoroastrianism.

The new belief involved far more than just the question of how many divine beings were to be worshiped. The one God was thought of as eternal, almighty, all-knowing, the creator of the whole universe, infinitely good, pure spirit yet somehow masculine. He would give humans prosperity and happiness so long as they worshiped and obeyed him alone, rejected all other gods and goddesses, and behaved righteously toward each other. If they did not, he would punish them with misfortune and misery, and for unsearchable reasons he also allowed evil to befall even those who were righteous in his sight. One day, however, he would send a mighty redeemer who would deliver the righteous from all evil, to live in blessedness forever. Meanwhile, his worshipers would form a community united in knowledge of him and obedience to his commands, and guided by holy writings and by specially qualified believers.

Several peoples had beliefs that were forerunners of monotheism and may have influenced its rise. About 1800 B.C., the Egyptian pharaoh Akhenaten had worshiped a single divine power that ruled the whole universe, though his innovations had been rejected after his death (p. 25). A thousand years later, the Persians saw the world as a place of struggle between mighty good and evil forces (p. 35). But above all, monotheism developed out of the beliefs and practices of the Jews and their experiences of triumph and disaster as their region of the world collapsed into chaos, recovered from the crisis, and came under the rule of universal empires.

One Land and Many Gods: The Israelites

For many centuries of their early history, the Jews lived in a single territory, the land of Palestine on the eastern shore of the Mediterranean Sea (Map 2.2). With its rocky landscape, its hot, dry summers, and its cold, wet winters, Palestine had only a limited amount of agricultural wealth to provide a foundation for civilized life. Over many centuries from about 3000 B.C. onward, however, farmers in Palestine and many other Mediterranean lands had learned to get the most from their soil by growing grain together with olive trees and grapevines.

The peoples of Palestine and nearby lands had learned from the ways of life of Anatolia, Egypt, and Mesopotamia, and in recent centuries the Hittites and the Egyptians had fought many wars for empire over them (p. 28). They spoke and wrote Semitic languages (p. 17), and they had links of trade and travel with nearby and distant lands. They had their own pantheon of gods and goddesses, whose chief and father, El, was called by such names as "the Most High" and "El of the Covenant." The ideas of a supreme god and of covenants (formal promises of protection and loyalty binding together the god and the communities that worshiped him) were seemingly important ones in this traditional religion.

> **monotheism**
> The belief in a single, all-powerful, and all-knowing God.

"United yet diverse, enriched by many different cultural traditions that had grown up over the centuries, the Persian Empire was a high point of three thousand years of civilization in the lands between the Indian Ocean and the Mediterranean Sea."

Israel and Its Gods

When the great regional upheaval began, Palestine was caught in the general turmoil. Archeological surveys indicate that the region's thinly populated hill country, lying inland from the Mediterranean coast, filled up with settlers. The remains of their tools and buildings suggest that the newcomers came from the coastlands of Palestine itself as well as from other nearby lands, probably to escape troubles in these less sheltered regions. By 1200 B.C., many of the settlers formed a distinct people. Their name is first mentioned in a monument that an Egyptian pharaoh set up about that date, listing them among defeated enemies: Israel.

The Israelites, as they were usually called at this time,[1] had traditions of much older origins, which were recorded many centuries later in the Hebrew Bible (the Old Testament of the Christian Bible). These traditions spoke of lengthy travels from Mesopotamia to Egypt, beginning with a first forefather,

---

[1]Israel ("He Who Strives with God") was a name taken, according to tradition, by Abraham's grandson. Until about 500 B.C., it was the name used by the people that claimed descent from him, though sometimes they were called Hebrews (from a Semitic word meaning "wanderer"). The name Jews (from the part of Palestine known as Judah) came into use after 500 B.C. The language of the Jews at all periods is known as Hebrew.

Abraham; and of escape from oppression in Egypt and wanderings in the desert that lay to the south of Palestine, led by a great prophet, Moses. Both as a wandering and as a settled people, the Bible says, the Israelites were guided and protected by a mighty god, Yahweh, who had covenanted with them to bring them prosperity and victory so long as they served and honored "no other gods before me."

The Bible also records, however, that the Israelites regularly "lusted after other gods." At first, these deities were probably the traditional gods and goddesses of the nearby lands from which the Israelite settlers came, whom they saw nothing wrong in worshiping alongside Yahweh. As the Israelites developed into a separate people from their neighbors, however, their traditions of distant origins and Yahweh's guidance became increasingly important to them. They called him sometimes Yahweh and sometimes El, as if they thought of the two supreme gods as one and the same. But in time his name became too holy even to speak, and usually he was called simply "the Lord."

Even so, many or most Israelites did not give up the worship of other deities. Instead, they continued to follow the polytheistic tradition that it was righteous and prudent for humans to worship not just the chief deity of their own community but all gods and goddesses who might influence their destinies (p. 15). Priests and prophets might speak of "The Lord, whose name is Jealous," and ask, "Who is God, except the Lord?" But it took many centuries for the Israelites to decide that the priests and prophets were right.

David, Solomon, and the Temple

Initially, the Israelite settlers led a simple village way of life without central government. As their region recovered from the crisis, however, their society became more complex. In the power vacuum left by the collapse of the Hittite kingdom and the weakening of Egypt, they fought, allied, and intermarried with neighboring peoples, led by war chieftains who grew into hereditary kings. Finally, about 1000 B.C., there came a time of triumph, when King David conquered the important settlement of Jerusalem and made it his seat of government.

 **(http://www.pbs.org/wnet/heritage/episode1/presentations/1.6.1-1.html)** Listen to a biblical account of the Israelites' conquest of Canaan in the late thirteenth century B.C. and discover how archeologists investigate that story.

As in every other kingdom, the royal city became the home of the god that the rulers served. David's son Solomon built the Temple in Jerusalem—a magnificent house for Yahweh, where priests served him with plentiful offerings and sacrifices like any other leading deity. Like other deities, too, Yahweh was present in his Temple—but not in the usual form of a "graven image," for he had forbidden his people to make any such objects of worship. Instead, in the midst of the Temple there stood the Ark of the Covenant, a wooden chest sheathed in gold that was at once a container for writings of Yahweh's covenant with Israel and the throne and footstool of the unseen god. But Solomon also made

sure not to neglect other mighty deities. He built several other sanctuaries near Jerusalem, among them one for Ashtoreth, the local version of the ancient fertility goddess Ishtar (p. 18).

Kings and Prophets

As Israelite society became more complex, it also became more liable to conflict. Resentment grew against its newly powerful kings, and when Solomon died about 950 B.C., most of Israel rebelled. Yahweh's people were divided between two kingdoms: a larger one, Israel, under new rulers; and the southern kingdom of Judah, including Jerusalem, still ruled by kings of David's line.

With kings now ruling as servants of divine power, questions of which divine power they were to serve became more urgent and divisive than before. Most rulers continued to worship other deities alongside Yahweh, but time and again, Yahweh's prophets openly resisted the traditional-minded kings and

Map 2.2 **The Israelites and Their Neighbors**

About 1200 B.C. the Israelites lived mostly inland from the eastern Mediterranean coast. They were a farming people, unlike their seafaring neighbors, the Phoenicians, and their rivals the Philistines, who controlled most of the actual coastline. By 800 B.C. they had expanded but also divided into two kingdoms, Israel and Judah, which then became victims of the conquering Assyrians and Babylonians. © Cengage Learning

 Interactive Map

threatened them and their subjects with Yahweh's wrath. The prophets also denounced such features of social life in Israel and Judah as kings who stole the property of their subjects, judges who sold verdicts, and rich landowners who took over the farms of debt-ridden peasants. Prophets were sometimes deeply involved in power struggles within the two kingdoms, and one of them, Elisha, even sponsored the bloody overthrow of a dynasty in Israel.

But what motivated the prophets was always the belief that Yahweh was not being properly worshiped and obeyed. Above all, they condemned idols—the images and other objects on which worshipers of the gods and goddesses focused their love and fear of divine power. Idols, said the prophets, were "abominations"—not just forbidden by Yahweh's "jealousy" but unworthy of worship because the beings they represented were evil or powerless. Yahweh's people, the prophets declared, must finally choose between him and the rival deities. The prophet Elijah, reproaching worshipers in the kingdom of Israel who turned to the weather-god Baal in time of drought about 850 B.C., asked them: "How long will you go limping with two different opinions? If the Lord is God, follow him; but if Baal, then follow him."

> ❝*How long will you go limping with two different opinions? If the Lord is God, follow him; but if Baal, then follow him.*❞

Many Lands and One God: The Jews

Yahweh's people went on "limping with two opinions" all the same, until Mesopotamian world conquerors reached out to destroy the Israelite kingdoms. In 722 B.C., the Assyrians conquered the kingdom of Israel and made it a province of their empire. After Assyria's fall, the Chaldeans invaded Judah, and in 587 B.C. they captured Jerusalem and destroyed the Temple. Both disasters were followed by massive deportations to Mesopotamia, and when Judah fell, many of its people left for Egypt. Villagers in Palestine still worshiped Yahweh, but they were leaderless and mixed with settlers brought in by the conquerors. Priests, scribes, warriors, landowners, and many people of lower rank were now in exile.

God, His People, and the Nations

It was exactly these disasters that first made the monotheistic belief in Yahweh the dominant religion of his people. Most of the exiles from Israel and many from Judah lost their identity as Yahweh's people and merged with the nations among whom they were scattered. The only worshipers left to him were those who truly believed that he was the one almighty God that the prophets had proclaimed him to be. The true believers now listened to new prophets, who declared that, far from proving Yahweh's weakness, the disasters were proof of his worldwide power. The deportations and the Temple's destruction were God's punishment of his people for breaking their covenant with him. According to "the word of the Lord" as proclaimed by Isaiah about 700 B.C., even the mighty Assyrian king was merely "the rod of my anger."

diaspora
The dispersion of Jews to countries outside of Palestine.

Furthermore, he who punished could also forgive. If the Israelites turned their hearts back to God and fulfilled their covenanted duties to him, then sooner or later, in the words of Jeremiah (600 B.C.), "He who scattered Israel will gather him." Prophecies said to be by Isaiah declared that God would send a great king of David's line to deliver his people from oppression and evil, or perhaps a "suffering servant" who would take their sins upon himself. When that day came, the Temple would be rebuilt as "a house of prayer for all peoples," evil and suffering and war would cease, and "the earth shall be full of the knowledge of the Lord, as the waters cover the sea." The conquering universal empires that had destroyed the traditional Israelite nation would give way to a benign universal empire ruled by an Israelite king, in which all nations would unite in the worship of the one God.

Sure enough, when the Persians overthrew the Chaldeans and established the largest and most tolerant empire so far, they permitted the exiles to return to Palestine. By 515 B.C., the Temple was rebuilt, and again Yahweh was served with offerings and sacrifices in the city of David—though the "Holy of Holies" was now an empty chamber, since the Ark of the Covenant had not survived the troubles.

Many prophecies were still unfulfilled, however. God had not restored his people to their whole land, but only to Judah, from which they took their name as Jews. Instead of a God-sent king, the Jews were governed by the high priests of the Temple, appointed by the Persian rulers. Furthermore, most Jews did not return but continued to live in what came to be known as the **diaspora (dahy-AS-per-uh)**. In Mesopotamia, and later in Judah as well, they gave up Hebrew as their everyday tongue in favor of the internationally spoken Aramaic language, and in Egypt, they eventually came to speak Greek.

If the scattered Jews were to survive as the chosen people of the one God until the day of full deliverance arrived, they must make drastic changes in their religious practices so as never again to break their renewed covenant. These changes began among the exiled remnant in Babylon, were enforced on the villagers of Judah by returning exiles, and eventually spread to Egypt to form a new pattern of worship and life for Jews in every land.

The Holy Writings

To make sure that they strictly observed their covenant with God, more than ever before the Jews needed to put in writing the terms of the covenant and the history of God's dealings with

JERUSALEM BESIEGED: THE ASSYRIAN KING SENNACHERIB'S ACCOUNT

Sennacherib had the story of his royal deeds written down in many copies, one of which was found in A.D. 1830 in the ruins of his palace in Nineveh. Here he describes how in 701 B.C. he crushed a widespread rebellion by his vassal kings in Palestine and Syria, supported by Assyria's rival "great power," Egypt. One of the rebels was King Hezekiah of the Israelite kingdom of Judah. Sennacherib could not take Jerusalem, but he inflicted great casualties on the Israelite army and forced Hezekiah and other rebels into submission. Sennacherib is rather vague about the events at Jerusalem; for a contrasting account by the Jewish prophet Isaiah, see the document link below.

"Tamartu-presents" are gifts given by a defeated enemy; "katru-presents" are gifts by way of regular tribute.

In my third campaign I marched against Hatti. Luli, king of Sidon, whom the terror-inspiring glamour of my lordship had overwhelmed, fled far overseas and perished. The awe-inspiring splendor of the "Weapon" of Ashur, my lord, overwhelmed his strong cities such as Great Sidon, Little Sidon, Bit-Zitti, Zaributu, Mahalliba, Ushu, Akzib and Akko, all his fortress cities, walled and well provided with food and water for his garrisons, and they bowed in submission to my feet. I installed Ethbaal upon the throne to be their king and imposed upon him tribute due to me as his overlord to be paid annually without interruption.

As to all the kings of Amurru—Menahem from Sam-simuruna, Tubalu from Sidon, Abdiliti from Arvad, Urumilki from Byblos, Mitinti from Ashdod, Buduili from Beth-Ammon, Kammusun-adbi from Moab and Aiarammu from Edom, they brought sumptuous gifts and—fourfold—their heavy tamartu-presents to me and kissed my feet. Sidqia, however, king of

Ashkelon, who did not bow to my yoke, I deported and sent to Assyria, his family-gods, himself, his wife, his children, his brothers, all the male descendants of his family. I set Sharru-ludari, son of Rukibtu, their former king, over the inhabitants of Ashkelon and imposed upon him the payment of tribute and of katru-presents due to me as overlord—and he (now) pulls the straps of my yoke!

In the continuation of my campaign I besieged Beth-Dagon, Joppa, Banai-Barqa, Azuru, cities belonging to Sidqia who did not bow to my feet quickly enough; I conquered them and carried their spoils away. The officials, the patricians and the common people of Ekron—who had thrown Padi, their king, into fetters because he was loyal to his solemn oath sworn by the god Ashur, and had handed him over to Hezekiah, the Jew and he [Hezekiah] held him in prison, unlawfully, as if he [Padi] be an enemy—had become afraid and had called for

them. Documents already existed that told of God's promises and commands to his people and his dealings with them before the exile. Probably during and not long after the exile, these writings were combined and edited to produce books that in time came to be accepted as holy by Jews everywhere. Many new works, mostly telling of God's utterances through his prophets and his raising up and casting down of rulers and nations, were written from the time of the exile onward that also came to be considered as truthfully revealing God's deeds and will.

By sometime after 200 B.C., all the books of the present-day Hebrew Bible had been written, though it took until after A.D. 200 for Jewish leaders to settle on the **canon**—the exact list of works to be considered holy. In this way, the Hebrew Bible came into being—not as a single book, but as a collection of books that grew over many centuries.

Partly because the Hebrew Bible evolved in this way, it often makes contrasting statements about the one God. In one

book, for example, Yahweh insists to Moses on getting his share of every slaughtered animal, yet in another God declares to a prophet after the exile: "I desire steadfast love and not sacrifice, the knowledge of God rather than burnt-offerings." And many Bible stories depict Yahweh as a relentless war-god, while other stories tell of God's goodness to all nations, including even the terrible Assyrians.

"In the Beginning . . .": The Hebrews Explain Creation Read the Bible story of how God created the world.

Many of the features of God as portrayed in the Hebrew Bible were not new. Other peoples in the lands between the Indian Ocean and the Aegean Sea had already worshiped mighty creators of heaven and earth, inconceivably ancient and mysterious holy beings, dreadful judges of the righteous and the wicked, loving "shepherds" of individual humans, majestic wielders of supreme divine power, and deities to whom they were bound by covenants (pp. 15, 18, 25). But no earlier god had had all these features at once, and few had been without

help upon the kings of Egypt and the bowmen, the chariot-corps and the cavalry of the king of Ethiopia, an army beyond counting—and they actually had come to their assistance. In the plain of Eltekeh, their battle lines were drawn up against me and they sharpened their weapons. Upon a trust-inspiring oracle given by Ashur, my lord, I fought with them and inflicted a defeat upon them. In the melee of the battle, I personally captured alive the Egyptian charioteers with their princes and also the charioteers of the king of Ethiopia. I besieged Eltekeh and Timnah, conquered them and carried their spoils away. I assaulted Ekron and killed the officials and patricians who had committed the crime and hung their bodies on poles surrounding the city. The common citizens who were guilty of minor crimes, I considered prisoners of war. The rest of them, those who were not accused of crimes and misbehavior, I released. I made Padi, their king, come from Jerusalem and set him as their lord on the throne, imposing upon him the tribute due to me as overlord.

As to Hezekiah, the Jew, he did not submit to my yoke, I laid siege to 46 of his strong cities, walled forts and to the countless small villages in their vicinity, and conquered them by means of well-stamped earth-ramps, and battering-rams brought thus near to the walls combined with the attack by foot soldiers, using mines, breeches as well as sapper work. I drove out of them 200,150 people, young and old, male and female, horses, mules, donkeys, camels, big and small cattle beyond counting, and considered them booty. Himself I made a prisoner in Jerusalem, his royal residence, like a bird in a cage. I surrounded him with earthwork in order to molest those who were leaving his city's gate. His towns which I had plundered, I took away from his country and gave them over to Mitinti, king of Ashdod, Padi, king of Ekron, and Sillibel, king of Gaza. Thus

I reduced his country, but I still increased the tribute and the katru-presents due to me as his overlord which I imposed later upon him beyond the former tribute, to be delivered annually. Hezekiah himself, whom the terror-inspiring splendor of my lordship had overwhelmed and whose irregular and elite troops which he had brought into Jerusalem, his royal residence, in order to strengthen it, had deserted him, did send me, later, to Nineveh, my lordly city, together with 30 talents of gold, 800 talents of silver, precious stones, antimony, large cuts of red stone, couches inlaid with ivory, nimedu-chairs inlaid with ivory, elephant-hides, ebony-wood, boxwood and all kinds of valuable treasures, his own daughters, concubines, male and female musicians. In order to deliver the tribute and to do obeisance as a slave he sent his personal messenger.

EXPLORING THE SOURCE

1. What methods did the Assyrians use to bring the rulers of the region back into line?

2. Why does Sennacherib take full responsibility for and boast openly of the brutal deeds of his armies? How does this contrast with present-day behavior of commanders whose armies commit brutal deeds?

Source: James B. Pritchard, ed., *Ancient Near Eastern Texts Relating to the New Testament*, 3d ed. (Princeton, N.J.: Princeton University Press, 1969), pp. 287–288.

Jerusalem Besieged: The Prophet Isaiah's Account of Sennacherib's Siege Read a contrasting account of the siege by the prophet Isaiah.

---

humanlike weaknesses and vices or been considered the only deity to be worshiped.

Men and Women in the Bible

One divine feature that the Hebrew Bible leaves no doubt about is that God is best described as masculine and that he is to be served by male priests. All the same, the Bible's creation story says that humans were made by God "male and female" in his own image. In the Bible, both women and men share a likeness to God.

A vast range of different relationships between men and women appears in the Bible. In early wars in Palestine, the Bible says, Deborah the prophetess and Barak the warrior jointly led Israel to victory—but the treacherous Delilah used womanly wiles to coax the mighty Samson into revealing the secret of his strength, and then betrayed him to Israel's enemies. A rapist and his victim, God-given law decreed, must both be stoned to death unless the woman had cried out for help. A good wife

is "far above rubies," said a proverb—that is, a wife who could run a large farm on her own while her husband spent his time as a prominent citizen "sitting among the elders of the land."

These and many other proverbs, laws, and stories provided examples of relations between men and women to be imitated or avoided in many future centuries of Western civilization. All of them took for granted a prevailing inequality that was much the same as in any other society at the time.

Where the Bible is exceptional, however, is in telling a story of how inequality began. God formed Eve, the first woman, says the Bible, from the flesh of Adam, the first man. It was Eve who gave in to temptation and persuaded Adam to eat the fruit of the tree of knowledge against God's command, and as part of her punishment, God decreed that her husband would rule over her. Scholars disagree about the exact meaning of the story, but it does seem to say that some kind of male dominance is God-given. The story does not say that Eve's disobedience was worse than Adam's, however, and nowhere does the Hebrew

Bible say that women as a group are weaker or more sinful than men as a group because they are "daughters of Eve." These ideas were developed from the Bible story in later times.

A People Apart: The Law

The single most important part of the Hebrew Bible was its first five books, called the Torah ("Instruction" or "Law"). Much of the Torah was a vast legal code, collecting all the laws that Yahweh was said to have given to Moses. The code covered every field of life, including crime and punishment, marriage and divorce, debt and credit, the conduct of worship, ritual purity (bodily cleanliness in the presence of God), and righteousness in general. Included in the Law were the Ten Commandments, the punishment of some offenses on the principle of "eye for eye, tooth for tooth" as in Hammurabi's code (p. 18), the requirements of male circumcision and the purification of women after childbirth, and the prohibition on eating the flesh of animals considered unclean.

Many of the laws were generally similar to those of other peoples, but the laws of ritual purity were exceptionally strict. It was normal for polytheistic worshipers to purify themselves before sacrificing, but the Jewish laws applied to the whole

> "*Monotheism was one of the two longest-lasting legacies to later civilizations from the changing world between the Indian Ocean and the Aegean Sea after 1200 B.C.*"

people all the time. The reason was that God's covenant was with the whole people, and they must all obey his commands if he was to fulfill his promises. Accordingly, the Jews now began rigorously obeying the Law. And because obeying the Law was so important, for the first time the Jews took to keeping apart from Gentiles (non-Jews)—refusing, for instance, to intermarry or eat with them.

In addition, to avoid any influences from Gentile religious practices, the worship of God with offerings and sacrifices was now supposed to take place only in the Temple in Jerusalem. Outside the holy city, the religious practice of the Jews came to consist mainly of study of the holy writings and prayer and praise to God. It became customary for them to meet for these purposes on the Sabbath, the seventh day of the week, which God had commanded to be kept holy. The buildings where they met for prayer and study, and the congregations that met in these buildings, came to be known as **synagogues** (from the Greek word for "meetinghouses"). An elite of synagogue leaders grew up—men who could read and write and who were respected in their congregations for obeying, understanding, and interpreting the Law. These religious guides replaced the prophets, and gradually came to rival the Temple priests, as leaders of the Jews.

Heedful of the Bible and obedient to the Law, the Jews became what they had never been before, a people separate and apart from other peoples and forming their own widely scattered but closely knit community, the "House of Israel." But

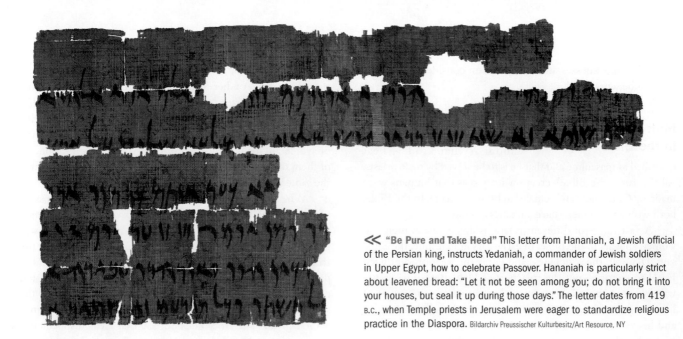

« **"Be Pure and Take Heed"** This letter from Hananiah, a Jewish official of the Persian king, instructs Yedaniah, a commander of Jewish soldiers in Upper Egypt, how to celebrate Passover. Hananiah is particularly strict about leavened bread: "Let it not be seen among you; do not bring it into your houses, but seal it up during those days." The letter dates from 419 B.C., when Temple priests in Jerusalem were eager to standardize religious practice in the Diaspora. Bildarchiv Preussischer Kulturbesitz/Art Resource, NY

their apartness, the Jews believed, would not last forever. The prophecies of the advent of a redeemer-king and the conversion of the Gentiles found their way into the Bible as authoritative statements of what God had in store for the human race as a whole. Meanwhile, Gentiles could "join the House of Israel" by accepting all the obligations of the Law. Gentiles could even live as "God-fearers" on the margins of Jewish congregations, believing in the one God without full observance. The Jews saw themselves as preserving and deepening a closeness between humans and God that would one day be shared by all nations.

In these ways, many present-day features of Judaism came into existence in Persian times, and some of these features were inherited by Christianity and Islam. These monotheisms, too, would have authoritative holy writings, and ministers of religion who acted as leaders of congregations and interpreters of the writings. Both would despise the gods and goddesses as imaginary or evil. They would expect the conversion of the human race to one belief in one God. They would look forward to the advent of a God-sent man of power who would rule in blessedness forever. And they would await the day of his coming as organized worldwide communities of believers.

For the moment, these were the beliefs of a scattered minority in a world where most people worshiped the traditional gods and goddesses. Still, monotheism was one of the two longest-lasting legacies to later civilizations from the changing world between the Indian Ocean and the Aegean Sea after 1200 B.C. The other was the adoption of a civilized way of life by a European barbarian people living on the region's northwestern edge: the Greeks.

 Listen to a synopsis of Chapter 2.

CHAPTER 3

THE FIRST EUROPEAN CIVILIZATION: THE GREEKS, 2200–400 B.C.

LEARNING OBJECTIVES

AFTER READING THIS CHAPTER, YOU SHOULD BE ABLE TO DO THE FOLLOWING:

LO¹ Describe the way of life of the barbarian peoples of Europe after the Agricultural Revolution.

LO² Discuss the evolution of early Greek civilization through a series of contacts with other peoples of the lands between the Mediterranean Sea and the Indian Ocean.

LO³ Compare the city-states of Sparta and Athens, and describe how the Athenian form of democracy operated.

> "WITHIN CLASSICAL GREEK CIVILIZATION THERE APPEARED IDEAS, ART FORMS, AND TYPES OF GOVERNMENT WHOSE INFLUENCE ON WESTERN CIVILIZATION HAS LASTED DOWN TO THE PRESENT DAY."

The Greeks began as one of many European **barbarian** peoples—that is, they had a distinctive way of life, based on farming and warfare, that was widespread in western Europe. About 2000 B.C., they began to migrate into Europe's southeastern region, within easy reach of the peoples of Asia Minor, Mesopotamia, and Egypt. As a result, the Greeks began to share in and adapt the more advanced ways of life of the peoples they encountered—something that would happen to European barbarian peoples over and over again in the next three thousand years.

The earliest Greek civilization was very much an offshoot of the ways of life of their eastern neighbors. It shared in the crisis and recovery of the lands between the Mediterranean Sea and the Indian Ocean (pp. 32–33) and finally emerged as "classical" Greek civilization about 800 B.C. Every feature of this renewed Greek civilization was still deeply influenced by their neighbors, but this time, the Greeks had created something new and distinctive. Within classical Greek civilization, there appeared ideas, art forms, and types of government whose influence on Western civilization has lasted down to the present day.

In particular, Greek city-states were the first to practice citizen participation in government—on a restricted basis in oligarchies like Sparta and on a much freer and wider basis in democracies like Athens. The city-states also traded and colonized along the northern coastlands of the Mediterranean Sea, and brought their distinctive civilization to many barbarian peoples of Mediterranean Europe—above all, Italy. They were also innovators in warfare, developing methods of fighting by land and sea that, shortly after 500 B.C., enabled them to preserve their independence against the mighty kings of Persia, the universal rulers of the time (pp. 35–36)—a role in which the Greeks would eventually replace them.

Test your knowledge before you read this chapter.

What do you think?

The practice of citizen participation in government is the most important legacy of ancient Greece.

Strongly Disagree						Strongly Agree
1	2	3	4	5	6	7

≪ Citadel and Shrine The Athenian Acropolis was already ancient when its temples were rebuilt after Persian invaders destroyed them in the fifth century B.C. The Parthenon (right) was the "Place of the Maiden"—the "home" of the city-state's virgin goddess, Athena. The Erechtheum (left) was named after Erechtheus, a mythical early god-king whom democratic Athens still venerated. The fortress wall dates from the Middle Ages, but follows the line of one built shortly before the temples.

Kevin Schafer/Corbis

45

barbarian
A term used to describe the distinctive way of life based on farming, warfare, and tribal organization that became widespread in Europe beginning around 2500 B.C.

megaliths
Massive rough-cut stones used to construct monuments and tombs.

tribe
A social and political unit consisting of a group of communities held together by common interests, traditions, and real or mythical ties of kinship.

LO¹ The European Barbarians

Over three thousand years up to the time of the Persian Empire, civilization had spread from its Sumerian and Egyptian homelands right across southwestern Asia and northeastern Africa, and other regions of civilization had also arisen in India, China, and the Western Hemisphere. Elsewhere, however, most people still lived the prehistoric village life that had emerged from the Agricultural Revolution (pp. 8–11), including in the lands stretching two thousand miles northwestward from the eastern Mediterranean Sea that we today call Europe.

The rulers, priests, and scribes of lands between the Indian Ocean and the Mediterranean Sea probably thought of these early Europeans merely as distant suppliers of raw materials and slaves and as occasionally troublesome raiders and invaders. Yet, it was out of the encounter between the peoples of prehistoric Europe and their southeastern neighbors that Western civilization would eventually be born.

The Earliest Europeans

Even before this historic encounter, the way of life of the peoples of Europe had undergone many changes and advances. By 4000 B.C., farming and village life had spread throughout the continent. With them came an increase in population and wealth, and by 3500 B.C. there were peoples in western Europe who were numerous and well organized enough to construct ceremonial monuments consisting of circles and rows of huge upright boulders, as well as massive earthen tombs and fortifications. Many of these **megalithic** structures (from the Greek words for "large boulder") have survived to the present day. Underneath some of the earthworks, archaeologists have discovered traces of furrows in the soil on which they were originally built—evidence that the peoples of this region were the first to use a revolutionary agricultural tool, the plow (p. 9).

Perhaps the most impressive single early European achievement was Stonehenge, a huge open-air monument built by a prosperous farming and trading people in the west of England, probably as a religious center. It was repeatedly rebuilt over a

An interactive exploration of life in Europe during the Iron Age, created by the BBC (http://www.bbc.co.uk/history/ancient/british_prehistory/launch_gms_ironage_life.shtml) Explore life in prehistoric Europe in this interactive game.

CHRONOLOGY

3500 B.C.	Megalithic structures constructed in Europe
2500 B.C.	Indo-European nomads from the steppes migrate into Europe; European barbarian way of life evolves
2200 B.C.	Minoan civilization takes root in Crete; Greeks arrive in southeastern Europe
1600 B.C.	Greek fortified settlements along the Aegean develop Mycenaean civilization
1400 B.C.	Destruction of Minoan towns
1200 B.C.	Mycenaean civilization falls; beginning of "Dark Ages" of Greek history
800 B.C.	Recovery in the Aegean; Greek city-states form
494–445 B.C.	Persian Wars
460–430 B.C.	Golden Age of Athens

period of several hundred years, until it reached its final form about 2000 B.C. The monument consists of about 160 massive boulders, weighing up to 50 tons each, all of which had to be dragged many miles to the site. Forty of the largest boulders were trimmed with stone tools to form neatly rectangular structural components. These were set upright with others placed horizontally on top of them as crosspieces. Together with the other boulders, they were arranged in four circular or horseshoe-shaped groups one inside the other, all carefully aligned to the movements of the sun and the moon. The structure, much of which is still standing today (see photo on page 47), is testimony to the level of wealth, organization, and skills reached by the peoples of prehistoric Europe.

Stonehenge Decoded, a National Geographic Special on New Findings (http://channel.nationalgeographic.com/episode/stonehenge-decoded-3372#tab-Overview)] Learn about the latest discoveries and theories regarding the mystery of Stonehenge.

The Barbarian Way of Life

The early Europeans cannot have had any sense of a common identity, but in time most of them came to share a distinctive way of life. This was probably the result of migrations of Indo-European nomads from the steppes (grasslands) that bordered Europe on the east (p. 20). From about 2500 B.C. onward, Indo-European peoples moved into Europe just as they did into Asia Minor and Persia, and under the influence of the newcomers, the settled peoples of the region began to form into new ethnic

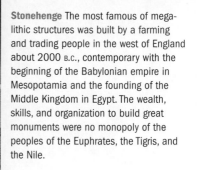

Stonehenge The most famous of megalithic structures was built by a farming and trading people in the west of England about 2000 B.C., contemporary with the beginning of the Babylonian empire in Mesopotamia and the founding of the Middle Kingdom in Egypt. The wealth, skills, and organization to build great monuments were no monopoly of the peoples of the Euphrates, the Tigris, and the Nile.

Royalty-Free/Corbis

groups whose way of life was a mixture of their traditional patterns and Indo-European influences.

Instead of their earlier tongues, the peoples of the region began to speak languages of Indo-European origin that were the distant ancestors of Greek and Latin, as well as of most European languages today. In other ways, too, their way of life underwent important changes. Throughout much of Europe, there appeared elites of warriors—often Indo-European–style charioteers and horsemen—whose lives centered around strength and courage, comradeship and loyalty, contests and battle. In addition to the deities of earth and fertility and the dominant mother-goddesses that many European peoples had traditionally worshiped, the warriors turned to gods of fatherhood and thunder, metalworking and war. When a leading warrior died, his horses and chariot, his bronze (or later, iron) swords and daggers, and his gold and silver drinking cups would all go to the grave with him—presumably so that he could go on riding, fighting, and drinking as a comrade of the gods in the afterlife.

> *"When a leading warrior died, his horses and chariot, his bronze (or later, iron) swords and daggers, and his gold and silver drinking cups would all go to the grave with him—presumably so that he could go on riding, fighting, and drinking as a comrade of the gods in the afterlife."*

Next to the warrior would lie his wife, with her jewelry and her fine textiles and utensils, so that she, too, could go on fulfilling her role in the afterlife—that of presiding over a household made wealthy by farming and war. She may even have been thought of as sharing in her husband's delights. To judge from the reports of Greek and Roman writers about the barbarian peoples of their time, women shared the warrior values of their menfolk. They went to war along with the men—not only to bring them food and bind their wounds but also to force them back into the fight if they panicked, and sometimes to join in the fighting themselves.

Even for the most warlike Europeans, however, the main business of life was farming, adapted in various ways to the different regions of the continent. They lived in villages or in big farmsteads that housed several related families; generally, the settlements were widely scattered, for the population was much thinner than in Egypt or Mesopotamia. Groups of villages or farmsteads formed **tribes**, held together by common interests, traditions, and real or mythical ties of kinship. A tribe would meet from time to time to conduct its business and celebrate the festivals of local deities, and would often build itself a massive earth and timber hilltop stronghold. Tribes would often have more or less powerful hereditary chieftains, whom Greek and Roman observers thought of as kings or (more rarely) queens.

Tribes, in turn, formed loose alliances under warrior kings or queens of exceptionally powerful tribes, together with their battle comrades. In good times, the tribal groupings fought each other for metals, slaves, and other items that brought prestige to their possessors or could be exported to Asia Minor, Mesopotamia, or Egypt in return for some of the luxuries of civilization. In bad times, overpopulation and famine sometimes drove them to massive armed migrations such as those of the Sea Peoples (p. 32). Either way, these groupings were mostly temporary. Tribes would join or leave them as suited their hopes and needs, and defeat—or disputes over the rewards of victory—often caused them to fall apart.

In this way, Europe came to be inhabited by peoples who spoke mostly Indo-European languages; who were skilled in farming, metalworking, trade, and warfare; and who were fairly well organized on the local level, but had no cities, written records,

Map 3.1 **The Greek Homeland**

The Greeks settled in mainland Greece from about 2000 B.C. onward, coming as migrants from somewhere farther north. Between 1200 and 800 B.C. they spread to the islands and eastern coastlands of the Aegean Sea. In later times, Greeks continued to migrate across Europe and Asia from the western Mediterranean to the borders of India, but the Aegean region remained the center of the Greek world. © Cengage Learning

Interactive Map

or fixed structures of government. The prehistoric peoples who followed this way of life are customarily called the European barbarians. The word comes from the Greek *barbaros*, which originally meant "non-Greek." Today, people often use the words "barbarian" and "barbaric" to describe those they believe to be less intelligent, refined, or humane than themselves. Scholars, however, use the word with no contemptuous overtones to mean the tribal groups and the way of life that emerged in Europe from about 2500 B.C.

One by one, over a period of three thousand years from 2000 B.C. right down to A.D. 1000, the European barbarian peoples came into contact with civilization. As with the earlier spread of civilization to the farming and nomad peoples of Mesopotamia and Anatolia (pp. 17, 19), the contacts were sometimes peaceful and sometimes warlike, and if the contacts were warlike, the barbarians were sometimes the conquerors and sometimes the victims. But the results were always the same: one by one, the barbarians adopted the ways of life of the civilizations they encountered. The chieftains and warriors of one era became the leaders of civilization in the next, often adapting and changing the form of civilization they had acquired. In this way, civilization eventually spread throughout Europe.

The first such European barbarian people to make contact with civilization were the Greeks. As a result of their encounter with peoples to their south and east from 2000 B.C. onward, the Greeks developed a distinctive civilization of their own—the first to emerge in Europe, and the first that counts as definitely "Western."

LO² The Aegean Encounter

The scene of this encounter was a region stretching from mainland Greece across the Aegean (eh-GEE-uhn) Sea, with its many islands, to the western coastlands of Asia Minor (Map 3.1). The farming wealth of the Aegean region, like that of Palestine (p. 37), came from a combination of grain fields, vineyards, and olive groves that was common throughout the Mediterranean lands. In addition, southeastern Europe was rich in metals and in timber for shipbuilding, so that the Aegean peoples also lived from metalworking, lumberjacking, trade, and piracy. Well before 2000 B.C., the Aegean had come to be a fringe region of civilization, inhabited by relatively advanced and prosperous peoples—none of whom, as yet, were Greeks.

Minoan Civilization

About 2200 B.C., a distinct civilization, known today as Minoan (from Minos, a legendary king), arose on the Aegean island of Crete. Minoan civilization drew its wealth from control of the surrounding seas and from thriving trade with many eastern Mediterranean lands, above all Egypt. As in Egypt, trade was controlled by the rulers, whose business records were written in a script developed locally under Egyptian influence. The ruins of luxurious palaces, as well as elegant jewelry and other surviving objects (see photo), suggest a wealthy and pleasure-loving society in which women played a prominent role—a society devoted to spectacular games resembling present-day bullfights.

Francesco's Mediterranean Voyage, Crete Tour the archeological sites of Minoan civilization in this video.

Artifacts from Minoan Crete in the Heraklion Museum's Collection (http://ancientgreece.org/images/museums/heraklion-mus/index.htm) Explore the art of the Minoans.

(above, center) **The "Master of the Animals"** This Cretan gold pendant, made about 1700 B.C., shows a powerful being with geese in each hand, and bull's horns looming behind him. The depiction of his body and the lotus flowers at his feet show Egyptian influence. The elegance of this piece of jewelry, and no doubt its luck-bringing power, were valued far from its homeland. It was found in the Greek island of Aegina, 200 miles across the sea from Crete. The Ancient Art and Architecture Collection

The Arrival of the Greeks: Mycenaean Civilization

At the time that Minoan civilization arose, great changes were taking place in the lands that stretched for thousands of miles to the north and east of Crete. Many Indo-European peoples were on the move, and about the same time that the Hittites conquered Anatolia (p. 20), another Indo-European–speaking people arrived in the Aegean—the Greeks.

There is no way of knowing exactly when, where, or how the Greeks developed into a separate ethnic group, but at the time that they made their way into their new homeland, they seem to have been a European barbarian people much like any other. They settled among the people that they found in their new homeland, developed a way of life that combined their own traditions and local ones, and eventually came under the influence of nearby Crete. By 1600 B.C., Greek chieftains had established fortified settlements along the mainland's southern shore and on some of the islands, and these settlements had become the centers of a new civilization—the Mycenaean civilization, so called from Mycenae, the first site to be excavated in modern times.

The Mycenaean Greeks were a warlike people whose leading warriors rode into battle in horse-drawn chariots and who protected their settlements with massive walls. They buried their rulers in huge, stone-lined underground chambers together with rich treasures of bronze weapons, as well as magnificent gold and silver jewelry and eating and drinking vessels. The Mycenaeans also adopted many features of Minoan civilization, including its writing, which they adapted to their own early version of the Greek language.

But the Mycenaeans also struggled with the Minoans for control of the commerce of the eastern Mediterranean. The rivalry ended about 1400 B.C. with the destruction of the Minoan towns, perhaps as a result of Mycenaean conquest. Crete became Mycenaean in civilization and eventually Greek in language, and the riches of every land between Egypt and the Black Sea now came by ship to the Mycenaean chieftains of the Greek mainland.

The "Dark Ages"

Mycenaean civilization lasted until shortly after 1200 B.C., when it fell victim to the same regional crisis that involved the downfall of the Hittites and the attacks of the Sea Peoples on Egypt. Exactly what happened in the Aegean is unknown. Perhaps, as later Greek tradition declared, new groups of warlike Greeks overran the region, or perhaps the Mycenaean chiefdoms were weakened by overpopulation and war, and themselves supplied uprooted warriors to the Sea Peoples. What is certain is that around 1150 B.C. Mycenae was sacked and all the other fortified settlements were deserted. The population dropped, the ships

colony
In ancient Greece, a new city-state settled in an oversea territory by a group sponsored by a city-state located elsewhere.

oracle
A priest or priestess who was believed to give answers that were inspired by a god or goddess to questions from worshipers at a temple.

"The minstrels' listeners absorbed the traditional values that the heroic songs celebrated—the values of a warrior aristocracy that was at home on both land and sea."

no longer sailed, and writing fell out of use. The crisis led to the eclipse of civilization for nearly four centuries—a period known as the "Dark Ages" of Greek history.

But the Greeks themselves survived and even expanded their territory: many of them settled across the Aegean on the western coast of Anatolia, which became part of the Greek homeland. In addition, many earlier religious and cultural traditions lived on. Minstrels sang songs of heroic deeds done in the days of "golden Mycenae"—above all of a grand expedition of allied chieftains from Greece to besiege and capture the flourishing city of Troy on the northwestern coast of Anatolia. And the minstrels' listeners absorbed the traditional values that the

heroic songs celebrated—the values of a warrior aristocracy that was at home on both land and sea.

The Renewal of Greek Civilization

By about 800 B.C., the Aegean region, like the lands to its south and east was on the way to recovering from the crisis. Again the population expanded—so rapidly this time that it outran the food supply. Newly forming Greek city-states sent out expeditions to found **colonies**. For two centuries, emigration continued, until by 600 B.C., Greek city-states dotted the coastlines from the Black Sea westward to Spain, and the Greeks had joined the Phoenicians as the leading commercial and seafaring nation of the Mediterranean (Map 3.2).

All the same, the Greeks maintained a sense of oneness, which was expressed above all in their common religion. From all over the Mediterranean, Greek athletes came to compete in the Olympic Games, held every fourth year in honor of Zeus at Olympia in southern Greece. Warriors and statesmen visited the **oracle** of the sun-god, Apollo, at Delphi in central Greece to learn whether their undertakings would succeed. Ordinary

Map 3.2 **Greek and Phoenician Overseas Migration**

IIn the eighth and seventh centuries B.C., as their wealth and population grew, the Greeks joined the Phoenicians as traders, travelers, and settlers across the sea. By 600 B.C., Greek city-states flourished along the coasts of southern Italy and Sicily, Gaul and Spain, North Africa, and the Black Sea. As the philosopher Plato said shortly after 400 B.C., "We Greeks live around the sea like frogs round a pond." © Cengage Learning

Interactive Map

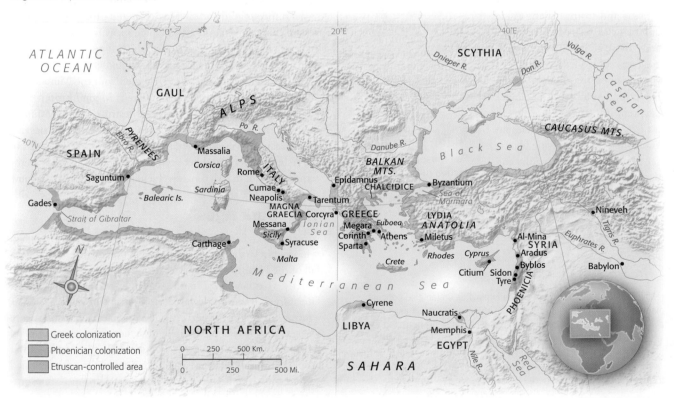

people went on pilgrimage to Eleusis, not far from Athens, to gain the hope of eternal life by sharing in the rites of the fertility goddess, Demeter. These practices, all dating from not long after 800 B.C., formed the main binding force in the renewed civilization of the Greeks.

As much as it inherited from the Aegean past, this renewed civilization was very different from the old one—mainly as a result of new influences from the changing lands to the south and east. From wealthy kingdoms that had arisen in Anatolia on the ruins of the Hittite state, Greek settlers on the coast learned the use of iron tools and weapons as well as coined money. From the Phoenicians, Greek sailors imitated the latest shipbuilding and naval warfare techniques. From the Phoenicians, too, the Greeks relearned the art of writing—this time in its new alphabetic form, with adaptations to fit the needs of the Greek language (for all these innovations, see Chapter 2). Greek mercenary soldiers, serving in the armies of Egyptian pharaohs defending their independence against Assyria (p. 34), came home with stories of huge stone temples and lifelike stone statues, which stirred the architectural and artistic ambitions of the increasingly wealthy rulers of the homeland. And Greeks who fought in the Babylonian armies that destroyed Jerusalem and scattered the Jews (p. 39) brought back knowledge of Babylonian astronomy, as well as of supposedly reliable ways of discovering the will of the gods from the shape and size of inner organs of sacrificed animals.

> **Speak like an Ancient Greek: The Ancient Greek Alphabet with Audio Files** (http://www.pbs.org/empires/thegreeks/igreeks/speak.html) Hear what the ancient Greek alphabet sounded like.

In the early development of their civilization, the Greeks began by doing what the Babylonians, the Hittites, and countless other peoples had done before them. After migrating into a region that brought them into contact with the civilizations that had begun in Mesopotamia and Egypt, they learned from these civilizations and then adapted what they learned to their own needs. But the Greeks went on to change what they learned so drastically that they created something new and different. Alongside Mesopotamia and Egypt there now appeared a third great civilization: that of classical Greece.

LO³ Citizens and Communities: The Greek City-States

With the recovery of Greek civilization, the tribal communities of the Dark Ages began to develop into city-states. Communities of this kind had often arisen before, for example, among the Sumerians and Phoenicians at times when there was no powerful kingdom or empire to limit their independence (pp. 12, 32). But the social and political development of the Greek city-state (often known by its Greek name, *polis*) took this type of community in unprecedented new directions.

Greek city-states were small places, generally consisting of no more than a town and a few square miles of surrounding countryside. Athens and Sparta, each about the same size as a couple of U.S. counties, were giants among city-states. The population of both town and country ordinarily numbered only a few thousand, though Athens may have reached as many as 250,000. Where possible, the town was built around a hill, at the top of which stood an **acropolis**—a combination of fortress and temple precinct.

> **acropolis**
> The high fortified citadel and religious center of an ancient Greek town.

Both fortresses and temples were vitally important to the Greek city-states. They were fiercely competitive communities that continually fought one another, and their single most important civic activity was the worship of the god or goddess on whom each community was thought to depend. Athens, for example, was the city of the goddess Athena, and from the Athenian acropolis her temple, the Parthenon, or "Place of the Maiden" (since mythology said that she was a virgin), overlooked the whole city (see photo on page 44).

In their small size, their competitiveness, and their reliance on community gods and goddesses, Greek city-states were much the same as those of the Sumerians or Phoenicians, but they differed in one important respect: for the Greeks, the city-state was a community in which all of its members had a share and in which all were entitled to participate to a greater or lesser extent. The Greek language is the first that is known to have had a specific word for a member of such a community: *politēs*, or "citizen."

City-States and Citizens

The notion of citizen participation seems to have originated partly in geography. The Greek city-states first developed at exactly the time that the Assyrians were reaching for power westward from Mesopotamia (pp. 33–34), but Greece was protected by many miles of land and sea. With no universal empire to keep them in order, the city-states were free to struggle among themselves. Furthermore, they occupied a land that was far less wealthy than Mesopotamia or Phoenicia. In their conflicts with one another, they could not afford professional soldiers or large cavalry forces.

An Athenian "Owl" That was the slang name of this tetradrachma (four-drachma coin), because of the owl, the sacred bird of Athena, on the reverse ("tails" side). On the obverse ("heads" side) the goddess herself wears a warrior's helmet. The coin, the size of a U.S. dollar, is pure silver—four days' pay for a skilled Athenian worker. Tetradrachmas were mass-produced in wealthy fifth-century B.C. Athens, and became the main international currency of the Mediterranean. Courtesy of the Trustees of the British Museum

hoplite
A heavily armed and armored citizen-soldier of ancient Greece.

phalanx
A unit of several hundred hoplites, who closed ranks by joining shields when approaching the enemy.

monarchy
A state in which supreme power is held by a single, usually hereditary ruler (a monarch).

oligarchy
A state in which supreme power is held by a small group.

triremes
Massive fighting vessels with three banks of oars, used to ram or board enemy ships.

tyranny
Rule by a self-proclaimed dictator (a tyrant).

democracy
In ancient Greece, a form of government in which all adult male citizens were entitled to take part in decision making.

Instead, they came to rely mainly on infantry armies made up of their own male citizens.

Citizens who could afford to serve as **hoplites** ("men-at-arms") equipped themselves with bronze helmets and armor, round shields, long spears with iron blades, and short iron swords.

> " *Alongside Mesopotamia and Egypt there now appeared a third great civilization: that of classical Greece.* "

They fought in formidable shock units of several hundred men each, known as **phalanxes**, or "rollers." Poorer citizens fought as light-armed infantry, harassing the enemy ahead of the phalanx's charge or covering its vulnerable flanks. This way of fighting was not new; in fact, much of the hoplites' equipment seems to have been modeled on that of Assyrian heavy infantry. But among the Greeks, it was ordinary male citizens fighting in this way on whom the city-states depended for survival. In the words of the poet Alcaeus about 600 B.C., "Not stone and timber, nor skill of carpenter, but brave men who will handle sword and spear—with these you have city and walls." And if sword- and spear-handling men wanted to participate in other community activities besides warfare, they could not very well be told to mind their own business.

The sense of the city-state as a community of all its citizens was reinforced by tradition and myth. Each city-state was believed to have been founded and developed by a family or clan descended from a divine or semidivine founder—in the case of Athens, King Theseus, the offspring of the sea-god Poseidon and the mortal princess Aethra—and most of its citizens claimed to trace their ancestry back to common forefathers. Citizenship was in fact a matter of birth: the status of a father usually determined that of his children. Thus, the citizens could think of themselves as distantly related members of one big family. They saw no more reason for conflict between the individual and the state than between the individual and the family. The "good life" for the individual was a life of active participation in civic affairs—including the government of the city-state.

Monarchy, Oligarchy, Tyranny, Democracy

In the earliest times of classical Greek civilization, the communities that would become city-states were ruled by kings (tribal chieftains) and their leading companion warriors, as described in the epics of Homer (p. 68). But with the development of citizen armies, **monarchy** (government by kings) gave way to new forms of government that distributed power more widely among male citizens. One of these forms was **oligarchy** (from the Greek for "rule by a few"). In this form, a minority of citizens dominated the government, and the power of the majority was limited in various ways. Many city-states in mainland Greece were oligarchies, above all Sparta.

But other city-states, particularly those that developed into large commercial centers, gave far more power to the majority. In such cities, the common people (in Greek, the *dēmos*) were too numerous and active to ignore, and the ruling groups were often divided among factions that competed for the commoners' support. Besides, big commercial cities needed navies as well as armies and depended in wartime on even the poorest citizens as oarsmen in the **triremes**. These were massive fighting vessels that fought in the Phoenician style, by ramming or boarding enemy ships, but had three banks of oars instead of two. Since each trireme needed 170 men to row it, there was no way that a city-state could maintain a powerful fleet without the willing cooperation of the commoners.

In these large city-states, social conflicts sometimes led to the emergence of **tyranny**—the rule of a "tyrant," or self-proclaimed dictator who held power partly by force, partly by exploiting internal divisions, and partly by providing efficient government. But tyranny was often only a passing phase on the way to **democracy** (literally, government by the common people), in which all government decisions were made by the majority of male citizens. The most powerful and successful of democratic city-states was Athens, but there were many others, particularly among the Greeks of Asia Minor and elsewhere on the Mediterranean coastline.

Like most tight-knit communities, Greek city-states were in many ways narrow and exclusive. Women generally participated in the community's affairs on a much more limited basis than men, immigrants were almost never awarded citizenship, and slavery was widespread. When a city-state sent some of its citizens overseas to found a colony, the new settlement became a separate, independent state. And when one city conquered another, it extended its control but not its citizenship. In the end, these tiny states exhausted one another through endless rivalry, jealousy, and war. But in the course of their warfare, they developed exceptional organizational and fighting skills that enabled them to hold their own even against the world-conquering Persians.

Although the Greek city-states had many features in common, each was individual in character and had its own personality. That was true, in particular, of the two communities that dominated much of the Greek world during the heyday of the city-states in the fifth century B.C., Sparta and Athens.

Sparta: The Military Ideal

The Spartans were the descendants of Greeks who had conquered part of the southern mainland, the territory of Laconia (see Map 3.1 on page 48). By the eighth century B.C., they were a minority of landholders (less than ten thousand adult males) ruling over a majority of **helots**, descendants of earlier Greek immigrants who were bound to the land by the Spartan state and compelled to work for the landholding citizens. Since much of the land in their territory of Laconia was infertile, the Spartans pushed westward into the broad and fertile plains of Messenia and turned the Greek inhabitants of that region into helots as well. As a result, the Spartan citizens were outnumbered by the noncitizens about ten to one.

The conquerors became prisoners of their own success. Though the Laconian helots were relatively well treated and even fought in the army, the Messenians were harshly exploited, never accepted their defeat, and often rebelled. To hold down the helots, the Spartan citizens had to accept a government system that put them under almost total domination by a few among themselves.

When and how the Spartans developed their government system is unknown, but by the fifth century B.C., policy decisions had been taken over by a council of elders—some thirty men from leading families who had to be at least sixty years of age and were chosen by the citizens for life. There were also two "kings"—actually high priests and army commanders—whose positions were hereditary in different families. The main executive authority, however, was held by five officials, elected annually and usually also elderly, who were called *ephors* (overseers). Although there was an assembly that was open to all adult males of the citizen minority, those who attended were not even permitted to debate. Instead, the council of elders drew up all proposals and then presented them to the assembly for approval or disapproval only—and this was given not by vote but by a shout. Thus, the Spartan government was a leading example of oligarchy.

The Spartan Way of Life

Along with this government system there went a way of life that dedicated male citizens entirely to the service of the state. The citizens' farms were worked by the helots, and a middle class of immigrant aliens took care of industry and trade. Meanwhile, the citizens devoted themselves to the one calling that was permitted to them by law: that of full-time hoplite warriors. Boys were taken from their families by the state at the age of seven; they were taught manly behavior and reading and writing and were started on a lifelong routine of physical toughening and military training. They were permitted to marry after age twenty—in fact, bachelors were punished—and the state encouraged the mating of the best human specimens. Even married men, however, were required to live in barracks until they reached the age of thirty. They might then have some home life, but they still had to take their chief meal each day at a soldiers' mess.

helots
Noncitizens forced to work for landholders in the ancient city-state of Sparta.

Spartan Practices of Child Rearing Read how Spartans raised their children.

Girls were also required to participate in drills and exercises that were designed to develop them into healthy, child-bearing women. But the state did not control women as rigorously as men, and for long periods they lived apart from their husbands, so that they led relatively free and active lives. As in all other city-states, however, they could not take part in assembly meetings or hold government positions.

The freedom of Spartan women aroused both admiration and disapproval among other Greeks, depending on how they thought it affected the power of the city-state. Sometimes, Spartan women won praise for sharing the militaristic ideal of their menfolk. The story was told of the Spartan mother whose parting words to her son, as she sent him off to battle, were that she expected him to return to her either with his shield (that is, as a victor) or on it (as a corpse). But in the fourth century B.C., when Sparta began to lose battles, the philosopher Aristotle claimed that the women, neither disciplined by the state nor controlled by their husbands, thought only of private and family interests and were useless in time of war.

To protect their harsh and rigid way of life, the Spartans tried to seal off their city-state from outside influences. Sparta had little contact with foreigners; it discouraged trade and showed

A Winner in the Heraean Games? This bronze statuette of a female runner is looking backward, as if at other runners behind her. Perhaps she is ahead in one of the women's foot races in honor of Zeus's consort Hera that were held alongside the Olympic Games. Most likely she and most of her rivals were Spartans—the only city-state where women regularly underwent athletic training. Courtesy of the Trustees of the British Museum

visitors little hospitality. But most Spartans were willing to pay a high price to preserve their system. With its well-trained and highly disciplined citizen army, Sparta not only held down the helots but was for several centuries the leading city-state of mainland Greece.

Many other city-states, including important centers like Corinth and Thebes, were also oligarchies, but their way of life was more easygoing. The power-holding "few" were generally the wealthiest citizens, who monopolized public office. But there were middling and poor citizens as well as wealthy ones, and the assemblies in which the "many" gathered had more power of debate and initiative than in Sparta. But even the most liberal oligarchy gave far less power to the majority of citizens than the main alternative form of government, democracy, as practiced most famously in Athens.

Athens: Freedom and Power

To the Athenians, the Spartan life was not worth living. One of their favorite jokes was that the life led by the Spartans explained their willingness to face death. The contrasts between the two cities are endless. Sparta was agricultural and landlocked; Athens carried on a prosperous commerce and had direct access to the sea. Sparta had the more powerful army; Athens's chief strength was its navy. Sparta sought cultural isolation; Athens welcomed foreign ideas and visitors. Sparta was a tightly controlled society; the Athenians were proud of their free way of life. The Spartans cultivated physical fitness and military courage; from Athens flowed daring inventiveness, glorious literature, and stunning creations of mind and hand.

But Athens was also a warlike community—and exactly because it had wider horizons than Sparta, it was more ambitious for conquest. Athenian democracy not only brought freedom for ordinary citizens and stimulation for artists, writers, and thinkers; for a time, it also brought exceptional power for the city-state in its struggles with its rivals.

Aristocrats and Commoners

The Athenian homeland was the peninsula of Attica in the central region of mainland Greece (see Map 3.1 on page 48). In the period of renewal of

> " *Instead of softening their feet with shoes, his rule was to make them hardy through going barefoot. . . . Instead of pampering them with a variety of clothes, his rule was to habituate them to a single garment the whole year through, thinking that so they would be better prepared to withstand the variations of heat and cold.* "
>
> —Xenophon, describing the rules of the Spartan Lycurgus, ca. 400 B.C.

Greek civilization about 800 B.C., many old-established communities in Attica merged to form a single city-state that was known by the name of the most important community, Athens.

Over the next three centuries, Athens grew to become the wealthiest and one of the most powerful of Greek city-states—largely thanks to the growth of its overseas trade. Attica's large area (by Greek standards) of fertile countryside made it a producer and exporter of wine and oil, and this helped Athens to become a trading and manufacturing center. Workshops sprang up where Athenian citizens, immigrants, and slaves worked side by side to produce weapons, pottery, and articles of silver, lead, and marble. Ships from Athens and many other Greek and Phoenician cities carried these products to lands stretching from Spain to Palestine and from Egypt to the south of present-day Russia. The ships returned with metal, timber, and grain, for as the city grew, the countryside could no longer supply the food and raw materials that it needed.

With more people and greater wealth came social and political conflicts. The disputes were usually between the increasingly powerful and wealthy **aristocrats**—descendants of prominent and long-established Athenian families that had traditionally ruled the city-state—and the increasingly numerous *dēmos*. It was out of these conflicts that democracy was born.

Athenian aristocrats prided themselves on being exceptionally excellent human beings—"the fine and noble ones," as they called themselves—as a result of both breeding and education. They were not a closed caste, but their families married mostly among themselves. Their boys were trained for physical fitness with exercises and sports, and as young men of eighteen, they were assigned to special companies for two years of military and civic training. But they were supposed to be outstanding in mind as well as body, and private schools or tutors taught them public speaking, music, and the works of Homer and other poets.

Some aristocratic girls also got an education, particularly if they were sent off to live for a few years before marriage with one of the groups of young women who served in the temples of various goddesses. But most were kept at home without formal education until they were handed over in their middle teens to aristocratic husbands in their early thirties to continue the "fine and noble" bloodlines.

Besides their feeling of superiority, however, Athenian aristocrats had a strong sense of citizenship and responsibility to the community. The best way to show their distinction,

AN ATHENIAN SPENDTHRIFT

In ancient Athens there were no district attorneys, and it was the business of the individual male citizen to prosecute a crime that had come to his knowledge by publicly accusing the perpetrator in a speech before a court. In 345 B.C. a citizen by the name of Timarchus intended to charge the well-known orator Aeschines with accepting bribes from King Philip of Macedonia. However, Timarchus had a bad reputation for loose living, and under Athenian law, such men could not speak in public. In his own law court speech Aeschines charged Timarchus with loose living and painted a very unflattering portrait of a man who had squandered his inheritance. In the process Aeschines gave a picture of the way of life of a not so "fine and noble" upper-class Athenian man.

The demes that Aeschines mentions were wards in the city of Athens or townships in the nearby countryside. Liturgies were public duties, such as maintaining and commanding warships, that wealthy men were expected to carry out at their own expense. A drachma was a silver coin equivalent to a day's pay for a skilled worker; there were 6 obols to a drachma and 100 drachmas to a mina.

When this (property) [which had come to his use through his connections with a certain Hegesander] too had disappeared and had been squandered in gambling and gluttony . . . and his abominable and wicked nature always maintained the same appetites, and in an excess of incontinence imposed command upon command and dissipated wealth in his daily life, then he turned to consuming his paternal estate. Thus not only did he eat it up, but if one may use the expression, he even drank it up. Not for a proper price did he alienate his several possessions, nor did he wait for the opportunity of gain or advantage, but he used to sell for whatever price a thing would bring, so strenuously did he pursue his pleasures. His father had left him an estate from which another man might even have discharged the expensive and gratuitous public functions [liturgies], but he could not even maintain it for his own advantage. He had a house behind the Acropolis, another in the outlying district, in the deme Sphettus; in the deme Alopece another place, and in addition slaves who were skilled in the shoemaker's trade, nine or ten of them, each of whom brought this man an income of two obols a day, and the foreman of the shop three obols; also a woman slave who understood how to weave the fibre of Amorgos, and a man slave who was a broiderer. There were some, too, who owed him money, and besides he possessed personal property. . . . The house in town he sold to Nausicrates the comic poet, and afterward Cleaenetus the trainer of choruses bought it of Nausicrates for twenty minas. The estate in the country was sold to Mnesitheus of the deme Myrrhinus. It was a large farm, but fearfully run to weeds under the management of the accused. As to the farm at Alopece, which is eleven or twelve stadia distant from the walls (of Athens), when his mother entreated and begged him, as I learn, to let it alone and not sell it, but if nothing else, to leave it for her to be buried in,—for all that, even from this place he did not abstain, but his farm too he sold, for 2000 drachmas. Furthermore of the woman slaves and the domestic slaves he left not one, but has sold everything.

EXPLORING THE SOURCE

1. What can we learn from the speech about the kind of property and activities that provided the wealth of upper-class Athenians?

2. Is there any reason to suppose that Aeschines may be exaggerating this man's irresponsible behavior?

Source: G. W. Botsford and E. G. Sihler, eds., *Hellenic Civilization* (New York: Columbia University Press, 1915), pp. 508–509.

they thought, was by fighting as leading warriors in the citizen army and navy and by paying for many city-state expenses, notably religious festivals and warships, out of their own pockets. In addition, the aristocrats needed the commoners as willing rank-and-file warriors, and they also had their own bitter rivalries that led them to look to the commoners for help against each other. In conflicts with the aristocracy, the *dēmos* could generally find aristocrats to lead them whom they respected and who wanted their support.

From Monarchy to Democracy

As a result, Athens passed through several stages of political growth, beginning with monarchy and including both oligarchy and tyranny. But the upshot was the extension of political power to all adult male citizens, with the aristocrats becoming leaders instead of rulers.

In the century after the coming of democracy, there were two turning points in the life of Athens and the rest of Greece.

SEVERAL FACTORS CONTRIBUTED TO THE DEVELOPMENT OF DEMOCRACY IN THE ATHENIAN CITY-STATE:

Class conflicts led to Solon's reforms, a first step in extending power beyond wealthy landholders

- The aristocrat Solon was appointed about 600 B.C. at a time of crisis when poorer citizens were losing their farms through debt. They demanded a share of political power.

- Solon altered the constitution to give decision-making power to the Assembly, open to all male citizens.

- Aristocrats retained the sole right to public office.

Rivalries within the upper class led one of the rivals, Cleisthenes, to introduce full democracy

- Cleisthenes opened public office to all adult male citizens.

- The Assembly of all male citizens was given ultimate power to make government decisions.

- The newly empowered commoners increased their commitment to the state by agreeing to man a new fleet of warships.

- Wealthy and educated men continued to serve as military and political leaders.

- Democracy unleashed the enthusiasm and commitment of all social groups, and it was this that for a time would make Athens a "great power."

The first was the Persian Wars, in which Athens led the Greek city-states to victory. This success was followed by Athens's Golden Age (460–430 B.C.), a period of the highest confidence, power, and achievement. That period was cut short by the second turning point, the Peloponnesian (pel-uh-puh-NEE-zhuhn) War between Athens and Sparta, in which Athens was defeated and never recovered its earlier confidence and power. Still, Athens continued as a democracy right down to 338 B.C., when it came under the control of Macedonia (mas-i-DOH-nee-uh), and it remained a center of historic achievements in art and thought even after it lost its independence.

The Persian Wars

In the sixth century B.C., the Persians conquered a realm that stretched from the border of India to the Nile and the Aegean. For the first time, a universal empire had come within striking distance of the Greeks, and the Persians were able to bring the Greek city-states in the west of Asia Minor under their rule. When the Athenian upstarts aided a rebellion by these city-states, the Persian king, Darius I, determined (about 494 B.C.) to extend his control into mainland Greece.

Darius, and later his son Xerxes I (zurk-seez), sent two expeditions by land and sea against the mainland Greeks; the Persians lost the first decisive battle to the Athenians at Marathon in 490 B.C. Ten years later, in a sea battle off the island of Salamis near Athens, the Athenian navy smashed the Persian fleet (supplied mainly by the Phoenician city-states, the former rulers of the sea). On land, a small Spartan force held up Xerxes' army in their renowned suicidal stand at Thermopylae (480 B.C.), and the main body of Spartan hoplites later routed the Persians in the pivotal land battle of Plataea. But it was Athens that went on to liberate the Greeks of Anatolia from Persian rule, and by 445 B.C., when final peace was made with Persia, Athens was the controlling power of the Aegean Sea.

The courageous and resourceful little state had demonstrated surprising capacity in fighting the Persian forces. At the height of the wars, the Athenians had fled their homes and watched the enemy burn their city to the ground, but they had come through victorious. With their victory came a new-felt power. How had they, so few in number, turned back the power of the King of Kings, with his millions of subjects? To the Athenians, there could be only one answer: they and their free institutions were superior. Democracy, it seemed, could not only nurture thinkers and artists; it could also win wars.

The leader of democratic Athens after the victory over Persia was another aristocrat, Pericles. By virtue of his personal influence and his long tenure in important elective offices, he held power during much of the thirty-year period of Athens's Golden Age, and it was in his time that democracy flourished

Greece Endangered: The Persians Cross the Hellespont Read how the Persians built a bridge to cross from Asia Minor into Greece.

Interactive Demonstration of Persian Bridge Construction (http://edsitement .neh.gov/PersianBridge_ flash_page.asp) See how the bridge to Greece was constructed.

most in Athens. Though the government system worked very differently from those of twenty-first-century democratic states, it nevertheless provided a precedent and example of democracy in action that have lasted—like the word itself—down to the present day.

The Workings of Democracy: The Assembly

In Athenian democracy, ultimate government power rested in the Assembly of adult male citizens. All major decisions were made there: for peace or war, for sending out expeditions, for spending public money, and for every other aspect of public affairs. Even the building of the Parthenon was decided not by any religious authority but by the Assembly. Meetings were held about once a week, and the number of citizens present was usually less than five thousand. Although many more were eligible to attend, men who lived in the country districts of Attica were often unable to come to town. At first, the Assembly met in the marketplace (*agora*) of Athens; later it met on the slopes of a nearby hill (the Pnyx). Voting was usually by a show of hands, and a simple majority determined the outcome. Anyone present could propose subjects for discussion, but most often, the Assembly debated proposals put before it by a smaller group, the Council of Five Hundred, which was also charged with executing the Assembly's decisions.

Debates in the Assembly were often spirited. Naturally, knowledgeable and convincing public speakers, distinguished battle commanders, patriotic contributors of triremes to the navy, and pious suppliers of animals for sacrifice to the gods were the most likely to be listened to. That was why most leading politicians were wealthy and well-educated aristocrats. But the ordinary members of the Assembly were highly critical and not always polite, and it took a shrewd and skillful leader like Pericles to win and hold the favor of the Assembly.

The Workings of Democracy: Officials and Courts

As an additional check on aristocratic power, the Council of Five Hundred and the roughly one thousand public officials that it supervised—tax collectors, building inspectors, and the like—were nearly all chosen annually by lot. Since these officials were paid for their services, poor men as well as rich could afford to serve, and the wealthy and well educated had no chance of monopolizing public office. The state covered the cost of official salaries by court fines, customs duties, an annual tax on aliens, and various sales taxes, since the rich preferred their contributions to go to more spectacular items that gained them credit with their fellow citizens.

The Athenians did not, however, trust to lot in selecting their chief military officers. These were the Ten Generals (*Stratēgoi*—literally "force commanders"), who were chosen each year by vote of the male citizens. They commanded the army and the navy, managed the war department, and exercised extensive control over the treasury. The Ten Generals chose their own chairman; the popular Pericles was elected general by the citizens and chairman by his fellow generals for sixteen years in succession. Since there were so many generals, there was little chance of a military takeover of power. And if any of them seemed to be becoming too ambitious, he risked **ostracism**: the Assembly could exile him or any other citizen for ten years by simple majority vote that required no proof of actual wrongdoing.

The Athenians also trusted to chance—or the will of the gods, as expressed by the drawing of lots—in the administration of justice. The court for each trial was made up of five hundred men chosen by lot from a long list of names. This made bribery or coercion difficult and guaranteed a broad cross section of citizen judgment. There was no judge to decide questions of law; the Athenian court was judge and jury combined. By majority vote, it ruled on all issues of procedure, legal interpretation, guilt or innocence, and type of punishment. There were no lawyers either, but every citizen argued his own case—though if he could afford it, he could hire some well-known orator to write his speech for him.

Civic and political participation was therefore part of the Athenian way of life for adult male citizens—but adult male citizens were a small minority of the population of Athens. Estimates suggest that during the Age of Pericles, out of Athens's quarter-million population, there were about 40,000 adult males who qualified. The rest of the population was made up of adult female citizens, adult noncitizens (resident aliens and slaves) who actually outnumbered the citizens, and of course children. Adult males probably made up no more than one-fifth of the total adult population, and the other four-fifths—female citizens, as well as aliens and slaves of both sexes—had no say in the city-state's democratic government.

Women in Athens

Most of what is known of the life of Athenian citizen women comes from surviving law court speeches composed by famous orators; in other words, it reflects conditions in families (from small farm and business owners up to the "fine and noble" elite)

> **ostracism**
> Banishment for ten years by majority vote of the Athenian Assembly.

> "*Where our rivals from their very cradles by a painful discipline seek after manliness, at Athens we live exactly as we please, and yet are just as ready to encounter every legitimate danger.*"
>
> —Pericles, according to Thucydides, ca. 404 B.C.

that could afford to hire speechwriters. In some ways, the relationships of women and men in these families showed much the same patterns of inequality as anywhere else; in other ways, the relationships were actually more unequal than elsewhere.

Within marriage, the sexual liberty of the husband was taken for granted. In addition to his wife, he had access to his household slaves as concubines, as well as to public prostitutes. If he found his wife boring and could afford to do so, the husband might take up with more engaging female companions (*hetaerae*). These women, usually noncitizens from Asia Minor, were schooled in the arts of conversation and entertainment. The most famous of them was Aspasia, the consort and mistress of Pericles.

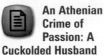

An Athenian Crime of Passion: A Cuckolded Husband Exacts the Ultimate Revenge Read an Athenian husband's tale of finding his wife with her lover.

In addition, the husband could without dishonor fall in love and have sexual relationships with teenage boys—preferably only one of them. When the boy grew up, a relationship of this kind was supposed to turn into ordinary friendship, and male homosexuality between "consenting adults" was regarded as unmanly (though not wicked). Within these limits, homosexuality played an important part in the lives of well-to-do Greek men.

These Athenian customs, including love between men and boys, were found among other ancient peoples. In some other respects, however, women from well-off families in democratic Athens led a more restricted life and had fewer rights than in many other Greek city-states, as well as in Persia and Egypt. They were not supposed to socialize with men other than their fathers, brothers, and husbands; male visitors to a house had to keep to a special "men's room." If a woman left the house, she had to be escorted by a close male relative or be in a group with other women; and she had to have a specific reason, such as buying supplies or taking part in public religious celebrations. Women held property under the control of a male "guardian"—usually a father, brother, or husband—and they could plead in the law courts only through these guardians.

On the other hand, women were highly visible in an area of family and community life that was just as important as politics and law—the worship of the gods. It was aristocratic Athenian girls and women who every four years wove a new robe for Athena's sacred image on the Acropolis and brought it to her temple in solemn procession—the high point of the community's service to its beloved goddess. And in 480 B.C., when the Athenians were evacuating their city ahead of the approaching Persians, it took the priestess of Athena to persuade the citizens to hurry by convincing them that the goddess herself had already left.

Women in Classical Greece (http://www.metmuseum.org/toah/hd/wmna/hd_wmna.htm) View images of women in ancient Greece.

Not much is known of women's life lower down the social scale or outside the city. *Hetaerae* were not despised, and they were entitled to generous gifts from their lovers. Sometimes they passed on their profession to their daughters, thereby forming independent though insecure female "dynasties."

Poor townswomen certainly worked in trades outside the home as weavers, innkeepers, and vendors in the marketplace. And rich or poor, no countrywoman could have done the "women's work" (p. 10) of the farms if she had lived under the same restrictions as well-off women in the city. In any case, no woman could take part in the proceedings of the Assembly or the law courts, let alone hold public office.

Aliens

The fifty thousand or so resident aliens were a very varied group. Some were wealthy businessmen, or independent women like Aspasia, who socialized on equal terms with the "fine and noble" citizens. Many were owners of stores and workshops, hardly different from citizens in the same lines of business. Many others were freed slaves who often went on working in the households of their former owners as artisans, laborers, domestic servants, concubines, and prostitutes.

Freeborn aliens were mostly Greeks and were still citizens of their city-states of origin even though their families might have lived in Athens for generations. If they were freedmen or freedwomen (ex-slaves), they were mostly non-Greeks or their descendants. Resident aliens in Athens bore all the obligations of citizenship but were entitled to only some of the benefits. They had to register with the government, pay taxes (including a special tax levied only on them), and (if male) do military service. They could sue Athenians in the law courts, and they shared on an equal footing in the community's worship of the gods, but they could not take part in Assembly meetings or hold government office. Their status was similar to that of resident aliens in the United States at the present day, except in one all-important respect: they had next to no chance of ever becoming citizens.

Still, freeborn aliens from elsewhere in Greece evidently preferred permanent second-class status in Athens to first-class status in their home city-states. And as resident aliens, ex-slaves gained a secure position in a community where they had lived for many years if not all their lives.

Slaves

The hundred thousand or so slaves in Athens were also a very diverse group, not all of them living lives of total subjection and powerlessness. "Fine and noble" citizens gave talented slaves an education and kept them as tutors to their sons; state-owned slaves worked as clerks in government offices, and even as policemen charged with such duties as corralling citizens from the marketplace to the meeting field on Assembly days.

Most slave owners were small businesspeople and farmers who kept only a few slaves and often worked side by side with them. Masters and (with the approval of their guardians) mistresses often freed their slaves: either they allowed them to work on their own account and save money to buy themselves free, or they freed them in their wills as a reward for faithful service. A slave concubine might even persuade her master to free her during his lifetime and make her his wife. Most Athenians did not expect deference from slaves. One of the few who did, an anonymous writer of Pericles' time or not long afterward, complained that slaves would not even get out of citizens' way on the streets.

But there were many for whom slavery was a truly inhuman condition. Slaves, both female and male and usually young, were kept as prostitutes in brothels or as domestic servants who had to double as concubines. Others—perhaps as many as ten thousand male slaves—worked in the silver and lead mines, where they were sure to die sooner rather than later from overwork, metal poisoning, or cave-ins. Most slaves were non-Greeks, or the descendants of non-Greeks, who had been uprooted from their homelands by war, and of course, all slaves were property that could be bought and sold. Their price ranged from ten minae (about ten pounds of silver, or a couple of years' wages for a skilled free worker) down to half a mina, depending on age, strength, skills, and looks. The slaves, therefore, represented an important part of the wealth of democratic Athens.

Democracy Within Traditional Civilization

The Athenian laws and customs concerning women, aliens, and slaves were not a special feature of democracy as such. They were the local version of traditional values and practices that the Athenians shared with most of the world at the time. But of course, democracy implies equality—yet so far as is known, no one in Athens ever complained that the treatment of women, aliens, and slaves was undemocratic.

The exclusion of female citizens from the community's decision making, for example, seems to have caused Athenian men no uneasiness whatever. Near the end of Athens's Golden Age, Pericles spoke at the funeral of citizen-soldiers fallen in the Peloponnesian War against Sparta (p. 80); and the historian Thucydides, following a Greek tradition of putting revealing words into the mouths of historical characters (p. 71), turned the speech into a famous proclamation of the values of Athenian democracy. Thucydides makes the Athenian statesman praise the democratic community for expecting all male citizens to be active in its service: "we regard him who takes no part in public duties not as unambitious but as useless." But the exact opposite applies to the widows of the fallen: they must remember that "the greatest glory will be hers who is least talked of among the men, whether for good or for bad." Thucydides was himself an Athenian, and the words he gives to Pericles certainly reflect the male citizens' way of thinking.

This was not because Athenian men failed to value women as members of the community. In narrating the destruction of

The Funeral Oration of Pericles Read Thucydides' version of Pericles' funeral oration.

an Athenian force in Sicily later in the war with Sparta, Thucydides lists three precious things of which Athenian generals always reminded their soldiers to stiffen their courage when defeat was looming: "wives, children, and the gods of the forefathers"—in that order. But tradition said that the community was made up of families—of partnerships between men and women in which men were the senior partners and the ones responsible for running the community. The fact that running the Athenian community had become the business of all the men was simply not seen as a reason to make it the business of women as well.

True, the playwright Aristophanes staged two famous comedies in which he depicted women making decisions for the democratic city-state. In *Lysistrata*, the women of Athens and Sparta go on a sex strike to force an end to the war that their husbands are fighting; in *The Assemblywomen*, the wives actually take over the government. But comic dramatists often made their point by imagining the world turned ridiculously upside down. Aristophanes was a critic of democracy who disapproved of war with Sparta, and he probably wanted to shame the male citizens by showing them what seemed to them and to him a grotesque and impossible scene: women running the city-state, and doing no worse than the men.

What Athenian women themselves thought of democracy is unknown. However, well-born ancient Greek women sometimes broke the bounds of custom by studying and teaching philosophy, and a few of them expressed their views on the female role in the family and the community. In what is left of their writings, even these thinkers took for granted that the public life of city-states was male territory that women should not enter. According to Phyntis, probably writing after 300 B.C., "The activities proper to man are to command armies, to govern cities, to lead the people with rousing speeches. Those which are particular to woman are to look after her house, to stay at home, to wait for and to serve her husband." No ancient Greek woman is known to have criticized the exclusion of women from public life—or the institution of slavery, or permanent second-class status for immigrants—as women and men began to do when democracy returned in the West more than two thousand years later.

But the modern revival of democracy was part of a whole series of massive changes in basic features of civilization—religious beliefs, cultural values, economic systems, and family and social life, as well as government structures. Ancient Greek democracy, by contrast, had a brief "window of opportunity" to exist within a traditional civilization most of whose other basic features remained unchanged. That is the greatest difference between ancient democracy and that of the present day.

Listen to a synopsis of Chapter 3.

(above, center) **Just Married** A sixth-century B.C. Athenian vase painting shows newlyweds riding a donkey-cart away from the bride's home, where the ceremony has taken place. They are going to the groom's home, where his mother is waiting to greet them. The best man, who has helped the bridegroom fetch the bride, rides with them; tonight he will stand guard outside the marriage chamber. Image copyright © The Metropolitan Museum of Art/Art Resource, NY

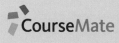

CHAPTER 4

NEW CREATIONS: GREEK RELIGION, ARTS, AND IDEAS, 800–300 B.C.

LEARNING OBJECTIVES

AFTER READING THIS CHAPTER, YOU SHOULD BE ABLE TO DO THE FOLLOWING:

LO¹ Describe the distinctive features of Greek religious belief and practice and the features that the Greeks shared with other polytheistic peoples.

LO² Explain the evolution of Greek architecture and sculpture.

LO³ Discuss Greek achievements in poetry, drama, and history.

LO⁴ Trace the development of Greek philosophy from the Pre-Socratics through Aristotle.

> **"THE RISE OF GREEK CIVILIZATION WAS ACCOMPANIED BY AN OUTBURST OF ARTISTIC AND INTELLECTUAL CREATIVITY."**

The rise of Greek civilization was accompanied by an outburst of artistic and intellectual creativity. Greek architecture, sculpture, literature, and philosophy grew from three sources: their religious traditions, their encounter with the peoples of the lands between the Mediterranean Sea and the Indian Ocean, and the community life of their city-states.

Greek religion had a great deal in common with the beliefs of other polytheistic peoples and was directly influenced by the Greeks' southern and eastern neighbors, but the Greek gods and goddesses had a lifelike and human quality that helped inspire a lifelike and human art and literature. The need to honor these gods and goddesses, the wealth of city-states like Athens, and the example of the temples and statues of Egypt produced architecture and sculpture that stressed grace and movement yet was also solemnly impressive. The imported skill of alphabetic writing made it possible to record Greek poets' direct and vivid views of adventure and war, gods and fate, and personal feeling; dramatists actually showed their city-state audiences the characters and events they presented. And Greek thinkers, reflecting on their nation's religious traditions, the turbulent politics of the city-states, and the diverse international region in which they lived, began a quest for explanations of divine power, the natural universe, community life, and human behavior that has lasted in the West down to the present day.

Test your knowledge before you read this chapter.

What do you think?

The arts of the Greeks are the standard by which all arts should be judged.

Strongly Disagree						Strongly Agree
1	2	3	4	5	6	7

Reunion des Musees Nationaux/Art Resource, NY

≪ **"Guest of My Holy Hearth and Cleansed by Me of Blood-Guilt"** In a vase painting, the god Apollo holds high a slaughtered piglet; the blood drips onto the hand of Orestes, which holds the sword he used to kill his own mother Clytemnestra. The deed was retribution at Apollo's command for Clytemnestra's murder of Orestes' father Agamemnon, but the stain of matricide must still be washed away. Revenge and justice, divine retribution, pollution and cleansing, and sacrifice were among features of Greek religion that inspired tragedies such as Aeschylus's *Oresteia* trilogy.

LO¹ Greek Gods and Goddesses

The Greeks, like other polytheistic peoples, had no single set of beliefs about how the gods and goddesses were to be worshiped or about their plans for and demands on the human race. Traditional myths of the deities' personalities and deeds were preserved in the works of early poets, among them Homer, and lived on in poetry and art for thousands of years. Above all, however, Greek religion was a way for people and communities to understand and if possible influence the workings of the universe and human destiny—a way that many generations of Greeks found consoling and compelling.

Gods and Goddesses

The Greeks worshiped countless deities, who they believed could wield their power for good or ill on individuals, families, and city-states, so that it was vital to win their favor. "Impiety"—openly denying or insulting a deity—was a crime punishable by death, for it might bring divine revenge upon the community that tolerated it.

The gods and goddesses lived close by—lesser ones in homes, fields, streams, seas, and forests, and many of the great ones on top of Mount Olympus, the highest peak of Greece (see Map 3.1 on page 48). There, behind a veil of clouds, Zeus, the ruler of the sky, presided over a divine family. Zeus shared overlordship of the world with two of his brothers: Poseidon, ruler of the sea, and Hades, or Pluto, king of the underworld—a dark, forbidding place where spirits of the departed lingered for an uncertain period.

Hesiod's *Works and Days* Assesses the Human Condition Read a Greek story of the gods' role in creating the human race.

The gods and goddesses displayed human frailties and emotions, including ambition, lust, pride, and vengefulness. Zeus, for instance, came from a line of divine fathers and sons who had struggled for power by such means as castrating and swallowing each other. All the same, the deities expected righteousness from humans. The king of the gods in particular was regarded as the upholder of such virtues as abiding by oaths and welcoming the stranger—as Homer said, "All wanderers and beggars come from Zeus."

As Zeus embodied the patriarchal (fatherly) principle, his wife Hera embodied the matriarchal (motherly) principle. She was regarded as the protector of womanhood and marriage, though in accordance with the belief that the gods were above mere human taboos (p. 15), she was also Zeus's sister. Zeus himself was far from a faithful husband. Greek poets told, for example,

(p. 15)

"The gods and goddesses displayed human frailties and emotions, including ambition, lust, pride, and vengefulness. Zeus, for instance, came from a line of divine fathers and sons who had struggled for power by such means as castrating and swallowing each other."

CHRONOLOGY

CA. LATE NINTH CENTURY B.C.	Homer's *Iliad* and *Odyssey*
SIXTH CENTURY B.C.	Poetry of Sappho; Pre-Socratic philosophers
FIFTH CENTURY B.C.	Parthenon constructed; works of Aeschylus, Sophocles, and Euripides
LATE FIFTH TO FOURTH CENTURY B.C.	Socrates, Plato, and Aristotle

how a lesser goddess, Leto, presented him with a splendid pair of twins—the handsome Apollo and his sister Artemis (Diana). Apollo, later associated with the sun, was widely worshiped as the god of poetry, music, art, and manly grace. Artemis, associated with the moon, was the goddess of wild nature, a hunter, and the model of athletic girlhood.

Illustrated List of Greek Gods and Goddesses (http://www.greek-gods.info/greek-gods/) Learn more about all of the Greek gods and goddesses.

Athena, another of Zeus's offspring, was an armed and warlike virgin, though also linked with skill and wisdom. Aphrodite, on the other hand, the goddess of beauty and love, had many lovers among gods and humans, including the fierce war-god, Ares. But the god of war, "the curse of men," preferred the thrill of killing to the pleasures of lovemaking. Hermes, though, was the "friend of man"—the messenger of the gods, gliding on winged sandals over land and sea and guiding humans in every undertaking as well as on the way to the underworld.

The Worship of the Gods

The temple, the chief place of worship, was designed as a "home" where the god or goddess could live among the community that he or she protected. The deity was deemed to be present in the temple, usually in the form of a holy image that was tended by priests or priestesses who were appointed by the community or inherited their positions.

Ceremonies were usually performed in front of the temple, where the worshipers presented the priest or priestess with gifts—pottery, garments, whatever might be pleasing to the god or goddess. They also offered up prayers and animal sacrifices to win divine favor and assistance. After an animal had been ceremonially slaughtered and roasted and the aroma had reached the nostrils of the deity, the priest or priestess and the worshipers ate the meat in a common sacred meal. The worshipers also followed the Mesopotamian practice of judging the attitude of the gods to important undertakings from the shape and size of the victim's inner organs.

Oracles

Another way to discern the divine will was to consult an oracle—a person through whom a god or goddess was deemed to speak directly to humans. The most trusted oracles in all Greece were the priestesses of Apollo who lived at Delphi (see Map 3.1 on page 48). Politicians, generals, heads of families went or sent to Delphi for advice on such matters as whether or not to undertake a military campaign or what they must do to end a plague. A priestess would fall into a trance, relay the question to Apollo, and then utter the answer received from him. The utterance was usually unclear and had to be interpreted for the questioner by a priest. The Delphic oracles won a high reputation for accuracy, partly because the advice and predictions were in such vague, ambiguous terms that they could be made to fit almost any later event.

Mysteries

In these ways, the gods and goddesses offered mortals a glimpse of their will and ways of gaining their favor and help. What most of them did not provide was any promise of life other than the one on earth. There was no general expectation of immortality for humans and no system of rewards and punishments after death.

But some deities were more generous—above all, the wine god Dionysus (dahy-uh-NAHY-suhs) and the fertility goddess Demeter. These deities were associated with the "death" and "rebirth" of grapes into wine and seed into grain crops, and their followers believed that they could share in this death and rebirth by experiences such as becoming intoxicated with wine or drugs, eating a sacred meal, and witnessing a dramatic representation of death and resurrection. At the end of such rites, the worshiper sensed a mystic union with the deity and the assurance of everlasting life.

The rites were called **mysteries** because worshipers had to be initiated (solemnly admitted) to take part in them and must never reveal what they experienced. But tens of thousands of people took part, and in Athens, festivals of Dionysus and Demeter were as thronged as those of Athena and Zeus. These mystical experiences had compelling power—so much so that in spite of the vast numbers of people who shared them over many centuries, the details of what happened in them are today mostly unknown.

The Glory of the Gods

The Greeks shared the general features of their religion, including oracles and mystery cults, with many other ancient polytheistic peoples (pp. 14–15). Some of their actual gods and goddesses, like Zeus, had come with them as they moved into their new homeland, but others were deities that they had come across in the course of their migrations and international contacts. Athena, for example, was worshiped in the territory of Greece before the Greeks arrived. Adonis, one of Aphrodite's divine lovers, was a god originally worshiped in Sumer (p. 14), who "died" each year and was ceremonially mourned by women in every city from Athens to Babylon—his name came from the Semitic word *adon*, meaning "lord."

But as with other features of their civilization, the Greeks made something distinctive out of what they learned from other peoples. Wherever their deities originated, the Greeks generally gave them lifelike personalities and a lifelike appearance, modeled on those of human beings but far more "glorious"—a favorite Greek word of praise for gods and goddesses. An ancient hymn called Athena "the glorious goddess, bright-eyed, inventive, unbending of heart, pure virgin, savior of cities, courageous"; Apollo was "strong-shouldered," Demeter was "rich-haired," Aphrodite was "laughter-loving." The need to honor beings like these, so splendid and yet so human, helped inspire an art and literature that sought to depict the human quality in gods and the godlike features of humans.

LO² Architecture and Sculpture

As the early Greeks grew wealthier and their society grew more complex, Greek builders grew ambitious—and since community activities were more important than private affairs, they put their best efforts into public structures. They built open marketplaces enclosed by covered **colonnades** (rows of columns); outdoor amphitheaters (see photo on page 69) for dramatic festivals; and open-air gymnasiums, race courses, and stadiums. But their supreme architectural achievement was the temple.

Up to the sixth century B.C., even the most important buildings were usually made of wood. Gradually, however, limestone and marble took the place of timber in public structures. Impressed by the splendid temples of Egypt, the Greeks borrowed the Egyptian system of building stone structures from horizontal beams resting on vertical columns, but they developed the system in a new direction—toward a blend of solidity with graceful proportions.

Temple Building: The Parthenon

Early Greek temples had a rather heavy appearance, as in the sixth-century temple at Paestum in Italy (see photo on page 64). Gradually, however, the proportions of the temple, and of the columns especially, were refined. The most splendid result of this development was the Parthenon of Athens (see photo). In this shrine for Athena, a perfect balance of architectural features was achieved.

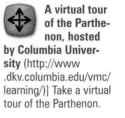

≪ An Early Temple This temple of the goddess Hera is one of a group of shrines, overlooking the sea not far south of Naples, that formed the religious center of a Greek colony, Paestum. The temple was built in the sixth century B.C., when Greeks were settling in large numbers in the fertile and thinly populated coastal lands of southern Italy and Sicily. It has the massive appearance typical of early Greek stone temples.

Nimatallah/Art Resource, NY

≫ The Parthenon Rebuilding the temple of Athena after its destruction by the Persians was a cherished project of Pericles. It was he who about 448 B.C. persuaded the Athenian Assembly to authorize its construction and to employ two well-known architects, Ictinus and Callicrates. They achieved a combination of solidity and gracefulness that has made the Parthenon a model of classic dignity and beauty from ancient times to the present day.

Art Resource, NY

The Parthenon was designed about 450 B.C. by the architects Ictinus and Callicrates (**cuh-LI-krateez**) as part of Pericles' plan for rebuilding the Acropolis after the Persians had destroyed the earlier sacred structures there. Though ravaged by time and war, it still embodies the Greek ideal of architectural perfection. It is not a huge structure, measuring only 100 by 230 feet, but it was perfectly suited to its purpose and position.

The exterior columns of the Parthenon form a continuous colonnade on all four sides of the temple. The interior consists of two rectangular chambers. The larger one was the actual chamber of the goddess, where she was present in the form of her holy image. The smaller chamber contained the treasury of Athens—as close as possible to the goddess herself, so that it would be under her protection day and night. The roof of the

building was gabled (slanted) and supported by a wooden framework. It was closed at each end by a triangular slab of marble, called the pediment.

The wonder of the Parthenon comes, in part, from the painstaking details of its design. Subtle curves, rather than straight lines, avoid any impression of stiffness. The diameter of each column, for instance, diminishes gradually as it rises to its capital (carved top) in a slightly curving line. The Greek builders had discovered that a perfectly straight profile makes a column look too rigid. They had also found that by adjusting the spacing between columns, they could improve the

A virtual tour of the Parthenon, hosted by Columbia University (http://www .dkv.columbia.edu/vmc/ learning/)] Take a virtual tour of the Parthenon.

visual effect of the entire structure. Hence, in the Parthenon, the space between each corner column and the column next to it is less than the space between other columns, and this gives a feeling of extra support at the points of extra stress. The fact that the designers went to such pains to satisfy the demands not only of engineering but of aesthetics as well is testimony to their desire for a building as glorious as the goddess who lived in it.

Images of Gods and Humans

The Greeks' passion for beauty and their interest in human forms are clearly reflected in their sculpture. Only a few originals—and these in mutilated condition—have come down to us. But hundreds of copies of Greek statues, produced in Roman times by Greek artisans, still survive, and have served through the centuries as models for Western sculptors.

 The Art of Classical Greece, ca. 48–323 B.C. (http://www.metmuseum.org/toah/hd/tacg/hd_tacg.htm) See more images of Greek gods and humans.

Early Greek statues, like their buildings, reveal an Egyptian influence. This is still seen in the many statues of young men, probably victorious athletes, that have been unearthed in Greece (see photo). Such statues were often placed in temples, thereby making the athlete into a personal "servant" of the god or goddess, in thanksgiving for victories in contests such as the Olympic Games. The pose of the statue, with arms hanging at the sides, fists clenched, and left foot forward, imitates Egyptian sculpture (compare photo on page 26). The nudity, however, and the smiling face—reproducing the nakedness of Greek athletes and expressing the joy of victory—are Greek innovations.

But Greek sculptors grew dissatisfied with this kind of representation and turned steadily toward greater naturalism, movement, and grace. The statues carved during the fifth century B.C. were chiefly of gods and goddesses; like the deities themselves, they resembled mortals—not actual individuals, but idealized men and women.

Phidias, the most highly respected sculptor of Athens in the Golden Age, was put in charge of the Parthenon sculptures. It was he who carved from wood the gigantic statue of Athena (some 35 feet tall) that was placed in the main inner chamber. Although the original was lost long ago, ancient descriptions tell us that it was richly decorated with ivory, gold,

> "The statues carved during the fifth century B.C. were chiefly of gods and goddesses; like the deities themselves, they resembled mortals—not actual individuals, but idealized men and women."

and jewels. Phidias also planned and supervised carvings on the marble pediments and the marble frieze (band) that ran around the outside of the inner chambers. Fragments of this sculpture are still in existence (see photo on page 66). They show a solemn procession to the Parthenon in honor of Athena—the high point of Athens's religious year. The sense of ease and motion and the splendid proportion and form are evident even in these fragments.

Better known is *The Discus Thrower* by Myron, another sculptor of the time of Phidias (see photo on page 66). The original bronze casting has been lost, but the figure was so much admired that many marble copies were made. In this statue, Myron chose to portray the athlete at the moment before he made his supreme effort, so that he would appear dynamically poised and in full self-control. The statue is not an accurate picture of a real discus thrower; rather, it is an ideal representation of the male figure—a masterpiece of line and form.

After about 400 B.C., Greek sculptors tended toward a more natural style, as well as a wider choice of subjects. The leading developer of this new style was Praxiteles (**prak-SIT-l-eez**). His most famous work, *Hermes with the Infant Dionysus* (see photo), shows Hermes smiling down at Dionysus and Dionysus reaching up toward Hermes, yet both of them are so perfectly and gracefully balanced that they seem lifelike and godlike at the same time.

It was probably also Praxiteles who broke with the tradition of portraying women and goddesses fully clothed and introduced an entirely new subject of sculptural art—the naked or half-naked female body. The famous *Aphrodite of Melos (Venus de Milo)* of about 100 B.C. (see photo) shows the goddess with her body slightly twisted, her weight on her right leg, and her left knee thrust forward, keeping her low-slung garment from slipping off her hips. Yet this complex pose is so perfectly balanced that it produces an effect of goddess-like serenity and power.

Along with the trend toward a more natural style there developed an interest in portraiture, emotional expression, and

The Parthenon Frieze The horsemen are riding in solemn procession to the Parthenon as part of the yearly festival of Athena. Ancient peoples often decorated temples with scenes of religious ceremonies, probably as a magical way of making sure that the deity would always be receiving worship. The carvers of the frieze, supervised by the renowned sculptor Phidias, brought to this tradition the freedom and gracefulness of the newly developed Greek style of sculpture. British Museum, London/The Bridgeman Art Library

The Discus Thrower This statue was much admired in the ancient world, and this is one of several marble copies made in Roman times. The bronze original, which does not survive, was made by Myron, a contemporary of Phidias, about 450 B.C. Unlike the early statue shown on page 65, with its conventional pose, this is an idealized study of the naked male body in action. Alinari/Art Resource, NY

>> Hermes with the Infant Dionysus This is the only surviving Greek statue known to be an original work by a famous master—the fourth-century B.C. sculptor Praxiteles. The statue was found in the nineteenth century A.D. in the ruins of the temple of Zeus at Olympia, exactly where the travel writer Pausanias had seen it 1,700 years earlier. Alinari/Art Resource, NY

representation of ordinary people—street vendors, dancers, and common soldiers. Exact likenesses became popular, and more and more statues showed intense emotion.

Probably the most famous example of this kind is the marble group known as *Laocoön and His Sons* (about 50 B.C.). According to legend, the Greeks had schemed to take Troy by hiding soldiers inside a giant wooden horse offered as a gift, and

the priest Laocoön **(ley-OK-oh-on)** had warned his fellow Trojans not to bring the horse into the city. But Athena, who favored the Greeks, sent two deadly serpents to crush the priest and his sons (see photo). The sculpture depicts the scene as one of desperate struggle and despair, yet also of perfect balance and proportion. In a distant future, this later style of sculpture would deeply influence the art of seventeenth-century Europe (compare photo on page 347).

LO³ Poetry, Drama, and History

As soon as the Greeks relearned writing (p. 51), they began using it to record traditional myths and tales. Later on, as their way of life developed, they wrote down poems praising winners in athletic contests and other matters of importance to an increasingly educated upper class. Then came dramatic performances and law court speeches that emerged from the life of city-states, above all Athens, as well as historical accounts of the conflicts among the city-states and between the Greeks and other peoples. The various kinds of poetry were exceptionally wide-ranging in their themes and expressive in their language; drama, speechmaking, and history were entirely new forms of the spoken or written word.

Epic and Lyric Poetry

The earliest type of Greek poetry was the epic—a long poem telling a story of gods and heroes in the national past. Such poems dated back two thousand years before the Greeks to the Sumerian *Epic of Gilgamesh* (p. 15), and many more were produced in the West for two thousand years afterward. Sometimes epics were based on ancient traditional tales that had been passed down orally (by word of mouth) before being written down, like the French *Song of Roland* (p. 238). Sometimes an epic was the written creation of a single author, like the *Aeneid* of the Roman poet Virgil (p. 108). Either way, the greatest epics became treasured possessions of the peoples among whom they originated—sources of national pride, of subjects for later poets, and of moral guidance.

Homer

The two surviving early Greek epics, the *Iliad* and the *Odyssey*, were believed by the Greeks themselves to be the work of a single author, Homer, who came from one of the Greek settlements in Asia Minor and lived perhaps about 800 B.C. Most likely, Homer worked with traditional tales sung with instrumental accompaniment by illiterate minstrels, who would have partly memorized and partly improvised them. Every minstrel and every generation had a different version, and what Homer probably did was to combine the tales into two great narrative poems, setting his stamp on them more than any minstrel before him. In addition, Homer or others soon after him had access to the new skill of alphabetic writing, so that his version became the standard, which has lasted for thousands of years.

The general setting of his poems is the Trojan War, a struggle between early Greeks and the defenders of Troy (Ilium) in Asia Minor that supposedly took place in the twelfth century B.C. The *Iliad* concentrates on the events of a few days in the tenth and last year of the war, telling the story of the wrath of the Greek hero Achilles and its consequences for the Greeks and Trojans. Homer's sequel, the *Odyssey*, skips the overthrow and destruction of Troy and tells the story of the ten-year journey home of one of the Greek heroes, the wily and brave Odysseus, king of the island of Ithaca off Greece's northeastern coast. The *Iliad* and *Odyssey* are not just tales of war and adventure. Like earlier epics, they also deal with deep questions about humanity and its place in the universe—with mortals and gods, morals and fate. In addition, more than any other epic poet before or since, Homer paints an unforgettable picture of human life as a whole.

Family life, for instance, is deeply important to Homer. The *Iliad*'s warrior heroes have aged fathers and mothers who love them and are afraid for them. They are happily married, and sometimes their wives wholeheartedly nurture any children they may happen to have had with slave women—a wifely deed that Homer evidently considered both praiseworthy and unusual. By contrast with this loving family life, the poem's scenes of strife and slaughter seem all the grimmer, and the heroes' bloody deaths are all the more tragic.

The Trojan Hero Hector Prepares to Meet His Destiny Read the moving story of the Trojan hero Hector's farewell to his family in the *Iliad*.

Likewise, Odysseus's adventures would not be so gripping without their longed-for goal of homecoming. His escape from a monster's cave, his defeat of a wicked enchantress, his survival through storm and shipwreck each take him a step closer to reunion with his wife and son—and to bloody revenge on strangers who have moved into his palace, tried to alienate his wife's affections, and plotted his son's death.

Furthermore, Homer's characters are no dim mythical figures, but human beings with many lifelike twists and turns of human nature. Priam, king of Troy, beside himself with grief and terror as he makes ready for a perilous nighttime journey to beg the body of his son Hector from the fierce Achilles, flies into a nervous rage at his remaining sons and cruelly tells them they are all worthless in comparison with the one he has lost. Penelope, Odysseus's faithful wife, dreams about his would-be rivals as her "pet geese," as if she cannot help being fond of the men who

> "*And her husband had pity to see her, and caressed her with his hand, and spoke and called upon her name: 'Dear one, I pray you be not of oversorrowful heart; no man against my fate shall hurl me to Hades; only destiny, I suppose, no man has escaped, be he coward or be he valiant, when once he has been born.*"
>
> —from the *Iliad*

have been keeping her company in his absence. And Homer shows his characters not only doing heroic deeds, but also taking care of the everyday business of life—building boats, washing laundry, roasting pork, making cheese. With their panoramas of adventure and war, their deep questions about human existence, their understanding of human nature, and their countless lifelike details, the *Iliad* and *Odyssey* have been an inspiration not only to the Greeks but to Western literature right down to recent times (p. 521).

Lyric Poetry

The Greeks created lyric poetry as well as epic poetry. It is called **lyric** because it was normally sung to the playing of a lyre (a plucked, harplike instrument). A lyric poem was a short work by a single author, who probably improvised it and improved it over time before writing it down. A good deal of lyric poetry was composed for public occasions—notably, praise of athletes and the wealthy backers who paid for their training and equipment. But much lyric poetry was also personal, expressing individual thoughts and feelings about life, love, patriotism—even the pleasures of wine.

An Illustrated Essay on Music in Ancient Greece, Metropolitan Museum (http://www.metmuseum.org/toah/hd/grmu/hd_grmu.htm)] Learn about lyres and the music of ancient Greece.

Solon, the Athenian lawgiver (p. 56), was as famous for his poetry as for his statesmanship. One of his verses is a proud defense of his record in politics. Referring to Athenians he had released from slavery, he wrote, "These I set free; and I did this by strength of hand, welding right law with force to make a single whole. So have I done, and carried through all that I pledged." But Solon's favorite subject was individual happiness and how it is won and lost. Foreshadowing later Greek dramatists, he advised his listeners "to call no man happy until the day of his death." Every life is uncertain, takes unexpected turns, and must be judged in its entirety.

One of the most admired of lyric poets was Sappho, an aristocrat from the Aegean island of Lesbos who lived about the same time as Solon. She spent much of her life away from home, in the neighboring land of Lydia in Asia Minor, where she had family connections, as well as in distant Sicily, where she spent years of exile after a local tyrant (p. 52) ousted her family from power.

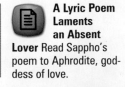
A Lyric Poem Laments an Absent Lover Read Sappho's poem to Aphrodite, goddess of love.

Many of Sappho's poems celebrate erotic love, especially of the young women living in the temples of various goddesses where she presided (p. 54). Hence the use of the word *lesbian* in referring to women of her sexual temperament, which was not disapproved by the ancient Greeks, any more than the accepted form of male homosexuality (p. 58). No doubt because of the many partings in Sappho's life, one of the themes of her poetry is that of love sharpened by distance: "Some say cavalry, and others claim infantry or a fleet of long oars is the supreme sight on the black earth. I say it is the one you love . . . Anactoria is far, and I for one would rather see her warm supple step and the sparkle of her face than watch all the dazzling chariots and armored hoplites of Lydia."

A New Art Form: Drama

Other peoples had epic tales and poems of personal feeling, but it was in Greece that drama began. In addition to being read or sung, drama was acted out, and its tighter structure gave it unity and impact. It enabled the audience to see with a sense of detachment the common destiny of themselves and others.

The comedies and tragedies were presented during the festival of Dionysus in open-air amphitheaters. The theater of Athens was located on a slope of the Acropolis. Rows of seats, arranged in a semicircle, descended from the top of the hill to the orchestra—a pattern that was repeated in many city-states, and is best preserved at Epidaurus, in the south of Greece (see

photo). Beyond the orchestra, across the open end of the theater, stood a *skéné*, or actors' building (the origin of the word *scene*); in front of it was a porch, or platform, from which the speakers usually recited their lines.

The Greek actors wore masks that identified their roles and were shaped to help them project their voices. All of them were men, though women seemingly were in the audience. The performances were colorful, with grand speeches, music, graceful dancing and singing, and rich costumes and headdresses. There was no curtain or lighting and very little scenery. The author himself wrote the music as well as the text and also trained the cast. During the standard three-day festival of Dionysus, dramatic performances began each morning and lasted until nightfall. Usually, three playwrights competed on successive days, and a prize of great honor was awarded to the one who was judged best.

 Ancient Greek Theater (http://www.richeast.org/htwm/Greeks/theatre/theatre.html) Learn more about Greek costumes, acting, and staging.

Tragedy: Gods and Humans, Morals and Fate

The three tragic playwrights most honored in ancient times, and still revered today, all lived in Athens in the fifth century B.C.

The Theater of Epidaurus Constructed by Polyclitus the Younger in the fourth century B.C. for dramatic contests in honor of the healer-god Asclepius, this theater is still in use today. The benches, seating about eight thousand people, surround the orchestra, and behind it are the foundations of the *skéné*. A person speaking in a normal voice from the *skéné* can be clearly heard seventy yards away in the rear of the theater. Robert Harding Picture Library/SuperStock 1890-20893

DRAMA EVOLVED IN ANCIENT GREECE IN TWO DIRECTIONS:

The Origins of Tragedy

- Greek tragedy grew out of ancient religious ceremonials. It began in the sixth century B.C. as part of the annual spring festival in honor of the god Dionysus.

- During the spring festivals, it was customary for a choral group to sing hymns about the gods and heroes of Greek legend. As the chorus sang, it danced in dignified fashion around a circular plot of ground called the *orkhēstra* (derived from the Greek word for "dance," and the origin of the word orchestra).

- Drama was born when the leader of the chorus was permitted to step out from the group and carry on a kind of conversation (in song) with the chorus.

- By the beginning of the fifth century B.C., the choral dramas might have several individual characters, although no more than three actors plus the chorus took part at any one time. Thus the ancient, repetitive ceremonial became a medium for expressing new ideas.

The Origins of Comedy

- The rites in honor of Dionysus included not only solemn dances and chants but also raucous processions and frenzied revels. It was out of these celebrations that Athenian comedy was born.

- The earliest comedies were crude slapstick performances, but gradually they became biting topical satires—though always heavily spiced with bedroom and toilet jokes.

- The most successful writer of Greek comedy was Aristophanes. He used his plays to make fun of local politicians, poets, and philosophers with whom he disagreed—as well as the politics and government of Athenian democracy, as in *Lysistrata* and *The Assemblywomen* (p. 59).

Aeschylus, Sophocles, and Euripides wrote nearly three hundred plays, although only about thirty have survived.

The earliest tragic dramatist was Aeschylus, whose plays transform suffering and death into inspiration and the will to live. In the Orestes trilogy—*Agamemnon*, the *Libation Bearers*, and the *Eumenides*—Aeschylus's central theme is the family crimes of the royal house of Atreus. The plot, well known in Greek legend, revolves around the murder of King Agamemnon by his wife Clytemnestra when he returns from the Trojan War. The murder is partly an act of revenge for Agamemnon's sacrifice of their daughter so that the gods will give a fair wind for the Greeks to sail to Troy at the beginning of the war; but in turn their son Orestes murders his mother. Father, mother, and son can all justify their acts, but all are nonetheless guilty. To Aeschylus, these crimes and the suffering they bring are divine punishment for violations of the moral order. In the final play of the trilogy, Athena herself intervenes to protect Orestes from pursuit by the Furies, the divine avengers of the murder of parents, and to stop the terrible cycle of crime and punishment (see photo on page 61). Revenge is transformed into the justice of the city-state, and Orestes is restored to respectability. Audiences left with the feeling that individuals pay for their crimes—that the gods and the moral law are hard but that one can face fate bravely and nobly.

Because Sophocles reflected the Greek ideal of "nothing in excess," he has been called the "most Greek" of the three playwrights. In the tragedy, *Oedipus the King*, Oedipus thinks he can avoid his fate, which has been foretold by the Delphic oracle of Apollo. A man of good intention, he tries to escape from the shocking prophecy that he will kill his father and marry his mother. But in the end, the truth of his moral crimes, which he has committed unknowingly, is brought to light by his own insistent searching. He realizes at last the folly of his conceit and savagely blinds himself as punishment for the foulness of his deeds.

Sophocles on the Wondrous Abilities of Human Beings Read a speech from Sophocles' tragedy, *Antigone*.

Euripides, the youngest of the great Greek tragedians, probably had the deepest insight into human character. He was also considered something of a radical, for he challenged the traditional religious and moral values of his time. He opposed slavery and showed the "other side" of war. In *The Trojan Women*, the battle ends with a broken-hearted old woman sitting on the ground holding a dead child in her arms. Euripides was keenly sensitive to injustice, whether of the gods or of mortals, and he pleaded for greater tolerance, equality, and decency.

History

All ancient peoples celebrated events and deeds of the past. Minstrels sang of epic deeds, rulers built monuments boasting of their victories, priests chronicled the doings of the deities they served. But Greek writers were the first to try to separate fact from fiction and to analyze in depth the human causes of events.

The "father of history," Herodotus (huh-ROD-uh-tuhs), was born in 485 B.C. in Halicarnassus, a Greek city on the shore of Asia Minor. A great traveler, he visited various parts of the Persian Empire—Mesopotamia, Syria, and Egypt. He also toured Greek colonies from the Black Sea to southern Italy. Having grown up in the time of the Persian Wars (p. 56), he decided to set down a record of that struggle and of the events that led up to it.

Herodotus called his work the *Historia*, which means, in Greek, "investigation," and he set out to separate fact from legend, to write an account based on direct observation and evidence. The sources he used were not all reliable, to be sure, but he usually warned his readers when he was passing along doubtful information. Most of the *Historia* is a survey of the entire region of eastern Europe, Egypt, and Persia that formed the background to the wars: political and military affairs, social customs, religious beliefs, and leading personalities. In the final portion of his work, he tells the story of the Persian Wars in a manner sympathetic to both Persians and Greeks, though presenting it as an epic contest between slavery and freedom.

A generation later, the Athenian Thucydides (thoo-SID-i-deez) took the writing of history to a higher critical level in his history of the long and cruel war between Athens and Sparta that had broken out soon after their joint victory over Persia (Chapter 5). An exiled general of Athens, he had traveled widely to gather information during the war. His subject matter is far more limited than that of Herodotus, but his account has greater unity and depth. And he excluded all suggestion of supernatural interference; history, he was convinced, is made by human beings, and human nature could be understood through careful study of the past. He presented his facts from both sides, showing the reader the causes, motives, and consequences of the war. But his work is more than military history; it deals with the still-relevant questions of imperialism, democracy, and the whole range of social relations.

Both Herodotus and Thucydides were influenced by existing traditions of Greek literature, especially the epics of Homer. For example, both historians put speeches into the mouths of leading figures like Pericles (p. 59) that were never actually spoken but reveal their personalities and motives, just as Homer did with many of his characters. But history also sprang from another source: the search by Greek thinkers for explanations of the world and humans that would be more logical and convincing than religious tradition provided.

LO⁴ The Founders of Philosophy

The earliest Greek philosophers (in the sixth century B.C.) began by looking for alternatives to the traditions about the gods and goddesses. They found it hard to believe that lightning was a bolt from Zeus, or that a god who repeatedly deceived his wife would care about humans abiding by oaths. But if not, what was the real cause of lightning? Why should people be righteous? And what were the gods really like? Greek thinkers did not reach final answers to questions like these and even argued fiercely whether final answers were possible at all. But they began a quest for answers that has influenced Western thought and science ever since.

> **"**O god—all come true, all burst to light! O light—now let me look my last on you! I stand revealed at last—cursed in my birth, cursed in marriage, cursed in the lives I cut down with these hands!**"**
>
> —from Oedipus the King

Thinking About the Universe: The Pre-Socratics

To answer questions about lightning and everything else that happens in nature, early Greek thinkers (now known as the **Pre-Socratics**) wanted to know what material things are made of. They were sure that everything they saw around them must be made of a few basic elements, but they could not agree on what these elements were. Around 600 B.C., Thales of Miletus (in Asia Minor) theorized that water was the basic element—it filled the sea, rivers, and springs; it fell from the sky; it was found in the flesh and organs of animal bodies. Though later philosophers rejected Thales' belief that everything can be reduced to water, they agreed that he was on the right track. Some believed the prime substance to be air or fire; others concluded that there are four basic elements: earth, air, fire, and water.

But during the fifth century B.C., Democritus of Abdera (in Thrace, a territory on the Aegean's northern coast) developed the theory that all things are formed by combinations of tiny particles, so small that they are both invisible and indivisible. He called them *atoms* (from the Greek for "can't be cut up"). Democritus's atoms are identical in substance but differ in shape, thus making possible the great variety of objects in the world. They are infinite in number, everlasting, and in constant motion. They account, said Democritus, for everything that has been or ever will be. Democritus offered no evidence to prove the

tragedy
A type of play in which the main character suffers a terrible downfall.

comedy
A type of play characterized by humor and a happy ending.

Pre-Socratic philosophers
The modern label given to ancient Greek philosophers before Socrates.

Sophists
A group of professional teachers who argued that truth is relative and that it was more important to have a persuasive argument than a sound one.

Socratic method
A form of inquiry involving questions and answers intended to lead from uncertainty to truth.

existence of atoms, but the fact that he could arrive at this idea demonstrates the far-reaching achievement of Greek reasoning.

Likewise, in the fifth century B.C., Hippocrates of Cos (an island in the Aegean) challenged traditional supernatural explanations of illness. He insisted that natural causes be looked for and that natural means be used to treat disease. He was one of the first physicians to stress the influence of the environment (climate, air, and water) on health. He also claimed that the human body contains four "humors" (fluids): blood, phlegm, yellow bile, and black bile. When these are in proper balance, the individual enjoys normal health. But when the balance becomes disturbed, the physician must use his skill to restore it. This theory was accepted in the West for more than two thousand years and was only proven incorrect in modern times.

Meanwhile, the philosopher Parmenides of Elea (in southern Italy) tackled the controversial issue of permanence versus change in the world. He convinced himself that everything in the universe must be eternal and unchangeable. Change requires motion, he reasoned, and motion requires empty space. But empty space equals nonexistence, which by definition does not exist. Therefore, he concluded, motion and change are impossible. Parmenides readily admitted that some things *appear* to move and change; but this must be an illusion of the senses, he said, because it is contradicted by logic. And logic, the Greek philosophers thought, is the most reliable test of truth.

Logic did not always lead to the same answers, however. In contrast to Parmenides, Heraclitus of Ephesus (in Asia Minor) insisted that the universe, instead of standing still, is in continuous motion. He declared that a person cannot step into the same river twice—a disturbing claim, for if everything is constantly changing (including ourselves), how can we gain true knowledge of anything? Heraclitus's answer was that the universe was ultimately understandable—that all its changes were governed by what he called Reason (in Greek, *logos*, from which the word *logic* derives), which was also present in the human mind. But so far as is known, he did not explain exactly how humans could use the Reason in their minds to understand the ever-changing universe.

> **"***Socrates did not believe it necessary to observe and collect data in order to find knowledge; on the contrary, he had a deep conviction that truth is implanted in the mind and cannot be seen in the changing world around us. The function of the philosopher is to recover the truth that lies buried in the mind.***"**

No Final Answers: The Sophists

Suggestions like these led many Greeks to abandon the effort to find certain knowledge of anything. A group of professional teachers, called **Sophists** because they claimed to make their pupils wise (*sophos*), played a leading part in this shift. Most of them visited various cities of the Mediterranean area to earn their living. When they settled in Athens, as many did, they held more cosmopolitan views about the world than did ordinary Athenian citizens. Prominent among the Sophists was Protagoras. He is famous for having declared, "Man is the measure of all things, of what is and of what is not." Completely skeptical (doubting) of general truths, even about the gods, he insisted that truth is different for each individual. What was true (or right) for a Spartan might well be false (or wrong) for an Athenian.

The Sophists thus rejected the established view that there existed a common, "objective" reality that all persons can grasp in the same way. They concluded, therefore, that it is pointless to look for certain knowledge about either nature or morals. Because truth is relative to each individual, it is important only to know what one finds agreeable and useful, such as the arts of persuasion or how to achieve success.

As news of these teachings circulated in Athens and elsewhere in Greece, the citizens were shocked and alarmed. Such ideas smacked of impiety (disrespect for the gods) and threatened to subvert the laws and moral code of the state. Protagoras protested that his theories did not call for the denial of authority and cautioned his pupils, "When in Athens, do as the Athenians." Social order, he agreed, requires reasonable conformity to the laws of the community, whether or not they are absolutely true or right. But the citizens were not reassured. It upset them to think that one person's ideas are as "true" as another's. And the laws of gods and mortals, they argued, cannot be properly respected and upheld unless people believe them to be genuinely true and just.

Truth Beyond This World: Socrates and Plato

The greatest teacher of the fifth century was Socrates, who met the Sophist view of how to get on in life with the full force of his intellect and will. He was convinced of the existence of a higher truth, though he did not claim to know this truth but spoke of himself only as a seeker after knowledge. He believed that knowledge must proceed from doubting, and he was forever posing questions and testing the answers people gave him. Because of this, the Athenians often mistook Socrates for a Sophist, and he shared in their unpopularity.

The Socratic Method

This "Socratic method" of questioning is simply a procedure for reaching toward truth by means of a dialogue or directed discussion. Socrates cross-examined his friends on their definitions of justice, right, and beauty, moving them constantly toward answers that seemed more and more certain. Socrates did not believe it necessary to observe and collect data in order to find knowledge; on the contrary, he had a deep conviction that truth is implanted in the mind and cannot be seen in the changing world around us. The function of the philosopher is to recover the truth that lies buried in the mind.

Socrates' search for truth sustained him in the face of death itself. In the dialogue of the *Phaedo*, his pupil Plato describes the final hours of his teacher. Condemned to death by an Athenian jury on charges of corrupting the youth and not worshiping the gods of Athens, Socrates faces his fate cheerfully. He does so because he believes the soul is immortal, though during life it is hindered by the troubles and "foolishness" of the body. Death brings release for the soul and the opportunity to see the truth more clearly than before. And for Socrates, the real aim of life is to know the truth, rather than to seek the satisfactions of the body.

Socrates: Death Is a Good Thing Read Socrates' thoughts on death as he hears his death sentence.

Plato: The Doctrine of Ideas

Almost all we know about Socrates' views comes to us through Plato, who wrote masterly literary works in the form of dialogues in which Socrates usually appears as the chief speaker. It is difficult to say where the ideas of Socrates end and those of Plato begin, but it seems clear that Plato took up and developed the main thoughts of his teacher. Plato was born in or near Athens, traveled widely through the Mediterranean lands, and founded a school at Athens in 385 B.C. The Academy, as it was called, became the most influential intellectual center of the ancient world. It endured after its founder's death for over nine hundred years, and it served as a model for similar schools in other cities.

Plato continued Socrates' attack on the Sophist theory of truth as changeable and different for each person. Returning to the controversies of earlier Greek thinkers about what things were made of and about the question of permanence and change, Plato felt that the imperfect surface of things conceals a perfect and eternal order.

In his famous "Doctrine of Ideas," Plato conceded that everything that we actually see around us is just what the Sophists suggested: imperfect, changeable, and different in appearance to every individual. But above and beyond it, Plato asserted, is the real world of perfect Ideas or Forms, which exist unchanged through all the ages. There are, for example, the Ideas of Man, Horse, Tree, Beauty, the State, Justice, and the highest of all Ideas—Goodness. These exist independent of individuals and can be known to them only through the mind. Plato speculated that the universe as we see it is the work of a *demiurge* (from the Greek for "craftsman")—a divine but imperfect being whose creation could only be a distorted reflection of the Ideas. Philosophers should turn away from things as we see them and focus on the discovery and contemplation of the perfect, the eternal, the real.

The Ideal Community

True to his belief in a perfect world beyond the world as we perceive it, in the best known of his dialogues, the *Republic*, Plato presented an image of the perfect city-state—which he probably never expected to replace imperfect existing ones. Such a community, according to Plato, would need to be guided by truthful principles as interpreted by philosophers. An aristocrat who grew up during the Peloponnesian War, which brought Athens's Golden Age to an end (pp. 80–81), Plato admired Spartan institutions and had contempt for democratic ways. The institutions of a perfect community should aim not at complete individual freedom and equality but at social justice and order. In the community, just as in the human body, every part should do the job it was designed to do. The foot should not try to become the head—nor the head the stomach. Only then would friction, envy, and inefficiency—the chief sources of human and social sickness—be eliminated.

To reach this objective, Plato felt, the city-state must be structured according to natural capacities. The bulk of its citizens would make up the class of Workers (producers), who would be sorted into various occupations according to their aptitudes. Above them would be the Guardian class, which would be trained in the arts

"Snub-Nosed and Pop-Eyed" This portrait bust, believed to date from about twenty years after Socrates died, is true to Plato's description of his teacher and friend. Plato also compared Socrates with Athenian statues of the pot-bellied, balding god Silenus—which, however, opened up to reveal that they contained golden images of the noblest deities. Vatican Museums/Art Resource, NY

PLATO ON THE EQUALITY OF WOMEN AND MEN IN HIS IDEAL CITY-STATE

Like Plato's other works, his description of the ideal city-state, the *Republic*, is written in the form of a fictional dialogue (conversation) between Socrates and his friends. Here, the subject is the "virtue" (the excellence as human beings) of women and men—especially in the guiding elite of Guardians—and the activities that women should share with men as Guardians. Socrates and his friend Glaucon are discussing how Socrates would argue against someone who disapproves of women being active alongside men in such pursuits as government, warfare, and athletics.

Next, we shall ask our opponent how, in reference to any of the pursuits or arts of civic life, the nature of a woman differs from that of a man?

That will be quite fair.

And perhaps he, like yourself, will reply that to give a sufficient answer on the instant is not easy; but after a little reflection there is no difficulty.

Yes, perhaps.

Suppose then that we invite him to accompany us in the argument, and then we may hope to show him that there is nothing peculiar in the constitution of women which would affect them in the administration of the State.

By all means. . . .

And can you mention any pursuit of mankind in which the male sex has not all these gifts and qualities in a higher degree than the female? Need I waste time in speaking of the art of weaving, and the management of pancakes and preserves, in which womankind does really appear to be great, and in which for her to be beaten by a man is of all things the most absurd?

You are quite right, he replied, in maintaining the general inferiority of the female sex: although many women are in many things superior to many men, yet on the whole what you say is true.

And if so, my friend, I said, there is no special faculty of administration in a state which a woman has because she is a woman, or which a man has by virtue of his sex, but the gifts of nature are alike diffused in both; all the pursuits of men are the pursuits of women also, but in all of them a woman is inferior to a man.

Very true.

Then are we to impose all our enactments on men and none of them on women?

That will never do.

One woman has a gift of healing, another not; one is a musician, and another has no music in her nature?

Very true.

And one woman has a turn for gymnastic and military exercises, and another is unwarlike and hates gymnastics?

---

of government and war. From this disciplined class would be chosen, with the greatest care, the rulers of the state.

The Guardians would be no privileged upper class, but would lead austere and regulated lives of total devotion to the state. Matings among them would be arranged by the state, to ensure the production of superior offspring. Any infant showing a physical defect would be left to die of exposure, and healthy infants would be taken from their mothers and placed in a community nursery. Parents would not be permitted to know their own children, nor would they be allowed to possess personal property. The education of the Guardians was to be closely controlled. Only the "right" kind of music, art, and poetry would be taught, so that pupils would receive the desired moral indoctrination. Those selected to be the rulers would have additional training in philosophy and would serve a period of political apprenticeship before taking their places as directors of the state. All this was necessary, thought Plato, if they were to become truly selfless and dedicated to the welfare of the whole community.

The Abolition of the Family

The Guardians would be both male and female, and among the rulers there would be both "philosopher-kings" and "philosopher-queens." This was not because Plato found the existing treatment of women oppressive. On the contrary, he believed that the existing system was too

Certainly.

And one woman is a philosopher, and another is an enemy of philosophy; one has spirit, and another is without spirit?

That is also true.

Then one woman will have the temper of a guardian, and another not. Was not the selection of the male guardians determined by differences of this sort?

Yes.

Men and women alike possess the qualities which make a guardian; they differ only in their comparative strength or weakness.

Obviously.

And those women who have such qualities are to be selected as the companions and colleagues of men who have similar qualities and whom they resemble in capacity and in character?

Very true.

And ought not the same natures to have the same pursuits?

They ought.

Then, as we were saying before, there is nothing unnatural in assigning music and gymnastic to the wives of the guardians—to that point we come round again.

Certainly not. . . .

Well, and may we not further say that our guardians are the best of our citizens?

By far the best.

And will not their wives be the best women?

Yes, by far the best.

And can there be anything better for the interests of the State than that the men and women of a State should be as good as possible?

There can be nothing better.

And this is what the arts of music and gymnastic, when present in such manner as we have described, will accomplish?

Certainly.

Then we have made an enactment not only possible but in the highest degree beneficial to the State?

True.

Then let the wives of our guardians strip, for their virtue will be their robe, and let them share in the toils of war and the defence of their country; only in the distribution of labours the lighter are to be assigned to the women, who are the weaker natures, but in other respects their duties are to be the same. And as for the man who laughs at naked women exercising their bodies from the best of motives, in his laughter he is plucking a fruit of unripe wisdom, and he himself is ignorant of what he is laughing at, or what he is about;—for that is, and ever will be, the best of sayings, *That the useful is the noble and the hurtful is the base.*

EXPLORING THE SOURCE

1. How did Plato justify allowing women to participate as Guardians in the governance of his ideal city-state, and what kind of activities did he want them to take part in?

2. Why did Plato think that it was desirable for women to share fully in the activities of his ideal city-state?

Source: Plato, *Republic* 5, trans. Benjamin Jowett, *Dialogues of Plato*, 3d ed. (London: Macmillan, 1892), 3:147–150.

easy on women, because it exempted them from the main burdens of citizenship. Women were well able to bear these burdens, Plato believed, because their abilities—including as warriors—were basically the same as those of men. On the average, he thought, women's abilities were not so strong as men's, but this made no difference to the fact that a city-state that did not make use of women in the same way as it made use of men "is only half a state, and develops only half its potentialities."

Plato applied this idea only to the Guardians, among whom breeding and education would produce superior females and males as thinkers, fighters, and rulers. For the Workers, whose tasks and abilities were on a lower level than those of the Guardians, he though that traditional family life was still best.

And in another work, the *Laws*, where Plato was more interested in making recommendations for existing city-states than in imagining ideal alternatives, he advised that women should be deliberately educated in the belief that their abilities were different from men's, so that traditional family and community life could run smoothly.

Plato was the first thinker to imagine an alternative to the way of life based on communities made up of families that had grown up with the Agricultural Revolution (pp. 9–10). At least among a restricted elite, his alternative involved the abolition of the family, the equality of women and men, and the complete subordination of the individual to the community. The belief that these three things go together has inspired many radical social reformers—and horrified their opponents—over the centuries. Plato was also the first thinker to claim that the idea of a fundamental difference in abilities between men and women is a socially convenient myth—a claim that is basic to much of modern feminism.

Analyzing This World: Aristotle

Born in Stagira on the Aegean's northern coast, Aristotle made his way early to Plato's Academy in Athens; years later, he founded a school of his own there—the Lyceum (335 B.C.). Far more than his teacher, Aristotle was interested in the evidence of the senses. He was, in fact, the greatest collector and classifier in antiquity. His interests ranged from biology to poetry, from politics to ethics.

Aristotle accepted Plato's general notion of the existence of Ideas or Forms, but he held that the things around us are also a part of reality, a kind of raw material given their different shapes and purposes by the Forms. By logical thinking, people can gain knowledge of these purposes, and thereby approach closer to God—whom Aristotle conceived as pure spirit and the source of the Forms. For this reason, he worked out systematic rules for logical thinking that have been respected by philosophers for centuries.

Classifying Human Beings

In accordance with his theory that all things have a purpose, Aristotle taught that every organ and creature should function according to its design—including human beings. Like Plato, he thought that different human beings were designed for different functions. For each of them, "virtue" (human excellence) consisted in perfectly fulfilling these functions, so that virtue meant different things for different types of humans. But Aristotle worked out in much more detail than Plato what this meant for existing communities, and unlike his master, he accepted as true the idea that men and women have basically differing abilities.

The highest kind of human excellence, Aristotle believed, was to be found in the activities of ruling over other humans and pursuing knowledge of the Forms and of God. This, he thought, calls for a harmonious balance of faculties (abilities) of both body and mind. In general, excellence in a particular activity lies somewhere between extremes. True courage in battle, for example, lies somewhere in between cowardice and foolhardiness. Likewise, a truly beautiful work of art is one that is "just right"—it cannot be improved either by adding something or by taking something away. Aristotle warned that his advice did not apply to things that are good or bad in themselves. Truth and beauty, for example, should be sought in the highest degree, while murder, theft, and lying are evil in any degree. But in most activities, each man should find, through trial and self-criticism,

the desired mean (midpoint) between extremes. This has come to be called the **Golden Mean**—not a pale average or a mediocre standard, but the best performance of mind and body working together in harmony.

This kind of virtue, however, was only to be achieved by a small minority of the human race, namely, freeborn Greek men with at least some wealth and education. The virtue of other humans lay in performing various lower, though still essential, functions. Non-Greeks, for instance, were not designed for highest excellence, and that was what made them suitable as slaves. For them, virtue meant willingness to perform dull and heavy tasks, thereby freeing their masters to pursue higher forms of excellence. Likewise, Aristotle said that "the male is by nature superior, and the female inferior," and that though both possessed virtue, their virtue was of different kinds; for instance, "the courage of a man is shown in commanding, of a woman in obeying." In this way, Aristotle used the new methods of philosophical reasoning to claim that the existing Greek pattern of community and family life was no hardship and did not need to be replaced by an ideal alternative society, but was part of the proper order of the universe.

Real-World Communities

Aristotle believed that communities, too, had a purpose. Their function was to create the conditions in which virtue could flourish, but there was no single way of doing this. In his classic work, the *Politics*, Aristotle examined existing city-states, analyzed and evaluated the major types of political organization, and recognized that there are differences in local conditions and classes of inhabitants. He considered government by one man, by a few, and by many all legitimate, if devoted to the general welfare; each needs to serve the interests of all social groups if it is to survive; and any type of government becomes a "perversion" when the rulers pursue their own interest alone. (The worst government of all, he thought, is a perversion of rule by the many.) Under whatever constitution, Aristotle favored a strong role for the middle class of citizens. The more numerous poor, he stated, lack experience in directing others; the very rich are not used to obeying. The middle class knows what it is both to command and to obey and may be counted on to avoid political extremes.

Aristotle on Politics Read a passage in which Aristotle analyzes different forms of government.

Aristotle's explanation of the order of the universe and human inequality had vast influence on Western philosophy, science, and everyday thinking for many centuries until recent times. His ideal of a highest human excellence that only a few can reach—though with the few no longer consisting of well-to-do men of a particular nation—is still influential today. And his method of analyzing and comparing the features and development of government systems is basic to modern political science.

Listen to a synopsis of Chapter 4.

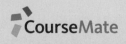

{ Listen Up! }

CHAPTER 5

GREATER GREECE: THE HELLENISTIC ERA, 400–30 B.C.

LEARNING OBJECTIVES

AFTER READING THIS CHAPTER, YOU SHOULD BE ABLE TO DO THE FOLLOWING:

LO¹ Trace the crisis of the Greek city-states and the rise of Macedonia.

LO² Explain how Hellenistic-era Greek culture gained international leadership but was also influenced by the peoples the Greeks ruled.

LO³ Contrast the Epicurean and Stoic philosophies of the Hellenistic era.

"THE GREEKS HAD EVOLVED FROM A BARBARIAN PEOPLE ON CIVILIZATION'S NORTHWESTERN EDGE TO BECOME THE DOMINANT NATION OF A REGION THAT STRETCHED FROM ITALY TO PRESENT-DAY AFGHANISTAN."

Throughout history, clusters of independent city-states have sooner or later come under the power of stronger neighboring rulers, and the Greek city-states were no exception. The longest and most brutal of their many conflicts, the Peloponnesian War between opposing alliances under Athens and Sparta, led to the end of the heyday of the city-states around 400 B.C. As a result, they eventually fell under the rule of the Greek-influenced northern kingdom of Macedonia.

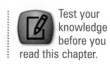

Test your knowledge before you read this chapter.

This did not mean the end of Greek civilization or of Greek power in the world, however. On the contrary, King Alexander of Macedonia led the Greeks to the conquest of Persia, and though his empire split up after his death, its separate territories came to be ruled by spectacularly wealthy and powerful Greek kings.

What do you think?

Greek civilization would have endured longer if the Greeks had not overreached.

Strongly Disagree						Strongly Agree
1	2	3	4	5	6	7

By 300 B.C., Greek civilization had entered a new phase, the Hellenistic (**hel-uh-NIS-tik**) era, in which theirs was the leading international culture but their way of life was also influenced by the peoples they ruled. And the Greeks themselves had evolved from a barbarian people on civilization's northwestern edge to become the dominant nation of a region that stretched from Italy to present-day Afghanistan.

≪ **A Hellenistic Buddha** This carving was made in Gandhara, in the borderland between present-day Pakistan and Afghanistan, about A.D. 100. Buddha is guarded by Vajrapani, the heroic symbol of his spiritual power. But Buddha's hairstyle, and his gown with its delicate folds, are Greek; and Vajrapani has the nude pose and the club of a Greek hero, Heracles. Following Alexander's conquests, Greeks had long ruled this region, and Buddhist art still felt their influence.

LO¹ The Crisis of the City-States

After several centuries of growing confidence and power, the Greek city-states were caught up in a massive conflict growing out of rivalry between Athens and Sparta. The Athenians called it the "Peloponnesian" war because their chief enemies were Sparta and its allies in the southernmost region of mainland Greece, the Peloponnesus, and neighboring areas (Map 5.1). There had been earlier conflicts between Sparta and Athens, but the long struggle that opened in 431 B.C., and lasted until 404 B.C., ended with the defeat of Athens and the weakening of Sparta.

The Peloponnesian War

Like all competitive city-states, those of Greece continually fought each other, with the more powerful ones struggling to dominate the others. Sparta, with its well-trained army, was traditionally the most powerful city-state in mainland Greece. The Persian Wars, however, made Athens first Sparta's equal partner and then its rival.

Map 5.1 **The Peloponnesian War**

The war was a conflict between the land power of Sparta and its allies, mainly in southern Greece, and the sea power of the Athenian alliance of city-states in the coasts and islands of the Aegean. It was hard for either side to strike a decisive blow until Athenian naval losses in Sicily, as well as money and supplies from the still mighty Persian Empire, enabled Sparta to build a navy that could defeat Athens. © Cengage Learning

Interactive Map

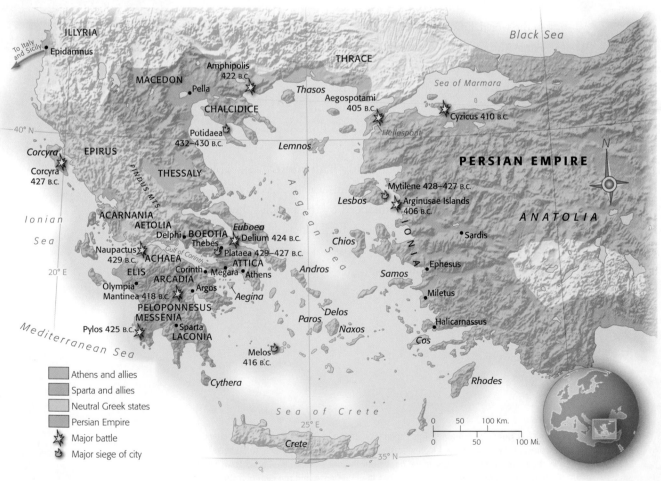

SEVERAL FACTORS CONTRIBUTED TO ATHENS LOSING THE PELOPONNESIAN WAR:

Natural Disaster and Poor Leadership

- In 430 B.C., a terrible plague struck Athens, killing thousands of inhabitants, including Pericles himself.

- Athens recovered, but leadership of the city passed to reckless politicians who spurned Sparta's offers of compromise and "peace without victory."

Damaging Losses

- In 413 B.C., Athens lost two-thirds of its fleet in an expedition against Sparta's ally Syracuse.

- With help from Persia (which considered Athens their greatest threat), Sparta built a navy to challenge Athens's now smaller fleet.

- The Spartans crushed the Athenian fleet in 405 B.C. at the battle of Aegospotami in the straits between the Aegean and the Black Sea.

- Their navy destroyed and needing grain supplies from overseas, the Athenian citizens were starved into surrender (404 B.C.).

 The Plague Strikes Athens Read a vivid account of the plague's toll.

Once the defeat of Xerxes' invasion in 480 B.C. made mainland Greece safe from attack, Sparta dropped out of the fighting. Athens, however, formed an alliance of city-states to go over to the offensive, which most of the Greek city-states on the Aegean coasts and islands eventually joined (Map 5.1). Members agreed to contribute money annually for the construction of triremes (p. 52), which were placed under Athenian command. The city thus gained control of several hundred vessels with their crews—by far the largest fleet to sail the Mediterranean at the time.

Athens Demands Tribute from Its Allies Read how the Athenians planned to collect tribute from their allies.

In 445 B.C., after the Greek city-states of Anatolia had been freed from Persian rule and the Persians had accepted defeat, Athens nevertheless forced its allies to go on sending money, thereby turning them into tribute-paying subjects. Many of the city-states of mainland Greece were provoked by the Athenians' behavior—especially as these city-states were generally ruled by oligarchies, and the Athenians usually insisted that their subject cities practice democracy. The smaller mainland cities appealed to the Spartans to put a check on Athens. At last, the Spartans decided to support their ally, Corinth, which had become involved in a naval war with Athens, and the Athenians took up

> "*To the north of Greece, a power was rising, the kingdom of Macedonia, that would soon put an end to the independence of the city-states. But under Macedonian leadership, the Greeks would enjoy a brief moment of unity that would enable them to replace the Persians as the dominant nation of the lands stretching from Asia Minor and Egypt to the borders of India.*"

the challenge. In the words of the historian Thucydides, what had brought on the conflict was the fact that "the Athenians had grown great and inspired fear in the Spartans, thereby compelling them to war."

In the course of the war (431–404 B.C.), the Athenians, under the guidance of Pericles, at first showed caution and sound strategy. The city of Athens and its nearby harbor, Piraeus, formed a single stronghold. The Spartans, unbeatable on the battlefield but not equipped for siege warfare, often raided Attica but could not capture the city itself or cut its links with the sea.

Meanwhile, the Athenians used their navy to guard the sea routes that supplied them with grain and to raid Sparta and its allies. Despite its strengths, however, Athens would eventually fall to Sparta.

Defeated, the Athenians gave up all their outlying possessions, pulled down their defensive walls, and became forced allies of Sparta under a harshly ruling oligarchy. But Sparta, too, had lost both men and resources, and could not prevent Athens from eventually returning to democracy and regaining its independence. With both rivals weakened, the city-states returned to their traditional pattern of continual struggle. Thebes tried unsuccessfully to replace Sparta and Athens as the dominant city-state, and even Persia, for a time, wielded effective influence in mainland Greece.

Meanwhile, Greek civilization continued to flourish. The works of Plato and Aristotle, for instance, date from the era that followed the end of the Peloponnesian War. Plato's search for an ideal city-state was perhaps partly inspired by the doubts and questionings in Athens following defeat—but in spite of the upheaval, Aristotle did not doubt or question the superiority of the Greeks in human excellence to all other peoples. In fact, the Greeks and their way of life were about to become more important in the world than ever before. To the north of Greece, a power was rising, the kingdom of Macedonia (**mas-i-DOH-nee-uh**), that would soon put an end to the independence of the city-states. But under Macedonian leadership, the Greeks would enjoy a brief moment of unity that would enable them to replace the Persians as the dominant nation of the lands stretching from Anatolia and Egypt to the borders of India.

The Rise of Macedonia

Macedonia was a border territory between Greece and still-barbarian peoples farther north in Europe, and though the Macedonians were probably native Greek-speakers, they and the Greeks regarded each other as different nations. The country was ruled in the traditional manner, by kings and warrior nobles. But it was also larger and richer in resources than any city-state, and its kings had always admired the Greeks and longed to associate themselves with them.

In 359 B.C., Macedonia came under the rule of King Philip II, a ruler of broad vision who was determined to gain control of the city-states and to lead the Greeks and Macedonians in a united force against the weakening empire of Persia. In the course of fighting against barbarian peoples to the north, he strengthened his army by adopting Greek phalanx tactics, improving the weapons of his hoplites, and building up a stronger cavalry force than any city-state possessed. Meanwhile, he made careful plans for infiltrating and conquering Greece. Philip's agents worked to prevent the city-states from joining forces against him. One eloquent Athenian, Demosthenes, recognized the peril and repeatedly warned his fellow citizens. But the traditional reluctance of the city-states to work together, combined with their failure to take the new menace seriously, played into Philip's hands.

At last, he was ready to move. Through diplomacy and military pressure, Philip thrust into northern and central Greece. The Athenians, aroused at last, formed an alliance with the Thebans in an attempt to stop him. It was too late. At the battle of Chaeronea (338 B.C.), the Macedonians won a decisive victory. What remained of Greek independence was left for Philip to decide.

The Macedonian king used his newly won power wisely, letting the Greek city-states govern themselves so long as they installed oligarchies and acted as loyal allies. Philip, now at the head of a powerful alliance, vowed to avenge the insults and injuries inflicted on Greek temples and sanctuaries by the invading Persians more than a century before (p. 64). But as he stood at the very brink of fulfillment, he was assassinated in 336 B.C. His son, Alexander III, only twenty years old, succeeded him and proceeded to carry out his father's grand design.

LO² The Greeks as a Ruling Nation

In 334 B.C., Alexander crossed into Asia Minor to launch the campaign that would make him one of the greatest conquerors in history. True, the Persian Empire had declined in military power, but the combination of heavily armed phalanxes, fast-moving cavalry, and Alexander's

《 **The Stag Hunt** This 6-foot-by-6-foot mosaic, dating from the late fourth century B.C., is part of a townhouse floor in the Macedonian capital, Pella. The lettering says "Gnosis made this." Only a very wealthy house owner could have ordered this luxurious walking surface, and only a very fashionable artist would have been allowed to sign it so conspicuously. Wealthy clients and fashionable artists were prominent features of the Hellenistic era.

HIP/Art Resource, NY

daring and genius succeeded beyond anyone's expectations. His army of about 35,000 Macedonians and Greeks—small in comparison with what it accomplished, though far larger than that of any individual city-state—broke the power of the Persian king within four years. Asia Minor, Syria, Egypt, and Mesopotamia fell before him (see Map 5.2 on page 84). Pushing on through Persia to the frontiers of India, Alexander was checked only by the grumbling and protests of his own men. At the age of thirty-three, he died from the combined effects of fever (perhaps cholera) and a drinking bout—in the city of Babylon, which he had chosen for his imperial capital.

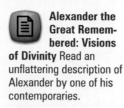

Alexander the Great Remembered: Visions of Divinity Read an unflattering description of Alexander by one of his contemporaries.

Biography of Alexander the Great http://www.biography.com/articles/Alexander-the-Great-9180468?part=0) Learn more about Alexander's life and conquests.

Alexander's Empire and Its Breakup

Alexander had hoped to found the latest in the succession of universal empires (pp. 33–37). This one would be held together by common values and a common way of life, in which Greek influences would predominate but would be blended with features of the local civilizations. He founded cities in the regions he conquered and sent Greeks or Macedonians to colonize them. Their military garrisons would serve to maintain order in the surrounding countryside, and the cities themselves would serve as cultural "melting pots." He made Greek the official language and distributed Greek books and works of art throughout his empire, hoping to spread Hellenic ideas and values. He also encouraged intermarriage and led the way himself by marrying a Persian princess, Roxana.

But after Alexander's death, his empire was soon divided. Though he left a son, the boy fell victim to power struggles among his father's leading generals. In twenty years of bitter warfare, three major states emerged, each ruled by a dynasty of kings descended from one or other of the Macedonian commanders Antigonus, Ptolemy, and Seleucus. The Antigonid kingdom was based on Macedonia itself; the Ptolemaic kingdom held Egypt and nearby lands; and the lands stretching eastward from Syria formed the Seleucid kingdom. Alongside these three dynasties, other rulers, Macedonian, Greek, and non-Greek, carved themselves smaller shares of territory (see Map 5.2).

> **"** *He accomplished greater deeds than any, not only of the kings who had lived before him but also of those who were to come later down to our time.* **"**
>
> —Diodorus of Sicily on Alexander's legacy

An Unfortunate Method of Royal Succession: Imperial Rule Shall Go "To the Strongest" Read an account of Alexander's death and his words on succession.

The three leading dynasties continued to be rivals and, from time to time, fought each other on a scale that dwarfed even the Peloponnesian War. As a result of these rivalries, the city-states of Greece itself managed to regain some freedom of action. But their citizen armies and navies were no match for the massive forces of Greek mercenary soldiers and slave-rowed warships that the "great powers" maintained, and the city-states generally bowed to whichever was strongest at any given time. Only in the western Mediterranean did truly independent city-states survive—many of them Greek, but others non-Greek, like the Phoenician outpost of Carthage and the native Italian community of Rome.

Hellenistic Refers to the "international" period of Greek history, when much of the Mediterranean and southwestern Asia was under Greek rule.

The Hellenistic Kingdoms

In the centuries of the emergence of the city-states, Greeks had already emigrated westward across the Mediterranean. Now, summoned by Alexander's successors, who needed them as soldiers, officials, and traders, they migrated eastward as well. By 200 B.C., Greeks were scattered across the world from the coasts of Spain to the borders of India.

Greeks and Non-Greeks

In Mesopotamia and Egypt in particular, the Greeks now lived side by side with ancient civilizations from which their own had partly arisen. A new era in the history of Greek civilization had begun—one for which historians have invented the term **Hellenistic** (from a Greek word meaning "to behave like a Greek").

Actually, few non-Greeks behaved completely like Greeks. Greek became the international language of business and government, which ambitious non-Greeks would learn so as to get ahead in those fields. But ancient local traditions of civilization continued to flourish. In Egypt, for example, temples were built and decorated, and gods and goddesses were tended within them, all according to age-old tradition, as if the several hundred thousand Greeks who now lived in the country had never arrived; even the Greek kings were venerated and obeyed by the Egyptians as native pharaohs. As for the Greeks, they were mostly content to study Homer by the banks of the Nile, or to applaud Athenian tragedies performed by traveling actors in amphitheaters in Syria and Lebanon that looked exactly like those of Greece itself (see photo on page 69)—or of Sicily and Spain.

Oppression in Alexander's Empire: Cleomenes, Satrap of Egypt Read a description of the misdeeds of a Greek official in Egypt.

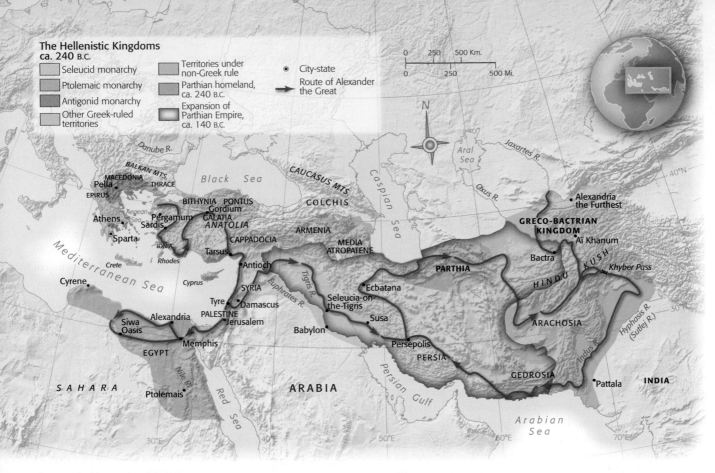

Map 5.2 **The Hellenistic Kingdoms**

With the conquests of Alexander, the Greek world expanded 2,000 miles eastward. Even though Alexander's empire fell apart after his death, much of it remained under the rule of Greek kings, and Greek cities sprang up from Egypt to the borders of India. The Greeks and their culture remained a dominant influence in much of the region for a thousand years until the rise of Islam in the seventh century A.D. © Cengage Learning

Interactive Map

Still, in the long run, the fact that the Greeks were now an internationally dominant nation could not help but bring about changes in their way of life. With the immense resources at their disposal, the Greek rulers were able to support researchers in many fields and to build libraries that preserved the legacy of their nation for future generations. With their new and wider horizons, Greek scholars studied the past and present of many of the lands they now lived in, and non-Greek scholars sometimes wrote the histories of their nations in Greek. Hellenistic civilization achieved great things in science and technology, geography, history, and literary scholarship, as well as carrying on the earlier achievements of the Greeks in philosophy and the arts.

In the long run, too, the Greeks could not help absorbing influences from the nations they now dominated—above all, in the field of religion. The Hellenistic world abounded with international gods and goddesses—for example, the Egyptian deities of the underworld and fertility, Isis and Osiris. The Greeks believed such deities to be the same as their own, only in foreign guise: thus, Isis was identified with Demeter, who had much the same powers among the Greek gods and goddesses (p. 63). But the foreign versions of the gods and goddesses came to seem to the Greeks themselves more powerful, holy, and helpful to humans than the native ones. Later these international deities were even

more widely worshiped in the Roman Empire, and their worship was a precedent for the spread of Christianity (p. 119).

Kings, Queens, and Cities

The political forms of the Hellenistic world were also different from those of the Greek past. The city-states of Greece still had strong community traditions, and wherever Greeks emigrated eastward they founded new cities that kept up many of these traditions. The fate of communities now depended not on citizen armies, navies, and governments, however, but on good relations with the monarchs who ruled the world.

The monarchs, for their part, needed vigorous Greek local communities to underpin their power. However, they preferred these communities to be run by citizens who were few enough to be easily controlled and rich enough to keep the rest of the people satisfied by paying out of their own pockets for religious festivals, public entertainments, and other community business. Wealthy citizens hungry for local prestige and power were glad to take on the responsibilities and expense, so that narrow oligarchies

The Art of the Hellenistic Age and the Hellenistic Tradition (http://www.metmuseum.org/toah/hd/haht/hd_haht.htm) View the artistic legacy of the Hellenistic Age.

A FEMALE PHILOSOPHER: HIPPARCHIA OF MARONEIA

This account of Hipparchia comes from a collection of biographies of notable thinkers written in the third century B.C. by Diogenes Laertius. Hipparchia, her brother, and her husband lived shortly before 300 B.C. in a town in the north of Greece that was under the rule of King Lysimachus of Macedonia. They belonged to the Cynic school of philosophy, which believed in striving for virtue by living a simple and natural life rather than chasing after the socially approved goals of wealth, fame, and power. The school's name came from the Greek word for "dogs," because conventionally minded people scorned the Cynics for their "doglike" existence.

"Leaving the shuttle near the warp" means suddenly breaking off from work. A shuttle is a device used to interweave a thread (called the warp) with other threads to make cloth.

Hipparchia, the sister of Metrocles, was charmed along with others by the doctrines of this school. She and Metrocles were natives of Maroneia. She fell in love with the doctrines and the manners of Crates, and could not be diverted from her regard for him either by the wealth or the high birth or the personal beauty of any of her suitors; but Crates was everything to her. She threatened her parents to make away with herself, if she were not given in marriage to him. When entreated by her parents to dissuade her from this resolution, Crates did all he could; and at last, as he could not persuade her, he arose and placing all his furniture before her, he said: "This is the bridegroom whom you are choosing, and this is the whole of his property. Consider these facts; for it will not be possible for you to become his partner, if you do not apply yourself to the same studies and conform to the same habits as he does." The girl chose him; and assuming the same dress as he wore, went with him as her husband, and appeared with him in public everywhere, and went to all entertainments in his company. Once when she went to sup at the house of Lysimachus, she attacked Theodorus, who was surnamed the Atheist. To him she proposed the following sophism: "What Theodorus could not be called wrong for doing, that same thing Hipparchia could not be called wrong for doing. But Theodorus does no wrong when he beats himself; therefore Hipparchia does no wrong when she beats Theodorus." He made no reply to what she said, but only pulled her gown. Hipparchia was neither offended nor ashamed, as many a woman would have been; but when he said to her:

> Who is the woman who has left the shuttle So near the warp? [Euripides]

She replied: "I, Theodorus, am the person; but do I seem to you to have come to a wrong decision, if I devote that time to philosophy which otherwise I should have spent at the loom?" These and many other sayings are reported of this female philosopher.

EXPLORING THE SOURCE

1. In what ways did Hipparchia's and her husband's way of life go against the expected behavior of women and married couples at the time? Why should Cynic spouses in particular have broken the rules in this way?

2. Why should an exceptionally famous, wealthy, and powerful man like King Lysimachus have invited a female Cynic? Given her principles and way of life, was it right for her to accept?

Source: G. W. Botsford and E. G. Sihler, eds., *Hellenic Civilization* (New York: Columbia University Press, 1915), p. 665.

became the commonest form of Greek community government. Democracy passed out of existence, not to be revived in the West for two thousand years.

Royal courts rather than citizen assemblies were now the real centers of government and politics, where officials, generals, and members of ruling families competed to reach the highest levels of power, wealth, and fame. As in earlier monarchies, women wielded power as wives, concubines, mothers, and sisters of kings, and occasionally as rulers on their own. In Greek cities, property-owning women contributed generously to community expenses alongside men, though in smaller numbers. Like men, they were honored with public monuments and public acclaim, thereby bringing prestige to their families. In this way, monarchy and oligarchy enabled some women to gain fame by doing what democracy had frowned on—getting themselves talked about by men (p. 59).

The Greeks venerated their mighty kings and queens as living gods and goddesses, with divine titles that proclaimed them doers of good, protectors from harm, members of harmonious families, and visible to humans: the Revealed God, the Father-Loving God and Goddess, the Savior God, the Benefactress Goddess (see photo). In Egypt, where the rulers were also pharaohs, they took up the local tradition of marriage between royal brother and royal sister, as myth declared was customary among gods and goddesses. But in Greek religion, too, the dividing line between humans and gods had always been porous, and incest was considered a mark of divinity (p. 62). The Greek version of divine rulership built on their own as well as non-Greek beliefs, and reflected both the self-confidence and the insecurity of a people that had so suddenly risen to international power.

The economy of the Hellenistic age was also different from that of earlier times. Large kingdoms encouraged large-scale production and trade. The Greeks had carried on a far-flung commerce, ranging from the Black Sea to Gibraltar, but now the gates were opened eastward as far as India. The vast new market stimulated enterprise: huge fortunes were made, banking and finance were expanded, and a kind of capitalism took shape. The rulers of the great states had a keen interest in business affairs. They promoted commerce by aiding navigation and transport and made up their expenses by taxing the enterprises. Although wages and general living standards remained low, the growth of industry and trade created many new jobs in the cities. As a result, thousands of peasants moved from the countryside into the urban centers of the eastern Mediterranean.

Large seaport cities such as fifth-century B.C. Athens were nothing new, but some cities—especially those that were centers of royal government as

The Benefactress Goddess On this ritual wine jug, Queen Berenice II of Egypt holds a horn of plenty, the symbol of royal beneficence, and pours out an offering to the gods. Berenice II married King Ptolemy III, the Benefactor God, in 249 B.C and seemingly shared his royal power. That was probably why her son King Ptolemy IV, the Father-Loving God, had her poisoned when he took over in 221 B.C.
The J. Paul Getty Museum, Villa Collection, Malibu, California Unknown, Fragmentary Oinochoe, about 243-221 B.C., Faience, Object: H: 22.2 (8³/₄ in.)

well as of trade and industry—now grew to unprecedented size. The biggest and most famous such **metropolis** ("mother-city") was Alexandria, founded by the conqueror himself near the delta of the Nile River, in Egypt. Alexandria soon outgrew Athens in size and wealth and came to rival it as the cultural hub of the Greek world. For centuries, its marvelous library and "museum"—a kind of research institute endowed by the rulers—were centers of scholarship and scientific study.

Tour the Sites of Ancient Alexandria (http://www.egyptologyonline.com/alexandria.htm) Take a virtual tour of Alexandria.

> *"The Greek version of divine rulership built on their own as well as non-Greek beliefs, and reflected both the self-confidence and the insecurity of a people that had so suddenly risen to international power."*

The End of the Greek Kingdoms

From about 200 B.C. onward, the Greeks began to lose their position as international rulers. They lost their hold on the lands stretching eastward from Mesopotamia to the borders of India, which were taken over by invaders from the steppes (p. 20), most notably the Parthians, who formed a sizeable empire on the territory of present-day Iran (see Map 5.2 on page 84). Unsuccessful Egyptian rebellions and a successful Jewish one (p. 125) further weakened Greek rule. Meanwhile in the west, a non-Greek city-state was growing more powerful than Athens had ever been, and more powerful even than the Hellenistic kingdoms—Rome. The Romans gradually took over Greece itself, Anatolia, and other eastern Mediterranean territories, and in 30 B.C. they conquered Egypt, the last surviving Greek-ruled kingdom.

Even so, Hellenistic culture lived on under Roman rule. It was among the Greeks that the Romans found the philosophy, science, literature, and art that were to inspire their own achievements, as well as the political forms of universal monarchy and divine rulership that they adopted in their own empire (pp. 104–105). Within the Roman Empire, the eastern Mediterranean remained a distinct region dominated by Greek civilization. When that empire finally divided, its Greek-dominated eastern half continued for several centuries until the Muslim conquest. Even then, the Greek legacy was preserved by the empire of Byzantium, acquired by Arab conquerors, and ultimately taken over by Christian Europe.

LO³ Hellenistic Thinkers: The Individual and the Universe

Even in the Hellenistic world, Athens continued to be the headquarters of philosophy. Earlier arguments about the workings of the universe continued, but they were given a new twist. Perhaps because the small world of the city-state now seemed to thinkers less important than the larger world beyond it, they were more concerned than before with the place of individual humans within the vastness of the universe.

Epicureanism

One answer to this problem was **Epicureanism (ep-i-kyoo-REE-uh-niz-uhm)**, a philosophy based on the teachings of Epicurus **(ep-i-KYOOR-uhs)**, who taught in Athens around 300 B.C. Epicurus's view of the universe was based on that of Democritus of Abdera (p. 72), who had declared that all matter is made up of atoms. Epicurus claimed that the shape and character of every living and nonliving thing result from the chance motions of these tiny particles, and there is no governing purpose on earth or in the heavens.

In such a universe, Epicurus believed, the only logical aim for the individual is to strive for personal happiness. As a guide in the search for happiness, Epicurus proclaimed the principle that happiness equals pleasure minus pain, and that the best way to secure happiness is by decreasing pain rather than by increasing pleasure. And the deepest source of human pain, Epicurus taught, is fear, the "ache of mind and heart."

 **Materialist Ethic: The Principal Doctrines of Epicureanism** Read some principles for a happy life from Epicurus.

Fear, in turn, feeds on ignorance and superstition, which for Epicurus included all forms of worship of the gods. The gods, he thought, are themselves chance groupings of atoms who live far from humans and have no concern for them. They certainly do not grant humans eternal life, for when the atoms that we are made of go their separate ways, there is nothing left of us. But that is exactly why death is not to be feared: "Death, usually regarded as the greatest of calamities, is actually nothing to us; while we are here, death is not, and when death is here, we are not."

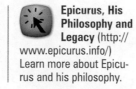 **Epicurus, His Philosophy and Legacy** (http://www.epicurus.info/) Learn more about Epicurus and his philosophy.

The pursuit of pleasure is more difficult than the avoidance of pain. Epicurus warned that what he called "dynamic" (restless) pleasures such as eating and drinking are usually self-defeating, for these pleasures only stimulate the appetite for more of them, which acts as a fresh source of pain. Rather than feed such appetites, he thought it wiser to discipline them and instead cultivate the "passive" (quiet) pleasures, such as literature, recollection and meditation, personal friendship, and the enjoyment of nature. He shunned the pursuit of wealth or public office, for it often brings disappointment, trouble, and pain. Epicurus valued, above all, calmness, poise, and serenity of mind.

Stoicism

A rival Hellenistic philosophy was **Stoicism** (STOH-uh-siz-uhm), named after the porch (*stoa*) in Athens where Zeno, the founder of Stoicism, taught about 300 B.C. Zeno believed that far from being the result of chance motions of atoms, the universe is pervaded and upheld by a living force, which he called by various names: "Divine Fire," "Providence," "God," and "Reason" (in Greek, *logos*). This idea came from an earlier thinker, Heraclitus (p. 72), but Zeno made it much more of a guide for understanding the place of the individual in the universe than Heraclitus is known to have done.

The Reason of the universe, Zeno and his followers thought, was present in everything orderly and good—the movement of the stars in their courses, the growth of seeds into plants, the righteousness and wisdom of human beings. Harmony and happiness, declared the Stoics, are achieved by understanding this Reason, accepting it by self-discipline, and living in accordance with it, all of which means striving for virtue rather than pleasure. Virtue of this kind is not the possession of any particular nation, gender, or social class, because all human beings share the spark of Reason that upholds the universe. The only qualification is to study philosophy so as to understand the "natural law"—the mutual rights and duties that make it possible for individuals and communities to live in accordance with Reason. And all human beings are capable of this study. An Athenian Stoic, Chrysippus, is supposed to have said around 250 B.C. that "both slaves and women must be philosophers."

Stoicism and Epicureanism were very different ways of thinking, and their supporters argued fiercely for many centuries. Both views made sense in different ways in the vast and diverse world of the Hellenistic kingdoms, and they continued to make sense in the even vaster and more diverse world of the state that followed them, the Roman Empire.

 Listen to a synopsis of Chapter 5.

CHAPTER 6

THE RISE OF ROME,
800–30 B.C.

LEARNING OBJECTIVES

AFTER READING THIS CHAPTER, YOU SHOULD BE ABLE TO DO THE FOLLOWING:

LO¹ Trace the evolution of the Roman Republic and describe its values.

LO² Explain how the Roman Republic was able to expand beyond the Italian peninsula.

LO³ Describe how the impact of war and conquest led to the overthrow of the Republic.

"MANY GREAT EMPIRES HAD COME AND GONE BEFORE THAT OF ROME, BUT NO CONQUERING KING, AND CERTAINLY NO CITY-STATE, HAD ACQUIRED SUCH A VAST DOMAIN AND HELD IT FOR SO LONG."

The rise of Rome began as a continuation of Greece's early westward expansion through the Mediterranean Sea, which brought the Greek model of civilization to the peoples of Italy during the eighth century B.C.

The Romans not only imitated Greek civilization but also improved on it, at least so far as government and warfare were concerned. About 500 B.C., Rome became a Greek-style city-state that was no longer ruled by kings, but the Roman government system—the Republic, as they called it—was for several centuries more stable and more effective than any in Greece. The war-fighting methods of Roman armies were more consistently successful than those of the Greeks, and Rome's treatment of conquered enemies was usually more generous. As a result, in five centuries Rome became the center of an empire that stretched from the borders of Mesopotamia to the Atlantic Ocean. But by that time, endless expansion had also led to social conflict, political crisis, civil war, and unstable rule by powerful army commanders—until one of these commanders, Augustus Caesar (**SEE-zer**), managed to turn military rule into a workable system of government by one man.

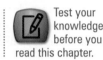
Test your knowledge before you read this chapter.

What do you think?

Rome built a great empire because of the exceptional virtue and public spirit of its citizens.

Strongly Disagree						Strongly Agree
1	2	3	4	5	6	7

≪ **Taking the Census** The Roman Republic held five-yearly censuses, in which the citizens had to come in to be counted. A carving from about 100 B.C. shows a citizen carrying a folded writing tablet in case he needs to look up the detailed information about his household and property that the census taker is asking him for and writing down. On the citizen's answers will depend his tax liability, his military service, and his actual membership in the Roman People, the united citizenry of the city-state.

LO¹ City-State and Empire: The Roman Republic

Many great empires had come and gone before that of Rome, but no conquering king, and certainly no city-state, had acquired such a vast domain and held it for so long. What features of the government and way of life of the Romans enabled them to outdo all that had gone before them?

Italy and Its Peoples

In the era of Indo-European migrations, when the Hittites moved into Asia Minor and the Greeks into the Aegean, other tribes moved into Italy. They arrived in a Mediterranean land with farming resources that were basically similar to those of Greece or Palestine (pp. 37, 49), but able to support a larger population—and in time, larger armies. In addition, Italy was situated astride the Mediterranean, commanding every direction: southward and eastward to the territories of Greek, Egyptian, and Mesopotamian civilization, northward and westward to the lands of barbarian Europe.

The Indo-European settlers formed various tribal groups, among them the Latin people of central Italy. Some of the Latins settled near the mouth of the Tiber River (see Map 6.1), building a cluster of dwellings on low-lying hills along the river—the famed "Seven Hills." Around 750 B.C., these settlements joined to form a single city-state, Rome. The Latins, of course, were only one of many peoples that lived in Italy, two of which were

to have a decisive influence on the growth of Roman civilization: the Etruscans and the Greeks.

The Etruscans were non–Indo-European immigrants who arrived in Italy from somewhere to the east about the ninth century B.C. They gained control of territory to the north of the Latins that the Romans called Etruria, established city-states under the rule of kings, and built up a civilization that combined native features and influences from Greece and farther east (see photo). In the seventh century B.C., they conquered Latium, and

≪ Etruscan Gold This foot-long gold cloak clasp comes from the tomb of an Etruscan warrior-noble who died about 650 B.C. Lions, an animal not found in Italy but often seen on art objects from ancient Anatolia and Mesopotamia, walk across its upper plate. The perfect workmanship, the weight of precious metal, and the exotic beasts are testimony to the skills, wealth, and international contacts of a people who deeply influenced Rome and for a long time ruled it. Scala/Art Resource, NY

for a time, Etruscan kings ruled Rome itself. From the Etruscans, the Romans adopted such features as a gridiron street plan for cities, gladiatorial combats, and the masonry arch.

The Romans also borrowed directly from the Greeks. As part of their expansion across the Mediterranean (p. 50), the Greek city-states had begun to plant colonies in southern Italy as early as the eighth century B.C., and these spread northward up the coast almost to the borders of Latium (see Map 6.1). It was from these neighbors that the Latins first learned the alphabet and gained knowledge of the life of Greek city-states.

Illustrated Essays on the Etruscans (http://history-world.org/etruscans.htm) Learn more about the ancient Etruscans.

The Roman Republic: The Senate and the People

Under the influence of the Etruscans and the Greeks, the Romans acquired the skills that enabled them to build their unique political institutions. At first, their city-state was ruled on the Etruscan model by powerful kings, including actual Etruscan conquerors. The king was advised by a council of elders called the Senate (from the Latin *senex*, meaning "old man"), whose members he appointed. Usually, he chose from among the **patricians** or "men with fathers"—that is, with fathers who already belonged to this hereditary group of leading families. When a king died, his suc-

patricians
Upper-class citizens who belonged to the oldest and noblest Roman families.

Map 6.1 **Rome in Italy**

Rome began as one among many Italian city-states, located in Latium, the territory of one among many Italian ethnic groups. In 250 years, Rome united Italy under its leadership by a system of alliances, by migration and settlement, and by roads that speeded the movement of goods, news, and above all armies. Rome would later apply these methods of unification in many lands of Europe, Africa, and Asia. © Cengage Learning

 Interactive Map

Republic

In reference to ancient Rome, the system of city-state government in which decision-making power was shared between the Senate and assemblies of male citizens.

plebeians

The Roman common people, including workers, small farmers, and wealthy people who were not patricians.

Senate

In ancient Rome, a government assembly appointed by the king, and under the Republic by the consuls; originally all members were patricians, but in time wealthy plebeians were appointed as well.

consuls

In the Roman Republic, two senators who led the government and military for one-year terms and appointed their own successors.

dictator

In the Roman Republic, a single leader with full decision-making powers, appointed for a maximum six-month term during times of emergency.

tribunes

Magistrates elected by the plebeians, who eventually gained the power to initiate and veto laws.

cessor was chosen by the Senate from among its own members, subject to approval by an assembly of all male citizens. The assembly's approval, however, was automatic, for apart from the king, it was the Senate and the patricians who dominated the city-state.

Around 500 B.C., Rome overthrew its Etruscan rulers, and the monarchy was also abolished. The government of the Roman city-state became officially the "people's business"—in Latin, *res publica*, from which the word *republic* is derived. Like Greek city-states, the Roman **Republic** underwent a long and turbulent development under the influence of social struggles between aristocrats and commoners. The result, however, was a system of government that was neither a Greek-style democracy nor an oligarchy, but a mixture of both.

Patricians and Plebeians

The aristocratic side in the conflicts of the Republic was of course the patricians. On the other side were the **plebeians** (from the Latin *plebs*, meaning "the common people")—everyone who did not belong to patrician families, including workers, small farmers, and even quite wealthy citizens.

In the earliest times of the Republic, the "people's business" was in practice run by the **Senate**, an assembly of about three hundred heads of patrician families. Two among the senators functioned as **consuls** ("colleagues"), wielding for a year at a time the military and government power that had formerly belonged to the kings. The consuls now appointed senators, and they also chose their own successors, though they were careful to choose men who would be acceptable to the Senate. The one-year terms of the consuls, and the fact that there were two of them (each empowered to veto the other's lawmaking proposals), were a guarantee against a revival of monarchy. The Romans were so eager to avoid this possibility that the practice grew up of appointing two or more men for one-year terms to every magistracy (public office). This slowed down government decisions and actions, but in time

of emergency the consuls, on the advice of the Senate, could appoint a **dictator**, with full power to give orders and make laws for a maximum period of six months. With this exception, the Republic's original government system kept power in the hands of the patrician group as a whole.

The plebeians at first deferred to patrician rule, but as Rome grew and the plebeians became more numerous and often wealthier, they began to resent being treated as second-class citizens. They put pressure on the patricians in various ways, including through acts of passive resistance and threats to secede and start a rival settlement. The conflicts were often bitter, but the plebeians never lost the feeling that they depended on the leadership of the Senate. Furthermore, Rome, like the Greek city-states, relied on its own citizens as fighting men, so that the Senate could not forever deny the plebeians a share in government. As a result, over more than two hundred years, the Republic developed a government system that both maintained the leadership of the Senate yet also admitted the plebeians to power.

Among the chief complaints of the plebeians was that they lacked legal protection. Before the fifth century B.C., there had been no written code of law. Instead, the sacred traditional laws were passed down orally and interpreted by judges, who were, of course, patricians. About 450 B.C., in response to the plebeians' demand, the laws of Rome were set down in writing. The new code was said to have been engraved on twelve slabs of wood or bronze and mounted in the chief public square, the Forum, for all to see. These "Twelve Tables" (so called from the old-fashioned English word for such a slab) served as the foundation for the elaborate system of Roman law that grew up in later centuries.

A Tour of the Roman Forum (http://www.italyguides.it/us/roma/rome/ancient_roman_empire/roman_forum.htm) Take a tour of the Roman Forum.

Not long afterward, new plebeian assemblies came into being alongside the existing one that soon gained far greater power. One of the new bodies, in which residents of the city of Rome predominated, won the right to elect consuls subject to confirmation by the Senate. The other, in which farmers from outside the city had a larger say, began electing their own magistrates, called **tribunes**. The tribunes eventually gained the power to initiate laws in their assembly and veto laws passed by the Senate.

Step by step, the patricians gave way to the plebeians, until by 250 B.C. the distinction between the two groups no longer much mattered in politics and government. By then, plebeians were eligible for all public offices including that of consul, they had won admission to the Senate itself, and they had even acquired the right to marry into patrician families.

"Mixed" Government

The struggles and compromises between patricians and plebeians produced a system of government that was bafflingly complex. Instead of abolishing an old institution, the Romans usually found it politically less divisive to install a counterweight—the two plebeian assemblies alongside the old one, or the tribunes alongside the consuls. But the resulting system showed extraordinary flexibility and resilience. The Roman "mixed" government, as it was called on account of its combination of oligarchic and democratic features (p. 52), was widely admired in ancient times and continues to influence government systems today. The separation of powers in the U.S. Constitution derives ultimately from the checks and balances between different branches of government in the Roman city-state.

But ultimate leadership of the Republic still rested in the hands of the Senate, and though plebeians could now join the Senate, only the wealthy could afford to do so. In yet another precaution against abuse of office, senators and would-be senators had to follow a complex career path from lower-ranking magistracies to higher ones, in which leapfrogging ranks was frowned upon or was actually illegal. Many of these magistracies were elective, and to get votes, a candidate had to spend large sums for displays and popular entertainments. In addition, he needed to follow the long-standing Roman practice of supporting **clients** ("hangers-on"). These were normally less wealthy citizens, who were protected and paid by a rich **patron** in return for personal services and campaigning. And once a candidate got himself elected, he had to pay the costs of his magistracy out of his own pocket, since it carried no salary. In this way, the Senate, originally an oligarchy of birth, became an oligarchy of wealth.

No matter how restricted a group the Senate might be, however, until the final centuries of the Republic, it governed firmly and effectively. The senators set long-range policies and made immediate decisions on pressing matters, appointed and instructed the military leaders of the Republic, received foreign ambassadors, and concluded treaties. They supervised finances and investigated high crimes. In all these ways, they exercised wide powers with general consent.

> **"** *The separation of powers in the U.S. Constitution derives ultimately from the checks and balances between different branches of government in the Roman city-state.* **"**

Republican Values

The "mixed government" of Rome, like Athenian democracy and Spartan oligarchy, was not just a government system but part of a way of life. The values that inspired this way of life were expressed in traditional stories of the heroic deeds of early times that were mostly fictional, and in laws like the Twelve Tables that were no doubt often broken. All the same, for many centuries the Romans judged themselves according to these values, which thereby influenced their behavior and achievements.

The Roman Republic (http://www.metmuseum.org/toah/hd/romr/hd_romr.htm) See republican values reflected in the arts.

The City and the Gods

Some Roman values were common to all ancient city-states—notably the belief that even more than on government systems, the community's survival and prosperity depended on a god or goddess who was thought to take a particular interest in its destiny. As the Romans came into closer contact with neighboring peoples, they came to see some of these gods and goddesses as wielding worldwide power, though foreigners might worship them under different names and tell different stories about them.

By the time of the Republic, Rome had a special relationship with three deities, whose joint temple stood on the Capitol, the city's fortified citadel and equivalent of a Greek city-state's acropolis (p. 51). These deities were the sky-god Jupiter, whom the Romans believed was the same as the Zeus whom nearby Greek city-states worshiped; his consort, the fertility goddess Juno (the same as Hera); and Minerva (Athena), goddess of skill and wisdom. Responsibility for maintaining the "peace of the gods"—Rome's good relationship with these and many other deities—belonged to the **pontiffs**, a group of priests headed by the supreme pontiff (*pontifex maximus*), who were leading magistrates of the Republic.

Citizens and the Community

The Romans shared other values specifically with Greek city-states. These values included the belief that it was the right and duty of the men of the community to fight its wars, and hence also to share in its government; and the community solidarity that came from the fact that high-born as well as low-born citizens bore the burden of war (pp. 52, 54–55). As in Greek city-states, too, the men took it for granted that the women of Rome had no right or duty to share in politics and government, and that women needed guardians for all legal transactions—"because of their light-mindedness," as the Twelve Tables declared.

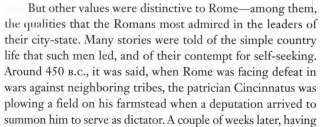
Law in Early Roman Society: The Regulation of Women and Family Read some laws concerning women in ancient Rome.

But other values were distinctive to Rome—among them, the qualities that the Romans most admired in the leaders of their city-state. Many stories were told of the simple country life that such men led, and of their contempt for self-seeking. Around 450 B.C., it was said, when Rome was facing defeat in wars against neighboring tribes, the patrician Cincinnatus was plowing a field on his farmstead when a deputation arrived to summon him to serve as dictator. A couple of weeks later, having

client
A person who provides personal services in return for money and protection from a patron.

patron
A wealthy person who supports others with money and protection in exchange for personal services.

pontiff
In ancient Rome, one of the Republic's leading priests.

paterfamilias
The "family father" in ancient Rome, who had unlimited power over his household.

matron
Title of honor given to a married woman in ancient Rome.

led the citizen-soldiers to victory, he resigned his office and went back to finish the plowing on which his family's survival depended.

The Community and the Family

Instead of devoting his life directly to the city-state as in Sparta, a Roman man belonged first of all to a family and a clan (a group of families descended from a real or mythical forefather). Clans and families, in turn, were held together by fathers—in particular by men who had the status of *paterfamilias* (**pey-ter-fuh-MIL-ee-uhs**) or "family father." The paterfamilias wielded unlimited power—including the power of life and death—over everyone in his household, as well as over sons and daughters who left his household upon marriage. Only his wife might not be completely subject to him—if she was still subject to the authority of her own father. The *genius* of the paterfamilias—the life-giving and life-upholding fatherly power that he embodied—was sacred and was worshiped by all in the household, including himself (see photo).

The Romans revered the power of fatherhood not only in family life but also in the community life of their city-state. The senators addressed each other in session as "conscript fathers"— men recruited to wield fatherly authority for the good of the Republic. In fact, Roman community life was seen as a kind of family life on a larger scale. One of the Republic's most important deities, besides those worshiped on the Capitol, was Vesta, the goddess of hearth and home. In every household, the fire in the hearth was sacred to Vesta and was only put out if the family moved. In addition, the Vestal Virgins, a group of six patrician women, devoted thirty years of their lives to tending the goddess's everlasting fire in her temple on the Forum, on behalf of the out-sized "household" of Rome itself.

 **Cato the Elder Educates His Son** Read a glowing description of how a paterfamilias treated his family.

Motherhood, too, was revered in Rome. A married woman bore the title of **matron**—in Latin, *matrona* or "lady mother." Her "Juno"—the divine force of fertility and nourishment that she embodied—was worshiped in the household alongside her husband's genius. She was supposed to live in subordination to her husband, but through strength of personality and authority with her menfolk, she was also expected to contribute to the community as well as the family.

The founding myth of the Republic itself told how Rome's uprising against its Etruscan king began when a matron, Lucretia,

was raped by the king's son and killed herself—just as a Roman man might do if he faced unbearable shame. As the historian Livy told the story five centuries later, Lucretia first made clear to her husband and brother that she expected them to avenge her—"if you are men." The ideal matron demanded from the men of her family hard work, courage as warriors, devotion to duty—all the moral qualities that the Romans summed up in the word *virtus*, or "manliness." In this way, women were expected to help make sure that men had the qualities they needed to keep the Republic strong.

LO² Roman Expansion

The Romans were, above all, a military people—patriotic farmer-soldiers. Their first wars were against the neighboring Etruscans, competing Italian tribes, and barbarian invaders. Then, as the Romans secured their position at home, they began to reach out for territories and allies. One of Rome's main assets in this effort was its superior army.

Allies and Colonies

The Romans were shrewdly generous in their treatment of defeated enemies. More often than not, these were given the status of allies, keeping their local laws, government systems, and armies under ultimate Roman authority. The Romans also

>> **A Household Shrine** A temple painted on an inside wall of a house in Pompeii, south of Rome, is the dwelling place of powerful beings. Two *lares* (**LAH-rayz**—protective gods), dance and brandish drinking horns. A fatherly genius holds an incense box and a ritual wine-pouring dish, and covers his head in preparation for sacrifice on behalf of the household. A snake, symbol of the fertility of the soil, wriggles along the ground. Alinari/The Bridgeman Art Library

THERE WERE SEVERAL REASONS WHY THE ROMAN ARMY WAS SO EFFECTIVE:

Better-Prepared Soldiers

- At the beginning of the Republic, the citizens usually served for short periods and without pay. But in the course of numerous wars that were fought ever farther from home, the Romans began to pay their citizen draftees so as to permit longer campaigns and better training.

Better Military Tactics, Adapted from the Enemies They Encountered

- They wore light armor and carried large, oblong shields.

- Rather than using long thrusting spears like the hoplites (p. 52), they attacked their enemies from a distance with javelins before closing in for hand-to-hand fighting with swords.

- By 250 B.C., Roman soldiers fought in small units of about one hundred men (centuries), each under the command of a centurion.

- The centuries were combined into bigger units, of which the largest was the legion, of about four thousand; thus Roman armies were highly maneuverable yet also well coordinated, unlike the unwieldy Greek phalanxes.

A Strong Military Culture

- The Roman army combined iron discipline with treatment of the soldiers as citizens who deserved respect.

- The soldiers elected their own centurions, yet once chosen, a centurion had almost absolute power.

- Penalties for cowardice or neglect of duty were harsh; on the other hand, there were generous rewards and promotions for the brave and victorious.

---

tightened their control over the Italian peninsula by creating a network of colonies of settlers from Rome—generally discharged citizen-soldiers and their families. Both the colonists and the allies raised soldiers on the same scale as Rome itself, and the allies often provided light infantry and cavalry, which the Romans lacked. In this way, the Roman forces increased in strength and striking power in step with their conquests—an important advantage for an expanding empire. Rome had its share of incompetent commanders and panicky soldiers, but however disastrously its armies might be defeated, there were always other armies to take their place.

The Roman colonists enjoyed rights of citizenship that were almost equal to those of citizens who lived in Rome itself. In time, the allies began to demand full integration with Rome, and early in the first century B.C., some of them took up arms when the demand was at first denied. Following these Social Wars ("Wars against the Allies," from the Latin *socius*, "ally"), most non-Romans in Italy gained Roman citizenship, and the status of "ally," separate from the Romans, disappeared. Thus, Rome, unlike the exclusive Greek city-states, became an expanding, absorptive political entity.

The Punic Wars

Roman methods of conquest and administration paid handsome dividends, for by 250 B.C., all of Italy south of the River Po (see Map 6.1 on page 91) was in Roman hands. But this success brought Rome into collision with a rival city-state beyond the sea: Carthage, on the north coast of Africa.

Founded about 700 B.C. by Phoenician colonists (pp. 32-33, 50), Carthage had become an oligarchic and empire-building republic similar to Rome and had spread its influence across North Africa, southern Spain, Sardinia, Corsica, and Sicily (see Map 6.2). It was the Carthaginians' interest in Sicily, lying between Africa and Italy, that brought them into conflict with the Romans. The Greek city-states of Sicily had for centuries been struggling with Carthage for control of the island, and the Romans had inherited the struggle when they took over responsibility for protecting their Greek allies. But ultimately what was at stake was the command of the whole western Mediterranean.

The Punic Wars (from *Poeni*, the Latin name for the Phoenicians) were waged on land and sea in three vicious rounds between 264 and 146 B.C. In the first phase of the struggle, after many years of exhausting warfare, Rome was able to force Carthage out of Sicily, but the North African city kept the rest of its empire. In the second (and decisive) phase, the Carthaginian general Hannibal invaded Italy, defeated several Roman armies, and brought Rome to the brink of defeat. But the loyalty of the Romans' allies, the perseverance of their own forces, and their greater manpower—for they were able to draw citizen and allied soldiers from all of Italy, while Carthage relied on smaller mercenary armies—enabled them to triumph. At the end of the Second Punic War in 202 B.C., Carthage was disarmed and helpless.

Eventually, fearing a Carthaginian revival, Rome provoked a third war, and in 146 B.C., Carthage was captured after bitter fighting. In a final act of vengeance, the Senate ordered the city

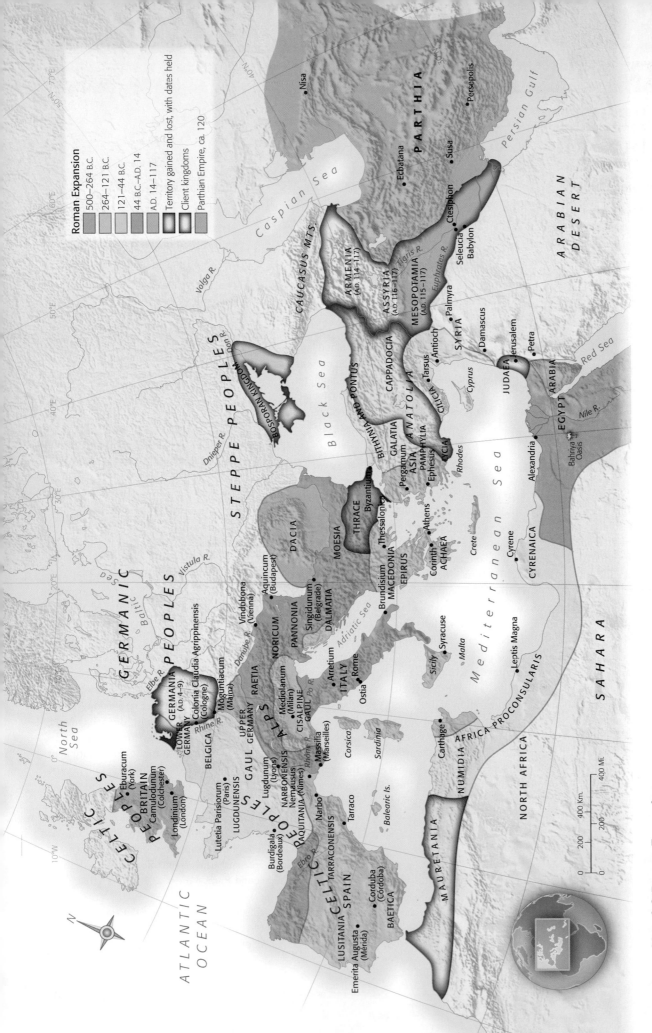

Roman Expansion

Roman Expansion
500–264 B.C.
264–121 B.C.
121–44 B.C.
44 B.C.–A.D. 14
A.D. 14–117
Territory gained and lost, with dates held
Client kingdoms
Parthian Empire, ca. 120

Interactive Map

Map 6.2 Roman Expansion

Notice the rhythm of Rome's expansion: 250 years to unify Italy (50C–264 B.C.); 140 years of much faster growth from the outbreak of the Punic Wars to the death of Gaius Gracchus (264–121 B.C.); 140 years of triumphant conquest even as the Republic collapsed (121–44 B.C.) and Augustus took over (44 B.C.–A.D. 14); and in the following century of imperial monarchy, the gradual end of conquest (A.D. 14–117). © Cengage Learning

to be leveled, its people sold into slavery, and even the ground on which it had stood to be solemnly cursed. But this was only an epilogue to the main struggle. Already in 202 B.C., Rome had won control of the western Mediterranean.

Conquering an Empire

The former possessions of Carthage in Sicily, Spain, and Africa became the first Roman provinces. These administrative units did not enjoy the status of Rome's allies in Italy; instead, they were ruled as conquered lands by proconsuls (governors—from the Latin words for "stand-in for a consul") appointed by the Senate. They paid tribute to the Roman state, contributed "auxiliary" units of cavalry and light infantry to the Roman forces, and provided opportunities for influential Roman citizens to build up private fortunes. It was not until the time of Augustus, after 27 B.C., that the provinces began to share in the benefits of Roman order. In addition, some local rulers survived by becoming client kings, bound to Rome by ties of allegiance and support like those between Roman patrons and clients, though in the first century A.D. their kingdoms were mostly absorbed into the empire as normal provinces. One way or another, for the Romans the conquest of the western Mediterranean meant an enormous increase in both resources and military power.

The result was a spectacular increase in the pace of expansion. In the previous 250 years, from 500 B.C. to the outbreak of the Punic Wars, the Romans had unified most of Italy; in the next 250 years, they would spread their rule from the eastern Mediterranean to the British Isles (see Map 6.2).

In Spain and neighboring territories in the south of Gaul, Rome for the first time gained a substantial foothold among the peoples of barbarian Europe, which they soon began to expand. But even before the final defeat of Carthage, venturesome Romans were looking also to the eastern Mediterranean for new areas to exploit. The prospects in that direction were promising, for the Hellenistic kingdoms (pp. 86–87) were beginning to lose their grip.

Rome's first involvement was in Greece, and it grew out of a special invitation. Around 200 B.C., ambassadors from various Greek city-states appealed to Rome for aid in resisting the king of Macedonia, who had been allied with Carthage. Moved by admiration for Hellenic culture as well as by greed, the Romans

Cato the Elder: "Carthage Must Be Destroyed" Read Greek historian Plutarch's account of who instigated the third war against Carthage.

replied by sending an army. Their professed aim was to secure the liberties of the proud and quarrelsome Greek cities and then to withdraw. But they soon began to actively intervene in the politics and conflicts of the Hellenistic kingdoms. In the course of endless maneuvering and fighting, the Romans carved one province after another out of the eastern Mediterranean and made many a local ruler into a client king, until by the late first century B.C., they were supreme in the region. From Gibraltar to Jerusalem fell the shadow of mighty Rome.

proletarian
In ancient Rome, a propertyless but voting citizen.

> "*In the course of endless maneuvering and fighting, the Romans carved one province after another out of the eastern Mediterranean and made many a local ruler into a client king, until by the early first century B.C., they were supreme in the region. From Gibraltar to Jerusalem fell the shadow of mighty Rome.*"

LO³ The Overthrow of the Republic

Already by the end of the Punic Wars, Rome ruled an empire far larger than that of any earlier city-state, yet the Republic's decisions were still supposed to be taken in person by arms-bearing citizens. The Senate, the people's assemblies, and the magistrates they chose now wielded unchecked power over millions of people—both non-citizens who had no right to a share in government, and citizens who lived far from Rome and mostly had no voting rights. Furthermore, war and conquest had disrupted the traditional social order in Italy, the heartland of the newly arisen empire, while the political leaders and ordinary voters in Rome used their power mainly in their own interests. As a result, Rome's city-state government system gradually broke down, and a universal monarchy replaced it like those that ruled every other vast empire.

The Impact of War and Conquest

Rome's triumphs abroad had a profound effect on society at home. In former days, the farmer-soldier had been the backbone of the state. But the social and economic revolution that followed the Punic Wars changed all that.

Proletarians, Profiteers, and Slaves

The Punic Wars and then the endless further conquests enormously increased the burden of military service on the Roman farmer-soldiers. Once drafted, they now served for years at a time until the particular conflict for which they had been called up came to an end. Many never came back; those who did often found their farms spoiled by neglect. Some farmers remained stubbornly on their land, but most gave up, sank to the status of **proletarians** (mere "producers of offspring"—the lowest class of Roman citizens), and drifted into the cities. There they could expect to receive free food and public entertainments at the expense of well-to-do citizens who thereby won prestige and power. Rome itself, with its wealthy rival politicians eager to gain the support of these propertyless but voting citizens, was particularly generous with "bread and circuses," and grew to become one of the Mediterranean's great metropolis cities (p. 86).

Meanwhile, a new social group was rising to prominence in Italy. It consisted of war profiteers of various sorts—contractors to the armed forces and dealers in loot and slaves. They used their wealth to buy up ruined farms, restock them, and turn them to new purposes. Small plots on which independent farmers had raised grain were often merged into large estates for use as vineyards, olive groves, or pasturelands for livestock. The new owners, who operated their holdings as capitalistic enterprises, had little interest in the displaced farmers, either as tenants or as hired hands, when they could use gangs of slaves, who had become plentiful and cheap as a result of Rome's conquests overseas.

By 150 B.C., slaves made up nearly one-third of the population of Italy. They labored mainly on the large estates, where they were often treated little better than beasts of burden. In the cities, slaves were secretaries and tutors in the households of the rich and powerful, domestic servants, and workers in every kind of business, including prostitution. A slave owner had a right to a slave's earnings, but he or she sometimes permitted the slave to withhold a portion. By this means, some slaves saved enough money to purchase their freedom and with it Roman citizenship. In addition, during their lifetimes or in their wills, owners often freed their slaves as a reward for loyal service. These freedmen or freedwomen were expected to continue in the service of the former owners or their families, but ex-slaves sometimes succeeded in business and became founders of wealthy families themselves.

The Aristocracy

At the topmost levels of society, patrician families still enjoyed the highest social prestige, but they now mingled with successful plebeian families to form a single, fabulously wealthy and powerful aristocracy.

Some of these "noble Romans" combined traditional virtues with a newly refined and cultured way of life, providing models that aristocrats and would-be aristocrats would imitate for many centuries. Such was Scipio Aemilianus, the conqueror of Carthage in 146 B.C. Scipio was a descendant of an ancient patrician clan and a battle-winning general who, in the best Roman tradition, passed up the limitless money-making opportunities offered by his military commands and other high offices. In addition, he

was well read in Greek philosophy and literature and generously sponsored early Latin poets and dramatists.

Such, too, was Cornelia, patrician wife of a plebeian, Tiberius Gracchus. She lived up to the ideal of a Roman matron as a *univira*—a "one-husband woman"—spending her life as a widow after Tiberius's death and seeing to the education of her sons in the manly virtues. But the household that she headed without a husband (and seemingly without a guardian) was a center of social life and Greek culture, and her letters to her sons were much admired as early examples of elegant Latin writing.

Even the noblest Romans had to scramble to make sure they got their share of the spoils of empire, however, and the traditional stability of households sometimes gave way to the interests of aristocratic "dynasties." Regardless of the ideal of fatherhood, men with sons to spare gave them up for adoption by men without sons. In this way, the givers of sons saved themselves the vast expense of launching young men on a political career and forged alliances with the aristocrats whose families they saved from extinction. The ideal of matronhood, too, was sometimes sacrificed to politics. Husbands divorced wives for the sake of more profitable family alliances—and wives, sure of the backing of fathers and brothers for more politically useful marriages, did the same to their husbands.

In general, aristocratic women seem to have had more choice than before over whether to observe the traditional constraints. They shared in the social life of their husbands in a way that would have been unthinkable in Greece. "Who among the Romans is ashamed to take his wife to a supper party? And which mother of a family does not hold the first place in the house and does not go out among crowds of people?" asked Cornelius Nepos, a writer of the first century B.C., comparing Roman customs to the segregated social life of the Greeks (p. 58).

> **"** *The ideal of matronhood was sometimes sacrificed to politics. Husbands divorced wives for the sake of more profitable family alliances—and wives, sure of the backing of fathers and brothers for more politically useful marriages, did the same to their husbands.* **"**

The Gracchi

Caught up in the scramble for the spoils of empire, the wealthy aristocrats in the Senate had little interest in finding ways to solve the Republic's problems. On the contrary, toward the end of the second century B.C. the Senate put a violent end to the Republic's most determined reform effort, that of Tiberius and Gaius Gracchus (the Gracchi brothers).

Tiberius and Gaius, the sons of the famous Cornelia, thought that a partial solution to Rome's troubles would be to resettle many of the city's poor, as well as discharged army veterans, on small farms and to provide a public subsidy of grain for those who remained in Rome. Such a program, they hoped, would raise the number of independent farmers and reduce the gap between rich and poor. Though unable to win Senate support for these measures, the Gracchi proposed them directly to a plebe-

ADVICE ON MANAGING SLAVES

Columella, an agricultural writer of the first century B.C., wrote a handbook for landowners on agricultural techniques and estate management. One of the key components of estate management was the effective control and exploitation of the labor force, most of whom were slaves. With the decline of the traditional free farmer, Roman cities became increasingly dependent upon the agricultural output of large estates worked by such labor forces. Thus Columella's advice was of importance not only to individual landowners but also to Roman society at large.

After all these arrangements [for buildings, tools, etc.] have been acquired or contrived, especial care is demanded of the master not only in other matters, but most of all in the matter of the persons in his service; and these are either tenant-farmers or slaves, whether unfettered or in chains. He should be civil in dealing with his tenants, should show himself affable, and should be more exacting in the matter of work than of payments, as this gives less offence yet is, generally speaking, more profitable. . . .

The next point is with regard to slaves—over what duty it is proper to place each and . . . what sort of tasks to assign them. So my advice at the start is not to appoint an overseer from that sort of slaves who are physically attractive, and certainly not from that class which has busied itself with the voluptuous occupations of the city. . . .

But be the overseer what he may, he should be given a woman companion to keep him within bounds and yet in certain matters to be a help to him; and this same overseer should be warned not to become intimate with a member of the household, and much less with an outsider, yet at times he may consider it fitting, as a mark of distinction, to invite to his table on a holiday one whom he has found to be constantly busy and vigorous in the performance of his tasks. He shall offer no sacrifice except by direction of the master. Soothsayers and witches, two sets of people who incite ignorant minds through false superstition to spending and then to shameful practices, he must not admit to the place. He must have no acquaintance with the city or with the weekly market, except to make purchases and sales in connection with his duties. . . .

In the case of the other slaves, the following are, in general, the precepts to be observed, and I do not regret having held to them myself: to talk rather familiarly with the country slaves, provided only that they have not conducted themselves unbecomingly, more frequently than I would with the town slaves; and when I perceived that their unending toil was lightened by such friendliness on the part of the master, I would even jest with them at times and allow them also to jest more freely. Nowadays I make it a practice to call them into consultation on any new work, as if they were more experienced, and to discover by this means what sort of ability is possessed by each of them and how intelligent he is. Furthermore, I observe that they are more willing to set about a piece of work on which they think that their opinions have been asked and their advice followed.

EXPLORING THE SOURCE

1. How does Columella advise the landowner to treat slaves, and why?

2. What class of people does Columella expect the overseer to come from, and what possible problems with overseers should the landowner guard against?

Source: Reprinted by permission of the publishers and the Trustees of the Loeb Classical Library from COLUMELLA: ON AGRICULTURE - VOLUME I, Loeb Classical Library Volume 361, translated by Harrison B. Ash, pp. 79-93, Cambridge, Mass.: Harvard University Press, Copyright © 1941 by the President and Fellows of Harvard College. Loeb Classical Library® is a registered trademark of the President and Felllows of Harvard College.

ian assembly. Tiberius, who was elected tribune of the people in 133 B.C., initiated the reform effort. But his term as tribune, limited by custom to one year, did not allow sufficient time to carry through his long-range program. Moreover, the Senate attacked him as a dangerous troublemaker. Tiberius decided to stand for reelection as a tribune, which gave his opponents an excuse to instigate and condone his murder, along with the murder of hundreds of his supporters. His younger brother, Gaius, carried forward the reform crusade, but he, too, fell under attack by the Senate and met a violent death in 121 B.C.

The reform movement was defeated, but for the first time, it had brought into question the traditional government system of the Republic and the power of the Senate. Soon the Senate would face new challengers who were not so easy to eliminate: the armies that had conquered Rome's empire, and the commanders who led them.

Soldiers, Warlords, and Civil War

With the changes in Rome's society and politics, the character of its armies and their commanders also changed. Instead of the farmer-soldiers of old, it was now landless and propertyless proletarians who were drafted to fill the ranks of the legions. This new type of soldier proved just as courageous and tough as the old one, and throughout the first century B.C., Rome's empire expanded faster than ever (see Map 6.2 on page 96). But Rome's citizen-soldiers were now "semiprofessionals" who fought largely in the hope of bettering themselves through pay, loot, promotion, and above all grants of land or money to provide them with a living when they were discharged. And small farms for veterans were precisely what the Senate had shown itself too greedy and shortsighted to provide.

Instead, the soldiers began looking for these benefits to their own commanders. As in the past, the commanders were mostly senators themselves, but now they stood to gain an edge in the scramble for wealth and power. Many army commanders turned into what amounted to independent warlords, sure of the personal loyalty of their soldiers and hence more powerful than the Senate itself. Since there was usually more than one such warlord at any given time, their rivalries led to bouts of destructive civil war, in each of which the winner became the one and only supreme warlord and hence the one and only ruler of Rome—a tyrant like the strongman rulers of the Greek city-states (p. 52), but on a vastly larger scale. But government by supreme warlords was bound to be brief and unstable—unless one of them could turn military dictatorship into legitimate power.

The first of the civil wars took place between 88 and 82 B.C. The main contenders were two rivals for political influence and army command, Gaius Marius and Lucius Sulla. Marius, a plebeian, claimed to represent the interests of the people and the common soldiers, while the patrician Sulla had the support of the Senate. In fact, both warlords set aside the republican government while they settled their dispute by military force. After vicious fighting in Greece, Italy, and Spain, and after Marius had sickened and died, there was no one left to challenge Sulla, and he was appointed to the unprecedented position of dictator for an indefinite term (see photo).

Sulla abolished the traditional limits on the power of the Senate but also made sure to pay off his soldiers with generous land grants. In reality, the only unlimited power in Rome was his own. He ruled by terror, making systematic use of proscription—an outlawry procedure involving the public posting of the names of those selected for death and the confiscation of their property. The victims included many senators as well as men of lower standing—opponents, possible opponents, and anyone who was rich enough to make it worthwhile to eliminate him. After two years, Sulla felt safe enough to retire from office, and he died in 78 B.C.

Rome's first experiment with one-man rule had not been encouraging, and the Senate and the other institutions of the Republic returned to their traditional functioning. Soon, however, a new generation of army commanders and would-be army commanders was struggling for power. Among them was the man who would become Rome's most spectacular warlord and its second and more statesmanlike, though ultimately unsuccessful supreme ruler, Julius Caesar.

Julius Caesar

Julius Caesar came from an old patrician family that had come down in the world, and he entered the city's politics as a young man determined to regain the fame and power of his ancestors. As he grew in maturity and experience, however, he also came to identify Rome's key problems at home and abroad. In the social struggles, he sided with the poorer citizens and used his influence with them to advance his own cause. But he was also a flexible politician, and in 60 B.C. he began to collaborate with Gnaeus Pompeius (Pompey), an officer promoted by Sulla who had conquered many eastern Mediterranean lands. The two allies formed a **triumvirate** ("Three-Man Board"), together with another former henchman of Sulla, Marcus Crassus, that was for a time the dominant political force in Rome.

Foreign Conquest, Civil War, and Supreme Power

With the help of his new friends, Caesar won an appointment as proconsul of a province that included the southern regions of Gaul, a territory stretching all the way from northern Italy and the Mediterranean coast to the Rhine River and the Atlantic Ocean (see Map 6.2 on page 96). The Gauls, as the inhabitants were called, were a branch of the Celtic peoples, the predominant barbarian ethnic group across most of western Europe and the British Isles. The Gaulish tribes outside the Roman-ruled areas were powerful enough that they might one day become dangerous to Rome and were wealthy enough to be a tempting target. In eight years of brilliant and brutal campaigns, Caesar conquered Gaul and even made forays into Britain and Germany. By 50 B.C., most of western Europe was under Roman rule, and Caesar had built a powerful army personally devoted to himself.

Meanwhile, on Rome's eastern frontier, Crassus had led an army to crushing defeat by the neighboring empire of Parthia (p. 86), while Pompey had stayed in Rome, growing increasingly jealous of Caesar's success. Finally, with Pompey's support, the Senate ordered Caesar to disband his army and return to Rome.

>> **"To Lucius Cornelius Sulla the Fortunate, son of Lucius, Dictator, from the Fundanian Reservoir Ward."** The Romans believed that a man's good fortune was a sign of divine favor, which people could share in by honoring and obeying him. By installing a statue of Sulla and carving this dedication on its pedestal, prominent citizens in a district of Rome could at least hope to avoid the very bad fortune of becoming victims of his reign of terror. Departmento de Historia, Universidad de Navarra, Pamplona/Visual Connection Archive

Instead, he decided to come back with part of his army, in defiance of Roman law. It was the beginning of another round of far-flung civil wars.

Pompey was hastily commissioned to defend the Senate, but his forces were no match for Caesar's veterans. Forced to flee from Italy, Pompey was later defeated by Caesar in Greece and murdered in Egypt, where he had taken refuge. After subduing supporters of Pompey and other opponents in Egypt, Anatolia, Africa, and Spain, Caesar returned to Rome in triumph in 46 B.C. The Senate now hailed him, however reluctantly, the Father of the Fatherland—a title recently invented for the Republic's most admired statesmen.

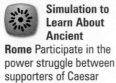

Simulation to Learn About Ancient Rome Participate in the power struggle between supporters of Caesar and Pompey in an online historical simulation.

Caesar moved swiftly to make himself supreme ruler of the Republic. He had himself appointed to most of the leading magistracies, either simultaneously or in quick succession: tribune, supreme pontiff, consul, and dictator for a ten-year term. The people's assemblies continued to exist, but they did little more than endorse Caesar's proposals. The Senate, now enlarged by his own appointees, paid him noble compliments, and its members vowed to risk death in defense of his person. For his part, Caesar showed respect to the Senate but treated it as a mere advisory body.

Caesar used his new powers to attack the grave problems facing Rome. He took care to keep the loyalty of the soldiers and prevent the rise of rival warlords, by resettling war veterans on farmlands in Italy and the provinces. He extended Roman citizenship to parts of Gaul and Spain and appointed citizens from the provinces to the Senate. He gave the Romans splendid public buildings and roads, and introduced reforms into every department of administration.

Assassination and Another Caesar

Romans at home and abroad applauded Caesar's deeds, but there remained a stubborn core of senators who were disturbed by his successes. Their concern deepened further when in 44 B.C. he secured a vote from the Senate making him dictator for life. Caesar never ruled by terror like Sulla, but he also showed no sign of giving up his high position as Sulla had done. On the contrary, he raised himself even higher, permitting a religious cult to be established in his honor and wearing the purple robe of the ancient Roman kings. In the view of the diehard senators, Caesar had become a Greek-style tyrant—and there was a traditional and honorable way of getting rid of tyrants. On the Ides of March (March 15), 44 B.C.,

Caesar appeared in the Senate house, unarmed and unguarded, according to his custom, and a crowd of senators struck him down with their daggers.

Caesar's murder did not restore the Republic; instead, his death produced yet another crop of warlords and yet more bouts of civil war. The main contenders were Mark Antony, once a commander under Caesar and now a consul; the leading assassins, Brutus and Cassius; and Caesar's grandnephew and adopted son, the youthful Octavian Caesar.

Mark Antony and Octavian were rival loyalists of Caesar, and each managed to attract some of Caesar's legions, which they used to fight a brutal war against each other in Italy. Then, however, they joined forces against Caesar's assassins; formed another triumvirate together with a lesser warlord, Marcus Lepidus; eliminated opponents in a new reign of terror in Rome; and defeated Cassius and Brutus in battle in Greece. The triumvirs declared that they intended to "restore the Republic," but they also had the Senate proclaim Julius Caesar a "Divine Being" (*divus*)—not quite a god like Jupiter, but far above any ordinary mortal. The murdered dictator had become a founding hero, whose memory would inspire all future supreme rulers of Rome.

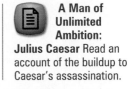

A Man of Unlimited Ambition: Julius Caesar Read an account of the buildup to Caesar's assassination.

The partners then divided the Roman world, with Octavian based in Rome, Lepidus in North Africa, and Mark Antony in Alexandria. Their cooperation soon turned to rivalry, however, and the balance of power began swinging toward Octavian. Antony's passionate love affair with Queen Cleopatra, one of the last descendants of the Greek rulers of Egypt, made him unpopular in Rome, and his efforts to win prestige by making conquests on the eastern frontier ended in failure. Meanwhile, Octavian pushed Lepidus out of power and successfully began expanding Rome's frontiers northward toward the Danube (see Map 6.2 on page 96).

Finally, in 31 B.C., the rulers of the two halves of Rome's empire went to war. Octavian's forces defeated those of Antony and Cleopatra in a decisive naval battle near Actium off the western coast of Greece. Antony and Cleopatra returned to Egypt, and within a year, both had committed suicide. Octavian was now the supreme warlord—the third to rule Rome, and the one who finally managed to turn military dictatorship into legitimate and permanent monarchy.

> *"But that which brought upon him the most apparent and mortal hatred was his desire of being king; which gave the common people the first occasion to quarrel with him, and proved the most specious pretence to those who had been his secret enemies all along."*
>
> —Plutarch, from *The Life of Julius Caesar*

Listen to a synopsis of Chapter 6.

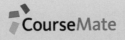

CHAPTER 7

THE ROMAN PEACE,
30 B.C.–A.D. 235

LEARNING OBJECTIVES

AFTER READING THIS CHAPTER, YOU SHOULD BE
ABLE TO DO THE FOLLOWING:

LO¹ Explain how the Augustan settlement led to stable
monarchy within the Roman Empire.

LO² Discuss the themes and concerns of writers and
philosophers in the Roman Empire.

LO³ Trace the evolution of Roman law.

LO⁴ Describe the distinctive features of Roman
architecture and engineering.

LO⁵ Analyze the social and cultural changes that took
place during the Roman Peace.

"THE ERA OF THE ROMAN PEACE WAS ONE OF MASSIVE SOCIAL, RELIGIOUS, AND CULTURAL CHANGES THAT WOULD FORM A NEW PATTERN OF WESTERN CIVILIZATION."

Augustus's new system of government kept many features of the Roman Republic, allowed subject peoples a good deal of self-rule, and brought Rome's destabilizing expansion to a halt. The result was two hundred years of stability that modern scholars call the Roman Peace.

Within the empire, the Roman version of Greco-Roman civilization prevailed in the Western territories, and the Greek version was dominant in the East. Roman literature and art, philosophy and law, architecture and engineering were often inspired by Greek models, but Roman achievements in these fields eventually equaled or surpassed those of the Greeks and became just as much an inspiration and model for future Western development.

In many ways, the dominant international civilization undermined the traditions of other peoples of the empire. In the West, the native languages of conquered European barbarian peoples began to be replaced by Latin; in the East, Egyptian hieroglyphic writing fell out of use. But the empire's most revered international gods and goddesses came from Egypt and other lands of the eastern Mediterranean or beyond the empire's eastern frontier, and the language of new Latin speakers began a lengthy evolution into the Latin languages of the present day. The era of the Roman Peace was one of massive social, religious, and cultural changes that would form a new pattern of Western civilization.

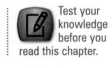

Test your knowledge before you read this chapter.

What do you think?

The era of the Roman Peace was a high point in the history of Western civilization.

Strongly Disagree						Strongly Agree
1	2	3	4	5	6	7

David Ball/Corbis

≪ Hadrian's Wall Constructed at the order of the emperor Hadrian between A.D. 122 and 128, this frontier wall was originally ten feet or more high. It ran for seventy miles right across the island of Britain, between the Roman Empire (on the right) and what the Romans called the *barbaricum*—barbarian territory. The barrier helped keep barbarians out, but it also marked a self-imposed limit on Roman expansion.

princeps
"First citizen," a traditional Roman name for prominent leaders who were considered indispensable to the Republic that came to be used by Augustus and other early emperors.

LO¹ The Rule of the Emperors

Soon after Octavian's triumph at Actium, the Senate conferred on him a new title, Augustus ("Revered One"), the name under which he has gone down in history. Now that he was supreme ruler, Augustus intended to stay in power, reconstruct the failed government of the Roman city-state, and keep its empire together. The main lines of the "Augustan settlement" had emerged by 27 B.C., the year generally accepted as the end of the Republic and the beginning of the rule of the Roman emperors.

The Augustan Settlement

At the time, Augustus did his best to make it seem as if no such historic change was under way. He again proclaimed the goal of restoring the Republic (p. 100) and set about consolidating his supreme rule as much as possible within the traditional government and political framework.

The First Citizen

Unlike Sulla and Caesar, Augustus refused the offer of a long-term dictatorship and referred to himself simply as **princeps** ("first citizen"), a traditional name for prominent leaders who were considered indispensable to the Republic. From time to time, he served terms in leading magistracies such as consul, censor, and supreme pontiff, though the only one that he continuously held, and used as the legal basis of his power, was that of tribune of the people.

By arrangement with the Senate in 27 B.C., Augustus was confirmed as commander in chief (*imperator*, from which the English word *emperor* is derived) of the armed forces, which included civil and military control of all provinces with garrisons. In return, he permitted the Senate to supervise Italy and the city of Rome, as well as provinces where no soldiers were stationed. On his way to supreme power, he had proscribed and put to death many opponents in the Senate and replaced them with his friends and allies. Now he could afford to consult the Senate frequently and give it genuine government power.

The people's assemblies, on the other hand, lost what remained of their power to elect magistrates and make laws. The people of Rome did not oppose this, for they had lost confidence in the traditional system and trusted Augustus to rule in their interests as they had trusted Caesar before him. True to his policy of not breaking openly with tradition, Augustus still summoned the assemblies from time to time, but later emperors did not bother even with this formality. In "restoring" the Republic, Augustus

 **The Roman Empire: In the First Century**
(http://www.pbs.org/empires/romans/index.html) Learn more about the Roman Empire in the first century in this interactive site.

CHRONOLOGY

29–19 B.C.	Virgil composes the *Aeneid*
27 B.C.	End of Roman Republic and beginning of rule of Roman emperors
A.D. 14	Augustus dies and Tiberius takes over without challenge
A.D. 62–70	Jewish revolt against Rome
A.D. 117	Under Emperor Trajan, the Roman Empire reaches its greatest extent
A.D. 126	Pantheon built in Rome
A.D. 212	All free inhabitants of the Roman Empire are declared Roman citizens
A.D. 529	Justinian's law code begins to be published, systematizing the laws of Rome

was careful not to bring back the "mixed" government that had once been the source of its stability and vitality.

The Divine Being

In spite of avoiding Caesar's open exercise of supreme power, Augustus followed the dictator's even more arrogant-seeming example of accepting religious worship of himself.

After Augustus won supreme power, Greek cities in Anatolia began building shrines and sacrificing to "Rome and Augustus"—worshiping Rome itself as divine, and Augustus as a god-sent human being who embodied Rome's beneficent rule. Augustus was not the first powerful Roman to be worshiped in this way, but this time the practice spread well beyond Anatolia—with Augustus's permission and often with his encouragement. Shrines of Rome and Augustus sprang up throughout the empire, with prominent local citizens competing to serve as priests. Finally, when he died, the Senate declared him a Divine Being like Julius Caesar. It soon became customary for emperors to be worshiped in their lifetimes and to be deified (declared divine) when they died.

Augustus also acquired the title of Father of the Fatherland and took seriously the fatherly duty of supervising the behavior of his "household"—especially of the upper classes in Rome. He had laws passed against adultery by women and against both men and women who failed to marry; another law exempted mothers of more than three children from the requirement of guardianship. Poets and artists depicted him and his wife Livia as models of Roman family life, with Livia in the role of chaste and strong-minded "matron" of the Fatherland. Livia, who outlived Augustus, was also deified upon her death—the first of several emperors' wives to be honored in this way.

Of course, there was a good deal of make-believe in all this. The Roman upper classes went on living their free and easy way of life in spite of the moralizing from on high. As a matter of fact, Augustus and Livia themselves both got divorced in order to marry each other, and they never managed to have children together. And emperors themselves did not always take their divinity seriously. A later ruler, Vespasian (**ve-SPEY-zhuhn**), who was known for his cynical sense of humor, is supposed to have said on his deathbed: "Oh no, I think I'm turning into a god!"

Still, the Romans already believed that there was something divine about every paterfamilias and every matron; and they regarded community life as a kind of large-scale family life (p. 94); and most other peoples of the empire had similar beliefs. For Romans and non-Romans alike, the rule of one man was actually easier to accept if they could think of him as worthy of divine worship as well as human honor, and as a traditional paterfamilias married to a traditional matron. Augustus's claim to divinity and his fatherly moralizing strengthened his own rule, as well as the whole new system of monarchy that he founded.

A Critical Assessment of the Reign of Augustus Caesar Read a vivid contemporary account of how Augustus handled power.

Reform, Reconstruction, and the End of Expansion

Ensuring peace and stability involved not only changing the way the Roman city-state worked but also reorganizing the whole of Rome's empire. There must be no more grasping governors and dishonest officials arousing fury among the subject peoples, and no more ambitious commanders making themselves into independent warlords with the help of discontented soldiers. Accordingly, Augustus began a whole series of large-scale reforms.

First, he brought the system of government appointments under his personal control. Here, too, he avoided breaking with tradition. Just as before, ambitious men from wealthy families made their way up a ladder of civil and military ranks in Rome and the provinces, and many of them were still appointed to their positions by the Senate. But none of them got far unless he performed competently, honestly, and loyally to the satisfaction of the princeps.

Second, Augustus showed respect for local institutions and encouraged provincial leaders to fulfill their responsibilities. He kept control over the affairs of the empire as a whole in Rome, but he left local affairs to the individual provinces, which in turn delegated a great deal of power. Greek city-states, Roman colonies, Celtic tribes, and countless other communities all ran their own day-to-day business, and it is estimated that the entire empire needed no more than a couple of thousand Roman officials to run it. Over several centuries and across a vast empire, corrupt and oppressive government was still common enough, but seemingly not so systematic and outrageous as under the Republic.

Third, Augustus reorganized the army to ensure the loyalty of the rank-and-file soldiers. After the battle of Actium, Mark Antony's troops came over to Augustus, who found himself at the head of a combined army of 600,000 men. Half were Roman citizens serving in about sixty legions, and the rest were noncitizens serving in auxiliary units (p. 97). Such a large army was impossible to pay for or keep under control, so Augustus quickly cut the troop strength in half and paid off the men he discharged with grants of land and money.

Then Augustus gradually brought about his single most drastic reform. Previously, soldiers had been mostly draftees who served for the duration of any particular war in units that were disbanded when a war ended. But by the end of his rule, all his soldiers were volunteers, serving for fixed terms of twenty-five years in permanent units. In this way, he hoped to make the army stable and reliable, since every man served by his own choice and knew exactly when to expect his release and his discharge grant. Soldiers in auxiliary units, which still made up about half the army, were not entitled to discharge grants, but later emperors began giving them something just as valuable: Roman citizenship (see photo on page 121). And every soldier swore obedience to the princeps personally and looked to him for pay and veterans' benefits.

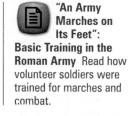

"An Army Marches on Its Feet": Basic Training in the Roman Army Read how volunteer soldiers were trained for marches and combat.

In this way, Augustus and his successors broke with the Roman tradition of citizen-soldiers to create the world's first professional standing army. The new model army was never completely proof against mutinous soldiers and treasonous commanders, but on the whole, it was loyal enough to the reigning princeps to give him a monopoly on military power.

The End of Roman Expansion

Even after Augustus's troop cuts, his army was still far larger than the forces that Rome had usually maintained in the past. He kept part of his army—the legion-sized Praetorian (**pree-TAWR-ee-uhn**) Guard—in Rome to back up his power at the empire's center, but he moved most of his forces to the frontiers of the empire, for he fully intended to continue Rome's tradition of seemingly endless conquest. Egypt, the lands stretching from Italy and Greece to the River Danube, a wide swath of Germany to the east of the Rhine (Map 6.2, p. 96)—all these territories were added to the empire by Augustus's legions. However, toward the end of his reign, Augustus turned against any further expansion—a change that had momentous long-term consequences for Rome's empire.

> **"** *Augustus and his successors broke with the Roman tradition of citizen-soldiers to create the world's first professional standing army.* **"**

THE ADVENT OF MONARCHY BROUGHT FIVE CENTURIES OF ROMAN EXPANSION TO AN END:

A military disaster prompted new thinking on expansion

- In A.D. 9, recently conquered peoples in central Europe and Germany beyond the Rhine rebelled against the Romans, and an entire Roman army was destroyed by German barbarian insurgents.

- This loss forced Augustus to realize that his army had been overstretched by conquests and that a still larger army would be so expensive and so uncontrollable as to endanger his power.

Augustus advised his successors not to expand

- After his death in A.D. 14, Augustus's will was found to contain a recently added clause advising the Senate and his successors that the empire should be confined within its existing boundaries.

- Most of Augustus's successors followed his advice because they, too, found expansion too risky and destabilizing. In the next century, only a few large independent territories were permanently added to the empire (Map 6.2, p. 96).

The army's mission was changed from conquest to defense

- The army's 300,000 men were stationed in hundreds of permanent encampments along what came to be thought of as the permanent frontiers of the empire.

- Though Roman forces often campaigned beyond the frontiers, it was nearly always to deter or punish attackers from the other side.

 Historical Simulation of a Soldier's Life on the Roman Frontier Experience life as a soldier on the Roman frontier.

>> **Marcus Caelius, First Centurion** This senior officer served for thirty years in Augustus's reformed army before perishing in the German rebellion of A.D. 9. His body was not found, but the inscription on this monument built by his brother says hopefully: "His bones may be interred here." He holds his centurion's baton and wears his many battle honors. Also commemorated are his two freedmen (ex-slaves) who died with him. Evidently his bond with them was close. LVR-LandesMuseum Bonn

Permanent Monarchy

Augustus was convinced that if Rome's new peace and stability were to last, the changes he had made in its government system must continue after his death. For that to happen, he must settle in advance on someone to replace him—and this chosen successor must come from his own family. He himself would never have come to power if Julius Caesar had not made him his son, and the soldiers of the army, who were represented in Rome by the Praetorian Guard, felt a hereditary loyalty to the descendants of Caesar. Given the importance to the Romans of clan and family ties—which could be by adoption as well as by blood (p. 98)—if the position of princeps were to last, it must be hereditary.

Having no sons of his own, Augustus finally settled on Tiberius, Livia's son from her first marriage, as the next princeps. Tiberius was already experienced in government and trusted by the army, for Augustus had made sure that men of his family got their share of leading magistracies and high military commands. In addition, Augustus adopted Tiberius as his own son so as to give him the necessary hereditary standing, and he had the Senate grant Tiberius the same power as commander in chief that he held himself. When Augustus died in A.D. 14, Tiberius took over without challenge.

At first, the emperors who succeeded Tiberius during the first century A.D. emerged—usually after vicious family infighting—from among the descendants of Julius Caesar and were then accepted by the Senate as Tiberius had been. Eventually, Caesar's last descendant, the notorious Nero, was overthrown after a tyrannical reign, but by that time, the Romans had become so used to one-man rule that no one seems to have thought of restoring the Republic. Instead, after a brief and brutal civil war among rival army commanders in A.D. 69, the winner—the humorous but also able and determined Vespasian—founded another dynasty, the Flavians (from Vespasian's full Latin name, Titus Flavius Vespasianus).

Near the end of the first century, the Flavian dynasty, too, came to an end following the assassination of another tyran-

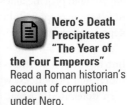 **Nero's Death Precipitates "The Year of the Four Emperors"** Read a Roman historian's account of corruption under Nero.

nical emperor, Vespasian's son Domitian (**duh-MISH-uhn**). Again, there was no thought of restoring the Republic, and the Senate appointed as princeps one of its own members, the aged and highly respected Nerva. Since Nerva had no sons and was unknown to the army, to avoid another civil war he adopted a leading general, Trajan, who took over peacefully upon Nerva's death in A.D. 98.

Subsequent rulers for much of the second century happened to have no sons by blood who survived them, so they, too, adopted sons whom they also designated (proclaimed) as their successors. Such an adopted son immediately became a junior emperor with what had by now become the imperial title **caesar**, and when his senior colleague died, he took full charge as **augustus**. This custom of "adoption and designation" produced a long series of outstanding emperors: Trajan, "the best of rulers," as he was called; the cultured and energetic Hadrian; the wise and dutiful Antoninus; and the philosopher-statesman Marcus Aurelius (**aw-REE-lee-uhs**).

Toward the end of the second century, however, the line of emperors by adoption and designation came to an end when Commodus, Marcus Aurelius's son by blood, outlived him, ruled irresponsibly, and was eventually murdered. Once again, civil war brought a new dynasty to power—this one founded by a capable and ruthless general of North African origin, Septimius Severus. His male descendants clung to power well into the third century in spite of rival generals and their own murderous quarrels, mainly thanks to their shrewd and determined mothers. All these women were close relatives of Septimius's wife Julia Domna, who came from a wealthy and cultured Syrian family. Some of them were publicly honored as "mother of the Senate," "mother of the camps," and even "co-ruler." Never before had Rome, with its reverence for public fatherhood (p. 94), paid the same honor to public motherhood—let alone to that of women from an eastern province.

In this way, Augustus's governing structure endured until the troubled times of the late third century (pp. 135–136). In spite of occasional upsets, the system always righted itself, for the soldiers, the ordinary Roman citizens, and the subject peoples all found a single all-powerful ruler far more helpful to their interests and needs than a greedy oligarchy. Even the upper classes found their pursuit of wealth and power on the whole safer and more predictable when it was supervised by the princeps. In this way, the Augustan settlement brought two hundred years of relative stability and prosperity that have gone down in history as the *Pax Romana*, the era of the **Roman Peace**.

LO² Literature and Thought in the Roman Empire

As Rome's conquests brought it into closer contact with the Greek world, the Romans began to share in the cultural traditions of Greece, and Latin joined Greek as a language of literature and thought. In the empire's eastern provinces, there was a great deal of writing in other languages such as Egyptian, Hebrew, and Aramaic, but most of it was for everyday and business purposes

or dealt with religious belief and worship. Anyone who wanted to write in the literary forms and the fields of thought and study developed by the Greeks nearly always wrote in one or other of the international languages.

Literature in Latin and Greek

The rise of Latin began with a Greek ex-slave, Livius Andronicus, who in the third century B.C. translated Homer's *Odyssey* and several Greek dramas. Very soon, native Roman authors began to write in these and other traditional Greek literary forms, but they used these forms to express distinctively Roman values and experiences. Their works became in turn revered models for expressing the values and experiences of future European nations.

caesar
The imperial title given to the designated successor of a reigning emperor.

augustus
The imperial title given to a reigning emperor.

Roman Peace
(*Pax Romana*) A term used to refer to the relative stability and prosperity that Roman rule brought to the Mediterranean world and much of western Europe during the first and second centuries A.D.

The Republic

Most of the earliest Latin literary works no longer exist, but many comedies staged in the third and second centuries B.C. by Plautus and Terence are still performed today. Their works were based on Greek comedies of the Hellenistic era, adapted to the rough-and-tumble tastes of Roman audiences.

Like their models, Plautus and Terence did not deal with topical subjects as Aristophanes had done (p. 70). Instead, they concentrated on the timeless themes of love and money. Their plays had complicated plots involving such characters as skinflint fathers, spendthrift and lovelorn sons, disillusioned but good-natured *hetaerae* (p. 58), beautiful young slave women who turn out to be the long-lost daughters of fabulously wealthy foreigners, and fast-talking slave men who juggle everyone else through to happy endings. What gave the Roman comedies their charm was their clever variations on the standard formulas, their humorously wise reflections on ordinary life and human nature, and the fact that audiences enjoyed being beguiled by what they knew perfectly well was wishful thinking. Terence himself had one of his characters say: "My life isn't like the comedies, where everything turns out well!"

The troubles of the first century B.C. were disastrous for the Republic but inspiring for writers. Men who were themselves involved in political feuding and military adventures produced notable works of history. Julius Caesar, for instance, wrote narratives of his own campaigns that were impressively sober and factual, and thereby convincingly advertised his battlefield genius. Outside politics, Catullus, a translator of Sappho (pp. 69–70), learned from her how to express deep passions in a brief space—but the passions he expressed were bitter as well as beautiful. "I hate and I love!" began one of his poems, inspired by a tempestuous affair with a free-living aristocratic woman.

The widest-ranging literary achievement of the late Republic was that of Cicero (**SIS-uh-roh**), an opponent of Caesar and a sympathizer with the dictator's assassins who was proscribed and killed on the orders of Antony and Octavian (p. 101). Trained as an orator in Athens, he put his skills to use in Rome, making magnificent Latin speeches in political and high-society trials and in Senate debates on matters of state. He was also a fascinating letter writer, a skill that was traditionally linked with oratory, since letters were often written to instruct and persuade. Besides serious reflections on life, however, his letters were full of news, gossip, and personal feeling. In addition, he wrote longer works on government, morals, and theology in which he explained and evaluated the ideas of Hellenistic philosophers, and thereby made Latin into a language of philosophy on a level with Greek.

The Empire

With Augustus's creation of a stable monarchy and the Republic's troubles still recent, writers found two themes both politically timely and genuinely inspiring: nostalgia for the supposedly simple and virtuous Roman past, and celebration of Rome's destiny as ruler and lawgiver of a peaceful world. These themes were most famously dealt with by a historian, Livy, and a poet, Virgil.

Livy's vast work, *From the Founding of the City*, narrated the entire eight hundred years of Rome's history up to the rise of Augustus. Its story was a patriotic but also a tragic one, of the community values and personal qualities that had made Rome great and the gradual decay of those values and qualities up to

The Power of Myth: Livy and the Rape of Lucretia Read Livy's retelling of the Roman legend of Lucretia.

Livy's own times, when "we can bear neither our diseases nor their remedies." Livy told a majestic story with memorable vividness, and his basic understanding of the Republic's history has survived to the present day.

Virgil's great epic poem, the *Aeneid* (**ih-NEE-id**), retells a Roman myth of the exile hero Aeneas (**ih-NEE-huhs**), who fled the destruction of Troy by the Greeks, wandered across the sea like Homer's Odysseus (p. 100), and redeemed Troy's defeat by making a new home in Italy that became the city of Rome. The myth expressed both Rome's need for a link with the traditions of the Greeks and its sense of rivalry with them, but Virgil's version is also a prophecy of Rome's imperial destiny. One of the stopping places on Aeneas's journey is the underworld, where he is shown a vision of his heroic descendants. These men are destined to take his city from humble beginnings to worldwide rule that "will bring good order joined to peace."

Besides triumph, however, the *Aeneid* is also full of what its hero calls "unspeakable woe": exile and separation; deaths of beloved kin and comrades and of worthy foes; the suicide of the queen of Carthage, whom Aeneas loves and leaves on his way to found the city that will one day destroy hers. Virgil's moving images of grief and pain, and his sense of the tragedy and cruelty of conquest, give depth and solemnity to his celebration of empire and make his tale truly heroic (see photo on page 109).

Two other poets of Augustus's reign, Horace and Ovid, were also eloquent spokesmen of Roman tradition and the blessings of empire, as well as of less momentous concerns. Many of Horace's lyric poems celebrate simple pleasures shared with friends, or comment ruefully on human foolishness. But for Horace, always aware of the shortness of human life, these seemingly trivial matters are deeply important. He conveys the joy and sadness that lie behind them in memorable images that make them, as he said of his own poems, "more lasting than bronze."

Ovid wrote long poems that told of such matters as Greek nymphs changing shape to escape lustful gods, lucky and unlucky days for Roman officials to issue laws, advice to men on how to seduce women, and advice to women on how to be seduced by men. Ovid was a master of shifting moods—irony and humor, sorrow and despair, cynical relish, and delight in human and natural beauty. His "how to" poems on seduction, celebrating the manipulative ways of men and women in Roman high society, displeased Augustus in his role as guardian and model of Roman family life, and Ovid spent his last ten years banished to a remote town on the west coast of the Black Sea.

In the century after Augustus, when one-man rule came to be taken for granted, writers became more detached and critical about Rome. The historian Tacitus (**TAS-i-tus**), for example, wrote disillusioned analyses of the workings of the imperial monarchy, as well as respectful treatments of barbarian

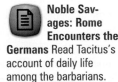

Noble Savages: Rome Encounters the Germans Read Tacitus's account of daily life among the barbarians.

peoples that Rome encountered. Following the ancient convention of inventing speeches for historical characters (p. 71), he made a British chieftain rally his warriors against a Roman army with a devastating condemnation of Rome's hypocrisy and oppression: "They call robbery, slaughter, and plunder by the lying name of empire; they make a desert, and they call it peace!" It was a very different view of Roman imperialism from Virgil's.

At about the same time, Juvenal brought to a new level of bitterness the tradition of lamenting Rome's moral decline, in a series of satirical poems on life in the capital. In Juvenal's Rome, aristocratic fathers of families go slumming in bars and brothels: meanwhile, their

> **"***But this is the kernel of my advice: Treat your inferiors as you would be treated by your betters. And as often as you reflect how much power you have over a slave, remember that your master has just as much power over you.* **"**
>
> —Seneca, ca. 50 A.D.

"Some God Preserves Your Life for Greater Deeds" This wall painting from Pompeii shows a scene from the *Aeneid*. Aeneas has been struck by a javelin in a battle in Italy, and he comforts his young son Ascanius while his comrade Iapyx tries to remove the blade. Invisible to them, Aeneas's divine mother Venus swiftly heals her son's wound, and Iapyx tells him that this must be a god's work, so that Aeneas may fulfill his high destiny.

Erich Lessing/Art Resource, NY

wives enjoy the same pleasures at home, in between meddling in "matters of men's concern" like athletics, politics, and literature. Jumped-up freedmen elbow aside respectable Romans in the crowded mansions of the rich and famous, the lower classes are anesthetized with "bread and circuses," and foreigners—especially Greeks, Syrians, and Jews—are overrunning the natives. With scornful relish, Juvenal portrayed a city that in gaining an empire, had lost its traditions and identity to the peoples it ruled.

Greek Writers

Like the Romans, authors writing in Greek—which included both native Greeks and non-Greeks from the eastern provinces—both worked within their own traditions and had to come to terms with powerful foreign influences. In their case, however, the foreign influences were those of Rome itself.

The first Greek writer to encounter Rome in this way was the historian Polybius, who came to Rome as a hostage in the course of the conquest of Greece during the second century B.C. He befriended leading Romans, and his history sought to explain Rome's rise to supremacy over the Mediterranean world. Like Livy (who based a good deal of his history on Polybius), he admired Roman community values and personal qualities, but he also stressed the balance of power between Rome and its rivals, its style of warfare, and its city-state institutions. It was Polybius who first described the Republic as a "mixed government," combining the democratic commitment of all

citizens to the state with the experience and farsightedness of a stable oligarchy.

Two centuries later, another victim of Rome who became its friend, Josephus, wrote the history of the great Jewish revolt against Rome and its bloody suppression in A.D. 62–70 (p. 125). Josephus was himself a leader in the revolt who changed sides but remained a Jewish believer. Traditionally, the Jews had explained disasters as punishment by God for their sins (p. 39), but Josephus narrated this one much as Thucydides had narrated Athenian defeats in the Peloponnesian War (p. 71), as a human event resulting from human causes. Roman oppression, he thought, had fostered Jewish extremism and vice versa. Oppression and extremism had finally exploded into a disaster that had prevented or delayed the Jews from getting what Josephus believed God intended for them: an honored position under the Romans, whom God had raised up as world-ruling protectors of the Jews just as he had earlier raised up the Persians.

The broadest-ranging of Greek writers was Plutarch, who in the late first and early second centuries wrote well over a hundred short works on history, philosophy, and religion. Plutarch believed in the Stoic philosophy of achieving happiness by striving for virtue (p. 110), and in his most famous work, *Lives of the Noble Greeks and Romans*, he "compared and contrasted" the moral qualities of pairs of famous soldiers and statesmen of both nations. He explained the different strengths and weaknesses of his characters, but usually avoided finding a Greek generally more virtuous than a Roman or vice versa. In this way, Plutarch celebrated the partnership between Greece and Rome without taking sides in their rivalry.

Later in the second century, Lucian of Samosata, a Syrian from the Euphrates frontier who thoroughly mastered Greek culture, made fun of every kind of folly and pretentiousness in every class of society. Among his many targets were wealthy Romans who hired Greek philosophers as hangers-on to make themselves look well educated—as well as the philosophers they hired, for allowing themselves to be used in this demeaning way. His depiction of life in the mansions of the Roman rich and famous was much the same as Juvenal's, but it was seen from the opposite viewpoint—with Romans as the exploiters and Greeks as the foolish victims.

Epicureanism and Stoicism

In the era of the Roman Peace, Greeks and Romans came to share common traditions in philosophy as well as literature. These traditions originated with Plato, Aristotle, and other early Greek thinkers, but in Hellenistic times, Greek thinkers had become more concerned with the place of the individual within the universe (p. 86), and it was these later ideas that strongly influenced the Romans.

Epicureanism

One Hellenistic thinker widely revered in Rome was Epicurus, who claimed about 300 B.C. that everything in the universe was formed by the chance motion of atoms with no ultimate purpose, and that people should learn to live without fear, cultivate peace of mind, and accept the nothingness of death (p. 86).

The chief Roman promoter of Epicurus's teachings was Lucretius (**loo-KREE-shuhs**) (first century B.C.), who articulated them in a long poem *On the Nature of Things*. The poem is also a hymn to Epicurus himself, whom Lucretius praises for having liberated the human mind from superstitious fears. Later on, many poems of Horace celebrating private pleasures temperately enjoyed among friends, and many satires of Lucian targeting gullible religious believers, were also influenced by Epicureanism.

Epicureanism was not just a way of thinking but a way of life—one that involved giving up excitement, ambition, and sensual pleasure, and that needed training to live it properly. Groups sprang up across the Greek world and later the Roman world to study and follow Epicurus's example under the guidance of experienced practitioners, with the motto: "We will be obedient to Epicurus, according to whom we have made it our choice to live." It was a choice for a disciplined and directed life like that of Christian monks and nuns (p. 132), but one without immortality or gods.

Stoicism

The Hellenistic philosophy that most deeply influenced Rome, however, was Stoicism, with its belief in a purposeful universe functioning according to a plan of goodness that all humans can understand through reason, and that all humans must obey by living virtuously (p. 87).

The followers of Stoicism ranged from the orator and statesman Cicero, through Epictetus, a Greek freedman who had been a learned slave in Nero's court, to an actual emperor, Marcus Aurelius, who sought to embody Plato's dream of the philosopher-king (see photo on page 144). Day by day, while commanding his legions in fierce frontier wars, he set down his innermost thoughts in a little book, called *Meditations* (thoughts to himself). Stoicism, as formulated by Marcus Aurelius, was quite in accord with the ancient Roman virtues. "Let it be your hourly care," he advised, "to do stoutly what the hand finds to do, as becomes a man and a Roman, with carefulness, unaffected dignity, humanity, freedom, and justice." All people, whether emperors or slaves, must do their duty as it falls to them. Thus nature's plan is served, and the individual's life is blended with that of the universe.

In accordance with this principle, some writers of Roman times stressed the equal abilities and mutual duties of men and women. Plutarch wrote a lengthy essay, *On the Virtue of Women*, to prove the truth of Plato's doctrine that male and female virtue were the same (pp. 74–75). Seneca, tutor and adviser to Nero, even proclaimed in a letter to a friend the untraditional belief that "a man does wrong in

A Wealthy Stoic Urges Humane Treatment of Slaves Read Seneca on the just treatment of slaves.

> **"***The earth occupies the central position in the cosmos, and all heavy objects move toward it.***"**
>
> —Ptolemy, ca. 50 B.C.

requiring chastity of his wife while he himself is having affairs with the wives of other men."

But Stoic philosophers expected that women, unlike Plato's philosopher-queens, would usually exercise their virtue within their traditional duties. Musonius Rufus, a Roman thinker of the first century A.D., believed that because philosophy involved the study of human groups including households, "a woman shaped by philosophy" would better understand "household management, the good provision of family needs, and the command of servants." The notion that sharing in traditionally male activities would make women more skillful at traditionally female tasks had a long history ahead of it, right down to the beginnings of modern feminism.

Roman Women: Following the Clues (http://www.bbc.co.uk/history/ancient/romans/roman_women_01.shtml) Learn more about the roles of women in ancient Rome.

Science and Medicine

Unlike literature and philosophy, science under the Roman Empire remained mostly a Greek pursuit, and Alexandria continued as the hub of scientific and medical works. It was there, in the second century A.D., that the Greek astronomer and geographer Claudius Ptolemy (**TOL-uh-mee**) compiled his *Almagest*. The title is Arabic, meaning "the greatest," for the book was neglected in Europe after the fall of Rome but continued to be studied and admired by Muslim scholars. Bringing together the accumulated learning of the Greeks about the earth and the heavenly bodies, Ptolemy set forth a model of the universe that was generally accepted in the West until the Scientific Revolution of the seventeenth century (pp. 357–359).

A Geocentric Explanation: The Earth Must Be Stationary Read a selection from Ptolemy's description of the universe.

Of equal influence was a series of books written about the same time by a Greek physician, Galen of Pergamum (in Asia Minor). Galen stressed the importance of personal hygiene to health, and his views on anatomy and physiology were accepted until the emergence of scientific biology in the seventeenth century.

Women of Substance: Midwifery Training Read a passage from another Greek physician, Soranus, on the training of midwives.

LO³ Roman Law

The Romans were vigorous originators in the field of law, and their most enduring contribution to Western institutions lay in legal theory and practice. Beginning as a city-state guided by its own unwritten customs, the Romans gradually developed the idea that the law should not simply follow the traditions of a particular community but should reflect "universal reason"—what human reason discovers to be right at all times and in all places.

The Evolution of Roman Law

Rome's first written law code, the Twelve Tables (p. 92), remained the basis of Roman law for centuries, but it was continually adapted in accordance with Rome's increasingly complex needs. After 366 B.C., a special magistrate, called a praetor (Latin for "person in charge"), was elected annually to administer justice to the citizens of Rome. He was expected to follow the Twelve Tables, but at the start of his term, he was required to announce his own interpretation of the law. Through this decree and through his daily decisions, he adapted the original laws to the cases before him.

By 246 B.C., another praetor was established to deal with disputes between Roman citizens and noncitizens under Roman jurisdiction. This official could draw on the various foreign laws, as well as on Roman law, in arriving at fair decisions and settlements. Thus there grew up, in the days of the Republic, two distinct bodies of law: the "law of citizens," or *jus civile*, and the "law of peoples," or *jus gentium*.

But by the first century A.D., with Rome's empire much larger and dealings between citizens and noncitizens more intensive, the basic provisions of the two bodies of law had been brought close together. After 212, when all free inhabitants of the empire were declared Roman citizens (p. 121), the dual system disappeared. By then, the law recognized a class distinction between "worthier" and "humbler" citizens, but one system prevailed throughout the empire.

Under the empire, the laws of the Republic were further expanded by the decrees and interpretations of rulers and also by the writings of legal experts. The praetors of the Republic, who were not professional lawyers, had begun consulting men who were "skilled in the law" (*jurisprudentes*), and emperors regularly appointed outstanding legal scholars in this role. The opinions of these experts on individual cases, and their commentaries (explanations of existing laws), had much the same authority as actual laws.

The Idea of Natural Law

Most of the jurists were well-educated men who felt at home with Stoic philosophy. They observed that the laws of nations had many elements in common and that the laws themselves were gradually fusing into the single law of the empire. This similarity in legal ideas among the peoples of the empire coincided nicely with the Stoic belief that the just and orderly plan of the universe as a whole also applied to human communities.

From this, the jurists argued that the laws of actual communities should operate according to this "natural law." Cicero, in the *Laws*, observed, "Law and equity have been established not by opinion but by nature." The regulations of states that do not conform to

reason, he declared, are not truly laws and do not deserve obedience. This doctrine of natural law gives added authority to laws that citizens regard as right but opens the door to rebellion in the case of laws they believe to be wrong. It has repeatedly been used both ways in the history of the West—most notably, in the U.S. Declaration of Independence (pp. 381–382).

aqueduct
A channel or tunnel used to convey water across a distance, usually by gravity.

> "*Cicero, in the Laws, observed, 'Law and equity have been established not by opinion but by nature.*"

Codification of the Laws

Roman law grew naturally over many centuries, and it was only very late in the empire's history, after several earlier efforts, that the sixth-century emperor Justinian succeeded in combining the long-standing accumulation into a single orderly code. To do justice to the law's complexities, Justinian's *Corpus Juris Civilis* (*Body of Civil Law*) consists of several parts. The *Digest* summarizes judicial opinions and commentaries; the *Code* is a collection of statutes from Hadrian to Justinian himself; the *Novels* ("additions") include imperial statutes enacted after the publication of the *Code*; and the *Institutes* ("instruction") summarize the basic principles of Roman law. Justinian's great codification became the foundation for the legal systems that were later developed throughout Europe. Hundreds of millions of people today live under systems that are modeled, in whole or in part, on Roman law as found in Justinian's code.

LO⁴ Architecture and Engineering

There is no more impressive proof of the Romans' sense of power and permanence than their architecture. After centuries of erosion and vandalism, the ruins of Roman buildings still stand across the empire's former territories, all the way from the Euphrates to the Atlantic. Egyptian pharaohs and Hellenistic rulers had already built vast buildings, but the Romans outdid them in the sheer amount of construction and their combination of grandeur, elegance, and display.

Arches, Vaults, and Domes

For truly impressive buildings, the Romans found the Greek style of columns and beams (p. 63) inadequate. Instead, they preferred the arch, vault, and dome. All these forms dated back to ancient Sumer, but the Romans exploited and developed them on an unprecedented scale.

The Romans realized that an arch formed of bricks, stones, or poured concrete could carry a far heavier load than a stone beam supported at either end by a column. And they discovered that a row of arches built side by side, and more rows built on top of the first one, could carry a bridge or an **aqueduct** across a deep valley (see photo on page 115).

vault
An arch made deeper to produce a tunnel-shaped enclosure.

A **vault** is an arch made deeper to produce a tunnel-shaped enclosure, which can be of any desired length but admits light only at the two ends. To overcome this difficulty, Roman architects devised the cross-vault, which permits light to enter from the sides as well. It consists of one or more short vaults intersecting the main vault at right angles. This kind of structure can be carried to a great height and can be made to enclose a huge space with no need for supporting members between floor and ceiling (see photo).

The dome, resting on a cylindrical wall or on a circle of supporting arches, could also be used to create a vast and uncluttered interior. A large dome was built from a series of progressively smaller horizontal rings of brick, stone, or concrete. When completed, the parts formed a single unit firmly set in place (see photo).

Wealthy Romans lived in townhouses and country mansions that were extremely comfortable and luxurious, as we can tell from the remains of the splendid houses at Pompeii, not far south of Rome, which was buried by an eruption of Mount Vesuvius in A.D. 79. Excavations have revealed homes designed on an Etruscan plan, with a central court (*atrium*) partly open to the sky, as well as fountains, sculptures, wall paintings, mosaics, and metalware. The great mass of the urban populations, however, lived in *insulae* ("islands")—crowded and often shoddily constructed apartment buildings with half a dozen or so floors. Examples of these have been uncovered at Ostia, a port and suburb of Rome.

Cross-Vaulting: The Baths of Diocletian The *frigidarium* ("cold-water hall") of public baths built in Rome by the emperor Diocletian about A.D. 300 was remodeled by Michelangelo nearly thirteen hundred years later as a church. The Renaissance architect was able to make use of the vast space created by the Roman cross-vaults—the intersecting arches of the ceiling.

≪ The Pantheon "Thanks to its dome it resembles the vault of heaven itself," said a Roman writer of this building. That was what the emperor Hadrian and his architect Apollodorus of Damascus wanted, in order to build a temple that would be worthy of "all the gods." The result was this unprecedented dome, which remained the world's largest for more than a thousand years after it was built about A.D. 120.

Forums, Basilicas, and Temples

The grandest Roman buildings were public ones. Every major city of the empire had a public square—a **forum**—that served as a civic center. The Roman Forum, for example, was a marketplace in the early days of the Republic, but it was gradually transformed into an impressive meeting place with handsome statues, temples, and halls of government. Overlooking the Forum was the sacred Capitoline Hill, topped by the temple of Jupiter, Juno, and Minerva, while across the Forum, on the Palatine Hill, stood the palaces of the emperors.

Several emperors constructed their own forums in Rome as memorials to themselves. One of these, the Forum of Trajan, was built early in the second century A.D. on a spacious site near the Capitoline Hill. Symmetrically laid out, it included a large area for shops, an imposing public hall, a library, and a temple dedicated to the deified emperor. Dominating all the rest was the towering marble Column of Trajan, with a spiral sculptured band 3 feet across and 650 feet long depicting the emperor's conquest of Dacia (present-day Romania), the last substantial addition to the empire.

Most of the public meeting halls in Rome and the other cities of the empire were built in the style of the **basilica** (buh-SIL-i-kuh) or "imperial hall" (from *basileus*, the Greek word for "emperor"). This was a long rectangular building with a wide central aisle or "nave" and narrower side aisles. By lifting the roof of the center aisle higher than the roofs of the side aisles, the architects were able to admit light through a series of "clerestory" windows. At one or both ends was a semicircular structure called an apse, which was frequently walled off from the center aisle and used as a chamber for courts of law. In the fourth century, when Christians began building public houses of worship, they adapted the basilica to their own needs. The congregation stood in the open rectangular area, and the apse was used to house the altar and sacred objects. This plan of church architecture persisted for centuries (see photo).

The usual Roman temple was built on much the same plan as Greek ones, but the most impressive of all Roman temples, the Pantheon (Temple of All the Gods) in Rome, has a different design. The Pantheon consists of a round central hall capped by a vast concrete dome (see photo on page 112). To carry the great weight of the dome, the rotunda wall was built 20 feet thick. The height of the dome and its diameter are identical (140 feet), and the dome is pierced by a 30-foot hole or "eye" at the top that serves as the source of light. The single doorway is approached through a Greek-style porch. From the outside, the Pantheon has a squat, heavy appearance, but the interior gives a dramatic impression of space and buoyancy.

forum
A public square that served as a civic center in ancient Roman towns.

basilica
A type of building with a wide central aisle (nave), narrower side aisles, and a semicircular chamber (apse) at one or both ends of the nave; originally used for government halls and later for churches.

Sant'Apollinare in Classe This church in the Italian seaport of Classe was built by the local bishop about A.D. 540 to honor his predecessor Saint Apollinaris. It is modeled on a traditional Roman type of public building, a basilica, but it dates from sixty years after the last emperor reigned in Rome. The church's construction was a sign of the town's continuing prosperity in spite of the empire's troubles. Siepmann/Photolibrary

Baths and Arenas

Elaborate structures were erected in the empire's cities to satisfy the recreational needs of the people. Particularly popular were the public bathhouses, which were equipped with steam rooms and small pools filled with hot, lukewarm, or cold water. The emperors also courted popular favor by donating magnificent pleasure palaces that housed not only baths but also large indoor and outdoor swimming pools, gymnasiums, gardens, libraries, galleries, theaters, lounges, and bars. Because these recreational centers were especially attractive to the lower classes and to idlers, their reputation in polite society was not altogether respectable.

 Public Space in an Urban Setting: The Sounds of a Roman Bath Read a short humorous account of the sounds coming from a Roman bath.

The best-preserved pleasure palace in Rome is the complex of buildings known as the Baths of Diocletian, built in the late third century A.D. One of its surviving halls, constructed on the cross-vault principle, is 300 feet long, 90 feet wide, and 90 feet high (see photo on page 112). It is estimated that the baths could accommodate three thousand bathers in lavish surroundings of gilt and marble.

One of the most popular pastimes of the Romans was watching the chariot races of the circus and the gory combats of the arena. Although every city of the empire had places for these mass entertainments, the most famous arena was the Colosseum of Rome (see photo). This huge structure, which covers about six acres and seated more than fifty thousand spectators, was the largest of its kind. The crowds made their way to their seats through some eighty entry vaults, and the stairways were arranged so that the stadium could be emptied in minutes.

Animation: The Colosseum: Building the Arena of Death (http://www.bbc.co.uk/history/ancient/romans/launch_ani_colosseum.shtml) Get a closer look at the Colosseum in this interactive animation.

A variety of materials was used in the construction of the Colosseum. Key areas of stress, such as archways and vaults, were generally of brick; other sections were of concrete and broken stone. The outer enclosure was built of three rows of arches topped by a high wall of stone blocks. Sockets set inside the high wall held great poles, on which protective awnings could be mounted. A coating of marble originally covered the exterior of the Colosseum, but the marble (and other building material) was carried off over the centuries for use in other structures.

Underneath the arena floor, which was made of wood covered with sand, lay a maze of corridors, chambers, and cells where animals and people (mainly slaves or criminals) awaited their turn at combat. The entertainments were lengthy affairs, lasting from early morning until dark. Wealthy donors seeking popularity—above all, emperors themselves—usually paid the bills, including the cost of food and refreshments.

 **Art of the Roman Empire 27 B.C. to A.D. 393** (http://www.metmuseum.org/toah/hd/roem/hd_roem.htm) View the art of the Roman Empire.

Statues and Portraits

Like forums, baths, and arenas, works of sculpture were also used by the Roman rulers as a medium of propaganda. They might relate the events of a military campaign like Trajan's conquest of Dacia, or they might proclaim an ideal of imperial rule, like a famous bronze statue of Marcus Aurelius on horseback (see photo on page 115). The strength and eagerness of the horse express the power and authority of the rider who controls

The Colosseum A new imperial dynasty, the Flavians, built this arena about A.D. 80 to win popularity in the city of Rome by providing mass entertainment on a spectacular scale. The entertainment—mainly gladiatorial combats, wild beast hunts, and mock sea battles—continued until A.D. 523, when the city's decay ended them. The Colosseum then served as a "stone quarry" for newer buildings, but the structure was so huge that it took a thousand years to reduce it to the size seen here.

Qwentes Italia srl/TIPS Images

The Pont du Gard Completed in 19 B.C. as part of a 30-mile aqueduct supplying the city of Nemausus in southern Gaul (present-day Nîmes, France), this bridge carried a water channel for 300 yards across the 160-foot valley of the River Gard. The bridge is built of accurately cut stones that hold together by their own weight without cement, yet the structure is so strong that the bottom row of arches carries a roadway used by modern motor vehicles.

it, and the rider's high-browed, bearded face (modeled on depictions of Greek philosophers) and his outstretched arm speak of wisdom and mercy.

Most Roman portraits, however, are extremely lifelike, and sculptors carried farther than ever before the Hellenistic tradition of making a portrait bear the mark of an individual personality. A bust from about 80 B.C., for instance, depicting an unknown patrician, is a fine study of character in this case, an aged but strong-minded, shrewd, and perhaps grimly humorous noble Roman (see photo on page 116).

Aqueducts and Roads

More than any other Western people until recent times, the Romans were builders of infrastructure—works other than actual buildings that served practical needs. To supply their cities with water, they built great aqueducts leading down from distant mountain springs. Much of the way, the water descended through pipes or channels in the mountains or hills, but across a valley or a plain it flowed in a channel carried by an aqueduct, engineered so that the water flowed steadily by force of gravity alone. The famous Pont du Gard (see photo) is part of a Roman aqueduct that once carried water in a 900-foot covered channel 160 feet above a river valley in southern Gaul.

Perhaps the most impressive infrastructure achievement of the Romans was their wide-ranging network of roads. Like the Assyrians and Persians before them (pp. 34, 36), they needed a swift and reliable means of overland movement to control, defend, and expand their empire. Over the centuries, they built or improved some 50,000 miles of roads, reaching out from Rome to the farthest corners of the empire. The typical roadbed was about 15 feet wide and 5 feet deep. Broken stone and gravel were packed down to form a foundation and then carefully graded to ensure solidity and good drainage. The surface was usually of dirt, except in the neighborhood of towns, where traffic was heaviest and thick blocks of hard stone were used.

The army, government officials, and the emperor's messengers had priority in the use of the strategically planned system of roads, but roads were also open to the public in general. The roads were regularly patrolled, and on the major arteries there was a stable every 10 miles and a hostel every 30 miles for the use of official travelers. Land travel under Rome's rule was easier than it had ever been before or than it would be again for nearly fifteen hundred years.

Emperor Marcus Aurelius This bronze equestrian (horse-riding) statue has inspired many other masterpieces since it was set up in Rome about A.D. 165 (see photo on page 299). Michelangelo, who designed the statue's present pedestal, was supposedly so taken with the horse's lifelike quality that when the pedestal was ready he commanded the animal to walk forward onto it.

LO⁵ Rome and Its Peoples

For two centuries, Rome's imperial monarchy brought unaccustomed government stability to the peoples living between the Euphrates and the Atlantic. But the era of the Roman Peace was also one of massive social and cultural change, which continued in the far less peaceful and stable two centuries that followed. Under the rule of the emperors, ancient traditions withered and died, new religious beliefs emerged that spread through the empire and beyond, new languages came into use that today are spoken across the world. The Roman Peace was an era of creative and destructive encounters among the peoples of the empire that permanently altered their patterns of civilization.

The Empire's Size and Structure

At the time of its greatest extent during the second century A.D., the Roman Empire measured nearly 3,000 miles from east to west and nearly 2,000 miles from north to south (Map 7.1), and its population was perhaps as high as 70 million. At the time, only the empire of China had a population as large as Rome's (though probably not larger), and no other human group under a single government was as large as these two.

The Empire and the World

As large as it was, the empire included less than half of Europe and far smaller amounts of Africa and Asia. Its survival therefore depended partly on the balance of power among nearby and distant peoples across the Eastern Hemisphere.

In spite of its name, the era of the Roman Peace saw plenty of frontier wars, but there were no enemies strong enough to make permanent breaches in Rome's defenses. To the south, the desert tribes of northwestern Africa were no more than small-scale raiders; in the Nile Valley, the Nubian rulers were mostly friendly. The Germanic barbarian tribes beyond the European

frontier (p. 135) were still not powerful enough to invade the empire. The chief antagonist in the east was the empire of Parthia, carved by nomadic invaders out of territories beyond the Euphrates that had once been conquered by Alexander. On the eastern frontier, Parthia was a serious rival, but it was a mere "regional power" compared with the intercontinental empire of Rome.

Beyond Parthia, the Romans had sea links to India and Ceylon (**si-LON**), and on the lower Danube, they were in touch with the horse-riding nomads of the steppes (p. 20). But for the time being, the steppe peoples fought mainly with each other or with Rome's Asian counterpart, the empire of China. As for China itself, then enjoying power and prosperity under the Han dynasty as great as those of Rome itself, it was a distant land, known to the Romans only through the reports of middlemen in the overland silk trade. Thus, the intercontinental balance of power among the peoples and states of Asia, Africa, and Europe for the moment favored the peace and stability of the Roman Empire.

Cities of the Empire

Although the empire was administered through some forty provinces, the basic unit of government and of social and economic life was the city. Where cities existed in conquered territories, the Romans strengthened them as centers from which to control the surrounding districts; where there were no cities, the Romans created new ones in the image of Rome.

The cities of the empire were bound together by a network of sea lanes and highways, with Rome, the magnificent capital, at the center. During the prosperous second century, nearly a million people lived there. Augustus is said to have found Rome a city of brick and to have left it a city of marble. And the emperors who followed him lavished gifts on the capital, building temples, forums, arenas, monuments, public baths, and palaces to honor themselves and to please the populace. There were, in addition, the elegant private estates of the wealthy, both in the city and in its suburbs. True, most of the people lived in overcrowded tenements. But Rome gave a stunning impression of affluence and grandeur.

In the empire's eastern territories, the old-established Greek metropolis cities of Alexandria in Egypt (p. 86) and Antioch in Syria were not much smaller than Rome. Hundreds of smaller Greek or Greek-dominated cities of the eastern Mediterranean led their

> "*Since the city was not adorned as the dignity of the empire demanded, and was exposed to flood and fire, Augustus so beautified it that he could justly boast that he had found it built of brick and left it in marble. He made it safe too for the future, so far as human foresight could provide for this.*"
>
> —Suetonius, first century A.D.

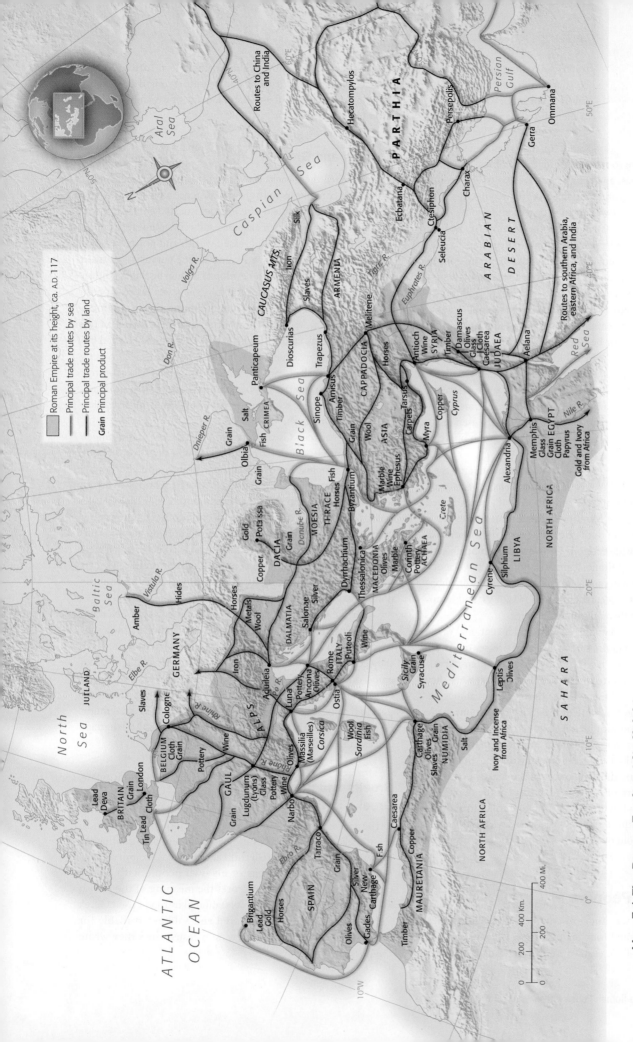

Map 7.1 The Roman Empire at Its Height

The map shows the empire at the beginning of Hadrian's reign. The road network stretches from Britain to the Middle East. But transport by water is even more efficient, and the Mediterranean, the Rhine, and the Danube are highways, not barriers. The network of trade and travel does not stop at the empire's frontiers but stretches deep into barbarian Europe, down the Red Sea to Arabia and India, and across the Middle East and central Asia all the way to China. © Cengage Learning

Interactive Map

Roman Empire at its height, ca. A.D. 117
Principal trade routes by sea
Principal trade routes by land
Grain Principal product

traditional community life, ruled by oligarchies that now obeyed the Roman emperor instead of Hellenistic monarchs (pp. 84–85). The cities of the West—Italy, Gaul, Spain, Britain, and northwestern Africa—strove to become miniature Romes. Each had its forum, baths, arenas, and temples, as well as its governing council of wealthy townsmen modeled on the Roman Senate.

Unlike in Rome, however, in many of these cities, the governing elite still had to struggle for the votes of the people. In Pompeii (p. 112), professionally painted election signs on houses excavated by archeologists bear witness to hard-fought campaigns. "Terentius Neo asks your vote for Cuspius Pansa as Commissioner of Streets, Temples, and Public Buildings!" announced a well-off bakery owner. Women had enough public standing among the townsmen to join in campaigning, though they could neither vote nor be elected. "Fabia asks your vote for Caius Secundus for the Two-Man Judicial Board. He's worthy!" said a sign at the doorway of a respected matron. And sometimes campaigns went negative: "Marcus Cerrinius Vatia for Streets, Temples, and Buildings Commissioner—the small-time hoodlums ask your vote for him!" In this way, traces of the Republic's "mixed" government survived under Rome's imperial monarchy.

The Imperial Economy

As the Romans conquered their empire, they were able to expand along far-flung networks of trade and travel that already linked the lands surrounding the Mediterranean and nearby areas of western Europe. In the era of the Roman Peace, these networks grew into an empire-wide economy. Olive groves in Spain supplied oil to the citizens of Rome; legions stationed on the Danube received part of their grain rations from North Africa; workshops in Gaul turned out cheap earthenware bowls, jugs, and lamps for use in households throughout the empire.

Large markets also encouraged technical invention. Water-powered mills to grind grain, screw-operated presses to extract oil from olives and juice from grapes, light wooden barrels instead of heavy earthenware jars to carry oil and juice once they were pressed—these and many other devices first came to be commonly used in the Roman Empire. Such inventions made production and transportation easier and more convenient, but perhaps the single most notable Roman contribution to ease and convenience came in the field of reading and writing. Sometime in the first century A.D., the Romans began to make books with pages that could be turned as one read, instead of the traditional lengthy scrolls that had to be wound from one roller to another. By the end of the empire, the new reading device was on the way to replacing the old one, and has remained standard in the West ever since.

The Empire's Peoples

The Roman Empire was home to countless different peoples, but broadly they formed four main groups: Romans, Greeks, non-Greek peoples of the eastern Mediterranean, and the less

complex societies of Europe and northwestern Africa. Out of the relationships, both friendly and hostile, among these groups there arose new forms of civilization, many of which have lasted down to the present day.

Romans and Greeks

The Romans owed many basic features of their civilized life to Greece. When the Greeks came under Roman rule, their influence on the conquerors only grew, for Greece alone could satisfy the intellectual tastes, the desire for sophisticated entertainment, and the need for models of elegance and refinement that developed in Rome along with increased wealth and power.

Like many peoples who come under pervasive outside influences, the Romans also developed a long-lasting tradition of fear and resentment against the foreigners who were supposedly diluting their identity and undermining their traditional way of life. Cato, an aristocrat of the same generation as the admirers of Greek culture Scipio and Cornelia (p. 98), called the Greeks "a quite worthless people. . . . When that race gives us its literature, it will corrupt all things." Two and a half centuries later (about A.D. 100), the poet Juvenal proclaimed, in effect, that Cato's prophecy had come true: "I can't stand a Rome that's turned into Greece!"

But in between Cato's time and Juvenal's, the Latin tongue had been enriched by borrowings and adaptations from Greek to become a sophisticated language of literature and philosophy; Roman writers had been inspired by Greek traditions to create works of prose and poetry that often outdid what the Greeks were producing at the time; and Roman officials governing eastern provinces had the advantage of knowing the international language of the region. The Romans had become partners and rivals of the Greeks in a common civilization that today is often called "**Greco-Roman**"—one that was also the empire's dominant international civilization.

For the Greeks, too, partnership between themselves and the Romans brought many benefits. True, they were now a subject people in a foreign empire, but in cultural matters, at least, they could feel themselves to be senior partners. All-powerful emperors often prided themselves on their fluent knowledge of Greek, but the Greeks never felt that knowledge of Latin was essential to being an educated person. Cato and Juvenal might resent this—but they, too, made sure to master the language and culture of the nation they resented.

Greeks and non-Greeks in the East

Partnership with the Romans meant that imperial rule actually safeguarded Greek dominance in the empire's eastern territories. Throughout those lands, the Greek language and culture wielded compelling influence on non-Greeks. The Jewish thinker Philo of Alexandria combined the sacred traditions of his own people with Greek philosophical thought to interpret the meaning of the Jewish holy writings. Roman army units stationed in Egypt used Greek for their lists of supplies ordered and soldiers available for duty—and so did Jewish believers in Jesus when they wrote the gospels.

For some eastern Mediterranean peoples, the combined impact of Greek culture and Roman power brought wrenching changes. Among the Jews, it gave rise to disputes and power struggles out of which both present-day orthodox Judaism and Christianity emerged (see Chapter 8). In addition, the empire's international civilization undermined the three-thousand-year-old traditions of Egypt. The Egyptian belief system, centered on the pharaoh as the upholder of the entire universe (p. 22), no longer made sense now that their country was a mere outlying province of a foreign empire. Perhaps for this reason, many other Egyptian traditions faded away—for example, their writing system. Shortly before A.D. 400, hieroglyphs were carved on a temple wall for the last time, and not long after, no Egyptian could read the ancient writing. But the Egyptians produced more documents and books than ever before, now that they read and wrote their language in the easily learned Greek alphabet.

The ways of Greece and Rome also changed under the impact of non-Greek ways, however—especially in the all-important field of religion. The international civilization needed international deities, and during the era of the Roman Peace, the most widely beloved and worshiped of these was the Egyptian goddess, Isis. Mighty and mysterious queen of the dead, yet also loving and merciful protectress of the living, she was approachable through secret rites in which rich and poor, men and women, slave and free could all gain her help in this world and her gift of eternal life.

The worship of Isis spread widely through the eastern Mediterranean lands in the centuries of Greek rule and Roman takeover (p. 84). Eventually, it reached Rome, where the Senate and the first emperors issued prohibitions against what seemed to them a subversive and un-Roman cult. By A.D. 100, however, Isis had a splendid temple in Rome, fitted out with genuine hieroglyphic carvings from Egypt—though Greek and Roman images of her generally played down her foreign origin (see photo). By A.D. 200, her worship had spread throughout the western half of the empire. Lucius Apuleius, a Roman lawyer from North Africa and author of works on philosophy as well as of a famous tale of magical adventure, *The Golden Ass*, praised Isis as the mightiest of deities: "The gods above adore you, the gods below do homage to you, you set the orb of heaven spinning around the poles, you give light to the sun, you govern the universe, you trample down the powers of Hell." It was the first but not the last time

that the empire's rulers resisted and then accepted a religion that originated among one of their subject peoples.

Romanization

The process of cultural change in which non-Romans adopted Roman ways.

Romans and Conquered Barbarians

From Spain, Gaul, and Britain all the way eastward to the Black Sea, Rome ruled a vast region of European barbarian peoples (Map 7.1 on page 117). Many of them were wealthy and highly skilled—especially the widespread Celtic tribes of western Europe (p. 100)—and the Romans had learned a great deal from them. Much of the armor and weaponry used by Roman armies, for instance, was adapted from the equipment used by Celtic warriors in Gaul and Spain. Town life and the use of writing had spread among some tribes, and if they had kept their independence, in time they would probably have developed their own local versions of Greco-Roman civilization.

Instead, the barbarians were conquered, and Roman soldiers, officials, and colonists moved in, bringing with them their language and culture. The Romans were perfectly willing to share all this on equal terms with wealthy native chieftains, landowning warriors, and traders, so long as they accepted imperial rule. The result was a wide-ranging and mostly peaceful process of cultural change known as **Romanization**.

Already under Augustus, according to the Greek geographer Strabo, the native people in prosperous riverside towns of southwestern Spain were known as "toga wearers" (clothed in Roman-style robes), who had "completely changed over to the Roman way of life, not even remembering their own language anymore." Four centuries later, the language of country dwellers as well as townspeople, in most of the European barbarian lands that Rome had conquered, was Latin.

But the international Latin language had many native words in it—not because the new speakers were slow learners, but because the way the Romans themselves spoke their language changed to accommodate what they learned from the peoples they conquered. The Celtic peoples of Gaul, for instance, used a kind of four-wheeled horse-drawn wagon called a *carros*, which could transport far more and far heavier goods than the flimsy two-wheeled Roman carts. The Romans began to use these wagons, and having no word for them, used the Gaulish one, pronounced Latin-style: *carrus*. Many of the peoples ruled by Rome went on speaking Latin after the empire fell apart, though the pronunciation changed yet again: two thousand years later, speakers of Spanish, Portuguese, and Italian call a wagon a *carro*—and English speakers, whose language is heavily influenced by Latin (p. 238), call an automobile or a railroad vehicle a *car*.

>> **A Roman Image of Isis** In token of her origin, the goddess holds up a sistrum, a kind of rattle that was used in Egyptian temple processions, but her headdress and hairstyle, her clothing and her ritual wine jug, are all Greek (compare an Egyptian depiction, p. 27). Isis has been repackaged to meet Greek and Roman ideas of what a goddess should look like—thereby inspiring reverence from the emperor Hadrian, who kept this image in his mansion near Rome. Vanni/Art Resource, NY

TURNING CONQUERED PEOPLES INTO ROMANS: GNAEUS JULIUS AGRICOLA

Gnaeus Julius Agricola was governor of the Roman-held part of Britain late in the first century A.D., put down rebellions there, and conquered additional territory. He was the father-in-law of the historian Tacitus, who wrote his biography. In this selection, Tacitus describes Agricola's peacetime activities as governor of the province. Tacitus's depiction is probably too good to be true, but it shows how he thought high Roman officials ought to behave when dealing with recently conquered and still rebellious "provincials" (non-Roman peoples), and what he thought of the process of Romanization itself.

The mention of "dancing attendance at locked granaries" refers to abuses of the practice of collecting taxes in the form of grain for the needs of the army. Tribes were forced to buy the grain from distant granaries and deliver it to distant army camps, which evidently enabled corrupt officials and grain dealers to make a profit.

Agricola was heedful of the temper of the provincials, and took to heart the lesson which the experience of others suggested, that little was accomplished by force if injustice followed. He decided therefore to cut away at the root the causes of war. He began with himself and his own people: he put in order his own house, a task not less difficult for most governors than the government of a province. He transacted no public business through freedmen or slaves: he admitted no officer or private to his staff from private feeling, or private recommendation, or entreaty: he gave his confidence only to the best. He made it his business to know everything; if not, always, to follow up his knowledge: he turned an indulgent ear to small offences, yet was strict to offences that were serious: he was satisfied generally with penitence instead of punishment: to all offices and positions he preferred to advance the men not likely to offend rather than to condemn them after offences.

Demands for grain and tribute he made less burdensome by equalising his imposts: he cut off every charge invented only as a means of plunder, and therefore more grievous to be borne than the tribute itself. As a matter of fact, the natives used to be compelled to go through the farce of dancing attendance at locked granaries, buying grain to be returned, and so redeeming their obligations at a price: places off the road or distant districts were named in the governor's proclamations, so that the tribes with winter quarters close at hand delivered at a distance and across country, and ultimately a task easy for everyone became a means of profit to a few. . . .

In order that a population scattered and uncivilised, and proportionately ready for war, might be habituated by comfort to peace and quiet, he would exhort individuals, assist communities, to erect temples, market-places, houses: he praised the energetic, rebuked the indolent, and the rivalry for his compliments took the place of coercion. Moreover he began to train the sons of the chieftains in a liberal education, and to give a preference to the native talents of the Briton as against the plodding Gaul. As a result, the nation which used to reject the Latin language began to aspire to rhetoric: further, the wearing of our dress became a distinction, and the toga came into fashion, and little by little the Britons were seduced into alluring vices: to the lounge, the bath, the well-appointed dinner table. The simple natives gave the name of "culture" to this factor of their slavery.

EXPLORING THE SOURCE

1. Describe the policies of Agricola in Britain. How do they compare with those of recent and present-day conquerors in dealing with peoples under their control?

2. In Tacitus's view, how far did Agricola succeed in turning conquered peoples into the best kind of Romans, and how far was Romanization an improvement in their way of life?

Source: Tacitus, *Agricola* 19–21, trans. Maurice Hutton, Loeb Classical Library (London: Heinemann, 1914), pp. 203–207.

>> **Proof of Citizenship** This bronze plaque is one of a pair recording a grant of citizenship to Reburrus son of Severus (third line from bottom), upon his discharge from the Roman army on January 19, A.D. 103. Reburrus, a native of Spain, served in a cavalry unit in the west of Britain, and retired in the rank of decurion—commander of a thirty-man troop. The document lists many other locally stationed units whose new veterans became new citizens that day, gives the names of witnesses, and adds that it is an authentic copy of an original kept in Rome. For Reburrus, this was important proof that he had risen into the empire's ruling nation. Archaeological Museum Carnuntum, Austria

In ways like these, out of the encounter between the Romans and conquered barbarians there began to grow many worldwide languages of the present day.

Citizenship and Identity

Under the Republic, Rome had learned to be generous in awarding its citizenship to the peoples of Italy, but in the provinces, only a scattering of people were Roman citizens. Under the emperors, however, many provincials of middle-class social rank or higher were granted citizenship. These included important people who made themselves useful in local government, children of legally recognized marriages between male citizens and noncitizen women, and veterans of auxiliary army units (see photo).

Non-Romans who became citizens gained valuable advantages, such as the right of appeal against decisions of Roman officials, immunity from torture if they were suspected of crimes, and entry to government and army careers that might take them as far as the Senate. Above all, new citizens gained a new identity as Romans while remaining leading members of their non-Roman communities. About A.D. 150, Aelius Aristides, a Greek orator and Roman citizen, told an audience in Rome that included the emperor Antoninus: "You have divided all the people under your rule into two parts, ... making citizens of all those who are more cultured, noble, and powerful, indeed making them your own kin, while the rest are in the position of subjects and the governed." And of course, the rulers expected these "more cultured, noble, and powerful" people to be guided by their identity as Romans in governing "the rest."

In A.D. 212, the emperor Caracalla (**kar-uh-KAL-uh**) extended citizenship to all freeborn inhabitants of the empire. Probably he wanted to make it easier to levy taxes on poorer people and draft recruits into the army at a time when new outside threats and internal conflicts were bringing the Roman Peace to an end. But by Caracalla's time, a legal distinction was already growing up in regions like Italy, where most free inhabitants had long been citizens, between "worthier" citizens—aristocrats, government officials, and the military, including common soldiers—and "humbler" ones, which meant everyone else. Once the great majority of people throughout the empire were granted citizenship, the legal distinction between "worthier" and "humbler" citizens became all the more important.

In this way, the population of the empire continued to be "divided into two parts." The wealthy, educated, arms-bearing, and mostly town-dwelling few, with their common identity as leading Romans, held the empire together. The unprivileged, mostly country-dwelling majority, on the other hand, paid heavily for the splendor of the emperor, the upkeep of the army, and the beautification of the cities. At least among the elite, however, citizenship in a vast empire undoubtedly inspired a new sense of belonging to the human family. As Aristides told his hearers: "You have given the best proof of the ever-repeated saying: 'The earth is everyone's mother and everyone's common fatherland.'"

Which vision of Rome was closest to the truth—Aristides' worldwide fatherland or Juvenal's city swamped by its subject peoples, Virgil's bringer of order and peace or Tacitus's empire of plunder and slaughter? All these visions reflected different realities of an empire that forced itself on many peoples, made them live together more or less peacefully, and brought great changes to both rulers and ruled—changes that continued for centuries after Rome's peoples went their separate ways.

> "*Once the great majority of people throughout the empire were granted citizenship, the legal distinction between 'worthier' and 'humbler' citizens became all the more important.*"

Listen to a synopsis of Chapter 7.

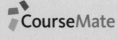

CHAPTER 8

THE CHANGING WORLD OF ROME: EMPERORS, CHRISTIANS, AND INVADERS,
200 B.C.–A.D. 600

LEARNING OBJECTIVES

AFTER READING THIS CHAPTER, YOU SHOULD BE ABLE TO DO THE FOLLOWING:

LO¹ Describe the effects of Roman rule on the development of Judaism.

LO² Trace the development of Christianity during the Roman Peace.

LO³ Explain the problems facing the Roman Empire beginning in the third century, describe how the emperors responded, and discuss how their efforts failed in the Western half of the empire.

LO⁴ Discuss how Christianity became the dominant religion of the empire, and describe how the Church became a powerful organized community in partnership and rivalry with the state.

"INSTEAD OF DYING, THE MEDITERRANEAN CIVILIZATION OF GREECE AND ROME BEGAN TO SPREAD AMONG MANY STILL-BARBARIAN NORTHERN PEOPLES, UNTIL IT BECAME THE CHRISTIAN EUROPE OF THE MIDDLE AGES."

The greatest single change that began among the peoples of the empire during the era of the Roman Peace was the spread of a new form of monotheistic religion, Christianity. The new religion began as a group within Judaism at a time of division and uncertainty among the Jews arising out of their encounter with the international civilization of Greece and Rome. In two centuries, Christianity developed away from Judaism to establish its own scattered, empire-wide community, the Catholic Church, which was already well on the way to forming the beliefs and practices that it would keep for centuries to come.

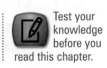 Test your knowledge before you read this chapter.

Meanwhile, the empire helped bring changes to peoples living outside as well as inside its borders. In particular, the Germanic barbarians of northern Europe became wealthier, more highly organized, and militarily stronger as a result of living as Rome's

What do you think?

A decline in morals and values led to the fall of Rome.

Strongly Disagree						Strongly Agree
1	2	3	4	5	6	7

neighbors during the era of the Roman Peace. From about A.D. 200, they became such a formidable threat that the emperors could hold them off only by building up the army, replacing self-rule by centralized government, and openly ruling as absolute monarchs—changes that, in the long run, failed to hold the empire together, but had lasting results for the future development of the West.

In addition, the empire was still strong enough to bring about the last and greatest of the changes in civilization that took place under its rule. As long as Rome had prospered, the emperors had taken little notice of Christianity's growth and spread; in the empire's time of troubles, they sometimes harshly persecuted it and sometimes deliberately tolerated it. Now, in the course of the empire's restructuring, they took Christianity into partnership as the official and majority religion.

Eventually, the burden of government and the army became too heavy to bear, the barbarian attacks grew too fierce to be resisted, and the empire began to collapse.

≪ **Christ Victorious** This mosaic in a chapel in the Italian city of Ravenna dates from about A.D. 500, when Rome was beset by invaders and Christians were bitterly divided over belief. Christ is shown as a youthful and steadfast Roman soldier, wearing the purple cloak of an emperor, and carrying his cross like a shouldered weapon. His open Bible proclaims: "I am the way, the truth, and the life."

Gentiles
A term for non-Jews; Christians used it to refer to worshipers of the gods and goddesses.

Over about a century down to A.D. 500, the entire western half was gradually taken over by Germanic invaders. But the Germanic rulers of the West accepted the Latin-speaking culture and Christian religion of Rome, and Rome's territories in the East survived as the long-enduring, Greek-ruled empire of Byzantium. Instead of dying, the Mediterranean civilization of Greece and Rome began to spread among many still-barbarian northern peoples, until it became the Christian Europe of the Middle Ages.

LO¹ The Jews in the World of Greece and Rome

Christianity began as one of many Jewish religious groups, each of which had its own answer to a disturbing question that faced the Jews as a whole: What was the will of God for his people in a world that was dominated by the international civilization of Greece and Rome?

True, the Jews believed that God had already revealed his will to them through prophets and holy writings (pp. 39–43). God, it seemed, wanted the Jews to live scattered through the world under the rule of more powerful peoples, but united in his worship as a single community under the ancient name of Israel. Around them, God would raise up and cast down world-ruling nations, but he would preserve and protect his people as long as they obeyed his Law. They must live righteously, structure their social institutions such as marriage according to his requirements, observe strict practices of ritual purity such as circumcision, and worship him in his Temple in Jerusalem.

But the worship of the one God was not for the Jews alone. One day, God would send his people a mighty redeemer—his Messiah (from the Hebrew for "Anointed One"), as the redeemer began to be called after about 200 B.C. There was no way of knowing when that day would come, but when it did, all the Jews would be gathered in their homeland and all peoples would come to the knowledge of the one true God.

Meanwhile, the Jews were a prominent people both inside and

> *"One day, God would send his people a mighty redeemer—his Messiah (from the Hebrew for 'Anointed One'), as the redeemer began to be called after about 200 B.C. There was no way of knowing when that day would come, but when it did, all the Jews would be gathered in their homeland and all peoples would come to the knowledge of the one true God."*

CHRONOLOGY

63 B.C.	Jewish kingdom comes under Roman rule
CA. A.D. 30	Death of Jesus
A.D. 50–60	Paul's letters to Christian communities
A.D. 70	Temple in Jerusalem destroyed by Romans
A.D. 235–284	Series of short-reigning Roman emperors
A.D. 285	Diocletian takes control, begins reforms
A.D. 313	Edict of Milan formally ends persecution of Christians
A.D. 370	Huns enter eastern Europe; barbarians forced from frontier into empire
A.D. 378	Visigoths defeat Romans at the Battle of Adrianople
A.D. 410	Alaric and the Visigoths loot Rome
A.D. 476	Last Western Roman emperor deposed

outside the Roman Empire. Many were townspeople and peasants in the homeland of Judaea in Palestine, but the majority lived in the Diaspora ("dispersion"): their congregations thrived in the cities of every Mediterranean land and beyond the empire's frontiers in Mesopotamia. They did not go out of their way to make converts, but **Gentiles** (JEN-tie-uhls) (non-Jews) sometimes either became full Jews or shared Jewish beliefs as "God-fearers" without complete obedience to the Law. Both in Judaea and the Diaspora, leaders of prayer to God and study of the holy writings held wide authority. The Temple in Jerusalem, with its long-lived dynasties of priests and its endless round of sacrifices, was one of the world's most magnificent shrines.

In all these ways, the place of the Jews in the world, and their future role in leading the human race to God, seemed assured. But in recent times, the world had begun to change, and the old answers had come to seem less certain.

Jewish Disputes in a Changing World

The change began in the second century B.C., when the Greeks started to lose their place as rulers of the lands between the Mediterranean Sea and the Indian Ocean, and for the first time since the days of David and Solomon almost a thousand years before, a powerful Jewish kingdom arose. The new state emerged from a heroic and brutal twenty-five-year struggle against a Greek king of Syria who had tried to prohibit Jewish worship. The struggle was led by the priestly family of the Maccabees, who became the new kingdom's rulers.

Eventually, the dynasty fell victim to family disputes, and the Romans stepped in, capturing Jerusalem in 63 B.C. Even so, the kingdom survived, and its most famous ruler, Herod the Great, reigned as a client king (p. 97) in allegiance to the new masters of the world for more than thirty years.

Yet the new kingdom produced discontent and division among the Jews. Most of the kings also held the office of chief priest of the Temple and used it to bolster their power. In addition, they made the Jewish peasants pay heavily for their building projects and their wars. Furthermore, they were deeply influenced by the international Greco-Roman civilization, even in religion. Herod, for instance, rebuilt the Temple to be more splendid than ever before, but in Caesarea, his kingdom's Mediterranean seaport, he built another temple—of the emperor-worshiping cult of Rome and Augustus (p. 104).

Many of the leaders of prayer and study who were now so influential with ordinary Jews distrusted the rulers and the Temple priests. They usually called on the people to obey the rulers and their Roman overlords and to make offerings in the Temple, but to some extent, they stood apart from other Jewish authorities. Perhaps for this reason, they came to be known as Pharisees, from a Hebrew word meaning "separators." Other groups separated themselves far more drastically from the rulers and the Temple, and set up communities in which they led lives of rigorous ritual purity and self-denial. Many of these groups believed that the Messiah would come sooner rather than later. He would be no peaceful uniter of the human race in the worship of the one God, but a warlike divider who would sweep away Greeks, Romans, Jewish kings, and all other Jews who did not accept him, leaving his loyal followers to live forever in blessedness under his rule.

Eventually, the Romans broke up the Jewish kingdom and made Judaea a province of the empire. Rome respected Jewish religion as the Greeks and Persians had mostly done, but its taxation was heavy and its governors were corrupt, inspiring hatred among the peasants and hope among those who expected that these troubles heralded the

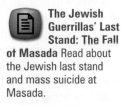

The Jewish Guerrillas' Last Stand: The Fall of Masada Read about the Jewish last stand and mass suicide at Masada.

advent of the Messiah. The result was two massive uprisings that were crushed by the legions and also resulted in religious disaster. The first ended in A.D. 70, with the destruction of the Temple, and the second in A.D. 135, with Jerusalem turned into a Roman city—complete with a shrine of Jupiter on the Temple site—that Jews were not allowed to enter. The traditional Temple worship had come to an end, never to be resumed.

Jewish Revolt Against Romans, A.D. **66–70 (7:11)** (http://www.pbs.org/wgbh/pages/frontline/video/flv/generic.html?s=frol02p584&continuous=1) Learn more about the Jewish revolt of A.D. 66–70 in this video.

Rabbinic Judaism

The end of the Temple worship was far from meaning the end of Judaism, however. Instead, the Jews continued the life of prayer, praise, and obedience to the Law that had grown up alongside the Temple worship and that now completely replaced it as the heart of Jewish religion.

The Pharisee leaders of prayer and study in Palestine had opposed both revolts, and events had proved them right. Favored by the Romans, who still tolerated Jewish religion even while they crushed the strivings for independence, the leaders of prayer and study became more revered than ever among the Jews. It became customary to address them as "My teacher!"—in Hebrew, *rabbi*.

The rabbis strove to end the disputes among the Jews by enforcing a consensus on belief and practice that all should follow. About the middle of the second century, they established the canon (authoritative list) of religious writings that Jews were to accept as written at God's command. Out of over fifty works that were more or less widely revered, the rabbis agreed on thirty-nine that were to be regarded as genuinely holy—the ones that make up the present-day Hebrew Bible. Meanwhile, their interpretations of and additions to the Law themselves acquired binding legal authority, and were collected about A.D. 200 in a book known as the "Repetition" (*Mishnah*). Later on, two enormous works explaining and expanding the Mishnah appeared, each of which was known as a "Commentary" (*Talmud*).

Judaism was now entirely based on the Bible and the rabbis' interpretations of the Law rather than on the Temple worship, and it was the rabbis who from now on led the Jews, rather than priests, prophets, or kings. This new, "rabbinic" form of belief and practice has remained the basic pattern of Judaism down to the present day. Rabbinic Judaism still foretold the future coming of the Messiah, the gathering of God's people in the homeland, and the turning of the entire human race to the true worship of the one God. But the spread of monotheism to become the dominant belief of the Roman Empire and many other lands began with a Jewish splinter group that believed that the Messiah had already arrived.

"The Priesthood Shall Be Theirs by a Perpetual Ordinance." This painting from a third-century A.D. synagogue in the eastern frontier town of Dura Europos shows the consecration of Moses's brother Aaron and Aaron's sons as hereditary priests during the Israelite wanderings in the desert. Aaron's name is in Greek letters, and the tabernacle, God's movable dwelling place, looks like a Greek temple. The Jews of Dura Europos could not escape contemporary influences, but the ancient covenant with God was still the center of their faith.

Princeton University Press/Art Resource, NY

LO² Christianity in the Era of the Roman Peace

In its first two hundred years, Christianity acquired many lasting features of its belief and practice. The development of the new religion involved not only the Christians themselves, but also the Jews among whom it began, the Gentiles whom it sought to convert, and the environment of the Roman Empire through which it mainly spread.

Jesus

It was during the period of Jewish conflict and dispute leading up to the destruction of the Temple in A.D. 70 that Jesus lived and taught. What is known of him is found in the gospels (books of "good news") named after his followers Matthew, Mark, Luke, and John, which are thought to have been written between forty and seventy years after he died about A.D. 30. Most likely the gospel authors retold stories about Jesus that they found in earlier documents, or that had come down to them by word of mouth. Scholars debate how much these stories reflect Jesus's actual words and deeds, but some basic gospel traditions about him certainly dated back to his lifetime or not long afterward.

In any case, the authors of the gospels felt no need to set down all the details of Jesus's life, but focused on his birth, the brief years when he was a wandering preacher in Judaea, and his death and its aftermath. This was all that was necessary to show Jesus in two roles: as teacher explaining God's purposes, and as Messiah sent by God.

The Teacher

The gospels, written at a time when the Jewish majority and the believers in Jesus were turning against each other, portray him as an outright opponent of other Jewish groups. What is known of the teachings of these groups, however, suggests that Jesus had much in common with them, though with shifts of emphasis that made his message very much his own.

Like the Pharisees, Jesus obeyed the Law, visited the Temple, and called for acceptance of Roman rule, while standing apart from the Temple priests. Like the Pharisees, too, he appealed to a long-standing Jewish tradition of warning that true righteousness meant more than just obeying the strict ritual commands of the Law. However, Jesus took this tradition farther than ever before. He taught that even the most faithful righteousness according to the Law fell far short of what was necessary to please God. One must love not only one's friends but one's enemies; one must refrain not only from adultery but from lustful

The Gospel According to Matthew: The Sermon on the Mount Read Jesus's teaching from the Sermon on the Mount.

thoughts; one must not only avoid coveting one's neighbor's goods but give away all possessions and trust in God to "give us this day our daily bread." In short, one must "be perfect, as your heavenly Father is perfect."

Exactly because of this, Jesus made a point of associating with people whom sticklers for the Law thought of as highly displeasing to God—"prostitutes, tax collectors, and sinners." Furthermore, the entourage of eager hearers that accompanied him on his travels included women who broke the bounds of custom by leaving their homes and families to follow him. Sinners, Jesus taught, longed for God's forgiveness, which alone could admit them to his kingdom; and in God's kingdom, marriage and family would count for nothing. For Jesus's biggest difference with the Pharisees, as the gospels describe it, was that, like the radical Jewish groups, he proclaimed that "the kingdom of God has come near"—in fact, that, with himself, it had already arrived.

The Messiah

The gospels tell of Jesus's many signs and wonders. His birth to the Virgin Mary in fulfillment of prophecy; the descent upon him of the Spirit of God, which in Jewish belief had given life to Adam and guided the prophets; his miracles of healing that filled the crowds who saw and heard of them with joy and sometimes with terror—all are reported in the gospels as proof that he was Israel's redeemer.

But the Jesus of the gospels is a different kind of redeemer from the one that most other messianic (Messiah-expecting) Jewish groups hoped for—in some ways more benign, but in other ways even more terrible. He has not come to deliver just the Jews, but to fulfill the traditional prophecy that the whole human race will turn to the one God. He will redeem his people, Jew and Gentile, not as a warrior king but as a victim, by offering himself for one of the traditional purposes of sacrifice: to reconcile sinful humans with the divine power that they have displeased. But he also warns that "I have not come to bring peace, but a sword," and that when he comes again he will separate the righteous and the sinners "as a shepherd separates the sheep and the goats." Those who have believed and repented will live with him forever; for those who have rejected or ignored him, there will be eternal "weeping and gnashing of teeth."

Furthermore, in the gospels, Jesus calls himself both "Son of Man"—an ancient term for a human as against a divine being—but also "Son of God," and he proclaims that "The Father and I are one." He seems to be saying that he is both human and divine, and that he and God are somehow different and yet the same. And Jesus sometimes calls God's guiding Spirit "he," as if the Spirit were not just God's "breath"—the original meaning of the word—but a divine being in his own right. In these ways, the gospels announce a drastic change in the traditional Jewish understanding of the one truth about the one God.

To the Temple priests and the Roman rulers, popular preachers and miracle workers were a dangerous nuisance, particularly if they were suspected of claiming to be the Messiah. Accordingly, the priests arrested Jesus and the Romans crucified him, their standard method of executing the most despised criminals.

But then, say the Gospels, came Jesus's most spectacular signs and wonders of all: an empty tomb, appearances to witnesses, return to God who had sent him, and the descent of God's guiding Spirit upon his closest followers. For these followers, the age of the Messiah had already begun, when the Gentiles would finally turn to the God of Israel; and they saw themselves as the Messiah's **apostles** (from the Greek word for "messenger")—sent out by him to fulfill his command: "Go into all the world and proclaim the good news to the whole creation."

But what exactly was the "good news" that they were to proclaim? What did it mean in practice for the worship and daily life of believers? And who had the authority to proclaim the good news and tell believers how to live? Very soon, Jesus's followers started to wrestle with these questions. Out of their arguments and soul-searching there grew a movement that would change the religious outlook and the power structure of Western civilization.

apostles
Jesus's followers and messengers of his teachings.

From Jesus to Christ: The First Christians (http://www.pbs.org/wgbh/pages/frontline/shows/religion/) Find out what archaeologists and others have discovered about the life of Jesus and the rise of Christianity.

Paul

In the thirty years after Jesus's death, his apostles worked hard to proclaim his "good news." Groups of believers sprang up in cities where Jews and Gentiles lived side by side—from nearby Antioch and Damascus, across Anatolia and Greece, all the way to Rome itself. This success brought Jesus's believers face to face with a first momentous question: To be accepted into the Messiah's coming kingdom, must Gentiles obey the Law's requirements of ritual purity?

Gentiles and the Law

In heated debates among leading apostles a few years after Jesus's death, the most forceful advocate of freedom from the Law was a Jew from a city in Anatolia, Paul of Tarsus. Paul had recently come to Judaea as a studious Pharisee and opponent of the new belief, but a vision made him a passionate believer in Jesus as Messiah and in his own work as an apostle—above all to the Gentiles. In a quarter-century of hard journeys by land and sea, he founded many groups of believers in Anatolia and Greece, driven on by the conviction that there was not much time for the Gentiles to turn to God before the Messiah would come again.

During his travels, Paul kept in touch by letter with distant groups of believers. Some of his letters, written between about A.D. 50 and A.D. 60 in Greek, the international language of Jews and Gentiles alike, are the earliest surviving documents of the new belief. In them, Paul gave guidance, tried to settle quarrels, and argued against the views of rival missionaries—including about the still disputed question of Gentiles and the Law.

For Paul, freedom from the Law was part of the changes that God had in store for the whole human race in the age of Christ—his Greek word for the Messiah. It was no longer "circumcision"—Paul's shorthand term for strict obedience to the Law—that made a person righteous in the sight of God. Instead, a person must have faith in Christ—in his self-sacrifice, his resurrection, and the day of his coming again. In the short time until that day came, let Jewish believers by all means live under the Law and Gentile believers not do so, so long as both understood that living or not living under the Law was beside the point. As Paul wrote to believers in Galatia, an inland territory of Anatolia: "in Christ Jesus neither circumcision nor uncircumcision counts for anything; the only thing that counts is faith working through love."

But how was it that not all who heard the gospel believed it? Paul himself had come to see the light; others seemingly no wickeder than he had rejected that light. This must be the doing of God himself: as Paul said in a letter to believers in Rome, "So then he has mercy upon whomsoever he chooses, and he hardens the heart of whomsoever he chooses." In that case, faith must be a gift granted or withheld by God for his own secret reasons, so that God determined in advance who would be saved and who would be damned. This doctrine of **predestination** was to become a feature of Christianity that many believers rejoiced in, others tried to soften, but few rejected outright (pp. 143, 318).

The Life of Early Believers

When writing to a group of believers in a particular city, Paul often called it by a Greek name used by Jewish congregations outside Judaea—*ekklēsia*, which literally means "assembly," but when used for believers in Jesus is usually translated as "church."

Within these earliest churches, there was no formal structure of authority and power. Apart from Paul himself, who claimed that his guidance was to be heeded because Christ had chosen him as an apostle, the main leaders were relatively wealthy heads of households in whose homes the worshipers met. Alongside these "house-church" leaders, however, there was room for many others who claimed special "gifts" from the Holy Spirit—such as prophets who gave guidance directly from God, and deacons (from the Greek for "servants") who organized festivities and helped the poor and sick. As befitted groups that saw themselves as fore-runners of Christ's kingdom, women acted alongside men in every role from house-church leaders to deacons. Paul spoke of women who "have struggled beside me in the work of the gospel"—though he was also nervous about their becoming too prominent in worship.

> "*There is no longer Jew nor Greek, there is no longer slave nor free man, there is no longer male nor female; for all of you are one in Christ Jesus.*"

Already the churches' worship included two formal services, both centering on Jesus as Messiah: baptism and a sacred common meal that came to be called the Eucharist ("Thanksgiving").

Baptism, the dipping of converts in water to purify them before God and admit them to the community of his worshipers, was a long-standing Jewish tradition. For believers in Jesus, however, it had a new meaning, the washing away of sin itself and becoming members of Christ's kingdom. For this reason, not only converts were baptized but also adult people who had been brought up as believers. In the Eucharist, the worshipers shared bread and wine in accordance with Jesus's command to his disciples at the Last Supper before he was crucified. In this way, believers were united with each other and with Christ, and celebrated his death as the central event of the age of the Messiah.

The Churches and the World

The believers in Jesus belonged not only to churches but also to other human groups—families, cities, the Roman Empire. They therefore faced a difficult problem of how they should live their lives from day to day. Should they live as part of "this world"—human society, with its imperfect human institutions, such as government and marriage? Or should they live as if Christ's kingdom had already arrived, recognizing no rule except his, and freed from Adam and Eve's burden of marriage and toil?

Paul gave guidance on this problem too, usually trying to find compromises between the way of life of this world and that of the coming kingdom. Both men and women, he said, should best live unmarried—that is, as virgins—but those who had no gift to do so must marry and not deny each other sexual satisfaction, for "it is better to marry than to be aflame with passion." Likewise, believers should not "take each other to court before the unrighteous," but they must accept government authority, for governments "have been instituted by God." Other differences of power and status in human society were also God-given: "Wives, be subject to your husbands as you are to the Lord. . . . Slaves, obey your earthly masters . . . as you obey Christ."

Yet Christ would soon return and do away with these differences—in fact, where believers gathered, his kingdom was already here. As believers were told at baptism services in Paul's churches, "There is no longer Jew nor Greek, there is no longer slave nor free man, there is no longer male nor female; for all of you are one in Christ Jesus."

The Break with Judaism

Even during Paul's lifetime, he reproached his fellow Jews for distrusting his vision of Jews and Gentiles "all one in Christ Jesus," and after he died about A.D. 60—probably beheaded in Rome as a Jewish troublemaker—the vision faded.

To most Jews, the belief in a crucified Messiah who was himself divine seemed insulting to God, and the majority of new believers were Gentiles. Then came the Temple's destruction in A.D. 70, which most believers in Jesus took as God's abandonment of the Jews for rejecting the Messiah. Not long afterward, the believers in Jesus began calling themselves by a name originally given them by Gentile disbelievers, but which was now useful to mark them as a separate group—"Christians." For the Christians, the human race was now divided into three groups: the Jews, God's former chosen people; the Gentiles, a word that Christians still often used to describe worshipers of the gods and goddesses; and themselves, who were Gentiles no longer but God's new chosen people.

Still, by proclaiming faith rather than the Law as the bond between God and his people, Paul opened the way for a community of believers in one God to grow up that was drawn not from one but from many nations. Furthermore, Paul showed how this international community of believers could coexist with everyday human society, yet still think of itself as part of Christ's coming kingdom. This would become increasingly important as another part of Paul's vision faded, and it came to seem likely that Christ would not be returning, and everyday human society would not be ending, anytime soon.

The Church

As the years passed and Christ did not return, his believers did not lose their faith that he would one day come—and meanwhile, there was more time for them to proclaim his good news. But as Christianity grew and spread, this faced the churches with yet another problem: How could they be sure that they were truly obeying Christ's commandments and rightly proclaiming his good news when there were more churches scattered over wider regions, and when Christ's first coming was fading into a distant past?

Clergy and Laity

Early in the second century, out of the shifting leadership exercised in the earliest churches by whoever was deemed to have some special "gift," types of leaders began to appear who wielded firmer authority. Churches began to choose bishops (from the Greek word for "overseers") as permanent chiefs; priests (from the Greek for "elders") who assisted the bishops in teaching and worship; and deacons, who now also gained official standing.

Partly, this organization developed because churches were growing larger than before, but the new officials were far more than just managers. Early in the second century, Bishop Ignatius of Antioch, traveling under arrest to Rome to be put to death as a Christian, wrote to believers in the Anatolian port city of Smyrna: "Follow, all of you, the bishop, as Jesus Christ followed the Father; and follow the priests as the apostles. Moreover, revere the deacons as appointed by God. . . . Whatever the bishop approves is also pleasing to God, so that everything you do will be secure and valid." Surely, Ignatius thought, Christ would not leave his people without guides and rulers whom they should obediently follow until his second coming—and deacons, priests, and above all bishops were those Christ-appointed guides and rulers.

In the course of the second century, this "threefold ministry" spread through the churches. All male believers had a say in choosing ministers, though the ministers themselves, especially the bishop, and wealthy and prominent church members often had the largest say. Bishops as well as priests and deacons were usually married men who in poorer churches had to earn a living in some business or profession. All the same, the ministers came to form a group apart, the **clergy**—from a Greek word meaning "allotment," probably indicating that they specially belonged to God—as against the **laity**, from the Greek word for "people."

Now that the churches had formal rulers, women lost some of the share of leadership that they had held in the earliest churches. They still worked as deacons taking care of the poor and the sick, and wealthy women wielded weighty influence as owners of houses where Christian gatherings were held—for until the fourth century, there were no purpose-built Christian places of worship (see photo on page 130). Women as well as men were revered if they fell victim to persecution or lived lives of Christian self-denial. But women did not rule churches as priests or bishops—since formal rulership, according to the standards of everyday human society that the churches now observed, belonged in principle only to men.

The Canon of Scripture

For Christians to be sure of God's purposes and commands, they also needed writings that they could rely on as truthfully revealing his deeds and will. To begin with, all they had were the Jewish writings, which they continued to accept as holy. But of course, though these were deemed to foretell the coming of Christ, they did not record the actual deeds and sayings of Jesus or of the apostles who were next to him in holiness.

Collections of Jesus's sayings were probably compiled within twenty years of his death, and the four present-day gospels were written in the second half of the first century, as believers became more widely scattered and living memory of Jesus faded away. Meanwhile, churches that received letters from Paul preserved some of them, passed on copies to other churches, and revered them as the work of an inspired apostle. Many other gospels, letters, and prophecies appeared in the late first and early second centuries that claimed to be the work of this or that apostle.

By the end of the second century, some of these works, above all the present-day gospels and Paul's letters, were so revered that readings from them and sermons explaining the readings had become a regular feature of Christian worship services, and they were beginning to be thought of as a new group of holy writings alongside the Jewish ones—the "New Testament." The name came from the Latin *testamentum* or "covenant," since these writings were deemed to tell of God's "new covenant" with the Christians, as opposed to the Old Testament, which told of his "old covenant" (pp. 37, 38) with the Jews.

clergy
Church ministers—bishops, priests, and deacons—who guide the laity.

laity
Those members of the Church who are not clergy.

"The One Who Believes and Is Baptized Will Be Saved" A few blocks from the Dura Europos synagogue (photo on page 126), Christians met in a converted house. This reconstruction of their baptistry (christening room) includes original paintings and decorations. Catechumens ("persons under instruction," usually adults) kneel in the tub under the arch as water is poured on them from the pitcher. The wall images show women approaching Jesus's empty tomb: through baptism believers will share in his resurrection. Yale University Art Gallery, Dura-Europos Collection

Like the rabbis with the Hebrew Bible, the bishops had to decide which of many would-be holy writings truly deserved to be part of the New Testament. Since there was no way of knowing for certain which works had been written by apostles, the bishops usually accepted works that had been long revered by many churches. On the other hand, if a work went against their understanding of what Christian writings "ought" to say, they rejected it. In this way, they took until about A.D. 400 to settle on the present-day New Testament canon of twenty-seven books.

The Catholic Church

Apart from the churches that Paul and others founded in this or that city, his letters speak of "the Church" founded by Christ himself, meaning the entire body of believers awaiting Christ's second coming. As the Christian churches broke away from the wider community of Israel that bound together the Jewish congregations, they became increasingly aware of belonging to this wider body of their own. Early in the second century, they began to speak of it as the Catholic (from the Greek for "world-wide") Church.

During the second century, this "worldwide" Church came to operate as a fairly well coordinated network within the Roman Empire. Bishops wrote to each other a great deal and visited each other when they could, and sometimes came together in groups to discuss and decide on matters of common concern. But the Catholic Church was more than just a way for widely scattered bishops to keep in touch. Only by following the Catholic consensus, the bishops came to believe, could they be sure that they were acting rightly as guides and rulers—for the Church as a whole was guided and ruled by God himself. Late in the second century, Irenaeus, bishop of Lyon in southern Gaul, declared: "Where the Church is, there is the Spirit of God, and where the Spirit of God is, there is the Church."

Orthodoxy and Heresy

Sizable minorities of Christians, classified by modern scholars as Gnostics (from the Greek word for "knowledge"), did not agree that Christ must have appointed guides and rulers for his people. Instead, they said, believers must look for knowledge of God inside themselves, and to do so, they must give up unspiritual human activities like marriage and children, and lead a life of strict self-denial. Those who did not lead such a life must expect to spend eternity with God more or less hidden from them.

Furthermore, the Gnostics thought, Jewish traditions were no guide to knowledge of God. Jesus's perfect heavenly father

THE TRUTH ABOUT CHRISTIAN WORSHIP

As Christianity spread in the first two centuries after Jesus, it earned the suspicion of the Roman state and of worshipers of the gods and goddesses throughout the empire. Many misunderstood the act of communion as an act of ritual (or even real) cannibalism, and since the empire's welfare was thought to depend on the "peace of the gods," Christianity's rejection of the traditional deities seemed to endanger the whole of society as well as the state. In this document, dating from about A.D. 150, the well-educated convert Justin of Caesarea offers a description of early Christian practices in an effort to allay some of these suspicions.

All who are convinced and believe that what is taught and said by us is true, and promise that they are able to live accordingly, are taught to pray and with fasting to ask forgiveness of God for their former sins; and we pray and fast with them. Then they are brought by us to where there is water, and they are reborn in the same manner as we ourselves were reborn. For in the name of God, the Father and Lord of the universe, and of our Savior Jesus Christ, and of the Holy Ghost, they then are washed in the water. . . .

After thus washing the one who has been convinced and has given his assent, we conduct him to the place where those who are called the brethren are assembled, to offer earnest prayers in common for ourselves, for him who has been enlightened, and for all others everywhere, so that we, now that we have learned the truth, may by our works also be deemed worthy of being found to be good practitioners and keepers of the commandments, and thus be saved with eternal salvation. When we end our prayers we greet each other with a kiss. Then bread and a chalice of wine mixed with water are brought to the one who presides over the brethren; and he takes it, and offers up praise and glory to the Father of the universe, through the name of the Son and the Holy Ghost; and he gives thanks at length for our being deemed worthy of these things by Him. When he has finished the prayers and thanksgiving, all the people present express their assent, saying "Amen." . . . And when he who presides has celebrated the eucharist [thanksgiving], and all the people have expressed their assent, those called among us deacons allow each one of those present to partake of the bread and wine and water for which thanks have been given, and they bring it also to those not present. And this food is called among us the eucharist. . . .

And on the day called Sunday there is a gathering in one place of all who dwell in the cities or in the country places, and the memoirs of the Apostles or the writings of the prophets are read as long as time allows. Then when the reader is finished, he who presides gives oral admonition and exhortation to imitate these excellent examples. Then we all rise together, and offer prayers; and, as stated before, when we have ended our praying, bread and wine and water are brought. And he who presides similarly offers up prayers and thanksgiving, as far as lies in his power, and the people express their approval by saying "Amen." And each receives a share and partakes of the food for which thanks have been given, and through the deacons some is sent to those not present. The prosperous, if they so desire, each contribute what they wish, according to their own judgment, and the collection is entrusted to the one who presides. And he assists orphans and widows, and those who are in need because of illness or any other reason, and those who are in prison, and strangers sojourning with us; in short, all those in need are his care.

EXPLORING THE SOURCE

1. What were the main worship practices in early Christian communities?

2. How similar do the worship practices seem to those of the present day?

Source: From Roman Civilization: Selected Readings by Naphtali Lewis and Meyer Reinhold, eds. Copyright (c) 1955 Columbia University Press. Reprinted with permission of the publisher.

could not have created either the imperfect everyday world or the imperfect human race that lived in it. That had been the work of a lesser and perhaps even evil divine being—and it was this being, not the true supreme God, whose deeds and commandments were described in the Jewish holy writings. Jesus, in the Gnostic view, had been sent by the supreme God, but he, too, was not really part of this imperfect world. His life in the

body, troubled by hunger in the wilderness and suffering the agony of crucifixion, was mere appearance. He had not come to sacrifice himself for the whole human race, but to provide mystical knowledge of the supreme God to a minority of devotees.

The belief in a perfect spiritual world that people could only find inside themselves, and an imperfect outer world formed by an imperfect creator, came from a non-Christian

orthodoxy
In Christianity, religious practices, customs, and beliefs proclaimed by a Church authority to be righteous or true.

heresy
In Christianity, religious practices, customs, and beliefs proclaimed by a Church authority to be wicked or false.

ascetic
A person who practices a life of self-denial as a way to God.

philosopher, Plato (p. 73), but it fit in with the Christian belief in God working on the soul from within. Gnosticism was a strong movement throughout the second century and beyond, and Gnostic and Catholic Christianity may well have developed out of conflict with each other. But Christians who believed that Jesus was the longed-for Messiah of the Jews, that he had fully shared in the everyday human condition, and that everyday believers could become equal members of his kingdom naturally made the most converts. It was Catholic Christianity that became the predominant version of the new religion.

All the same, the Gnostics were active and articulate, and the disputes between them and the bishops were as fierce as between Christians and Jews, for in both cases, what was at stake was the one truth about the one God. The bishops, said the Gnostics, were "empty ditches," with no water of truth flowing in them; the Gnostics, said the bishops, were "wolves" preying on Christ's flock. In their struggle against Gnostic "ravings," the bishops insisted all the more on their authority as guides and rulers backed by the Catholic consensus, and they barred from the New Testament canon many would-be holy writings expressing Gnostic views. This, the bishops believed, was their duty as guardians of **orthodoxy** (from the Greek words for "right opinion") against **heresy** (from the Greek word for "school of thought"), which the bishops redefined to mean "false belief."

Philosophy and Faith

In this way, the bishops held on to much of the inheritance of Jewish tradition—disputing ownership of it with their rival heirs, the rabbis, and defending it against the Gnostics who wanted to renounce it. Still, with their belief in the divinity of Christ, orthodox Christians had themselves departed from the Jewish understanding of the one truth about the one God. For guidance in the search for a new understanding, these Christians, too, were tempted to turn from Jewish tradition to the wisdom of the Gentiles—to Greek philosophers whose own search for truth had led them away from the traditional gods and goddesses. But did the Gnostic use of Plato mean that the wisdom of the Gentiles could only lead Christians astray?

Tertullian, a successful lawyer from Africa who became a fierce advocate for Christianity late in the second century, certainly said so. "Heresies," he said, "are themselves instigated by philosophy. . . . What has Athens to do with Jerusalem? What has the Academy [the school where Plato taught] to do with the Church? What have heretics to do with Christians? We have no need of curiosity once we have Christ Jesus, nor of inquiring once we have the Gospel."

But the fact was that in their quest for a truthful understanding of divine power the Greek philosophers had developed ideas that orthodox Christians could not do without. Most notably, many Greek thinkers believed that the entire universe was upheld by a living divine "Reason" or "Word" (in Greek, *logos*) that was present also in human beings (pp. 72, 87). This concept fit in well with orthodox belief. It helped explain how such a distant and mysterious being as God could be involved in every detail of the universe, and could even take human form: Christ must be none other than the *logos* through whom God created and upheld all things.

Already about A.D. 100, John's gospel hailed Christ as the *logos*, and Tertullian himself used the same idea to argue that Christ was both God and man. So did Justin of Caesarea, a Roman citizen from Palestine who became a Greek-style philosopher and then a Christian, but who always admired the Greek thinkers and their search for truth. They had lived, he said, "according to the *logos*"; in fact, philosophers like Socrates, whom the Athenians had put to death for not worshiping their gods, "are Christians, even though they were thought atheists." Eventually Justin followed Socrates' example: he was put to death in Rome about A.D. 165.

Asceticism

Whatever they thought about the Greek philosophers, orthodox Christians could not ignore the idea that self-denial was the best way to God. Paul himself had said that virginity was better than marriage, and the bishops gladly admitted that it was right for Christians to live in this world as they would in Christ's kingdom, by denying the demands and passions of the body—just so long as such exceptional strivers did not claim that Christ would bar from his kingdom believers who lived the everyday life of society.

By the end of the second century, there were many such orthodox self-deniers or **ascetics** (from the Greek word for the strenuous training of an athlete). The Greek physician Galen, an opponent of Christianity, reported that Christian ascetics stood comparison with followers of non-Christian philosophers like Epicurus who strove for mastery over the passions (p. 110). Christians, he said, "include not only men but also women who refrain from sexual intercourse all through their lives; and they also number individuals who, in self-discipline and self-control in matters of food and drink, and in their keen pursuit of righteousness, have reached a level not inferior to that of genuine philosophers."

Christianity and Rome

Judaea had strong links to Jews in two empires—eastward in Parthia and westward in Rome. However, Paul and many other early missionaries came from the world of the eastern Mediterranean, where both Jews and Gentiles were influenced by the international culture of Greece. Probably for this reason, in the era of the Roman Peace, Christianity spread mainly westward, and its destinies became entangled with those of Rome and its rulers.

The Spread of Christianity

By the end of the first century, there were about fifty Christian churches, mostly in the towns and cities of Syria, Palestine, and western Anatolia. Probably these churches included many people who still considered themselves Jews, as well as Gentile doubters of the power, goodness, or existence of the gods and goddesses.

As the rabbis created a new consensus within Judaism, the numbers of Jewish converts tapered off, and Christianity drew for its growth mainly on Gentiles. Mostly it seems to have spread through face-to-face contacts. Neighbors grew curious about the way of life of people next door; wives wore down husbands, and husbands exerted authority over wives; traders from distant cities chatted with business acquaintances after bargaining was done; slaves followed along willy-nilly with masters and mistresses; parents brought up their children as believers and began baptizing them as newborns. As a result, by the end of the second century, the network of churches in the original eastern territories had grown denser, and there were expanding footholds in Egypt and North Africa as well as toeholds in Italy and Gaul (Map 8.1).

For those who converted, the idea of Jesus as the Messiah was a life-changing truth that gave hope of eternal blessedness. Christianity was not the only international religion that offered this hope, and probably far fewer people became Christians than joined in the worship of Isis, for example (p. 109). But the crowds who took part in the Egyptian mysteries went their separate ways after the ceremonies were over, and did not stop worshiping other gods and goddesses. Christian converts, on the other hand,

became lifelong members of close-knit communities and were lost to the worship of the gods and goddesses—as were their offspring after them. As long as Christianity gained a more or less regular trickle of converts, it was bound to grow and spread.

As often happens with close-knit minorities that share and seek to spread religious hope, Christians were exceptionally generous and helpful toward each other and outsiders, notably honest in their business dealings, and impressively courageous in the face of persecution. That, at least, was what they boasted, and Lucian of Samosata (p. 109), a second-century Greek writer who was no lover of any kind of religion, agreed with much of what they claimed.

The activity of these people, in dealing with any matter that affects their community, is something extraordinary; they spare no trouble, no expense. You see, these misguided creatures start with the general conviction that they are immortal for all time, which explains the contempt of death and voluntary self-devotion which are so common among them; it was impressed on them by their original lawgiver [Jesus] that they are all brothers

Map 8.1 The Spread of Christianity

The map shows areas in which Christian churches were thickly scattered at different dates. Christianity spread slowly during the Pax Romana down to A.D. 200, much faster in the troubled times between A.D. 200 and 300, and fastest of all in the era of imperial favor and barbarian invasions between A.D. 300 and 600. © Cengage Learning

Interactive Map

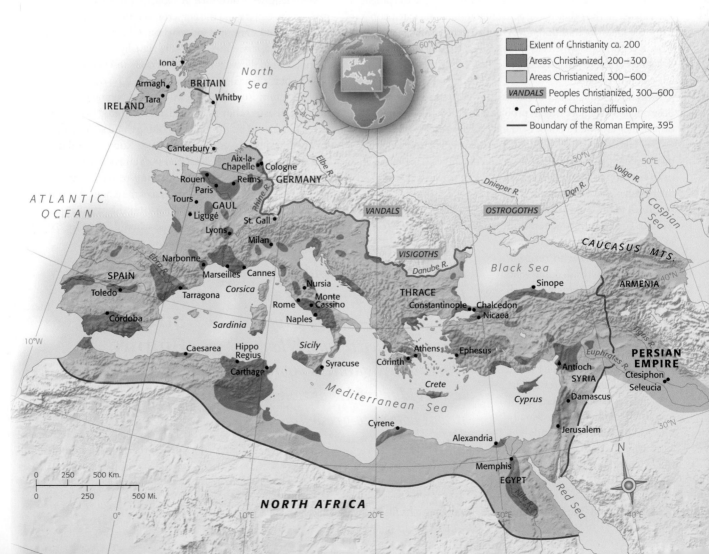

from the moment that they are converted, and deny the gods of Greece, and worship the crucified man of wisdom, and live after his laws.

It was this solidarity based on shared hope that gave Christians the self-confidence to call themselves the "Catholic Church" even though they were a small and scattered minority—fewer than the Jews, disliked by most Gentiles, and harassed by the rulers.

The Rulers and Christianity

As soon as the rulers of Rome became aware of Christianity, they viewed it with deep suspicion—as did the majority of worshipers of the gods and goddesses. Christians were disturbers of the "peace of the gods" (p. 93), who refused to take part in the traditional public worship on which the safety of communities and of the empire was thought to depend, and they refused to venerate the emperor as representative of divine power (pp. 104–105). Instead, they worshiped a man who had died a criminal's wretched death on the orders of lawful Roman authority; and they did so behind closed doors, with ceremonies that were said to include loathsome practices such as ritual cannibalism.

True, the Jews also denied the gods and goddesses, but theirs was an ancestral belief that they did not usually try to spread. Christians, on the other hand, actively sought to alienate people from the empire's traditional worship and to recruit them into what a high Roman official, Gaius Pliny, writing to Emperor Trajan early in the second century, called "a grotesque and deviant cult movement."

To begin with, however, Christians were a tiny minority, and busy officials had more urgent problems to deal with. On imperial orders, they followed a policy of "Don't ask, don't tell," acting only against Christians who were denounced to them by accusers who openly identified themselves. The action that officials took in such cases was extraordinarily mild, from their point of view: any suspect who sacrificed to the gods was released with no further investigation into his or her past conduct.

For a suspect who refused, however, the penalty was death—and the reward, Christians believed, was eternal blessedness with Christ whose suffering the suspect had shared. The church of which the steadfast victim had been a member would yearly commemorate the day of his or her death and revere the burial place—since the remains of executed criminals were usually released to family or friends—as a "victory monument." Word of the "victory" would go to other churches, the "victorious one" would be honored by Christians across the empire as a **martyr** (from the Greek for "witness"), and the martyr's church would gain in standing within the Catholic Church as a whole. In this way, persecution gave Christianity a sense of struggle and triumph, without being systematic enough to crush it.

Late in the second century, as Christianity became more widespread, so did persecution. Across the empire, from Smyrna in Asia Minor to Lyon in Gaul, Christians were dragged to amphitheaters and sadistically tortured or devoured by wild beasts, for the entertainment of crowds whose fury against the "atheists" often forced the hands of Roman officials. These crackdowns were local and generally short-lived, but they were a sign that the rulers and the majority were taking Christianity more seriously.

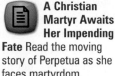

A Christian Martyr Awaits Her Impending Fate Read the moving story of Perpetua as she faces martyrdom.

Defending Christianity

In response, Christians began writing "apologies"—from the Greek word for a law court defense, in this case against the charge of disturbing the "peace of the gods."

Apologists countered this charge in two ways. First, they poured scorn on the gods and goddesses as nonexistent or (more often) as wicked demons. But secondly, in line with Paul's statement that governments were instituted by God, they insisted that Christians revered the empire and the emperor, and that they prayed to God for both—and since the God to whom Christians prayed was the only true one, it was they who were actually upholding Rome. As Tertullian told the worshipers of the gods and goddesses: "Caesar is more ours than yours, appointed as he is by our God." True, at Christ's return Rome and the world would come to an end amid hideous disasters, but as Tertullian admitted, "We [Christians] have no desire to go through such things, and so long as we pray for them to be delayed, we are helping Rome to endure." After two centuries in which Christ had not returned, Christians were beginning to have a stake in the survival of the empire that persecuted them—and this was happening at a time when the empire itself was coming under threat.

LO³ The Struggling Empire

Early in the third century A.D., a new and harsher era began for Rome. Already under Marcus Aurelius (p. 107), there had been signs of trouble to come, as epidemic disease spread through the empire and on the Danube frontier barbar-

> **"** *Christian converts became lifelong members of close-knit communities and were lost to the worship of the gods and goddesses—as were their offspring after them. As long as Christianity gained a more or less regular trickle of converts, it was bound to grow and spread.* **"**

ian peoples mounted larger and better-organized attacks than ever before. Then, the emperors themselves began to lose their secure hold on power.

The Problems of the Empire

Following Marcus's death and the murder of his son Commodus, the new ruling dynasty founded by Septimius Severus (p. 107) gradually fell apart. The men and women of Severus's family struggled among themselves and were challenged by ambitious army commanders. In hopes of keeping their soldiers loyal, both they and their rivals faithfully followed the deathbed advice that Severus was said to have given his sons, to "pay off the soldiers and forget about everyone else."

The resulting gifts and pay raises had to be paid for by increasing taxes and debasing the coinage (cutting its gold and silver content). "Humbler" citizens paid more for the upkeep of the "worthier" elite than ever before, at the same time that prices were rising in step with the decreasing value of money. Insecure rulers, expensive armies, and poverty-stricken citizens, in turn, made it all the harder for the empire to deal with renewed attacks by the unconquered barbarian peoples who lived to the north of its European frontiers.

The Germanic Barbarians

These were the Germanic peoples, the latest ethnic group of European barbarians to live on the fringes of civilization and grow in skills, wealth, and power, just like the Celts, the Romans, and the Greeks before them.

The Germanic peoples seem to have originated in Scandinavia and northern Germany, but by the time of Caesar they had spread into the broad area between the Baltic and North Seas and the Rhine-Danube frontier. In the third century A.D., they moved into eastern Europe as well. The Romans called this whole region *Germania*—a much larger area than the Germany of the present day (see Map 6.2 on page 96).

Like all European barbarians, the Germanic peoples were not just fierce warriors but also hard-working farmers, shrewd traders, and skilled craftspeople (pp. 46–48). Roman writers, notably Tacitus, describe them as having a relatively free way of life, with villages run by assemblies open to all free males. Groups of villages formed tribes, which often fought for control of land and trade under the leadership of war chieftains and their **war bands**, groups of leading warriors who pledged themselves to follow a chieftain and defend him with their lives. The chieftain, in turn, supported the warriors and gave them a share in the spoils.

After Germanic resistance in Augustus's time brought the empire's expansion to a halt, the two sides became permanent neighbors (p. 106). There were many frontier wars, but Romans and barbar-

ians also lived peacefully side by side. Germanic stockbreeders sold meat and hides to Roman army supply officers, important chieftains received subsidies and were awarded citizenship, and warriors fought in the legions as well as the war bands. Ironically, the more the Germanic barbarians came under Roman influence, the more dangerous they were to the empire.

The Crisis of the Empire

When Severus's dynasty finally collapsed shortly before the middle of the third century, the combination of overstrained resources, power struggles, and growing barbarian strength brought about a crisis that almost destroyed the empire. Again and again, provincial armies fought to advance their favorite candidates, and many of the battle-hardened generals who came to power in this way proved to be effective leaders. But this did not save them from violent death, and their terms of office were generally short. In the half-century after the end of Severus's dynasty, the emperorship changed hands on average once every two and a half years.

Meanwhile, barbarian tribal confederacies devastated the empire's European territories from Gaul to the Black Sea. Even lands far from the frontiers, such as Spain, Greece, and Italy itself, were looted by barbarian war bands. Farther east, the Parthian kingdom (p. 116) had been overthrown by a revived Persian kingdom, whose rulers looked to rebuild the great empire of earlier centuries (pp. 34–37) at Rome's expense and now devastated the empire's eastern frontier territories.

Sometimes, barbarian and Persian invaders profited from each other's attacks and from the empire's civil wars. At other times, failure to cope with invaders caused the downfall of emperors and civil wars among rival would-be replacements. Either way, ordinary citizens were being ruined by taxes, rising prices, looting by invaders, and supply requisitions by Roman armies. The empire seemed caught in a vicious downward spiral.

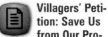 **Villagers' Petition: Save Us from Our Protectors** Read a village's plea to the emperor for relief from the demands of Roman armies and officials.

<< **The Gundestrup Cauldron** The metal workmanship of this two-foot-wide first-century B.C. silver cauldron is Thracian (from present-day Bulgaria). The images of a bearded god holding humans in his hands are probably Celtic (of the then-dominant ethnic group in Europe north of the Alps). It ended up buried in a field in Denmark, at the other end of Europe from its place of manufacture—evidence of the skills, wealth, and long-distance contacts of European barbarian peoples. Erich Lessing/Art Resource, NY

INCREASED CONTACT WITH ROME MADE THE GERMANIC TRIBES STRONG ENOUGH TO CHALLENGE THE EMPIRE:

- Whether they fought for or against Rome, the Germanic warriors learned the empire's methods of fighting and adopted its weapons.

- In the second century A.D., the tribes began to form larger confederacies (tribal groupings) led by powerful chieftains and their war bands.

- Thriving on warfare, wealthy from loot or Roman subsidies, and eager to spend their wealth on the luxurious trappings of the upper-class Roman way of life, the members of the war bands became an elite that stood apart from the average Germanic warrior-tribesmen.

- With the ability to field armies as large as twenty thousand warriors, the tribal confederacies had formidable war-making capacity, both against each other and against Rome.

Restructuring the Empire: Diocletian

At last, in A.D. 284, a ruler came to power who had the shrewdness and good fortune to avoid sudden death and the vision and determination to rescue the failing empire. Diocletian was born in Illyria—a territory to the south of the middle stretch of the Danube that had become a main recruiting ground for the empire's overstretched armies (see Map 7.1 on page 117). He was the son of a freed slave who enlisted in the ranks, worked his way up, was at last proclaimed emperor by his troops, and subdued all rivals who contested his claim to the throne. After a reign of some twenty years, he retired voluntarily to a palatial estate at Split, in his native Illyria.

Already before Diocletian, hard-pressed emperors had found Augustus's power-sharing arrangements with the Senate, the aristocracy, and the cities to be a nuisance (pp. 104, 105). But they had mostly improvised new arrangements during their brief reigns, and

>> **All for One, and One for All** These contemporary sculptures show Diocletian, Maximian, Constantius, and Galerius, the four emperors who jointly ruled Rome from A.D. 293 to 305. The statues, set into an outside corner of Saint Mark's Cathedral in Venice, previously stood in separate pairs on a building in Byzantium. But their identical appearance and soldierly clothing, their embraces and their hands on their sword hilts, all convey a message of forces united to uphold Rome's empire come what may. Scala/Art Resource, NY

Diocletian was the one who systematically reorganized the Augustan settlement to build a new government structure—one based on the imperial bureaucracy, the army, and his sacred imperial authority.

The Government and the Army

Partly because the empire was threatened from so many directions, and probably also to win the support of commanders who might become his rivals, Diocletian made unprecedented use of the old system of senior and junior emperors (p. 107). He ruled the empire's eastern territories from Nicomedia, close to the Bosporus (see Map 7.1 on page 117). In 286, he appointed a fellow general, Maximian, as joint ruler to govern the empire's western territories from Milan, which was closer than Rome to the threatened frontiers. From then on, emperors only rarely ruled from Rome, though they still honored it as the empire's founding city. In 293, these two senior emperors or *augusti* each acquired a junior colleague (a *caesar*), who was entrusted with his own region carved out of his augustus's territories and who would one day become an augustus in his turn (see photo).

The most urgent problem that Diocletian and his colleagues faced was that of coping with more numerous and better-armed Germanic barbarian raiders, as well as with Persian attacks spearheaded by forces of heavily armed and armored cavalry. Diocletian began a series of reforms to meet these threats that, by early in the fourth century, produced what amounted to a new Roman army. The old legions were broken up into smaller units; infantry arms and armor were lighter and fortifications much stronger than before. Cavalry—in particular, Persian-style heavy cavalry, the forerunners of the knights of the Middle Ages—was far more important than in the days of the legions.

All this required an increase in troop strength to perhaps 400,000 men—one-third higher than in Augustus's time. To reach these numbers, more and more of the soldiers had to be recruited from the barbarians, and in time many of them became loyal Romans and rose to positions of high command.

The emperors also strengthened their grip on their territories by dividing them into more and smaller provinces—about a hundred in all—with much greater power over local affairs than before. Cities were made strictly responsible to the provincial authorities, and leading citizens were compelled to take over government duties, above all tax collection—and made personally responsible for shortfalls. The provinces were grouped into twelve units called **dioceses** (from the Greek word for "administration") that were in turn grouped into the four regions that the augusti and caesars ruled. It is estimated that the new government structure employed perhaps as many as 20,000 officials—ten times the number under Augustus. One of its main tasks was to carry out regular surveys of the empire's population and wealth and thereby ensure a higher tax yield to provide for Rome's larger army.

Diocletian knew that if the empire was to bear the increased burden of his army and bureaucracy, he must restore its prosperity. A tough old soldier, Diocletian tried to deal with economic problems by giving orders, many of which were ineffective or pointless. To check inflation, he issued an edict freezing the price level of all basic commodities, and to reduce tax evasion and banditry, he ordered that important occupations such as those of soldier, baker, and farmer be made hereditary. Both these sweeping decrees were widely disregarded and probably hindered Rome's recovery from war and invasion, if they had any effect at all.

All the same, Diocletian, his colleagues, and his successors managed to restore order in the empire and on the frontiers. They did so by breaking the limits on the size of the bureaucracy and the army that every emperor since Augustus had more or less kept to, and by imposing on the citizens a heavy burden of tax payments and supply deliveries. A thousand years later, their innovations would be studied and imitated by many European rulers when they, too, wanted to collect more taxes to pay for larger armies.

Sacred Monarchy

As a pious Roman, Diocletian believed that army and government reforms were not enough: the empire also needed to keep the support of divine power, which for him meant the traditional gods and goddesses of Rome. He built or restored many temples, and unlike earlier emperors, who had merely accepted veneration of themselves as sharing in the larger divinity of Rome (p. 104),

Diocletian called himself "Jupiter-like," while Maximian was "Hercules-like." The rulers believed themselves to be specially linked to these two gods, and expected the empire's citizens to revere them accordingly.

Diocletian's court ceremonial matched his new divine status. In Nicomedia, Diocletian built a two-thousand-room palace, set in a vast park. On state occasions, he sat on an immense throne beneath a canopy of Persian blue and the glittering emblem of the sun, wearing a crown of pearls. Visitors lay flat on the floor before his sacred person, and reported proudly, in documents describing their life histories, that they had "adored the purple"—that the emperor had actually let them kiss the hem of his purple robe. In this way, Diocletian's efforts to add majesty and mystery to the emperorship were successful. Whatever all-too-human struggles might have brought him to his high position, he deserved reverence as a representative of divine power.

The Palace of Diocletian at Split (http://www.croatiatraveller.com/Heritage_Sites/Diocletian'sPalace.htm) Take a tour of Diocletian's palace at Split, a UNESCO World Cultural Heritage site.

Among the emperor's subjects, only two groups refused to accept that the emperor was himself divine. One was the Jews, whose devotion to the one God was respected as part of their ancient national traditions. The other was the Christians, who had newly turned against the gods and goddesses of Rome and whose numbers had increased spectacularly in the empire's time of troubles.

Christianity in Rome's Time of Troubles

By A.D. 300, there were several million Christians among the 60 million people of the empire, so that they were perhaps as large a minority as the Jews. Probably the empire's misfortunes made Christianity seem more convincing than before, and this gave continued momentum to a natural process of growth. More Christians meant more face-to-face contacts, more conversions, and more offspring, so that the increase in numbers grew continually larger and faster.

The increase was not the only change in Christianity. The new religion spread to the Western half of the empire, with many churches in prosperous towns of Africa and Spain, Italy and Gaul, and the Danube and Rhine frontiers (see Map. 8.1 on page 133). Most Christians still lived in the East, but Latin joined Greek and various tongues of the empire's eastern borderlands as a language of Christian literature and church services. Bishops of larger cities with larger churches gained authority over bishops of smaller cities with smaller churches, and bishops of the largest cities became leaders of "blocs" of bishops throughout whole regions of the empire. The bishops of Antioch and Alexandria wielded this influence in the eastern parts of the empire, and the bishops of Rome in the western territories.

Furthermore, Christianity was reaching into Rome's ruling elite, and the new religion's leaders were themselves becoming

diocese
An administrative unit in the Roman Empire; the term would later refer to the churches under a bishop's charge.

an elite. According to the renowned Egyptian thinker and teacher Origen, Christianity now attracted "even rich men and persons in positions of honor, and ladies of refinement and high birth"—probably ladies in particular, since they did not have public careers that might be endangered by unwise conversion. Big-city churches became large-scale organizations: about the middle of the century, Bishop Cornelius of Rome claimed that his church had more than 150 full-time clergy and supported 1,500 widows and other poor people. And complaints surfaced that Christian leadership was becoming an object of worldly ambition and pride. "In many so-called churches, especially in large cities," said Origen, "one can see rulers of the people of God who do not allow anyone, sometimes not even the noblest of Jesus' disciples, to speak with them on equal terms."

In these ways, Christianity was not just spreading within the empire, but growing together with it. That, in turn, faced the rulers with a choice. Should they try to uphold the "peace of the gods" by more systematic repression of Christianity, or should they take the Christians at their word and let them alone to pray to their God for the safety of the empire?

Given the overwhelming problems that the emperors had to cope with, the second course was much the easiest, and most of them followed it. In the half-century before Diocletian, two of the many short-reigning emperors launched empire-wide campaigns of persecution, but each was more or less formally called off by the next emperor. The numerous Christians who had not been steadfast could repent, though there were fierce disputes over how far this applied to priests and bishops. Christians who had lain low could come into the open, churches had their confiscated property returned by the government, and those who survived were inspired by the memory of the martyrs who had borne witness to the faith. Both persecutions ended with the Christian churches becoming larger and more numerous than ever.

Diocletian, too, left the Christians alone until near the end of his reign, when he undertook the most systematic persecution of all. The persecution continued for several years after he left office in 303, but to be successful, it would have taken a united long-term effort by all his fellow emperors. Instead, not all of them agreed that repression was the best way to deal with Christianity, and in any case, power struggles broke out among them as soon as he retired from office. After years of warfare, by 324 one among the various claimants to power, Constantine I, had defeated all rivals and became the founder of a new dynasty.

Restructuring the Empire: Constantine

Constantine carried forward most of Diocletian's government and army reforms. He built up the army to perhaps as many as half a million troops, some in mobile armies inland and others in central reserve forces in the imperial capitals. To help pay for the extra soldiers, he introduced a new gold coinage that kept its value for many centuries. Like Diocletian, he shared power with fellow emperors, though in his case, they were his sons; and he began building an Eastern capital, the city of New Rome, later called Constantinople, strategically located on the straits between Europe and Asia.

Constantine and Christianity

Constantine's one historic innovation was in the empire's relationship with Christianity. In 313, when he already ruled the empire's Western territories, he and the incumbent Eastern emperor issued the Edict of Milan, once again formally ending persecution and proclaiming complete freedom of worship throughout the empire. As between repressing and tolerating Christianity, the emperors had again made the second choice. But Constantine went on to make a third, and entirely new choice. He began to actually favor Christianity, thereby opening the way for it to become the religion of Rome.

Exactly how and when Constantine came to believe in the Christian God is unknown. His own story was that during the wars that brought him to power, he began using the cross of Jesus as a battle standard—because, he said, he had one day seen the cross hovering above the sun with the words written on it, "Conquer by this sign!" In any case, just like Diocletian, Constantine wanted to win for the empire the support of the divine power that ruled the universe, and to strengthen his authority as emperor by identifying himself with that power—only the power he had in mind was the one God whom the Christians worshiped. Of course, as a Christian, he could not expect to be venerated as a god himself. Still, he retained the majesty and mystery of Diocletian's court, and bishops themselves expressed reverence for him. In a speech before the emperor, his friend and biographer Bishop Eusebius of Caesarea once made a point-by-point parallel between Constantine as ruler of Rome and Christ himself as ruler of the universe.

The Burden of Empire

The Christian version of sacred monarchy had a long history ahead of it. Right down to the nineteenth century, European monarchs would claim to wield power as the chosen ones of God. But Christianity could not solve the urgent problems of the Roman Empire. Rivalries and warfare among emperors and would-be emperors, and frontier wars against barbarians and Persians, continued regardless of religion.

Above all, Christianity did not alter the fact that the empire of Diocletian and Constantine was drawing too heavily from its most precious asset: the willingness of the citizens to bear the burden of keeping it going. Particularly in the West, high taxation and rising prices were as destructive and demoralizing in the long run as the most savage barbarian attacks.

In the third century, many cities of the Western empire had become heavily fortified outposts whose citizens had lost all real self-government. In the fourth century, the cities became centers of social life for wealthy landowners and of Christian religious life, and they found a new source of civic leadership in the clergy. But urban life no longer flourished as it had in the days of the Roman Peace.

Meanwhile, the country dwellers, bankrupted by the endless demands of the tax collectors, came under the domination of a tiny elite of landowners—those who were wealthy enough to carry the burden of taxes or influential enough to gain tax exemptions. The debt-ridden peasants sold out to these wealthy men and became sharecroppers or laborers—giving up part of their harvest or doing farmwork in return for continuing to occupy their holdings. Though they were not human property like the slaves who worked alongside them (p. 98), the peasants became bound to their landlords by ties of personal obedience and subjection. The landowners usually dealt with the government on behalf of their peasants, often shielding them from the tax collectors as best they could, if only in order to exploit the peasants more effectively themselves (see photo).

In spite of their power and wealth, there were limits to the sacrifices that the landowners were willing to make for the emperor. Ever since the troubled times of the third century, emperors had kept them out of the most important government positions. Lower-ranking officers, common soldiers, and barbarian chieftains were promoted to high army commands and leading official positions, while landowners had to be content with wielding local power as counts—officials in charge of a city and its surrounding territory—and as bishops.

Both as counts and as bishops, the landowners were strongly attached to the ideal of Rome and far from disloyal to the emperors, but in practical politics, what counted most for them was not the empire as a whole but their local power and local responsibilities. In reaction against the overmighty state of Diocletian and Constantine, some of the features of the western Europe of the Middle Ages were already beginning to appear—notably the institution of serfdom (p. 193) and the involvement of the Church in matters of worldly government.

The Germanic Invasions of the West

Thanks to the reforms of Diocletian and Constantine, the empire held off barbarian attacks for most of the fourth century. During this time, there was plenty of brutal and exhausting warfare between the Romans and their barbarian neighbors, but in many ways, they were becoming increasingly alike. Leading Romans began to take up barbarian ways: even the

A Year on Lord Julius's Country Estate A fourth-century A.D. mosaic shows a North African mansion surrounded by scenes of country life. At bottom, left to right, a garden boy offers spring flowers to his mistress while she chooses jewelry; a secretary hands his master a scroll addressed "To Lord Julius"; and a fruit picker carries the fall plum harvest. At top, children in winter hoods beat olives out of trees; the mistress fans herself as she arranges a summertime table, and grain grows tall.

Bardo Museum Tunis/Gianni Dagli Orti/The Art Archive

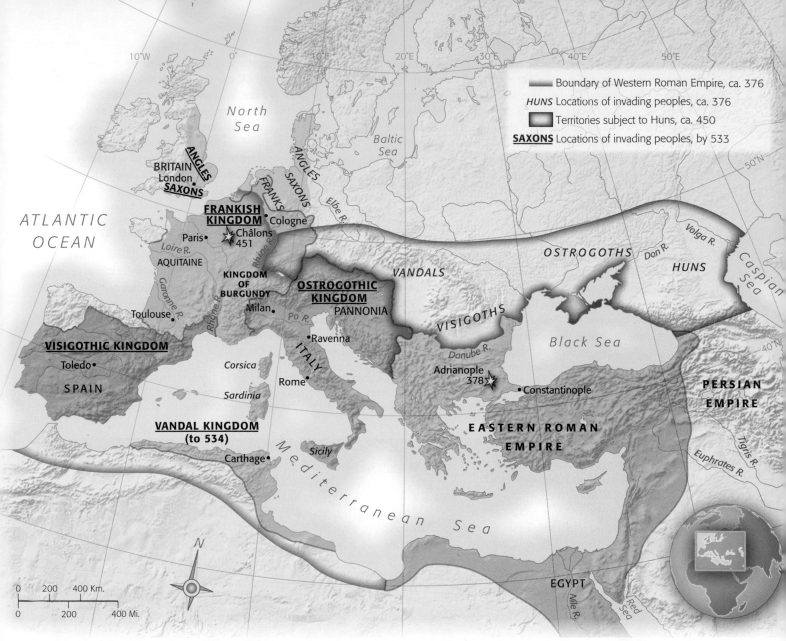

Map 8.2 **Invasions of the Western Empire**

The map shows the locations of the main invading groups when the invasions started in A.D. 376, and the regions that they came to occupy in A.D. 533—after 150 years of struggles with the Romans, with each other, and with less successful invading groups, and just before Eastern Roman efforts at reconquest began. © Cengage Learning

Interactive Map

emperors, when not dressed for court ceremonies, now wore the cloak, tunic, and pants of Germanic chieftains. Some tribal confederacies became Christian, though in the bitter fourth-century conflicts over Christian belief, they mostly adopted the Arian version of the new religion that Rome itself eventually rejected (pp. 145–146).

In this way, the stage was being set for a "merger" between Rome and the barbarians. When it came, the merger involved the entire Western half of the empire and took more than a century to accomplish. Sometimes it took the form of bloody conquest; sometimes, too, it resembled a peaceful takeover.

The Opening Moves

The Germanic barbarians began to move in on the empire not because of any deliberate plan of invasion but as a result of a shift in the intercontinental balance of forces that had helped Rome endure for so long (p. 116). Shortly before the beginning of the Christian era, a nomadic people living to the north of China, the Huns, had been defeated in conflicts with other nomads who were backed by the Chinese emperors. As a result, they began to move away westward across the steppes, and as often happened with nomad peoples, once they had left their homeland, they gradually migrated and fought their way farther westward, picking up other tribes on the way.

Finally, in 370, they burst into Europe. Though earlier nomad conquerors had ruled parts of Eastern Europe, none had been so well organized, ruthless, and ambitious as the Huns. For three-quarters of a century, they dominated a region stretching from Europe's eastern borders all the way to the Rhine (Map 8.2), causing turmoil among the barbarian peoples of the region. Some tribal confederacies joined the Huns, others were destroyed, and others migrated away from them.

Among those who migrated were the Visigoths, a Christian tribal confederacy living on the lower Danube who in 376 begged to be admitted to Roman territory. Their plea was granted, but the starving tribespeople were ruthlessly oppressed by corrupt Roman officials and provision merchants. Finally, the Visigoths went to war, and at the battle of Adrianople, their horsemen won a crushing victory over the imperial foot soldiers, killing the emperor Valens. His successor, Theodosius I, decided to make the best of the situation. First, he gave the Visigoths a substantial grant of land, and then he used them as allies against a rebellious army commander in the West.

When Theodosius died in 395, he left the empire to his two sons, one ruling the West from Milan and the other ruling the East from Constantinople. It was by now traditional for emperors to arrange for more than one successor to rule within what they still thought of as a single empire, but from now on, there were two continuous lines of rulers in East and West. Meanwhile, the Visigothic chieftain Alaric began to exploit the weakness of Theodosius's successors to gain even more land and power in the empire. Sometimes he played off the Eastern against the Western emperor, sometimes he helped them both against Roman foes, and sometimes he made or threatened to make war on them. Sensing the greater weakness of the West, Alaric finally concentrated his efforts there, and in 408 he led the Visigoths into Italy.

Meanwhile, the West was being penetrated from another direction. In 406 and 407, taking advantage of the Western emperor's problems with the Visigoths, several other Germanic tribal confederacies crossed the frontier on the Rhine River. By 410, they had spread far and wide into Gaul and Spain. In that year, too, the Visigoths, angered by what Alaric saw as the Western emperor's unreasonable refusal to grant them land and Roman civil and military titles, captured and looted Rome itself. Such a thing had not happened in eight hundred years, but it would happen twice again in not much more than a century.

The Crumbling of the Western Empire

During the fifth century, the story of these opening moves in the barbarian takeover was repeated over and over again. The leaders of the tribal confederacies were not deliberately trying to destroy the empire but rather to extract concessions from its rulers. Depending on circumstances, they would fight the Romans or each other or make deals with emperors or local Roman commanders—and the Romans were ready to deal. Rival emperors or would-be emperors sought the help of the invading tribal confederacies in wars against each other, and Eastern emperors troubled by barbarian armies persuaded them to move to the West. Even when the Romans defeated some barbarian group, they simply settled the invaders within the frontiers. And in 451, at the battle of Châlons, Romans and Germans fought side by side to hold off an invasion of Gaul by the Huns under their famous ruler Attila. Within two years, Attila was dead and his people began to retreat back into Asia and disperse.

In any case, by the time the Huns disappeared, not much of the Western empire was left to save. The last Western emperor, Romulus Augustulus, was a teenage boy installed in 475 by his father, a rebellious Roman general, and deposed the next year by a barbarian mercenary commander who did not even bother to kill him.

By the early sixth century, the Western empire had been carved up into a number of territories, each dominated by one or another Germanic tribal confederacy. The Visigoths had moved right across the empire to occupy Spain; the Ostrogoths now held Italy; Africa belonged to the Vandals; the Franks were supreme in most of Gaul as well as across the Rhine, in the western lands of barbarian Germany; and the Angles and Saxons had sailed across the North Sea to conquer Britain (see Map 8.2). Most of the Germanic ruling chieftains had won some kind of recognition and official titles from the Eastern emperors in Constantinople and were in theory the emperor's subordinates. In practice, however, they ruled as independent kings. The kings gave their leading warriors vast landholdings, and the mass of tribal fighters received freehold homesteads.

All the same, Roman normality continued, and the empire's international civilization lived on. Except for the Angles and Saxons in Britain, the invaders were a small minority of the population, and their chieftains and leading warriors revered Rome's way of life. Roman institutions continued to function in the service of the Germanic kings. Roman landowners had to give up a great deal of land to Germanic settlers, but they still had enough left to live cultured lives in their country mansions. Bishops, emperors, and Germanic kings built splendid new churches (see photo on page 113), and in Rome itself, crowds still enjoyed bloodthirsty entertainments in the Colosseum. The main change was that, to the relief of ordinary citizens, tax collectors and army requisition officers came around less often than before.

Meanwhile, in the East the Roman Empire lived on: the emperors in Constantinople still saw themselves as successors of Augustus, and were deferred to as such by the barbarian kings of the West. And in both East and West, Christianity kept the position it had won since Constantine, as the imperial religion of Rome.

LO⁴ Imperial Christianity

In the two hundred years after Constantine, regardless of the empire's problems and the barbarian takeover, Christianity won and kept its position as the religion of the rulers and the masses. But the issues that it had faced in earlier centuries did not go away, and some of them became more urgent and divisive than before. Christian arguments and soul-searching continued, and Christianity developed features as a majority religion many of which have lasted to the present day.

The Twilight of the Gods

Roman rulers had persecuted the Christians as disturbers of the "peace of the gods," but Christians had all along claimed that the truth was exactly the other way around: it was the one true

God with whom Rome must be at peace, and it was the traditional worshipers who were disturbing the peace. Nearly all emperors after Constantine were Christians, who therefore felt responsible to God and the empire for discouraging what they now began to call pagan worship. (In Latin, *paganus* meant a country dweller or a civilian, and most Christians were town dwellers who often thought of the Church as a kind of army.) But actually eliminating traditional religion took time.

The Shift to Christianity

To start with, Constantine began honoring the one God in the same way that emperors had used to honor the gods and goddesses—with splendid buildings. Magnificent Christian places of worship built on the model of imperial basilicas (public halls—p. 113) rose at the burial places of martyrs to rival the temples—for example, the Basilica of St. Peter in Rome (see photo). Temple funds were confiscated to help pay government expenses—which now included subsidies to churches for their charitable work. Meanwhile, bishops devised splendid public festivities to compete with celebrations of gods and goddesses. For instance, Western bishops began celebrating Christmas on December 25—a date not mentioned in the gospel accounts of Jesus's birth that was the same as that of a joyous sun-worshiping festival that greeted the lengthening of daylight. Now that Christianity was prominent and respectable, it seemed much more convincing to many more people than before.

But Christian emperors, like pagan ones before them, had too many other problems to try to systematically crush by force the worship they viewed as disturbing the peace. "Let them have, if they please, their temples of falsehood," said Constantine of the traditional worshipers, and the old and new religions continued alongside each other for several decades after he died in 337. In the 380s and 390s, however, there came a tipping point. The emperor Theodosius issued a series of decrees on such matters as canceling pagan holidays and closing temples—and by that time, Christians were numerous and powerful enough in the cities to save him the trouble of systematic enforcement. Mobs, often egged on by bishops, began smashing images, attacking worshipers, and demolishing temples or commandeering them for use as churches. The Parthenon in Athens, for instance, the 800-year-old temple of the virgin goddess Athena, became a church of the Virgin Mary.

By early in the fifth century, open worship of the gods and goddesses was unusual in the cities, and in the fifth and sixth centuries, it retreated in the villages as well. Regardless of the barbarian takeover of the West, landowners built village churches, appointed parish (local) priests, gave land to support the priests and maintain the churches, and used their power to deter their dependent peasants from the traditional rites. "Beat them . . . cut off their hair . . . bind them in iron shackles," advised Caesarius, a sixth-century bishop of Arles in southern Gaul. One way or another, by A.D. 600 the Church organization was well established in the countryside, and Christianity was probably the religion of the majority in most of the territories that belonged or had once belonged to the Roman Empire (see Map 8.1 on page 133).

The Jews in a Christian World

For the Jews, the shift to Christianity made no difference to their belief in themselves as a minority living among Gentiles who did not know the one truth about the one God. Christians by now mostly believed that God himself was punishing the Jews for rejecting the one truth about him, by scattering them across the earth and depriving them of his presence in the Temple, while they misguidedly submitted to the burden of the Law. Thus, by actually suppressing Judaism, Christians would be going against the judgment of God.

Saint Peter's Basilica, Rome This painting of the church constructed at Constantine's command in the mid-fourth century A.D. was made by assistants of the Renaissance artist Raphael just after the building was demolished to make way for the present one. The scene, showing Constantine "donating" to the pope the power to rule the West, is fictional (pp. 292-293), but the view of the thronged and splendid interior is authentic. Compare the modest house-church of only a century earlier (see photo on page 130).

Scala/Art Resource, NY

Christian mobs did sometimes attack Jews as well as pagans (p. 147), but Theodosius ordered that Jewish religious practices be tolerated, and the bishops did not oppose him. All the same, Jews were forbidden to seek converts or to build new synagogues, intermarriage between them and Christians was severely punished, and they were excluded from government service. In this way, there began an ambivalent Christian policy toward the Jews that was to continue for centuries to come—one of harassing, restricting, and humiliating them while not usually seeking to convert or destroy them as a people.

Christian Thinkers and the Shift to Christianity

Coercion of pagans probably worked because, from the pagan point of view, Constantine and his successors seemed to have broken the "peace of the gods" and gotten away with it. The gods and goddesses, it seemed, were weak, or evil, or did not exist—in which case, what was the point of resisting Christianity?

But then the Western frontiers started to give way, and though no one at the time knew how far that process would go, it was accompanied by a deeply troubling event, the sacking of Rome by the Visigoths in 410. If the God whom the Christians worshiped held worldwide power, both pagans and Christians asked, how was it that he allowed the Roman Empire, which was now so devoted to him, to suffer such a blow?

The Two Cities: Augustine

The thinker who answered this question was a pagan convert and bishop from North Africa, Augustine of Hippo (see Map 8.1 on page 133).

Augustine's conversion was not an easy one. In his *Confessions*, he describes it as a long struggle to turn away from rival philosophies to which he was strongly attracted, as well as from a life of pleasure to which he was compulsively addicted. Like Paul, Augustine believed that his change of life and belief was the work of Christ himself: "For so completely didst thou convert me to Thyself that I desired neither wife nor any hope of this world, but set my feet on the rule of faith."

Like Paul, too, Augustine believed that God predestines those who are to belong in his kingdom and those who will be excluded. Late in his life, he spelled this out. Humans, he argued, cannot influence God's choice of whom to save and whom to damn, for hopeless sinfulness is part of their biological inheritance, passed down from Adam by sexual intercourse. It is God alone who enables his chosen ones, though undeserving, to do good, avoid evil, and receive a place in his kingdom. Augustine's explanation became the classic statement of the doctrine of predestination for future generations of believers.

In his monumental book, *The City of God*, Augustine assured the faithful that the sack of Rome was a spectacular confirmation of basic Christian teachings. All of humanity, he said, is divided into two communities. The first is the "Earthly City" of those who are moved by love of self; the second is

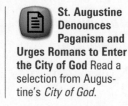 **St. Augustine Denounces Paganism and Urges Romans to Enter the City of God** Read a selection from Augustine's *City of God.*

the "Heavenly City" of the saved, who are moved by love of God. The members of these two communities live mixed together in the present world, but the first will suffer everlasting punishment with the devil, while the second will live eternally with God.

The Heavenly and Earthly cities were not the same as the Church and the empire. Augustine thought that many Christians would not be saved and that God had raised up Rome as a protector of both earthly life and orthodox Christianity. But in an era when Christian worldly evildoers lived alongside Christian zealous believers, and when the empire was struggling to survive, Augustine's arguments made sense. He had adapted to Christianity the ancient Jewish understanding of their place among the Gentiles. Scattered through the world, the citizens of the Heavenly City should live within whatever empires God might raise up and cast down, but they could never fully belong to these. As the Roman Empire continued to fall apart in the West, Augustine's belief only became more compelling.

"Plundering the Egyptians": Christianity and Greco-Roman Culture

Even while emperors and bishops were suppressing the traditional worship, educated Christians faced the problem of what to do with the art and literature with which it was so closely connected. Already Christians had differed over whether they should rely on Greek philosophers for guidance in understanding their own beliefs. But what about the poetry of Homer and Virgil, the oratory of Demosthenes and Cicero, and the art of Phidias and Praxiteles?

In the fourth century, this question became more urgent than before, as pious Christians struggled for the allegiance of the educated elite. How could they command the respect of the elite without being knowledgeable in Greek and Roman culture, and how could they argue persuasively without the skills of eloquence in speech and writing that were a basic part of that culture? But, as the Egyptian Christian ascetic Antony (p. 144) said, "in a person whose thought is pure there is no need for writing"—and it was hard to study Greek and Roman culture without taking a worldly delight in it that might taint the purity of one's thoughts.

To solve this dilemma, learned Christians turned to Old Testament stories of how the Israelites had taken and used the possessions of their enemies—for instance, when they escaped from oppression in Egypt they had "plundered the Egyptians" of gold and silver and fine clothing. In the same way, Christians must plunder all that was good and useful in the international culture of Greece and Rome, and reject all that was useless and wicked.

Among those who followed the Israelite example was one of the greatest of Christian scholars, Jerome, who lived about the same time as Augustine. Born in Illyria (see Map 7.1 on page 117), he went to Rome, studied Latin and Greek, and developed a guilty love of pagan literature; but at the orders of the pope, he also used his knowledge to revise the existing Latin translation of the New Testament by comparing it with the original Greek version. That left the Old Testament, however, which had originally been written in Hebrew and had been translated into Latin from a Greek version originally made by Jewish scholars.

hermit
An ascetic who lives alone, removed from ordinary society.

monastery
The residence of an ascetic community.

Finally, Jerome decided he must be either a "Ciccronian" (an admirer and imitator of Cicero, the renowned orator, thinker, and letter writer of the Roman Republic—p. 108) or a Christian. He left Rome for the Holy Land, where he learned Hebrew—a rare accomplishment for a Gentile. Then he harnessed his new knowledge to the mighty Christian task of translating the Old Testament directly into Latin. His new version eventually became part of the Vulgate (the "commonly used version"), the standard Bible of the Church in the West. Meanwhile, Jerome wrote Latin letters to his friends that combined the intimacy and eloquence that he had learned from Cicero's letters with Christian guidance—as well as not-so-Christian malice against people he disliked. In ways like these, Jerome and other learned Christians were able to distance themselves from the pagan culture of Greece and Rome yet also preserve and benefit from its legacy.

"White Martyrdom": Hermits, Monks, and Nuns

There had always been Christian men and women who lived an ascetic life, breaking the ties that bound them to this world—pleasure, comfort, marriage, and children—and living a life of prayer and self-denial that bound them to the world to come. Usually, they had lived their lives in families and households and had helped out with tasks such as teaching and charity in the churches to which they had belonged.

As Christianity grew in the third century, many more people followed the path of "white martyrdom" (without the shedding of blood, as opposed to "red martyrdom"). Furthermore, they did so more radically, withdrawing from family, household, and everyday church life. And when Christianity became the imperial religion, this kind of asceticism became a mass movement.

Partly, this was because many more wealthy people than before were pious believers. A rich gentleman like Anthony, who late in the third century gave all his possessions to the poor, lived alone in the Egyptian wilderness, and dug himself a garden plot like a field hand, was obeying the commandment of Jesus and imitating his humility. Likewise, Macrina, a well-off lady in Anatolia in the mid-fourth century, used her property to set up a community of like-minded virgins who shared the work, food, and bedding of the maidservants. And poorer believers welcomed a life where toil, hardship, strict obedience, and floggings—all normal features of ascetic communities—were not just a result of injustice or bad luck but steps on the narrow path to God's kingdom.

Men and Women Alone with God; Ascetic Brothers and Sisters

Many ascetics were solitary seekers after God or **hermits** like Anthony—or like Mary the Egyptian, a free-living young woman from Alexandria in the fourth century who took a pleasure trip to Jerusalem, repented of her way of life in the holy city, and heard an inner voice: "If you cross over Jordan you will find real peace!" She crossed the river eastward out into the desert and lived there for forty-eight years, often struggling with sexual thoughts "as though with wild beasts." In the fourth and fifth centuries, many believers moved out into the eastern deserts, as well as into the forests and mountains of Italy and Gaul, hoping through hardship and inner struggle to come to the joyful awareness that "I and God—we're alone in the world."

Hermits tended to attract followers, however, and not everyone who wanted to live an ascetic life was eager to do so completely on their own. Women's ascetic communities or **monasteries** dated back to the third century, and one of the earliest monasteries for men was founded early in the fourth century on an island in the Nile by Pachomius, a former soldier. He laid the place out like an army camp and imposed a strict schedule, hard manual work, and fierce discipline on his "recruits."

In the centuries of the shift to Christianity and the barbarian takeover, many revered ascetics founded monasteries across the Mediterranean lands and western Europe, and two in particular devised ways of life for ascetic communities that were disciplined but more varied and harmonious than that of Pachomius and came to be followed by women as well as men. About 360, Basil of Caesarea, a younger brother of Macrina, founded a monastery on one of his family's estates in Anatolia. In 529, after the Western empire's collapse, an Italian nobleman, Benedict of Nursia, founded the monastery of Monte Cassino on a towering hilltop south of Rome.

The Rule of St. Benedict: Work and Pray Read a short passage from Benedict's *Rule.*

Both Basil's and Benedict's monks combined regular services of prayer and praise to God by day and night with labor in the fields, at handicrafts, or in study—for as Benedict said, "Work is prayer." New members had to spend a period as "novices," to make sure that they were up to the ascetic life, before taking perpetual vows of poverty, chastity, and obedience. They were to live in harmony as "brothers" under an abbot (from the Hebrew word for "father"), whom they were bound to obey but whom they would themselves elect. Within a few centuries, Benedict's rule (regulations for ascetic community life) became the model for both monks and nuns in the West, and Basil's rule became the model in the East.

Ascetics and the World

In the age of imperial Christianity, however, even those who sought distance from the world could

> "*Idleness is the enemy of the soul. And therefore, at fixed times, the brothers ought to be occupied in manual labour; and again, at fixed times, in sacred reading.* "
> —Benedict of Nursia, A.D. 529

not help remaining a part of it. The religion whose founder had said that "Many are called, but few are chosen" was now the faith of millions, and believers could no longer look to the gods and goddesses in the daily business of life. For help in finding a place in the world to come as well as for guidance in this world, ordinary Christians often looked to ascetics.

The ascetic feats of hermits, for example, gave them compelling authority over ordinary Christians. The deserts of Egypt and Syria were not far from the river valleys with their towns and villages, so hermits were actually easy to visit and consult. One of the most famous hermits of the fifth century was Simeon Stylites (the "Pillar-Dweller") of Syria. In an effort to limit his contacts with visitors who wished to witness his holiness, he lived for many years on a small, unenclosed platform at the top of a pillar (see photo). This did not prevent crowds of pilgrims—including the Eastern emperor himself—from seeking Simeon's advice on personal and business matters as well as spiritual ones.

When Simeon died, the nearby city of Antioch fought off an effort by distant Constantinople to get hold of his body, and preserved it in a splendid building, according to what was by then a well-established custom of venerating "white martyrs," like "red martyrs," after their deaths. The dead Simeon was a **saint** (literally, a "holy person") who was both close to God in his kingdom and yet watched over the city where his body was preserved, and who could intervene with God at the request of humans, as a favored official might intervene with the emperor at the request of ordinary citizens.

Monks and nuns, too, had their saints, and their communities came to be considered essential to the well-being of Christianity as a whole. Ordinary Christians could be helped into heaven by their prayers—or by giving a son or daughter to God, so that in time, the majority of monks and nuns came to be "draftees" rather than volunteers. At the command of bishops, rank-and-file monks swarmed out of their monasteries to destroy temples or intimidate believers in rival versions of Christianity. And leading monks often became bishops, for their closeness to God made it seem likely that they would best withstand the money-making and power-abusing opportunities that were now open to rulers of the Church.

Rival Orthodoxies

Ever since the first disputes over Gentile converts and the Jewish Law, Christians had argued over the beliefs and practices of their religion. After the second-century rise of the Catholic Church, the arguments became for a while less bitter and widespread, but exactly in the era of Constantine they became fiercer than ever before.

Partly, this was because the arguments concerned basic and long-held ideas about the God and the Christ in whom Christians believed. God, they thought, was not just the almighty

Creator and Father. God was also the world-upholding and world-redeeming Son, and the Holy Spirit, the guide of individual believers and the whole Church. Furthermore, the eternal divine Son was also Jesus the mortal human being. Yet Christians also believed that there was only one true God, and that there was an infinite divide between God and humans. Was there some logical way in which God could be both one and three, and Christ could be both God and human?

The Arian and Nicene Faiths

On the whole, Christians had managed to live with this problem until about the time that Constantine came to supreme power, when a learned priest in Alexandria, Arius, proposed a solution. The Son, said Arius, was indeed divine, but since he was also human, he was not the equal of the Father, but had been brought into being by the Father as part of his plan for the universe. This view was acceptable to many bishops and ordinary believers in the Eastern empire. To many others in the East, however, and to the vast majority in the West, it seemed a wicked heresy that made Christ more human than divine. And if the bishops could not agree among themselves, who was to say which view was orthodoxy and which was heresy?

This was a tormenting situation for believers who needed to be sure of the one truth about the one God, including for the newly Christian emperor Constantine. Accordingly, in A.D. 325 he took the unprecedented step of summoning the bishops to a general council at Nicaea in Asia Minor. He hoped that the Holy Spirit would guide them to the truth, which they would then proclaim with their united authority.

Pushed by the emperor's longing for consensus, the bishops drew up a formal **creed** (statement of belief) restating the traditional beliefs in a way that rejected the Arian view—in particular, the Son was "of the same being as the Father" and yet "was made flesh, becoming human." But not long after the council broke up, this "Nicene" consensus (as proclaimed at Nicaea) began to unravel. Eastern bishops sympathetic to Arius felt that this wording suggested there was no difference between the Father and the Son, and once back in their cities they in turn opposed the creed as a heresy. The disputes soon restarted, and continued for nearly three centuries.

> **saint**
> A holy person believed to reside in heaven and to intervene with God on behalf of the living.
>
> **creed**
> A statement of religious belief.

<< **"In Thanks to God and Saint Simeon, I Have Made This Offering"** So says the lettering on this silver plaque, donated to a Syrian church about A.D. 600. A ladder leans against the saint's pillar for visitors to climb in search of advice and help. He is absorbed in a holy book, oblivious of a huge snake which (so the story went) is waiting for him to notice it and miraculously remove a stake from its eye—another beneficiary of the saint's influence with God. Reunion des Musees Nationaux/Art Resource, NY

Three Centuries of Conflict

What kept the arguments going was not just the importance of the actual issues but also the new position of Christianity itself. Divisions among Christians now involved whole populations and their powerful bishops, as well as rivalries among the bishops themselves. The emperors were also involved, both as Christian believers with their own views and as rulers who needed the Church's support—and rival emperors were liable to have differing views. And most Christians by now agreed that there ought to be a Catholic consensus on belief, so that the rival faiths battled all the more fiercely to capture the consensus for themselves. A fourth-century observer, Ammianus Marcellinus, himself a pagan but mostly respectful of Christianity, said of the disputes: "No wild beasts are such dangerous enemies to man as Christians are to one another."

History of Arian Doctrine (http://www.earlychristianhistory.info/arius.html) Learn more about the Arian doctrine and its followers.

By the end of the fourth century, the arguments and power struggles had played out in such a way that most bishops in the empire were prepared to reject the Arian faith. But the fifth-century Germanic invaders had mostly been converted to Christianity by Arian missionaries, and as rulers of the West, they kept their faith for a century or more until they finally adopted the Nicene faith of their Roman subjects. Meanwhile, many eastern bishops who opposed the Arian faith swung to the opposite extreme, and declared that since Jesus was the divine Son of God, he was not really or only secondarily a human being—and they, too, proclaimed their faith to be orthodoxy and other faiths to be heresy.

Christian arguments and power struggles continued in Egypt, Syria, and other eastern lands until the seventh century, when the Arabs conquered the region and brought a new monotheism, Islam. The overwhelming majority in the remaining Christian lands was committed to the Nicene faith, and in this way it became more or less unchallenged orthodoxy. In spite of all objections, Nicene Christians insisted that the only way to describe God and Christ was by fully accepting the seemingly opposed ideas of one and three, divine and human. God was a Trinity of three separate "persons" who were nevertheless a single "being." Jesus was the almighty and eternal Son, but he was just as much a human being subject to change and death. This understanding of God, as above and beyond what seems logical to the human mind, has remained basic to Christianity ever since.

Bishops and Emperors

Already before Constantine, Christianity had been growing together with Rome, but now, with the shift to Christianity, Rome had two closely interlocking power structures. One was that of the empire, headed by emperors, officials, and army commanders, and the other was that of the Church, headed by the bishops.

The Bishops

The Church's power structure or **hierarchy** (from the Greek words for "sacred government") from deacons to bishops was already well developed before Constantine, but now it grew several new layers. Big-city bishops were formally recognized as "metropolitans" or "archbishops" with authority over bishops of neighboring smaller cities. The authority of the bishops of Rome, Antioch, and Alexandria over wide regions of the empire was also formally accepted, and in the fifth century, the bishop of the empire's new Eastern capital of Constantinople gained the same status. Together with the bishop of the holy city of Jerusalem, these leading bishops acquired the title of **patriarch**, which had earlier only been used for Abraham and other revered early Israelites (from the Greek for "forefather"). These arrangements were mostly legislated by councils of the whole Church, six of which met in various Eastern cities from the fourth to the sixth centuries. All of them were called in connection with the struggles over belief, but they also dealt with questions of Church organization.

Within their cities, bishops were now just as important as the local imperial officials, the counts. They presided over awe-inspiring services in imposing public buildings. They controlled massive resources of land and money, built up by contributions from wealthy donors and supplemented by government subsidies. This wealth enabled them and their clergy to live comfortably and to provide society's main safety net for sick and poor people. They socialized with local landowning families, to which they themselves often belonged; a bishop's position was a valuable family asset, and in any case, many landowners now felt the same devotion to the Church that they had traditionally felt for the empire. Bishops also wielded strong influence over ordinary believers, who still had a say in choosing them alongside the local clergy and wealthy and prominent local men and women. They could unleash riots against pagans, heretics, Jews, and sometimes each other: in A.D. 366, fighting between supporters of two rival candidates to become bishop of Rome left 137 dead in a single day.

Naturally, there were bishops who valued their positions, as Ammianus Marcellinus put it, because "they are sure of rich gifts from upper-class ladies, they can ride in coaches, dress splendidly, and serve such lavish dishes that their cuisine outshines royal banquets." But he also allowed that there were bishops "whose extreme frugality in eating and drinking, their simple clothing, and their downcast eyes, prove to the eternal deity and his genuine worshipers the purity and modesty of their lives." Corrupt and unworthy bishops,

> "*Corrupt and unworthy bishops, and zealous and saintly ones, would be among the most hated and the most beloved figures in the public life of Christian peoples for many centuries to come.*"

and zealous and saintly ones, would be among the most hated and the most beloved figures in the public life of Christian peoples for many centuries to come.

The Emperors

Apart from the actual clergy, there was now one more level in the hierarchy—the emperors. The Christian rulers of Rome considered themselves instruments of God and responsible to him for the welfare of their subjects, including in the world to come. That gave them the right to a large say in the Church's doings, and besides, the Church had become so powerful that they could not rule effectively without this influence.

It was emperors, not bishops, who called general councils, which often fell into line with the version of the faith that the incumbent ruler preferred. Arian-leaning emperors banished and replaced Nicene-leaning bishops and vice versa. Bishops hung around imperial courts, hoping to persuade emperors to favor their version of the faith or to appoint their friends and family members to well-paid government jobs. A succession of Eastern emperors was able to build up the bishops of their capital city, Constantinople, to patriarch status against the resistance of the bishops of Rome, Alexandria, and Antioch. And in cities like Constantinople that were close under the eye of an emperor, it was he, rather than the local clergy and people, who chose the bishop.

Bishops did sometimes defy emperors. Bishop Athanasius of Alexandria, for example, was an unbending supporter of the Nicene faith about the middle of the third century. He spent years in hiding from Constantine's Arian-leaning son Constantius, writing attacks on the emperor as a heretic and persecutor who interfered in Church matters that were none of his business. Near the end of the century, Bishop Ambrose of Milan on two famous occasions made the emperor Theodosius actually do his bidding. First of all, he refused to continue with a service that Theodosius was attending until the emperor agreed to drop punishments he had ordered for a Christian mob that had destroyed a synagogue in a town on the Euphrates frontier. Later, he persuaded the emperor to repent humbly and publicly for having ordered an army massacre of rioters in a town in Greece.

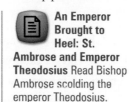

An Emperor Brought to Heel: St. Ambrose and Emperor Theodosius Read Bishop Ambrose scolding the emperor Theodosius.

When emperors stepped out of line by favoring heretics, giving Jews equal protection with Christians, or committing atrocities against Christian citizens, the balance of power between them and bishops could shift. Furthermore, the barbarian takeover and the end of the rule of the emperors in the West led to a larger shift in the balance, not only between emperors and bishops, but also among the bishops themselves—the growing authority of the bishops of Rome.

The Popes

In the East, where Christianity began, many cities could claim a connection with Jesus himself and his most revered early followers. In the West, there was only one such city, Rome. Rome was the place of martyrdom not only of Paul, the apostle to the Gentiles, but also of Peter, whom Jesus had called "the rock on which I will build my Church." As a result, the bishops of Rome were uniquely respected by Christians in the West, and other bishops often accepted their advice and instructions. But most Christians were still to be found in the empire's Eastern lands, where the bishops took most seriously the advice and instructions of the bishops of Antioch and Alexandria. In case of dispute, the Easterners usually "agreed to differ" with the distant Roman bishops.

The fourth-century changes in Christianity brought the Roman bishops greater authority in the West than ever before. There were more believers to look up to them, the hierarchy that took their advice and instructions was more powerful and better organized, and since emperors no longer governed from Rome, there was no one in the city itself who outranked them. Above all, in the disputes over belief the Roman bishops and the Western hierarchy were usually Nicene believers, while Eastern bishops argued and general councils wavered. Surely, thought many in the West, the best judge of orthodoxy and heresy was no council, and no emperor to whose wishes a council might bow. About the middle of the fourth century, the Roman bishops began quoting Jesus's words to Peter as proof that they were the supreme Christ-appointed guides of the whole Church, East and West.

In the fifth century, as the Western empire collapsed and the Eastern empire continued to be troubled by disputes over belief, the Roman bishops insisted more and more on their guiding role in the Church. At the end of the century, Bishop Gelasius told an Eastern emperor: "Twofold are the ways in which this world is mainly ruled: by the sacred authority of bishops and by the imperial power. The burden on the priests is heavier, because they will be accountable to the Lord at his judgment even for the souls of rulers . . . in matters of religion you should not take the lead but rather submit." And when Gelasius spoke of bishops, he had in mind "specially the Vicar [deputy] of the blessed Peter." Not long after Gelasius's time, the Vicars of Peter acquired a title that marked how special they were. Traditionally, Christians had often respectfully called priests and bishops "daddy" (in Latin, *papa*), to show their childlike love for their spiritual fathers. Now, Westerners stopped using that name except for the bishop of Rome, who became the one and only *papa*—the pope.

Meanwhile, the Eastern emperors went on taking the lead in religious matters in the lands they ruled, and rather than submitting to the popes, they built up the patriarchs of Constantinople to become leading bishops in the Eastern empire. The popes and the patriarchs shared the Nicene faith and considered themselves to belong to one undivided Church. In both West and East, the power structures of the rulers and the Church continued to be tightly interlocked. Patriarchs sometimes resisted Eastern emperors, and popes sometimes deferred to Western kings. But in the East, the rulers reigned over an empire where they were just as responsible for their subjects' salvation and the orthodoxy of the Church's beliefs as the clergy—and in the West, the popes were beginning to carve out for themselves and the clergy a separate and higher realm.

Listen to a synopsis of Chapter 8.

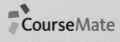

PART II

MEDIEVAL CIVILIZATION,

500–1300

The conversion to Christianity of the peoples of the Roman Empire and the Germanic invasions of the empire's western territories were completed by about the year 500. Together with the conquest of lands stretching from Spain to the borders of India by Islam in the seventh century, they bring us to a new phase of Western history. These shifts in civilization opened the thousand years of the Middle Ages—the "in-between times" separating the ancient from the modern period (p. 2).

Geographically, the Middle Ages were the European phase of Western development, when a new and distinctive civilization emerged on the soil of Europe, spread throughout that region, and reached the highest levels of cultural achievement. In religion, this was the era when the Christian faith and Church spread through all of Europe and set the tone of Western civilization in every activity. In government and social life, it was the heyday of an elite whose power came mainly from the fact that its members were owners of land and leaders of warriors—the social group that came to be known, on account of its overwhelming prestige, as the nobility. It was also a time when Western civilization came into closer touch with the other civilizations of the Eastern Hemisphere than before, but was inferior to them in wealth, practical knowledge, and social organization.

In these ways, the Christian Europe of the Middle Ages was very different from the secular-minded, democratic, and world-dominating West of the present day.

The modern West is separated from the Middle Ages by a new series of spectacular shifts in civilization that began about two hundred years before 1500 (the "official" end date of the Middle Ages), went on for more than a century afterward (see Part Three), and were followed by yet more shifts that have continued down to the present (Parts Four and Five). Because of these shifts, Christian Europe is often regarded today as the most alien of the Wests of the past. The word *medieval* (from the Latin for "Middle Ages," *medium aevum*) is often used to mean the same as "brutal," "superstitious," "closed-minded," "unhygienic," and other unpleasant adjectives that people today like to think no longer apply to Western civilization.

In fact, many of the things that are thought of today as typically "medieval" in the bad sense were widespread features of traditional civilization in general. Disease, poverty, and torture were just as common in ancient Greece and Rome, for instance, as in the Middle Ages, and in reality they are also normal features of present-day civilization. Christian Europe also shared many of its more praiseworthy features with other civilizations. It inherited many of its cultural and intellectual traditions from ancient Greece and Rome and developed these traditions in many creative ways. In spite of religious hatreds, Christian Europe also learned a great deal from the neighbor and rival civilization of Islam. But the civilization with which Christian Europe has the most in common, in spite of all shifts and changes, is the present-day West.

The list of basic features of the West of today that originated in medieval times is a long one. It was in the Middle Ages that Western civilization first came to be made up of many ethnic groups, each with its own version of a common culture, and of many independent states, all competing fiercely with each other. English, Spanish, and most of the other languages of the West were first spoken and written in the Middle Ages. England, France, Russia, and many other present-day European countries first came into existence and practiced the earliest forms of representative government. Christianity itself remains the overwhelmingly predominant religion of the West. Everyday practices of today, such as arranging lists in alphabetical order so as to make the items easy to find, or putting hops into beer to make it taste interestingly bitter, also began in medieval times. In all these and many other ways, the modern West is still the child of the Christian Europe of the Middle Ages.

CHAPTER 9

AFTER ROME,
500–700

LEARNING OBJECTIVES

AFTER READING THIS CHAPTER, YOU SHOULD BE
ABLE TO DO THE FOLLOWING:

LO^1 Describe the way of life of the Germanic barbarians,
and discuss their role in preserving and spreading
Roman and Christian civilization.

LO^2 Trace the expansion and contraction of the Eastern
empire, and explain how Byzantium served as the
main custodian of ancient Greek culture while also
sponsoring new art and architecture.

LO^3 Discuss the emergence of Islam as a new religion
and culture, and explain why the rise of Islam was an
important event for European peoples.

>**"The upheaval of the early Middle Ages ended not in a collapse of civilization but in its renewal, and the first two early medieval centuries set the patterns for how this renewal would later take place in western and eastern Europe."**

The two centuries after the fall of Rome were a time of turmoil in Europe that would continue for five hundred years—a half-millennium that counts as the "early" part of the Middle Ages. As with the upheaval in ancient civilization two thousand years before (pp. 32–33), the upheaval of the early Middle Ages ended not in a collapse of civilization but in its renewal, and the first two early **medieval** centuries set the patterns for how this renewal would later take place in western and eastern Europe.

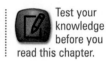 Test your knowledge before you read this chapter.

In the Germanic kingdoms that had taken over the western half of the Roman Empire, Roman institutions gradually stopped working, cities ceased to be centers of trade and social life, and warfare became more important than education and culture in the lives of the upper classes. But missionary-monks brought Christianity and Roman traditions to peoples beyond the empire's old frontiers, and in the largest Germanic kingdom, carved out of Roman and barbarian lands by the Franks, the kings ruled in partnership with warrior-landowners and Church leaders. Both the missionaries and the Frankish rulers created precedents for spectacular later renewal in western Europe.

Meanwhile, the Roman Empire's surviving eastern half contributed to western Europe's chaos by efforts at reconquest, and then itself came under attack by newly powerful neighbors. By 700, the emperors in the eastern capital, Constantinople, ruled only Anatolia and a few patches of land in Europe, and their state had become more Greek than Roman. To mark the difference, the remaining empire is today usually called by its capital's original Greek name, Byzantium (bi-ZAN-tee-uhm).

What do you think?

The early medieval period was a "dark age" in Western history.

Strongly Disagree						Strongly Agree
1	2	3	4	5	6	7

«**The Baptism of Clovis** An ivory plaque made about A.D. 900 depicts the founding event of the Kingdom of the Franks four centuries earlier. The conquering chieftain Clovis is humbly naked and up to his waist in water. The Roman aristocrat Remigius, bishop of Reims, touches Clovis's head as he speaks the words of baptism. Clotilde, Clovis's already Christian queen, looks on; the Holy Spirit, in the form of a dove, brings holy oil in token of God's blessing upon the fusion of Frank, Roman, and Christian.

The Granger Collection, New York

151

medieval
Refers to the distinctive civilization of the Middle Ages, which developed in Europe after the disintegration of the Roman Empire and before the emergence of the modern West.

noble
A member of the warrior-landowner group that formed the elite of medieval Europe.

However, Byzantium was still a powerful state and a center of Christianity and Greek culture. From Byzantium, renewal would spread to the ethnic group of barbarians that took over most of eastern Europe, the Slavs, and Byzantine cultural impulses would reach both halves of Europe. And the empire kept up links of trade and travel across the Middle East and northern Africa, in spite of losing those regions to the Arabs with their new monotheism, Islam.

The Muslim conquest of Christian Syria, Palestine, and North Africa redefined Christianity as geographically European for the rest of the Middle Ages, and it led to many centuries of warfare between Christians and Muslims. But as Europe renewed itself, it would also find in Islam a source of trading wealth and cultural inspiration, and a gateway to more distant civilizations of the Eastern Hemisphere. Apart from Christianity, the religion that would have the greatest impact on medieval Europe in war and peace would be Islam.

LO¹ The Germanic Kingdoms of the West

The Germanic invaders of the West were a small minority who in time were mostly assimilated by the Roman peoples they conquered. All the same, some of their traditions lasted, and these same traditions persisted more strongly among Germanic peoples farther north in Europe who did not enter the empire. Either way, the way of life of the Germanic barbarians influenced various features of civilization in western Europe, alongside Roman culture and institutions and Christianity.

The Germanic Barbarians

Over several centuries of close contact with Rome, the Germanic peoples had developed an elite of powerful chieftains and their war bands of leading warriors (p. 135). When they took over the empire's western territories in the fifth century, the chieftains shared newly acquired land with

FIFTH CENTURY	Angles and Saxons invade Britain
486	Clovis leads Frankish confederacy against Romans and rival Germanic invaders in Gaul
527–565	Reign of Emperor Justinian in the Eastern empire
542	Plague hits Egypt, then spreads throughout the Mediterranean area and much of western Europe
568	Lombards conquer most of northern Italy
570–632	Life of Muhammad
595	Missionaries sent by the pope begin to convert the pagans of England
711	Muslim invasion of Spain
800	Slavs occupy almost all of eastern Europe

the members of their war bands, who became owners of vast properties. They took up Roman ways and often intermarried with Roman aristocrats, but they also changed the way of life of the relatively unmilitary Roman landowners to form a new elite of warrior-landowners. Landownership and war leadership came to be marks of what came to be called the **nobles** for the next thousand years.

More "democratic" tribal institutions, notably regular assemblies of rank-and-file warriors and farmers (p. 135), did not long survive the move into the Roman Empire. Even among the tribes that did not move into the empire, the spread of Christian and Roman civilization increased the power of chieftains and their favored warriors at the expense of tribal assemblies. All the same, a tradition of popular participation in government continued, especially in the field of law and justice. In many western European countries in the early Middle Ages, groups of ordinary freemen would be summoned and sworn to reveal their collective knowledge of the truth, in such matters as identifying the originator of a blood feud, establishing ownership of property, or accusing wrongdoers.

Many Germanic pagan traditions persisted in folklore and symbolism even after the adoption of Christianity. Thus, in the English language, the names of Tiu, the Germanic war god;

> "*The Germanic takeover actually led to the spread of Roman and Christian civilization beyond Rome's frontiers.*"

Woden, who was thought to take a special interest in the affairs of the human race; Thor, the thunder god; and Frigg, the fertility goddess, are still honored in the names of four days of the week: Tuesday, Wednesday, Thursday, and Friday. Even the climactic day of the Christian calendar received its name, in many northern lands, from Eostre, the ancient Germanic goddess of spring.

Perhaps the most important result of the Germanic takeover was that, in the long run, it led to the disappearance of the already crumbling frontier between Roman and barbarian Europe. In Germany, the Low Countries, and the Scandinavian lands farther north, there remained many Germanic peoples who had not moved into the Roman Empire. These barbarians now began to look southward in their turn for trade, conquest, Roman culture, and Christianity. Meanwhile, the Germanic rulers of former Roman lands were less cautious than the Romans had been about expanding their power north and east of the Rhine and Danube Rivers. In this way, the Germanic takeover actually led to the spread of Roman and Christian civilization beyond Rome's frontiers.

The Kingdom of the Franks

In not much more than two centuries, many of the Germanic kingdoms fell victim to Byzantine efforts at reconquest, to the power of Islam, or to each other. However, two Germanic groups that established themselves for the long term, the Anglo-Saxons and the Franks, together with the non-Germanic Irish, played a leading role in preserving and spreading Roman and Christian civilization.

England and Ireland

From the area that is now Denmark and northwestern Germany, two tribal groups, the Angles and the Saxons, sailed over the North Sea and invaded Britain during the fifth century (see Map 8.2 on page 140). They overran the native Britons and established several kingdoms of their own. Unlike in other conquered regions of the Roman Empire, it was the natives who were assimilated by the invaders, except in outlying territories that came to be known as Wales and Scotland. In the rest of Britain, Germanic dialects and customs took firm root, and the country came to be known as "the land of the Angles," or England. Though pagan when they first settled, most of the Angles and Saxons became Christian during the seventh century, partly as a result of missionary efforts sponsored by the papacy from 595 onward and partly under the influence of two neighboring, already Christian nations: the Irish and the Franks.

Ireland was the first territory outside the frontiers of Rome to which Christianity spread when the empire collapsed. A remnant of the Celtic peoples who had dominated much of western Europe centuries earlier (p. 100), the Irish had never been conquered by Rome. In the turmoil of the fifth century, Patrick, a native Briton who had been captured by Irish raiders, brought Christianity to the island, and Christian monasteries soon came to dominate the tribal life of the country. Under their influence, a unique Irish civilization grew up, based on the Christian faith, Roman literature, and the heritage of Irish barbarian culture. This civilization, in turn, came to influence much of western Europe during the early Middle Ages.

Clovis and the Franks

The most powerful Germanic kingdom was that of the Franks, who were to give their name to modern France. The Franks were originally a loose tribal confederacy along the lower Rhine River, just outside the Roman frontier. In 486, as the Western empire was falling apart, a Frankish chieftain, Clovis, led the confederacy in campaigns against the Romans and rival Germanic invaders in Gaul. From then on, Clovis's family, the **Merovingians** (from the Frankish word for "children of Merovech," their mythical forefather), were the ruling dynasty of all the Franks. Clovis and his successors pushed southward and also eastward from their original homeland, until they ruled all of present-day France and much of western and southern Germany (see Map 8.2 on page 140). As the Franks became Christian and adopted Roman ways, so also did some of their subject tribes to the east of the Rhine. In this way, the spread of Christian and Roman civilization beyond the empire's former frontiers began on the mainland of western Europe.

In Search of Ancient Ireland (http://www.pbs.org/wnet/ancientireland/index.html) Explore the truth behind Irish legends and learn more about Irish influences on western Europe.

Anglo-Saxon Treasure Shortly after A.D. 600 a local ruler was buried aboard a ship in a mound at Sutton Hoo, near the eastern English seashore. Among the treasures buried with him was a locally made purse covered by this eight-inch-long lid, decorated with images of men, wolves, and eagles and delicate abstract patterns, all made of gold, garnets, and colored glass. Anglo-Saxon England was a land of skilled craftspeople and of wealthy rulers who were at home on both land and sea.
Courtesy of the Trustees of the British Museum

THE CONVERSION OF ENGLAND: INSTRUCTIONS TO MISSIONARIES

In 595, Pope Gregory I the Great sent a Roman monk, Augustine, to convert the Anglo-Saxon kingdom of Kent, a territory in southern England. About 150 years afterward, the Anglo-Saxon monk Bede of Jarrow included in his *Ecclesiastical History of the English People* a letter from Gregory to the leader of a later group of missionaries, giving instructions to be conveyed to Augustine on how to make Christianity easier for pagans to adopt. Gregory's strategy involved building the new faith by using the foundations of the old one.

When Almighty God shall bring you to the most reverend Bishop Augustine, our brother, tell him what I have, after mature deliberation on the affairs of the English, determined upon, namely, that the temples of the idols in that nation ought not to be destroyed, but let the idols that are in them be destroyed; let holy water be made and sprinkled in the said temples; let altars be erected, and relics placed. For if those temples are well built, it is requisite that they be converted from the worship of devils to the service of the true God; that the nation, seeing that their temples are not destroyed, may remove error from their hearts and, knowing and adoring the true God, may the more familiarly resort to the places to which they have been accustomed.

And because they have been used to slaughter many oxen in the sacrifices to devils, some solemnity must be substituted for them on this account, as, for instance, that on the day of the dedication, or of the nativities of the holy martyrs whose relics are there deposited, they may build themselves huts of the boughs of trees about those churches which have been turned to that use from temples, and celebrate the solemnity with religious feasting, no more offering beasts to the devil, but killing cattle to the praise of God in their eating, and returning thanks to the Giver of all things for their sustenance; to the end that, whilst some outward gratifications are permitted them, they may the more easily consent to the inward consolations of the grace of God.

For there is no doubt that it is impossible to efface everything at once from their obdurate minds, because he who endeavors to ascend to the highest place rises by degrees or steps and not by leaps. Thus the Lord made himself known to the people of Israel in Egypt; and yet he allowed them to use the sacrifices which they were wont to offer to the devil in his own worship, commanding them in his sacrifice to kill beasts to the end that, changing their hearts, they might lay aside one part of the sacrifice, whilst they retained another; that whilst they offered the same beasts which they were wont to offer, they should offer them to God, and not to idols, and thus they would no longer be the same sacrifices.

EXPLORING THE SOURCE

1. What would have been the benefits of this method of conversion as opposed to using more aggressive tactics? What would have been the disadvantages?

2. Are you familiar with any present-day Christian practices that originated from pagan roots?

Source: James Harvey Robinson, ed., Readings in European History (Boston: Ginn, 1904), 1:100–101.

Clovis now began to build a stable system for governing his territories. He shared the conquered land with his leading warriors but made sure that the lion's share went to himself and his descendants. He let the existing Roman elite of landowners, counts, and bishops keep much of their property and their positions in church and state. He further strengthened his rule by converting to the Nicene Christianity (p. 145) of his Roman subjects (see photo on page 150). At a time when many Germanic invaders were Arian Christians, this won him the enthusiastic support of the bishops, who revered him as a God-sent ruler—a Frankish Constantine. The imperial partnership of bishops and rulers continued, with two important changes from Roman times:

the kings always obeyed the bishops and never commanded them in matters of faith, but from now on it was the kings, not the local clergy and people, who chose the bishops.

Kings, Warrior-Landowners, and Bishops

History of the Franks: An Early Frankish King and His Wives Read the story of Frankish King Lothar's romantic entanglements.

When Clovis died, however, much of what he had done to restore stability was destroyed. Following Germanic custom—and the example of the Roman emperor Constantine—he divided his territories among his sons, each of whom became the king of his share of the royal inheritance. But what worked well enough in a loosely organized tribal society, and in an empire with a strong government structure, spelled trouble in a Germanic kingdom, where leading warriors and Roman landowners were merging into a powerful new elite. The local kings often quarreled over their shares of the royal inheritance, and this gave leading warrior-landowners a chance to play off one king against another. To win their support, the kings had to appoint them to positions as counts and bishops, grant them royal lands, and give them the right to control their lands without royal interference.

As a result, a vicious circle set in. As the rulers' lands, revenues, and control over the government and the Church gradually dwindled, they were forced to depend still more on the leading warrior-landowners and to concede them still more land and power. By the end of the seventh century, the Merovingian kings were mere puppets of their chief officials, the **mayors of the palace**. The mayors were themselves usually the heads of powerful factions among the warrior-landowners. But these factions feuded ferociously with each other, and there was usually more than one rival mayor, each associated with one or another rival king, so that even the power of the mayors was insecure. In consequence, the authority of the central government became increasingly weakened, with each warrior-landowner family acting as a power unto itself.

> *"The imperial partnership of bishops and rulers continued, with two important changes from Roman times: the kings always obeyed the bishops and never commanded them in matters of faith, but from now on it was the kings, not the local clergy and people, who chose the bishops."*

Compared with the Roman Empire in its most glorious days, the Frankish kingdom was a feeble political structure, yet its role in the building of European civilization was important. The Merovingian kings and warrior-landowners were Christian believers and respecters of Roman culture. True, in the sixth and seventh centuries, they gradually ceased to be the well-educated rulers and aristocrats of imperial times; in fact by 700, they were usually illiterate. But they invested a great deal of their resources in monasteries that harbored learning, culture, and religion, and they sent many of their own sons and daughters to become monks and nuns. The Franks passed these beliefs and practices on to neighboring Germanic peoples to the east and north, often with the help of Anglo-Saxon and Irish missionaries.

Furthermore, in spite of the Frankish kingdom's history of conflict and disintegration, it set important precedents for later European government and politics. Within the kingdom, the main elements of the feudal state, with its decentralized authority and its constant interplay

> *"In one form or another, monarch, nobles, and churchmen would dominate political and social life in most European countries down to the nineteenth century."*

of monarch, powerful nobles, and leading churchmen, were already coming into existence. In one form or another, monarch, nobles, and churchmen would dominate political and social life in most European countries down to the nineteenth century.

LO² The Eastern Empire and Its Neighbors

While Germanic kings ruled the West, the emperors in Constantinople still ruled a mighty empire in the East, stretching from the Danube to the Euphrates and the Nile (Map 9.1 on page 156). The Eastern empire still worked on the pattern laid down by Diocletian and Constantine. It had an all-powerful emperor surrounded by a splendid court, a centralized bureaucracy, and massive armies and navies recruited from within the empire and from neighboring barbarian peoples. Unlike the Western lands, the Eastern empire's territories were wealthy enough to support this burden. The Eastern emperors still saw themselves as Roman, and claimed authority over East and West alike. But when they seriously tried to enforce this claim, instead of growing, their empire began to shrink.

From "Eastern Empire" to "Byzantium"

Reconquest and New Invasions

In the fifth century, the Eastern emperors were too busy holding their existing frontiers and dealing with Christian religious disputes to try to reconquer territory in the West. But in 527 Justinian came to power—a ruler of extraordinary talent and determination, with a program of what he called "renewing the empire." Part of his program was peaceful and long-lasting—notably the codification of Roman law, the *Corpus Juris Civilis* (p. 111), which still forms the foundation of the legal systems of most Western countries today. But Justinian was also intent on restoring the empire to its traditional

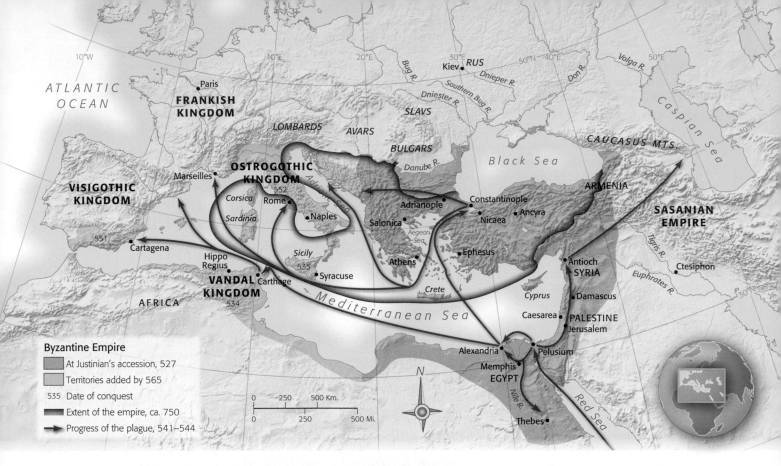

Map 9.1 From "Eastern Empire" to "Byzantium," A.D. 527–ca. 750

In the mid-sixth century after Justinian's campaigns of reconquest, he seemed to be on the way to regaining much of Rome's universal empire, but in 750 Byzantium was struggling to hold the Balkans and Anatolia. Most of Byzantium's losses were to the new universal empire of Islam. To the north, Byzantium confronted a combination of Asian nomadic invaders and European barbarian peoples—above all the Slavs, who became predominant across most of central and eastern Europe. © Cengage Learning

Interactive Map

size—an endeavor that involved years of destructive warfare and only short-lived success.

By the middle of the sixth century, Justinian's armies and navies had regained Italy, northwestern Africa, and some of Spain. But it was at the cost of massive devastation, made worse by the effects of bubonic plague. Since this rat-borne disease was new to the Mediterranean world, the population was especially vulnerable to it. The plague first reached Egypt from Ethiopia or India in 542, and from there it spread throughout the Mediterranean area and to much of western Europe. The toll was staggering, equaling that of the later Black Death (p. 247). Far more than the original Germanic invasions, sixth-century disease and warfare were responsible for the loss of population, the emptying of towns and cities, and the decay of Roman government and education in the West.

Furthermore, late in the sixth century, new attacks on the empire's overexpanded frontiers began. The first invasions came from Europe, where barbarian nations were once again set moving by nomadic invaders from Asia, as in the time of the Huns and the Visigoths (pp. 140-141). This time the Avars, a people akin to the later Turks, followed the trail blazed by the Huns and set up an empire in central and eastern Europe. In 568, a Germanic tribal group in flight from the Avars, the Lombards, conquered most of northern Italy. The Lombards stopped there, and like other Germanic invaders, they became the rulers of a fragile Christian kingdom. But it was the end of the empire's efforts to reconquer the western lands that had once been ruled by Rome.

The Slavs

Also caught up in the Avar invasion was an entire ethnic group of European barbarians who would eventually come to dominate eastern Europe just as the Germanic barbarians dominated the West: the Slavs.

There is no way of knowing when and where the Slav tribes first formed a distinct group, though they certainly had a language and customs of Indo-European origin (p. 20). By the time of the fall of the empire in the West, however, they lived in an area stretching between two eastern European rivers, the Vistula and the Dnieper (see Map 9.1). This was a fertile region of forest and grassland, sandwiched between the lands of Germanic peoples to the west and the eastern steppes where nomads roamed. More than once, the Slavs were conquered by these neighbors, but they did not lose their identity. Instead, they served their various overlords in peace, fought under them in war, followed them on campaigns of conquest all over eastern Europe, and finally inherited their dominion.

The Slavs began their warlike expansion as foot soldiers of the Avars. Under Avar leadership, in the sixth and early seventh centuries, they moved south from their homeland, crossed the Danube River, and broke the defenses of the Eastern empire. They took over most of the empire's provinces in southeastern Europe—the region known today as the Balkans—including, for a time, Greece itself. In the same period, other Avar campaigns took Slavic tribes north and west until they reached the

Baltic Sea and threatened the eastern frontier of the Frankish kingdom. More slowly and peacefully, Slavs also settled the vast forest region that stretched for hundreds of miles northeast of their homeland. By 800, the Slavs had occupied almost all of eastern Europe.

Whereas the Germanic tribes had been absorbed and lost their identity nearly everywhere they migrated, in eastern Europe it was the Slavs who assimilated the earlier peoples of the region. As a result, most of the peoples of eastern Europe are still ethnically Slavic at the present day. But as the Slavic tribal confederacies scattered, they began to divide into different groups, each with its own version of the original Slav language. There was a western group, the forerunner of such modern nations as the Czechs and Poles; a southern group, including tribes that already called themselves Croats and Serbs; and an eastern group, out of which the Russians, Ukrainians, and other nations would in time evolve.

Here and there, old-established peoples managed to avoid assimilation by the Slavs. In swamps and forests along the shores of the Baltic Sea, earlier Indo-European settlers survived to become the Baltic nations of today. In mountain valleys on the east coast of the Adriatic Sea, tribes that had never been fully assimilated by Rome eventually developed into the present-day Albanians. Along the lower Danube, where the Latin language had been spread by Roman soldiers and settlers, it continued to be spoken by mountain shepherds and by farmers in the plains, the ancestors of the Romanians. And in Greece, where persistent Byzantine efforts of reconquest eventually succeeded, it was the Slavs who were absorbed and turned into Greeks. In these ways, with the Slavic invasions there began to come into existence the present-day ethnic pattern of eastern Europe and the Balkans.

> "*The yellow-haired nations are rash and dauntless in battle when it is a question of liberty. Being daring and reckless, they look disdainfully on even a short retreat as a sign of cowardice, and they calmly despise death, fighting violent hand-to-hand combat either on horse or on foot.*"
>
> —Byzantine emperor Maurice on the Slavs, ca. 800

Byzantine Strategy Against the Slavs and Avars Read a Byzantine emperor's military analysis of the Slavs and how to defeat them.

Persian and Muslim Invasions

Italy and southeastern Europe were not the only regions where the Eastern empire was under attack. Late in the sixth century, the empire of Persia, continuing its feud with Rome (p. 135), launched an assault on Justinian's successors. In a series of vicious wars, the Persians conquered both Syria and Egypt but were eventually driven out in 630. But both sides were so exhausted that the empire's territories in Syria, Palestine, Egypt, and North Africa, as well as Persia's entire empire, fell to the Arabs a short while later. By 650, all that was left to **Byzantium**—the present-day name for the changed and shrunken empire—was Anatolia, Constantinople and its outskirts, a few other coastal footholds in the Balkans, and its possessions in Italy and Sicily (see Map 9.1).

Byzantium
The present-day name for the changed and shrunken Eastern Roman Empire of Justinian's successors.

The Survival of Byzantium

The Byzantine rulers were upheld, in spite of all disasters, by a mystical faith in themselves and their empire. Though ethnically Greek, they still thought of themselves as Roman emperors. But their Rome, they believed, was not a passing "Earthly City" as it had been considered earlier by Augustine (p. 143). Rather, it was a true reflection on earth of the Heavenly City of God, which would never perish. And as rulers of that city, the emperors—like Constantine and Theodosius before them—saw themselves as rulers of the Church as well as the state. The Byzantine emperors appointed the patriarch of Constantinople and intervened in disputes over belief and the enforcement of clerical discipline.

Meanwhile, the Roman popes had no emperor to rely on or contend with, and in and around the shrunken city of Rome, they wielded power as rulers as well as bishops. The popes' decisions on issues of faith and their guidance on the conduct of religious ceremonies were accepted throughout the West, though as yet they had very little power over the appointment and behavior of the clergy. As successors of Peter, they claimed the same authority in the East as well—a claim that Constantinople rejected. The Eastern or Greek Church and the Western or Latin Church, as they were coming to be called, still saw each other as part of one and the same all-embracing Christian Church, but they were beginning to drift apart.

Justinian's successors managed to restructure the government to support the armies and navies that would enable them to hold on to what was left of their empire, and they even regained lost territories in the Balkans and eastern Anatolia (Map 9.1). Warfare and diplomacy held off Asiatic nomads, Slav barbarians, and Muslim conquerors. And Persians and Arabs, Slavs and Avars were still brought to a halt before the gates of Constantinople, which stood on a peninsula projecting from the European side of the Bosporus and was defended by massive walls against attack by both land and sea (see photo on page 158). It was not until the eleventh century that the empire again began to shrink, and it took until 1453 for Constantinople to fall to another nation of Muslim invaders, the Turks (pp. 213, 214, 251). Meanwhile, Byzantium was still the wealthiest and

URBS CONSTANTINOPOLITANA NOVA ROMA.

>> **"The City of Constantinople, New Rome"** Landward and seaward walls protect the city on its triangular spit of land. An equestrian statue of Constantine commemorates the city's founder. The dome of a church (predating Justinian's as yet unbuilt Hagia Sophia) dominates the urban landscape. This illustration, from a list compiled about A.D. 400 showing the locations of Roman government agencies and army units, presents an image of Constantinople as an impregnable fortress of Christianity and empire that would remain truthful for many centuries. Bodleian Library Oxford/The Art Archive

best organized of European states—a model of civilization for eastern European peoples, and in spite of religious differences, a source of cultural inspiration for western Europe.

Byzantine Culture and Architecture

Byzantium inherited from the Hellenistic past the internationally dominant Greek culture of the eastern Mediterranean, and even when the Greeks lost their cultural leadership to the new, Arab-dominated civilization of Islam, Byzantium continued to serve as the main custodian of Greek culture, pagan as well as Christian. Much of the literature of ancient Greece was conserved in archives and libraries, and Byzantine scholars added their own commentaries and summations. Greek learning continued to serve as the foundation of education. Though Justinian closed the schools of Athens, one of the last outposts of pagan philosophy, a great Christian university grew up in Constantinople.

Byzantium also contributed to the education of western Europe. All through the Middle Ages, there was constant interchange between East and West—by way of clergy, warriors, pilgrims, traders, and scholars. There was not much love lost between "the Greeks" and "the Franks," as they called each other. But right down to the Renaissance (Chapter 16),

 **The Glory of Byzantium** (http://www.metmuseum.org/explore/Byzantium/byzhome.html) Learn more about the art of Byzantium.

western European scholars looked to Byzantium for knowledge of Greek language and literature, and in the Middle Ages, many western European artists and architects looked up to those of Byzantium as their masters.

Visitors from the West were dazzled by the artistic treasures and the magnificent churches and palaces of Constantinople, the "city of cities." Above all, they were impressed by Justinian's mighty cathedral of Hagia Sophia (Holy Wisdom) with its huge main dome resting on four giant arches (see photo). Never had so large a dome been supported in this way until the Greek architect-mathematicians Anthemius of Tralles and Isidorus of Miletus designed this structure. The dome was described by the historian of Justinian's reign, Procopius of Caesarea, as "marvelous in its grace, but . . . utterly terrifying. For it somehow seems to float in the air with no firm support, but to be poised aloft to the peril of those inside it."

Hagia Sophia: The Heart of Constantinople Read another description of how Hagia Sophia appeared to sixth-century viewers.

Built in only six years' time under the urging of the impatient emperor, Hagia Sophia is one of the world's architectural wonders—proof of the Eastern empire's exceptional cultural vitality, engineering skill, and religious commitment. The building inspires, in its own way, the sense of marvel and holy mystery that the cathedrals of Europe were to achieve centuries later, and it has served as a model for countless religious buildings—both churches and mosques.

The Cathedral of Hagia Sophia Justinian's cathedral, later a mosque and now a museum, was the work of two architect-mathematicians, Anthemius of Tralles and Isidorus of Miletus. Using their knowledge of the geometry of curves, they designed a dome supported by arches high in the air that remained a model for both church-builders and mosque-builders for more than a thousand years.

LO³ A New Monotheism and a New International Civilization: Islam

At the same time that Rome and Byzantium were beginning to evolve different versions of European civilization, the largest single section of the old Roman Empire, its lands in northern Africa and on the eastern shore of the Mediterranean, developed in an entirely different direction. This region became the seat of a new and different form of civilization as a result of another great invasion—this time, from Arabia. The Arabs brought a militant faith and succeeded in building a brilliant and distinctive culture—both known by the name of Islam.

The Arabs and Muhammad

At the opening of the seventh century, most of the Arabs were nomadic tribespeople. Because they conquered and adapted to

> *"Built in only six years' time under the urging of the impatient emperor, Hagia Sophia is one of the world's architectural wonders—proof of the Eastern empire's exceptional cultural vitality, engineering skill, and religious commitment."*

an advanced civilization, there is a parallel between their role in the Mediterranean world and that of the Germanic invaders in western Europe. But the Arabs, instead of being converted by the Christians they conquered, were fired with a monotheistic zeal of their own, and most of the peoples they overcame eventually accepted their version of the one truth about the one God.

Muhammad, the founder of the faith, was born about 570 in Mecca, a trading center near the western coast of Arabia. He apparently grew up with no formal education, but he did learn something of the teachings of Judaism and Christianity, which had sifted down from Palestine and Syria. When he was about forty years old, he turned from his life as a merchant to become a hermit. Spending days in solitary meditation, he began to experience visions that he believed to be direct revelations from God—in Arabic, *Allah*. In one of these visions, the archangel Gabriel directed him to carry these messages to his people, and from that time on, he abandoned all other activities.

Most Arabs, however, were polytheists, and Muhammad's insistence that "there is no God but Allah, and Muhammad is his Prophet" proved offensive to them. He became especially unpopular in the city of Mecca, where a building known as the Kaaba housed images and a black stone considered holy by the Arabs. When he denounced this shrine, he was branded a blasphemer and a disturber of the peace. Faced with this opposition, Muhammad left Mecca in 622 and fled northward to Yathrib (later renamed Medina, "City of the Prophet"). This event marks the beginning of the Islamic calendar and is known as the **Hegira**.

The Constitution of Medina: Muslims and Jews at the Dawn of Islam Read a selection of Muhammad's rules for the community of believers in Medina.

In Medina, Muhammad was able to preach freely, and his band of disciples began to grow and to follow his example of preaching complete submission to the will of Allah as revealed to him. The Arabic word for submission is *islam*, and the word for one who has submitted is *muslim*. These are the terms used to identify, respectively, the faith and the believer.

Like Abraham and Moses, the Israelite servants of the one God whom Muhammad revered, he was a warrior and ruler as well as a prophet. He was persuaded through revelation that the use of force, if necessary, against unbelievers was one of many forms of religious "striving" (in Arabic, *jihad*) that were approved by Allah. (Other forms of *jihad* included everything from unwarlike efforts to convert unbelievers, through the struggle for justice in society, to the individual's striving for personal righteousness.) Soon Muhammad was

caliph
The successor to Muhammad as leader of the Islamic religion and people.

caliphate
The empire of the caliph.

mosque
A Muslim house of worship.

Koran
The sacred book of Islam (the scholarly letter-for-letter version of the spelling in the Arabic alphabet, *Qur'an*, is also used in English today).

Five Pillars of Faith
The fundamental religious duties of Muslims, as stated in the Koran.

minaret
A slender, free-standing tower next to a mosque from which a muezzin (crier) calls the faithful to prayer.

leading his followers in successful warfare against the Meccans, and the Prophet returned to Mecca in triumph. He ordered that all the images in the city be destroyed, but he preserved the Black Stone as a symbol of the new faith. Attracted by his militant methods and by his vision of bringing the whole world under Islam, the desert tribes began to flock to his leadership. By the time of his death in 632, he had extended his personal control over a large portion of Arabia.

The Arab Empire

Once the pattern of expansion had been established, the movement spread with lightning speed. Muhammad had left no son to inherit his mantle, so his disciples chose a successor (**caliph**) from among his close relatives. Family connection with Muhammad was accepted from the beginning as a mark of political legitimacy, in the same way that Jewish Temple priests had claimed descent from Moses's brother Aaron.

Under the first two caliphs, Abu Bakr and Omar, the Arabs carried their holy war to neighboring lands. Commanders and warriors alike were driven on by a religious sense of mission and contempt of death, expansion helped hold together the recently united Arabs, and each victory brought hope of yet more conquests. Besides, the Arabs' main opponents, Byzantium and Persia, were weakened by their endless wars against each other, and Christian religious disputes were causing many bishops and ordinary believers in Egypt and Syria to turn against their rulers in Constantinople. Within a decade after Muhammad's death, the hard-riding Arab horsemen conquered Persia and took Egypt and Syria from the Byzantine Empire, and within a century, their empire (**caliphate**) (from the Arabic word for "successor" of the Prophet) stretched from Persia to Spain (Map 9.2).

Finally, Islam's warlike expansion came to a halt. In 718, Arab besiegers gave up a year-long blockade of Constantinople after suffering huge casualties from starvation and disease; in 732 a Muslim raiding army that had moved far into the Frankish kingdom was intercepted and forced to retreat (p. 167). But where the warriors stopped, the traders took over. By 1000, Arab merchants, looking in distant lands for exotic goods to bring to the centers of the Islamic world, had spread the religion of

Islam: Empire of Faith/Jewels of Architecture (http://www.pbs.org/empires/islam/featuresjewels.html) Take a video tour of Islamic architecture.

the Prophet to gold- and ivory-producing kingdoms in western Africa, to the spice islands of East Asia, and to empire-building Turkish nomads in Central Asia.

Though determined to drive out paganism and eager to convert all peoples to their faith, the Arabs offered toleration to Jews and Christians (upon payment of a special tax). Within a few generations, however, most Christians in the conquered territories embraced Islam. There were legal and social advantages in becoming Muslims, and the religion appealed to many Christians. The conversion was to prove lasting; except for Spain, the lands that fell to the Arabs are still lands of the **mosque**.

Islam and Christianity

What were the teachings of this new faith? A radical monotheist, Muhammad never claimed divinity for himself but insisted only that he was the last and greatest of Allah's prophets, for Allah was the same God that Jews and Christians worshiped and who had already spoken through prophets from Abraham to Jesus. Instead of claiming that he was introducing a new religion, he insisted that his work was the fulfillment of the old, just as Jesus had claimed that his work was the fulfillment of Judaism. His message, as recorded in the **Koran**, might be viewed in this light as a sequel to the Old and New Testaments. But in the same way that Christians believed that the Jews had gone astray from the one truth about the one God, Muslims believed that Christians had also gone astray. From the Muslim viewpoint, Christians were worshipers of three or more divine beings, who endlessly wrangled over doctrine and had tainted Jesus's message with pagan superstition.

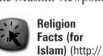
Religion Facts (for Islam) (http://www.religionfacts.com/islam/index.htm) Learn more about the Muslim faith.

The central spiritual appeal of Islam is its stress on the oneness of God. Most of the Koran is given over to describing and praising Allah, who alone is the supreme reality, all-knowing and all-powerful. The true believer must submit unreservedly to Allah's will as expressed through the Prophet. This can be done simply and without doubting; unlike Christianity, Islam raised no questions concerning the nature of God (pp. 145–146).

Similarly, there were no arguments over what made up the sacred canon (authorized holy books). Muhammad's revelations were memorized by his disciples and written down in final form shortly after his death; this original Koran, in Arabic, remains the only version studied by Muslims, whatever their native language. Shorter than the New Testament, it is a poetic book, which millions have memorized (hence its name, which in Arabic means "Recitation").

Islamic Social and Ethical Ideas

Muhammad's ethical teachings are in the tradition of Judaism and Christianity, and the Koran repeats many of the proverbs and stories of the Bible. Because the Prophet had a practical mind, the model life that he described is within the reach of the faithful. While stressing love, kindness, and compassion, he did not insist on self-denial beyond the powers of most people. He

Map 9.2 The Expansion of Islam

The swiftest Muslim conquests came in the century after Muhammad, when Islam united under its rule nearly all the lands once held by Alexander and nearly half the lands once held by Rome. Thereafter, resistance on the western and eastern fringes of Islam, as well as its own disputes and power struggles, slowed further expansion. All the same, a new world of religion and culture had come into being, stretching from Spain to the borders of India. © Cengage Learning

Interactive Map

saw no particular virtue, for instance, in sexual abstinence. He did, however, try to moderate the ancient practice of polygamy by declaring that a man should have no more than four wives at a time. No limit was set on the number of concubines a man might have. Though women possessed some property rights, Muslim society was (and is) a "man's world."

Still, in Islam, both men and women stand as equals before Allah—though in practice, religious scholars and holy men enjoy special respect and authority. There are no saints mediating between humans and God , and because there are no priests, there are no mysterious rites that only priests can perform. To increase the worshiper's concentration on Allah, statues and images are banned from Muslim art. In the mosque (from an Arabic word meaning "to worship"), there is nothing that resembles an idol.

Obligations of the Faithful

The religious duties of Muslims, known as the **Five Pillars of Faith,** are clearly stated in the Koran. The first is the familiar profession of belief, "There is no god but Allah, and Muhammad is his Prophet." By accepting and repeating these words, the convert is initiated into the faith.

Daily prayer—at dawn, midday, midafternoon, sunset, and nightfall—is the second duty. At the appointed hours, from atop slender **minarets** (towers), the muezzins (criers) call upon the

faithful to bow down, turn toward Mecca, and say the prayer in Arabic. The prayer itself usually includes the short opening verse of the Koran, praising Allah and asking for guidance along the "straight path." This formula is repeated many times each day. The only public religious service is the midday prayer on Fridays, which must be attended by all adult males (and is closed to females). Inside the mosque, standing in self-ordered rows, the congregation prays aloud in unison; then the leader, a layman, delivers a brief sermon. After the service, normal everyday activities may be resumed.

The third duty is giving to the poor. At first, almsgiving was practiced as an individual act of charity, but it gradually developed into a standard payment. In the Islamic states, the money was collected through regular taxation and was used to help the needy and to build and maintain the mosques. The usual amount was one-fortieth of the individual's income.

Fasting, the fourth pillar of faith, ordinarily is confined to *Ramadan,* the ninth month of the Muslim lunar (moon-based) calendar (p. 16). It was during Ramadan that Allah gave the Koran to the archangel Gabriel for revelation to Muhammad. For thirty days, no food or drink may be taken between sunrise and sunset. Fasting, which was not practiced by the Arabs before Muhammad, was adopted from Jewish and Christian custom.

Finally, every Muslim who can afford it must make a pilgrimage to the Holy City of Mecca at some time during his or her

A New Monotheism and a New International Civilization: Islam **161**

EUROPEANS BENEFITED IN A NUMBER OF WAYS FROM CONTACT WITH ISLAM:

- Islam spread in every direction from its Arabian origin, forming an intercontinental region of trade and travel that linked the peoples beyond its borders more closely than before. Europe thereby became part of a group of civilizations that stretched all the way to China and Japan.

- Arab traders traveled between Spain and western Africa and between Egypt, Syria, China, and the East Indies; as a result, exotic goods came within reach of merchants from Europe.

- Scholarly and scientific discoveries from other civilizations reached Europe through Islam as well. For example, what we now call Arabic numerals came to Europe from India by way of Islam, and this innovation freed mathematicians from the awkward Roman system.

- Muslim scholars also made advances in knowledge that came to be known in Europe. In the field of medicine, a noteworthy contribution was the *Canon* of Avicenna (ibn-Sina), a summary of the medical knowledge of his time (eleventh century).

- Great centers of learning sprang up in the Islamic world, notably at Cairo (Egypt), Toledo (Spain), and Palermo (Sicily), and western European scholars made their way to Spain and Sicily. From Arabic translations—retranslated into Latin, the scholarly language of western Europe, by Spanish and Sicilian experts—the scholars recovered many of the treasures of Greek philosophy and science that had been forgotten in western Europe for centuries.

- Western artisans and builders were also impressed by what they discovered in Muslim countries. Muslim architects devised a graceful variation on the traditional rounded Roman arch that was also a technical improvement by making it pointed (see photo on page 163)—a form that was taken up by their western European colleagues to produce some of the noblest Christian houses of worship ever built, the Gothic cathedrals.

---

life. Over the centuries, this practice has had a unifying effect on the different peoples that embrace Islam. Rich and poor, black and white, Easterner and Westerner—all come together in the Holy City.

In the early stages of Muslim history, a sixth duty was required of all able-bodied men: participation in *jihad*, in the sense of war against unbelievers. It was this requirement that sparked the first explosive conquests of the Arabs. Each caliph believed it his obligation to expand the frontiers of Islam and thus reduce the infidel "territory of war."

The Qur'an: Muslim Devotion to God Read the description of the Last Judgment from the Koran.

The Five Pillars of Faith are only the minimum requirements of Islam. In all things, true believers must seek to do the will of Allah as revealed in the Koran. They must also believe that God has *predestined* the ultimate fate of all humankind, to be revealed in the Last Judgment. Muhammad left vivid descriptions of hell and heaven. Unbelievers will burn eternally in a great pool of fire; believers who die in sin will also suffer there for a time but will finally be released. In the end, all Muslims (male and female)—who have accepted Allah—will enjoy the pleasures of paradise. Muhammad, drawing from Persian sources, pictured paradise in sensual terms as an oasis of delight, with sparkling beverages, luscious fruits, and dark-eyed beauties.

Religious and Political Divisions

In spite of the comparative simplicity of Muhammad's teachings, they were open to conflicting interpretations as the years passed. The major disagreements arose over the principle of succession to the caliphate, religious doctrines, and the proper way of life for Muslims.

The main division was between the **Sunni** and the **Shia**, a division that still disturbs the Muslim world. The Sunni (from the Arabic word for "example"—followers of the example of the Prophet) were associated with the Umayyad dynasty, which seized the caliphate in 661 and moved the capital of Islam from Medina to Damascus, in Syria. They accepted as valid certain traditions that had grown up outside the Koran. On the other hand, the Shia (from the Arabic

> *"Lo! the Day of Decision is appointed—the day when there shall be a blowing of the trumpet, and ye shall come in troops, and the heavens shall be opened, and be full of gates, and the mountains shall be removed, and turn into [mist]."*
>
> —from the Koran

The Ibn Tulun Mosque, Cairo Pointed arches, more stable than round ones of the same height, were a feature of Muslim architecture that developed from about A.D. 800 in what is now Iraq. They were used in the courtyard of this mosque, built on the orders of an Egyptian ruler, Ahmed ibn Tulun, shortly before A.D. 900. Italian traders visiting Cairo would have brought word home of this new style of arch construction, so that Ibn Tulun's mosque is an ancestor of medieval Gothic cathedrals.

for "followers"—followers of their founder, Muhammad's cousin Ali), held strictly to the Koran and insisted that only descendants of the Prophet could become caliphs. The Abbasid family, who were Shia Muslims, gained power in 750 and moved the capital again, this time to the new city of Baghdad (see Map 9.2) on the River Tigris in Mesopotamia.

After the eighth century, the Arab empire began to break up. The ousted Umayyad family established itself in Spain and broke off political connections with Baghdad. Similarly, a descendant of Muhammad's daughter Fatima later declared himself an independent caliph in control of Egypt, Syria, and

Morocco. Provinces in Arabia and India also fell away, until by 1000 the Abbasid ruler controlled only the area surrounding Baghdad.

In spite of these religious and political divisions, Muslim civilization reached its height in the ninth and tenth centuries. The Islamic achievements of this period built on earlier Greek, Syrian, and Persian traditions. But out of this blend there emerged a distinctive new international culture that replaced those of Greece and Persia in the lands stretching from northern Africa to the borders of India, and eventually spread, with Islam itself, to a vastly larger area.

The Muslim Legacy to the West

The rise of Islam was almost as important an event for European peoples who remained Christian as for those of Africa and Asia who actually became Muslims. The Islamization of North Africa and much of the eastern Mediterranean lands had the effect, for many centuries, of confining Christianity, and many traditions of Greco-Roman civilization, to the territory of Europe. The Christian European peoples now lived on the fringes of a mighty intercontinental civilization that was inspired by an opposing version of the one truth about the one God, and that included many more lands with ancient traditions of civilization, and many more centers of wealth and power, than half-barbarian Europe.

 Córdoba (History and Culture) (http://www.muslimheritage.com/topics/default.cfm?ArticleID=454) Learn about Córdoba, the largest city in medieval Europe after Constantinople.

It was no wonder, then, that for Europe, Islam was a formidable enemy. For a thousand years, Christians and Muslims fought bitter wars against each other. The warlike prowess of medieval European society was steeled by the continual conflict; European states such as the Frankish kingdom and Byzantium devoted much of their energies to it; and the struggle with Islam eventually led to European overseas exploration and empire building (Chapter 15). Yet Islam was also a neighbor from which Europe benefited in many peaceful ways, and the rise of Islam furthered the renewal of civilization in Europe.

 Listen to a synopsis of Chapter 9.

> "*The rise of Islam was almost as important an event for European peoples who remained Christian as for those of Africa and Asia who actually became Muslims.*"

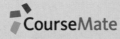

CHAPTER 10

EUROPE TAKES SHAPE, 700–1000

LEARNING OBJECTIVES

AFTER READING THIS CHAPTER, YOU SHOULD BE ABLE TO DO THE FOLLOWING:

LO¹ Trace the rise of the Carolingian dynasty and explain the significance of the Carolingian Renaissance and the coronation of Charlemagne.

LO² Describe the collapse of Charlemagne's empire and the rise of western Europe and Byzantine eastern Europe in the ninth and tenth centuries.

" By 1000, civilization had spread throughout Europe, and the three-thousand-year-old European barbarian way of life had come to an end—the victim of its own success. "

Shortly after A.D. 700, the renewal of European civilization in the West began with the rise to power of a new dynasty in the Frankish kingdom, the Carolingians. In the Frankish ruling partnership of kings, nobles, and the Church, the Carolingians made themselves very much the senior partners. Around A.D. 800, the Carolingian warrior-king Charlemagne was able to conquer barbarian peoples in central Europe, encourage a revival of education and scholarship among the clergy, and take the title of Roman emperor. In the end, Charlemagne's empire fell apart, but the rulers of its easternmost section soon became powerful in their own right, as the Holy Roman emperors.

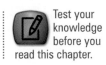
Test your knowledge before you read this chapter.

Meanwhile, the renewal also got under way in the East, where Byzantium regained some of the ground it had lost to Arab, Slav, and nomad invaders. Where it could not reconquer, it began to project its influence well beyond its frontiers by converting many eastern European peoples to Christianity—sometimes on its own initiative, and sometimes at the plea of their increasingly powerful rulers.

What do you think?

The popes acted in the best interest of the Church when they allied with the Frankish kings.

Strongly Disagree						Strongly Agree
1	2	3	4	5	6	7

During the era of renewal, barbarian and nomadic peoples, notably the Norsemen and Hungarians, continued to raid, conquer, and settle in lands that had once belonged to Rome or where Roman influence had already spread. As with earlier invasions, however, what enabled these peoples to make such inroads was the fact that they were already growing in organization and skills, and they ended by adopting the way of life of the peoples they attacked. By 1000, civilization had

Scala/Art Resource, NY

≪ Charlemagne The mighty Frankish ruler appears on his coffin enthroned, and only a little lower than Christ. Churchmen stand respectfully beside him: Pope Leo III (left), who crowned him Emperor of the Romans in A.D. 800, and Archbishop Turpin of Reims, his warrior-companion in medieval epic. The Holy Roman Emperor Frederick II had the coffin made in 1215, but Charlemagne himself would probably have been pleased with this image. Certainly this is how medieval emperors, competing with the popes for supremacy in Western Christendom, wanted to see him.

Carolingian
The Frankish dynasty founded by Charles Martel in the eighth century, as successors to the Merovingians.

spread throughout Europe, and the three-thousand-year-old European barbarian way of life had come to an end—the victim of its own success (pp. 46–49).

Because they were conquerors rather than conquered, however, most of the once-barbarian peoples formed separate kingdoms that were independent of the older civilized lands. As a result, the renewed European civilization was one of many vigorous ethnic cultures and many powerful competing states. And it renewed itself in two variant forms, named after the different branches of ancient traditions and Christianity that inspired them—the "Latin" West and the "Greek" East.

LO¹ The Carolingians

By A.D. 700, the kingdom of the Franks, once the most powerful state in western Europe, was seemingly falling apart. It was divided among rival kings of the Merovingian dynasty, each controlled by a "mayor of the palace" (head of the royal household) who wielded whatever government authority was left, while competing factions among the nobles scrambled for wealth and power (pp. 154-155).

 The Decline of the Merovingians Read a critical description of the powerless Merovingian kings.

Finally, however, one particular family that had become exceptionally wealthy and powerful in the continual factional struggles gained the hereditary position of one and only mayor of the palace throughout the Frankish kingdom. Like the kingship, the mayoralty was liable to be divided between heirs, but in 714, an out-of-wedlock son of the family by the name of Charles laid claim to the position and won it in several years of civil war. He thereby became the ancestor of a new dynasty, the **Carolingians** (from the Frankish word for "children of Charles").

The Carolingians rebuilt the Frankish kingdom, and although their power melted away in its turn, their achievements outlasted them. It was they who began the rise of western Europe to become the heartland of Western civilization.

The Rise of the Carolingian Dynasty

Charles was a ruthless and warlike ruler who went down in history as Charles Martel ("Charles the Hammer"). But in the power struggles of Frankish warrior-landowners it was important to reward followers as well as to crush opponents. Rewarding followers meant giving them gifts of land—but not from one's own family possessions, the main source of a ruler's wealth and power. Some of the land could come from defeated opponents,

CHRONOLOGY

732	Charles Martel forces an Arab army to retreat from Frankish kingdom
751	Pope Zachary approves the transfer of royal power from the Merovingian king to Pepin, a Carolingian
756	Donation of Pepin seals the alliance between the Frankish kingdom and the papacy
768–814	Reign of Charlemagne
780	Charlemagne sets up a palace school in Aachen
800	Pope Leo III crowns Charlemagne "Emperor of the Romans"
CA. 800	Charlemagne conquers the barbarian peoples in central Europe; Norsemen begin raids along coastline of western Europe; Byzantium regains control of Greece, begins to push against Slavs and Arabs
843	Treaty of Verdun divides the Frankish kingdom among Charlemagne's three grandsons
871	King Alfred leads the Anglo-Saxons of England against the Danish Viking invaders
911	Last direct descendant of Charlemagne dies in eastern Frankish kingdom
962	Otto I of eastern Frankish kingdom is crowned emperor in Rome; beginning of Holy Roman Empire
987	Hugh Capet replaces last Carolingian in western Frankish kingdom (France)
988	Prince Vladimir of Kiev converts to Christianity
1000	Viking journeys across Atlantic to Iceland, Greenland, and "Vinland" (North America)
1066	Norman conquest of England

but to be truly generous, it was necessary to find some additional source of property to distribute, and Charles found it in lands belonging to the Church.

Charles was a generous donator of land to favored monasteries, but bishops and abbots often belonged to noble families that he distrusted. Surely, he felt, it was right for him to take Church property that might be misused for a bad political purpose, namely to oppose him, and use it for a good political purpose, namely to strengthen him as a Christian ruler. Charles was not the first powerful believer to think this way, and he would not be the last. But he commandeered Church resources on an unprecedented scale—not only to reward supporters, but also to give land to foot soldiers who served him in peace and war (see photo on page 168).

Not long after Charles took power, he faced a historic challenge—and a historic opportunity—when Arab invaders from Spain took over some of the kingdom's southern borderlands. In 732, an Arab army moved out of the occupied territory on a large-scale raid far north into the Frankish kingdom. Charles intercepted them near the town of Tours and forced them to retreat. The Christian nobles of the south, who had been practically independent rulers of their lands, accepted the authority of their rescuer, and in hard campaigning over the next twenty years, the invaders were forced back into Spain. The expansion of Islam had come to a halt, and the whole of the Frankish kingdom was under a single effective rule—though the rule was that of a mayor of the palace who called himself "chief and army commander of the Franks," and not that of a king.

> "*Except for his empty title, and an uncertain allowance for his subsistence, . . . there was nothing that the king could call his own, unless it were the income from a single farm, and that a very small one, where he made his home, and where such servants as were needful to wait on him constituted his scanty household. When he went anywhere he traveled in a wagon drawn by a yoke of oxen, with a rustic oxherd for charioteer.*"
>
> —Einhard, on the last Merovingian kings, ca. 825

The Alliance of the Franks and the Papacy

Charles Martel's son, Pepin, decided that the time had come for the actual power in the kingdom to be recognized as the legal power. But it was not a simple matter to take the crown from the Merovingian descendants of Clovis. Though they were only figureheads, they were respected as the rightful possessors of the kingship, and all the powerful men of the kingdom—bishops, nobles, and mayors of the palace—had sworn loyalty to them.

In search of a way to take over the kingship that would be seen as legitimate (rightful and lawful), in 751 Pepin turned to the generally accepted highest religious authority, Pope Zachary. For a pope to be consulted on a transfer of royal power actually widened the papacy's authority, and a grateful new Frankish king might be a valuable ally. With papal approval, the last Merovingian king was sent to live out his life as a monk, the assembled Frankish nobles chose Pepin to replace him, and Pepin was anointed (holy oil placed on him) by Archbishop Boniface of Fulda, a monk and missionary in the kingdom's eastern lands who was close to both Pepin and the pope.

This was the first time in the history of any western European kingdom that a king began his reign with a solemn religious ceremony. The ceremony was patterned after the inauguration of Byzantine emperors, which in turn imitated the consecration of the Israelite kings at God's command as described in the Old Testament. It is not certain that Pepin also underwent coronation (placing a crown on his head) like the Israelite and Byzantine rulers. But against the hereditary legitimacy of the Merovingians, Pepin certainly now claimed a special holiness and authority from God. Both coronation and anointing soon became the normal inauguration ceremony for kings throughout Europe. In this way, kings proclaimed that their power came from God, though in the Middle Ages, the popes always stressed that this divine authority was conferred by the Church.

A few years later, Pope Stephen II came in person to the Frankish court and anointed Pepin as well as his two sons—an additional precaution to make sure that the Carolingians could legitimately continue as a royal dynasty. In return, Stephen won promises of military help against the papacy's Italian neighbors, the Lombards, whose king was trying to take over the lands around Rome that the popes ruled (p. 157). Accordingly, in 756 Pepin crossed the Alps, defeated the Lombards, and transferred a strip of territory right across central Italy to the governing authority of the pope (Map 10.1 on page 169).

By the so-called Donation of Pepin, the popes acquired a legal basis for authority over a much wider region than before, and they ruled their new territory for over a thousand years—until the unification of Italy in 1870. But at about the same time as Pepin's gift, the papacy began to claim far wider power. The papal court produced a document that had supposedly been issued by the Roman emperor Constantine when he left Rome for a new capital in the East (p. 138). In the document, Constantine made over to the popes the rule of the entire West, acknowledged their supremacy over the entire Church, and recognized their superior dignity to emperors. In the fifteenth century, the Donation of Constantine, as it came to be called, was shown to be a forgery (pp. 292-293), but as late as the sixteenth century, popes used it as a basis for claiming power over emperors and kings.

Meanwhile, however, the Donation of Pepin sealed the alliance between the Frankish kingdom and the papacy, the two

>> Carolingian Foot Soldiers
A picture in the Utrecht Psalter, a book of psalms made in a northern French monastery about A.D. 830, illustrates Psalm 27: "Though an army encamp against me, my heart shall not fear." Soldiers with spears and round shields, some helmeted, some bareheaded, but otherwise unarmored, spill out of tents and brandish their weapons at a church, where a priest welcomes a believer to take sanctuary. Charles Martel's soldiers would have looked much the same a century before. Bibliotheek der Rijksuniversiteit, Utrecht

strongest forces in the West. The outcome of this alliance was the "Roman" empire of Charles the Great.

Charlemagne

Charles, Pepin's son and Charles Martel's grandson, was a towering figure, celebrated in history and legend under the name of Charlemagne—the French version of "Charles the Great." Through the force of his personality and the challenges of a forty-six-year reign, he contributed mightily to the evolution of western Europe.

Charlemagne (http://www .youtube.com/ watch?v=qJBKGVR dhy8) Watch a short film on Charlemagne's legacy.

Descendant of Frankish barbarian invaders, warrior against heathens and Muslims, and holder of the revived office of emperor, Charlemagne personified the merging of Germanic, Christian, and Roman elements in western European civilization.

Conquests: Italy, Germany, Spain

Charlemagne was almost constantly at war. Ruthless and cruel in battle, he fought not only for territory and spoils but also for what he considered the higher goals of Christianity and universal order. As a result, he expanded the boundaries of both Christianity and Frankish power outward in all directions by military force.

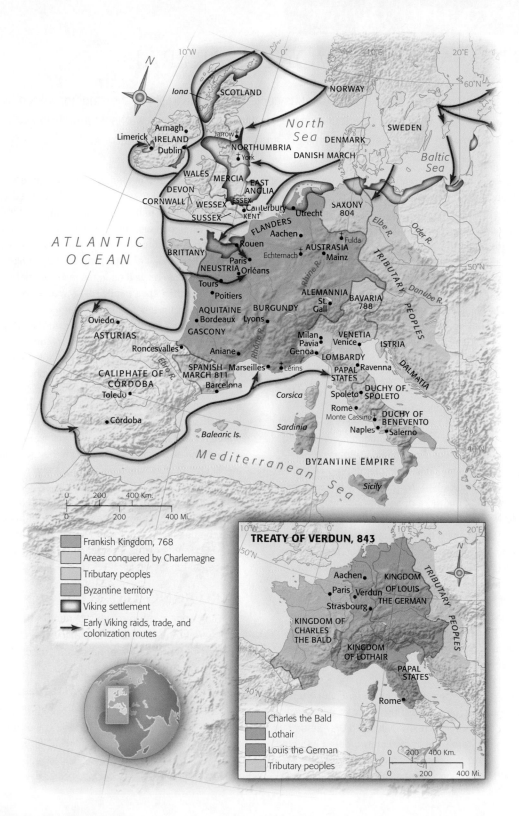

Map 10.1 **Charlemagne's Empire**

Charlemagne ruled far less territory than the original Roman emperors, but he widened the strip of Christian lands that stretched between the Islamic world and the pagan barbarians and nomads of northern and eastern Europe. Furthermore, his empire was twice the size of contemporary Byzantium. Even after his death and his empire's gradual collapse, the new boundaries of Christendom did not shrink, and the balance of power within Christendom did not swing back to the East. © Cengage Learning

Interactive Map

CHARLEMAGNE: A WORD PORTRAIT

This description of Charlemagne's behavior and habits comes from a biography of the emperor written by a well-educated courtier, Einhard, who knew Charlemagne well. It gives an intimate view of someone who seemed larger than life in his own time and was celebrated in history and legend for centuries afterward.

Charles was large and robust, of commanding stature and excellent proportions, for it appears that he measured in height seven times the length of his own foot. The top of his head was round, his eyes large and animated, his nose somewhat long. He had a fine head of gray hair, and his face was bright and pleasant; so that, whether standing or sitting, he showed great presence and dignity. Although his neck was thick and rather short, and his belly too prominent, still the good proportions of his limbs concealed these defects. His walk was firm, and the whole carriage of his body was manly. His voice was clear, but not so strong as his frame would have led one to expect. . . .

He took constant exercise in riding and hunting, which was natural for a Frank, since scarcely any nation can be found to equal them in these pursuits. . . .

He wore the dress of his native country, that is, the Frankish; [and] he thoroughly disliked the dress of foreigners, however fine; and he never put it on except at Rome. . . .

In his eating and drinking he was temperate; more particularly so in his drinking, for he had the greatest abhorrence of drunkenness in anybody, but more especially in himself and his companions. He was unable to abstain from food for any length of time, and often complained that fasting was injurious to him. On the other hand, he very rarely feasted, only on great festive occasions, when there were very large gatherings. The daily service of his table consisted of only four dishes in addition to the roast meat, which the hunters used to bring in on spits, and of which he partook more freely than of any other food.

While he was dining he listened to music or reading. History and the deeds of men of old were most often read. He derived much pleasure from the works of St. Augustine, especially from his book called *The City of God*. . . .

While he was dressing and binding on his sandals, he would receive his friends; and also, if the count of the palace announced that there was any case which could only be settled by his decision, the suitors were immediately ordered into his presence, and he heard the case and gave judgment as if sitting in court. And this was not the only business that he used to arrange at that time, for he also gave orders for whatever had to be done on that day by any officer or servant.

He was ready and fluent in speaking, and able to express himself with great clearness. He did not confine himself to his native tongue, but took pains to learn foreign languages, acquiring such knowledge of Latin that he could make an address in that language as well as in his own. Greek he could better understand than speak. Indeed, he was so polished in speech that he might have passed for a learned man.

He was an ardent admirer of the liberal arts, and greatly revered their professors, whom he promoted to high honors. In order to learn grammar, he attended the lectures of the aged Peter of Pisa, a deacon; and for other branches he chose as his preceptor Albinus, otherwise called Alcuin, also a deacon,— a Saxon by race, from Britain, the most learned man of the day, with whom the king spent much time in learning rhetoric and logic, and more especially astronomy. He learned the art of determining the dates upon which the movable festivals of the Church fall, and with deep thought and skill most carefully calculated the courses of the planets.

Charles also tried to learn to write, and used to keep his tablets and writing book under the pillow of his couch, that when he had leisure he might practice his hand in forming letters; but he made little progress in this task, too long deferred and begun too late in life.

EXPLORING THE SOURCE

1. Biographers often make the people they write about seem better than they actually were. Does Einhard's portrayal of Charlemagne seem "touched up" or lifelike, and why?

2. Which of Charlemagne's activities described here had the greatest importance for the European future, and why?

Source: James Harvey Robinson, ed., *Readings in European History* (Boston: Ginn, 1904), 1:126–128.

Not all of Charlemagne's victims were pagans or Muslims. When advised by the pope that the Lombards were again threatening papal territory, he led his armies into Italy in 774 and broke the Lombard power. Now, he called himself king of the Lombards as well as king of the Franks, and gained control of northern Italy (see Map 10.1 on page 169).

His hardest campaigns, which lasted some thirty years, were against the Saxons. Some of these Germanic barbarians had crossed the North Sea to Britain in the fifth century, but the rest still lived on the northeastern boundary of the Frankish kingdom (see Map 10.1 on page 169). Unlike the Saxons in England, they clung stubbornly to their heathen religion. Charlemagne, encouraged by the Church, was determined to transform the Saxons into Christian subjects. He succeeded, but only after laying waste to Saxony, massacring countless captives, and deporting thousands of families in other parts of his empire. At last, the Saxons accepted Christianity, and the Frankish clergy moved in to establish bishoprics and monasteries.

Christianity at the Point of a Sword: The Saxon Settlement Read Charlemagne's harsh orders for dealing with the pagans of Saxony.

Farther south, Charlemagne attacked the nomadic nation of the Avars, who had invaded central and eastern Europe in the sixth century (p. 171). As with the Huns before them, the defeat of the Avars caused most of them to retreat and disperse, but they left behind Slavic tribes who had accompanied them on their campaigns of conquest. The eastern borderlands of Charlemagne's empire now marked an ethnic divide between Germanic and Slavic peoples that has lasted, more or less, to the present day.

Government: The Church and the State

Charlemagne concerned himself with domestic matters as well as with military campaigns. As a Christian ruler, he worked to strengthen the leadership of the Church and extend its activities. He did not intervene in matters of belief like the Byzantine rulers, but he appointed bishops and issued reform orders to the clergy. In addition, like every ruler since Constantine, he needed the help of the Church to reinforce his own power. He treated bishops and abbots as agents of his government and saw to it that they received copies of all his decrees.

Like earlier rulers back to late Roman times, Charlemagne governed through local officials called **counts** (p. 139). Each count represented the crown in a given region, his *county*. He presided over a court that met once a month, collected fines, and in time of war called out the warriors of his county. Sometimes,

> *"If any one of the race of the Saxons hereafter concealed among them shall have wished to hide himself unbaptized, and shall have scorned to come to baptism and shall have wished to remain a pagan, let him be punished by death."*
>
> —Charlemagne

count
In Charlemagne's time, a local official who represented the crown in a given region (county), presiding over the local court, collecting fines, and, in times of war, calling out the warriors of the county. Later, leading lords would take over these royal offices and convert them to hereditary titles.

duke
A royal official in charge of several counties; came to be a hereditary title.

for purposes of defense, several counties were grouped into a larger unit headed by a **duke**.

Counts and dukes traditionally came from the local landed nobility, and their positions were a valuable asset that they might use in the interest of their own families rather than in the service of the ruler. As a check on these officials, Charlemagne appointed royal inspectors, who visited all his territories once a year. Traveling in pairs (a nobleman and a clergyman), they investigated the performance of the counts and dukes and reported their findings to Charlemagne. By acting vigorously in response to this intelligence, he succeeded in holding together his far-flung empire.

Because there was no general system of taxation, Charlemagne had to draw most of his revenue from the crown lands, which he kept as his own. He held thousands of estates, most of them concentrated between Paris and the Rhine River (see Map 10.1) where his noble ancestors had first built up their power. Understandably, he was keenly interested in the efficiency with which his properties were managed, and he prepared detailed instructions for the guidance of his royal stewards (estate managers).

Inspecting the Imperial Domains: The Capitulary de Villis and an Estate Inventory Read Charlemagne's detailed instructions for managing his estates.

Art and Literature: The Carolingian Renaissance

Charlemagne made his capital at Aachen, which was surrounded by productive crown lands in the heart of the ancient Frankish territories. His palace chapel, which still stands, was the first important stone building to be erected north of the Alps after the fall of Rome (see photo). This fact in itself indicates the slow recovery of the West. The chapel was modeled on the church of San Vitale in Ravenna, a Byzantine outpost on Italy's east coast. The king was so impressed when he first saw San Vitale, with its dome supported on arches and its glistening mosaics, that he directed his builders to duplicate the plan in his own capital. Thus,

Bildarchiv Steffens/The Bridgeman Art Library

Charlemagne's Palace Chapel Built about A.D. 800 in Charlemagne's capital at Aachen in the west of present-day Germany, the chapel imitates an earlier Byzantine building in Italy. However, the designer was a Frankish architect, Odo of Metz, who evidently possessed sophisticated knowledge and skills. The chapel remained for many centuries an imperial shrine and a monument to the dream of a revived Roman Empire.

the art of Constantinople found its way to Aachen and the Frankish heartland.

Charlemagne was also concerned over the low level of education and scholarship in his realm and issued a decree instructing bishops and abbots to improve the training of the clergy. In Aachen itself, around 780, he set up a palace school that would become a center of intellectual activity.

  An Illustrated Guide to the Aachen Cathedral (http://www.sacred-destinations.com/germany/aachen-cathedral) Tour Charlemagne's chapel in Aachen.

The school came under the guidance of a monk named Alcuin, the leading scholar of his day, whom Charlemagne had called from the cathedral school of York, the finest in England. The students, like most of those who received any kind of schooling at the time, all belonged to the clergy. It was still unusual even for high nobles and rulers to be literate: Charlemagne himself only learned to read as an adult and never mastered the art of writing.

Alcuin trained a staff of expert scribes (copyists), who brought back the monastic tradition of reproducing ancient

BOTH THE POPE AND CHARLEMAGNE DESIRED CHARLEMAGNE'S CORONATION:

The Pope's Reasons

- The pope needed a strong protector in Italy, and there was also the possibility that the Franks themselves might prove dangerous.

- By crowning the emperor, the pope defined the relationship between the restored (Western) empire and the Church.

- Charlemagne received the crown from the hand of the pope, thereby putting the emperor under obligation to the papacy—and what the papacy had given, it also had a right to withdraw.

Charlemagne's Reasons

- Though Charlemagne may have been surprised by the circumstances of his crowning, there is no evidence that he was displeased.

- Under his rule, the Frankish state had become large and strong enough to lay claim to being a restored version of the Roman Empire. The coronation ceremony seemingly confirmed the truth of this idea.

- The coronation gave Charlemagne even greater power as a ruling figure. He could claim a special holiness and authority from God.

---

manuscripts. Most of the ancient Roman works that survive today have come down from Carolingian copies preserved in monastery libraries, and the easily readable handwritten letters designed by the Carolingian scribes still form the basis of today's lowercase letters. In copying, the monks naturally concentrated on Christian authors, but they also preserved pagan literature. Christian tradition encouraged the reading of pagan works that were morally and intellectually improving (pp. 143-144), but monks sometimes stretched the limits of what was allowed. Alongside works on philosophy and morals by the high-minded Cicero, they also carefully copied the how-to poems on seduction of the disreputable Ovid (p. 108).

Alcuin also established a course of studies, based on that of the monastic and cathedral schools, for selected young men of the Frankish nobility. The faculty of the school at Aachen was made up of distinguished scholars drawn from all over Europe. Many of their pupils became outstanding teachers themselves in other intellectual centers of present-day Germany and France. Though Charlemagne's empire barely survived him, the "Carolingian Renaissance" of the arts and scholarship provided a lasting impetus to the cultural development of Europe.

The Restoration of the "Roman Empire"

The most dramatic event of Charlemagne's rule was his coronation as "Charles Augustus, Emperor of the Romans." The event took place on Christmas Day, 800, while the Frankish king was attending Mass in Saint Peter's Basilica in Rome. Supposedly, he had not planned the coronation beforehand; his biographer, Einhard, reports that Pope Leo III, without warning, placed the crown on his head and declared him emperor.

The restored empire in fact had a very different structure from the old one. It was much smaller than the Western half of ancient Rome; missing were North Africa, Sicily, Spain, and Britain, though lands east of Rome's Rhine frontier were part of Charlemagne's realm. In Charlemagne's territories, there was no single citizenship, no unified law, no professional civil service, no standing army, and few cities, and the roads had fallen into disrepair.

Even so, Charlemagne's coronation was a truly historic event. There was, after all, another "Roman emperor" in Constantinople. At the time, an empress, Irene, was reigning over Byzantium, contrary to strict Roman tradition under which females were considered ineligible to rule. The pope may therefore have seized the moment to elevate Charlemagne to a "vacant" throne. But in any case, by accepting the title of emperor, Charlemagne was not just restoring the old empire. For the first time, a barbarian-descended western European king was claiming equality with, or even supremacy over, the Eastern emperors. Between the Byzantine East and the barbarian West, the balance was beginning to shift.

LO² The New Pattern of Europe

After Charlemagne died in 814, the promise of order and stability that his rule had held out faded in the dusk of renewed civil

serf
A peasant bound to work for a landowner—a lifelong hereditary status—as a condition for hereditary possession of a small farm.

vassal
A warrior who agreed to serve a greater warrior in exchange for secure possession of land.

wars and invasions. Yet, out of the collapse of his empire emerged the main features of medieval European civilization that would govern Western life and thought until the fifteenth century.

The Collapse of Charlemagne's Empire

One of the main reasons for the Carolingian rulers' success so far was that they had escaped having to follow the custom of sharing the mayoralty and then the kingship with other heirs. Both Pepin and Charlemagne had brothers, but Pepin's brother voluntarily became a monk and Charlemagne's brother conveniently died. Likewise, it was good for the dynasty's future that Charlemagne had only one surviving son, Louis. The new emperor reigned well enough to go down in history as Louis the Pious, but unfortunately for the dynasty, he had three sons who survived him. During his lifetime, he tried to break with custom and hand on most of his inheritance to his eldest son, Lothar, but this effort led to warfare with his younger sons.

Renewed Division and Renewed Invasions

Finally, after Louis's death, his sons arrived at a settlement that marked an important early stage in the development of the countries of western Europe. By the Treaty of Verdun (843), Lothar was confirmed as emperor and given a middle section of the empire stretching from present-day Holland to northern Italy. The second son, Louis, received the section east of the Rhine, which would one day become Germany. Charles, the youngest son, inherited the western section, the nucleus of France. But the treaty did not prevent continued fighting among Louis's sons and their descendants. The middle section soon disappeared, with most of its territory ultimately taken over by the rulers of the eastern section.

Collapse of the Carolingian World: Partition and Invasion Read a medieval account of the events surrounding the Treaty of Verdun.

The disintegration of Charlemagne's empire was accelerated by ferocious attacks from outside. In the Mediterranean, Muslim raiders from North Africa had taken over Sicily and Sardinia. They preyed on shipping, struck at the coastal towns of Italy and southern France, and made off with everything they could carry. In 846, they captured Rome and looted Saint Peter's Basilica, the central church of the Christian West.

On the eastern frontier, there appeared yet another nation of Asiatic nomads, the Magyars or Hungarians (Map 10.2). They took over the same territory that the Huns and Avars had occupied before them—a large plain about halfway along the course of the River Danube, which still makes up present-day Hungary. From here, they sent raiding expeditions throughout Germany, sometimes striking as far as the Netherlands and southern France. For much of the tenth century, they kept central Europe in turmoil.

The Norsemen

The strongest blows came from Scandinavia, home of the Norsemen or Vikings ("men of the North" or "pirates" in their own language). The Norsemen were the northernmost branch of the Germanic peoples, and with the northward spread of Christianity and Roman culture, it was their turn to live on the fringe of civilization. By the ninth century, like the Greeks in their encounter with the people of the eastern Mediterranean many centuries before (pp. 49-53), they had become a formidable nation of seafarers, traders, and warriors, and their population had grown beyond what the harvests of their northern homeland could support. Consequently, they struck out on what proved to be the last great barbarian invasion of civilized Europe.

From 800 on, the high-prowed longboats of the Norsemen began to appear all along the coastline of western Europe (see photo on page 176). The warriors who leaped ashore demanded tribute from the inhabitants and carried off what they could. From the coasts, they moved up the rivers and carried their raids deep into the interior. Finally, the Viking raids turned into regular campaigns of conquest in which they seized and settled whole territories.

The western Viking tribes, the Norwegians, mainly sailed westward and took over much of Scotland and Ireland; by 1000, their westward urge had taken them across the Atlantic to Iceland, Greenland, and "Vinland" (North America). The southernmost tribes, the Danes, generally moved southward to the coastlands of the North Sea and the Channel: England, France, and the Netherlands. The Anglo-Saxons were forced to surrender the eastern half of England (the Danelaw) to the invaders, and the Frankish rulers were compelled to yield a large territory along the Channel that was called, after the Norsemen, the duchy of Normandy (see Map 10.2).

Meanwhile, the eastern Vikings, the Swedes, traveled across the Baltic Sea and then upriver to a watershed region far inland, where other rivers led them hundreds of miles south to the Black Sea. They won power over the Slavic tribes who had settled this vast region of eastern Europe, and in 860 their longboats attacked Constantinople.

The Great Lords

Throughout the territory of Charlemagne's empire, the struggles among his descendants, as well as barbarian and Muslim attacks, made violence and danger more than ever a normal condition of life. Everywhere, people turned from the distant and helpless rulers to whoever was near enough and strong enough to offer them some protection. Free peasants bound themselves and their descendants to labor on the lands of local warriors as **serfs** (p. 193). Lesser warriors agreed to serve greater ones in war and peace as their **vassals** (pp. 184–185) and in turn received from the greater warriors secure possession of land. Everywhere, effective power came to be exercised by the strongest warrior nobles who could gain the allegiance of the largest number of lesser warriors to swell their armies. They could then use their armies to win control of the most important resources: land, the labor of peasants, and the goods and treasure obtainable by trade or looting.

The leading warrior-nobles also increased their power at the expense of the rulers. Partly by grants from Carolingian rivals who sought their support, and partly by simple seizure from feeble kings, the leading nobles took over royal lands, collected royal revenues, and exercised royal powers of justice. And they treated all these new resources and powers, as well as the rights they acquired over lesser warriors and peasants, as family property. The hereditary possessor of such a property was known as a **lord**. The leading lords also took over such former royal offices as duke and count and converted these into hereditary titles.

Finally, in both the eastern and the western Frankish kingdoms, the succession to the kingship itself came to be settled through election by the great lords. When the direct descendants of Charlemagne died out—in the eastern kingdom in 911 and in the western kingdom in 987—the great lords chose

> **lord**
> The hereditary possessor of lands, revenues, and powers over lesser warriors and peasants.

Map 10.2 **Invasions of the Ninth and Tenth Centuries**

Muslim sailors attacked the Christian coastlines of the western Mediterranean. Magyar horsemen raided westward from the middle Danube, the traditional staging area for nomad invaders of Europe. Norsemen traveled the coasts and rivers of western Europe, made lengthy river voyages across eastern Europe to the Black Sea, and "island-hopped" across the Atlantic to North America. But converted Norse and Magyar settlers in parts of eastern and western Europe eventually helped to strengthen Christendom. © Cengage Learning

Interactive Map

new (and powerless) kings from among themselves.

The Rise of Western Europe

The collapse of Charlemagne's empire did not mean the end of civilization in Europe. On the contrary, as with the fall of Rome in the fifth century, the end of empire and barbarian invasions actually led to civilization's wider spread.

Government itself did not simply disintegrate but developed into new and, in the long run, more effective forms. The great lords, eager to pass on their newly acquired powers and possessions to their descendants, began to give up the custom—previously followed by nobles as well as kings—of dividing their properties among their children. Instead, during the eleventh century, the custom grew up of handing the bulk of the property to the eldest son. This was known as the right of **primogeniture** (from the Latin for "firstborn"). As a result, dynasties of great lords emerged that were able to control fairly stable blocks of territory over several generations.

Sooner or later, any individual dynasty would usually fall victim to defeat in war or failure to produce male heirs. As a group, however, the great lords came to constitute a class of regional potentates, presiding effectively over a chaotic but dynamic warrior society. They defended their possessions against Norsemen, Hungarians, and Arabs; they undertook counteroffensives, such as the reconquest of Spain or the Crusades; and they fought continually against each other.

But these lords did more than wage wars. They generously endowed monasteries and supported movements of reform and reorganization in the Church. They pushed the peasants on their lands to carve new farms and villages out of the wilderness

The Gokstad Ship This Viking longboat was buried with its owner in Norway about A.D. 900 and was dug up and restored in 1870. It has a mast to hoist a sail and 32 oar holes along the top edge of the hull. The 75-foot-long boat probably carried 64 warrior-oarsmen rowing in shifts, with wooden chests for their clothes and bedding that doubled as rowing benches, on lengthy open-air trips on stormy seas and treacherous rivers. In 1893, a replica of this vessel crossed the Atlantic. University Museum of Cultural Heritage, Oslo

that at that time covered much of Europe, and they took a hand in founding towns as centers of trade and industry. The role of these leading nobles in the building of medieval European civilization was an important one.

Barbarian Conquerors and the Spread of Civilization

Even where barbarian invaders conquered and settled, as so often before, they ended by adopting the civilization of their new homelands. Furthermore, the very same Norse and Hungarian attacks that helped demolish the power of the Carolingians also led to the appearance of new forms of royal government to defend whole countries against the invaders (p. 178).

In the main western European territories seized by the Vikings—the Danelaw and Normandy—the Norse settlers agreed to become Christian in return for recognition of their conquests by the English and French kings. In England, Danes and Anglo-Saxons—both ethnically Germanic—became so mixed in language and customs that within a few generations they were hard to tell apart; in Normandy, the sons and daughters of the invaders already spoke the language into which the Latin of that region had evolved in the centuries since the fall of Rome—French. From England and France, and under the influence of the Holy Roman Empire, Christianity and Roman civilization spread back to the Norse homelands, so that by 1000 Norway, Denmark, and Sweden were on the way to becoming Christian kingdoms.

Among the Norse conquerors, the Normans in particular had a great impact on the development of civilization in the West. In 1066, Duke William of Normandy conquered the Anglo-Saxon kingdom of England, coming not as a barbarian invader but with his banners blessed by the pope, as a claimant to the country's Christian kingship. Building on the institutions of the Anglo-Saxon kingdom, the Norman conqueror and his successors made innovations in the fields of administration and justice that have influenced the laws and government of England, and of countries inheriting English traditions, down to the present day (pp. 189–190).

The Bayeux Tapestry (http://www.bayeuxtapestry.org.uk) Explore the Bayeux Tapestry, depicting the Norman invasion of England.

Losing to William the Conqueror: One Abbey's Experience Read an account of one abbey's hardships after William conquered England.

Meanwhile, other Normans acting independently of their dukes wrested Sicily from Muslim control, and together with warriors from other parts of France, they reinforced Christian efforts at the reconquest of Spain. In this way, the descendants of pagan barbarian conquerors became the leaders of the western European counteroffensive against Islam.

In central Europe, barbarian conquerors were absorbed in much the same way as farther west. After their defeat by Otto I in 955, the Hungarians still held a large region between the Holy Roman Empire and Byzantium (see Map 10.3). Instead of retreating and dispersing as earlier defeated nomads had done, the Hungarians held on to the territory they had conquered, and won acceptance from the Holy Roman Empire by adopting its Western Christianity and culture. During the ninth and tenth centuries, so did the rulers of various groups of Slav tribes that in earlier centuries had settled in the lands on the empire's eastern borders (pp. 156-157): the Poles, Czechs, and Slovaks, and farther south, the Slovenes and Croats.

For many barbarian peoples, contact with civilization was divisive. Leading warriors often clung to traditional pagan beliefs, and they rightly suspected that their rulers would swell from mere chieftains into kings who would demand obedience in peace as well as war. In Scandinavia, Poland, and Hungary, the coming of Christianity led to rebellion and civil war, and the triumph of the new religion was military as well as spiritual. But the upshot was that the ninth- and tenth-century invasions ended with the boundary of Western Christianity expanding northward into Scandinavia and a long way into eastern Europe and the Balkans (see Map 10.3).

The Rise of Byzantine Eastern Europe

Beyond the boundary of Western Christianity, the same general pattern prevailed, of successful barbarian peoples attacking civilized states yet also reaching toward the religion and way of life of their victims. The difference was that the Christianity and civilization they were reaching for were those of Byzantium.

In Byzantium, as in western Europe, central power grew stronger under the stress of external attack from the seventh century onward as the emperors reorganized their administrative and military system. By about 800, Byzantium had regained control of Greece from the Slavs, and its rulers were experts in playing the Slav tribes and nomadic invaders of eastern Europe against each other. During the ninth and tenth centuries, with many setbacks, Byzantium gradually pushed northward against the Slavs and eastward against the Arabs.

The Conversion of the Slavs

In dealing with the Slavs, the Byzantines did not rely on warfare and diplomacy alone. Among the Slavs, like the Germanic tribes before them, migration and war had fostered a wealthy and powerful elite of chieftains and warriors. This elite might fight against Byzantium, but also wanted to participate in its way of life. Byzantine armies and navies could never banish the Slav threat, but the Christian religion and the Greek heritage might at least bring the Slavs under the empire's spiritual and cultural sway.

In the ninth and tenth centuries, the Byzantine emperors and leading clergy of the Eastern Church deliberately set about the task of bringing Christianity and Greek culture to the Slavs. So eager were the Byzantines to make their message acceptable that they even allowed the Slavs to worship in their own language, rather than in Greek—unlike the Western Church, which usually insisted that no other language than Latin be used in public worship. Byzantine monks also adapted the Greek alphabet to the sounds of the Slav language. The result was the Cyrillic alphabet

NEW FORMS OF ROYAL GOVERNMENT AROSE IN ENGLAND, THE HOLY ROMAN EMPIRE, AND FRANCE IN RESPONSE TO THE NORSE AND HUNGARIAN ATTACKS:

England

- In the ninth century, King Alfred of the southern kingdom of Wessex led all the Anglo-Saxons in resistance to the Danes. Even though he had to concede the Danelaw to the invaders (see Map 10.2 on page 173), it remained under his overlordship.

- Alfred's tenth-century successors were able to recover the lost territory and, for the first time, build a united English kingdom.

Holy Roman Empire

- In the eastern Frankish kingdom, the great lords badly needed strong leadership against the Hungarians, and finally, they permitted the most powerful family among them, the dukes of Saxony, to fill the office of king.

- The ablest of that family, Otto I, defeated the Hungarians decisively in 955, ending their raids into Germany.

- Otto next reclaimed the "Roman" imperial title, which had fallen into disuse, and was crowned emperor by Pope John XII at Rome in 962. Actually, Otto's holdings included only Germany and the northern and central regions of Italy, and the empire he founded came to be known as the Holy Roman Empire of the German Nation, or the Holy Roman Empire (Map 10.3).

- The Holy Roman emperors were never consistently able to enforce the principle of hereditary succession against that of election by the great lords, but they remained powerful down to the later Middle Ages, and the empire itself lasted until 1806.

France

- In the western Frankish kingdom, Hugh Capet, count of Paris, replaced the last Carolingian king in 987.

- Though Hugh wielded little power outside the area of northern France that he controlled as count, he did at least succeed in persuading the great lords to elect his son king during his own lifetime.

- Later Capetian rulers managed to get rid of election altogether and hand on the kingship—whole and undivided, like the rest of their possessions—by hereditary right.

- Having thereby won "independence" from the other great lords, the Capetians would lead the way, by the thirteenth century, to the establishment of a strong hereditary monarchy in France (pp. 187–188).

---

tsar
The Slav term for emperor, from the Latin *caesar*.

(named for the missionary Cyril, one of the leaders in the project of converting the Slavs); it has remained the standard script in Russia and several other Slav countries ever since.

These Byzantine gifts of religion, culture, and literacy were usually combined with others that were just as appealing: military alliances, commercial treaties, and prestigious imperial titles for the Slav chieftains. In the long run, the combination proved irresistible. One by one, the chieftains invited Byzantine missionaries to their lands or came in person to Constantinople to be baptized. As in

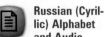 **Russian (Cyrillic) Alphabet and Audio Pronunciations** (http://listen2russian.com/lesson01/a/index.html) See the Cyrillic alphabet and hear the Russian pronunciations.

western Europe, pagan warriors often clung to their traditional customs, but their opposition faded away or was crushed. More serious competition came from the Western Church, which was able to attract the westernmost Slav tribes into its orbit. Elsewhere, it was Byzantium that triumphed.

The Balkans

In the Balkans, for a time, Byzantium had a formidable rival. North of Byzantium's recovered territory of Greece, many Slav tribes had been united into a powerful state by yet another nation of nomadic invaders, the Bulgars. The Slav majority eventually assimilated their overlords and accepted Christianity from Byzantium. Even so, the Bulgarian **tsars** (the Slav version of the Latin title *caesar*, inherited by Byzantium from ancient Rome) struggled with the Byzantine emperors for control of the Balkan region. Around 1000, in the last of many brutal wars,

Map 10.3 Europe About 1000

The division between Christian Europe and pagan barbarian Europe has almost vanished. Slavs, Norsemen, and Magyars have formed Christian kingdoms on the model of their neighbors and former victims. More convert peoples have followed the model of the Latin than of the Greek Church, so that the boundary between the two runs a long way east. To the south, the rival monotheism of Islam has yielded little ground. Europe is taking shape between the Atlantic, the Mediterranean, and the River Volga. © Cengage Learning

Interactive Map

Byzantium finally conquered Bulgaria, though in language and culture the Bulgarians remained Slavic.

To the west of the Bulgarians there lived another Slavic tribal group that had become Christian under Byzantine influence, the Serbs. Long overshadowed by the powerful Bulgarians, the Serbs were now able, for the first time, to build a unified state, whose rulers soon came into conflict with the rulers of the neighboring Slav people to the west, the Croats. In addition, between Serbia and Croatia there now ran the dividing line between Western and Eastern Christianity; and while the Serb rulers counted as subject to Byzantium, from about 1100, Croatia was ruled

> " *Then we went on to Greece, and the Greeks led us to the edifices where they worship their God, and we knew not whether we were in heaven or on earth. For on earth there is no such splendor or such beauty, and we are at a loss how to describe it. We know only that God dwells there among men, and their service is fairer than the ceremonies of other nations.* "
>
> —A Russian visitor to Constantinople, A.D. 987

by the kings of Hungary. Thus, although the Serbs and Croats were closely related tribal groups whose descendants still understand each others' languages today, they eventually developed into separate and sometimes rival nations.

Russia

Byzantium's greatest success was with the Slavs of northeastern Europe, between the Baltic and Black Seas. These Slavs came to be known by the name of a group of Swedish Vikings who conquered them in the ninth century: the Rus or Russians. The Swedish conquerors formed their territories into a powerful state that they ruled from the important commercial center of Kiev (see Map 10.3). Like the Norse conquerors of Normandy, those of Russia quickly adopted the language and customs of their subjects (in this case, Slavic), but they did not lose their Viking appetite for trade and warfare.

The main trading partner of the Russians, and the target of many of their raids, was Byzantium. Either way, the Russian rulers admired the empire's way of life and respected its ancient glory. Finally, in 988, Prince Vladimir of Kiev made a bargain with Byzantium: in return for the exceptional honor of marriage to the emperor's own sister, he threw down the pagan idols of Kiev and was baptized into the Eastern Church. Thus Russia became the easternmost of the states that shared in the religious and cultural heritage of Byzantium.

By 1000, most of the eastern European peoples formed a religious and cultural community like that of western Europe—but one that looked to Constantinople instead of to Rome. What held this community of Byzantine-influenced states together was not, as in western Europe, the inheritance of Roman civilization, the Western Church, and obedience to the pope. Instead, it was the inheritance of Greek civilization, the Eastern Church, and reverence for the Byzantine emperor (or in some cases his actual overlordship). In this way, as Europe took shape, it developed different variants of a common civilization in its western and eastern regions.

> *"Christianity and the inheritance of Greece and Rome, in spite of all divergences between Rome and Byzantium, gave European civilization its basic unity. Numerous different ethnic groups and independent states supplied the vigor of diversity and competition, as well as the destructive urge to conflict and domination."*

Holy Russia/ The First Flowering of Christianity (http://mini-site.louvre.fr/sainte-russie/EN/html/1.2.html Holy Russia) View the earliest Christian art of Russia.

Religious Competition in Kievan Russia Read the medieval story of Vladimir of Russia's conversion to Christianity.

The End of the Barbarian Way of Life

By 1000, the turmoil of the ninth and tenth centuries had produced a surprising result. For three thousand years, Europe had been both the meeting place and the arena of conflict between civilized and barbarian peoples; and now this lengthy era had more or less come to an end. It took another four centuries for the last remaining pagan tribes along the southern and eastern coastlands of the Baltic Sea to be converted. But otherwise, all of Europe had come within the orbit of civilization, and this civilization had already developed distinctive features that have characterized it ever since. Christianity and the inheritance of Greece and Rome, in spite of all divergences between Rome and Byzantium, gave European civilization its basic unity. Numerous different ethnic groups and independent states supplied the vigor of diversity and competition, as well as the destructive urge to conflict and domination. All these features would be inherited to a greater or lesser extent by the modern West.

Listen to a synopsis of Chapter 10.

≪ **"He Fell in Battle, in the East In Garthar"** This carved stone commemorates Torstein, the leader of a Swedish warrior band that fought in "Garthar"—Russia—probably for Yaroslav the Wise, a warlike ruler of Kiev about 1050. The inscription is written in runes, the ancient alphabet of pagan Scandinavia, but the monument is marked with a cross. At a time when Christian kingdoms were forming across northern Europe, converted Vikings were fighting and dying in the service of their rulers. Swedish National Heritage Board/Visual Connection Archive

CourseMate Access to the eBook with additional review material and study tools may be found online at CourseMate for WCIV. Sign in at www.cengagebrain.com.

{ Learning Your Way }

89% of students surveyed found the interactive online quizzes valuable.

We know that no two students are alike. *WCIV* was developed to help you learn Western Civilization in a way that works for you.

Not only is the format fresh and contemporary, it's also concise and focused. And, *WCIV* is loaded with a variety of supplements, like Chapter in Review cards, flash cards, a robust eBook, and more.

At **CengageBrain.com**, you'll find plenty of resources to help you study no matter what your learning style!

CHAPTER 11

MANORS, TOWNS, AND KINGDOMS, 1000–1300

LEARNING OBJECTIVES

AFTER READING THIS CHAPTER, YOU SHOULD BE ABLE TO DO THE FOLLOWING:

LO¹ Describe how feudalism worked to govern social and political relationships in the Middle Ages.

LO² Discuss the operation of a manor.

LO³ Explain how the rural-based civilization of the early Middle Ages became a city-based civilization.

> **"BESIDES NEW PEOPLES AND NEW KINGDOMS, THE FIVE HUNDRED YEARS OF UPHEAVAL THAT FOLLOWED THE FALL OF ROME ALSO PRODUCED NEW SKILLS AND NEW SOCIAL STRUCTURES."**

Besides new peoples and new kingdoms, the five hundred years of upheaval that followed the fall of Rome also produced new skills and new social structures. The new kingdoms continued to be ruled in partnership by rulers, warrior-landowners, and Church leaders, but in many of them, the interplay of these power wielders came to be regulated by rules and customs so formal and binding that they had the force of law. In this way, a new pattern of social life and government arose—that of feudalism. Between 1000 and 1300, feudalism enabled some of the new kingdoms to become well-organized states.

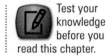

Test your knowledge before you read this chapter.

Meanwhile, turmoil in the countryside gave rise to the institutions of serfdom (an unfree but farm-holding peasantry) and the manor (a type of agricultural estate). These institutions gave both peasants and landowners an incentive to grow more crops, at the same time as inventive ironworkers were developing new and more effective farming tools. The result was three centuries of growth in population and wealth, which kings, nobles, and Church leaders were able to use for purposes of government, warfare, religion, and culture.

What do **you think?**

Feudalism fostered greater inequality than we experience in contemporary society.

Strongly Disagree						Strongly Agree
1	2	3	4	5	6	7

The increase of farming wealth, together with closer contacts with the world outside Europe, in turn led to an increase in trade and a revival of urban life. Roman towns revived, new ones grew up in once-barbarian lands, the network of trade routes and commercial centers grew extensive and close-meshed, and in regions where rulers were weak, independent city-states appeared for the first time since the rise of Rome.

≪ Sir Geoffrey Luttrell A fourteenth-century English knight prepares for the battle or the joust. His wife, Agnes de Sutton, hands him his helmet; his daughter-in-law, Beatrice le Scrope, holds his shield. The shield, and the clothing of the rider and the horse, display the Luttrell coat of arms; on Agnes it is combined with the Sutton coat of arms, and on Beatrice with that of the Scropes. The three families form a warrior-landowner network linked by marriage, and the married ladies approve and support their knightly warrior.

These changes affected all of Europe, but the "Greek" East still contended with nomad invasions and Muslim expansion. For this reason, change was most spectacular in the "Latin" West, which now rose to become the heartland of a renewed civilization, as brilliant as any in the past.

LO¹ Feudalism

The word **feudalism** was coined by historians long after the end of the Middle Ages, to describe the type of government institutions, as well as the general social and political relationships, that existed at that period among warrior-landholders in much of Europe. Feudalism originated in northern France during the tenth century, following the breakup of the Carolingian empire. Warrior-landholders elsewhere who found that it met their needs, as well as conquering Norman warriors (p. 177), brought it to many other countries. By the twelfth century, not only France but also England, the Holy Roman Empire, Spain, Sicily, and even Byzantium were governed according to feudal principles.

Feudalism was not a tidy unified system, but it always worked according to two basic principles, each affecting one of the two things that were of most concern to warrior-landholders—warfare and land.

As warriors, feudalism bound them by personal ties of mutual trust and loyalty. Lesser warrior-landholders were supposed to show loyalty to a greater one, enabling him to rely on them as his personal army; but the greater warrior-landholder was expected to show them loyalty in turn, protecting and helping them individually so that they would not have to stand against enemies on their own.

As landholders, feudalism bound members of the upper class together by giving them mutual rights over and interests in the most important of all resources, the land and the peasants who worked it. Lesser warrior-landholders did not actually "own" their land but "held" it on condition of doing military and other service to a greater one, who in turn was obligated to guarantee and protect the lesser ones in the secure hereditary possession of their estates.

For leading warriors to provide for their soldiers by giving them land was nothing new, but the soldiers who now had to be provided for were not just the infantry of Charles Martel's time (p. 167), but heavily armed and armored horse warriors (see photo on page 182). Heavy cavalry warfare was first practiced by the Persians and spread to the Romans and then the Arabs, who in turn "taught" it to their European opponents. Along the way, it was made easier by the invention of stirrups—iron foot rests hanging from a saddle—which were brought to the Middle East and Europe by nomad invaders. Stirrups gave horsemen a more stable platform from which to wield their weapons. As a result, during the eleventh century, heavy cavalry became the main striking force of armies.

In English, these warriors came to be called *knights*, from a Germanic word meaning "servant." But to provide for just one such "servant," with all his training and equipment, took a good deal of land and and a good many peasants. Through feudal ties, kings and great lords could assure themselves of the services of knights by guaranteeing them the hereditary control of land and peasants that made them, too, part of the ruling warrior-landholder class.

Relationships of the same kind also existed between rulers of countries and the great lords within the countries they ruled. Since the great lords had taken over so much of the powers of government (p. 175), it was only through these ties that monarchs were able to hold their countries together. In any country, in fact, there existed a host of miniature governments, each ruled by one or another great lord and loosely associated under the monarch by the ties of feudalism. In spite of its decentralized operation, feudal government afforded some measure of security and justice for millions of Europeans, and held many countries of Europe together as political units, for five hundred years. It even succeeded in producing powerful states, in which effective central authority was grafted onto the decentralized feudal structure with its stress on mutual rights and responsibilities between holders of power and those subjected to them.

The Feudal Compact

At first, the practice of exchanging property for personal service was extremely vague, consisting of unwritten agreements among greater and lesser landholders that were subject to a wide range of interpretations. By the eleventh century, however, the **feudal compact**, or contract, as this aspect of feudalism is called, had evolved into a fairly standard arrangement. Whoever granted land to someone stood in the position of lord; the grantee was his vassal (from another word for "servant"); and the land granted was called a **fief** (from a word for "property"—in Latin, *feudum*, from which *feudalism* is derived).

Besides possession of land, the fief carried with it government responsibility and power. The vassal was expected to protect the inhabitants of his fief, collect revenues, and dispense justice. In this way, political authority was linked to landholding. In addition, each vassal, in return for the benefits of his fief, owed important obligations to his lord.

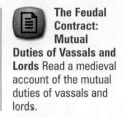

The Feudal Contract: Mutual Duties of Vassals and Lords Read a medieval account of the mutual duties of vassals and lords.

Chief among these was military service. A vassal was expected to serve his lord in person, and the holder of a large fief was required, in addition, to furnish knights—his own vassals—as well as foot soldiers. In this way, the kings and the great lords, who found it impracticable to pay for standing armies, were able to raise fighting forces when needed. At first, the vassal's obligation to fight when called on by his lord was unlimited, but gradually, it was set by custom at about forty days' service each year.

The holder of a fief was also obliged to serve on the lord's court, which was usually held once a month. This court heard disputes among the lord's vassals, often over land and interpretations of feudal rights, as well as criminal charges. The lord presided in all cases, and his vassals acted as judges. It then became the lord's duty to enforce their decision, but should the losing party refuse to accept it, armed conflict could result. In this way, a lord and his vassals formed a community, with shared responsibility and power.

Under the feudal compact, a lord had no general right to collect taxes from a vassal or the peasants who lived on the vassal's fief, but in some strictly defined circumstances, a vassal was required to make payments to his lord. After receiving his fief, he normally paid its first year's income to the lord. When the lord's eldest son was knighted (see next section) or his eldest daughter was married, or if the lord was captured in battle and had to be ransomed, the vassal had to make payment. In addition, for a given number of days each year, the lord and his family and attendants could demand food, lodging, and entertainment from the vassal.

Homage and Knighthood

The granting of a fief, with all its requirements, was accompanied by the vassal's doing **homage** to his lord (see photo on page 196). Usually, the vassal knelt down, put his hands between those of his lord, and offered himself as the lord's "man" (in Latin, *homo*). The lord accepted the vassal's homage, told him to rise,

and embraced him. Next, it was customary for the vassal to make a Christian vow of fealty (faithfulness). The lord, in exchange for the declaration of vassalage, customarily presented his vassal with a clod of earth or some other object symbolizing the right to govern and use the fief.

With its use of symbol and ritual, its hand-clasping and embracing and taking of vows, the act of homage was not unlike a wedding. In fact, the intention was much the same: to reinforce a legally binding contract between two individuals by a strong personal bond—one that would survive disputes, conflicts, and even the occasional breach of the terms of the contract.

The feudal contract remained in effect so long as lord and vassal honored their mutual obligations or until one of them died. By the custom of primogeniture (p. 176), their eldest sons then inherited the positions of lord and vassal. But whenever one of them died, new ceremonies of homage were necessary.

Since kings and great lords led their forces in person as heavy cavalry soldiers, they, too, came to regard themselves as "knights," and by the eleventh century, knighthood came to be an honorable status shared by the entire feudal elite. Before a young man could qualify for this status, he had to serve an apprenticeship as squire to a respected knight—preferably someone other than his own father, so that he could forge loyalties and friendships beyond his own family. The young man would then be knighted—initiated into the professional caste of warriors, usually by being presented with a sword by an already qualified knight.

This ceremony soon developed spiritual and religious overtones. By the middle of the twelfth century, the knight's sword was usually placed on an altar before the presentation, implying that the knight was obliged to protect the Church. By the thirteenth century, the ritual was normally performed in a church or a cathedral, rather than in a manor house or a castle. The initiate spent a night of vigil and prayer before the day of the ceremony, emerging from the ritual as a "soldier of Christ."

When a vassal died and left an heir who was not a qualified knight, special arrangements had to be made. If the heir was a son who had not yet attained his majority, the lord would normally serve as guardian until the youth could qualify as a knight and become his vassal. If the sole heir was a daughter, the lord would serve as guardian until he found her a knightly husband. Then her husband, through the act of homage, would receive the fief as the lord's new vassal. Such marriages were one of the chief means of expanding individual and family power during the feudal age, and women continued to fulfill one of their ancient traditional functions in family politics, of binding

feudal compact
An arrangement between a lord and his vassal involving the exchange of property for personal service.

fief
A grant of land and accompanying government responsibilities and power.

homage
A vassal's act of promising loyalty and obedience to his lord.

Doing Homage These pictures from the *Saxon Mirror*, a thirteenth-century German law book, illustrate sections on rights of giving and holding fiefs. In the second picture down, kneeling vassals and seated lords clasp each others' hands. One vassal has the shaven head of a clergy member, and the givers of fiefs are clergy and ladies—groups for whom the law made special provision. In the third picture down, a vassal swears allegiance to a lord (both laymen) on a casket containing relics, and dutifully welcomes the lord into his house.

together higher-ranking and lower-ranking power wielders. When a vassal died leaving no heir, the fief reverted to the lord, who could keep it for himself or grant it to a new vassal on the same terms.

The Feudalization of the Church

Because of the close interlocking of the Church hierarchy and the ruling power structure, land held by the Church was naturally also bound up in the feudal pattern. Church lands were held as fiefs by archbishops, bishops, and abbots who had sworn fealty to counts, dukes, princes, or kings. But how could clergymen be warriors on the field of battle? They were not trained knights, and Church law forbade the shedding of blood by the clergy.

The higher clergy were usually the sons of noblemen and familiar with the ways of war. During the ninth and tenth centuries, in fact, they often ignored the Church prohibition and fought in person. Archbishop Turpin, in the epic *Song of Roland* (p. 238), wields his sword against the infidel and dies a hero's death along with Charlemagne's lay vassals. However, with the reform movement of the eleventh century (pp. 208-211), clerical vassals were directed to satisfy their military obligations by assigning portions of their properties as fiefs to vassals who pledged to perform the required military services.

Feudal States

Feudal relationships also existed between rulers of countries and the great lords within the countries they ruled. Since the great lords had taken over so much of the powers of government, however, any feudal monarch who wanted to be truly the ruler of his country faced daunting problems. It was only in his hereditary family territories within his kingdom that he was entitled to do justice, levy taxes, recruit knights, and in general, exercise government authority. Outside these territories (the "royal domain"), it was the great lords, or **barons**, as they were called, who held these powers. Of course, all the barons were vassals of the monarch as overlord, holding their properties as fiefs on condition of doing him military service and bound to him by the personal tie of homage. But it was hard for the monarch to compel them to meet their obligations, given that their combined knightly armies—and often those of individual barons—were larger than his own.

All the same, a feudal monarch did have certain assets on which to build. One was the fact that the barons actually needed an effective overlord to settle their quarrels and lead them in war. A king could use the authority he gained in this way to favor cooperative vassals and undermine obstructive ones. He would use every chance to increase the size of the royal domain so that his personal wealth and power would grow to outweigh those of his vassals. And if things went wrong, the barons rebelled, and he was defeated, he was almost certain not to be killed or overthrown. For of all the warrior-landholders in his country, he alone was holy: chosen by God, crowned, anointed like King David of old, and even credited with the miraculous power to heal disease by his mere touch.

A feudal monarch who built up his assets in this way could not only be a powerful ruler but also create government institutions to ensure that his power would outlive him. In this way, there developed within feudalism effectively governed states, of which the most important were the Holy Roman Empire, France, and England. All of these states were vulnerable to disruptions of various kinds—above all, resistance and rebellion on the part of barons and disputes with the Church, which was both a partner and a rival institution. As a result, throughout medieval times and beyond, the balance of power in the ruling partnership of kings, nobles, and Church leaders constantly shifted. In one and the same country, kings might be feared and respected rulers in one generation, and helpless figureheads in the next.

But only the Holy Roman Empire was permanently weakened by these problems. France and England, in spite of many ups and downs of royal power, survived as strong states into modern times and provided models of statehood for other European countries.

> *"Of all the warrior-landholders in his country, the king alone was holy: chosen by God, crowned, anointed like King David of old, and even credited with the miraculous power to heal disease by his mere touch."*

France: The Strengthening of Monarchy

In France, the homeland of feudalism, for more than a century the descendants of Hugh Capet (p. 178) had enough to do ensuring that the kingship would remain in their family and strengthening their control of the royal domain, a 50-mile stretch of countryside around the city of Paris. Outside that area, the barons governed their territories—often ably and effectively—and struggled for power among themselves, paying little heed to the wearer of the crown.

In the twelfth century, however, the power of the rulers began to grow—mainly because outside threats caused the barons to cluster more closely as vassals around their overlord, the king. The Holy Roman emperors coveted territory in eastern France and even dreamed of restoring the united empire of Charlemagne. In the south, militant heretics, the Albigensians (al-bi-JEN-see-uhns) (p. 212), challenged Catholicism and feudalism alike. Above all, France was threatened with gradual takeover by rival foreign rulers who were also overmighty French vassals: the kings of England.

THE HOLY ROMAN EMPERORS LOST POWER AS FEUDAL MONARCHS GRADUALLY OVER TIME:

- Their control of Church positions was disrupted when the Church reasserted its independence.

- The great lords lost the habit of looking to the emperors for leadership.

- The emperors diverted energy and resources in a vain attempt to

establish power bases in Italy, from which they hoped to overawe both their German vassals and the popes.

- The great lords gained the power to elect emperors, and from the middle of the thirteenth century onward, they chose emperors who would leave them alone.

- Each fief, bishopric, and city in the empire became in practice a small independent state. While individual states might be fairly powerful, none would be as formidable as the large feudal states of France and England.

It was in the duel with the English kings that a powerful French monarchy was forged. Ever since Duke William of Normandy (a territory that was part of France) had conquered England in 1066, his descendants had been fully independent kings of England yet also, so far as their French possessions were concerned, vassals of the king of France. In the twelfth century, by marriage and inheritance, the English kings added to Normandy a whole series of other fiefs that gave them control of the entire western half of France. Although they were vassals, they were easily powerful enough to destroy their overlords. Therefore, as a matter of survival, their overlords set out to destroy them.

It was King Philip Augustus who finally succeeded in this undertaking. Patiently, late in the twelfth century, he exploited his powers as overlord against his dangerous vassals, rallying other French barons against them, and hearing appeals from the English king's own French vassals against high-handed acts by their overlord. He even encouraged the disobedient and warlike sons of his English rival, Henry II, in rebellions against their own father. The climax of Philip's campaign came in 1204. Using feudal procedures, he declared one of Henry's successors, King John, a rebellious vassal in his capacity as duke of Normandy. Philip then confiscated that territory and summoned his other vassals to come with their knights to enforce the judgment. Normandy and other French pos-

> "*Each prince shall possess and exercise in peace according to the customs of the land the liberties, jurisdiction, and authority over counties and hundreds which are in his own possession or are held as fiefs from him.*"
>
> —Emperor Frederick II, 1231

sessions of the English kings were conquered—and many of them were added to the French king's royal domain. Though the English kings still held extensive fiefs in southwestern France, it would be more than a century before they again challenged the French monarchy.

The French kings had become the most powerful warrior-landholders in their country, to whom even the greatest barons looked for leadership, and this, in turn, gave them the chance to build a strong state. The thirteenth-century King Louis IX, courageous crusader, generous giver to the poor, fighter against injustice and corruption in his own government, who was eventually recognized by the Church as a saint, was also the mightiest ruler in Europe. His royal courts were open to all free subjects, regardless of the courts maintained by barons in their fiefs. Paid officials throughout the country enforced the king's decisions, carried out his orders, and saw to it that the central power of the king overrode the local power of the barons. Even so, Louis kept the barons' support—because he personally was a model of the Christian warrior virtues that they admired and because on the whole he stayed within the limits of feudal custom and tradition. Louis and later thirteenth-century French kings still operated in many ways as feudal overlords, but they also laid the foundations of the absolute monarchy of later times.

The Holy Roman Empire: The Weakening of Monarchy

In the same centuries that the kings of France changed from figurehead rulers to truly powerful monarchs, the Holy

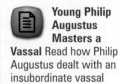

Young Philip Augustus Masters a Vassal Read how Philip Augustus dealt with an insubordinate vassal early in his reign.

Roman emperors moved in exactly the opposite direction. The empire's founder, Otto I (p. 178), and his tenth-century successors had been able to exploit from the start the kind of assets that it took the French kings generations to acquire. The emperors already owned massive domain territories, and the great lords needed their leadership against outside enemies, above all the Slavs and Hungarians. In addition, the emperors controlled the Church, thus ensuring that bishops and abbots, with their extensive properties and large knightly armies, would be agents of the ruler's power throughout the empire.

True, for a long time, the lords were outright owners of their territories, rather than holding these on condition of service to the ruler. But the twelfth-century emperor Frederick I Barbarossa ("Red-Beard"), a contemporary of Philip Augustus and Henry II, remedied this. He obliged the great lords to accept the status of vassals to him as overlord, holding their territories as fiefs. Like Philip Augustus, he deprived an overmighty vassal, Duke Henry the Lion of Saxony, of his fief, and then drove him into exile. The empire, too, it seemed, was on its way to becoming a powerful feudal state.

However, the emperors faced a persistent and formidable adversary: the popes. In Charlemagne's time and for long afterward, the popes had been willing to accept the protection of the emperors and often their supervision. But with the eleventh-century Church reform movement, the popes began to seek independence from and even supremacy over the emperors. In the long run, the monarchy became weak and the Holy Roman Empire was fragmented.

 **Concessions to the German Princes** Read the list of concessions that a thirteenth-century Holy Roman emperor had to make to the German princes (local rulers).

England: The King's Government and the Common Law

In England, feudalism from the start actually favored the growth of royal power. It was Duke William of Normandy who introduced feudalism when he conquered England. As the leader of a victorious army, he could structure his relations with his vassals to his own advantage as king. He kept no less than one-sixth of the country in his own hands as royal domain. He also set up his leading Norman vassals as barons in England, with generous fiefs; however, these mostly consisted not of solid blocks of territory but of smaller areas scattered across the country. As a result, they were practically impossible to govern

"Walter Trenchebof was asserted to have handed to Inger of Faldingthrope the knife with which he killed Guy Foliot, and is suspected of it. Let him purge himself by water that he did not consent to it. He has failed and is hanged."

—from a document of the English Royal Courts (ca. 1201–1214)

without central government services that only the king could provide. Furthermore, earlier native English rulers had already devised a fairly efficient government system. The whole country was divided into counties, or *shires*, with a royal official, the *shire reeve* (sheriff), transacting business in accordance with written royal orders or **writs**.

William's successors, particularly the contemporary and rival of Philip Augustus, King Henry II, built on this basis the most complex and efficient of medieval states. On the whole, they got the cooperation of the barons because the state provided both the barons and lesser folk with services that they could not provide for themselves. Most notably, by the beginning of the thirteenth century, the king was providing his subjects with standardized justice operating according to standardized rules and precedents (the "common law").

A Sampling of Criminal Cases Read a sampling of criminal cases and jury decisions.

The king's legal experts, or *justices*, regularly traveled the country to hear cases. When a justice would arrive in a county to hold a court session, the sheriff would summon sworn groups of freemen known as *juries* (from the Latin *jurare*, "swear an oath"), to give truthful evidence before the justice that would establish the rights and wrongs of disputes over property, or to present before him those suspected of serious crimes.

Criminal suspects were normally sent for trial by **ordeal** (from a Germanic word meaning "judgment"). Ordeals involved such procedures as "purging oneself by water"—being tied up and lowered into a pit full of water after a priest had blessed it and asked God to reveal his judgment. Suspects who sank were thought to have been miraculously "accepted" by the water and therefore to be innocent; those who floated had been "rejected" and were therefore guilty. Ordeals were common throughout Europe and dated back at least to the ancient Babylonian King Hammurabi (p. 18). Early in the thirteenth century, however, the Church paralyzed the criminal justice systems of many countries by declaring ordeals superstitious and ungodly. Most governments responded by reviving investigative methods of Roman law,

> "*No free man shall be arrested or imprisoned or disseised [dispossessed] or outlawed or exiled or in any way victimized, neither will we attack him or send anyone to attack him, except by the lawful judgment of his peers or by the law of the land.*"
> —from Magna Carta, 1215

including torture, but in England the king's legal experts thought up a new procedure. From now on, the guilt or innocence of suspects would be determined by summoning juries of a new kind, who would render a verdict, under the guidance of the justice, on the truth of testimony given by others. In this way, the feudal English state inaugurated the modern jury system.

With these and other changes in law and administration, the English kings extended their power over everyone throughout their country. But they were still feudal rulers whose power came from their overlordship of vassals, and their innovations also led to problems and tensions that exploded early in the thirteenth century into a major political crisis.

The Crisis of English Feudal Monarchy: Magna Carta

The English rulers used their new government machinery not just to benefit their subjects but also to exploit the resources of the country to the fullest—above all, to maintain armies that would protect their possessions across the sea in France. Henry II and his elder son Richard I (the "Lion-Hearted") made their English subjects pay heavily for these wars. They even stretched their powers as overlords to demand money as well as military service from their vassals. But at least they were mostly victorious—an important quality in a feudal overlord. In 1204, however, Richard's younger brother, King John, lost Normandy and other French lands to Philip Augustus and subsequently failed to win them back. As a result, he lost the respect of his vassals— "Lackland," they scornfully called him—and he had to rule by increasing oppression and terror.

Between overlords and vassals, outright oppression and terror were always counterproductive: the end result, in 1215, was a rebellion on the part of many leading barons in which the king found himself deserted and alone. But the barons, true to feudal tradition, could not bring themselves to kill or depose their crowned and anointed king. Instead, following complex negotiations, the armed barons came to an agreement with their king that was enshrined in a famous document: **Magna Carta,** the "Great Charter."

 **Magna Carta: The Great Charter of Liberties** Read a selection from Magna Carta.

What the barons wanted from the king was not for him to dismantle his efficient government machine. Rather, they wanted him to ensure that it worked to their benefit, by operating within the traditional feudal framework of mutual rights and responsibilities between overlord and vassals. Some of the king's concessions were of historic importance. He promised that in the future, should he need to collect money from his vassals other than for the traditional feudal purposes of knighting his eldest son, marrying his eldest daughter, or ransoming himself, he would do so only with the consent of a council composed of the vassals themselves. And he also promised that he would not deprive any free man of life, liberty, property, or protection of the law, "unless by lawful judgment of his peers or by the law of the land."

Of course, King John granted all this because he could only get the armed barons to demobilize by promising whatever they demanded. He and the barons were soon at war again, and conflicts of this kind continued to break out regularly during the thirteenth century. But at the end of every conflict, as a trust-building gesture, the Great Charter would be solemnly renewed, and in time, it became part of the political instincts of kings and barons alike.

Only a powerful king heading an effective government, they came to believe, could ensure peace, justice, and prosperity in the kingdom. But as overlord, the king must respect the rights of his vassals—including their right to share with him the responsibility for governing the country—and he must strictly observe his own legal procedures. The king, then, was under the law, and he needed the consent of at least his leading vassals before taking measures that were not expressly part of his legal rights. In this way, out of the collision between the newly powerful state and the traditions of feudalism, England took its first steps toward constitutional and parliamentary government.

Time Traveller's Guide to Medieval England (http://www.channel4.com/history/microsites/H/history/guide12/part02.html) Learn more about the politics, culture, and society of medieval England.

LO² Peasants and Lords

In the Middle Ages, society was often thought of as being divided into three **estates** (social groups), each making its particular contribution to the welfare of the whole. Highest were "those who pray"—the clergy, whose lives were the most honorable because they were the guardians of people's souls. Next came "those who fight"—the feudal nobility, from mighty kings to simple knights, who protected life and property. Lowest in status were "those who work"—the common people in town and countryside, including everyone from wealthy merchants and lawyers to landless farm workers, whose labors supported the clergy and nobles as well as themselves.

The people of this low estate had little political voice and even less social prestige, but it was they who made possible the achievements of medieval civilization. Like every great civilization before it—those of Sumer and classical Greece, for example (pp. 11-12, 50)—the civilization of medieval Europe owed its rise to an increase of population and agriculture and a growth of cities and trade. These developments provided the wealth for a complex society, a well-organized government, and a brilliant culture. Accordingly, it is to the life, labor, and forms of community of "those who worked" that we now turn—beginning with the most numerous group, probably forming 90 percent of the population in most countries: the ones who worked in the countryside.

The Manorial Estate

In medieval Europe, most of the agricultural population worked as members of families that occupied small farms—that is, they belonged to the type of rural social group that is known as peasants. But the peasant families did not work their farms individually, nor did they own them as private property. Instead, the principal farming property and social unit was the **manor**, usually belonging to a member of the feudal nobility or to a Church institution. A relatively humble member of the nobility—a simple knight, for instance—might possess no more than a single manor or even a fraction of one. A great fief, on the other hand, consisted of hundreds of manors. And so far as the peasants were concerned, anyone who owned a manor, no matter how high or low his status in the feudal hierarchy, was their lord.

Manors ranged in size from about 300 acres to perhaps 3,000. The average manor was probably about 1,000 acres, supporting some two or three hundred people. It had to be large enough to

manor
The principal farming property and social unit of a medieval community, usually belonging to a member of the feudal nobility or to a Church institution.

>> **A Wheeled Plow** This one belonged to a peasant in Moravia (present-day Czech Republic) in the eighteenth century, when such plows were still standard equipment. As the plow moves, the colter (the vertical blade behind the wheels) slices through the earth; the plowshare then rips the earth up from underneath; and the moldboard (beneath the handles) shoves against the earth, turning it over so tht it settles as loose and fertile soil. The wheels make it easier for animals to pull this complex earth-breaking device.

"The rise of trade and the growth of cities, the emergence of national states, the struggles between religious factions—all seem to have had slight effect on the basic patterns and rhythms of rural life."

support the people who lived in it and to enable its lord to fulfill his feudal obligations, but it could not be so large as to be unmanageable as a farming unit.

Farming Methods: Wheeled Plows and the Three-Field System

The productive heart of the manor consisted of crop-growing fields (arable fields or plowland). Crop yields were tiny by today's standards, but they had been boosted by technical innovations that had spread widely through much of western Europe since the fall of Rome, regardless of the turmoil of the times.

Ironworking had become so common that blacksmiths were to be found on most estates, turning out sturdy tools that made it easier to clear forests and work the soil. In particular, iron was used to make soil-cutting parts for big wheeled plows that turned over the wet, heavy soils of northern Europe far more thoroughly than earlier types of plow (see photo on page 191). Iron horseshoes and new types of harness made it possible to use horses as work animals, though the less powerful but hardier oxen were more often used. Water-powered grain-grinding mills, first used on a large scale in the Roman Empire and widespread throughout much of Europe by 1000, relieved peasant women from endless hours of grinding grain by hand—time that they could devote to more productive women's work (p. 10) such as taking care of farmyard animals, spinning, and weaving (see photo on page 194).

The most important innovation that increased the agricultural wealth of western Europe was the **three-field system** of cultivation. The manor's plowland was divided into three large, unfenced fields. In a given farming year, one of these fields would be planted in the fall with crops, mainly wheat and rye, that took about nine months to grow and ripen; another in the spring, with crops such as barley and oats that needed six months or less; and the third would be left fallow (unplanted), to regain its fertility. Late in the summer, the fall and spring crops would all be harvested, and in the fall, the fallow field would be planted. In the following spring, the previous fall field would be planted, and the previous spring field would be left fallow for the whole year; and in the third year, the three fields would be rotated yet again. Thus, each year, two-thirds of the arable lands were in use while one-third was lying fallow. This simple conservation measure helped to maintain the fertility of the soil.

Individual peasants did not have compact farms assigned to them. Instead, they held long, narrow strips in each of the three fields. In this way, peasant families had a regular supply of fall crops and spring crops each year, more fertile and less fertile land was evenly distributed among families, and plowmen could work more efficiently because they did not have to turn their teams so often. This layout, together with the regular crop rotation, meant that the peasants must farm cooperatively, planting and harvesting the same crops in the same field at the same time.

Land and Buildings

Besides plowland, a manor needed woodland for fuel, meadowland (grass-grown areas to provide hay for work animals), and pasture where sheep and cattle grazed. Only a small section of the estate was occupied by the homes of the village, with thatched or tiled roofs and timber, brick, or plaster walls according to local conditions and the wealth of the peasants; windows were shuttered but not glazed, since glass was an expensive luxury. Around these cottages were sheds and gardens where the village women raised vegetables, hens, rabbits, and pigs.

The Medieval Village of Wharram Percy (http://loki.stockton.edu/~ken/wharram/wharram.htm) Take a guided tour of the archeological site for Wharram Percy, a medieval village.

Many villages had a manor house for the lord, as well as a church or priest's house. If there was no church or the lord did not actually live in the manor—or if the "lord" was not an individual person but an institution such as a monastery or bishopric—there would at any rate be barns to collect the produce that was the lord's due. Then there were the mill and the smithy, as well as a bake oven and a wine press. All were provided by the lord for a fee, usually paid in the form of produce—for example, a share of the grain that a peasant brought to be ground, or of the resulting flour. In addition, the priest, the miller, the blacksmith, and the baker had their own holdings.

Alwalton Manor: An Inventory Read an inventory of a manor belonging to an abbey, including the people who lived on it and the days of labor and payments in goods and money that they owed the abbot.

The People of the Manor

The records of village life prior to the thirteenth century are meager. But we do know that in those mute centuries, the basic habits of work, law, worship, and play evolved into established custom. And we have abundant evidence that village life as it existed in the thirteenth century persisted with little change for the following five hundred years. The rise of trade and the growth of cities, the emergence of national states, the struggles between religious factions—all seem to have had slight effect on the basic patterns and rhythms of rural life.

The Lord and His Family

The lord of the manor was presumably guided by the rules of God and by custom; in any case, his word was law. Whether a simple knight or a noble of high degree, he was often away from home for long periods of time. He was a warrior as well as a landlord and had his feudal obligations to fulfill. When he was not performing those duties, his favorite pastime was hunting. He typically took little direct interest in farming and left the management of his lands and local justice to his overseers (*stewards* or *bailiffs*). The lord's wife spent most of her days in the manor house supervising the servants, household operations, and entertainment of guests. If she was a lady of high rank, she might also act as a partner in the conduct of her husband's political and administrative affairs.

The lord normally took about half the total production of the estate—mainly crops from strips in the open fields that the peasants cultivated for him, and also payments from them of household and garden produce. He also maintained a reserve of grain in his barns so that in years of crop failure he would be able to provide the peasants with food and seed. He could not allow them to starve, for aside from humane considerations, they represented his labor force.

Peasants and Serfdom

Most of the peasants were serfs (from Latin *servus*), whose special status and ties to the soil were inherited. The origins of serfdom can be traced back to the western provinces of the Roman Empire in the third and fourth centuries (pp. 138-139); by 1000, serfdom had spread beyond the empire's former frontiers and was normal throughout most of Europe. During the turbulent times of the early Middle Ages, whole communities of farmers had placed themselves under powerful warriors for protection (p. 174). In addition, in territories that had once belonged to the Roman Empire, many serfs were descended from earlier generations of slaves who had worked on the estates of great landowners (p. 98)—*servus*, in fact, originally meant "slave." In their case, serfdom represented an improvement in status. Nevertheless, a serf was legally unfree.

Life in Medieval Europe (http://www.youtube.com/watch?v=pypbyC548dw) Watch a re-creation of peasant life in medieval Europe.

The main duty of the serfs was to cultivate the strips in the open fields that belonged to the lord. In addition, they could be called on to build roads, clear forests, and do other work.

Their work obligation or **labor service** was usually reckoned in time rather than specific duties, and mostly varied between two and three days in the week. In addition, they had to give the lord fixed amounts of any valuable items that they produced, such as spun yarn or poultry (see photo on page 194). The serfs'

labor service
The work that a serf was required to do as a condition of holding a farm. It included cultivating the lord's crops and performing other tasks such as building roads or clearing forests.

children were likewise bound to the manor; no members of their families could leave the estate or marry without the consent of the lord. A serf's eldest son normally inherited the rights and duties of his father.

Peasants whose ancestors had managed to avoid serfdom had the status of *freemen*. This did not necessarily mean that they were better off; some, in fact, lived on the edge of starvation. If the freeman farmed land, he did so as a farm tenant, paying rent to the lord in the form of a share of his crop. The lord could evict a freeman whenever he saw fit, whereas a serf could not legally be separated from his land.

Manors and serfdom were the medieval European way of fulfilling the traditional purposes of farming communities ever since the earliest civilizations—to provide for the needs of both the families who farmed the land and the elite who lived off their labors. Serfdom persisted in many countries until the nineteenth century; much is known about the life of serfs in these later times, and there is no reason to suppose that in the Middle Ages it was basically different. Kings and nobles might look down on peasants as a mass of humble toilers, but each village had its own hierarchy of families with larger and smaller holdings, as well as families with no land at all. Better-off families married into each other, dressed up for family and religious occasions, and lent each other tools and work animals. They gave handouts of food and clothing to landless families, became godparents to their children, and hired them as farmhands—whom they then sent to labor on the lord's land, rather than perform this humbling duty themselves. For serfs, too—at least, the better-off ones—had their pride.

Manorialism and Increasing Wealth

In its time, manorialism was a highly successful form of economic and social organization. More secure than freemen, with far greater property rights than slaves, and benefiting from a relatively productive farming system, the serfs had an incentive to found families and increase the amount of land they farmed. Partly for these reasons, the emergence of manorialism by 1000 was followed by three centuries of agricultural boom. Throughout Europe, the serfs cut down forests, drained swamps, and brought grasslands under the plow. Thousands of new villages sprang up, and by 1300 the population of Europe had risen from roughly 40 million to about 100 million.

Women's Work A fourteenth-century peasant woman feeds chicks and a hen, part of the labor around the house and farmyard that was done by women in medieval Europe as in every traditional agricultural society. Under her arm she carries a distaff for spinning raw linen or wool into yarn, so that the moment she is finished with the chickens she can get back to spinning—slow but money-earning work, as she will sell the yarn, or cloth that she will weave from it, to a traveling merchant. © British Library Board, Add. 42130, f. 166v

This **internal colonization**, as it is called, was very much in the interests of the lords, as it increased the amount of productive land that they controlled. Usually, it was they who founded new manors on uncultivated land and moved serfs into them. But to get the cooperation of the serfs, the lords had to offer them concessions, such as larger holdings, smaller crop deliveries, and fewer days of labor service. In time, the lords even found it preferable to turn their serfs into free tenants, paying rent in produce or cash. (The lords, however, usually retained manorial powers of government and justice, as well as ultimate ownership of the land.) In western Europe, this eventually led, by the end of the Middle Ages, to the almost complete disappearance of serfdom (p. 255).

In addition, European society became much wealthier and also more complex and diverse. As the population swelled and peasants and lords both prospered, commerce and industry also began to grow, and the number of people who made a living by these activities increased. Alongside the manor, the typical community of peasants and lords, there appeared another type of community, formed by merchants and craftspeople: the town.

LO³ Trade and Towns

As the towns grew, an expanded cast of medieval characters appeared there, consisting of merchants, bankers, lawyers, artisans, and unskilled laborers. As was normal in even the wealthiest societies before modern times, these groups made up only a fraction of the population (on average probably less than 10 percent by 1300), but their importance in medieval Europe was out of all proportion to their numbers.

In some areas, notably northern Italy, where trading opportunities were particularly rich and the authority of the feudal ruler, the Holy Roman emperor, was usually feeble, the towns grew into cities. They extended their power over the neighboring countryside, acquired their own armies and navies, and thus became true city-states. More commonly, the towns had to find themselves a place within the existing structure of feudal monarchy. But their place was an important one: it was in the towns that kings set up their government offices, bishops built their cathedrals, and scholars gathered to form universities (pp. 233-235). Thus, the rural-based civilization of the early Middle Ages became a city-based civilization, like those of earlier Greece and Rome—or neighboring Byzantium and Islam.

The Growth of Trade

As the medieval agricultural boom got under way, the lords of manors and even better-off peasants had more to spend on the luxuries that the towns had to offer. Likewise, with some assurance that crops could be marketed in the towns, peasants and lords had an additional incentive for increasing farm output. Church lords and nobles, instead of consuming all the food and supplies that the peasants produced for them, sold some of the produce in the towns in return for cash; or instead of receiving their income in goods and services, they freed their serfs and charged them rents to be paid in money—for money was now seen as the key to new comforts and delights.

Long-Distance Trade

Many luxuries came from the Mediterranean world and the wider intercontinental world to which the Mediterranean gave access. Byzantium and Islam, which dominated the sea's eastern and southern shores, were vigorous commercial societies and manufactured elegant articles for export; in addition, they controlled trade routes that led overland across Central Asia to China and by sea across the Indian Ocean to India and the spice islands of East Asia (pp. 271-272). Their merchandise was brought to western Europe

> "*Throughout Europe, the serfs cut down forests, drained swamps, and brought grasslands under the plow. Thousands of new villages sprang up, and by 1300 the population of Europe had risen from roughly 40 million to about 100 million.*"

overland through Spain or, more commonly, through Venice and other port cities of northern Italy (Map 11.1 on page 198). Constantinople was the main source of luxury goods, which found a growing market among European aristocrats. Those who could afford them sought spices (pepper, ginger, and cinnamon); silks and satins; precious jewels; statues; and rugs and tapestries.

In return for these imports, the Europeans began to export woolens and linens, horses, weapons and armor, timber, furs, and slaves. (The word *slave* is derived from *Slav* because Slavs, captured in wars among themselves or with their German and Hungarian neighbors, often ended up being sold by Italian merchants in the slave markets of Byzantium and the Muslim world.) From all parts of Europe, caravans carried goods across the Alps, chiefly to Milan, Pisa, and Venice, for transshipment further east. Northern Italy thus became the commercial gateway between western Europe and the rest of the Eastern Hemisphere.

Industry and Technology

The wool and textile industries provided the bulk of European exports. These industries centered in the Low Countries, where conditions were favorable for sheep raising. In time, this region gained fame also for its manufacture of woolen cloth, and Flemish producers finally had to turn to outside sources of raw wool to satisfy their needs. After the thirteenth century, both in England and on the mainland of Europe, there was a growing cash market for wool. English farmers and landlords met this demand by converting more of their holdings into pastureland, and in this way, became participants in the new trading economy.

The increase in wealth brought about by the growth of agriculture and trade also fostered a spirit of technical progress, which was shared not only by "those who worked" but also by "those who fought" and "those who prayed."

Enterprising craftsmen, wanting to save labor and increase production in their workshops, devised ingenious mechanisms to adapt the waterwheel, long used for grinding grain, to all sorts of other tasks. Hammering raw iron to remove impurities, beating rags into pulp to make paper, stamping on woolen cloth to thicken it—all these and many other manufacturing processes came to be done by water-powered machinery. Feudal lords wishing to besiege the castles of their rivals equipped their forces with trebuchets—huge wooden contraptions that

Famous Makers and European Centers of Arms and Armor Production (http://www.metmuseum.org/toah/hd/make/hd_make.htm) Learn more about arms and armor production in medieval Europe.

FROM MERCHANT TO HERMIT: THE CAREER OF *ST. GODRIC OF FINCHALE*

Godric of Finchale, who lived in the eleventh and twelfth centuries, began as a trader and ended his life as a hermit (a solitary seeker after God) in the north of England. His biographer Reginald of Durham describes the steps by which Godric rose from being a small-time peddler to a successful and wealthy merchant, and then turned away from the world, in an era when the medieval economy was growing and commerce was turning into big business.

When the boy had passed his childhood years quietly at home, then, as he began to grow to manhood, he began to follow more prudent ways of life, and to learn carefully and persistently the teachings of worldly forethought. Wherefore he chose not to follow the life of a husbandman [farmer] but rather to study, learn, and exercise the rudiments of more subtle conceptions. For this reason, aspiring to the merchant's trade, he began to follow the chapman's [peddler's] way of life, first learning how to gain in small bargains and things of insignificant price; and thence, while yet a youth, his mind advanced little by little to buy and sell and gain from things of greater expense. For, in his beginnings, he was wont to wander with small wares around the villages and farmsteads of his own neighbourhood; but, in process of time, he gradually associated himself by compact with city merchants. Hence, within a brief space of time, the youth who had trudged for many weary hours from village to village, from farm to farm, did so profit by his increase of age and wisdom as to travel with associates of his own age through towns and boroughs, fortresses and cities, to fairs and to all the various booths of the market-place, in pursuit of his public chaffer [bargaining]. He went along the highway, neither puffed up by the good testimony of his

conscience nor downcast in the nobler part of his soul by the reproach of poverty. . . .

Yet in all things he walked with simplicity; and, in so far as he yet knew how, it was ever his pleasure to follow in the footsteps of the truth. For, having learned the Lord's Prayer and the Creed from his very cradle, he oftentimes turned them over in his mind, even as he went alone on his longer journeys; and, in so far as the truth was revealed to his mind, he clung thereunto most devoutly in all his thoughts concerning God. At first, he lived as a chapman [peddler] for four years in Lincolnshire, going on foot and carrying the smallest wares; then he travelled abroad, first to St. Andrews in Scotland and then for the first time to Rome. On his return, having formed a familiar friendship with certain other young men who were eager for merchandise, he began to launch upon bolder courses and to coast frequently by sea to the foreign lands that lay around him. Thus, sailing often to and fro between Scotland and Britain, he traded in many divers wares and, amid these occupations, learned much worldly wisdom. . . .

Then he purchased the half of a merchant-ship with certain of his partners in the trade; and again by his prudence he bought the fourth part of another ship. At length, by his skill

used the counterweight principle to hurl boulders weighing as much as a ton. And bishops and abbots, desiring their cathedral and monastery towers to be heard as well as seen across miles of countryside, urged on metalworkers to develop methods of large-scale bronze casting that would produce monster bells. The spurt of technical progress that began in the Middle Ages continued and accelerated without a break until it ended in the Industrial Revolution of the eighteenth and nineteenth centuries (pp. 256-258, 422-425).

The Location and Appearance of Towns

Towns usually appeared at places where land and water routes converged: sheltered harbors, junctions of highways, or conflu-

ences of rivers. Often, there were already settlements at these places that welcomed merchants and craftspeople—government centers of kings and great lords, cathedrals of bishops, Viking trading posts, and ancient cities that had survived the fall of Rome. In some parts of Europe, particularly "frontier" areas such as eastern Germany, new towns were deliberately founded. Kings and nobles cooperated in founding them on account of their strategic value, but rarely took part in their actual government. In other regions, the townspeople had to struggle for many generations to win from the rulers, great lords, and bishops a degree of self-government for their communities.

However a town came into being, it needed walls—in fact, the word *town* derives from the Anglo-Saxon *tun*, meaning "fortified enclosure." If an existing settlement grew into a town,

in navigation, wherein he excelled all his fellows, he earned promotion to the post of steersman. . . .

For he was vigorous and strenuous in mind, whole of limb and strong in body. He was of middle stature, broad-shouldered and deep-chested, with a long face, grey eyes most clear and piercing, bushy brows, a broad forehead, long and open nostrils, a nose of comely curve, and a pointed chin. His beard was thick, and longer than the ordinary, his mouth well-shaped, with lips of moderate thickness; in youth his hair was black, in age as white as snow; his neck was short and thick, knotted with veins and sinews; his legs were somewhat slender, his instep high, his knees hardened and horny with frequent kneeling; his whole skin rough beyond the ordinary, until all this roughness was softened by old age. . . .

And now he had lived sixteen years as a merchant, and began to think of spending on charity, to God's honour and service, the goods which he had so laboriously acquired. He therefore took the cross as a pilgrim to Jerusalem, and, having visited the Holy Sepulchre, came back to England by way of St. James [of Compostella]. Not long afterwards he became steward to a certain rich man of his own country, with the care of his whole house and household. But certain of the younger houschold were men of iniquity, who stole their neighbours' cattle and thus held luxurious feasts, whereas Godric, in his ignorance, was sometimes present. Afterwards, discovering the truth, he rebuked and admonished them to cease; but they made no account of his warnings; wherefore he concealed not their iniquity, but disclosed it to the lord of the household, who, however, slighted his advice. Wherefore he begged to be dismissed and went on a pilgrimage, first to St. Gilles and thence to Rome the abode of the Apostles, that thus he might knowingly pay the penalty for those misdeeds wherein he had ignorantly partaken. I have often seen him, even in his old age, weeping for this unknowing transgression. . . .

Godric, when he had restored his mother safe to his father's arms, abode but a brief while at home; for he was now already firmly purposed to give himself entirely to God's service. Wherefore, that he might follow Christ the more freely, he sold all his possessions and distributed them among the poor. Then, telling his parents of this purpose and receiving their blessing, he went forth to no certain abode, but whithersoever the Lord should deign to lead him; for above all things he coveted the life of a hermit.

EXPLORING THE SOURCE

1. How did Godric start out as a trader, and what were the main stages of his commercial career? What does this tell about the ways of achieving business success around 1100?

2. Does Godric's decision to give up the life of a merchant seem to you reasonable or foolish, and why?

Source: Reginald of Durham, "Life of St.Godric of Finchale," in *Social Life in Britain from the Conquest to the Reformation,* ed. G. G. Coulton (Cambridge: Cambridge University Press, 1918), pp. 415–420.

its fortifications were lengthened to make room; if a town was newly founded, it soon acquired walls. The remains of these town walls may still be seen in many of the old cities of Europe, notably Carcassonne in France, Avila in Spain, and Rothenburg in Germany.

Rothenburg, Germany's Model Medieval Village (http://www.roadstoruins.com/rothenburg.html) Tour the medieval town of Rothenburg, Germany.

Understandably, space was at a premium in these towns. Streets and passageways were kept as narrow as possible so that a maximum number of buildings could be erected within the walls, and the buildings themselves had as many stories as safety would permit. Even so, as the numbers of townspeople increased, many of them took the risk of living outside the walls, and towns grew *suburbs* (from the Latin for "beneath the walled town"). Both inside and outside the walls, housing was painfully cramped—tighter, sometimes, than the space in peasants' cottages. There was very little town planning, and sanitation was notoriously poor. From the very earliest times, European cities faced problems of congestion, traffic jams, infectious diseases, slums, and devastating citywide fires.

Nevertheless, there was a certain order in most medieval towns. By the thirteenth century, a typical pattern had appeared. The town was usually dominated by the towers or spires of its main church. Next in importance were the town hall and the buildings of the various trading and industrial organizations, the guilds. The heart of the town was the central marketplace with its stalls selling produce from the nearby countryside,

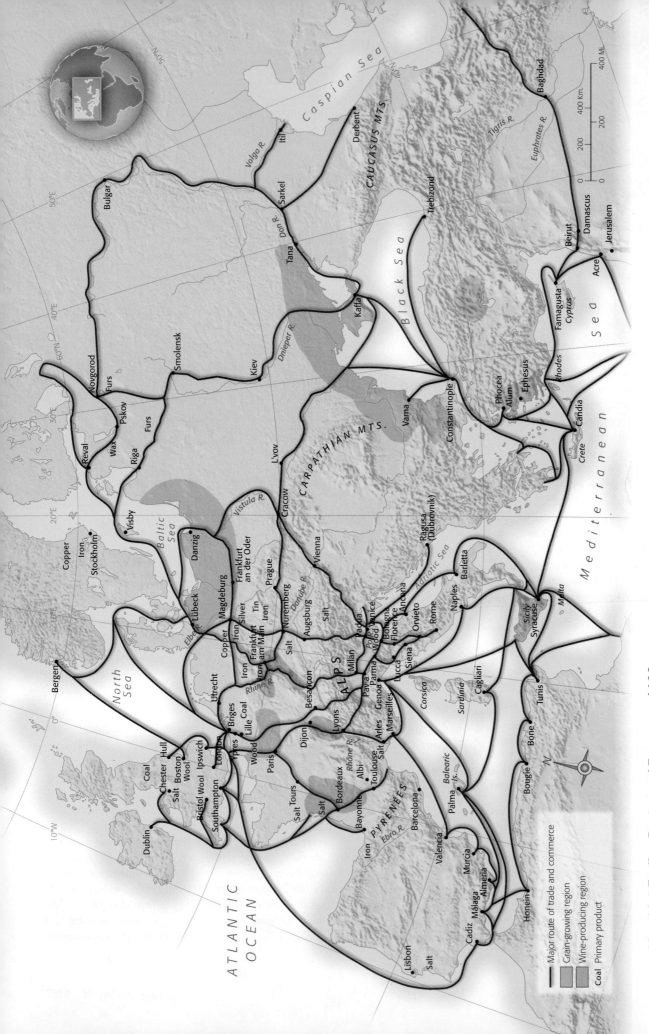

Interactive
Map

Map 11.1 Trading Routes and Towns, ca. 1100

With Europe's medieval economic boom well under way, the network of land and sea routes and important towns is still densest in areas that once belonged to the Roman Empire—through southern and western Europe and across the Mediterranean to the Islamic world. But the network has also extended to places that were far from civilization in Roman times—Scandinavia and the Baltic, and eastern Europe as far as Russia. © Cengage Learning

Major route of trade and commerce

Grain-growing region

Wine-producing region

Coal Primary product

locally manufactured goods, and luxury items from distant lands (see photo). The marketplace and nearby streets were likely to be lined with houses where families lived, worked, and sold what they made—all in the same building, since most industry and commerce, like farming, was carried on by small family businesses.

The Life of Townspeople

Unlike the peasants, all townspeople were legally free, but the towns had a social structure of their own. At the top were the leading merchants and moneylenders and the heads of the guilds.

Beneath them were skilled artisans and clerks, and at the bottom were apprentices and unskilled laborers.

The members of the highest group dominated civic affairs and constituted a new element in European society, which gained in wealth and power as the centuries passed. But except in regions like northern Italy where the cities were truly the dominant force in society, even the wealthiest and most powerful townspeople were regarded as legally and socially inferior to the clergy and the nobility.

Because the whole pattern of life in the towns was different from that of the feudal estate, a new plan for government had to be devised for the new communities. The townspeople

≪ **The Ravenna Gate Market, Bologna** An early fifteenth-century picture shows a market specializing in textiles just inside the walls of a north Italian city. Cloths are displayed on counters, hang from ceilings, and lie around in unopened bales. A porter bends under his load and a storekeeper waits for customers; one woman inspects merchandise and another has made up her mind to buy. A crucifix presides in its shrine over the busy commercial scene.

Scala/Art Resource NY

Trade and Towns **199**

charter
A document granting rights and privileges to a person or institution—in particular, a document permitting the establishment of a town and allowing the townspeople to establish their own rules and government in exchange for regular payments of money to the grantor.

guild
An organization of merchants or craftspeople who regulated the activities of their members and set standards and prices.

master
A craftsman who had the right to operate workshops, train others, and vote on guild business.

journeyman
A licensed artisan who had served an apprenticeship and who was employed by a master and paid at a fixed rate per day.

apprentice
A "learner" in the shop of a master.

> "*In the first place, that no one of the trade of spurriers shall work longer than from the beginning of the day until curfew rings out at the church of St. Sepulcher, without Newgate; by reason that no man can work so neatly by night as by day. . . . And further, many of the said trade are wandering about all day, without working at all at their trade; and then, when they have become drunk and frantic, they take to their work, to the annoyance of the sick, and all their neighborhood as well.*"
>
> —from regulations of the Spurriers' Guild (makers of spurs for horses) of London, 1345

sought special **charters**—documents that would free them from the customary obligations of the feudal relationship and would permit them to establish appropriate rules of their own. These charters, granted by the king, nobleman, or bishop holding authority over the area, recognized the citizens of the town as a collective group or *corporation*, with legal privileges and powers. In return for these privileges, and in place of feudal services, the corporation made regular payments of money to the grantor. The form of government differed from one town to another, but in most places, control rested in the hands of a governing council and a mayor. Though voting rights (for adult males only) were often quite liberal, it was uncommon for any but the leading families to hold important offices.

 New Regulations: No Work After Sundown Read a sampling of regulations from the spurriers' (spur makers) guild.

The Guilds

The governing council imposed strict political control on the community. Legally, the citizens of a town were free individuals, but the idea of collective responsibility and regulation was accepted in town and countryside alike. Merchants and craftspeople formed special organizations called **guilds**. The guilds limited production and sale of goods to their members, upheld standards of business practice and quality of merchandise, and set prices for every commodity.

The principal organization in most towns was the merchant guild, which established rules for the times and places at which goods could be sold, weights and measures, and grades and prices of goods. At first, the merchant guild included most of the tradespeople in a given town. With growing specialization, however, one group after another split off from the parent unit to form independent craft guilds: weavers, dyers, tailors, carpenters, masons, silversmiths, bakers, barbers, and the like. By the thirteenth century, there might be as many as thirty or forty guilds in a single town.

The primary function of a craft guild was to supervise the production of goods and the training of artisans. Craftsmen were classified as **masters**, **journeymen**, and **apprentices**. Only masters had the right to operate workshops and train others; they alone were voting members of the guild and directed its policies, and their coveted status was won by other craftsmen only after long experience and proof of excellence. Before the masters admitted a journeyman to their rank, they customarily required him to submit an example of his workmanship—his *masterpiece*. Journeymen were licensed artisans who had served an apprenticeship. They were employed by the masters and were usually paid at a fixed rate per day (in French, *journée*). Before becoming a journeyman, an individual was obliged to work for a specified period of time, ranging from two to seven years, as an apprentice (learner) in the shop of a master. In return for their labor, apprentices received only food and lodging. Though women of the towns were permitted to perform some skilled and unskilled services, they were generally excluded from guild membership.

The guilds also performed charitable and social functions. If a member fell sick, was put in jail, or got into some other kind of trouble, he could count on help from the guild brotherhood. The guilds provided proper ceremonies on the occasions of births, marriages, and funerals; they conducted social affairs; and they celebrated Church festivals as a body. Each one, moreover, honored a particular saint who was associated by tradition with a given craft—Saint Joseph, for example, was honored by carpenters. The guilds often dedicated altars or chapels in the town church to their special saints. In all their varied activities, they embodied the corporate and community spirit so characteristic of medieval society.

Listen to a synopsis of Chapter 11.

CHAPTER 12

WESTERN CHRISTENDOM AND ITS NEIGHBORS, 1000–1300

LEARNING OBJECTIVES

AFTER READING THIS CHAPTER, YOU SHOULD BE ABLE TO DO THE FOLLOWING:

LO¹ Describe the changes in the Church during the Middle Ages, and explain how those changes were related to society and government.

LO² Discuss the goals and outcomes of the Crusades.

LO³ Describe the challenges facing eastern Europe as western Europe grew stronger.

> **"THE SINGLE MOST IMPORTANT INFLUENCE ON MEDIEVAL EUROPE WAS RELIGION—SO MUCH SO THAT EUROPEANS AT THE TIME USUALLY CALLED THEIR PART OF THE WORLD NOT BY A GEOGRAPHICAL NAME BUT BY A RELIGIOUS ONE—'CHRISTENDOM.'"**

As with earlier civilizations, the single most important influence on medieval Europe was religion—so much so that Europeans at the time usually called their part of the world not by a geographical name but by a religious one—"Christendom." In the early Middle Ages, two regions had developed within Christendom: a western region looking to Rome, and an eastern one looking to Constantinople (p. 180). Christians in both regions still saw themselves as belonging to a single Church, and in both regions, the conversion of barbarian peoples, the rise in population, the agricultural boom, and the revival of trade brought the Church more territory, believers, and wealth. But as with other features of the renewal of European civilization, the renewal of Christianity brought the greatest changes in the West.

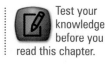

Test your knowledge before you read this chapter.

One feature of this Western renewal was an upsurge of new developments in the Church's beliefs, practices, and organization. More humanly appealing forms of devotion appeared that made heaven seem more accessible to believers and strengthened the authority of the clergy who controlled this access. New groups of monks and nuns were founded—some to make up for the failings of existing groups that had been spoiled by increasing wealth, and others to adapt to the needs of the growing towns.

All these changes gained approval and backing from the popes, who were striving to bring the whole Church under their central control. Their efforts ran into determined resistance from their partners and rivals, the rulers of the western European feudal states. All the same, the popes acquired such authority that they became for a time the most powerful rulers in western Europe.

What do you think?

The Crusades are an example of the misuse of religion.

Strongly Disagree						Strongly Agree
1	2	3	4	5	6	7

≪ Krak des Chevaliers The "Fortress of the Knights" was built in the twelfth-century Holy Land by crusading warrior-monks, the Knights Hospitalers. To the east beyond the castle lay Muslim-held land; this side belonged to the County of Tripoli, a crusader foothold on the Mediterranean coast that the castle helped protect. With its double walls, its state-of-the-art round towers that had no vulnerable corners, and its 2,000-strong garrison, the castle withstood besiegers such as the renowned Muslim commander Saladin for more than a century.

Nick Ledger/Alamy

Religious renewal and that of civilization in general also combined to produce two other features of Western Christendom: bitter internal conflicts and an urge toward outward expansion. New heresies arose that denied the authority and holiness of the clergy. Christian resentment of Jews in the growing towns led to frequent explosions of anti-Jewish violence. And beyond the frontiers of Western Christendom stood yet more religious enemies—above all, Islam.

Accordingly, Western Christendom also invested its newfound skills in formidable attacks on its religious foes. The Church tribunals of the Inquisition devised complex procedures of investigation and punishment to enforce religious conformity. Rulers of powerful feudal states used their government machinery to expel the Jews from entire countries. And the main forces in medieval society—the Church, the feudal warriors, and the towns—combined to undertake a series of unprecedented long-distance expeditions against religious enemies—the Crusades.

These holy wars failed in the most famous of the purposes for which they were fought: to regain the Holy Land permanently from Islam. They led to a split with Eastern Christendom, which came to be seen in the West as a religious opponent because it would not accept the rule of the pope. But the Crusades also brought colonists and missionaries to conquered territories in Muslim Spain and remaining pagan regions in eastern Europe, as well as traders to seaports in the eastern Mediterranean. In this way, the Crusades set a precedent of colonizing and converting non-Christian lands, and of long-distance overseas trade, which was to be followed by empire-building western European nations at the end of the Middle Ages.

LO¹ The Western Church

Both halves of the Church inherited their basic features from the early Christianity of the Roman Empire (Chapter 8), but within the Western Church, many of these features developed

CHRONOLOGY

910	Monastery of Cluny is founded; beginning of the Cluniac reform
1054	Disputes between the Eastern (Orthodox) and the Western (Catholic) Churches result in mutual excommunications
1095	Pope Urban II launches the First Crusade
1098	Abbey at Cîteaux founded; beginning of the Cistercian order
1099	Crusaders take Jerusalem; Latin Kingdom of Jerusalem established
1122	Investitures Dispute between the pope and emperor is settled in a power-sharing compromise
1170–1221	Life of Dominic, founder of Dominican order
1181–1226	Life of Francis, founder of Franciscan order
1187	Saladin crushes army of Latin Kingdom; regains Jerusalem for Muslims
1204	Constantinople looted by western crusaders; Latin Empire of Constantinople founded
1231	Pope Gregory IX establishes the Inquisition to find and try heretics
1261	Byzantine emperor regains Constantinople

in new ways—both shaping and responding to other changes in the government and society of western Europe.

The Church's Worship

Church worship took on even greater significance in the Middle Ages as a path to divine aid in this world and the afterlife.

The Sacraments

Ever since the earliest days of Christianity, believers had undergone ceremonies that they believed were necessary to admit them to Christ's kingdom (p. 128). Over many centuries, the number of these ceremonies had increased in East and West alike, but Western religious thinkers developed a specific theory of how many such ceremonies there were and how they worked.

The Western Church recognized seven **sacraments** (from the Latin word for "holy"). All of them were traced back to gospel commands and sayings of Jesus, who had established them as a means of **grace**—divine aid to sinful men and women without which they could not be saved.

Four of the sacraments must be undergone by all believers. Through *baptism* a person gained entry to Christ's kingdom (usually as an infant) and was cleansed of the stain of sin. *Confirmation* was administered to baptized people later on, to confirm them in their acceptance of baptism and strengthen them in faith. *Penance* involved confession to a priest and acceptance of a penalty, thereby cleansing believers of recently committed sins and making them worthy to receive the *Eucharist* ("Thanksgiving) or *Mass* (probably from the Latin for "dismissal," because the congregation was told to leave at the end of the service). The Church taught that at a certain moment in the rite, the bread and wine were transformed in their inmost nature ("substance") into the body and blood of the Savior, while keeping the outward appearance of bread and wine—a process known as **transubstantiation** ("transfer of substance"). The recipients, united with each other and with Christ himself, would be aided in doing good and resisting evil.

The other three sacraments were not compulsory for all believers. Through *extreme unction* ("final anointing") Christians in danger of death were granted final forgiveness of sins, but death was too unpredictable for everyone to receive this sacrament. *Ordination* was the sacrament whereby a bishop made a person a priest with the miraculous power to administer sacraments. The seventh sacrament was *matrimony*, the joining together of husband and wife so long as they both lived; the Church did not permit divorce, though widows and widowers could remarry.

Ever since Christianity began, believers had had to contend with the problem of how to keep their standing as members of Christ's kingdom if they sinned after baptism. The seven sacraments, guaranteeing believers divine aid and forgiveness throughout their lives, broadened the narrow path to salvation. And the actual sacraments were accompanied by many other practices and observances that made God and his kingdom more accessible to sinful humans.

Jesus the Human

It was a basic doctrine of Christianity that Christ the Son of God and Jesus the human being were one and the same person, but Christian worship had traditionally stressed the Savior's role as God. Early medieval art usually portrayed him as the risen Christ sitting in royal dignity upon the heavenly throne (see photo on page 206). Sometime after the year 1000, a new view began to prevail. It emphasized Jesus's human experiences—his struggles, humiliations, and sufferings. Both theologians (religious thinkers) and the common people drew fresh meaning from the suffering of their Lord, recognizing in his agony their own anguish and miseries. Artists increasingly showed the dying Savior hanging heavily from the Cross. Gradually, the crucifix, which aroused in pious hearts the deepest feelings of compassion and love, became the most popular devotional object (see photo on page 207).

Medieval Images of Christ from the Getty Museum (http://www.getty.edu/gettyguide/displayObjectList?sub= 2032280) View a gallery of medieval images of Jesus.

In the same way, the infant Jesus in early portraits appears as a kingly figure, but during the Middle Ages he was made to look like any infant held in the arms of a loving mother. And his mother, Mary, was presented in an ever more tender and human light.

The Virgin Mary and the Saints

The cult of the Virgin was exceedingly popular in the Middle Ages. The monasteries played a leading role in developing it, but ordinary people responded warmly to the appeal of Mary. Aside from her role as the Mother of God, she personified the Christian ideals of womanhood, love, and sympathy. During an upsurge of religious fervor in the twelfth and thirteenth centuries, many of the great new cathedrals were dedicated to Mary. A rich literature and a host of legends came into being that told of the countless miracles of the Virgin. She was pictured as loyal and forgiving toward all who honored her and ready to give earthly benefits and heavenly rewards to those who prayed to her. And the opinion gained ground among believers, though it was not yet officially accepted by the Church, that Mary, unlike all other humans, was completely free of sin.

Medieval Images of Mary from the Getty Museum (http://www.getty.edu/art/gettyguide/displayObjectList?sub= 2032407) View a gallery of medieval images of Mary.

No other human was considered sinless, but ever since early Christian times, it had been customary to revere apostles and martyrs as especially close to God. Later on, exceptionally devoted hermits, monks, and nuns, as well as exceptionally pious laypeople (ordinary believers), also came to be regarded as saints (holy people). In this way, the numbers of saints increased over the centuries, so that by medieval times, the Church revered several thousand of them. Most of them had first gained the reputation of sainthood in the places where they had spent their lives; local bishops and heads of monasteries had supported or led public opinion; and reverence for them had then spread more or less widely. In the thirteenth century, another step became necessary: the pope himself must canonize a person (formally identify him or her as a saint).

A Comprehensive List of Catholic Saints and Angels (http://www.catholic.org/saints/) Learn more about the lives and legends of Catholic saints.

Christians traditionally showed the saints the special honor of veneration (deep reverence). Veneration was not the same as worship (which was reserved for God), but it did include praying to saints for their favor and help. Saints, in turn, could intercede (plead with) God to miraculously grant a human need, whether

transubstantiation
In Catholic belief, the process of "transfer of substance" in the Mass, whereby bread and wine are transformed in their inmost nature ("substance") into the body and blood of Christ while keeping their original outward appearance.

Christ on His Throne This late-twelfth-century statue is carved in a tympanum (a space above a doorway) in the west façade of the cathedral of Saint-Trophîme in the southern French town of Arles. Christ is crowned as a king and seated upon a throne as he blesses the world and holds a Bible on his knee. He is surrounded by winged creatures symbolic of the Evangelists (authors of the Gospels)—an angel (Matthew), a lion (Mark), an ox (Luke), and an eagle (John). Scala/Art Resource, NY

recovery from sickness, rain in time of drought, or victory in battle. God was believed to grant such requests to show both his power and the holiness of the saint who made it.

Hardly any act was undertaken in the Middle Ages without first calling upon these Christian heroes who could influence God himself. Moreover, some of their power was thought to stay on earth in their real or alleged clothing, possessions, and bodily remains (*relics*) (see photo on page 208). Oaths and treaties were sworn on relics; townspeople carried them in religious processions, and knights often inserted them in the hilts of their swords. People traveled hundreds of miles on pilgrimage to the shrines of famous saints where their relics were preserved to ask for favors or give thanks for help received.

The Saints and Purgatory

Above all, the saints could also give benefits in the other world. Since early times, Christians had prayed for the dead, as if the path to salvation continued after death and souls still needed help to travel it. Out of this practice, there developed the belief in **purgatory**—a place where souls that were not hopelessly sinful would be cleansed of sin before entering God's kingdom. The cleansing process was long and painful, including fire that, in the words of the fourth-century thinker Augustine (p. 143), "will be harder to bear than anything a human being can suffer in this life."

>> **Christ on the Cross** The Gero Crucifix, a life-size wood carving made for Archbishop Gero of Cologne toward the year 1000, is one of the earliest appearances in art of the figure of Christ suffering on the Cross. Traditionally, artists had treated the Crucifixion as a scene of the divine Savior triumphing over death. Here, by contrast, Jesus is shown with his arms stretched back, his knees giving way, and his head hanging down—a human being in the last agony of a cruel death. Erich Lessing/Art Resource, NY

purgatory
In Catholic belief, a place where souls that are not hopelessly sinful will be cleansed of sin before entering God's kingdom.

indulgence
A reduction in the time a person must spend in purgatory, issued by the pope.

But God would shorten the suffering of the "Poor Souls" in response to the earnest prayers of believers, of monks and nuns whose way of life brought them closer to him, and above all, of the saints who surrounded him in heaven. In the eleventh century, the popes began issuing **indulgences**—reducing the time a person must spend in purgatory so long as that person demonstrated true repentance for sin. God, it was believed, would honor the pope's action in consideration of the accumulated holiness of the saints and of Christ himself, which made up for the failings of sinners. In ways like these, medieval practices made the path of salvation easier to travel.

The Clergy

Ever since Christianity became the religion of Rome, the clergy had been one of the most powerful groups in society, and events in Western Christendom since the fall of Rome had caused their power to grow greater still. As barbarian peoples became Christian, bishoprics, parishes, and monasteries sprang up among them. As bishoprics and monasteries accumulated land, bishops and abbots became full partners in government and politics with kings and great lords, and as feudal relationships developed, they became leading vassals like the barons (p. 187). As feudalism grew into a system of government, illiterate kings and great lords depended on the clergy to staff their government offices. And as the path to salvation became easier to travel, more than ever the clergy became guides and gatekeepers on the path. Practices grew up that symbolized their special status apart from and above the laity. At the Mass,

> "*Gradually, the crucifix, which aroused in pious hearts the deepest feelings of compassion and love, became the most popular devotional object.*"

laypeople received only bread, while the clergy received both bread and wine; popes and bishops insisted that ordained priests be celibate (unmarried).

Corruption in the Church

But exactly because the clergy were so wealthy and powerful, they were deeply entangled with the society that they were supposed to be guiding. The choice of bishops, abbots, and even parish priests was too important to be left to the Church. Instead, kings and great lords maneuvered relatives and political allies into bishoprics, and landowners who founded monasteries and parishes gained the hereditary right to appoint abbots and parish priests. Often, the appointers also took the Church's welfare into consideration, and the appointees turned out to be zealous religious guides—but often, too, the appointees turned out to be zealous political operatives or zealous devotees of the luxury and pleasure to which wealth and power gave access. The increased power of clergy as gatekeepers on an easier path to heaven likewise opened the way to moneymaking abuses—the sale of fake relics, and indulgences exchanged for cash without real repentance.

Medieval believers were well aware of these problems; in fact, throughout the Middle Ages, no one was more generally despised and detested than corrupt and unworthy members of the clergy. From time to time, public opinion would revolt against corruption in the Church, and there would be a cleanup campaign. As with every cleanup campaign in every era, sooner or later the hue and cry would die down and the problem would return. Still, medieval struggles against Church corruption were genuine movements of religious striving, and because the Church was so important in society, they also had

>> Saint Andrew's Sandal Gold, ivory, pearls, and precious stones cover this reliquary (relic casket), and a life-size hammered-gold sandaled foot tells of a revered object inside—the sole of a sandal said to have belonged to Jesus's disciple Andrew. Archbishop Egbert of Trier in western Germany, who commissioned the casket about A.D. 1000, used it as an altar for saying Mass when away from a church. Portable altars for important people, and reliquaries in the shape of the relics they contained, were common in medieval times. Scala/Art Resource, NY

massive social and political consequences—especially the first great struggle, in the tenth and eleventh centuries.

The struggle began at a time when the Carolingian empire was collapsing, and no ruler was able to wield wide-ranging power over the Western Church mainly for the Church's benefit, as Charlemagne had done (p. 171). Corruption in the Church was on the rise, and so were distrust and anger against the clergy—against bishops who bought their positions from great lords and let their parish priests live as illiterate drunkards; and against high-living abbots of wealthy monasteries who let their monks neglect their prayers and books and take the vow of chastity lightly. But it was also religiously devoted abbots, allied with earnest-minded great lords and conscientious bishops, who were the first leaders of the campaign for reform.

Cycles of Reform: Cluny and Cîteaux

The most far-reaching reform effort was undertaken by the monastery of Cluny (**KLOO-nee**), founded in Burgundy (in eastern France) in 910 by the duke of Aquitaine (**AK-i-teyn**). The first abbot, Berno, set out to revive the strictness of the Benedictine rule (regulations for monks and nuns—p. 144), which was followed by many monasteries in Western Christendom, and his efforts were carried on by a series of extraordinary abbots. Many new monasteries were founded and old ones were reformed on Cluniac principles throughout western and central Europe, with generous support from lords and bishops who were attracted by Cluny's reputation for holiness.

To protect individual monasteries from falling under local political influences, the Cluniac monks placed themselves under the direct authority of the pope. For the same reason, the abbots of Cluny did not allow newly founded monasteries to become independent, as Benedictine monasteries had traditionally been. Instead, they were "daughter houses" subject to the "mother house," and the priors (deputy abbots) who governed them were appointed by the Great Abbot of Cluny.

From Cluny, the movement for reform spread to all parts of the clergy. Cluniac monks became bishops, **simony** (the selling of Church services or offices) was exposed and reduced, and the behavior of parish clergy was more strictly controlled. But in the end, Cluny's very success brought about its decline as a model of reform. By the twelfth century, surrounded by mounting wealth and influence, the monks of Cluny slipped into the ways of material ease.

Repeating the Cluniac pattern, a new **religious order** (group of monasteries following the same way of life) now appeared. This order also arose in Burgundy, with the founding of an abbey at Cîteaux (**SEE-toe**) in 1098. Its daughter houses expanded spectacularly under the leadership of Bernard of Clairvaux (**KLER-voe**), who was to promote the Second Crusade of 1147–1149. The Cistercians (from *Cistercium*, the Latin name of Cîteaux) wore white robes to distinguish themselves from the black of the Benedictines. There was acute rivalry between the two orders, with the Cistercians at first deploring the riches of Cluny. But the white robes, too, became soiled by economic success, gifts, and worldly power. Within a century of the abbey's founding, the Cistercians had fallen to the comforts of wealth.

A New Kind of Holiness: The Friars

Early in the thirteenth century, a young Italian, Francis of Assisi, felt himself called to live his life in imitation of Christ. The son of a wealthy merchant, Francis followed Jesus's gospel command and gave up his home, his fine clothing, and the security of his family. For a thousand years, many strivers after holiness had done the same, but usually they had gone into the wilderness to live alone as hermits. Francis, however, walked the highways and city streets, begging for food and lodging and preaching as well as praying.

Soon he was joined by like-minded companions, forming a company of twelve who took over an abandoned building near Assisi as a base from which they continued to wander, preaching the ideal of Christian love and brotherhood. A wealthy lady, Clare, became Francis's disciple, and women as well as men followed his way of life of "holy poverty." Married people who could not join the actual Franciscan friars (from the French word for "brothers") and "Poor Clare" sisters joined Francis's "Third Order" to follow his example as best they could.

In this way, Francis founded a movement of religious striving of a new kind—one that did not withdraw from the world, but was very much part of it. Within a century, there were groups of Franciscans and Poor Clares in towns and cities throughout western Europe. To do their work, these groups needed permanent living quarters and places of worship, and they disputed fiercely whether their ideal of poverty allowed them to own land and buildings. But this did not prevent them from becoming the most important single influence on the religious life of the burgeoning towns of Western Christendom (see photo on page 210).

Francis himself was a mystic—one who seeks God's truth through inner inspiration and revelation. He and his fellow mystics were doubtful of book learning and human reason. Of a contrary view was the Spaniard Dominic, a contemporary of Francis. Dominic was an intellectual, who saw the Christian faith as a reasoned approach to truth, and the order of friars he founded was devoted chiefly to scholarship, teaching, and preaching—their official name was the "Order of Preachers." Alarmed by the spread of heretical doctrines in his time, Dominic believed he could best serve the Lord by guiding the thoughts and education of Christians. Francis appealed mainly to people's hearts; Dominic appealed more to their minds. But Dominican communities and churches spread as widely as Franciscan ones, Dominican scholars were prominent in newly founded universities, and Dominican inquisitors were in charge of preventing the spread of heresies.

> **The Franciscan Archive** (http://www.franciscan-archive.org/index2.html) Learn more about the life of Francis and his followers.

> **"My Last Will and Testament," Francis of Assisi** Read Francis's guidance to his followers about how to carry on after his death.

> ❝*Medieval struggles against Church corruption were genuine movements of religious striving, and because the Church was so important in society, they also had massive social and political consequences.* ❞

The Papal Monarchy

The greatest changes in the Western Church involved the papacy itself. Traditionally, the popes were obeyed throughout Western Christendom in matters of belief and worship but had little or no governing power, such as over the appointment of clergy. Furthermore, as bishops of Rome, they were themselves chosen by the traditional method of election by the clergy and male believers of their bishopric (p. 129). In practice, this meant that local nobles controlled the elections, and their rivalries and intrigues had produced many disreputable popes.

However, as the Holy Roman emperors became powerful rulers and began to take an interest in the affairs of Italy (p. 178), they sometimes intervened to appoint their own candidates—most of them worthy and conscientious churchmen. It was one such imperial appointee, Pope Leo IX, a German bishop much influenced by Cluniac ideals, who, toward the middle of the eleventh century, first put the papacy at the head of the movement for Church reform.

The Independent Papacy: Gregory VII

To the more radical reformers, however, it seemed a wicked defiance of the will of God that the successors of Peter (p. 147) should be under the control of any worldly ruler, even reform-minded emperors. The chief promoter of this idea was the Italian Hildebrand. As archdeacon of Rome, a key position in the Church's administration, he proved himself a shrewd planner and tactician.

In 1059, thanks largely to Hildebrand's efforts, a new system was brought into being for the election of popes. From now on, the right to vote was to be restricted to the **cardinal** clergy—a small number of the ranking priests of Rome. The cardinals were appointed by the pope, and when a pope died, they met in seclusion to name his successor. Because they usually chose from their own membership, the body automatically furnished select

> ❝*Francis founded a movement of religious striving of a new kind—one that did not withdraw from the world, but was very much part of it.* ❞

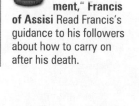

simony
The selling of Church services or offices—from Simon, reported in the New Testament to have offered money to the apostles for a share of their miraculous powers.

religious order
A group of monasteries following the same way of life.

cardinal
One of the ranking priests of Rome, appointed by the pope and authorized to name his successor.

candidates for the papal office. In this way, the voting process was to be insulated from any kind of lay influence, and the choice of the successor of Peter would hopefully be where it belonged—with the Holy Spirit, speaking through a group of clergy who were uniquely qualified to hear his voice.

The Popes and the Church

In 1073, the cardinals chose Hildebrand as Pope Gregory VII. Conditioned by his earlier training at Cluny, he applied himself to a sweeping reform of the Church. To bring this about, it was not enough for him to issue declarations; he must effectively govern the church to put reforming ideals into effect. He kept in touch with the bishops through continual correspondence—the papal letters run to thousands of volumes. He required bishops to make regular visits to Rome, which often involved weeks of arduous travel. He sent out papal legates (ambassadors) to conduct inquiries and see that the pope was being obeyed in the territories they visited. He also began hearing appeals against decisions of bishops on matters such as marriage and ownership of Church property.

All this activity needed an expanded headquarters in Rome. Under Gregory's guidance, the central administration of the papacy came to be handled through a number of bureaus, departments, and assemblies—called, collectively, the papal *curia* (court or council). The officers in charge of these agencies were usually chosen from among the cardinals and formed, in effect, a kind of "cabinet" for the pope. To finance the administration, countless payments started flowing to Rome: fees for appeals from bishops' courts, for dispensations (exemptions) from Church law, for acquiring Church positions, and for indulgences. In this way, Gregory and the popes who followed him built up what amounted to a complex international government system, financed by Church institutions and believers.

In building their power across Western Christendom, the popes were in some ways in the same position as rulers who were building their power across countries (p. 187). The popes, too, had certain assets to begin with—in their case, the Western consensus that they were the Christ-appointed guides of the whole Church. They also had means of compulsion against resisters. They could **excommunicate** opponents, thereby depriving them of the sacraments without which there was no salvation.

A Franciscan Preacher Bernardino of Siena, a fifteenth-century friar, is shown in a painting by a local artist, Sano di Pietro, preaching to a segregated crowd of men and women before his hometown's city hall. The gaunt-faced friar aims harsh words against their sins while holding up a symbol of hope—a plaque with the Greek letters $I H \Sigma$, the Holy Name of Jesus. Two centuries after Francis, his follower made crowds in Siena and throughout Italy kneel in shame and hope. Cathedral Treasury Trier, Photo: Rita Heyen

They could place whole regions under interdict, forbidding the conduct of Church services and thereby depriving whole populations of the sacraments. But these measures would not have worked if local clergy had not been willing to enforce them, and if local laity had not taken them seriously in the first place.

As with rulers, therefore, the main reason that the popes were able to grow powerful was that this seemed in the interest of the people over whom they wielded power—above all, because the popes were seen as leaders in the struggle for Church reform. Obedience to the papacy, it seemed, provided a guarantee that bishops and priests would be conscientious, monks and nuns would be saintly, and laypeople, whether kings and great lords or peasants and craftspeople, would honor the clergy. That suited both laypeople and clergy who wanted to see in the Church to which they belonged a true reflection within earthly society of God's heavenly kingdom.

But earthly society contained other powerful forces, notably the rulers who were also striving for increased power. And no ruler could be truly powerful without the influence in the Church that Gregory wanted to deny them.

Popes and Rulers

Ever since the time of Constantine, Christian teaching had given monarchs a sacred character as well as secular authority. The emperor Charlemagne, who was held up as a model, had appointed bishops and abbots to their offices and had employed churchmen as administrators and teachers in his palace school. The nobility and the clergy supported each other at all levels of feudal government. It was this relationship that Gregory and his successors sought to change.

The Investitures Dispute

By various historical arguments and documents, including the falsified Donation of Constantine (pp. 292–293), Gregory claimed to be the overlord of the rulers of western Europe. He declared, for example, that the Holy Roman emperor, Henry IV, was his vassal, on the grounds that Charlemagne, Henry's predecessor, owed his crown to Pope Leo III (p. 173). He objected particularly to Henry's control over the selection of German bishops, who were important fief-holders and vassals of the emperor. Henry was exercising a traditional right when he influenced their selection and invested (clothed) them with their symbols of office. Gregory insisted, however, that bishops were spiritual officers and could be invested with ring and staff, the symbols of their religious authority, only by the pope. What he sought, of course, was papal control over the elections themselves.

Gregory employed every means at his command to bring Henry down. He plotted with the emperor's enemies in Germany, excommunicated and deposed him (1076), and turned to the Normans in southern Italy for military assistance against Henry's forces. After his excommunication, Henry outmaneuvered his adversary by crossing the Alps in winter and appearing as a penitent before Gregory at the palace of Canossa in northern Italy. Standing barefoot in the snow, he begged the pope to forgive him for his offenses and restore him to communion with the Church. Gregory granted the request, but the contest shortly resumed, and the pope once again excommunicated Henry. In the long run, Gregory lacked sufficient armed power to transform occasional triumphs into lasting victory. The **Investitures Dispute**, as modern scholars call it, was settled later by compromise: Henry's successor agreed in 1122 to give to the pope the investiture of religious symbols, but he retained the emperor's traditional influence over the selection of German bishops.

The Concordat of Worms: Compromise Ends the Investiture Controversy Read a selection from the Concordat of Worms, the compromise that ended the Investitures Dispute.

> **Investitures Dispute**
>
> A conflict, originally between Pope Gregory and Emperor Henry IV, over who had the power to select the bishops of the Holy Roman Empire.

The Papacy at Its Height

Even so, the papacy's growing control over the Church gave it greater power against emperors and kings than ever before. During the reign of Innocent III, the papacy reached its height of prestige and power. Its strength was shown by the humbling of King John of England, who, after a bitter dispute with Innocent over the election of the archbishop of Canterbury, the kingdom's leading churchman, was forced to submit. In the course of the dispute, John was deposed; afterward, in 1213, he was granted the realm of England as a fief from Rome, but only after doing homage to the pope. Such was the international authority of Innocent III that John's subjection to the pope actually strengthened the king's hand in his disputes with his discontented barons (p. 190).

A century later, papal claims were carried even further by Pope Boniface VIII. He met his match, however, in King Philip (the Fair) of France. Philip, who was waging war against England, levied a tax on church properties in 1296. Boniface answered this bold move, which was contrary to existing law, with angry denunciations. The violent dispute reached its climax a few years later when Boniface issued a declaration titled *Unam sanctam*, which insisted that *all* secular rulers were subject to the pope and that the pope could be judged by God alone. (Papal declarations are named after their first two words in Latin, in this case "One Holy" [Catholic and Apostolic Church].) Boniface concluded, daringly, "We declare, state, define, and pronounce that it is altogether necessary to salvation for every human creature to be subject to the Roman pontiff." Yet Boniface's words did not prevail over Philip's deeds. Philip sent a military force across the Alps to seize the aged pontiff. Roughly treated and humiliated by the French soldiers, Boniface died soon afterward in 1303.

The popes had failed to win supremacy over secular rulers or even to put an end to the power of those rulers within the Church. In the partnership and rivalry of Church and state that had begun with Constantine, the balance would soon swing against them. Even so, the position of the papacy within the Church had permanently changed. The popes had won for themselves a position as true rulers of the Church, governing and supervising its operations, which they have kept to the present day.

Rebellion Against the Church

Rulers who opposed the increase in power of the papacy did not question the belief that Christ had founded the Church and appointed a clergy to guide it that was headed by the pope. As the Church grew stronger and better organized, however, there also appeared movements of rebellion against it—new or revived heresies that denied the Church's beliefs and despised the priests, bishops, and pope.

One of the most widespread of these, perhaps descended from the Gnostics of early Christian times (pp. 130–131), proclaimed that only spirit was good, whereas matter was by nature evil. It was the creation not of God himself but of a lesser or opposing being, the "King of the World," and it was this being that the Church served. Sexual intercourse, procreation, and the eating of meat, among other things, were forbidden to God's true devotees, the "Most Perfect Ones," though ordinary "Believers" were permitted an easier way of life. Beliefs of this kind spread widely in both Western and Eastern Christendom, and were always viciously persecuted. They were found in the Balkans throughout the Middle Ages; in the twelfth century, they were widespread in southern France, where they were called the "Albigensian heresy," named for the cathedral town of Albi.

Pope Innocent III proclaimed a crusade against the Albigensians (al-bi-JEN-seez), and French nobles from the north cruelly suppressed the rebellion by 1226. But heresy smoldered even after the crusade was over. To snuff out the remaining embers, Innocent's successor, Pope Gregory IX, established a permanent court for finding and trying heretics: the **Inquisition**.

The Inquisition

The pope's grand inquisitor was placed at Carcassonne (kar-kuh-SON), in the south of France. He sent deputies, drawn chiefly from the new Dominican order, to the towns and cities of the area. In the public square of each place, the deputies would announce their mission and then call for people to testify regarding suspected heretics. In pursuing their inquiries, the deputies followed common judicial practice of the period in using torture to wring confessions from uncooperative suspects and in denying accused persons legal counsel and the right to call or confront witnesses. Proceedings were usually conducted in secret. Lucky prisoners would confess early, repent, and forfeit only their property.

Those who proved stubborn or who lapsed again into heresy after repenting were excommunicated and turned over to the civil authorities for more severe punishment, since Church law forbade the clergy to take life. Because heresy was often associated with popular discontent or rebellion, the civil authorities regarded it as equivalent to treason and therefore set the penalty of death for convicted heretics. The most common means of execution was burning at the stake—a means that symbolized the flames of hell that awaited unrepentant heretics, but also gave heretics a chance to make a final repentance as the flames reached higher and higher. They might then have time to beg for God's forgiveness and the salvation of their souls. But in no case would the fire be quenched; the body of a "confirmed" heretic was already forfeit.

Links to Inquisition Sites (http://www.rarebooks.nd.edu/exhibits/inquisition/text/links.html) Delve into the trials and punishments of the Inquisition.

In the view of medieval churchmen, the end of rooting out heresy justified these cruel means. Even the "angelic doctor" of the Church, Thomas Aquinas (p. 236), held that extreme punishments were necessary to protect souls from the contamination of false beliefs, and the papacy established inquisitions in many regions suspected of heresy besides southern France. But the Inquisition was also open to the foulest abuses. To level the accusation of heresy became a convenient way of injuring or getting rid of personal enemies, and the accusers were never identified by the court. Besides, Church courts subject to the pope came to be unwelcome even to Catholic rulers after the end of the Middle Ages. Except in Spain and Portugal, where the Inquisition became in effect an arm of the government, rulers preferred to use methods of religious repression that were more safely under their control (p. 323).

> "We declare, state, define, and pronounce that it is altogether necessary to salvation for every human creature to be subject to the Roman pontiff."
>
> —Pope Boniface, 1302 (?)

LO² Western Christendom on the Offensive: The Crusades

To the south and east of Christendom, stretching from Spain to the Middle East and beyond, lay the lands of the rival monotheism of Islam. Before the Arabs had conquered them, most of these lands had been Christian, and as European civilization renewed itself, rulers and warriors in both halves of Christendom struggled to win some of them back. For several centuries, there was continual fighting on the borders of Christendom and Islam—in Spain, the Mediterranean islands, and Asia Minor. But late in the eleventh century, as Western Christendom became more powerful, skilled, and ambitious, it took aim at a more distant target—the Holy Land.

In the Christian understanding, "holy war" was a form of "just war"—and no war could be "just" unless it was declared by an authority with legitimate power over the entire community. Western Christendom in the late eleventh century had such an authority—the papacy. Once the popes took on the role of declarers of war against the enemies of Christendom, the stage was set for the most dynamic forces in western European civilization—the feudal warriors, the townspeople, and the Church—to cooperate in a vast but ill-fated enterprise: the **Crusades**.

Triumph and Tragedy in the Holy Land

Although crusades were proclaimed and fought in the Middle Ages against various religious enemies in different regions, the most important of them were directed against the Muslims in the Holy Land for the purpose of recapturing the birthplace of Christianity. These "great" Crusades were international mass movements that fired the imagination of all classes of society, mainly in the twelfth and thirteenth centuries. Though the Crusades in the Holy Land failed to achieve their aim, they provided a dramatic expression of the confidence and zeal of the renewed Western Christendom.

Western Christendom, Byzantium, and the Turks

The series of events that led to the Crusades had its beginning in Central Asia. In this period, when the civilizations and peoples of the Eastern Hemisphere were drawing closer together, Islam, like Christian Europe, was subject to invasion by increasingly powerful nomads of the steppes. During the ninth century, a nomadic people that had recently come to prominence in the steppes, the Turks, entered Persia from the north. They were quickly converted to Islam and, for more than a century, held control over a portion of the Islamic empire.

In the eleventh century, the Turkish Seljuk dynasty conquered Baghdad and won the title of **sultan** (ruler) from its caliph (p. 160). Members of this warlike family pushed westward from Baghdad into Syria, Palestine, and Anatolia. They established themselves as rulers of several small states in those areas and were less tolerant of Christian minorities than earlier Arab rulers had been. In particular, they began harassing the growing numbers of Christian pilgrims to the Holy Land.

While resentment mounted in western Europe against the infidels who ruled the holiest shrines of Christianity, to Byzantium the expansion of the Turks was a formidable new threat. It arose, moreover, at a time when its relations with Western Christendom were endangered by religious disputes. Various differences of belief and practice had grown up over the centuries between the two halves of the Church, but now a new and especially divisive issue appeared: as the popes built up their power in the West, they also insisted more than ever before on their supremacy over the whole Church. This brought them into collision with both the emperors and the patriarchs in Constantinople.

In 1054, in the course of these disputes, papal representatives in Constantinople formally excommunicated the patriarch, whereupon the document of excommunication was solemnly burned by the Greeks, and the patriarch in turn excommunicated

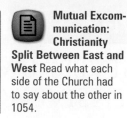**Mutual Excommunication: Christianity Split Between East and West** Read what each side of the Church had to say about the other in 1054.

the pope's representatives. At the time, neither side intended this as a complete break between the two halves of the Church. But they began to see each other, much more than before, as religious adversaries, and this eventually led to a lasting **schism** between the Catholic and Orthodox Churches.

Around this time, it became customary for the two halves of the Church to call themselves by different names, each of which had originally applied to the Church as a whole. The Eastern Church, which had overcome many internal disputes over belief, began to call itself specifically "Orthodox" ("rightly believing"). The Western Church, with its papacy that claimed to rule the whole Church, began to call itself specifically "Catholic" ("worldwide"). And the difference between the two halves was not just one of names. The Norman rulers of Sicily, having conquered the island from the Muslim Arabs, now went on to wrest southern Italy from Christian but "schismatic" (Church-splitting) Byzantium.

Now, on top of all these problems from its fellow Christians in the west, Byzantium suddenly found itself in deadly danger from its new Muslim neighbors to the east. In 1071, the Turks defeated a Byzantine army at Manzikert in eastern Anatolia (Map 12.1 on page 217) and then gradually moved westward toward the imperial capital itself. Finally, the eastern emperor, Alexius, decided to mend his relations with the Christian West and sent an appeal for help to Pope Urban II.

Preaching the Crusade

The pope heard the plea of Alexius's ambassador early in 1095 and found the idea of sending a rescue force to the East well suited to his own far-reaching aims. Heir to the Cluniac reform movement and to the policies of Gregory VII, Urban realized that a successful holy war against the Turks would do more than free the Holy Land and reopen the roads of pilgrimage. It would in all likelihood compel the Byzantine emperor, in repayment, to recognize the supremacy of the pope over the whole Christian Church. Moreover, the triumph would lift the prestige of the papacy to such a height that the ideal of Church supremacy over the state would surely be realized.

Inquisition
A Church tribunal that used complex procedures of investigation and punishment to enforce religious conformity.

Crusades
Holy wars declared by the popes against the enemies of Christendom.

sultan
A Muslim Turkish supreme ruler (from an Arabic word for "ruler").

schism
A division within the Christian Church mainly involving disputes over the powers of Church leaders rather than questions of actual belief.

THERE WERE SEVERAL MOTIVATIONS FOR THE WESTERN OFFENSIVE AGAINST ISLAM:

Religion

- War between Christians and Muslims and between Christians and pagans was already traditional, and the aim of offensive wars against Muslims was to reconquer lands that had been originally Christian.

- In the eleventh century, theologians redefined the Church's teaching about war against non-Christians.

- War against pagans and Muslims was no longer merely a necessary evil but a deed that was pleasing to God, and to die in the course of such a war was a form of martyrdom (similar to the Muslim doctrine of *jihad*, p. 162).

Feudal Land Hunger

- Kings and great lords were eager to enlarge their holdings and acquire land with which to reward their vassals.

- Among lesser warriors, many younger sons and landless knights dreamed of finding fiefs that would enable them to acquire the wealth and status of landholders.

- Therefore, feudal warriors went on the offensive, not just to eliminate enemies but also to conquer and colonize land. Any non-Christian nation, whether pagan or Muslim, was regarded as fair game for this purpose.

- During the tenth century, Norman warriors hastened to Sicily to reconquer it from the Arabs, and great lords and knights from all over Europe participated in the gradual reconquest of Spain.

Commercial Enterprise

- Conquest and colonization usually opened the way for trade and were therefore in the interests of townspeople as well as landholders.

- The pushing back of the frontiers of Islam cleared the western Mediterranean for the rising commerce of Christian Europe.

- In the eleventh century, while feudal knights were fighting to reconquer Spain and Sicily, the islands of Sardinia and Corsica were seized from the Arabs by an Italian city-state, Pisa.

Later in the year 1095, Urban used the Council of Clermont, in central France, as his forum for launching the First Crusade. Exactly what he said to the clergy who had gathered from all over France is uncertain. Different accounts, mostly written many years later, put different words into his mouth: about the blow to fellow Christians in the East whom the Muslims had "overcome in seven battles"; about the "base and bastard Turks" who had polluted Jerusalem, "the very city in which . . . Christ Himself suffered for us" (see photo); and about the opportunity for quarrelsome feudal warriors to save their souls by fighting for once in a just and holy war—"Let those who have been serving as mercenaries for small pay now obtain the eternal reward." Whatever the pope actually said, words like these must have been what the clergy in France and elsewhere in Western Christendom were saying—and what French feudal warriors and Italian seafaring traders were eagerly hearing.

Taking the Cross: The Path to the First Crusade Read how news of the crusade spread throughout Europe.

The crusading spirit possessed other classes of society as well. Early in 1096, a motley crowd of commoners set out from southern Germany for Constantinople. Their enthusiasm, sparked by the pope's call to arms, was whipped to a fury by a maverick preacher known as Peter the Hermit. The Peasants' Crusade, as it came to be called, distinguished itself chiefly by the massacre of Jewish communities along the way. Lacking provisions of their own, these commoners lived off the country as they marched. When they at last reached Constantinople, the Byzantine emperor grew alarmed and hastily ferried them across the Bosporus waterway to Anatolia. There, the Turks made quick work of the misguided peasants.

The First Crusade

Meanwhile, however, a more formidable force was assembling. French warriors, responding to the call of Urban (who was himself a French aristocrat), made up the main body of crusaders. Godfrey, duke of Lorraine, joined by other dukes, counts, and barons, set out in 1096 with an army of some fifteen thousand knights. It was this army of feudal warriors that fought and won the First Crusade, the only crusade that temporarily, at least, attained its goal.

The crusaders traveled down the Danube and then across the Balkans to Constantinople, where they met other groups of

≪ Jerusalem the Golden A map from about 1200 shows the city as a perfect circle surrounded by walls. Revered sites are labeled and imaginatively depicted, such as "Temple of Solomon" (top right in the circle); and "Golgotha," "Place of Calvary," and "Sepulcher of the Lord" with an empty coffin (lower left). Below the map, a crusader knight puts a Muslim knight to flight—the necessary bloodshed that will enable the Christian warrior to enter and possess the Holy City.

> The amount of blood that they shed on that day is incredible.... Some of our men (and this was more merciful) cut off the heads of their enemies; others shot them with arrows, so that they fell from the towers; others tortured them longer by casting them into the flames. Piles of heads, hands, and feet were to be seen in the streets of the city.... It was a just and splendid judgment of God that this place should be filled with the blood of unbelievers, since it had suffered so long from their blasphemies.

With the help of fleets from Venice, Genoa, and other Italian cities, the crusaders moved on to take the coastal towns of Palestine and Syria. (For this aid, the Italians received, as they had hoped, rich privileges in the trade of the Middle East.) The various conquered territories were then drawn together into a loose feudal state, the Kingdom of Jerusalem. Baldwin of Flanders was chosen as its first king and accepted the usual homage and services of the landholding nobility. The feudalism of western Europe was thus transplanted to Outremer (**OO-truh-mair**)—"Overseas," as the French called the Christian beachhead in the Holy Land.

Life as a Seljuk Turk During the First Crusade Experience life as a Seljuk Turk during the First Crusade.

Muslim Life Under Christian Rule Read a Muslim's account of life under Christian rule.

knights that had taken different overland routes, and then crossed into Anatolia to confront the Turks (see Map 12.1 on page 217). On the way across Anatolia, they suffered terrible hardships, disease, and some defeats, but they were at last victorious. Their leaders, having turned back the Turkish threat to Constantinople, moved on to establish dukedoms in eastern Anatolia and abandoned their original plan to march on to Jerusalem. The survivors of lesser rank, however, insisted that the crusade be resumed. Responding at last to their demands, Raymond, count of Toulouse, advanced on Jerusalem and took the city, after a six-week siege, in 1099.

The crusaders' entry into the Holy City was an orgy of looting and killing of Muslims and Jews. One crusader reported in his journal:

Frankish Arrogance in the Byzantine Court Read about the misbehavior of a Frankish knight in the Byzantine court of Constantinople.

The Struggle for the Holy Land

The First Crusade was followed by countless other expeditions, only some of which have been assigned a number by historians. Most of these later crusades to the Holy Land were intended not to expand the Christian territories but to defend them against fierce Muslim campaigns of reconquest. The Second Crusade (1147–1149)—called in response to Turkish success in recapturing part of the gains of the First Crusade—was inspired by a reforming monk, Bernard of Clairvaux. An extraordinarily persuasive man, he induced two leading feudal rulers, the king of France and the Holy Roman emperor, and thousands of fighting men to "take the Cross."

BERNARD OF CLAIRVAUX CALLS FOR A CRUSADE

In 1146, following Muslim gains at the expense of the Christian territories in the Holy Land, the widely revered Abbot Bernard of Clairvaux wrote an "open letter" to the clergy and people of Germany calling upon them to join a new crusade—what is now known as the Second Crusade. The letter would have been distributed widely enough to provide guidelines for local preachers. In this excerpt, Bernard explains how taking the Cross will be an aid to salvation, and discourages outbreaks against the Jews, which had been a feature of the First Crusade.

Behold, brethren, now is the accepted time, now is the day of salvation. The earth also is moved and has trembled, because the God of heaven has begun to destroy the land which is his. . . . And now, for our sins, the enemies of the Cross have raised blaspheming heads, ravaging with the edge of the sword the land of promise. . . . Alas! they rage against the very shrine of the Christian faith with blasphemous mouths, and would enter and trample down the very couch on which, for us, our Life lay down to sleep in death.

What are you going to do then, O brave men? What are you doing, O servants of the Cross? Will you give what is holy to the dogs, and cast your pearls before swine? How many sinners there, confessing their sins and tears, have obtained pardon, after the defilement of the heathen had been purged by the swords of your fathers?

What are we then to think, brethren? Is the Lord's arm shortened so that it cannot save, because he calls his weak creatures to guard and restore his heritage? Can he not send more than twelve legions of angels, or merely speak the word, and the land shall be set free? It is altogether in his power to effect what he wishes; but I tell you, the Lord, your God, is trying you. He looks upon the sons of men to see if there be any to understand, and seek, and bewail his error. For the Lord hath pity upon his people, and provides a sure remedy for those that are afflicted. . . .

But now, O brave knight, now, O warlike hero, here is a battle you may fight without danger, where it is glory to conquer and gain to die. If you are a prudent merchant, if you are a desirer of this world, behold I show you some great bargains; see that you lose them not. Take the sign of the cross, and you shall gain pardon for every sin that you confess with a contrite heart. The material itself, being bought, is worth little; but if it be placed on a devout shoulder, it is, without doubt, worth no less than the kingdom of God. Therefore they have done well who have already taken the heavenly sign: well and wisely also will the rest do, if they hasten to lay upon their shoulders, like the first, the sign of salvation.

Besides, brethren, I warn you, and not only I, but God's apostle, "Believe not every spirit." We have heard and rejoice that the zeal of God abounds in you, but it behooves no mind to be wanting in wisdom. The Jews must not be persecuted, slaughtered, nor even driven out. Inquire of the pages of Holy Writ. I know what is written in the Psalms as prophecy about the Jews. "God hath commanded me," says the Church, 'Slay them not, lest my people forget.'"

They are living signs to us, representing the Lord's passion. For this reason they are dispersed into all regions, that now they may pay the just penalty of so great a crime, and that they may be witnesses of our redemption. Wherefore the Church, speaking in the same Psalm, says, "Scatter them by thy power; and bring them down, O Lord, our shield." So has it been. They have been dispersed, cast down. They undergo a hard captivity under Christian princes. Yet they shall be converted at even-time, and remembrance of them shall be made in due season. Finally, when the multitude of the Gentiles shall have entered in, then "all Israel shall be saved," saith the apostle. Meanwhile he who dies remains in death.

I do not enlarge on the lamentable fact that where there are no Jews there Christian men *judaize* even worse than they in extorting usury,—if, indeed, we may call them Christians and not rather baptized Jews. Moreover, if the Jews be utterly trampled down, how shall the promised salvation or conversion profit them in the end? . . .

EXPLORING THE SOURCE

1. How does Bernard think that taking the Cross will help people to salvation?

2. What is Bernard's attitude to the Jews, and why does he think that it is wrong to use persecution and violence against them?

Source: James Harvey Robinson, ed., *Readings in European History* (Boston: Ginn, 1904), 1:33.

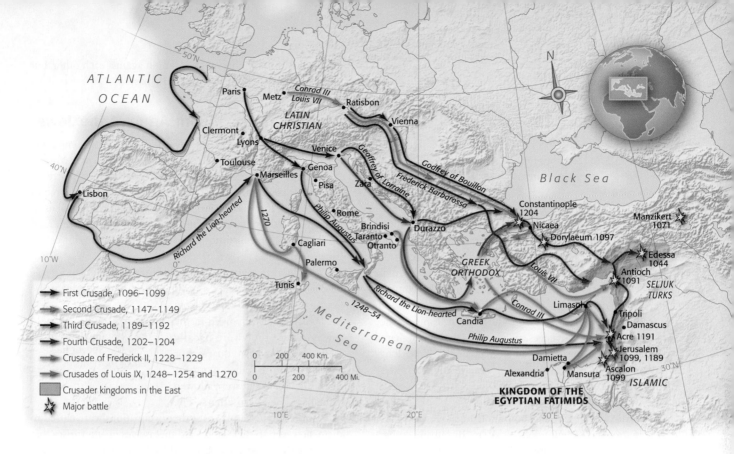

Map 12.1 The Crusades, 1095–1270

Western Christendom's efforts to conquer and hold the Holy Land, 2,000 miles away by land or sea, were on a vast scale. Large forces had not marched, sailed, and fought across such distances since the time of the Roman Empire—a sign of Western Christendom's growing wealth and skills. Crusades on this scale continued during the thirteenth century, but by 1300, the Muslims prevailed. © Cengage Learning

Interactive Map

The main force of this expedition was cut to pieces as it moved across Anatolia. Bernard, convinced that his cause was just, concluded that the failure must have been due to the sinfulness of the crusaders.

Bernard's view was accepted by his more ardent followers. Some of them went still further: they reasoned that if purity of the soul was a requirement for victory, young children would be the most favored of all crusaders. In accordance with this notion, thousands of innocent German and French boys marched off on the Children's Crusade in 1212. They never reached the Holy Land, however, for they fell victim to accident and disease or were captured by Christian slave dealers along the way—who mostly sold them to buyers in Muslim lands.

The climax of the struggles in the Holy Land came earlier, however, with the Third Crusade (1189–1192). Until not long before this crusade, most of the Muslim resistance to the invaders had come from Anatolia and Syria. Now, however, Muslim Egypt joined the struggle under its ruler Salah-ed-Din—Saladin, as the crusaders called him. Saladin was a pious Muslim, an ambitious statesman, and a formidable warrior who was a hero to Muslims and admired even by Christians. If he could expel the unbelievers from Jerusalem, to Muslims the "Glorious Place" from which the Prophet had ascended to heaven, he would both fulfill his duty of *jihad* and strengthen his position as the dominant Muslim ruler in the Middle East. Accordingly, in 1187, he crushed the army of the Latin Kingdom and went on to capture Jerusalem.

Once again, armies set out from the feudal kingdoms of western Europe—overland from the Holy Roman Empire and from France and England by sea routes that the Italian cities had opened across the Mediterranean (see Map 12.1). Saladin fought them all to a standstill, and finally, the most famous Christian warrior of the time, King Richard I of England ("the Lion-Hearted"; p. 190), had to make an agreement with the Egyptian ruler that left most of the Holy Land, including Jerusalem, in Muslim hands.

The Fourth Crusade and After

The Fourth Crusade, organized a few years later by leading French barons, involved a change of strategy: instead of going to the Holy Land, the barons made an agreement with the leading Italian seagoing city-state, Venice, to transport their army by sea to the center of Muslim

Life as a Crusader During the Third Crusade Experience life as a Christian warrior during the Third Crusade.

power in Egypt (see Map 12.1 on page 217). But Venice was ambitious to dominate the eastern Mediterranean, a deposed emperor in Constantinople appealed for help from the crusaders, the Orthodox Church was seen as a religious rival, and besides, Constantinople would be an easier prize than the Egyptian capital, Cairo. Accordingly, the crusaders changed their plans, and in 1204 the imperial capital was stormed by the very men whose forefathers had promised its rescue a century before.

Untold treasures of gold, silver, and holy relics were seized during the subsequent looting. Vandalism and fire consumed irreplaceable works of Greek art and literature. The city and the empire's European lands were then divided among the chieftains of the crusade, and these remnants were brought together as the Latin Empire of Constantinople. The count of Flanders was proclaimed its first emperor, and a new patriarch was installed—one who was loyal to the pope in Rome. Venice secured special trading privileges, and the farmlands were shared out in feudal fashion among the plundering knights. Thus, long-desired and ill-concealed goals were momentarily realized by the papacy, the Venetians, and the French aristocracy—all at the expense of Byzantium.

The Latin Empire of Constantinople had an even briefer life than that of the Kingdom of Jerusalem. Byzantine emperors carried on in exile, clinging to a small piece of territory in Anatolia, and in 1261 they managed to regain Constantinople and the area around it. But Christendom's southeastern gateway was no longer defended by a powerful empire, so that the Turks eventually made their way through it; and the rivalry between the Western and Eastern Churches hardened into outright hostility.

Additional crusades intended to maintain or expand the Christian presence in the Holy Land continued throughout the thirteenth century. They all came to nothing, however, and the last Christian foothold, the fortress of Acre, fell in 1291. After that, the popes continued to proclaim crusades—against eastern European pagan peoples, against Christian heretics, and even against local rivals in Italian power struggles. From the fifteenth century, however, as European rulers built up centralized governments and became the main focus of loyalty within their countries, they no longer needed or wanted to act under the authority of the pope. Christians and Muslims, and later on Catholics and Protestants, still fought wars of religion against each other, but formal crusades became a thing of the past.

Western Christendom Against the Jews

The Christian expeditions against the East were accompanied by rising hostility toward the Jews. During the early Middle Ages, the Jews had continued to live in communities scattered across Christendom under the terms of a grudging decree of toleration by the Roman emperor Theodosius I, as well as in Muslim North Africa and the Middle East. They remained small in numbers, constituting perhaps 1 to 2 percent of western Europe's population by the year 1000.

Medieval Jews were usually forbidden to hold land, serfs, or slaves and were in fact a group entirely separate from the Christian social order. Cut off from the land, they mainly lived in the towns, where they were usually confined to their own quarters or *ghettos* (from the Italian word for a Jewish quarter) but were allowed to manage their own affairs. The

A Charter for the Jews of Speyer Read about the rights of one medieval Jewish community.

professions, guilds, and most other occupations were closed to them, however, so they supported themselves in enterprises that were for the most part shunned by Christians—above all, moneylending.

Despite the limitations on their freedom of action, some Jews rose to positions of power and distinction in commerce and royal administration. These individuals, however, could not match the achievements of the Spanish Jews, who were able to take refuge with tolerant Muslim local rulers when Christian ones turned against them, and vice versa. Notable Sephardic (from the Hebrew word for "Spanish") scholars, poets, philosophers, and statesmen made a golden age of Jewish history. They contributed, at the same time, to the intellectual development of Christian Europe by helping bring the wisdom of the ancient Greeks into circulation in the West.

The Crusades, however, brought a disastrous end to the relative security of Jews in much of Western Christendom. The First Crusade, launched in 1096, set off a spasm of religious fanaticism and violence. During the next two centuries, as prejudices against Jews were stirred

> "*I have therefore collected some Jews and located them in a place apart from the dwellings and association of the other inhabitants of the city; and that they may be protected from the attacks and violence of the mob, I have surrounded their quarter with a wall.*"
>
> —The bishop of Speyer (Germany) on establishing a Jewish ghetto, 1084

up by Christian leaders, mob attacks on Jewish communities became commonplace.

Sporadic outbursts of anti-Semitic feeling had occurred in earlier times, but now the massacres became endemic. Ghetto laws became much stricter, and in 1215 the Fourth Lateran Council of the Church encouraged public humiliation of the Jews by ordering that they must wear a yellow patch or cap for identification. Punishment and intimidation often took the form of seizing and burning copies of the Talmud (ancient rabbinical commentaries on the Hebrew Bible; p. 125), on the ground that the contents were offensive to Christ.

At last, because they were thought to be an intolerable "contamination" to Christians, all Jews who refused conversion to Christianity were expelled from country after country: England in 1290, parts of Germany in 1298, France in 1306, Spain in 1492, and Portugal in 1498. Compelled to leave their property behind, thousands of Jews migrated to eastern Europe and Muslim lands.

 **Philip Augustus Expels French Jews** Read a medieval justification for expelling the Jews of Paris.

LO³ Western and Eastern Europe

In spite of their failure, the Crusades were mighty undertakings. In the Fourth Crusade, for example, 12,000 warriors and perhaps 1,000 horses sailed from Venice to Constantinople—as large a long-distance seaborne operation as the Romans themselves had ever undertaken. The crusade was a sign that in government effectiveness and industrial capacity, medieval western Europe was climbing back to the level of ancient Rome. On the other hand, eastern Europe was squeezed between nomad and Muslim invaders and the resurgent West. Europe was forming into two regions—a western heartland and an eastern periphery (outlying area) (see Map 12.2).

Byzantium and Orthodoxy

The differences between the two regions were partly religious and cultural, originating in the divergences between Roman and Byzantine civilization and the rivalry between the Catholic and Orthodox Churches, as they now usually called themselves. The Fourth Crusade and the capture of Constantinople in 1204 led to more than two hundred years of chaos in the Balkans, a region that Byzantium had earlier dominated, but which the Latin Empire of Constantinople and the restored Byzantine Empire were both too feeble to control.

Serbia and Bulgaria, both already important earlier in the Middle Ages (pp. 178–179), reappeared for a time as powerful independent kingdoms, but eventually they disintegrated as a result of disputes over the succession to their thrones and rivalries among their nobles. Other rulers held power over less prominent Balkan ethnic groups such as the non-Slavic Albanians and Romanians, which thereby took their first steps toward independent nationhood. Meanwhile, on the outskirts of the Balkans, powerful neighbors—Venice, Hungary, and the Turks—took advantage of the situation to gain power and influence in the region.

Yet the spiritual and cultural hold of Byzantium over the Orthodox peoples of eastern Europe was as strong as ever. The most successful Bulgarian and Serbian rulers took the title of tsar (emperor—p. 178), surrounded themselves with Byzantine pomp and ceremony, and dreamed of ruling in Constantinople. They established national "Bulgarian" or "Serbian" Orthodox (as opposed to "Greek Orthodox") churches and appointed "autocephalous" (independent) patriarchs to run these churches. They built splendid cathedrals and monasteries, where glowingly colored frescoes and icons (holy pictures) seemed to give believers a glimpse of the other world (see photo on page 221), and where monks wrote chronicles and lives of saints in the ancient Slavic religious language and the Cyrillic alphabet (pp. 177–178) used by all the national Orthodox churches. In many ways, the thirteenth and fourteenth centuries were the golden age of Slavic Orthodox culture.

As a result of the Fourth Crusade, this flourishing Orthodox world now viewed the Catholic Church as an enemy and a traitor to Christianity. The Bulgarian, Serbian, and restored Byzantine rulers sometimes struck bargains with the popes, submitting to papal religious authority in return for western military and political support. But these bargains never lasted, for suspicion and hatred of Rome were firmly anchored in the hearts of the Orthodox faithful. Thus the estrangement between the Catholic and the Orthodox Churches hardened into bitter religious hostility.

Eastern European States and Societies

The divergence between western and eastern Europe was also social, economic, and political. With the rise of a dynamic urban trading and industrial economy from 1000 on, western Europe forged ahead of the east. While the ruling families of western Europe came to accept the principle of primogeniture (p. 176) in the eleventh and twelfth centuries, those of eastern Europe continued to divide their lands among numerous heirs until the end of the Middle Ages, thereby weakening their dynastic power. Europe came to be divided into a group of politically and economically stronger western countries and a group of politically and economically weaker eastern countries. The second group included not only the Orthodox countries but also Catholic Poland and Hungary and the eastern territories of the Holy Roman Empire (see Map 12.2).

In the Middle Ages, the western countries gained many advantages from the countries on their eastern borders. For western Europe, the east provided territories for colonization and emigration and sources of foodstuffs and raw materials. In the twelfth and thirteenth centuries, crusaders from the Holy Roman Empire conquered many still-pagan tribes on the southern and eastern shores of the Baltic Sea (see Map 12.2). Throughout these eastern borderlands of the Holy Roman Empire and on into Poland and Hungary, masses of German colonists moved in, clearing the land for agriculture and founding new towns and cities—a migration that nationalist-minded German historians centuries later christened the "Drive to the East." Along with the migration of Germans, there was also a mass movement of Jews, fleeing eastward from western European persecution.

In the newly colonized territories, and throughout much of the rest of northeastern Europe, farmers grew grain and flax, and lumberjacks logged timber, for export westward. The towns functioned as trading outposts of German coastal cities that controlled the region's seaborne trade and eventually joined together in a cooperative trading organization, the *Hansa* (p. 253). Farther south, the commerce of Hungary, Serbia, Bulgaria, Byzantium, and the Black Sea regions (see Map 12.2) was controlled in the same way by the Italian city-states (p. 195).

Sometimes this western expansion into eastern Europe led to conflict. For more than two hundred years, the rulers of Poland vied for control of the Baltic coastlands with the Teutonic Knights, a group of crusading warriors that had led the German conquest of the pagan tribes of that region. The kings of Hungary likewise contested the hold of Venice on the eastern shores of the Adriatic Sea, Hungary's main outlet for seaborne commerce. In Bohemia, which was inhabited mainly by the Slavic Czechs, resentment at German immigration, along

Map 12.2 **Europe about 1230**

This small region of the world is crowded with kingdoms, princedoms, and self-styled empires. Many of these states will survive to the present through border changes, periods of foreign rule, and government and social revolutions; others, notably the Holy Roman Empire, will eventually disappear. One landmark of the early Middle Ages, Byzantium, has already almost vanished, and Islam is expanding into its former territories; at the other end of Europe, in the Iberian peninsula, Islam is retreating. © Cengage Learning

Interactive Map

The Lamentation of Christ Two Greek artists, Michael and Eutychius of Thessalonica, made this wall painting in 1295 for a church in a Balkan religious center, Ohrid. Disciples touch Christ's lifeless limbs, the Virgin Mary (at right) tears her hair, an angel clutches at his face. The painting shows human emotions and reactions in a manner quite new in Eastern Christendom—and new in Western Christendom when the Italian artist Giotto painted the same scene in the same manner ten years later (see photo on page 295).

with religious disputes, led eventually to a bitter internal and international struggle, the Hussite Wars (pp. 250-251).

But these conflicts were exceptional. So long as the rulers of eastern Europe did not feel directly threatened with the loss of their local power and independence, they usually accepted western immigration and commercial domination. The kings of Bohemia, Poland, and Hungary welcomed and even invited Germans and Jews to settle in their countries, for the sake of the increased prosperity—and increased tax revenues—that the newcomers brought. Noble landowners were glad to supply foodstuffs and raw materials to the west; and with the kings weakened by the division of their territories and family disputes, it was often the nobles who wielded the greatest share of power.

As a result of these migrations, social differences in eastern Europe came to be also ethnic. In any particular region, the peasants belonged to one ethnic group and the townspeople to other groups—usually German, Jewish, and in the Balkans, also Greek—and it was not unusual for the nobles and rulers to belong to yet another ethnic group. In the Middle Ages, eastern Europe was, on the whole, more tolerant of ethnic and religious diversity than western Europe. But in modern times, under the impact of religious, nationalist, and class ideologies of western European origin—combined, in the Balkans, with the lasting effects of Turkish conquest (p. 251)—eastern Europe would be torn by savage strife.

Mongols, Tartars, and Russia

There was another important difference between eastern and western Europe: the eastern countries, unlike the western ones, were constantly exposed to attack by the nomadic peoples of the steppes. This threat reached its height in the thirteenth

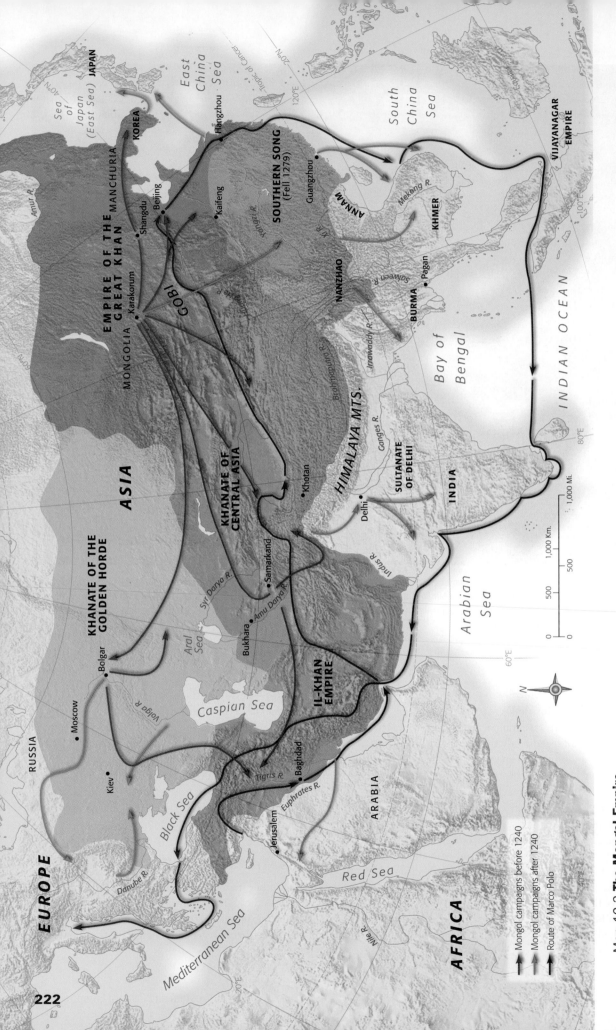

Map 12.3 The Mongol Empire

The Mongols built a larger empire than any conquering people before them, and held it securely for most of the thirteenth century. From his capital at Beijing, the Great Khan ruled China, Korea, and the Mongol homeland. Lesser khans, loosely subject to the Great Khan, ruled territories stretching across the steppes as far as Russia. For the first time in history, so far as is known, Europeans (including Marco Polo) could visit the eastern shores of Asia. © Cengage Learning

Interactive
Map

Mongol campaigns before 1240
Mongol campaigns after 1240
Route of Marco Polo

century when a pagan nomadic people from the Far East, the Mongols under Genghis Khan, built an empire that stretched from China to Europe (Map 12.3). Between 1237 and 1240, Genghis's grandson Batu Khan devastated much of eastern Europe and conquered Russia.

The Mongol Empire soon broke up, but Russia's ancient capital city of Kiev and most of the country's southern territories (present-day Ukraine) remained under the rule of a Muslim people ethnically related to the Turks and allied with the Mongols, the Tartars (known to the Russians, supposedly because of their luxurious encampments, as the "Golden Horde"). The northern regions, however, were held by native Russian vassals of the Tartars, most prominent among whom were the rulers of the city of Moscow and its surrounding territory.

Over the generations, even while acknowledging Tartar overlordship, Moscow extended its power over most of northern Russia. The new state was in close contact with the Byzantine-influenced Slavs of the Balkans and shared in their flourishing religious and cultural life, but its rulers already controlled far more people and territory than the Bulgarian and Serbian monarchs who so proudly called themselves tsars. Eventually, the Russian rulers would take—and keep—that title (pp. 251-252). In time, they would make their country as powerful as any of its western European rivals, but even they could not change the overall balance of power between the two halves of Europe, which has favored the West down to the present day.

 Listen to a synopsis of Chapter 12.

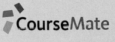

CHAPTER 13

THE CULTURE OF WESTERN CHRISTENDOM,
1000–1300

LEARNING OBJECTIVES

AFTER READING THIS CHAPTER, YOU SHOULD BE ABLE TO DO THE FOLLOWING:

LO¹ Describe the Romanesque and Gothic styles.

LO² Trace the renewal of intellectual life in medieval Europe.

LO³ Discuss the evolution of medieval literature.

"**AS THE RENEWAL OF MEDIEVAL CIVILIZATION REACHED ITS PEAK, THE INSPIRATION OF RELIGION, COMBINED WITH INCREASING WEALTH, TECHNICAL PROGRESS, AND THE REVIVAL OF URBAN LIFE, CREATED THE CONDITIONS FOR BRILLIANT CULTURAL ACHIEVEMENTS.**"

As the renewal of medieval civilization reached its peak, the inspiration of religion, combined with increasing wealth, technical progress, and the revival of urban life, created the conditions for brilliant cultural achievements. Western Christendom invested much of its newfound wealth and skills in magnificent religious buildings—the churches and cathedrals of the Romanesque and Gothic styles. New urban institutions of learning, the universities, supplied skilled professionals to meet the needs of a complex society and also nurtured advances in knowledge and thought. Literacy became normal for nobles and better-off townspeople, who provided authors and a public for masterpieces of literature in both Latin and the developing vernacular (native) languages of Europe.

Test your knowledge before you read this chapter.

What do you think?

Medieval artists, scholars, and writers were more concerned with the afterlife than this life.

Strongly Disagree						Strongly Agree
1	2	3	4	5	6	7

≪ **Understanding Aristotle** In a thirteenth-century copy of a work by an ancient Greek, Aristotle, with explanations by a medieval Arab, Averroës, a medieval-style "E" begins the Latin word *Ens* ("Being"—a philosophical concept). Inside the "E," a Christian scholar contemplates a model of the universe, representing "Being," with a smile of confident understanding—thanks to colleagues who have translated the original Greek and Arabic into Latin. Medieval Western Christendom is reaching for knowledge across barriers of language and religion to both the pagan past and the Muslim present.

LO¹ Architecture and Art

The creative force of medieval Christianity inspired spectacular achievements in the visual arts—above all, in architecture.

For several centuries after the Germanic invasions of the West, most new buildings north of the Alps were built of timber; the first stone structure of importance was Charlemagne's chapel at Aachen, completed around 800 (see photo on page 172). But the real beginning of medieval architecture came two centuries later. The end of invasions made it worthwhile to invest resources in large buildings with some assurance that they would not be looted and burned. There were more resources to invest as population, trade, and wealth increased. Greater security meant more travel, including by pilgrims visiting the shrines of saints, while reforming monks and pious rulers and nobles built hundreds of new monasteries. All of a sudden, great abbey and pilgrimage churches began to spring up.

CHRONOLOGY

ca. 1050–1120	Earliest Romanesque pilgrimage church, Conques, France
1140–1144	Earliest Gothic cathedral, Saint-Denis, France
ca. 1225–1274	Life of Thomas Aquinas, author of the *Summa Theologica*
1250	Robert de Sorbon establishes a college (the "Sorbonne") at the University of Paris that serves as a model for European universities
ca. 1265–1321	Life of Dante, author of the *Divine Comedy*
ca. 1343–1400	Life of Chaucer, author of the *Canterbury Tales*

The Romanesque Style

The style in which the new churches of the eleventh and twelfth centuries were built is known as **Romanesque** (Roman-like), because the church builders revived some basic features of ancient Roman architecture. But as usually happens when old traditions are revived, the builders of the Middle Ages used these Roman features in new ways to serve new purposes.

"Returning to the Cross"

Romanesque churches were ultimately based on the pattern of the Roman basilica (public hall), a long building with a nave (central hall) and side aisles, and an apse (a semicircular space) at one end. In late Roman times, Christians had used a

« Romanesque Structural Design As trade and travel revived after A.D. 1000, pilgrims on their way to the Spanish shrine of Jesus's disciple James at Compostela stopped off at the monastery of Vézelay in eastern France to honor relics said to be of another disciple, Mary Magdalene. The pilgrims' contributions helped the monks to build a splendid Romanesque church, completed in 1145. The light- and dark-colored round arches divide the ceiling into bays, and additional round arches running diagonally across the bays strengthen the structure. Dagli Orti/The Art Archive

more or less unchanged basilica plan for churches, (see photo on page 113) but in eleventh- and twelfth-century churches, chapels projected outward from the apse, and a transept ("cross-hall") intersected the nave at right angles. This "cruciform" (cross-shaped) plan provided more space for solemn Masses with many clergy; and in each chapel, worshipers could "talk one-on-one" with the saint to whom it was dedicated.

In addition, the cruciform plan had obvious symbolic meaning. When the faithful entered the church, they were "returning to the Cross." The façade (front) of the building usually had three main portals (entryways), symbolizing the Trinity. Whenever possible, the cross plan was located so that the nave ran from west to east, with the altar at the eastern end. Thus, the worshipers faced more or less in the direction of Jerusalem. Because of this symbolism and its suitability for changing religious practices, the cruciform plan remained the standard for large churches in Western traditions of Christianity until the rise of Modernist architecture in the twentieth century.

The actual structure of Romanesque churches also reused features of Roman models, notably high walls made of rows of rounded arches one on top of the other, and cross-vaults (diagonal arches intersecting each other) to lighten the weight of stone ceilings. Even so, ceilings were heavy. In the abbey church of Vézelay in eastern France, each cross-vault is made of 45 tons of stone. To carry this weight, the side walls have to be thick, with narrow slits for windows that widen on the inside so that shafts of light swing across the interior as the sun moves across the sky (see photo on page 228).

Build an Arch Animation, BBC History (http://www.bbc.co.uk/history/interactive/animations/arch/index_embed.shtml) Learn how medieval masons built cathedral arches.

Romanesque buildings often included a new architectural feature, the tower, from which bells called the worshipers to prayer. In Italy, the graceful *campanile* (**kam-puh-NEE-lay**) (bell tower) stood by itself a few feet away from the church; elsewhere in Europe, the tower was an integral part of the main building. It was sometimes built over the crossing of the nave and the transept, but more commonly, a tower or a pair of towers formed part of the front of the building. In some areas, bell towers were capped by a soaring spire. Church towers remain to this day a symbol of Western Christianity.

Bibles in Stone

The new churches needed painting and sculpture, not just for decoration, but above all for the glorification of God and the instruction of the faithful. Overcoming the barrier of illiteracy, each medieval church was virtually a "Bible in stone." Nowhere is the contrast between the early medieval world and the ancient world more sharply displayed than in Romanesque sculpture. The "idealistic" style of the Greeks and the "naturalistic" style of the Romans (pp. 65, 115) are both absent. Few ancient statues were available to the sculptors of the eleventh and twelfth centuries; they took as their models the illustrated figures of medieval manuscripts.

The tradition of furnishing written documents with illustrations dates back to ancient Egypt, where scribes most likely used it for magical purposes—to give additional force to the rituals and spells that their manuscripts contained. The idea of illustrating books for the sake of increasing the effect of the text on the reader—to give visual form to the ideas it contained or simply to break the monotony of the endless procession of words on a page—seems to have originated not long after the invention of books with pages (p. 118). In the early Middle Ages, this kind of illustration flourished. Bibles and prayer books, volumes of poetry, even philosophical works and law books—all were "enlumined" ("lit up") with pictures (see photos on pages 182, 186, 224, 240).

The strange animal figures that often appear in Romanesque sculpture came directly from the northern barbarian tradition. Numerous books were available describing hundreds of imaginary beasts, and sculptors copied them in stone. The upper walls of Romanesque churches were studded with *gargoyles* (from a French word for "throat")—frightening monsters and demons whose open mouths spouted water draining from the roof.

Medieval Gargoyles from Across Europe (http://quazen.com/arts/visual-arts/gargoyles-glorious-gruesome-grotesques/) View a gallery of medieval gargoyles.

Romanesque sculptors mingled the natural and the supernatural, the earthly and the unearthly. Hence, the real may look unreal and the unreal real. To ensure that the idea or story they were illustrating would be correctly interpreted, sculptors relied heavily on symbols. Although they might show Saint Peter in a number of poses, they always identified him by giving him a set of keys, because of Jesus's gospel saying that he would give Peter the keys of the kingdom of heaven. Matthew was consistently shown as an angel, Mark as a lion (see photo on page 206). Having identified a figure with its traditional symbol, the artist could then treat it in an individual manner.

This freedom presented an opportunity for creativity quite unknown in ancient art. Romanesque sculptors were not bound to exacting artistic rules or naturalistic representations. This also permitted them greater liberties in overall composition—a freedom shared by painters and other artists of the period.

The Gothic Style

In less than two centuries, out of the Romanesque came the later style of the Middle Ages—the **Gothic**. This style showed itself first in architecture around 1150 and reached its prime by 1300, though splendid Gothic structures were built as late as the sixteenth century.

The term *Gothic* (from the Goths, fourth-century barbarian invaders of the Roman Empire) was invented in the sixteenth

> **Gothic**
> A style of architecture and art that evolved in the twelfth century, characterized by spaciousness, height, glowing illumination, and naturalistic images.

cathedral
The head church of a bishopric—from the Greek word for "seat" (of a bishop).

flying buttress
A supporting structure on the outside of a Gothic cathedral that arches over the roof of a side aisle.

In the twelfth century, the era of the Crusades, the ruling papacy, and eager veneration of the Virgin Mary and the saints, the self-confidence and religious zeal of Western Christendom were on the rise. This mood found its outlet in Gothic churches, first of all, in new or rebuilt **cathedrals** (head churches of bishoprics) in the bur-

century, when Greek and Roman models of culture were the most admired. It was originally applied to the culture of the Middle Ages in general and meant much the same as "barbaric." The name continues to be used, without the contemptuous overtones, to describe the style of architecture and art that is now recognized as the grandest expression of medieval civilization.

Chartres Cathedral Nave Window (http://www.gigapan.org/gigapans/22895/) View a stained glass window from Chartres Cathedral and zoom in for a closer look.

geoning towns of northern France—structures as ambitious and daring as the finest buildings of Greece and Rome.

The cathedrals were also the most eloquent expression yet devised of Christian belief. Their architects sought to meet the desire of twelfth-century clergy for buildings that would be a true image of the universe as they believed it to be: a vast structure, designed by its creator to be perfectly harmonious in every detail and glowing with light that flowed from God himself. Only buildings of this kind, the clergy thought, would truly lead the worshipers to the knowledge and love of God.

 **Cathedrals** Learn more about medieval cathedrals.

Webs of Stone

Judged by this standard, Romanesque churches seemed inadequate. Their thick walls often gave a feeling of confinement, their massive arches seemed ill-proportioned, and their small windows did not provide a rich illumination. But any attempt to alter this pattern raised a difficult engineering problem. How could architects increase the spaciousness and height

≪ **Web of Stone** In Gothic cathedrals, structural stresses are transmitted mostly downward from intersecting stone ribs, shaped as pointed arches, to vertical pillars resting on bedrock. The spaces between the ribs and pillars are filled with brick or glass surfaces that carry no structural loads. At the thirteenth-century cathedral of Amiens in northern France, the system makes possible a nave that is 50 feet wide and 140 feet high. Angelo Homak/Corbis

of a building, reduce the thickness of the supporting walls and arches, and enlarge the windows, given that walls had to be thick and windows had to be small to support a massive stone ceiling?

Part of the solution was to lighten the weight of the ceiling, and twelfth-century Romanesque builders had already found a way to do this. They marked off each rectangular bay (building section topped by a vaulted ceiling) with four vertical stone pillars. From the top of each pillar, they connected ribs of arching stone to the tops of the other three; then they filled in the ceiling areas between these ribs with a thin layer of brick. The weight of the roof was carried to the ground through the ribs and pillars, and little or no force was exerted on the areas between the pillars (see photo on page 226).

Gothic architects developed the full potential of the new method with the aid of two further innovations. One of these was the graceful pointed arch. This hallmark of the Gothic style had originally been devised by Muslim mosque builders and had been learned from them by Christian church builders (see photo on page 163). It turned out to be perfectly suited to

> "*Gothic architects thought of a large church not as a stone mass enclosing static space but as a web of stone with space and light flowing freely through it.*"

cathedrals, since it accentuated the vertical lines of a structure and lifted its vaults to greater heights than could be achieved with the round arch. With the pointed arch, the direction of thrust was more downward than outward, decreasing the danger that the supporting pillars would collapse.

Even so, a further innovation was needed to keep the soaring vaults from falling down—massive external stone buttresses (props). These buttresses could not be placed directly against the pillars of the nave because the side aisles, with their separate, lower roofs, stood in the way, so they stood outside the side aisles. They rose almost to the level of the nave ceiling and were connected to the pillars of the nave by stone ribs (see photo). Since the ribs seem to "fly" over the side aisles, these structures are called **flying buttresses**.

This revolutionary plan of construction enabled Gothic

 **Amiens Animated Glossary, from Columbia University** (http://www.learn .columbia.edu/amiens_ flash/) Explore the plan of a Gothic cathedral in this interactive site.

Flying Buttresses At the east end of the thirteenth-century cathedral of Le Mans in northern France, flying buttresses help prop up the upper part of structure while straddling lower parts that project outward—essentially, they are outward extensions of the internal web of stone. The buttresses also draw the eye upward, making the building look higher but also less massive than it actually is. R.Lamb/Robertstock.com

architects to lift roofs to soaring heights and to make windows into broad, softly glowing sheets of stained glass. They thought of a large church not as a stone mass enclosing static space but as a web of stone with space and light flowing freely through it.

From outside, such a building was also overwhelmingly impressive. It stood high above the houses huddled in the town, symbolizing the commanding position of the Church in the life of the community. As travelers approached the town, the first sight they saw on the horizon was the spire (or spires) reaching hundreds of feet into the sky. Then the whole of the cathedral would gradually come into view, and its flying buttresses, with their tangle of tall stone pillars and slanting ribs, would make the building look even loftier than it actually was. If the travelers were pilgrims, they would approach the west façade and reverently prepare to enter.

Scala/Art Resource, NY

Gothic Sculpture The thirteenth-century Cathedral of Our Lady of Reims was the third to be built there since the Frankish chieftain Clovis had been baptized in the first one 800 years before (see photo on page 150). The west façade shows scenes from the Virgin's life in the new and lifelike Gothic style of sculpture. Left, the Annunciation: the Archangel Gabriel tells the Virgin Mary of the coming birth of Christ. Right, the Visitation: the Virgin (inner statue) is greeted by Saint Elizabeth, John the Baptist's mother.

Lifelike Images

Set into the façade were stone sculptures representing figures and scenes from the Bible, which the artists depicted in a much more lifelike manner than their Romanesque forerunners. Worshipers entering the northern French cathedral of Reims **(reemz)**, where the kings of France were crowned, would pass through a doorway above which a smiling Archangel Gabriel brought a solemn Virgin Mary the joyful yet awe-inspiring news that she would become the Mother of God, and the Virgin respectfully greeted the recognizably elderly Saint Elizabeth, the mother of John the Baptist (see photo). In keeping with the contemporary trend of emphasizing the human side of the beings whom Christians revered, Gothic sculptors were turning back to the aim of Hellenistic and Roman sculpture—to depict human emotion and interaction in stone.

Inside the cathedral, worshipers would be absorbed by the vastness, rhythm, and splendor of the interior, as well as by the many glowing colors in the stained-glass windows. These were huge "jigsaw puzzles" of pieces of glass that were colored while molten, cut to fit the design, and fastened together with strips of lead; important features like faces were then painted onto the surface of the glass. In the most renowned of French cathedrals at Chartres, worshipers would see "Our Lady of the Lovely Window," a seven-foot-high image of the Virgin Mary crowned and enthroned with the infant Jesus (see photo). The image proclaimed to them the contemporary cult of the Virgin as Queen of Heaven in a way that glowed with the light of divine

>> **"Our Lady of the Lovely Window."** Colored glass is an art form that dates back to ancient Egypt, and in the early Middle Ages both church builders and mosque builders began using it in windows. Muslim glassmakers devised complex abstract patterns, while their Christian counterparts created vivid representations of revered beings. This stained glass window in Chartres Cathedral depicts the Virgin Mary crowned and enthroned with the infant Jesus.

Giraudon/Art Resource, NY

UNIVERSITIES GRADUALLY TOOK OVER AS THE MAIN CENTERS OF EDUCATION AND STUDY:

Professional schools developed near Muslim and Byzantine centers of learning

- Medical instruction started at Salerno, in the south of Italy close to Muslim-ruled Sicily (and Muslim learning), in the ninth century.

- Late in the eleventh century, training in Roman law began in the northern Italian town of Bologna, not far from Ravenna, which had a long Byzantine tradition.

- The universities founded at these centers were professional schools that satisfied the demand for physicians and lawyers to serve Italian rulers and merchants, as well as the rising papal monarchy.

A new model university was established in Paris

- The university movement spread northward from Italy to Montpellier in southern France and to Paris.

- Europe's foremost institution of learning was established in Paris during the thirteenth century.

- Paris was the first to offer the four major curricula that were, for centuries, the main fields of university study: theology, law, medicine, and liberal arts.

New universities sprang up across Europe

- From Paris, the movement spread to England, Germany, and the rest of western Europe.

- By 1300, eighteen universities had been founded.

- By 1500, the total number of universities, many of which are still in existence, exceeded eighty.

---

revelation. And in its immensity, its harmonious beauty, and its glowing illumination, the cathedral as a whole conveyed to the worshipers something of the image of the universe and its creator that inspired the builders.

LO² Thought and Education

Medieval education, like the visual arts, was dominated by the Church. From the eighth to the twelfth century, members of the clergy made up the only literate and educated class of society, and even after that, they staffed virtually all the schools, libraries, and centers

> "*I have learned ... that you do not study in your room or act in the schools as a good student should, but play and wander about, disobedient to your master and indulging in sport and in certain other dishonorable practices which I do not now care to explain by letter.*"
>
> —Father to son, thirteenth century

of higher learning. But the feudalistic and local character of the times counterbalanced what was, in theory, the monolithic force of the Church. The methods of long-distance communication were primitive, and the Church itself was made up of many authorities, orders, and factions. Although basically only a Catholic point of view could be professed in western Europe, a wide range of intellectual inquiry and debate was still possible.

During the troubled centuries immediately after the fall of Rome, the monasteries had conserved precious manuscripts and provided at least the basics of education to the clergy, the only class of society

"THEY MAY GO IN SAFETY": IMPERIAL PROTECTION FOR SCHOLARS

Already in the twelfth century, increasing numbers of scholars and students in Western Christendom needed to travel long distances to study. Travel was often dangerous, and safety for academics did not always improve once they reached their destinations. As foreigners without local status, scholars and students could find themselves at the mercy of local officials, merchants, and landlords. At a meeting of nobles and high clergy of the Holy Roman Empire in the Italian city of Roncaglia in 1158, Emperor Frederick I Barbarossa issued an order of protection for scholars. The order was a sign of the high value that leaders of the church and the state put on education and scholarship, which would soon lead to the development of formal institutions of higher learning—universities.

After a careful consideration of this subject by the bishops, abbots, dukes, counts, judges, and other nobles of our sacred palace, we, out of our piety, have granted this privilege to all scholars who travel for the sake of study, and especially to the professors of divine and sacred laws, namely: that they may go in safety to the places in which the studies are carried on, both they themselves and their messengers, and may dwell there in security. For we think it fitting that, so long as they conduct themselves with propriety, those should enjoy our approval and protection who, by their learning, enlighten the world and mold the life of our subjects to obey God and us, his minister. By reason of our special regard we desire to defend them from all injuries.

For who does not pity those who exile themselves through love for learning, who wear themselves out in poverty in place of riches, who expose their lives to all perils and often suffer bodily injury from the vilest men,—yet all these vexatious things must be endured by the scholar. Therefore, we declare, by this general and ever-to-be-valid law, that in the future no one shall be so rash as to venture to inflict any injury on scholars, or to occasion any loss to them on account of a debt owed by an inhabitant of their province,—a thing which we have learned is sometimes done, by an evil custom. And let it

be known to the violators of this decree, and also to those who shall at the time be the rulers of the places where the offense is committed, that a fourfold restitution of property shall be exacted from all those who are guilty and that, the mark of infamy being affixed to them by the law itself, they shall lose their office forever.

Moreover, if any one shall presume to bring a suit against them on account of any business, the choice in this matter shall be given to the scholars, who may summon the accusers to appear before their professors, or before the bishop of the city, to whom we have given jurisdiction in this matter. But if, in sooth, the accuser shall attempt to drag the scholar before another judge, even though his cause is a very just one, he shall lose his suit for such an attempt.

EXPLORING THE SOURCE

1. What specific abuses does Frederick seek to protect scholars against?

2. Why does Frederick think that scholars and students are worthy of respect and valuable to society?

Source: James Harvey Robinson, ed., Readings in European History (Boston: Ginn, 1904), 1:452

---

that was thought to have need for it. Around 800, Charlemagne gave strong support to the revival of interest in intellectual matters (pp. 172–173), and by 1200, it was again normal for nobles and businesspeople to be mostly literate. The monasteries still provided elementary education, and cathedral schools were beginning to respond to a growing desire for education in the towns. But the most significant development was the rise of the universities.

Medieval Universities

Unlike the old monastic schools, nearly all of the universities were located in important towns and cities, reflecting the connection between the rise of universities and that of trade and towns. Each university operated under the protection of a charter granted by a ranking official of the Church or the state (usually the pope or a king). Thus, the universities were freed, for the most part, from the jurisdiction of local courts and local clergy. One justification for this exempted status was that teachers and students came from all over Europe, making the universities truly international. The Latin word *universitas* simply meant any kind of organized group including guilds, and universities were organized much like guilds (pp. 200–201), with "masters" (the faculty) practicing in their fields of knowledge and teaching "apprentices" (the students).

The basic curriculum that was followed in all universities was taken over from the monastic schools, which, in turn, followed late Roman educational practices. The course of studies consisted of the seven *liberal arts* ("fields of knowledge befitting a free man"): grammar, rhetoric, and logic (the *trivium*); and arithmetic, geometry, astronomy, and music (the *quadrivium*—the names came from the Latin for "three roads" and "four roads" to knowledge).

Grammar, of course, meant Latin grammar. This was the language used by members of the clergy, lawyers, physicians, and scholars all through the Middle Ages. But the trivium went beyond the mechanics of language; it included the study of works of philosophy, literature, and history. The quadrivium was based

A Fourteenth-Century Classroom Henry of Germany, an internationally respected expert on Aristotle, explains a work by the Greek thinker to a class at the University of Bologna about 1350. Students in the front rows follow his lecture attentively; students farther back have other things on their minds.

on the reading of ancient scientific and mathematical texts and was almost entirely theoretical.

Whatever subject they were studying, the students had few books and no laboratories. They scribbled their lecture notes on wax tablets and then transferred them to sheets of parchment. More stress was placed on memorizing and analyzing a small number of highly respected books than on extensive reading (see photo).

The faculty lectured in their homes or in hired halls, and students lived independently, according to their means and tastes, though wealthy clergy and laypeople donated lecture halls, libraries, and dormitories. The first notable "college" of this kind was established in Paris about 1250 by Louis IX's chaplain, Robert de Sorbon, and the "Sorbonne" is still part of the University of Paris today. Still, college students—all men, of course, since most women were thought to have no need for formal education and professional qualifications—had a reputation for wildness throughout the Middle Ages.

College Students Write Home: Parents Respond Read the correspondence between medieval students and their parents.

The students in medieval universities earned their degrees on the basis of comprehensive oral examinations. After attending lectures and reading for several years in the subjects of the trivium, a student would ask to be examined by the members of the faculty. If he performed satisfactorily, he was granted the preliminary degree of Bachelor of Arts, a prerequisite for going on to the quadrivium. After several additional years of study, the student would present himself for examination once again. If he passed, he was awarded the degree of Master of Arts, which certified that he was qualified to teach the liberal arts curriculum.

The Latin word *doctor* (teacher) was customarily used for higher degrees in theology, law, and medicine. Each of these degrees normally required four or more years of study beyond the master's and was also awarded on the basis of the candidate's performance in an oral examination. The candidate usually presented a *thesis* or *theses* (one or more statements about a subject), which he defended before a faculty board.

Scholastic Thought

University faculty, as well as earlier teachers in monastery and cathedral schools, not only taught but also contributed to their areas of study, especially in what they considered the most important areas—theology and its allied field of philosophy. Because these thinkers worked in universities and schools, they were known at the time as **schoolmen**, and medieval thought in general is today called **scholastic**.

Like other features of the renewed culture of Western Christendom, scholastic thought was nourished by impulses from Christianity's rival monotheisms, Islam and Judaism. In the twelfth and thirteenth centuries, Arabic versions of many works of Aristotle, as well as books of Hellenistic science, mathematics, and medicine, were translated into Latin. So also were original writings and commentaries (books explaining works of earlier thinkers and developing their ideas) by leading Muslim and Jewish scholars (see photo on page 224).

Chief among the Muslim commentators on Aristotle was the twelfth-century philosopher Averroës ((uh-VER-oh-eez)—ibn-Rushd), a Spanish-born Arab. But many Christians (and many Muslims) were disturbed by his doctrine, drawn from Aristotle, that the universe had always existed and was therefore not created. He also denied the immortality of the human soul. More acceptable were the writings of Averroës's Jewish contemporary, also born in Muslim Spain, Maimonides (mahy-MON-i-deez) (Moses ben Maimon). His *Guide for the Perplexed* addresses the "big" religious and philosophical questions that confront believing Jews, Muslims, and Christians alike: What is the purpose of God's universe? Will it last forever? How is God's will related to natural causes? Maimonides' answers to such questions consist of a closely reasoned mixture of Aristotle, the Hebrew Bible, and traditional Jewish authorities.

> "*Should human faith be based upon reason, or no?*
> *Is God the author of evil, or no?*
> *Did all the apostles have wives except John, or no?*"
>
> —Peter Abelard, ca. 1135

Reason and Faith

Like Maimonides, the scholastics wanted above all to use the recovered Greek thought to deepen their understanding of their religious beliefs. Thus, Anselm, a learned Italian monk who became archbishop of Canterbury in England, put together arguments to prove logically the existence of God. In another book, written about 1100, he explained why God had chosen to take on human form as Jesus. Understanding and believing, Anselm thought, belonged together, and one could not properly have one without the other—though believing came first: "I believe," he said, "so that I may understand."

In the twelfth century, the French scholar Peter Abelard argued that the authorities of the Church should not be read without questioning, for they often contradicted one another. He demonstrated this in an influential writing that put many such conflicting answers to theological questions alongside one another; he called this work *Sic et Non* (Latin for "Yes and No"). Abelard insisted, therefore, that all

Sic et Non: Is It or Isn't It? Read a selection of Abelard's questions.

writings be subjected to the light of logic. "By doubting," he observed, "we come to examine, and by examining we reach the truth." Thus Abelard had returned to the position of Socrates, who had sought knowledge through persistent questioning (p. 72).

Words and Things

Though theological matters remained the focus of scholastic concern, medieval philosophers debated every subject under the sun—some grand and divine, some trivial and worldly. One of the most absorbing issues was that of "universals." Do "Man," "Horse," "Beauty," and "Justice" exist independently of particular things? Or are these words merely convenient symbols for referring to various classes of objects and characteristics? The argument paralleled the ancient one between Plato and the Sophists (pp. 72–73). Plato believed that Ideas (Forms) have a perfect and independent existence, while the Sophists thought that only particular things exist. In the Middle Ages, those who held that universals are real were called *realists*; those who declared that they are just names (*nomina*) were called *nominalists*.

The extreme realists attached little importance to individual things, and sought, through sheer logic or divine revelation, to know the universals. The extreme nominalists, by contrast, saw only specific objects and refused to admit the existence of unifying relationships among particular things. The realists tended to ignore the observed world; the nominalists could scarcely make sense of it.

Most scholars took a middle position on this question. Among the moderates, Abelard expressed a view that is still widely held today. It is called *conceptualism*. Abelard held that only particular things have an existence in and of themselves. The universals, however, are more than mere names. They exist as *concepts in individual minds*—keys to an understanding of the interrelatedness of things. Thus, the concept "Horse" exists in our minds and adds something to our understanding of all four-footed animals of a certain general type. Once we have identified such a creature, we can assign to it the specific features drawn from our concept. By means of many such concepts, based on individual observations, we can make the world (to a degree) comprehensible, manageable, and predictable.

Harmony of Faith and Reason: Aquinas

Thomas Aquinas (**uh-KWAHY-nuhs**), the greatest of the scholastic philosophers, was a moderate realist. Born near Monte Cassino (Italy) of an aristocratic family, he joined the order of Dominican friars in 1244. A brilliant pupil, he studied at Cologne and Paris and spent his adult life teaching at Paris and Naples. He wrote an enormous number of scholarly works, in which he sought to harmonize various approaches to truth and to bring all knowledge together. In his most comprehensive work, the *Summa Theologica* ("Theological Summary"), he clarified Church teachings about the nature of God and humanity.

Summa Theologica: On Free Will Read a selection from *Summa Theologica*.

Following the lead of Anselm, Abelard, and other scholastics, Aquinas set a high value on human reason. By this time, the full impact of Aristotle (p. 76) had struck the schools and universities of Europe, and Christian teachings were being challenged, above all by Averroës . Instead of answering these arguments by denying the power of reason, Aquinas adopted Aristotelian logic and turned it to the defense of his faith. He sought to demonstrate that divine law—as revealed in the Bible—is never in conflict with logic, properly exercised. Both faith and reason, he argued, were created by God, and it is illogical to hold that God could contradict himself.

Aquinas's way of arguing involved dividing each major subject into a series of questions. For each, he explained the arguments for and against, in accordance with the usual scholastic method of presentation. The arguments are generally **deductive** in form—that is, they rely on reasoning from basic propositions assumed in advance to be true, because they are found either in the Bible or in the works of thinkers (both pagan and Christian) who are considered authoritative. He presented his own conclusion for each of the questions he posed—a conclusion that generally agreed with accepted Christian teachings.

The *Summa Theologica* is a masterful combination of quotations from Scripture, formal logic, and common sense. Aquinas's grand synthesis ("harmonization" of knowledge) stands as an impressive monument to the discipline and resourcefulness of the human mind.

Medieval Science

Besides the thought of Aristotle, the schoolmen also relearned from Muslim and Jewish experts the astronomy of Ptolemy and the medicine of Hippocrates and Galen (pp. 72, 110). Some became experts themselves and expanded on the ancient knowledge.

The German scholar Albert the Great (a teacher of Thomas Aquinas) wrote on the broad range of philosophical and theological questions that challenged thirteenth-century thinkers. But he also found time to observe systematically many of the animal species of western Europe, including bees, spiders, hawks, beavers, whales, and eels. Albert rejected medieval accounts of mythical animals like "griffins" and "harpies," simply because he had never observed any.

Robert Grosseteste, an outstanding English scholar of the same period, wrote commentaries on the Bible, Aristotle, and a wide variety of philosophical topics. But he wrote, too, about the sun, weather, tides, colors, comets, and other aspects of nature. Grosseteste was a pioneer teacher at the new Oxford University, where he helped establish the study of science and mathematics. A generation afterward, his pupil, Roger Bacon, continued to emphasize experimental methods. Bacon, who died in 1294, is remembered also for his predictions of such technological innovations as flying machines and powered ships.

The Legacy of Scholasticism

By the end of the thirteenth century, the intellectual life of Western Christendom had achieved a new vigor. The communities of university scholars had succeeded in their efforts to preserve and advance learning. The scholastic philosophers had refined the methods of logical thought and had laboriously collected, compiled, and classified sources of information. Above all, they had established the essentials of scholarship: comprehensive research and precise expression.

Modern thought owes much to these medieval seekers after truth. They built upon ancient Greek thought, reconciled it with Christian teachings, and absorbed new ideas from the Muslim and Jewish worlds. The twelfth-century thinker Bernard of Chartres once compared himself and his fellow scholars with the philosophers and scientists of ancient times. "We are dwarfs," he said, "standing on the shoulders of giants." There is modesty in this statement but also pride—pride in the fact that he and his colleagues could see a bit farther than their intellectual ancestors.

> "*We are dwarfs standing on the shoulders of giants.*"
> —Bernard of Chartres

LO³ Language and Literature

The international language of religion and thought, education and scholarship, and government and commerce in western Europe during the Middle Ages was Latin. Passed down from ancient Rome, it had been carried beyond the old Roman frontiers by the Church, and literary works were still written by and for people who knew Latin. But by now, no one knew Latin as their mother tongue, and in everyday life, people spoke local languages (**vernaculars**). These had developed in the early Middle Ages out of Latin itself and out of the languages of barbarian peoples in northern Europe. By the thirteenth century, the vernaculars were coming to be used in government and commerce, and they were already the main languages of literature.

Latin Writings

Medieval Latin did not usually follow the principles of ancient Roman "eloquence" (good style in speech and writing). Written and spoken Latin developed into a highly technical language of philosophy, administration, and law in which precision was more important than eloquence, and preachers and writers mostly used a modified Latin that itself became the medium for notable literary achievements.

The finest creations in medieval Latin were the prayers and hymns of the Christian worship services. Some of these were incorporated into the Mass and were notable for their poetic beauty, such as the *Stabat Mater*, the great hymn on the sorrows of the Virgin Mary: "At the Cross her station keeping, / Stood the mournful Mother weeping, / While her Son was hanging there."

Meanwhile, some ancient Roman authors were widely read. Christian writers who had lived at the time of the Roman Empire, such as Augustine and Jerome (pp. 143–144), were deeply studied for the religious guidance they offered. Some pagan authors, such as Cicero and Virgil (p. 108), were admired because it was felt that in spite of not possessing the faith, they taught valuable moral lessons. Furthermore, ancient eloquence was still admired. Hroswitha of Gandersheim (**hros-VIT-tuh, GAN-ders-hime**), a learned nun in tenth-century northern Germany, even confessed to preferring "the polished elegance of the style of pagan writers" to the Scriptures.

Furthermore, within the medieval "Age of Faith" there also flowed a powerful current of delight in earthly pleasures. According to Hroswitha, the most widely read of ancient writers was no Christian thinker or high-minded pagan but the playwright Terence (p. 107), in spite of the fact that his plays celebrated "the licentious acts of shameless women." In the tenth century, the vast majority of people who knew enough Latin to read Terence would have been monks and nuns—and it was monks and nuns who painstakingly copied his works and those of other "licentious" ancient authors like Ovid (p. 108), ensuring their survival alongside the works of Cicero and Virgil.

In this tradition, a great deal of medieval poetry in Latin celebrated eating, drinking, and lovemaking—often in a way that made fun of high-minded religious ideals. Many of these works were dedicated, tongue in cheek, to an invented holy patron, Saint Golias, and therefore are known as Goliardic poetry. The Goliardic poets were shy about revealing their names, but it is clear that they were men of learning, schooled in Latin and familiar with ancient literature. One of them looked forward to a boozily beautiful death: "Angels when they come shall cry, / At my frailties winking: / 'Spare this drunkard, God, he's high, / Absolutely stinking!'"[1]

 **Gaudeamus Igitur: Live While We Are Young** Read a poem in celebration of youth and pleasure.

---

[1]From George F. Whicher, *The Goliard Poets*. Copyright 1949 by George F. Whicher. Reprinted by permission of New Directions Publishing Corporation.

> **"Let us live then and be glad**
> **While young life's before us!**
> **After youthful pastime had,**
> **After old age hard and sad,**
> **Earth will slumber o'er us."**
> —from *Gaudeamus Igitur*,
> Anonymous, ca. 1175

Vernacular Writings

Literature in the vernacular tongues, however, spoke more directly even to those who knew Latin. In areas that had long been occupied by Rome, spoken Latin had evolved over many centuries into different local languages that already resembled such present-day Latin languages as Spanish, French, and Italian (pp. 119–120). In western Europe, north of the Roman imperial frontiers, former Germanic barbarian peoples (p. 135) spoke languages that were evolving toward languages of today like German, Dutch, and Swedish. Eastern Europe was occupied mostly by Slav peoples (pp. 156–157), whose speech was developing into present-day languages such as Russian, Polish, and Serbian.

European languages borrowed words from each other, as well as from Latin and Greek, and English borrowed more than any other language. English was originally the Germanic dialect of the Anglo-Saxon invaders of the island of Britain (p. 153). The later Danish and Norman conquests brought influences from Germanic languages spoken by the Vikings, as well as from French, which was spoken by the Normans. By the middle of the fourteenth century, Anglo-Saxon (Old English) had changed into what is now called Middle English. Out of this evolved modern English, a mixture of Germanic and Latin elements.

Epic and Romance

As with Homer's *Iliad* and *Odyssey* eighteen hundred years before, among the earliest medieval European vernacular written works were epic poems that grew out of traditional songs memorized and continually altered by generations of illiterate minstrels (p. 68). One of the most notable was the *Song of Roland*, written down around 1100 by an unknown author in northern France and based on *chansons de geste* (shahn-sawn duh ZHEST) ("songs of great deeds") about the hero-king Charlemagne and his companions. Like the epics of Homer, this poem about heroes of the past in fact expresses the values of the time at which it was written—in this case, the ideals of medieval Christian knights.

Its chief hero is Count Roland, nephew of Charlemagne. Roland personifies the warrior ideals of bravery, loyalty, and military prowess—and Christian faith in God and salvation. The field of battle runs red with the blood of the courageous, and Roland's fellow vassals observe strictly the code of honor and revenge. Many other national epics were written down in the eleventh and twelfth countries, such as the *Song of the Nibelungs* (NEE-buh-looongz) in Germany, the *Poem of the Cid* in Spain, and the *Lay of Igor's Host* ("The Ballad of Igor's Army") in Russia.

But the **troubadours** (nobles who created poems and accompanying music) did not confine themselves to epic tales. They also sang of "courtly" manners and romantic love (from *romance*, which originally meant a tale, as opposed to a learned work in Latin). For the first time since the days of the pagan authors, a poetry of passion appeared in Europe. Often, the passion was on an "elevated" plane. The romantic knight placed his ideal woman on a pedestal and adored her from afar—with thoughts of physical fulfillment repressed or postponed. Often, too, the knight was seduced by a female figure of power—King Arthur's unfaithful Queen Guenevere, or a well-wishing fairy lady in an enchanted castle—who found him irresistible for his beauty and "courtesy" (courtly manners). Either way, this "cult of love" also brought forth elaborate manuals of behavior for lovers. Courtly love, however, was a pastime for the nobility only; commoners were considered unsuited to the delicate art of romance. Even so, the code of conduct that held love as a noble ideal made a distinguishing mark upon the whole of Western culture.

 The Lay of Igor's Host: Warfare on the Russian Steppes Read a selection from the Russian national epic.

Clearly, the hearty masculine culture of the early Middle Ages was giving way to a more tranquil, confident, and leisurely society. The noble's castle was becoming less of a barracks for fighting men and more of a theater for refined pleasures. Aristocratic ladies were accorded more and more attention and were able to exercise greater control over the men. Most notable among such ladies was Eleanor, duchess of Aquitaine in southwestern France. Eleanor married King Louis VII of France, went on crusade with him, but agreed with him to have the pope annul the marriage, which had produced no sons. She then married King Henry II of England, had plenty of sons, but was imprisoned by him for supporting a rebellion against him by one of them. All the same, she ruled England for several years after Henry died while another son, King Richard the Lion-Hearted, went on crusade. Besides her deeds in politics, government, and war, Eleanor also reigned as the queen of courtly love and its laws of conduct.

The Rules of Love? Read some observations about courtly love.

The feudal society of the Middle Ages is splendidly portrayed in the so-called Arthurian romances, a cycle of verse tales composed in the twelfth and thirteenth centuries by French and Norman writers. The central figure of the romances is King Arthur, a Celtic chieftain of sixth-century Britain who fought against the Anglo-Saxon invaders, and the tales are based partly on ancient Celtic lore. But the legends of Arthur's Round Table are told in the manner of the Middle Ages; they are tales of forbidden love, knightly combats, and colorful pageantry.

Among the most popular of the romance writers were Chrétien de Troyes (kreh-t-YEN duh trwah) and Marie de France. Both of them lived in the late twelfth century, and both enjoyed the patronage of Eleanor of Aquitaine. Chrétien's romances of Lancelot, Percival, the Holy Grail, and other Arthurian characters and themes set a pattern for the lore of King Arthur and his knights and ladies that has lasted down to the present day. Marie composed "lays," shorter tales than Chrétien's romances, that also dealt with combat, seduction, and love among knights and ladies at Arthur's court. According to an English monk who admired her work, her poems were "dear to many a count, baron, and knight . . . and her lays please ladies too, who listen to them with joy and good will."

Realism and Satire

Toward the close of the Middle Ages, the narratives of chivalric love became less fanciful and more realistic than the Arthurian tales. Most successful was the work of Christine de Pisan, the first woman to support herself entirely from her earnings as an author. Born in Italy, she spent most of her years at or near the French court in Paris. Her best-known story, *The Book of the Duke of True Lovers* (ca. 1400), reads much like the earlier aristocratic romances. But it is based on actual events rather than legend, and its lovers act in response to common sense rather than to the dictates of passion and the cult of love.

> "*They died for the Russian land. The grass withered from sorrow, and the saddened trees drooped earthward.*"
>
> —from *The Lay of Igor's Host,* Anonymous, tenth century

As with works in Latin, there was also a far less high-minded form of literature, which also originated in France—the *fabliaux* (FAB-lee-ohz) (**fables**). Frank, sensual, and witty, they ridiculed both courtly and priestly life. One of the most popular fables was *Aucassin and Nicolette*, by an unknown author. Its hero, Aucassin, spurns knighthood in order to pursue his passion for a beautiful young Muslim captive. Indifferent to his soul's salvation, he subordinates everything to his desire for union with Nicolette. He even prefers hell to heaven, on the ground that the company there will be more attractive and entertaining.

Drama

Medieval drama, like that of ancient Greece (p. 70), grew out of religion—in this case, reenactments of scenes such as Christ's birth and death that were part of Christmas and Easter worship. In the twelfth and thirteenth centuries, as the clergy sought to stress the humanness of holy people and holy events (pp. 205–206), the reenactments developed into independent performances in vernacular languages. **Passion plays** showed Christ's suffering and death, with the Jews usually cast as collective villains; **miracle plays** had plots involving happy endings brought about by the Virgin Mary; in **morality plays**, the characters were torn between noble virtues and tempting vices; and **mystery plays** were edifying dramas staged by guilds ("mystery" being a medieval word for a guild or craft). These plays often used slapstick and satire to help make their point, and they were often staged outside churches by troops of semiprofessional actors.

passion plays
Dramatizations of Christ's suffering and death.

miracle plays
Dramas with plots involving miraculous happy endings brought about by the Virgin Mary.

morality plays
Dramas in which the characters were torn between noble virtues and tempting vices.

mystery plays
Dramas designed to edify and staged by guilds.

Chaucer and Dante

Two works of the late Middle Ages rise above ordinary classification. One is the *Canterbury Tales* of Geoffrey Chaucer, written in the fourteenth century. This collection of stories is in the general spirit of the fabliaux but includes all classes of society and a wide range of topics.

Born of a merchant family, Chaucer spent most of his life in the service of the English aristocracy. He read broadly, in Latin, French, and Italian as well as in English, and traveled extensively on the continent of Europe. His outlook was cosmopolitan and urbane, and he displayed a rare combination of scholarship, insight, and humor. In the *Tales*, a group of people exchange stories as they ride on a pilgrimage to the shrine of a revered saint, Thomas Becket, at Canterbury. The stories, of "good morality and general pleasure," appealed to all literate persons in fourteenth-century England. In them—and in the tellers of the tales, all of them typical people of the time (see photo on page 240)—they could see themselves and their society as in a mirror.

The other monumental work of the period is the *Divine Comedy* of Dante. A scholar and poet from the Italian city-state of Florence, Dante was deeply involved in the political and intellectual trends of his time, and his *Comedy* is a grand synthesis of medieval theology, science, philosophy, and romance.

Escorted by the Roman poet Virgil, Dante travels in his poem through the regions beyond the grave. He descends

>> **"Upon an Ambler Easily She Sat"** Geoffrey Chaucer's *Canterbury Tales* was already a best seller as a handwritten book—eighty-four copies, an unusually large number, still exist today. This illustration from a luxury manuscript of about 1400 shows one of the pilgrim storytellers, the Wife of Bath. Forceful, independent, and five times married and widowed, she is depicted as Chaucer describes her, with wide-brimmed hat, hair in a net, and riding astride, not side-saddle as was expected of medieval ladies.

> **"XV. Every lover regularly turns pale in the presence of his beloved. XVI. When a lover suddenly catches sight of his beloved his heart palpitates. XVII. A new love puts to flight an old one. "**
> —from Andreas Capellanus, *The Art of Courtly Love*, ca. 1175

into the terrible Inferno (hell), where the damned suffer eternal punishments that fit their crimes. Then he moves on to Purgatory, where pardoned sinners suffer for a limited time until they are cleansed of guilt. At last, he is permitted to enter Paradise (heaven), where the blessed enjoy, in fitting ways, the gifts of God. For this final portion of the journey, Dante must leave the pagan Virgil behind. Now he is guided by the pure Beatrice, his ideal of Christian womanhood, who represents the blending of romantic and spiritual love that leads Dante at last to a climactic vision of God.

Dante called his work a "comedy" because he believed the story suggests a happy ending for all who choose to follow Christ. (Later admirers added the compliment "divine.") But apart from his spiritual quest, Dante had strong opinions on subjects ranging from poetry and astronomy to city-state politics and the conflict of the

 ***The Canterbury Tales:* The Knight** Read the description of the Knight from the *Canterbury Tales*.

popes and the Holy Roman emperors (he sided with the emperors). At every turn of his narrative, Dante makes sharp comments on the real and mythical characters from ancient Israel, Greece, and Rome to his own time whom he meets in the other world, and who serve as dramatic symbols for his ideas. Readers may agree or disagree with Dante's judgments, but they will long remember the vivid images created by his words. The *Comedy* is an intensely personal story, yet it is also the finest expression of the ideals and conflicts, the hopes and resentments, the strivings and failures of the Western Christendom of the Middle Ages.

Listen to a synopsis of Chapter 13.

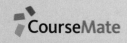
Huntington Library/SuperStock

{ More for Your Buck }

WCIV has it all, and you can too. Between the text and our online offerings, you have everything at your fingertips. Make sure you check out all that **WCIV** has to offer:

- Chapter in Review Cards
- Online Quizzing with Feedback
- Robust eBook
- Interactive Maps
- Western Civilization Resource Center

- Flash Cards
- Interactive Games
- BBC Motion Gallery Videos
- Audio Chapter Summaries
- And More!

Visit CourseMate to find the resources you need today! Login at **www.cengagebrain.com**.

Unlike the Roman world, the Christian Europe of the Middle Ages did not "fall." There were no waves of invading barbarians, no collapse of empires, no decline of trade and cities. Instead, many old-established and gradually developing traditions of medieval civilization reached "critical mass"—and gradual development turned into spectacular change.

Two of the most famous events connected with this change, Christopher Columbus's voyage of 1492 and the beginning of the Protestant Reformation in 1517, took place around the year 1500. As a result, that year has become the benchmark date of the "end" of the Middle Ages and the "beginning" of the modern period (p. 2). In fact, however, medieval civilization began to change as early as 1300, and it took 350 years for a recognizably more modern pattern of civilization to appear. A whole series of further changes then followed, which have gone on right down to the present. Unlike the ancient and medieval periods, the modern period has so far been one of continual shifts in civilization, each just as massive as the ones before it.

In the three and a half centuries of the first series of modern shifts in civilization, Europe's social and political structures, as well as its place in the world, were all transformed. Out of the booming agriculture and bustling cities of the Middle Ages came the freeing of the serfs in western Europe and the rise of international banking and capitalism. The competition of powerful feudal states led successful rulers to rely on royal bureaucrats, mercenary armies, and national taxation rather than on the services of warrior-landowners. Late in the Middle Ages, this led many rulers to seek backing from their subjects through representative institutions, but by 1700, the most successful states were those where rulers governed on their own authority as absolute (unlimited) monarchs. The one exception was Britain, whose limited monarchy combined representative institutions, guarantees of subjects' rights, and effective state power.

Meanwhile, stronger links with the other civilizations of the Eastern Hemisphere brought technical ideas from distant lands that fourteenth- and fifteenth-century Europe turned into revolutionary advances—firearms, printing, clocks. And out of the urge to make intercontinental links even stronger, as well as the need to counter the growing power of Islam, came exploration and overseas empires, so that Christendom replaced Islam as the world's farthest-flung intercontinental civilization.

The changes in culture and religion were just as drastic, and their roots in the past were just as deep. Medieval scholars and thinkers had always felt themselves to be the heirs of Greece and Rome, and this finally led them into a determined effort to revive all that was left of the ancient traditions—the Renaissance. Out of this encounter with the Greco-Roman past came new ideals of human personality and behavior, new philosophical ideas, new questions about Christian belief and practice, and new forms of art and literature.

Likewise, the Catholic Church of western Europe, for all its stress on unity of faith, had a long-standing history of inner conflict that finally exploded in the religious revolution of the Protestant Reformation. Protestantism failed to take over the entire Church or even to remain a united movement, but out of its disunity came many new forms of Christian belief and practice. The Reformation also strengthened the state in its partnership with both the Catholic and the Protestant Churches, and in the long run, it helped make religious diversity and freedom of conscience accepted Western values.

All these changes also strengthened the position that western Europe had won in the Middle Ages as the heartland of Western civilization. The Renaissance and Reformation began in western Europe and hardly affected the Orthodox countries of the East. The centers of finance, trade, and technical innovation, as well as the rulers with the best-organized governments and armies, were all to be found in the West. It was the western European countries that reached overseas for trade and empire, while eastern Europe served as their buffer zone against the expanding Islamic land empire of the Turks.

These shifts in civilization were far from being a triumphant progress toward modernity. The international capitalist economy brought bitter class struggles and vicious repression in town and countryside, and in eastern Europe, it helped serfdom grow ever more oppressive. The short-term result of the Reformation was two hundred years of religious hatred, persecution, and war. Europe's closer links with the rest of the world led to devastating intercontinental epidemics, the destruction of the civilizations of the Western Hemisphere, and the beginning of the Atlantic slave trade. In all these ways, the era was as tormented as any in history.

All the same, by 1650, a new kind of civilization, possessing unprecedented technical skills, worldwide power, and a willingness to deliberately alter its own ways of life, was coming into being. Christian Europe was on the way to remaking itself into the modern West.

CHAPTER 14

BEGINNINGS OF A NEW EUROPE: THE LATE MIDDLE AGES, 1300–1500

LEARNING OBJECTIVES

AFTER READING THIS CHAPTER, YOU SHOULD BE ABLE TO DO THE FOLLOWING:

LO¹ Detail the crises of the fourteenth century.

LO² Trace the evolution of capitalism in the late Middle Ages.

LO³ Describe the technical advances that, for the first time, gave Europe worldwide technological leadership.

LO⁴ Identify the changes in government and politics that began in the late Middle Ages.

"THE CRISES OF THE LATE MIDDLE AGES DID NOT STOP THE CONTINUING EVOLUTION OF CIVILIZATION IN WESTERN EUROPE, AND IN SOME WAYS THEY EVEN SPURRED IT ON."

In the late Middle Ages—the fourteenth and fifteenth centuries—Europe was shaken by a series of crises and disasters. The increase in population that had begun in the early Middle Ages broke through the limits of what existing farming methods could support, and the result was famine, social conflict, and peasant revolts. The Black Death, the famous mid-fourteenth-century outbreak of the plague, ravaged the entire Eastern Hemisphere and killed as much as a quarter of the people of Europe. The papacy became entangled in Church corruption and the rivalries of rulers, and the result was a long-enduring crisis of confidence in the holiness of the popes. Islam, now led not by Arabs but by convert peoples from the Asiatic steppes, once again went over to the offensive in its continual struggle with Christendom, and much of eastern Europe came under the rule of the Turks.

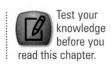

Test your knowledge before you read this chapter.

What do you think?

The Black Death was the worst catastrophe that Europe ever faced.

Strongly Disagree						Strongly Agree
1	2	3	4	5	6	7

But these crises did not stop the continuing evolution of civilization in western Europe, and in some ways, they even spurred it on. Merchants reinvested their profits in industry and banking as well as trade, so that a capitalist sector of the economy began to appear alongside the agrarian and guild-based economy of the Middle Ages. Partly in order to serve the needs of this new economy, and helped by its ability to mobilize resources and create markets, late medieval inventors came up with a series of world-changing devices: three-masted sailing ships, firearms, printing presses, and mechanical clocks. All these inventions built on inspirations from Islam and East Asia, but for the first time, they gave Europe technological leadership among the civilizations of the world.

Capitalism and new technology also helped change the way in which rulers governed their countries. Rulers began to rely on taxes from their subjects and on

≪ **Telling the Time** On a clock installed in 1410 on the city hall of the central European city of Prague, a hand points to numbers on the outer ring that show twenty-four-hour time beginning at sunset—but since sunset changes from earlier to later and back again through the year, the outer ring turns very slowly back and forth to compensate. The clock shows much more timekeeping and astronomical information, all automatically. Revolutionary devices like mechanical clocks were among the many new beginnings of the later Middle Ages.

Jacquerie
A large-scale uprising of French peasants in 1358.

loans from bankers as well as on the services of vassals. New infantry weapons overthrew the battlefield supremacy of mounted knights. The invention of cannon made the castles of nobles vulnerable to attack, as well as being too expensive for anyone but leading rulers to afford. The Italian city-states came under the rule of efficient despotic governments that practiced the naked pursuit and use of power. The rulers of western European countries began to build up centralized governments, hire mercenary soldiers, and collect taxes directly from their subjects.

However, the feudal notion persisted that subjects had rights against rulers and that rulers could not do things that affected these rights without their subjects' consent. Accordingly, to get the backing of their subjects for their new measures, rulers in many countries began to summon representative assemblies—most famously, the English Parliament.

LO¹ The Fourteenth-Century Disasters

Famine, rebellion, war, and disease have been regular features of human society from prehistory to the present. In the Middle Ages, conflict and corruption within Christendom, and reverses in the continual struggle with Islam, were nothing unusual. But in fourteenth-century Europe, all these things happened one after another and on a massive scale, with aftershocks that continued into the fifteenth century and long afterward.

Famine, Rebellion, War, Disease

About the year 1300, the lengthy agricultural boom that had caused Europe's population to more than double over three centuries (p. 193) came to an end. Early in the new century, arctic cold and heavy rains swept across Europe, flooding farmlands and shortening the growing season. Because of the earlier growth in population and farming, there was no more wild territory that could be turned into productive fields, and the available farmland had reached the limit of what it could produce with the methods in use at the time. The resulting famines led to hostility between peasants and lords, lowered human resistance to disease, and disrupted agriculture and commerce.

Rebellion and War

In 1320, a peasant uprising started in northern France. Its leaders expressed the grievances of the poor and a religious hope that the lowly would overthrow the highborn and establish a

"Christian commonwealth" of equality for all. Farmers and poor people from the cities joined excited mobs as they made their way across the countryside. The rebels seized arms, attacked castles and monasteries, and destroyed tax records. Finally, after Pope John XXII had condemned the outlaws, mounted bands of knights ruthlessly slaughtered the weary peasants (see photo). But the resentment and anger of the poor persisted.

Another uprising occurred about a generation later, in 1358. It was called the **Jacquerie** (zhahk-REE), (from Jacques, the French for Jack—a slang name for a peasant). Kindled in a village near Paris, the revolt spread like wildfire across the country. At its peak, perhaps 100,000 men, women, and children were on

≪ Crushing an Uprising This manuscript illustration shows the capture of a rebellious town in fourteenth-century France. Foot soldiers hack at rebels and throw them into a river; mounted knights patrol the streets, and noble ladies, dressed in the height of fashion, look on unconcerned. Snark/Art Resource, NY

the rampage. Though better equipped and better organized, the Jacquerie suffered the same fate as the earlier rebellions, with systematic burning, looting, and killing by both the peasants and the avenging nobles.

France was not alone in its ordeal. Similar uprisings occurred all over Europe throughout the century. In England, the Peasants' Revolt of 1381 followed the pattern of the Jacquerie. Marked by murders and burnings, it was finally crushed by the ferocity and treachery of the nobles and the king.

Adding to these miseries were lengthy struggles between the English and French kings, which began in 1338, continued with intervals for more than a century, and are known as the Hundred Years' War. The combats, which often consisted of large-scale English raids deliberately intended to inflict the maximum destruction, brought ruin to the farms and towns of France, the principal battlefield.

The Black Death

But the cruelest blow of all was the **Black Death**. This was the name given in Europe to a pandemic (universal) outbreak of a deadly disease, the bubonic **(byoo-BON-ik)** plague—from *buboes*, painful swellings that mark the disease's onset. The infection had already devastated much of Europe in the sixth century (p. 156). For several centuries, there were no more massive outbreaks, until one began in southwestern China about 1340 and spread in a few years throughout the Eastern Hemisphere (Map 14.1).

By about 1347, the plague reached the Black Sea region; from there, merchants from the city of Genoa brought it to Italy; and in about four years, it spread across Europe. Having had little or no prior contact with the infection, people were highly susceptible, and their capacity for resistance was weakened by widespread malnutrition. The plague killed perhaps a quarter of all the inhabitants of Europe during the fourteenth century (25 million out of a population of 100 million).

By the close of the fourteenth century, the effects of the plague had diminished, and life returned more or less to normal. But it was not until the sixteenth century that the population reached its earlier level, and the plague continued to flare up locally until the late seventeenth century. In addition to its toll in death and suffering, the plague had drastic economic, social, and psychological effects. Death became a universal obsession. Many people interpreted the plague as a punishment from God that called for severe personal penitence; some thought the end of the world was at hand. And the plague and the other catastrophes that had struck the people of Europe severely strained the medieval patterns of society.

The Plague Hits Florence Read an eyewitness account of life in Florence during the plague.

Black Death: The Lasting Impact (http://www.bbc.co.uk/history/british/middle_ages/black_impact_01.shtml) Learn how the Black Death changed life in England.

Simon Schama Hosts a BBC Motion Gallery on the Black Death (http://www.bbc.co.uk/history/interactive/audio_video/) View a short video on "King Death" in England.

The Crisis of the Papacy

Besides these human disasters, the fourteenth century was also an era of crisis in the leading religious institution of Western Christendom, the papacy. Since about the year 1000, the popes

"Babylonian Captivity"
The period in which the popes resided in Avignon rather than Rome and were thought to be controlled by the French monarchy.

Great Schism
The division of Western Christendom into two competing groups, each with its own pope and college of cardinals.

had gained a new position as rulers with international governing power over the Catholic Church. They had done so partly by building on their traditional position as generally accepted guides in matters of belief and worship, and partly by putting themselves at the head of the eleventh-century movement for Church reform (pp. 210–211). As a result, they had become both partners and rivals of feudal rulers in the power structure of Western Christendom.

Exactly because the Church was so powerful, rivalries between popes and feudal rulers were often intense. Should clergy who committed crimes be tried by Church or royal courts? Could rulers levy taxes on the clergy to help pay the expenses of governing their countries, and could popes collect fees from believers to help pay the expenses of governing the Church? Popes and rulers naturally tended to have very different views on matters like these.

Furthermore, in spite of their supreme position in Western Christendom, the popes were liable to all sorts of pressures from below. There was pressure, for example, to do favors for cooperative rulers—especially the kings of France, who were usually on good terms with the papacy. Thirteenth-century popes appointed many French churchmen as cardinals (pp. 209–210), so that the papal court became divided between a French bloc and an Italian bloc.

Furthermore, now that the popes headed an international government, their officials were eager to enrich themselves from fees and bribes. Like all rulers at the time, popes found it hard to stamp out this practice, since the chance of fees and bribes was exactly what made officials willing to work in government—in fact, able but corrupt Church officials sometimes rose to become popes. As a result, in the never-ending struggle against Church corruption, the papacy was no longer seen as part of the solution, but as part of the problem. Around 1300, the pious Catholic Dante, in his story of his journey through the afterlife, told of meeting the recently deceased Pope Nicholas III in hell—stuck forever upside down into a hole, just as during his lifetime he had stuck into his purse the money he had made from selling Church positions.

The Babylonian Captivity and the Great Schism

Late in the thirteenth century, the papacy's relations with France

In the fourteenth century, disputes and pressures like these led to a historic shift in the relationship of popes and rulers.

> **"** *And turn or tarry where I may, I encountered the ghosts of the departed.* **"**
>
> —from Boccaccio,
> *The Decameron*

temporarily soured, and in 1303, Pope Boniface VIII died after being humiliated by King Philip IV of France in a struggle arising out of a dispute over taxation of the clergy (p. 211). Shortly afterward, with powerful help from Philip, a French archbishop was elected as Pope Clement V. The new pope began by appointing nine new cardinals, all Frenchmen, giving the French bloc a majority at the papal court—and it was the cardinals who elected the pope. A few years later, Clement moved his court to Avignon, a papal holding on the Rhône River just east of the border of the French kingdom. For some seventy years, a succession of French popes reigned at Avignon.

Outside France, these popes were looked upon with suspicion and hostility. Because the pope holds office by virtue of his being the bishop of Rome, it seemed improper that he should reside anywhere but in the Eternal City, and the move confirmed a widespread feeling that the papacy had become a captive of the French monarchy. The Italian humanist Petrarch labeled the popes' stay at Avignon the **"Babylonian Captivity,"** a reference to the forced removal of ancient Jewish leaders to Babylon.

More serious embarrassments to the Church were yet to come. In 1377, Gregory XI decided to return the papal court to Rome; upon his death there, a Roman mob pressured the cardinals into choosing an Italian as pope. But the French cardinals then fled the city, pronounced the election invalid, and chose a pope of their own. This one, with his supporting cardinals, moved to Avignon, while the Italian pope, with his cardinals, stayed in Rome. Each declared the other to be a false pope and excommunicated him and his followers.

For the next forty years (1378–1417), Western Christendom had two popes and two colleges of cardinals, each supported by competing groups of rulers: France and its allies recognized Avignon, while England and the German princes recognized Rome. The **Great Schism** (split), as this division is called, was at last settled by a general council of the Church at Constance in Switzerland, which deposed both rival popes and elected a new one. That, however, raised a new danger to the papacy—that its supremacy over the Church might be challenged by bishops acting collectively in council and swayed by the rulers who backed them.

The Triumph of Conciliarism: End of the Great Schism Read a selection from the documents that announced the end of the Great Schism.

Powerful but Disrespected: The Fifteenth-Century Papacy

Fifteenth-century popes were able to fend off this danger. They astutely played rival rulers against each other and made compromises with them, whereby the rulers controlled leading Church appointments while letting the popes collect large sums from the Church in their countries. Meanwhile, the popes strengthened their control over the States of the Church, the territories that they ruled in central Italy. They made sure of a permanent Italian majority among the cardinals and became leading contenders in Italian power struggles.

But popes who made deals with rulers to skim off the Church's resources, and who acted as ruthless Italian power wielders, were in no position to restore confidence in the papacy's holiness. Halfway through the fifteenth century, the papacy repeatedly called for a crusade to liberate Constantinople, recently captured by the Turks, and no one responded. None other than Pope Pius II explained why not, in a speech to the cardinals: "People think all we want to do is to heap up gold. No

> "*People think all we want to do is to heap up gold. No one believes what we say. Like bankrupt tradesmen, we have no credit.*"
>
> —Pope Pius II

 The Downfall of the Church: Condemnation of the Papacy During the Great Schism Read a fifteenth-century description of the greed of the pope and cardinals.

one believes what we say. Like bankrupt tradesmen, we have no credit."

In an era when the pope himself called the papacy "bankrupt," the question was bound to arise: Was this situation simply the result of mistakes and failings that could be corrected, or was there something basically corrupt and unholy about a powerful clergy headed by a ruling papacy? Late in the fourteenth century, some dissident religious thinkers gave the second, more radical answer. In England, the followers of John Wiclif became, for a time, a widespread movement, and the Bohemian supporters of Jan Hus were able to take and hold an entire country.

John Wiclif

A leading Oxford scholar and teacher, Wiclif was among the first to question openly the need for a priesthood. After a lifetime of study, Wiclif concluded that the Church was suffering from

Map 14.1 **The Spread of the Black Death**

The map shows the spread through Europe and neighboring lands of a disease that affected most of the Eastern Hemisphere. It arrived in the Black Sea region by overland routes across Asia. From there it spread in two years (1346–1347) from seaport to seaport along both shores of the Mediterranean and Europe's Atlantic coast. In a few following years it spread farther by way of seaports and inland trading cities from Ireland across Scandinavia all the way to Russia. © Cengage Learning

Interactive Map

more than just the misbehavior of some of its clergy. He challenged the established role and powers of the clergy itself—arguing that God and Scripture (the Bible) are the sole sources of spiritual authority. To enable ordinary English people to read Scripture for themselves, he made an English translation of the Vulgate Bible (p. 144). Every individual, he said, can communicate directly with the Lord and can be saved without the aid of priests or saints.

For challenging the accepted doctrines of authority and salvation, Wiclif was condemned and forced to retire from teaching. Civil disturbances in England and the Great Schism in the Church saved him from more drastic punishment, and he had many followers in England, whom their opponents called Lollards (a slang word for "mumblers"—of prayers and foolish beliefs). The alarmed English Parliament introduced the penalty of burning for heresy, not previously known in the country, and systematic repression caused the Lollard movement to die out during the fifteenth century.

Jan Hus

The fate of the movement that began with Jan Hus was different. Hus was a priest and a professor at Charles University in Prague, in the central European kingdom of Bohemia (Map 12.2 on page 220). Already active in efforts to reform the clergy, he was inspired by the writings of Wiclif to launch stronger, more radical attacks. Hus had the support of most of his compatriots, partly because many of the clerics he criticized were Germans, whereas he himself and the majority of the population in Bohemia were Czechs (pp. 220–221).

Bohemia was part of the Holy Roman Empire, and Emperor Sigismund grew disturbed by the mounting agitation there. Hus was summoned by the Council of Constance in 1414 to stand trial on charges of heresy, and the emperor promised him safe conduct to and from the trial. After a long and cruel imprisonment in Constance, Hus was tried and found guilty. The emperor did not keep his promise of protection, and Hus, refusing to recant (withdraw) his beliefs, went to his death at the stake. The reaction in Bohemia was instantaneous. Anti-German and antipapal sentiments were inflamed. A bloody uprising erupted , which eventually took over the country and fought off Catholic campaigns against it. The Hussite armies carried on their banners the emblem of the chalice, the cup in which wine was offered at Mass, in token

 Czechs in History: Jan Hus, by Nick Carey for Radio Prague (http://www.radio .cz/en/article/37466) Read about present-day arguments over the still-controversial Jan Hus.

Map 14.2 **The Ottoman Empire about 1500**

The Ottoman dynasty began in 1300 as mere beys ("lords") of a hundred-mile stretch of land in northwestern Anatolia. By 1500, they had conquered their Muslim and Christian neighbors in Anatolia and the Balkans; the incumbent ruler now called himself *padishah* ("Lord of Kings"), and Christians, impressed by his power, called him the "Grand Turk." Yet this was only the beginning of Ottoman conquest; compare Map 14.5 on page 266. © Cengage Learning

Interactive Map

of what became their defining belief, that laity and clergy alike—not just clergy as in the Church's practice (p. 207)—should receive both bread and wine. In spite of internal divisions, the Hussite movement persisted for more than a century and finally merged into the Protestant Reformation.

In the rest of Western Christendom, the consensus still prevailed that Christ had appointed the clergy to guide believers to salvation under the supreme authority of the pope, but the question of how to bring the reality of the Church closer to the ideal was widely debated. Given the Church's importance in society, any answer to this question must have wide-ranging social and political as well as religious consequences.

The Turks in Europe

At about the same time that the Mongol Empire began to break up (p. 223), a Middle Eastern empire began to form that would reach far into Europe—that of the Turks. By origin yet another nomadic people of the steppes, the Turks had entered the Middle East and become Muslims in the ninth century. Under the Seljuk dynasty in the eleventh and twelfth centuries, they had already conquered most of Anatolia. Then, in 1299, they came under the rule of a new dynasty, the Ottomans.

The Ottoman Conquests

Combining warlike prowess with exceptional diplomatic and governing skills, the **Ottoman Turks** expanded their empire by stages rather than all at once like the Mongols—and their first target was the chaotic and divided Balkans (southeastern Europe).

The Turks first landed in Europe in 1352 and quickly took over most of the limited territories that the restored empire of Byzantium still possessed. Within fifty years, the Bulgarians and Serbs were conquered, and the Albanians not long after that. There followed Byzantium's final destruction. In 1453, the last outpost of the thousand-year-old empire, Constantinople itself, was taken. The city founded by Rome's first Christian emperor became the capital of the Ottoman sultan, and Justinian's cathedral of Hagia Sophia was turned into a mosque. Outlying areas of the Balkans, such as Greece and the Romanian territories, still had to be "mopped up" (see Map 14.2). But by 1500, the Turks were ready to turn their attention to new targets: Hungary, the lands surrounding the Black Sea, and a huge swath of Arab countries stretching right across the Middle East and North Africa. Once again, as in the early Middle Ages, Christendom confronted a huge and expanding Islamic empire.

 **The Fall of Constantinople to the Ottomans: A Lamentation** Read the anguished words of a Byzantine commander upon losing Constantinople.

Christian Peoples in a Muslim Empire

For the Christian peoples of the Balkans, life as subjects of this empire had its advantages. The Turks brought unity and peace such as the region had hardly ever known since Roman times, and with unity and peace came

prosperity, trade, and low taxes. Trade flourished and towns burgeoned. Constantinople, where a shrunken population had lived amid abandoned buildings at the time it was conquered, grew to a size of three-quarters of a million, thereby regaining its long-lost position as Europe's largest city.

Turkish rule even brought religious benefits, for the sultans, in accordance with Muslim principles (p. 160), tolerated other monotheistic religions. The Orthodox majority not only could practice their religion freely but were also sheltered by Turkish power from Catholic efforts to make them accept the supremacy of the pope. Furthermore, under Muslim law, the Orthodox faithful constituted a separate community, governed in secular as well as spiritual matters by their own religious leaders. As a result, the Orthodox bishops, headed by the patriarch of Constantinople, actually wielded greater worldly power under the Turks than they had ever enjoyed under the Christian emperors. Jews, too, fleeing Christian persecution around 1500 in Spain and Portugal, found the Turkish-ruled Balkans a haven of tolerance, and were far more prosperous and respected there than those who fled western Europe for Poland and Hungary.

All the same, most Christians in the Balkans now had a status of second-class citizens from which there was only one way of escape: conversion to Islam. Many people chose this escape, among them, noble landowners who wanted to maintain their privileged status; Christian heretics in Bosnia who were squeezed between the Muslim rulers and the traditional Orthodox persecutors; and Albanians moving out of their mountainous homeland along the Adriatic Sea into the nearby Serb-inhabited plain of Kosovo (pp. 601, 604).

There was one Christian group that was highly favored: the wealthy Greek upper class, which became a second ruling elite of the Balkans under the Turks. Now that they were freed from Venice's domination by Turkish power, Greek merchants and bankers controlled the region's trade and finance and provided men and ships for the Turkish merchant and war fleets. Likewise, Greek patriarchs and bishops held power throughout the Balkans, regardless of whether the local faithful were Greek or not. The other Orthodox nations of the Balkans now consisted almost entirely of peasants, with no leadership apart from their parish priests and monks.

In these ways, new religious and national divisions grew up in the Balkans. When Turkish rule grew weak and oppressive in the eighteenth and nineteenth centuries, and finally disappeared early in the twentieth century, this mixture would flare into frequent murderous conflicts.

Pushing Back Islam: Russia and Spain

The frontier between Christendom and Islam was a long one, and in spite of the Ottoman conquests, in other regions Christendom made gains. In the far northeast of Europe, Russian rulers in the city of Moscow had formed an extensive princedom as vassals of the Muslim Tartars

Europe's Largest Mosque The Selimiye (she-LEEM-ee-yeh) Mosque was built in the late sixteenth century at Edirne (eh-DAIR-neh), on the European side of the Bosporus, at the command of the Ottoman sultan Selim II. With its 200-foot minarets and its symmetrical structure topped by a dome that the architect, Mimar Sinan, intended to rival that of Hagia Sophia, the mosque symbolizes the splendor of the Ottoman Empire at its height. De Agostini/SuperStock

(p. 223), and in the fifteenth century, Ivan the Great threw off what has gone down in Russian history as the "Tartar yoke" and became an independent ruler—but not as a mere prince. He married Sophia, the niece of the last emperor of Byzantium, and took the title of tsar ("caesar"), the traditional Slav name for Eastern emperors. Those emperors had in turn been regarded as the legitimate successors of the emperors of ancient Rome, and accordingly, a Russian writer of Ivan's time referred to Moscow as the "third Rome." From Rome and Constantinople, the Christian imperial mission had passed to Moscow.

Meanwhile, at the other end of Europe, the Spanish rulers Isabella and Ferdinand completed another long-standing Christian mission. In 1492, they conquered Granada, the last Muslim territory in Spain, and soon inflicted on their Muslim subjects far more systematic repression than Balkan Christians endured under the Turks.

The Ottoman conquests outweighed these Christian gains, however—partly because the western European countries mostly left the Balkans to their fate. Western help was generally too little and too late, and was usually coupled with highly unwelcome demands that Orthodox rulers and their subjects submit to the pope. Up to 1500, what prevented the Turks from advancing still farther into Europe was mainly the huge size of their empire, which obliged them to fight wars on many other fronts besides Europe. With little effort of their own, the western countries were insulated from attacks from the east as they pursued the innovations that would create the modern West.

LO² The Birth of Capitalism

From about 1200 onward, European commerce began to develop a new feature: alongside guilds, craftspeople, and local traders, there began to appear international merchants who branched out into industry and banking. The troubles of the fourteenth century did not stop this development; in fact, they may even have speeded it up. Independent craftspeople, in trouble because of trade stoppages, might become employees of wealthy merchants who were better able to survive until times improved; kings fighting expensive wars, and popes moving money to Rome, both needed the services of bankers. An economic system began to come into being that was new to Europe: that of **capitalism**.

Trade and Capitalism

Italian merchants had taken the lead in the revival of trade in the eleventh century (p. 195), and in the thirteenth, they pioneered the development of capitalism. They dominated the profitable trade of the Mediterranean, and many of them made quick fortunes in their dealings. Finding that they could not spend all their profits immediately, they hit upon the idea of reinvesting the surplus.

This novel idea made it possible for successful traders to launch new, more ambitious enterprises. Soon, they were no longer traveling about as ordinary merchants but minding their account books at home. They extracted profits from their varied enterprises and reinvested them to gain yet more profits. Thus emerged the features that have characterized capitalism ever since: its boundless profit seeking and its dynamic spirit.

What the Italians achieved as the middlemen between Europe and Islam, the merchants of the port cities of Germany achieved in the Baltic Sea area. They found that by pooling their resources, they could build fleets and win joint trading privileges abroad, and by the fourteenth century, the leading towns of northern Germany had formed a commercial league, the *Hansa* (a German word for a group of merchants), which dominated the trade of northern Europe from England to Russia. The cities of the **Hanseatic League** monopolized the foreign trade of northern Germany and set up outlets in the trading centers of Russia, Poland, Norway, England, and the Low Countries. From these far-flung outposts, rich profits flowed to the capitalists of northern Germany.

The merchants of the Low Countries prospered too. The wharves of Antwerp and Bruges saw a steady stream of Italian ships carrying oriental spices and silks, as well as vessels from the Baltic loaded with furs, timber, and herring. The industries of England and western Germany also sent their products into the Low Countries. By the fifteenth century, a truly international commerce had developed—extensive enough to provide for the accumulation of profit surpluses and for the growth of a capitalist class.

Breaking Away from the Guilds

Traditionally, industry and commerce were locally regulated. Business owners ran their shops where they made and sold their products within a strict framework of rules set by the collective organizations to which they all belonged, the guilds (pp. 200–201). This system still worked well for businesses such as goldsmiths' and pharmacists' stores, which sold small amounts of items that took a great deal of skill and knowledge to produce. But with the growth of international trade, industries grew up that produced goods in large amounts and needed many semiskilled or unskilled workers. After about 1200, these industries began to cast off the shackles of the guilds.

In the woolens industry, for example, the traditional association of master weavers, journeymen, and apprentices had disappeared in many areas by 1400. The industry was taken over by enterprising merchants who bought the raw wool and put it out to semiskilled laborers for processing—first to spinners and then to weavers, dyers, and cutters in succession. The workers were paid by the piece or by measure, but ownership of the materials stayed with the merchants. They sold the finished cloth or garments in the international market at whatever price they could get. To avoid guild regulations, the merchants and their workers operated outside the cities—in suburbs beyond their walls, or actually in the countryside.

The wool merchants thus reaped the profits of both industry and commerce. They paid the laborers at a low rate and permitted them no say in running of the business. Moreover, the laborers were forbidden by law to organize or strike. This **"putting-out" or "domestic" system** destroyed the close relationship between master and journeyman that existed in the guilds. It made profit the sole concern of the entrepreneur and diminished the worker's sense of creativity. The antagonisms that grew up between these entrepreneurs and the workers, especially in Europe's biggest textile-producing region, the Low Countries, foreshadowed the fierce conflicts that were to mark the later industrial world.

International Banking

Large-scale international trade, wars, and movements of Church funds all required large-scale international methods of borrowing and transferring money. Merchants with extra capital on hand were glad to oblige, so long as they were well paid with interest and fees.

Moving Money

Often, the new methods of transferring money involved replacing actual gold and silver with paper (see photo on page 254). A Venetian who bought linen from Antwerp, for example, could avoid shipping cash to the Low Countries every time he placed an order by giving the cash to a Venetian merchant who had an office in Antwerp—with a bit extra for his trouble. In return, the merchant would give the linen buyer a **bill of exchange**—an order to the Antwerp office to pay the money to the linen seller. The buyer would then send the bill of exchange to the seller, who could get his cash from the Antwerp office—or he could endorse the bill (sign it on the back) and hand it over to someone else to whom he, in turn, owed money. Thus, the bill would become a kind of international paper money.

capitalism
An economic system that developed as entrepreneurs reinvested their surplus wealth (capital) in order to gain more profits.

Hanseatic League
A commercial league of the port cities of Germany that by the fourteenth century dominated the trade of northern Europe from England to Russia.

"putting-out" or "domestic" system
A system of production in which merchants supply workers with raw materials and pay them by the piece or by measure.

bill of exchange
A paper substitute for gold and silver used for long-distance business transactions.

Lending Money

Even more profitable than organizing money transfers for a fee was lending it at interest, and in the thirteenth century, large-scale moneylending became normal. In earlier times, moneylending had been on a small scale—partly because the economy was not so prosperous and partly because the Church condemned all interest-taking as usury (lending at an excessive rate). In consequence, lending at interest had been done chiefly by Jews, whose faith did not forbid it. This particular role of the Jews no doubt contributed to the periodic outbursts against them in Europe (pp. 218–219).

With the expansion of commerce, however, many people came to realize that lending was a useful and acceptable activity. The traditional argument against interest payments was based on a revulsion against taking high rates from individuals "in distress." But loans to businessmen engaged in profitable enterprises, or to kings and popes, were obviously of a different sort. These loans could be productive, and they exposed the lender to risks that justified some reward. Many theologians agreed that this kind of lending was not sinful, and the popes themselves were among the biggest borrowers. Consequently, small-scale Jewish moneylending was overtaken by large-scale Christian banking.

Keeping Track of Money

Moving and lending money was a complicated business, and to keep track of it Italian merchants about 1300 developed a new system of bookkeeping that involved keeping separate records or "accounts" for the resources and activities of a business, for example, cash in hand and items sold. Every transaction would affect two or more accounts and had to be subtracted (debited) in one account and added (credited) in another. Accounts had to be compared from time to time, and if debits and credits did not "balance" (equal each other), that indicated an error. The new system made it possible for owners to stay in control of their businesses from day to day and know how well they were doing over the long term. Without this method of **double-entry bookkeeping**, banks or any kind of large-scale business would have been very difficult to operate, and it is still the standard method of accounting today.

On Commerce and the Perfect Merchant: The Power of Bookkeeping Read the advice of an entrepreneur on the importance of bookkeeping.

A Genoese Loan with Interest Read a medieval loan document.

Banking Families

Large-scale financial business required a pooling of capital and of managerial talent. Merchants often formed **partnerships**—especially with their own relatives, or with business associates whom they made into relatives by strategic marriages. A group of relatives, well placed in cities across several countries, could best handle long-distance matters demanding secrecy and mutual trust, and could ensure the continuance of an enterprise.

In the thirteenth and fourteenth centuries, the largest of these international family businesses were based in Florence, which became the leading center of international finance. The Bardi and Peruzzi families, for example, lent huge sums to King Edward III of England, which financed the first campaigns of the Hundred Years' War. Later, Edward refused to repay the loans and thereby forced those families into bankruptcy—an occupational hazard for bankers who lent to rulers. But in the fifteenth century, a new house of bankers, the Medici (**MED-ih-chee**), emerged in Florence that restored the financial power of the city and came to dominate its political and cultural life as well.

Banking spread north from Italy to the rest of Europe. Jacques Coeur (**K-uh-r**), a French merchant who had made a fortune by trading in oriental

≪ Financial Innovation Fifteenth-century customers do business at a branch of Europe's leading firm of international bankers, the Medici of Florence. At right, a clerk hands out coins to a customer. At left, a clerk examines a piece of paper that a customer has handed him. Probably it is a recent financial innovation, a bill of exchange. This customer is having this Medici branch pay him money he is owed by another Medici customer in a foreign city, without the trouble and risk of shipping cash. The Granger Collection, New York

silks and spices, was appointed royal treasurer by King Charles VII of France in 1439, and he lent the king the money finally to expel the English from France. Taking advantage of his position at the court, Coeur acquired extensive holdings in mines, lands, and workshops and thus became one of Europe's most powerful international industrialist-bankers. In the end, rivalries at court caused his downfall, but the palace he built himself on a kingly scale still stands in his native town of Bourges.

The wealthiest banker of the era was Jacob Fugger of Augsburg in southern Germany, a region that in the fifteenth and sixteenth centuries was sharing in the prosperity of growing commerce. He invested in copper and silver mines in the Holy Roman Empire and Hungary—an industry where improved tools were enabling miners to dig more deeply and more efficiently. The leading entrepreneurs of the industry soon took control of smelting and metalworking as well as mining, concentrating the direction of all operations in a few hands, and the workers, who had formerly been independent producers, now became employees of capitalists like Fugger.

Jacob drew immense wealth from these and other enterprises and channeled the surplus into international banking. He ventured into buying, selling, and speculating in all kinds of goods, and he provided financial services to merchants, high clergy, and rulers. One of his most spectacular operations was to lend half a million florins (a sum of gold coins worth perhaps $60 million at today's value of gold) to King Charles I of Spain. The Spanish monarch used the money to become the Holy Roman emperor Charles V by bribing the imperial electors (p. 267). A good capitalist, Jacob was also a good philanthropist. He and his brothers built, as evidence of their piety and generosity, an attractive group of dwellings for the "righteous" poor of Augsburg. They still stand, near the center of the city, as a memorial to the Fuggers' wealth and charity.

> **Photos and Description of the Housing Complex Sponsored by the Fugger Brothers** (http://www.historicgermany.com/4244.html) Tour the Fuggerei of Augsburg, Europe's oldest social housing complex.

Capitalism and Society

Successful international bankers like the Medici and the Fuggers gained social and political influence, and sometimes actual government power, equal to that of counts or princes. All the same, the European social order was still dominated by kings, nobles, and Church leaders. Europe was still basically an agrarian region where land and its products remained the main forms of wealth. Merchants and bankers sooner or later took their profits out of trade and finance, put them into land, and sought to acquire noble titles.

> **A Lesson for Success in Business** Read a successful merchant's advice to his children on working within the social order.

Masters and workers in industries like woolen textiles that outgrew the guild system were powerfully affected by growing capitalism, though there were many other industries where the traditional system continued unchanged. The new economy's influence was felt most strongly of all, however, in the countryside, affecting western and eastern Europe in strikingly different ways.

> **partnership**
> A type of business organization in which a group of entrepreneurs pool their capital and talent.

Western Europe: The End of Serfdom

Traditionally, serfs were required to cultivate the lord's demesne, the land reserved for his benefit. From about 1000 to 1300, as the population grew, landowners had generally lightened the burdens on serfs to get their cooperation in bringing new land under the plow (pp. 193–194).

Toward the end of the medieval period, the nobles often found it advantageous to rent out their demesnes to free tenants, who were now able to sell their produce at nearby markets and pay their rents in cash. The serfs preferred this arrangement because it released them from extra work; the lords preferred it because they could usually find cheap day labor and still have cash left over from the serfs' payments.

The next step was the emancipation (freeing) of the serfs. Now that the nobles no longer depended on forced labor, they were willing to grant the serfs freedom. In most instances, freed serfs remained on the land as tenants and in exchange for freedom paid the lords a lump sum or extra rent. But in so doing, they normally lost their former hereditary right to stay on the land, which meant that they could be evicted when their leases expired.

By 1500, serfdom had become a rarity in western Europe. The medieval lord, with his rights to the produce and services of the peasantry, had become a landowner living off his rents. Though many of the great estates remained intact, the pattern of relationships had been changed. The spirit of commercial enterprise had spread to the countryside.

Eastern Europe: The Second Serfdom

In eastern Europe, too, so long as the population was growing and more land was coming under the plow, nobles had lightened the burdens of serfdom as in the western countries. But even so, eastern Europe was more thinly populated than western Europe, with fewer nearby towns to provide a market for farm products. Nobles therefore depended heavily for their income on grain exports to the big cities of Germany and Italy, which were too far away for most peasants to reach them. Unable to rely on peasants to sell produce and pay them cash rents, the nobles (or their farm managers) had to sell the grain themselves, so they needed serfs to grow it for them—and when the Black Death drastically reduced the numbers of serfs, the nobles began to make the burdens of serfdom heavier than before.

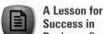

> *"By 1500, serfdom had become a rarity in western Europe."*

> *"Sea transport, warfare, book production, the measurement of time—all were revolutionized by the Europe of the late Middle Ages."*

This **second serfdom**, as modern scholars call it, prevailed in the eastern territories of the Holy Roman Empire, through Poland and Hungary, and on into Russia. In these countries, serfdom persisted down to the nineteenth century, further pushing apart the two halves of Europe.

LO³ Technology Breakthroughs

The rise of capitalism, like the rise of trade and towns earlier in the Middle Ages (pp. 195–196), went hand in hand with technical progress. Now, however, increased contact, both peaceful and warlike, with the intercontinental civilization of Islam exposed Europe to the often superior technology not only of the Arabs but of East Asia as well. Like many earlier peoples, the Europeans adapted and improved on advances that they learned from outside, and in this case, the result was a whole series of world-changing technical innovations. Sea transport, warfare, book production, the measurement of time—all were revolutionized by the Europe of the late Middle Ages.

Navigation and Ship Design

One of the basic needs of growing medieval trade, in an age when transport was far more efficient by water than by land, was for reliable methods of navigation—for sailors at sea to be able to know where they were and what direction they must sail in to reach the ports for which they were bound.

Building on geographical techniques developed by the Greeks and improved on by Arab scientists, European mapmakers began to produce accurate charts of the Atlantic and Mediterranean coastlines. New instruments of navigation came into use. One was the north-pointing **magnetic compass**, a Chinese invention that helped the navigator set and hold a ship's course. Another was the **astrolabe**, an astronomical instrument devised in ancient times and improved by Arab astronomers, which enabled the navigator to calculate latitude (a ship's position north or south of the equator) by determining the height of the sun and stars above the horizon. Both these aids to navigation were in com-

mon use on the seaways of Europe by the early fifteenth century. Soon they would help guide sailors across oceans to distant continents (see photos on pages 271 and 275).

Growing trade also needed ships that were large, strong, and easy to handle. Shipwrights in Venice and Genoa, whose craft had to be able to carry goods to and from western Europe, combined features of ship design from both the Mediterranean and the stormier Atlantic waters. They borrowed the triangular sails of their Mediterranean neighbors the Arabs, which made for easy maneuvering, as well as the stout hulls and square, wind-catching sails of Atlantic ships. The result was a new kind of vessel, the **carrack** (from the Arabic word for "merchant ship")—the first three-masted sailing ship, which appeared about 1400 and would soon become the workhorse of overseas exploration (see photo on page 268).

Carracks had a combination of speed, maneuverability, and seaworthiness that was unmatched by the vessels of the most advanced non-European civilizations. And eventually, three-masted ships would also become unbeatable fighting vessels, once they were equipped with another late medieval invention—the cannon.

Firearms

The Chinese invention of gunpowder first became known to Europeans in the twelfth century, when Christian warriors in North Africa and Spain found their Muslim foes using the quick-burning substance against them as an incendiary (fire-starting) weapon. The idea of confining the powder so that it would actually explode, and using the force of the explosion to hurl a projectile, seems to have been a European one. At any rate, "firepots" or "tubes" (Latin, *canones*) are first mentioned in Italian documents of the 1320s.

 **Ancient Chinese Technology** (http://library.thinkquest.org/23062/frameset.html) Learn more about Chinese inventions that were adapted by the West.

Up to around 1400, cannon were too small, inaccurate, slow to operate, and dangerous to their users to make much real difference to warfare, but in the fifteenth century, improvements came quickly. Makers of church bells began using their knowledge of large-scale bronze-casting methods to manufacture guns that were solid and safe to use. Ironworks started turning out cannonballs that were heavier in proportion to their size, more accurately spherical, and far quicker to make than stone ones. Carpenters devised wheeled gun carriages that made the weapons mobile and absorbed the recoil when they were fired. Water-powered hammermills were adapted to crush charcoal, sulfur, and dried animal droppings so as to produce gunpowder by the ton. Mathematicians tackled the problems of weight and motion involved in accurate aiming.

By 1500, cannon could be relied on to smash any stone castle or town wall—let alone the wooden hulls of sailing ships—and scaled-down versions of the big weapons were beginning to appear that were small and handy enough for a single soldier to load, aim, and fire.

Printing

European traders and warriors earlier in the Middle Ages had learned from the Muslims of peaceful as well as warlike Chinese inventions—most notably, of paper and woodcut printing. Paper, made mainly from rags that were beaten to a pulp with water and various chemicals and then dried into sheets in special frames, was much faster and cheaper to make than parchment (the skin of lambs or calves), the traditional European writing material.

Likewise, printing with woodcut blocks was faster than writing out books by hand. The process involved carving a whole page of text and illustrations in mirror image out of the surface of a single block of wood, then smearing the block with ink, and pressing a sheet of paper onto the block with a roller. By 1400, small books and items such as playing cards (an Arab pastime that had spread to Europe) were commonly produced in this way. But woodcut printing was an expensive way to produce large books with many pages, since hundreds of blocks had to be painstakingly chiseled and then thrown away when the job was finished.

Supposing, however, that each individual letter were made in mirror image on its own tiny block, many such blocks could then be put together to form the text of a page, and taken apart and reassembled any number of times to make new pages. The printing process would become fast and cheap, even for the longest books.

This had already occurred to printers in China and Korea, but the idea had never caught on there—partly because of the large number of characters in the Chinese writing system (used in both countries at the time), which made it hard to manage all the different blocks. When the same idea struck Johann Gutenberg, a businessman in the German city of Mainz, he had the basic advantage of living in a region that used an alphabetic writing system with relatively few characters (p. 33).

Even so, it took twenty years of tinkering and much technical wizardry to put the idea into practice. Gutenberg's greatest inspirations were to make the tiny single-letter blocks ("types") out of metal so that they could be quickly cast in molds rather than laboriously carved, and to adapt the centuries-old olive or grape press to apply quick and accurate pressure to the paper

lying on the ink-smeared type. By about 1450, he had developed a reliable system of printing with "movable" (reusable) type.

The new method of printing, with its drastically reduced costs, for the first time made it possible to mass-produce books, and the international trading and credit networks of early capitalism enabled books to find a mass market. By 1500, there were more than a thousand printers at work in Europe, and nearly 10 million books had been printed (Map 14.3). The influence of the printed word was far wider than that of the written word had been before. The spread of religious and cultural movements like Renaissance humanism and the Protestant Reformation, the growth of powerful centralized governments with their need for law books and bureaucratic form documents, the expansion of business firms which also benefited from standardized paperwork—all were helped along by the Gutenberg printing process (see photo).

Clocks

Along with printed books and firearms, the late Middle Ages also saw the introduction of history's first widely used automatically operating machine, the mechanical clock. Automatic machines that modeled the motion of the sun, moon, and stars across the sky and thereby measured time had a long history in ancient Greece, China, and Islam, but they were unwieldy devices powered by the flow of water. Medieval European clocks seem to have been inspired partly by astrolabes, which used dials with revolving pointers as sighting devices to measure the motion of the sun, moon, and stars across the sky. Sometime late in the thirteenth century, inventors in various countries began tinkering with ways to make the pointer actually "imitate" these sky objects—in particular the sun—by moving around the dial. Since the hours and days were reckoned by the motion of the sun, the effect would be that the motion of the pointer would measure the passage of time.

Of course, for this to happen, the pointer would have to be made to turn by itself. Rather than flowing water, a falling weight, attached to a cord wound around a spindle, could provide the necessary turning power. But there would also have to be mechanisms to slow the weight's fall and "wind it up" again when there was no more cord left to unwind, and gearwheels to slow the turning motion still more, so that the pointer would move round the dial no more than once in a day.

It seems to have been mechanically minded English monks, looking for improved ways of regulating their communities' complex daily routines of work and prayer, who first came up with practicable solutions to these problems around 1300—and made their pointer-turning gearwheels also actuate a bell-striking mechanism to summon brethren who were out of sight. Falling weights were a far more convenient source of power than flowing water, and it was not long before the lives of townspeople, with their hours

≪ **"We, the Undersigned Account-Masters in the Treasury of the United East India Company in Middelburg, Hereby Acknowledge . . ."** On a bond issued by a Dutch company to Jacob van Neck, mayor of Amsterdam, who lent it 2,400 guilders at 8 percent for six months on November 22, 1622, all standard wording is printed and only the details are written in. The company was a huge enterprise that borrowed large sums from many lenders; printing greatly speeded its business operations. Visual Connection Archive

Map 14.3 **The Spread of Printing**

The map shows the dates were printing presses were first set up in some of the most important of the 265 places where they are known to have been operating in 1500. Notice how fast printing spread, starting a dozen years after Gutenberg's press first went into operation in 1448. In the 1460s, 1470s, and 1460s, presses were established in 38 of the 53 places shown on the map. © Cengage Learning

Interactive Map

of work fixed by guilds or settled privately between capitalists and their employees, also came to be regulated by the new time-measuring machine. High in a tower of town hall or cathedral, it was visible to many as its hand (to start with, usually only one of them) moved, with no human intervention, in step with the movement of the sun itself; and everyone could hear the clock as it struck the changing hours of the day (see photo on page 244).

Clocks were machines that worked by themselves, printing presses turned out a complicated product in large quantities, and cannon released massive energy from small amounts of chemicals. In these ways, late medieval Europe set precedents for today's world of automation, mass production, and large-scale power generation. And already, by the end of the Middle Ages, firearms and new-style sailing ships were helping rulers to build stronger governments and sailors to explore and conquer across the world.

LO⁴ The New Politics

Economic and technical change enabled rulers to gain more control of their governments and armed forces than before (see Reasons Why).

Governments did not necessarily become more efficient as a result. Most officials were not paid from the central government treasury but were expected to charge the public fees, which they put directly into their own pockets. Tax collection was usually assigned to "farmers"—bankers who agreed to pay governments a fixed sum and were permitted to collect a larger amount and pocket the difference. Both practices were a license for every kind of fraud and corruption. Likewise, military contractors might take the money but not provide the soldiers—or they might provide the soldiers but not get their money, in which case the soldiers would mutiny for lack of pay.

THE GROWTH OF ROYAL POWER IN THE LATE MIDDLE AGES WAS FUELED BY SEVERAL DEVELOPMENTS:

The Rise of a Money-Based Economy

- Because all classes of society were able to make payments in money, it was easier for rulers to collect rents, levy tariffs on trade, and impose national taxes.

- Rulers had to decide what property to tax, hold kingdom-wide property surveys, and take measures against tax avoidance. Late Roman emperors had faced the same problems and recorded the solutions in their law codes (p. 137), which were eagerly studied by medieval lawyers.

- Rulers could also borrow large sums from bankers.

- With all this money available, rulers could buy the services of officials and mercenary soldiers rather than relying on help from their independent-minded vassals.

New Developments in Warfare

- New developments in warfare weakened the power of the feudal elite as it strengthened the rulers.

- With the invention of the longbow, the pike, and various types of axes, knives, and hooks on long poles, foot soldiers became more deadly (see photo on page 260).

- Cavalry soldiers were still needed in battle but were no longer the dominant force as in the era of knights on horseback.

- Cannon, which were so expensive that only governments could afford them, were able to smash through the walls of nobles' fortifications.

Furthermore, none of these developments deprived the nobles as a group of their leading place in society and government. In most countries, rulers found it too risky to tax the nobles and clergy, and the burden of national taxation was borne mainly by commoners. Officials and bankers usually invested their profits in land, and expected to be rewarded for their services to rulers with titles of nobility; and even men from ancient noble families could gain additional wealth and honor as royal officials or commanders of mercenary soldiers.

Sometimes, nobles were able to prevent the growth of royal government, as happened in the Holy Roman Empire, or to roll it back for a time, as in sixteenth-century France (p. 324). But countries that remained without strong central government for any length of time were bound to become dominated by more powerful neighbors, or even to be swallowed up by them. From the late Middle Ages on, the successful European countries would be ones where the traditional governing partnership of rulers, nobles, and Church leaders continued, but with rulers enjoying more direct control of their countries than under feudalism.

Building National Monarchies: France, England, and Spain

Among European rulers, those of France, England, and Spain took the lead in building nationwide power. Benefiting from the inheritance left by strong rulers of feudal times, helped by the increasing wealth and technical advancement of western Europe, and backed by growing national feeling, French, English, and Spanish rulers came into more direct control of their countries than ever before.

France: The Hundred Years' War

In France, the richest and most populous kingdom of Europe, with some 12 million inhabitants, the most powerful stimulant to national feeling was the **Hundred Years' War** (1338–1453). This lengthy off-and-on struggle with the English began when the king of England, Edward III, himself the grandson of a French king, laid claim to the throne of France. By 1420, the English had triumphed. Most of northern France was given to Henry V, now the English king, and the French also agreed to accept Henry as heir to their throne.

This humiliation at the hands of foreigners brought forth a surprising reaction among the French people, who had traditionally been indifferent toward feudal struggles. After the throne fell vacant, they found an inspiring leader in a peasant girl called Joan of Arc, who in 1429 persuaded Charles, the disinherited son of the former French king, to march to Reims, the ancient crowning place of French monarchs. Claiming divine guidance, Joan herself took command of a small military force and vowed to drive the English from the soil of France. The young prince, responding to Joan's appeal, was crowned in Reims Cathedral as Charles VII and went on to lead his armies to final victory over the English. Joan did not live to see that day, however. Soon after Charles's coronation, she was captured by the English, tried as a witch, and burned at the stake. The martyred Joan has been revered for centuries as the glorious symbol of French patriotism.

The Hundred Years' War was frightfully destructive to France and interrupted the growth of royal authority. But when it was over, Charles VII and his son, Louis XI, were able to build a stronger monarchy than ever before.

France: The King and the Nobles

In their efforts, the kings of France were able to take advantage of the new developments in warfare to build armies that were more than a match for any aristocratic opponent. Such armies required more revenue than the monarch had ever received through ordinary feudal dues, but Charles succeeded in raising this revenue. In preparing for his final thrust against the English, he summoned the **Estates-General** of France in 1439. This body, which represented the three estates, or groups making up society (p. 190)—the clergy, the nobles, and the commoners—had the sole power to authorize new taxes. In a burst of patriotic fervor, the Estates-General approved Charles's national army and voted a permanent tax for its support. This tax, called the *taille* ("cut"), was a kind of land tax levied mainly on commoners. With this substantial new revenue, supplemented by income from his own lands, Charles could now afford to act against nobles who opposed him. By deception, threats of force, and marriage alliances he brought the fiefs of powerful vassals back into the royal domain (his personal holdings).

Louis XI pursued his father's methods and more than doubled the size of the royal domain. His final victory was to win back the duchy of Burgundy, which had long been independent even though it was legally subject to the French crown. Its last duke, Charles the Bold, had tried to expand his holdings into a major state between France and Germany. But his plans had miscarried; and when he died without a male heir in 1477, Louis took over the duchy.

France: The King and the Church

While taming the nobility, Charles did not overlook the clergy. The archbishops, bishops,

The Granger Collection, New York

Infantry, Cavalry, and Artillery An early sixteenth-century woodcut shows state-of-the-art warfare. In front, opposing masses of foot soldiers wielding pikes and halberds (axes on poles) have come to grips; where they meet, there is a grim killing zone. Behind them, cannon are emplaced to bombard a walled town; to left of the town, more pikemen are shown, leveling their weapons for the charge. At rear, armored horsemen charge against each other in the traditional way.

and abbots themselves mostly came from noble families, and they wielded the vast wealth and power of the Church, which all Catholic rulers needed to have reliably on their side. But of course, Charles had a formidable competitor for control of the Church—the pope.

The French bishops and abbots had traditionally tended to act independently of Rome. They had no thought of overturning Catholic doctrines and institutions, but they resented the large proportion of Church revenues that was siphoned off by Rome, and the papal practice of filling important Church offices without consulting them. At the Council of Bourges in 1438, the clergy, with Charles's approval, formally declared the administrative independence of the "Gallican" (French) Church from the pope. The decree limited papal interference and forbade payments and appeals of local decisions to Rome. This move gave clear control of the Gallican Church to the French bishops under royal protection.

But the popes were too valuable as allies and too dangerous as opponents in international politics to be defied in this way. Louis XI revoked the decree, and his successor, Francis I, struck a new bargain with the pope. By the Concordat (treaty) of 1516, Francis secured the right to appoint French bishops

THE TRIAL OF JOAN OF ARC

As a teenage farm girl in the 1420s, Joan of Arc heard voices that she believed to be from Heaven telling her to drive out the English invaders who at that stage of the Hundred Years' War controlled most of France. She gained the confidence of the French king Charles VII, and in eighteen months of campaigning won a string of victories until she was finally captured. A French bishop allied with the English had a Church court convict her of a variety of religious offenses including witchcraft, and in 1431 she was burned at the stake. The trial was intended to discredit King Charles by showing that his armies' successes were the result of witchcraft. But the French eventually won the war, in 1455 the pope quashed the verdict on Joan, and in 1920 she was declared a saint.

This excerpt from testimony at Joan's trial mainly involves her victory over an English army that was besieging the city of Orleans, in which she took over from Count Jean de Dunois as leader of an assault on an English-held fortress commanded by Sir William Glasdale ("Classidas").

Joan [to her inquisitors]: When I was thirteen years old, I had a voice from God to help me govern my conduct. And the first time I was very fearful. And came this voice, about the hour of noon, in the summertime, in my father's garden. . . . I heard the voice on the right-hand side . . . and rarely do I hear it without a brightness. . . . It has taught me to conduct myself well, to go habitually to church. . . . The voice told me that I should raise the siege laid to the city of Orleans . . . and me, I answered it that I was a poor girl who knew not how to ride nor lead in war.

Jean Pasquerel [priest, Joan's confessor]: On the morrow, Saturday, I rose early and celebrated mass. And Joan went out against the fortress of the bridge where was the Englishman Classidas. And the assault lasted there from morning until sunset. In this assault . . . Joan . . . was struck by an arrow above the breast, and when she felt herself wounded she was afraid and wept. . . . And some soldiers, seeing her so wounded, wanted to apply a charm to her wound, but she would not have it, saying: "I would rather die than do a thing which I know to be a sin or against the will of God." . . . But if to her could be applied a remedy without sin, she was very willing to be cured. And they put on to her wound olive oil and lard. And after that had been applied, Joan made her confession to me, weeping and lamenting.

Count Dunois: The assault lasted from the morning until eight . . . so that there was hardly hope of victory that day. So that I was going to break off and . . . withdraw. . . . Then

the Maid came to me and required me to wait yet a while. She . . . mounted her horse and retired alone into a vineyard. . . . And in this vineyard she remained at prayer. . . . Then she came back . . . at once seized her standard in hand and placed herself on the parapet of the trench, and the moment she was there the English trembled and were terrified. The king's soldiers regained courage and began to go up, charging against the boulevard [line of defense] without meeting the least resistance.

Jean Pasquerel: Joan returned to the charge, crying and saying: "Classidas, Classidas, yield thee, yield thee to the King of Heaven; thou hast called me 'whore'; I take great pity on thy soul and thy people's!" Then Classidas, armed from head to foot, fell into the river of Loire and was drowned. And Joan, moved by pity, began to weep much for the soul of Classidas and the others who were drowned in great numbers.

EXPLORING THE SOURCE

1. Whose side are the witnesses testifying on, and how does their testimony support their case?

2. What image does the testimony give of Joan as a warrior?

Source: Used with permission of Madison Books from Joan of Arc, By Herself and Her Witnesses by Régine Pernoud, 1966; permission conveyed through Copyright Clearance Center, Inc.

and abbots. In return, the papacy was granted the first year's income of Church officeholders in France. The pope thereby gained additional revenue and the alliance of a powerful monarch; the king, outflanking his own clergy, brought the Church within his grip.

In these ways, French kings after the Hundred Years' War built up their power in their governing partnership with the nobles and the Church, but the partnership itself was as strong as

ever. Nobles who cooperated with the rulers kept their ancestral estates and inherited titles, were awarded favored positions as military commanders or civil officials, and were appointed to leading positions in the Church. Furthermore, the lands of nobles, together with those of the Church, were exempt from the *taille*. Wealthy bankers like Jacques Coeur gave financial aid to the kings and financed their military campaigns while townspeople generally favored the growth of royal power, but the ambition of

England: The King and Parliament

most successful commoners was to join the nobility themselves.

From time to time, the kings summoned the Estates-General, but now that it had granted the kings permanent tax authority, it was no longer a necessary partner in royal government, and in the end, the rulers stopped calling it together. Meanwhile, the English kings were relying heavily on their own national representative body, the Parliament.

In England, as in France, the Hundred Years' War had strengthened national feeling, but the eventual defeat weakened the position of the monarch. In addition, in order to raise the substantial sums of money needed for the expeditions to France, the kings of England had had to make concessions to **Parliament**.

The origins of Parliament go back to the thirteenth century. Already in 1215, the Magna Carta had expressed the idea that the king needed the advice and consent of his barons before taking measures such as the levying of unaccustomed taxes (p. 190). Later in the century, as both king and barons sought to enlarge their bases of support in the country, the custom grew up of inviting representatives of the shires (counties) and boroughs (towns) to such meetings.

In 1295, Edward I held the precedent-setting "Model Parliament," and during the next century, Edward's successors called Parliament frequently in their need for additional funds to carry on the war in France (see photo). Parliament evolved into two chambers: the House of Lords and the House of Commons. In the Lords sat the great barons and clerics of the country—the king's leading vassals together with bishops and important abbots. In the Commons sat representatives of the shires and of certain towns, elected on open ballots by a small minority of the male population. The Lords were the more important house for several centuries, but the Commons would ultimately have the upper hand in lawmaking. Parliament only met when the king decided to call it, but he needed its consent for approval of new revenues, and its members took advantage of that to gain privileges and redress of their grievances. Unlike the French Estates-General, England's Parliament granted the king no permanent tax and often gave the king less than he asked. The king benefited too, however: measures that he and the Parliament agreed on became laws that must be nationally obeyed, for they were enacted not just by himself, but also "by and with the advice and consent of the Lords Spiritual and Temporal and of the Commons."

At the close of the Hundred Years' War, England suffered a series of calamities. Confidence in the crown was shattered by the defeat in France, and civil war began between noble factions led the houses (family lines) of York and Lancaster, which had rival claims to the throne. The Wars of the Roses (from the heraldic emblems of the two sides) took place in several bouts of fighting for more than thirty years. A relative of the House of Lancaster, Henry Tudor, won the final bout in 1485, put a real end to the wars by marrying the Lady Elizabeth, heiress of the House of York, and as Henry VII began rebuilding royal power.

Henry and the rulers who followed him wielded unprecedented nationwide authority. But unlike the rulers of France, those of England continued to rely on Parliament, using it both as a safety valve for grievances and to give legitimacy to their actions. Parliament actually became more important and more deeply involved in government than before—a true partner of the rulers, though still the junior one.

The Unification of Spain

In the Middle Ages, the name "Spain" meant not a country but a region that included several separate countries, among them the Christian kingdoms (from east to west) of Aragon, Castile, and Portugal, and the Muslim

The English Parliament At a ceremonial opening session, King Edward I (about 1300) is surrounded by visiting rulers of Scotland and Wales and by archbishops and high officials. In the middle, the Law Lords (high judges) sit on sacks of raw wool, a symbol of England's wealth. To the king's right and in front sit the Lords Spiritual (high clergy). To his left sit the Lords Temporal (leading nobles). The Commons, not shown, would be farther in front, standing in the presence of their betters.

state of Granada in the south. In 1469, however, Queen Isabella of Castile married King Ferdinand of Aragon, and "Spain" soon came to mean those two linked kingdoms, as against the separate kingdom of Portugal.

Between them, Isabella and Ferdinand brought independent-minded nobles into line and reformed the Church in their kingdoms, gaining the right to name its bishops. They conquered Granada and soon broke promises of tolerance they made to Muslims, as well as viciously repressing the Jews, who were forced to convert or leave the country. The Inquisition was established under strict royal control, and for two centuries it enforced Catholic religious conformity that came to be linked with an idea of nationhood as confined to those who were "pure of blood"—not tainted by Jewish or Muslim ancestors.

Under the descendants of Isabella and Ferdinand, Castile and Aragon remained legally separate kingdoms sharing one ruler, but the rulers governed from the Castilian capital, Madrid, and gradually turned Aragon into a province of their Castilian-dominated kingdom. In this way, a whole new country was brought into existence from the top down, by the marriage of two powerful late medieval rulers and the policies of themselves and their descendants.

State Power in Miniature: Italy

Ever since the end of the Roman Empire, Italy had been the scene of continual struggles for power among barbarian, Muslim, and Norman invaders, Byzantine and Holy Roman emperors, and the popes. As a result, Italy had become a permanently divided country (Map 14.4). Instead of developing across the whole country, state power was wielded on a smaller scale by city-states, popes, and kings. But these rulers often governed more efficiently than those of the larger countries, and the theory of unchecked state power was pioneered by an Italian, Niccolò Machiavelli (**NICK-oh-loh mak-ee-uh-VEL-ee**).

City-States and Despots

Northern Italy was officially part of the Holy Roman Empire, but the emperors were weak and distant, and the leading commercial cities were exceptionally wealthy and powerful. In the Middle Ages, the region developed into a cluster of self-governing city-states struggling against each other for survival and mastery, like the Greek city-states two thousand years before. The Italians certainly had a sense of nationhood like the French and English, but their strongest loyalty went to their city-states.

The internal politics of the Italian city-states were generally turbulent. The usual source of trouble was rivalry among factions: bankers and capitalists, rising rapidly in wealth, tried to take political control from the more numerous small merchants, shopkeepers, and artisans. At the same time, wealthy families competed with one another for special advantage. Out of the struggle, political strongmen had emerged during the fourteenth century. Sometimes they were invited to assume power by one or another of the factions; sometimes they invited themselves.

Conflicts between the elite and the common people, vendettas among upper-class families, and takeovers of power by strongmen had also been normal features of city-state life in ancient Greece (p. 52). In Greece, such takers of power were called tyrants; in reference to medieval Italy, they are today usually known as **despots**. Like Greek tyrants, Italian despots were often enlightened rulers and eager patrons of the arts; they were liable to assassination and overthrow; and they hoped to gain legitimacy by becoming hereditary rulers and founders of dynasties. The main difference was that Greek tyranny sometimes led toward democracy, whereas in Italy, rule by despots became widespread and permanent.

Partly, this difference was because the merchants and bankers of medieval Italian city-states were far wealthier and more powerful than the well-to-do upper-class citizens of ancient Greece. Furthermore, in Greece, the commoners had had strong political leverage because their city-states needed them as part-time warriors in the armed forces. In medieval Italy, however, the city-states came to rely on professional mercenary soldiers, recruited and trained by enterprising warrior-businessmen known as **condottieri** ("contractors"). With no sentimental attachments, condottieri generally sold their services to the highest bidder. On occasion, they turned down all bids and seized power for themselves. Either way, they provided the armed force that was needed to gain and hold power regardless of the commoners.

One of the most famous condottiere-despots was Francesco Sforza (**SFORT-suh**), who made himself ruler of Milan in 1450. Assuming the title of duke, which an earlier despot had purchased from the Holy Roman emperor, he governed from his moated fortress-palace. Under the shrewd policies of Sforza and his heirs, Milan enjoyed a half-century of peace and prosperity, and his descendants continued to govern Milan as hereditary dukes well into the sixteenth century.

The city of Florence remained officially a republic during the fifteenth century, but in the course of many upheavals, it developed into a despotism in practice. In 1434, authority settled in the hands of Cosimo de' Medici, heir to Europe's wealthiest banking family. He and his successors generally held no major political office, but they controlled the machinery of government through persuasion, manipulation, bribery, and force. The Medici advanced their own financial interests and the interests of their supporters, and treated rival groups harshly. The most illustrious member of the family, Lorenzo the Magnificent, was a man of extraordinary ability and artistic taste. Under his rule, late in the fifteenth century, Florence reached its peak as the cultural center of Italy. Later Medici rulers turned Florence into a hereditary dukedom like Milan.

Venice, too, remained a republic, and never came under the rule of a single despot. Instead, it was ruled by a kind of collective despotism that had been securely in power since the beginning of the fourteenth century. A small group of rich merchants managed to keep political control over the city and saw to it that the rest of the citizens were excluded from participation. The constitution of Venice, the envy of its less fortunate rivals, provided that the city be governed by councils and committees elected from and by the merchants. The official head of state was the *doge* (duke), who was chosen for life by the leading families. Though the doge was treated with respect, he had no independent authority.

Despotism in Central and Southern Italy

In the middle of Italy, the States of the Church, originating in the eighth-century Donation of Pepin (p. 167), were under the rule of the pope. In the south of the peninsula was the feudal Kingdom of the Two Sicilies, ultimately descended from territories conquered by the Normans in the eleventh century.

In the States of the Church, the pattern of despotism was the same as that in the rest of the country. The popes hired condot-

tieri to strengthen their control of their territories, engaged in wars and alliances, enthusiastically sponsored scholarship and art, and used their office to further the wealth and rank of their families. Usually, the popes came from prominent families in Rome or elsewhere in Italy, and were the winners in intensive bouts of deal-making among the cardinals at each conclave (papal election). The process produced popes who were able politicians but not usually noted for holiness. Alexander VI, who reigned around 1500, wanted to found a dynasty like other despots. He and his out-of-wedlock son, Cesare Borgia, tried to carve out a territory for Cesare to rule, but Alexander's death and the election of a pope from a rival family put an end to the plan.

South of Rome, the Kingdom of the Two Sicilies was equal in area to all the rest of Italy (see Map 14.4 below). It was created in 1435 when King Alfonso of Sicily won a major victory in the Italian power struggle by acquiring the kingdom of Naples on the mainland and strengthened his control of his territories by the same methods as the popes. But Alfonso was also king

Map 14.4 **Fifteenth-Century Italy**

A thousand years after the fall of Rome, Italy is still in some ways the center of Europe. Two city-states, Milan and Florence, are Europe's main banking centers. Two others, Genoa and Venice, control Mediterranean empires and sea routes. The popes, rulers of the States of the Church, also govern the international Catholic Church. But the world of these "great powers" is threatened by still greater ones—the Ottoman Turks, France, and Aragon (in Spain), which already ruled the south of Italy. © Cengage Learning

Interactive Map

of Aragon, in the east of present-day Spain, and this link with a powerful outside kingdom in the end helped undermine the independence of the Italian states.

By the middle of the fifteenth century, the stronger Italian states had expanded their boundaries, absorbing weaker neighbors. A kind of balance of power developed among the three leading city-states, Milan, Florence, and Venice, together with the States of the Church and the feudal Kingdom of the Two Sicilies. It was the interplay of these states with each other and neighboring states, as well as the despotic methods of their rulers, that formed the background to the thought of Machiavelli.

The Theory of Absolutism: Machiavelli

In the late fifteenth and early sixteenth centuries, Italy was invaded by the kings of France and Spain, whose own governments were less efficient than those of the local despots but operated on a larger scale. For more than a century, the French and Spanish rulers fought each other for control of Italy and kept the country in turmoil. The Italian states were able to keep some of their independence by playing the rival invaders against each other, but Italy as a whole was more than ever before at the mercy of outsiders. Nearly two thousand years before, the crisis of the Greek city-states had helped inspire Plato and Aristotle to think deeply about politics and government; now, the crisis of the Italian states helped lead Machiavelli to the idea of **absolutism**, the theory that state power should be unlimited.

As a onetime diplomat and a close observer of Italian affairs, Machiavelli knew that despotic rule had put down internal dissension in Milan and his own city of Florence, but in relations among the Italian states, anarchy still reigned. If a despot could bring all of Italy under his rule, he believed, the country would benefit from effective government in the same way that individual states had done. But how to bring this about? In 1513, Machiavelli set down his basic views in a kind of how-to book, *The Prince*. At that time, the word *prince* was used to mean the ruler of a state, and Machiavelli intended his book as a guide for the despot who he hoped would one day liberate Italy.

 **The Prince: Power Politics During the Italian Renaissance** Read a selection from *The Prince*.

The Secularization of the State

Machiavelli's book marks a sharp turn in Western political thought. Medieval philosophers had seen government as one aspect of God's administration of human affairs: the Church and its officers direct Christians toward spiritual salvation, which is eternal; the state looks after their physical well-being, which is temporal (limited in time). Yet both branches of authority are subject to divine law.

Thomas Aquinas had discussed this matter in his *Summa Theologica* (p. 236). He reasoned that temporal power is invested by God in the people as a whole, who delegate it to suitable persons. The state, then, whether monarchical, aristocratic, or democratic, is not a power in itself. It receives its authority from God (through the people), and it must exercise its power for Christian purposes and in a Christian manner. To be sure, there were just as many ruthless and unscrupulous rulers in the Middle Ages as in any other era, but their practices were condemned as a perversion of the state's true purpose.

absolutism
The theory that state power is and should be absolute (unlimited).

Machiavelli met this doctrine head on and rejected it. He believed that Christian teachings, in general, did not contribute to good citizenship. In his *Discourses*, a commentary on the ancient Roman Republic, he claimed that the pagans had encouraged civic pride and service, whereas the early Christians had urged people to turn away from public affairs. The state, he thought, does not rest on any supernatural authority. It provides its own justification, and it operates according to rules that have grown out of the "facts" of human nature. He thereby removed politics from Christian belief and placed it on a purely secular (worldly) level.

The Pursuit of Power

Means, as well as ends, were a matter of concern to Machiavelli. As he saw it in *The Prince*, the central problem of politics is how to achieve and maintain a strong state. Much depends on the character of the citizens. He admired the Romans of the ancient Republic, but he concluded that a republican form of government could prosper only where the citizens possessed genuine commitment to the state. According to Machiavelli, the Italians of his day were "ungrateful and fickle, fakers, anxious to avoid danger, and greedy for gain; they offer you their blood, their goods, their life, and their children, when the necessity is remote; but when it approaches, they revolt." With citizens of such character, a strong state could only be founded and preserved by a despot.

Machiavelli advised that a ruler first turn his attention to military strength. He must devote himself to the training and discipline of his troops and must keep himself fit to lead them. Machiavelli had only contempt for the condottieri, for they had proved ruinous to Italy and incapable of defending the country from invasion. He advised the prince to build an army of citizens drawn from a reserve of qualified men under a system of compulsory military training, for their interests would be bound up with his own. Machiavelli thus introduced to modern Europe the ideas of universal male conscription (draft) and the "nation in arms."

Military strength is not enough in itself, however. For the prince must be both "a lion and a fox." The lion, Machiavelli explained, cannot protect himself from traps, and the fox cannot defend himself from wolves. A ruler, in other words, must have both strength and cunning. Machiavelli noted that the most successful rulers of his time were masters of deception. They made agreements to their advantage, only to break them when the advantage passed. He declared that the ruler should hold himself above normal rules of conduct—that the only proper measure for judging the behavior of a prince is his power. Whatever strengthens the state is right, and whatever weakens it is wrong; for power is the end, and the end justifies the means.

Machiavelli cautioned the prince never to reveal his true motives and methods, for it is useful to appear to be what one is

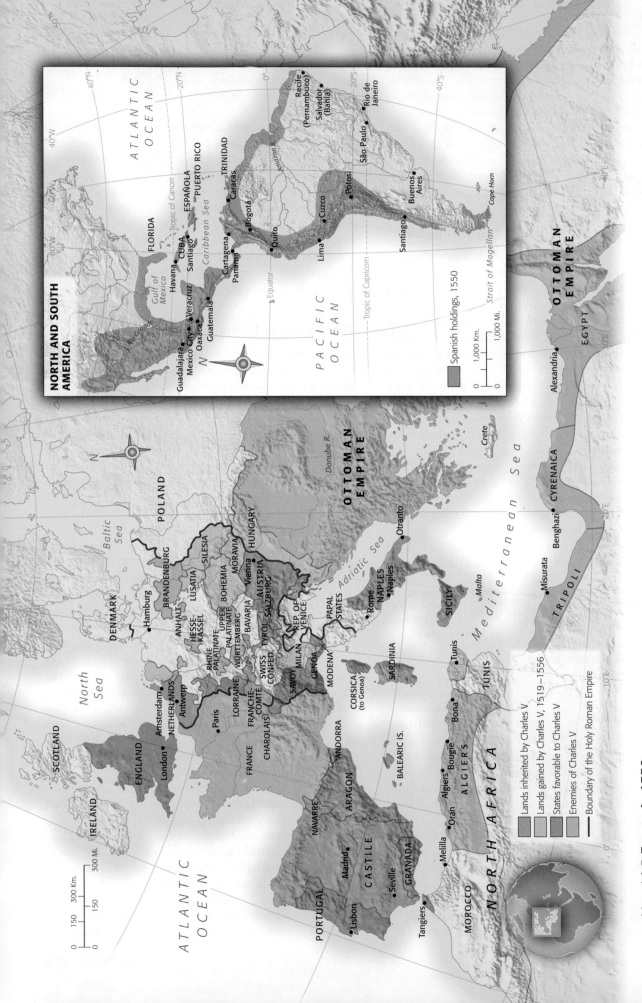

Map 14.5 Europe in 1556

In half a century, two dynasties have come to dominate Europe. The regional empire of the Ottoman Suleiman the Magnificent has expanded across southeastern Europe, North Africa, and Western Asia (compare Map 14.3 on page 259). Meanwhile, the Habsburg Charles V has acquired the first worldwide empire, with lands stretching from the Netherlands to Sicily, from Austria to Spain, and from California to Chile. The Habsburg-Ottoman rivalry also gives room for four competing middle-sized powers: England, France, Poland, and Russia. © Cengage Learning

 Interactive Map

(map labels, main map)

SCOTLAND
IRELAND
ENGLAND
London
North Sea
DENMARK
Hamburg
Baltic Sea
POLAND
Amsterdam
NETHERLANDS
Antwerp
BRANDENBURG
ANHALT
LUSATIA
SILESIA
Paris
FRANCE
RHINE PALATINATE
HESSE-KASSEL
UPPER PALATINATE
BOHEMIA
MORAVIA
LORRAINE
WÜRTTEMBERG
BAVARIA
HUNGARY
FRANCHE-COMTÉ
SWISS CONFED.
TYROL
AUSTRIA
SALZBURG
Vienna
CHAROLAIS
SAVOY
MILAN
REP. OF VENICE
GENOA
MODENA
CORSICA (to Genoa)
PAPAL STATES
Rome
NAPLES
Naples
Danube R.
OTTOMAN EMPIRE
Adriatic Sea
NAVARRE
ANDORRA
ARAGON
SARDINIA
BALEARIC IS.
Madrid
CASTILE
Seville
GRANADA
PORTUGAL
Lisbon
Tangiers
MOROCCO
Melilla
Oran
Algiers
ALGIERS
Bourgie
Bona
TUNIS
Tunis
SICILY
Malta
Crete
Mediterranean Sea
NORTH AFRICA
Misurata
TRIPOLI
Benghazi
CYRENAICA
Alexandria
EGYPT
OTTOMAN EMPIRE
Otranto

ATLANTIC OCEAN

N

0   150   300 Mi.
0   150   300 Km.

Legend

- Lands inherited by Charles V
- Lands gained by Charles V, 1519–1556
- States favorable to Charles V
- Enemies of Charles V
- Boundary of the Holy Roman Empire

Inset map: NORTH AND SOUTH AMERICA

ATLANTIC OCEAN
Gulf of Mexico
Rio Grande
Guadalajara
Mexico City
Oaxaca
Veracruz
Guatemala
FLORIDA
Havana
CUBA
Santiago
ESPAÑOLA
PUERTO RICO
Caribbean Sea
TRINIDAD
Cartagena
Panama
Caracas
Bogotá
Quito
Lima
Cuzco
Potosí
Santiago
Buenos Aires
São Paulo
Rio de Janeiro
Salvador (Bahia)
Recife (Pernambuco)
Amazon R.
Equator
Tropic of Cancer
Tropic of Capricorn
Strait of Magellan
Cape Horn
PACIFIC OCEAN

N

Spanish holdings, 1550

0   1,000 Km.
0   1,000 Mi.

not. Though the prince must stand ready, when necessary, to act "against faith, against charity, against humanity, and against religion," he must always *seem* to possess those qualities. Machiavelli summarized his advice to the ruler as follows:

> Let a prince therefore aim at conquering and maintaining the state, and the means will always be judged honorable and praised by everyone. For the vulgar [common people] is always taken in by appearances and the result of the event; and the world consists only of the vulgar, and the few who are not vulgar are isolated when the many have a rallying point in the prince.

Famous and Provocative Quotations from Machiavelli (http://www.brainyquote.com/quotes/authors/n/niccolo_machiavelli.html) Discover fifty-eight provocative sayings from Machiavelli.

Building Dynastic Monarchy: The Habsburgs

One of the factors that enabled the city-states of northern Italy to build their independent power was the failure of the region's highest feudal overlords, the Holy Roman emperors, to turn their territories into an effectively governed state (pp. 188–189). In the empire's much larger territories north of the Alps, including Germany and neighboring lands, many local power wielders likewise gained more or less independent authority, and one particular dynasty, the Habsburgs, rose from local to Europe-wide— and ultimately worldwide—power.

The emperor's vassals north of the Alps included nobles with a bewildering array of ranks and titles, wealthy trading and industrial cities, and leading archbishops, all of whom governed their territories more or less independently of the emperor himself. The ranking vassals—three nobles, three archbishops, and the emperor's highest vassal, the king of Bohemia—had the status of permanent **electors**. When an emperor died, these seven men met to choose his successor. In spite of his limited power, the Holy Roman emperor was still the first in honor of European monarchs, so an imperial election often involved lengthy bargaining.

However, in the fifteenth century, the electors developed a habit of choosing emperors from one ruling family, the Habsburgs. The family originated in southern Germany; in the thirteenth century, they had become leading nobles as dukes of Austria, in the southeast of the empire; and from 1438 until the end of the Holy Roman Empire in 1806, every emperor came from the House of Habsburg. Even so, each Habsburg would-be emperor had to win over the independent-minded electors, and the fam-

ily's efforts to revive the imperial power were generally unsuccessful. The Habsburgs therefore also looked to build their power by marrying into ruling dynasties outside the empire.

Every ruling family made dynastic marriages, both as a way of cementing alliances and in hopes of one day gaining territory by inheritance. Of course, inheritance depended on accidents of birth and death in the families involved, and in the inheritance lottery, the Habsburgs were luckier than any other dynasty— above all in the early sixteenth century.

From fifteenth-century dynastic marriages, the youthful Charles of Habsburg inherited the Netherlands, Spain, Sardinia, Naples, and Sicily, besides the family's original territory in Austria. In 1519, he bought the votes of the electors with the help of a huge loan from the Fugger banking firm and became Emperor Charles V, and in the 1520s, Spanish conquests in the New World made him the ruler of a vast transoceanic empire (Map 14.5). Meanwhile, Charles's younger brother Ferdinand married the sister of the king of Hungary and Bohemia, and when the king died in battle against the Turks in 1526, Ferdinand was elected king by the nobles of those two countries. No single dynasty had ever ruled so much of western and central Europe as the Habsburgs, and none in the history of the human race had ever ruled lands in both the Eastern and Western Hemispheres.

But these far-flung lands were exceedingly hard to control. The emperor encountered an endless series of political, military, and personal frustrations, and he at last retired to a monastery in 1556. Before abdicating, Charles divided the Habsburg lands between two heirs. His son Philip was given Spain, the dynasty's other territories in western Europe and the Mediterranean, and the Spanish overseas empire. His brother Ferdinand inherited Austria, Bohemia, and Hungary, and was elected Holy Roman emperor.

Far from weakening the Habsburgs, the division of their territory into more manageable portions actually strengthened them. Working closely together, the Spanish and Austrian branches of the dynasty dominated Europe for a hundred years. It was they who sustained the Catholic Church against the Protestant revolt, fought the Turks to a standstill, and organized the Spanish empire in the New World (pp. 278–279, 328, 335-337). In these ways, the Europe and the world of today still feel the effect of their power.

elector
One of seven high-ranking vassals of the Holy Roman emperor with the authority to elect the emperor's successor.

> **"No single dynasty had ever ruled so much of western and central Europe as the Habsburgs, and none in the history of the human race had ever ruled lands in both the Eastern and the Western Hemispheres."**

Listen to a synopsis of Chapter 14.

CourseMate Access to the eBook with additional review material and study tools may be found online at CourseMate for WCIV. Sign in at www.cengagebrain.com.

CHAPTER 15

WORLDWIDE EUROPE: EXPLORATION AND EMPIRE BUILDING,

1300–1800

LEARNING OBJECTIVES

AFTER READING THIS CHAPTER, YOU SHOULD BE ABLE TO DO THE FOLLOWING:

LO¹ Explain the developments outside and inside Europe that led to European efforts to find new routes to Asia.

LO² Discuss the stages of European exploration, from early voyages to overseas empires.

LO³ Describe the mutual impact between Europe and the rest of the world from the sixteenth to the eighteenth century.

"THE RESULT OF THE EUROPEAN CONQUEST OF THE AMERICAS WAS A HISTORIC CHANGE IN THE POSITION OF EUROPE AMONG THE CIVILIZATIONS OF THE WORLD."

The beginnings of European worldwide exploration and empire building were linked with other changes of the late Middle Ages—the renewed Muslim offensive against Christendom, the capitalist pursuit of profit, new seafaring and war-fighting technology, and the competitive ambitions of powerful rulers. The explorers originally hoped to find routes to East Asia that would bypass the Venetian and Arab traders who controlled the existing routes, and to find distant allies against Islam. The first of these hopes came true, while the second turned out to be false. But the explorers also came into contact with the civilizations of the Western Hemisphere, which lacked many technologies and resources—as well as diseases—shared by the peoples of the Eastern Hemisphere, and were therefore easy to conquer.

The result of the European conquest of the Americas was a historic change in the position of Europe among the civilizations of the world. The capitalists of western Europe gained worldwide profits. The region's governments fought worldwide wars against each other for control of worldwide trade and empire. The Christianity of western Europe, both Protestant and Catholic, became a worldwide religion, for the first time outreaching Islam. At the same time, the eastern European countries became strong enough to hold off the Turks, stabilizing the land frontier with Islam and reaching across northern Asia to the Pacific, while the western countries broke out from Europe across the oceans to spread their influence around the globe.

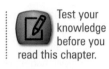

Test your knowledge before you read this chapter.

What do you think?

Columbus's voyage across the Atlantic was the most momentous undertaking of late medieval Europe.

Strongly Disagree						Strongly Agree
1	2	3	4	5	6	7

« **A *Nanban* Carrack** To the Japanese, Europeans were *nanban*—"southern barbarians," since they came by way of southern Asia and their manners were crude by local standards. Still, the *nanban* were in some ways fascinating, among other things on account of their large, fast-sailing, and easily maneuverable ships. This painting by Kanō Naizen, a fashionable artist about 1600, shows a Portuguese carrack, the workhorse vessel of European worldwide trade and exploration, leaving port with wind-filled sails and its crew in their exotic Western costumes.

Courtesy, Kobe City Museum

LO¹ Europe's Intercontinental Ambitions

Neither earlier Europeans nor fifteenth-century non-Europeans were ripe for long-term exploration and empire building in distant lands. A landing in North America by the Norwegian Leif Ericson in the course of the Viking migrations around 1000 made only a slight impression in Europe. Likewise, a fifteenth-century non-European venture, in which the Ming emperors of China sent several powerful fleets ranging across the Indian Ocean from the East Indies to the African coast, came in the end to nothing. But in the fifteenth and sixteenth centuries, Europe—or at least a group of leading western European countries—became hungry for contact with the outside world.

Wider Horizons

This hunger was partly the outcome of changes in the wider group of civilizations of which Europe had come to be a part. Ever since the rise of Islam and of the nomadic peoples of the steppes had linked the civilizations of the Eastern Hemisphere, Europeans had benefited in many ways from membership in this intercontinental grouping. They had tasted sweets, spices, and other luxuries from afar, and they had enjoyed exotic pastimes such as card games and chess. By the fifteenth century they were making use of non-European knowledge and inventions such as Arabic numerals, gunpowder, and printing—as well as mapmaking methods, navigational instruments, and models of ship design that would in time help them across oceans (pp. 256–258; see photos on pages 268, 271, and 275).

But until late in the thirteenth century, Europeans had known little of the distant lands from which these things came to them. The region they actually knew and lived in stretched from Greenland to North Africa and the Middle East. Revived knowledge of ancient Greek geography—another Arab import—had taught them more about the rest of the world than they knew before. They had a vague idea of the coastlines and islands of the Indian Ocean. They believed that Europe, Asia, and Africa formed a single huge landmass, surrounded by ocean that covered all the rest of the earth's surface. And they were well aware that the world as a whole was round. But the actual size of Asia and Africa, the geography of their interiors, and the peoples who lived in them were matters of fantasy and guesswork.

The Mongol Empire

In the thirteenth and fourteenth centuries, this European ignorance of the outside world began to change. The main reason was the rise of the intercontinental empire of the Mongols. As devastating as the Mongol conquests were to their victims in eastern Europe and to Muslim lands in Asia, once established, their empire maintained secure communications across the steppes for a hundred years (see Map 12.3 on page 222). For the first time, Europeans were able to visit the lands beyond Islam and return to tell what they had seen.

see Map 12.3 on page 222

CHRONOLOGY

1298	Marco Polo dictates his book of travels
1300s	Venice establishes a trading monopoly with Asia
1420s	Portuguese expeditions sponsored by Prince Henry the Navigator begin to chart the West African coastline
1488	Bartolomeu Dias rounds the southern tip of Africa
1492	Christopher Columbus leads an expedition across the Atlantic, reaches the Americas
1494	Treaty of Tordesillas between Portugal and Spain establishes boundary for each country's exploration, trade, and conquest
1497	John Cabot discovers Newfoundland for England
1498	Vasco da Gama reaches India by way of the African coastal route
1519–1522	Magellan's crew circles the globe
1521	Cortés completes the Spanish conquest of the Aztecs
1523	Beginning of trans-Atlantic slave trade
1531	Pizarro completes the Spanish conquest of the Inca
1540	Portuguese trading network extends along the coastline from West Africa to Japan; Jesuit Francis Xavier begins his mission to Asia
1571	Spanish-led Christian alliance defeats Turks at battle of Lepanto, ending Ottoman naval domination of Mediterranean
1600s	English, French, and Dutch begin colonizing North America and establishing trading posts in Asia

Marco Polo, a thirteenth-century merchant of Venice, contributed more than anyone else to Europe's awareness of the lands beyond Islam. Members of the Polo family, after establishing trading contacts with the Mongol Empire in western Asia, made the long trek from the Black Sea to Beijing, newly established as the Chinese capital by the Mongols. The Mongol ruler Kublai Khan welcomed the Polos with courtesy, and they later returned with Marco, who remained in China for many years before returning by way of Southeast Asia and the lands of the Indian Ocean. Once back in Italy, he wrote of his travels and revealed to astonished Europeans the fabulous wealth of **the Indies**—their name for the entire region of eastern and southern Asia.

Not long afterward, Europe received the same revelation about another hitherto unknown part of the world with which it did indirect business—West Africa (the lands in the bulge of Africa south of the Sahara). Early in the fourteenth century, Mansa Musa, the ruler of the powerful Islamic empire of Mali, fulfilling his obligation to visit Mecca, passed through Cairo, where there was a large Italian trading community. Soon the news reached Europe that the wealthy pilgrim had handed out so much gold by way of gifts that the gold-based Egyptian coinage had temporarily lost a quarter of its value. Much else was reported about Mansa Musa, his empire, and its resources (see photo).

 **In the Footsteps of Marco Polo: A Journey Through the Met to the Land of the Great Khan** (https://www.metmuseum.org/explore/Marco/index.html) View Marco Polo's journey through art and artifacts.

From this new knowledge of Asia and Africa, Europeans began to get a distinct idea of the distant lands and peoples of the Eastern Hemisphere—together with the uncomfortable but enticing feeling that among these lands and peoples, they were, so to speak, poor relations.

The Indies
The medieval European name for the region encompassing eastern and southern Asia.

Barriers to Trade and Travel

In the middle of the fourteenth century, the Black Death swept through Asia, Africa, and Europe, leading to an intercontinental decline in prosperity and trade. Disputes among the successors of Genghis Khan led to the gradual collapse of the Mongol

A European View of an African King The *Catalan Atlas* (about 1375) shows the African coastline with descriptions of harbors and landmarks; the radiating lines indicate compass directions, and the pebble-like band is the Atlas Mountains. Mansa Musa, "Lord of the Black People of Guinea" has a European-style crown and scepter; his right hand holds a gold nugget. A camel-riding Sahara nomad has his face wrapped against wind-blown sand. Just before exploration began, Europeans already had fair knowledge of some of the outside world. Art Gallery Collection/Alamy

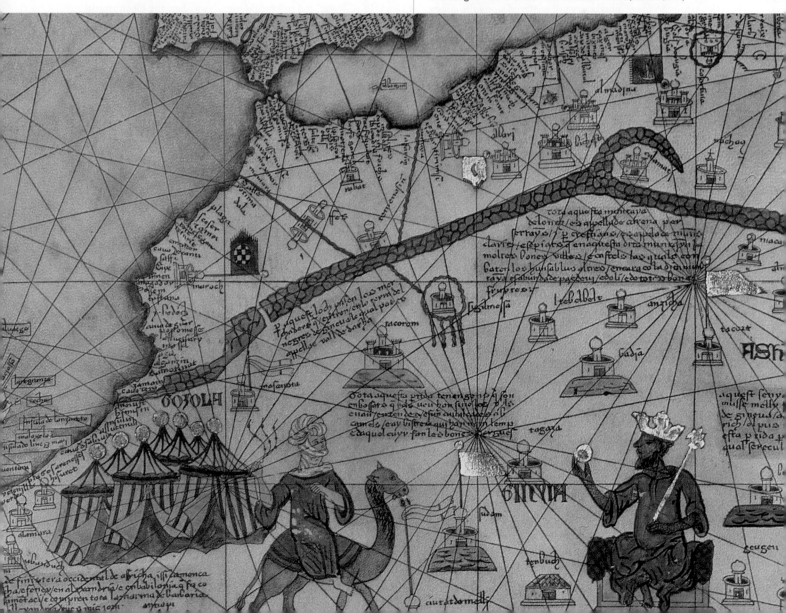

Empire, and the rising power of the Turks (p. 251) blocked off the western end of the overland routes to the Indies. Trade and other contacts between Europe and Asia came to be channeled mainly through Egypt, where Italian and Arab merchants exchanged European textiles against the spices of the Indies. Thus, as Europe gradually recovered from the Black Death, it found the door to the outside world partly closed. But in the countries of western Europe, the effect was actually to increase their hunger for contact with distant lands.

> "*Marco Polo, a thirteenth-century merchant of Venice, contributed more than anyone else to Europe's awareness of the lands beyond Islam.*"

Venice's Monopoly

Among the Italian city-states that had traditionally dominated the routes to the eastern Mediterranean (p. 195), competition to control the chief remaining link with the Indies grew intense. In the fourteenth century, the two largest cities, Venice and Genoa, fought a series of wars that ended in the victory of Venice. That city now became Europe's main gateway to the rest of the world. Venetian strongpoints and harbors were scattered along the coasts and islands of the eastern Mediterranean, guarding the sea routes, attracting the commerce of neighboring areas, and creating a Venetian trading monopoly in the region. But the Venetians not only traded; they also developed new resources. In the Venetian-owned island of Cyprus, a fabulously profitable crop of Middle Eastern origin, sugarcane, was grown on plantations worked by gangs of slaves imported from countries to the north of the Black Sea.

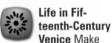 **Life in Fifteenth-Century Venice** Make choices and experience the consequences in the role of a young man in fifteenth-century Venice.

In these ways, Venice set an example of empire building and colonial exploitation that was carefully studied by the increasingly powerful and prosperous countries of western Europe—even while they envied the city's newfound monopoly of links with the Indies. Meanwhile, Genoa was confined to the western Mediterranean and the sea routes leading from there to the lands of Europe's Atlantic coast. It was no coincidence that Christopher Columbus came from Venice's Atlantic-oriented rival city.

The Muslim Offensive

The fifteenth century also saw a hardening in western European attitudes toward Islam. The Muslim world, for so long the connecting link between Europe and other civilizations of the Eastern Hemisphere, came to seem an irksome obstacle now that western Europeans had some idea of what lay beyond it. At the same time, the Turkish drive into eastern Europe left no doubt that Islam was a more formidable adversary of Christendom than ever before—one against which it would be most desirable to find non-European allies. Somewhere in the world beyond Islam, there might be powerful Christian rulers, or non-Muslim ones ripe for conversion to Christianity, who would join Christendom's struggle against the followers of the Prophet.

Merchants, Rulers, and Clergy

To break Venice's trading monopoly and to find allies against Islam, a way must be found linking western Europe directly with the Indies. The prizes for whoever found the way would be glittering indeed. Western European merchants would become as rich as or richer than those of Venice. The region's ambitious rulers would make money by collecting taxes on the new trade or sponsoring trading ventures of their own—and more money meant more mercenary soldiers, less dependence on the nobles of their kingdoms, and last but not least, more power against each other. And of course, the rulers and merchants of each country intended that they and they alone would find the way, excluding the rulers and merchants of every other country just as Venice monopolized the existing Mediterranean route.

In addition, the rulers and merchants had the blessing and encouragement of the Church for any efforts to find allies against Islam and spread the gospel. Even in the European religious turmoil of the sixteenth century (see Chapter 17), both Catholic and Protestant missionaries, as well as rival Protestant churches and Catholic religious orders, would strive against each other to baptize the maximum number of converts.

LO² Breaking Out

In this way, the clergy's Christian zeal, the rulers' hunger for power, the merchants' instinct for profit, and the competitive spirit of all three groups combined to sharpen their desire to find a new way to the Indies. But did this new way exist at all, and if so, where was it to be found?

Portugal and Africa

The little kingdom of Portugal was the first to begin looking for a new way to the Indies. Carved by Christian warriors out of formerly Muslim lands during the reconquest of Spain, Portugal was a relatively poor country of farmers and fishermen, sandwiched between the larger and wealthier kingdom of Castile to the east and the Atlantic to the west—and one thing that seemed certain about any new route to the Indies was that it must go by way of the western ocean.

If Portuguese sailors were to be the ones to find the route, their country's standing among Christendom's competing kingdoms would be changed out of all recognition. The merchants of Portugal's capital city and main seaport, Lisbon, would become as rich as those of Venice, and richer than their rivals in Castile's main Atlantic seaport, Seville. Portugal's rulers would be able to shift the balance between their kingdom and

Castile, while also winning glory as Christendom's leaders in its struggle with Islam.

Besides, Portugal was close to the most likely region of the ocean to look for a new way to the Indies, southward along the coastline of Africa. Sooner or later, the coastline must surely turn northward, allowing a ship to sail on eastward to the Indies. Of course, no one knew exactly where the turn in the coastline would come, but at least there would be a coastline to follow. Sailors could stay close to land, fill their holds with food and water whenever they ran short and keep on going, or turn back and find their way home to report. And well before they reached the Indies, they would arrive in West Africa and do profitable direct business with the wealthy peoples who were known to live there.

Early in the fifteenth century, these hopes filled the mind of a younger son of the Portuguese royal family, who sponsored many expeditions along the African coast and has gone down in history as Prince Henry the Navigator. By 1460, Henry's sailors had occupied the nearby Madeira Islands and the Azores (**AY-zorz**) and had opened trade for gold, ivory, and slaves along the coast of West Africa. But then the prince died and the African coastline turned from going eastward toward the Indies to going southward, away from them. As a result, exploration came to a halt.

Twenty years later, an ambitious new king of Portugal, John II, took up where Henry had left off. New expeditions sailed, and in 1488, Bartolomeu Dias sailed farther south than any earlier Portuguese sailor until the coastline finally turned northward—and was still trending northward at the point where his crew grew nervous and made him turn for home. Still, the turn in the coastline was encouraging news, which seemed to justify King John's decision a few years earlier to reject an unorthodox proposal for a different way to the Indies made by an Italian residing in his kingdom—Christopher Columbus.

Spain Looks Westward

Columbus grew up in Genoa as the son of a weaver, but he found work with a family firm of international merchants that took him to Lisbon. There, he went into the business of making sea charts and accompanied ship captains on voyages down the African coast. Meanwhile, he studied the works of Marco Polo and of Muslim and ancient Greek geographers, and came to the conclusion that the shortest sea trip to the Indies would be not southward round Africa, but westward across the Atlantic Ocean.

In 1485, Columbus asked King John II for ships and men to make the trip, but the royal advisers on geography and navigation pronounced his plans unsound. The reasons they gave are unknown, but they certainly did not say that Columbus would fall off the edge of the earth. Most likely they disagreed with Columbus's unorthodox view that, going westward on the surface of the round earth, the Indies were only about 2,600 miles away—near enough for a ship to arrive without resupplying with food and water. The orthodox view, based on the work of the ancient Greek geographer Ptolemy (p. 110), was that the world was indeed round, but that the westward distance to the Indies

must be at least 10,000 miles. In that case, the crew of a ship that sailed that way would perish of thirst and hunger in the middle of the ocean, and probably this assessment was what led King John to refuse Columbus's proposal.

Not being a man to give up, Columbus turned to Queen Isabella, the ruler of Portugal's neighbor and rival kingdom of Castile, whose marriage to King Ferdinand of Aragon had made the two of them joint rulers of Spain (p. 263).

The Spanish monarchs had recently made an agreement with the Portuguese king whereby, in return for various concessions, they agreed not to permit their merchants to compete with Portuguese ones on the West African coast. Columbus's offer to find a way to the Indies that would bypass Africa as well as Venice and Islam was therefore a tempting one. But their advisers, too, said that Columbus was wrong, and they hesitated for several years until 1492, when he was about to leave to put his idea to the king of France. Isabella and Ferdinand could not face the thought of giving up to a rival monarch even a slim chance of gaining a monopoly of a quick and easy route to the Indies.

Sure enough, after a five-week voyage, Columbus sighted land at precisely the point where he expected to find the shores of the Indies (Map 15.1). Most geographers remained convinced that the western ocean was wider than Columbus believed, and that he had stumbled across uncharted islands well short of the Indies. But even that was very encouraging: it gave hope that a ship could take on food and water in the western islands and sail on to the Indies. Columbus finding land in the middle of the ocean was like Dias rounding the southern tip of Africa. Both Spain and Portugal, it seemed, were within reach of the longed-for destination but not quite there.

1492: An Ongoing Voyage (http://www.ibiblio.org/expo/1492.exhibit/Intro.html) Explore the impact of Columbus's voyage of 1492 on the worlds of Europe, the Americas, and Africa in this online exhibit.

Fulfillment and Frustration

Now that it seemed possible that there were two routes to the Indies, the Spanish and Portuguese monarchs agreed to respect each other's regions of exploration, trade, and conquest. In 1494, by the **Treaty of Tordesillas (tor-duh-SEE-yuhs)**, these rulers of countries that together occupied about one-third of one percent of the earth's surface agreed to divide the other ninety-nine and two-thirds percent between them. They established a demarcation line—a circle that passed through a point approximately 1,500 miles west of Cape Verde, the westernmost tip of Africa (see Map 15.1) and continued north and south right around the globe. The Portuguese would stay within the hemisphere to the east of that line, while the Spaniards would limit themselves to the hemisphere west of the line. Secured from each other's

> **Treaty of Tordesillas**
> The 1494 agreement between Portugal and Spain that established the boundary for each country's new territorial claim.

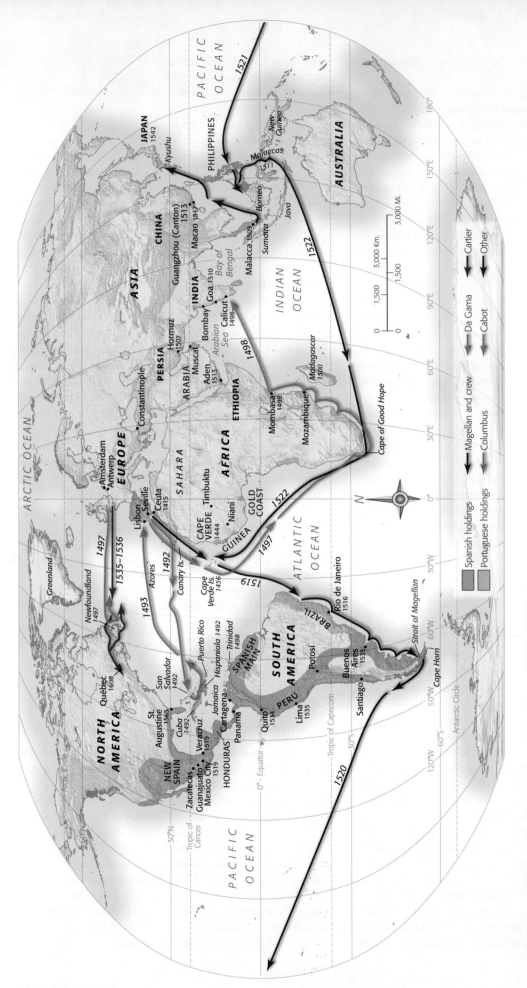

Interactive Map

Map 15.1 European Explorers and Empires, 1492–1535

In the early sixteenth century Portuguese eastward explorers sailed round Africa, spread out across southern and eastern Asia, and began building an intercontinental network of trading footholds among powerful peoples and states. Westward explorers inspired by Columbus's dream of a shortcut to the Indies ranged the coastlines of the Americas, across the Pacific, and eventually around the world. Vast New World territories fell to conquerors from the least wealthy and powerful of the civilizations of the Old World. © Cengage Learning

interference by this agreement, the rulers and sailors of both nations set about finally winning the prize.

Portugal Finds the Way

For the Portuguese, success came soon. In 1497, King John of Portugal sent Vasco da Gama to follow the same route as Bartolomeu Dias, but this time with four ships, two of them cannon-armed carracks (p. 256). Vasco continued beyond where Dias had turned back until he reached Arab trading cities in East Africa, and then sailed across the Indian Ocean to the west coast of India (Map 15.1). After almost a century, Portugal had found the way to the Indies.

> **"***Thirty years after Columbus, the Spaniards now knew that even the orthodox view of the westward distance to the Indies was an underestimate.***"**

Spain, the New World, and the Pacific

Meanwhile, Spain was not so lucky. With hopes so high, an international boom in exploration across the western ocean got under way. Columbus himself made three more expeditions and found many more islands before he died in 1506, still believing he had found the Indies but not having reached any of the wealthy lands described by Marco Polo. Meanwhile, regardless of the Treaty of Tordesillas, in 1497 King Henry VII of England sent out a Genoese mariner, known to the English as John Cabot, who made landfall in or near Newfoundland. Shortly after Cabot's voyage, Portuguese sailors sailing southwestward in the Atlantic toward the line of demarcation found land on their side of the line (present-day Brazil). Spaniards searching westward across the Caribbean reached a coastline that did not seem to be that of an island, and in 1513, Vasco Nuñez de Balboa made his way across the Isthmus of Panama, thereby becoming the first European to see the Pacific Ocean.

No one as yet gave up hope of finding a quick and easy westward route to the Indies, but it was clear that vast lands stretched for thousands of miles across the western ocean. In 1508, a colorful description of some of these lands was printed under the title *The New World*. The book was based on letters by Amerigo Vespucci (**ve-SPOO-chee**), a mapmaker from Florence who had sailed with various explorers. It became a bestseller, and shortly afterward, a German mapmaker gave this New World what became its standard name, the "land of Amerigo," or America.

The climax of the exploration boom came in 1519, when the Holy Roman emperor Charles V, in his capacity as king of Spain (p. 267), accepted a proposal by a sea captain of Portuguese origin, Ferdinand Magellan, to find a southern route past the New World to the Indies. Magellan guided his fleet of five ships down the coast of South America. He managed the hazardous passage around the southern tip of the continent and then sailed northwestward into the Pacific. Following a frightful three-month crossing, during part of which his men lived on leather and rats, Magellan reached the island of Guam. With fresh provisions, he sailed on to the Philippine Islands, where he got involved in a conflict between local rulers and was killed. But the expedition pushed on across the Indian Ocean and westward around Africa, and the one remaining vessel finally returned to Spain in 1522 (Map 15.1). So far as is known, the ship's eighteen surviving crewmen were the first human beings ever to travel right around the world.

>> **Finding the Way** On a sixteenth-century astrolabe (p. 256), a navigator sights along the pointer to determine the height above the horizon of the sun or a star, and thereby to find out a ship's latitude (its position north or south of the equator). The ring and the disk beneath it revolve to compensate for the seasonal movement of the sun and stars. Instruments like this one helped make long exploring voyages possible. Courtesy of the Trustees of the British Museum

Thirty years after Columbus, the Spaniards now knew that even the orthodox view of the westward distance to the Indies was an underestimate. The Indies were nearly 12,000 miles away, so that they lay mostly on the Portuguese side of the line of demarcation as it continued round the world from the Atlantic to the Pacific. But the New World, which had so far seemed a frustrating barrier to their westward search, was about to yield them wealth and power that more than made up for their disappointment in the Indies.

Conquering Overseas Empires

The Portuguese and Spanish discoveries were followed by empire building. A network of Portuguese harbors and citadels arose along the coastlines of the powerful peoples and states of the Old World, while Spain overthrew entire vulnerable civilizations in the New World.

The Portuguese in the Indies

As soon as Vasco da Gama returned to Lisbon with news of his success, the Portuguese began preparing to exploit their victory on the largest scale they could manage. In 1497, Vasco had set out with four ships; when he left Lisbon again in 1502, he commanded twenty, and from then on, Portuguese fleets regularly sailed the waters of the Indies. Within forty years, they made their way right across the Indies to the Spice Islands (Indonesia) and Japan.

On the way to the Indies, the Portuguese had encountered powerful West African kings and well-armed Arab city-states in eastern Africa. Now they met with fabulously wealthy local rulers in India and the Spice Islands, the well-run feudal state of Japan, and the huge empire of China. The few hundred soldiers aboard the Portuguese ships were no match for the local armies; their one advantage was at sea, with their cannon-armed carracks. The Portuguese negotiated for trading rights, seized outposts that were easy to defend against attack by land, and used their sea-fighting advantage against the Arab merchants who controlled the trade of the Indian Ocean.

By about 1540, the coastlines of the Eastern Hemisphere from western Africa to East Asia were dotted with Portuguese-controlled harbors, naval bases, and trading stations. The trade in spices, silks, and other luxury goods from India, the Spice Islands, and East Asia to Europe, as well as much of the regional trade of eastern and southern Asia, was in their hands. It was a repetition of what Venice had done in the eastern Mediterranean, only on an enormously larger scale—and, of course, to the great disadvantage of the Italian city. For it was the Portuguese who now monopolized the trade between Europe and the East, and it was Lisbon that was now Europe's gateway to the Indies (see Map 15.1).

Spain in the New World

While the Portuguese were building a far-flung imperial network in Africa and Asia, the Spaniards were founding modest farming settlements in the Caribbean islands and brutally enslaving the Native Americans of the region. Some of the newcomers moved westward, still hoping to find the way to the Indies but also attracted by rumors of nearby peoples rich in gold and silver. In 1519, the same year that Magellan set sail for the Indies, a former law student turned farmer and imperial official in Cuba, Hernán Cortés, finally came upon the reality behind the rumors, the Aztec Empire in Mexico.

An Aztec View of a Spanish Conquistador A traditional Aztec manuscript, one of the last to be made, shows a Spanish commander setting out to conquer a territory in western Mexico. A caption by an unknown Spanish writer explains: "In the year . . . 1529, Nuño de Guzmán left for Jalisco to subjugate that land; they claim that a snake came out of the sky saying that hard times were coming for the natives with the Christians going over there."

CORTÉS ON THE PEOPLES OF THE NEW WORLD: REPORTS TO CHARLES V

Hernán Cortés often had bad relations and even armed conflicts with local Spanish officials in the Caribbean and fellow conquistadors. It was therefore important for him to gain and keep the good will of the Holy Roman emperor Charles V, who was also king of Spain and its empire in the New World. In these excerpts, from the second and fifth of a series of lengthy reports that Cortés sent to Charles, he describes the former Aztec capital city of Tenochtitlán (present-day Mexico City) and his activities during an expedition to Honduras.

This great city of Tenochtitlán is built on the salt lake. . . . It has four approaches by means of artificial causeways. . . . The city is as large as Seville or Córdoba. Its streets . . . are very broad and straight, some of these, and all the others, are one half land, and the other half water on which they go about in canoes. . . . There are bridges, very large, strong, and well constructed, so that, over many, ten horsemen can ride abreast. . . . The city has many squares where markets are held. . . . There is one square, twice as large as that of Salamanca, all surrounded by arcades, where there are daily more than sixty thousand souls, buying and selling . . . in the service and manners of its people, their fashion of living was almost the same as in Spain, with just as much harmony and order; and considering that these people were barbarous, so cut off from the knowledge of God and other civilized peoples, it is admirable to see to what they attained in every respect.

It happened . . . that a Spaniard saw an Indian . . . eating a piece of flesh taken from the body of an Indian who had been killed. . . . I had the culprit burned, explaining that the cause was his having killed that Indian and eaten him which was prohibited by Your Majesty, and by me in Your Royal name. I further made the chief understand that all the people . . . must abstain from this custom. . . . I came . . . to protect their lives as well as their property, and to teach them that they were to adore but one God . . . that they must turn from their idols, and the rites they had practised until then, for these were lies and deceptions which the devil . . . had invented. . . . I, likewise, had come to teach them that Your Majesty, by the will of Divine Providence, rules the universe, and that they also must submit themselves to the imperial yoke, and do all that we who are Your Majesty's ministers here might order them. . . .

EXPLORING THE SOURCE

1. What is Cortés's attitude to the indigenous peoples of Mexico and Honduras, and how does he expect to make them obey him?

2. How would the information that Cortés gives in these letters help him gain the king's approval?

Source: Fernando Cortes: His Five Letters of Relation to the Emperor Charles V, trans. Francis A. MacNutt (Cleveland, Ohio: A. H. Clark, 1908), 1:256–257, 2:244.

Cortés's conquest of the Aztecs was both daring and cruel. The Aztecs were a civilized people who boasted rich cities, splendid temples and palaces, superb artistic creations, and a well-organized government. They suffered serious disadvantages, however. They had no iron weapons, no horses, and no firearms. The government was oppressive and constantly threatened by rebellious subject peoples. Finally, like all the peoples of the New World, the Aztecs had not been exposed to European diseases; they therefore lacked resistance to the deadly smallpox germs that the invaders brought with them.

As a result, Cortés was able to do in the New World what was impossible for the Portuguese in the Indies—with only a few hundred soldiers of his own, to overthrow an empire. By 1521, the last Aztec emperor, Moctezuma, was dead; his capital city of Tenochtitlán (**teh-noch-tit-LAN**), which was probably larger than all except a handful of European cities, had been destroyed and was being rebuilt as Mexico City; and Cortés was governing in the name of the distant Spanish king, with the title of captain-general and governor of New Spain.

Within a decade, Cortés and other **conquistadors (kon-KEY-stuh-dors)** (conquerors) expanded New Spain to include most of Central America, from the Rio Grande to Panama (see photo on page 209 and Map 15.1), and another, Francisco Pizarro, then moved into South America. Learning of gold and silver in the Inca territories, he organized an

 The Battle Between the Spanish and the Aztecs Experience the battle between the Spanish and Aztecs in your choice of role in this simulation

 "Ice Treasures of the Incas" (http://www.national geographic.com/features/96/mummy/) Learn more about the civilization of the Incas before their encounter with Pizarro.

EUROPEANS HAD CERTAIN ADVANTAGES OVER THE NATIVE AMERICANS:

Technologies Built Up by Many Old World Civilizations

- About 4,500 years had passed since the civilizations of Sumer and Egypt had first arisen, whereas it was only about 2,500 years since the earliest civilizations had appeared in the Western Hemisphere.

- European benefited from armor made of iron, a metal first worked in the Middle East, and the gunpowder for

their weapons had been invented in China.

- Europeans brought horses, which had first been domesticated in Central Asia.

Greater Resistance to Smallpox and Other Diseases

- The diseases that Europeans brought with them were common throughout

the Eastern Hemisphere but were unknown in the Americas.

- It is believed that, having no resistance to these diseases, the indigenous population was reduced by as much as 90 percent in the first hundred years of European rule—a staggering blow to their ability to resist.

---

expedition with royal approval. The Inca Empire, like that of the Aztecs, rested upon an advanced society; it stretched southward along the Andes Mountains from Ecuador through the modern states of Peru and Bolivia. Pizarro discovered, however, that the empire was torn by internal unrest and infected with smallpox—to which his own soldiers had greater resistance. Like Cortés, he made the most of the situation. Armed with superior weapons, Pizarro's men captured the ruler, Atahualpa (ah-tah-WAHL-pa) and held him for an extravagant ransom. After Pizarro had received tons of gold and silver, carried in from all parts of Peru, he had his prisoner baptized a Christian and then had him strangled. He next marched to the magnificent Inca capital of Cuzco (KOOS-koh), looted it, and took over the empire in 1534.

LO³ Europe Encounters the World

In 1580, thanks to an earlier dynastic marriage, the Spanish ruler King Philip II inherited the kingdom of Portugal. From the Spanish farming settlement of Valparaiso in the south of Chile to the Portuguese trading outpost of Nagasaki in Japan, people in every continent now acknowledged him as their ruler. Persia, Rome, and China had built mighty regional empires; never before had an empire stretched across the world. The empire lasted only sixty years until Portugal regained its independence, but still, it was a symbol of Europe's sudden

worldwide impact—an impact that took different forms in different regions of the world.

The Americas: The Triumph of Europe

In the sixteenth century, the impact of the Europeans was felt above all in the Western Hemisphere. The confrontation between the Europeans and the Native Americans was a clash between the Old World and the New World in which the advantage was overwhelmingly on the side of the former.

Building Spain's Empire

After the era of conquest and plunder was over, the Spaniards undertook two tasks—of exploiting the wealth of the conquered lands, and of making them Christian. Like the Portuguese in the Indies, they, too, had a model to follow, but in their case, it was not Venice but the empire in which they had themselves been a subject nation more than a thousand years before—Rome.

Like the Romans in Spain, the Spanish settled in the Americas by tens of thousands, bringing with them their language and their way of life and founding cities on the model of the cities of their homeland. Like the Romans, they were willing to intermarry and share their way of life with the indigenous elite, and a colonial upper class of Spanish or Hispanicized townspeople and landowners grew up, while most of the indigenous population lived as unfree peasants subject to compulsory labor and tribute payments. Like the Roman emperors, the Spanish kings governed their empire through a relatively small number of aristocratic officials, chief among them the **viceroys** of New Spain and Peru—"viceroy" meaning "stand-in for the king," just as in Rome "proconsul" had meant "stand-in for a "consul" (p. 97). And the Spanish New World, like Roman Spain, was a source of immense wealth to its owners. Central American farmers produced valuable crops like tobacco, cocoa, and dyestuffs, and the silver mines of Peru helped make the Spanish kings the strongest in Europe.

Meanwhile, Spanish bishops and clergy attended to the conversion of the people to Christianity, using, in the New World, the same methods that bishops and clergy had used in the Roman Empire after the conversion of Constantine (p. 142). The shrines of gods and goddesses were destroyed or turned into churches, and other traditions deemed idolatrous, such as the ancient writing system of the Maya people of Central America, were abolished. Devoted missionaries preached to New World peoples demoralized by conquest and disease, and encouraged cults of local saints, both Spanish and indigenous. Towns were centers of Christianity from the start, and more gradually, missionaries, soldiers, and landowners enforced it in the villages as well.

As in Europe, many traditional beliefs and practices survived in more or less Christian guise, especially in the countryside. But from now on, the accepted, respectable, and official religion of Spain's New World empire was Catholic Christianity, just as its accepted, respectable, and official language and culture were Spanish. On the ruins of the indigenous civilizations, a variant of Western civilization grew up that has flourished down to the present day.

The exploitation of empire took a different course in the Caribbean islands and in the Portuguese territory of Brazil. These regions were thinly populated, and the Native Americans quickly succumbed to the maltreatment and disease of the invaders. They were replaced, over time, by millions of Africans brought to the Western Hemisphere as slaves, and for that reason, their history is closely linked with that of Africa.

An Ambassador's Report: The Costs of Wealth from the Indies Read an account of how the Spanish profited in New Spain

Spanish Colonial Art from the Denver Art Museum (http://www.denverartmuseum.org/explore_art/collections/collectionTypeId—90) See how the Christian art of Spain was transformed in the Americas.

A Dominican Voice in the Wilderness: Preaching Against Tyranny in Hispaniola Read how a missionary urged the Spanish to halt the mistreatment of Caribbean peoples.

> *"The Europeans held no massive advantage that would have enabled them, as a handful of newcomers, to undermine the Asian civilizations."*

Asia: The Limits of European Power

While the impact of the Europeans in the Western Hemisphere was catastrophic, in Asia it was at first hardly noticeable. The reason, once again, was that the peoples of Asia and Europe belonged to the same group of civilizations. The Europeans had most of their knowledge and skills, and even their diseases, in common with the peoples they encountered; in fact, the wealth of India and the statecraft of China, for example, were superior to their own. Thus, the Europeans held no massive advantage that would have enabled them, as a handful of newcomers, to undermine the Asian civilizations. Apart from the Spaniards in the Philippines, Europeans were unable to conquer and Christianize any Asian territories other than their tiny commercial footholds.

Missionaries like the Jesuit father (pp. 321-322) Francis Xavier traveled incredible distances and learned many languages to preach the gospel throughout the Indies. But without the help of conquering armies, cultural shock, and deadly diseases as in the New World, the success of Christianity depended on whether the local rulers tolerated, accepted, or rejected it.

China and Japan

At first, many rulers tolerated Christianity, partly because the missionaries also brought new technology and science in an era when Europe was, for the first time, gaining an edge in these fields over the other Old World civilizations. But as in pagan Rome (p. 134), Christianity rejected practices on which the rulers and the people believed that the good order of the state, society, and the universe depended—such as the honor due to Hindu gods and goddesses, the veneration of the Chinese and Japanese emperors as divine, and the Chinese practice of ancestor worship.

Around 1600, the Japanese rulers began systematic persecution in regions where Christianity had taken hold, and soon drove the new religion deep underground. Meanwhile, Jesuits in China convinced themselves that reverence for ancestors and the emperor were not the same as worshiping them as divine, so that converts need not give up these basic traditions of Chinese civilization. But early in the eighteenth century, the papacy rejected the Jesuit compromise, and the Chinese government responded by banning Christianity. In both China and Japan, every other kind of European activity was also strictly controlled—a sure sign that the rulers took the Europeans seriously as a potential source of disruption. It was not until the nineteenth century that

viceroy
In the Spanish colonies of the Americas, a high-ranking official who governed as a "stand-in for the king."

Western countries became strong enough to force the rulers to change their policies (pp. 462–463).

Africa and the Slave Trade

In the last major area of the world where the Europeans were newcomers, Africa south of the Sahara, they also encountered civilizations and cultures that they could not destroy. In West Africa, powerful Islamic states had existed for centuries, and at the time of the arrival of the Europeans, central and southern Africa were also advancing in prosperity and sophistication.

Stable governments and powerful tribal chiefdoms, centered on permanent capital cities like Timbuktu in western Africa or Zimbabwe in the southeast, were an increasingly common feature of the region. Iron, horses, and of course Old World diseases were more or less familiar throughout most of Africa. Even with their firearms, when Europeans tried to conquer black African nations, they were generally defeated. Thus, they had to treat the rulers of the region as partners to be dealt with on the basis of mutual interest, rather than as victims to be destroyed.

Above all, this mutual interest lay in trade. Black African rulers had traditionally built their power partly on the control of those resources of their region that were most highly valued in the outside world, namely, gold, ivory, and slaves. European traders had originally been attracted to Africa, above all, by the lure of gold, but following Venice's example, they soon began buying slaves to work on sugar plantations—in this case, located in various newfound islands of the Atlantic.

The African Slave Trade Make choices and experience consequences in this simulation about life in Africa during the fifteenth century.

Then, in the sixteenth century, the rulers of the new European empires in the Americas turned from plunder to developing new sources of wealth. In Brazil, the Caribbean, and North America, there was land suitable for growing not only sugar but also other profitable crops like tobacco, coffee, and later cotton; but there were few indigenous inhabitants who could be compelled to grow them. However, all along the Atlantic coast of Africa were densely populated regions with rulers who continually fought for control of the region's resources.

The result was the appearance of the most massive and systematic traffic in human beings that the world had ever seen: the African slave trade (Map 15.2). Between 1523, when the first Africans were shipped across the Atlantic, and the 1880s, when

the trade finally came to an end, at least 12 million people were transported from Africa to the Americas.

This was also the most systematically brutal of all forms of slavery. Captured by enemy warriors in the course of plundering their villages, the victims—mostly young men, though young women were also taken—were marched down to the nearest coastal trading station and sold to European (mainly Portuguese, English, and Dutch) dealers. They were packed lying on their backs into the holds of the slave ships for a voyage of many weeks: at least one in six could expect to die on the way. Once arrived and sold to a plantation owner, another one in three could expect to be dead of overwork and underfeeding within three years. But that did not matter to the owners. Until competition among traders drove up the price in the late eighteenth century, new slaves could always be bought cheaply from the African suppliers.

An Eyewitness Describes the Slave Trade in Guinea Read a Dutch captain's account of the slave trade on African soil.

An African Slave Relates His First Impressions upon Boarding a Slave Ship Read an African's account of conditions on a slave ship.

The Impact of the Slave Trade

For Africa, the result of the slave trade was a debilitating loss of human resources. Many other warlike and rapidly advancing societies, including that of medieval Europe (p. 195), had profited by selling captives to foreigners as slaves. But to do so on such a vast scale helped bring to an end several centuries of social and political development in black Africa. For the Americas, the result was a corresponding gain, especially from the late eighteenth century, when the African survival rate began to rise. In the end, a distinctively African element emerged in the culture of many nations from Brazil to the United States.

For the western European countries that ran the slave trade, the result was enormous profits that helped make them the economic center of the world. In addition, the unchecked exploitation of Africans led to the growth of the belief in white racial superiority and the related feeling that the rest of the world was at Europe's disposal to do with as it wished. It was these notions that helped fuel the intensive imperialism of the nineteenth and twentieth centuries (p. 459).

> " *Between 1523, when the first Africans were shipped across the Atlantic, and the 1880s, when the trade finally came to an end, at least 12 million people were transported from Africa to the Americas.* "

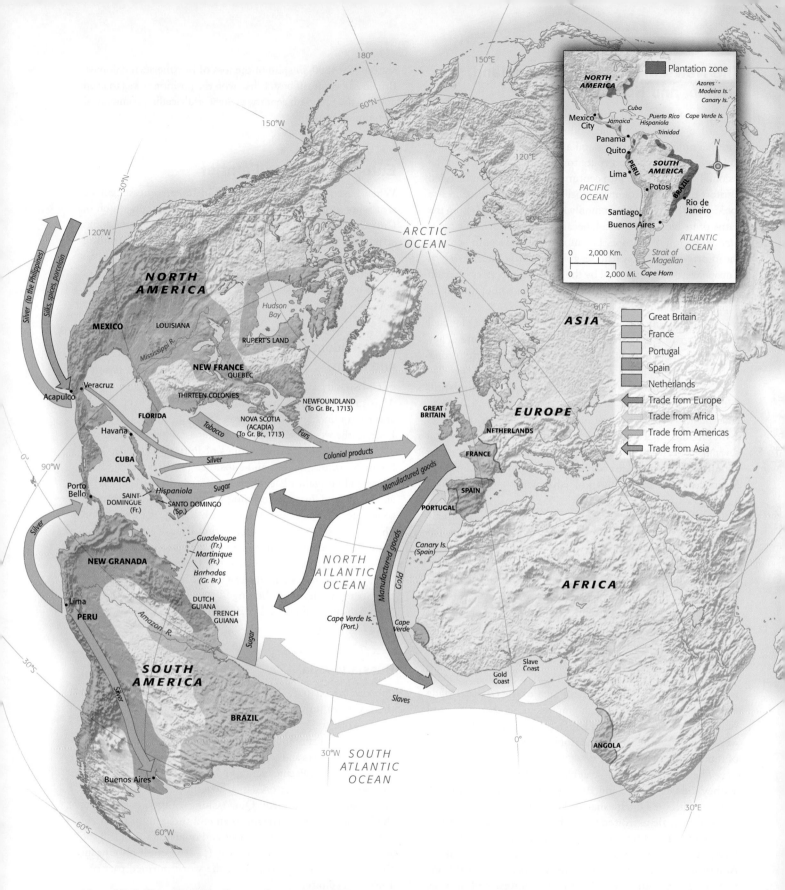

Map 15.2 **The Atlantic Economy about 1750**

A far-flung trading system has grown up across the western ocean. The system has three main components: the trade in sugar and tobacco from plantations in the eastern coastlands and islands of the Americas to Europe; the trade in slaves from western Africa to the Americas to work the plantations; and the trade in manufactured luxuries and necessities from Europe to the Americas and Africa in exchange for sugar, tobacco, and slaves. © Cengage Learning

Interactive Map

The New Empire Builders: England, France, and Holland

As soon as news of Columbus's and Vasco's successes arrived in Europe, the rulers, nobles, and merchants of the ambitious national monarchies of England and France began scheming to join in the search for a route to the Indies. Later on, in the second half of the sixteenth century, most of the Spanish-ruled territory of the Low Countries rebelled and won its independence (p. 324). The new state, commonly known as Holland (from the name of its largest province), became the most dynamic commercial nation of Europe. For most of the sixteenth century, the efforts of these powerful seagoing nations of northwestern Europe were overshadowed by the fabulous successes of Spain and Portugal. But three such competitors could not forever be kept on the sidelines.

Around 1600, the English, French, and Dutch redoubled their efforts to gain a share of world trade and empire. They explored the coastlines of North America and northern Europe, vainly searching for a "northwest" and "northeast passage"— routes to the Indies that would bypass the regions of the world controlled by Portugal and Spain, in the same way as those countries had bypassed Venice and Islam. (Though such routes do exist, they are too icebound to have been used by sixteenth- and seventeenth-century ships.) More successfully, the northwestern countries began to settle colonists in areas not yet occupied by Spain and Portugal, mainly in North America.

Europe's Worldwide Wars

In addition, the new competitors began to encroach on the trade and territories held by the Spanish and Portuguese themselves. An era of "world wars" began, in which European armies and navies fought for control of distant overseas lands (Map 15.3).

By the end of the seventeenth century, England, France, and the Netherlands had successfully stepped into the inheritance of Portugal and Spain. They dominated the trade of East Asia, and most of Portugal's possessions there were now in the hands of the Dutch or the English. They had taken over many Caribbean islands, and Dutch ships carried much of the overseas trade of the Portuguese and Spanish empires in South and Central America. English, French, and Dutch colonies in North America were thriving, with those of the English already harboring tens of thousands of settlers.

The three newcomers struggled as fiercely with each other as they did with Spain and Portugal. During the eighteenth century, with the Dutch exhausted by wars within Europe, the overseas struggle narrowed to one between France and Britain (the union formed by England and Scotland in 1707; p. 344). Every major eighteenth-century war, including those of the American and French Revolutions, was part of a worldwide conflict between these two most powerful western European nations. By 1800, in spite of the loss of its American colonies, Britain had come off best. It had won the position it was to keep down to the twentieth century, as the world's leading commercial and imperial nation.

Europe's Eastern Frontier

When Vasco da Gama first arrived in India, a messenger he sent ashore told local Arab merchants: "We came in search of Christians and spices"—in search of allies in Christendom's struggle with Islam as well as of intercontinental trading wealth. The explorers never found those religious allies, but all the same, by 1700 their efforts had helped shift the balance of power between Christendom and Islam, and Europe had broken out eastward on its land frontier as well as westward overseas.

Christendom and Islam

As a result of Spain's conquest and conversion of the peoples of the New World, the position of Christianity among the world's religions was transformed. After many centuries in which Christianity had been almost entirely confined within the narrow limits of Europe, it replaced Islam as the world's farthest-flung intercontinental religion.

In addition, the silver mines of Peru financed massive Spanish armies, navies, and subsidies to allies that helped Christendom against Islam in Europe itself. In 1571, Spain led an alliance of Christian seagoing states of the Mediterranean that defeated a Turkish fleet at the battle of Lepanto on Greece's western coast, ending a century of Ottoman naval domination of the Mediterranean. Likewise, Spanish money and troops stiffened resistance to the Turks in central Europe by the Austrian branch of the Habsburg dynasty to which the Spanish kings also belonged (p. 267). After 1600, the Ottomans pushed no farther into Europe, and by 1700, they were losing ground.

Russia in Asia

Farther north, the Russian tsars pursued their own Christian imperial mission (p. 252). In the sixteenth century, they conquered their Muslim former overlords, the Tartars, who lived on the borders of Europe and Asia. The vast eastward wilderness of Siberia, with a tiny indigenous population, was now open to Russian fur traders and settlers. By 1700, the tsar's rule stretched all the way to the Pacific Ocean, and Russians would soon enter the New World by way of Alaska. Together with contemporary conquests by the powerful Qing (Ching) emperors of China, the Russian advance brought to an end thousands of years of nomad domination of the steppes and nomad invasions of the settled peoples of Europe and Asia (p. 20). And it also meant that yet another huge region of the world formed part of a European empire.

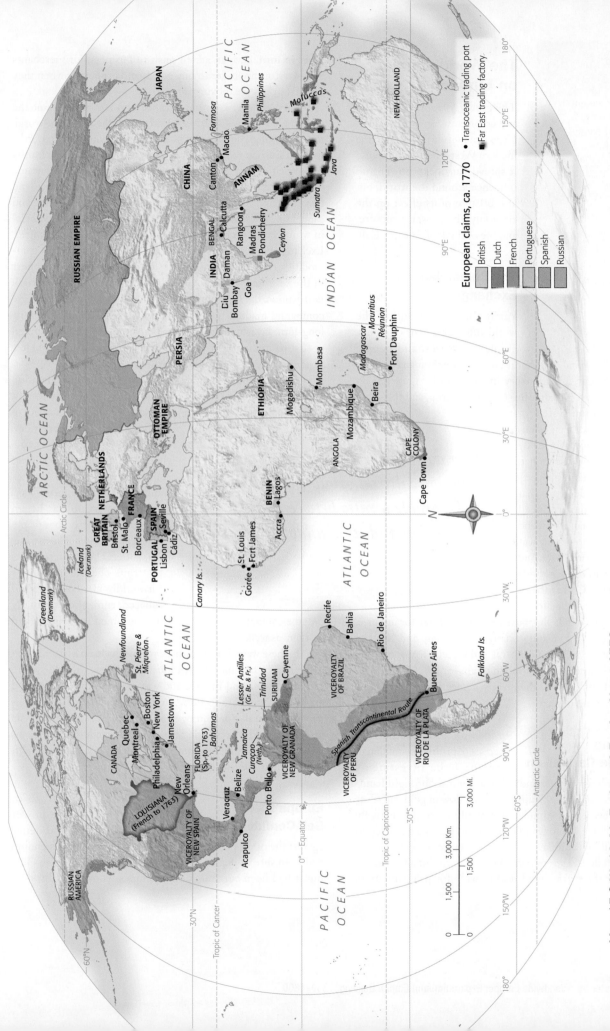

Map 15.3 Worldwide Trade and Empire About 1770

Three centuries after Columbus, European rule has spread through the Americas, Russia stretches eastward to Alaska, European trading footholds dot the coasts of Africa and Asia, and Britain has replaced Spain as the leading worldwide power. Soon there will be drastic changes in this global pattern centered on Europe: independence in the Americas, imperialistic conquest in the interior of Africa and Asia, and new centers of trade and empire in North America and East Asia. © Cengage Learning

European claims, ca. 1770

- British
- Dutch
- French
- Portuguese
- Spanish
- Russian

• Transoceanic trading port
■ Far East trading factory

Interactive Map

The World's Impact on Europe

The growth of worldwide trade and empire was one of the main forces that remade Europe into the modern West—not only because it spread European power and influence around the world, but also because of its effect on the economy, the power structure, and the outlook of Europe itself.

The Columbian Exchange

Partly this was a result of the worldwide movement of plants, animals, diseases, and people between the New and Old Worlds, which brought many changes to Europe. Sugar, a rare luxury in the Middle Ages, was an everyday item by 1700, after this Old World crop, and the slave-worked plantation system of cultivating it, had been established in the New World. By 1800, European peasants had taken to growing corn and potatoes—New World crops that were hardier and produced larger harvests than wheat and rye—and the population was growing faster than before. And this was only part of a worldwide process—the **Columbian Exchange**, as it is called today, because it began with Columbus's voyages. By 1800, for instance, "golden apples" had become a daily food in Italy and "fruit of Paradise" were common in central and eastern Europe, while in Iran people were eating "foreign plums" and in China, "barbarian eggplants"—all of them local names for another New World crop, tomatoes.

Europe and Worldwide Capitalism

In addition, as worldwide trade increased, profits accumulated; and the huge investments required for long voyages and colonial ventures brought handsome gains to bankers and capitalists. The flow of gold and silver from the New World stimulated general business activity. By 1600, the volume of money in existence in Europe had risen to nearly $1 billion (in today's terms). This larger supply of coins promoted trade and strengthened the incentive of all classes to produce for the market, and it also made for price inflation.

This, in turn, gave an added push to business, for merchants and investors are eager to buy goods and properties when they see that prices are moving upward.

Furthermore, as Britain, France, and Holland became the main trading gateways between Europe and the rest of the world, the center of prosperity and power shifted from Italy to northwestern Europe. Venice, Florence, and Milan were still wealthy trading cities, but Antwerp, Amsterdam, and London became the leading financial centers of expanding world commerce, and they took over as the leaders in the development of banking and capitalism. These cities had the first organized "money markets" in which large private and government loans were arranged. Exchange houses arose there for trade and speculation in commodities, currencies, bonds, and stocks. Stocks began to appear in the seventeenth century with the creation of **joint-stock companies**, the forerunners of the modern corporation; these companies made it possible to raise large sums of capital for long-term investment (see photo on page 257). Though limited at first to trading ventures, joint-stock companies were later formed in the mining and manufacturing industries.

The triumph of capitalism was assured by the acceleration of trade and production. The wealth of Europe mounted steadily, and the variety and quantity of goods increased with every day. New products and habits, formerly unknown in Europe, were introduced from both America and Asia. Oriental furnishings and exotic art objects began to appear in the homes of the privileged classes. Chinaware, tea, coffee, chocolate, and citrus fruits became necessities for middle-class people. And tobacco, rum, and eventually potatoes, tomatoes, and corn were consumed by peasants and workers as well.

In these ways, Europe, whose people made up a tiny fraction of humanity, became the headquarters of a worldwide system of trade, travel, and finance and was in a position to seize and exploit vast areas of the globe. In no other period of history has a major cultural group enjoyed so favorable a ratio between its population and its available resources. Although the Europeans were to squander this advantage on endless wars, it served to lift their standard of living and their sense of power.

> *"In no other period of history has a major cultural group enjoyed so favorable a ratio between its population and its available resources."*

Europe's New Self-Confidence

In addition, the growth of Europe's worldwide power increased its self-confidence against the other peoples of the world. Medieval Christendom had been sure of possessing the one truth about the one God, but it had been surrounded by peoples whose worldly skill, knowledge, and power were greater than its own. Now, Europe had not only spread its religion far and wide but had outdone the rest of the world in these nonreligious respects as well. For that matter, it had also outdone in worldly skill, knowledge, and power the non-Christian peoples of the past to whom even Christians had been accustomed to look upon with awe—the Greeks and Romans. This was not the first time that a people had felt itself superior to other peoples of the past and present, but it was the first time that this had happened on a worldwide scale.

 Listen to a synopsis of Chapter 15.

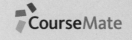 **Access to the eBook with additional review material and study tools may be found online at CourseMate for WCIV. Sign in at www.cengagebrain.com.**

CHAPTER 16

REVIVING THE PAST AND CHANGING THE PRESENT: THE RENAISSANCE, 1300–1600

LEARNING OBJECTIVES

AFTER READING THIS CHAPTER, YOU SHOULD BE ABLE TO DO THE FOLLOWING:

LO¹ Describe how Renaissance humanism offered a new set of values based on ancient models.

LO² Discuss how humanist ideals and the ancient past shaped the visual arts of the Renaissance.

LO³ Explain how humanist ideas were spread to a larger audience through vernacular literature.

> *"The best of Renaissance literature and art provides an ideal of beauty and an understanding of the human condition that will never cease to console and inspire."*

From about 1300 onward, scholars, thinkers, writers, and artists began taking to a new level the existing medieval habit of borrowing ideas and knowledge from ancient Greece and Rome. This endeavor began in Italy, but by 1600 most of the educated elite of western Europe had come to share in it. To those who took part in the endeavor, it seemed so exciting that they came to speak of literature, thought, and the arts as having been "reborn," and today we still call the movement by the French word for "rebirth"—the **Renaissance.**

The Renaissance involved far more than simply resurrecting the past, however, for there was no way that the admirers of Greece and Rome could separate themselves from the living civilization of their own day and age—the Western Christendom that had grown up in the Middle Ages. The Renaissance, in fact, was an encounter between Western Christendom and the Greek and Roman past—an encounter that brought about an extraordinarily diverse cultural achievement.

 Test your knowledge before you read this chapter.

What do you think?

The artists and thinkers of the Renaissance have had greater influence than any earlier age on the culture of today.

Strongly Disagree   Strongly Agree

| 1 | 2 | 3 | 4 | 5 | 6 | 7 |

Renaissance scholars rediscovered the ancient ideal of the fully developed human being whose character was formed by literary study and education, and traders and bankers, lords and ladies, and even popes and bishops tried to live up to this ideal. Thinkers looked for an ultimate truth that would reconcile the pagan wisdom of Greece and Rome with Christian faith, and sought to renew Christianity by bringing it back to its roots in the ancient world. Painters and sculptors used and improved on the methods of ancient artists to make saints and angels come alive before believers' eyes. Writers longed to "equal or surpass the ancients" in the beauty of their Latin style, but they wrote just as eloquently in French, English, and many other native languages of Europe. And most often, what they wrote about was the life and characters of their own or recent times—the hypocrisy and

≪ Scholars and Thinkers A painting by Domenico Ghirlandaio portrays four renowned leaders of the Renaissance in Florence about 1490. From left: Marsilio Ficino, reviver and adapter of the thought of Plato; Cristoforo Landino, writer on the much-discussed theme of the life of action versus the life of contemplation; Angelo Poliziano, scholar and poet in Greek, Latin, and Italian; Demetrius Chalcondylas, responsible for the first printed edition of Homer's *Iliad* and *Odyssey*.

Renaissance
From the French word for "rebirth," the term for the period beginning around 1300 when scholars, artists, and writers revived and adapted the traditions of the Greco-Roman past.

humanists
From the Latin *humanitas*, the word Renaissance scholars used to define themselves as seekers of human excellence through the study of Latin and Greek works.

virtù
Human excellence, as conceived by Italian humanists.

corruption of monks, for example, or the tragic flaws of an all too thoughtful prince of Denmark.

By reviving and adapting the traditions of the Greco-Roman past, however, the scholars, thinkers, writers, and artists of the Renaissance also changed the traditions of the European present—and thereby contributed in many ways to the remaking of Christian Europe into the modern West. Their efforts to renew Christianity helped bring about both the Protestant Reformation and the reform and reaffirmation of Catholicism. Their rediscovery of ancient mathematical knowledge and military tactics helped make possible the Western revolutions in science and warfare. Their ideals set precedents for basic cultural values of today—belief in the ennobling effect of education, literature, and art on the human personality; respect for unfamiliar ways of life and thought; and distrust of received wisdom and preconceived ideas. And though the writers and artists of the modern West have traveled far from the aims and methods of their Renaissance forerunners, the best of Renaissance literature and art provides an ideal of beauty and an understanding of the human condition that will never cease to console and inspire.

LO¹ The Humanist Enterprise

Throughout the Middle Ages, thinkers, writers, and scholars had looked up to "the ancients," as they called the Greeks and Romans, and had drawn on their achievements. Latin had never ceased to be the international language of Western Christendom, which most literate people knew well. Monks had carefully copied the works of Roman writers, and had sometimes imitated them in works of their own. Scholastic philosophers had leaned heavily on the thought of Aristotle. Dante told of being guided round the other world by Virgil; less high-minded readers had taken pleasure in the how-to poems on seduction of Ovid. But Renaissance scholars undertook to study and imitate the works of the ancients on an unprecedented scale, and actually to revive the way of thinking and living that they found in these works—above all, the values of what today is called *humanism*.

CHRONOLOGY

(time spans are life dates)

1266?–1337	Giotto, pioneering artist of the early Renaissance
1304–1374	Petrarch, poet and pioneer of humanist revival
1313–1375	Boccaccio, author of *Decameron* and humanist scholar
1377?–1446	Brunelleschi, architect and sculptor who revived the building traditions of ancient Rome and developed geometrical rules of perspective
1386?–1466	Donatello, pioneering sculptor of *The Feast of Herod* and statue of Gattamelata
1401–1428?	Masaccio, one of the first painters to apply Brunelleschi's rules of perspective
1440	Lorenzo Valla demonstrates that the Donation of Constantine is a forgery
1450	Cosimo de' Medici founds the Platonic Academy in Florence; scholars include Marsilio Ficino and Pico della Mirandola
1445–1510	Botticelli, Platonist and painter of *The Birth of Venus*
1447–1576	Titian, Venetian painter of *Venus of Urbino*
1452–1519	Leonardo, artist, inventor, and symbol of Renaissance ideal
1466?–1536	Erasmus, author of *In Praise of Folly* and corrected version of New Testament
1475–1564	Michelangelo, painter, sculptor, architect of Renaissance masterpieces
1490–1553	Rabelais, popular satirist whose works were condemned by authorities
1533–1592	Montaigne, influential French essayist and skeptic
1564–1616	Shakespeare, English playwright

The Appeal of Humanism

Cicero, the Roman orator, letter writer, thinker, and statesman (p. 108), had used the word *humanitas* as a shorthand term for the powers of reasoning, creation, and action that distinguish human beings from animals. Such human excellence, he thought, is best nurtured and expressed through literature (including his-

HUMANIST IDEALS APPEALED TO VARIOUS MEMBERS OF SOCIETY:

The Secular Elite

- Kings, nobles, bankers, and city-state despots hoped to imitate the elegance, refinement, and heroic achievements of the elite of Greece and Rome (see photo).

High-Ranking Clergy

- In an era when popes and bishops were also devoted to elegance, refinement, and worldly achievements, they, too, looked up the ancients with a new level of sympathy.

Middle Classes

- Middle-class people who could afford time and leisure for study had the satisfaction of feeling that their human excellence put them on a level with kings, nobles, bankers, despots, and bishops.

tory, philosophy, and oratory). Renaissance scholars, following Cicero's lead, took ancient Latin and Greek literature as a guide to human excellence, and accordingly, they described themselves as **humanists**.

This ideal of human excellence—*virtù*, as the Italian humanists called it—was generally earnest, high-minded, and optimistic about human nature. It overlapped with some traditional values of the Middle Ages, for example the ideal of the chivalrous warrior, but it ran counter to the ideal of the saintly ascetic and to the Christian view of the human race as utterly sinful and dependent on divine mercy. The new ideal certainly did not drive out the traditional ones. Many people rejected humanist values, and many people "compartmentalized," living as both humble and repentant Christians and self-confident imitators of the ancients.

In many ways, too, the urge to revive the ancients actually worked together with the urge to reinvigorate Christianity. Italian humanists often sought to combine Christian belief with ancient

(above, center) **The Triumph of Fame** The Florentine painter Giovanni Lo Scheggia depicts Fame as a living ancient Roman statue, greeted by horsemen in fifteenth-century war gear as trumpets sound fanfares in all directions. The scene appears on a birth tray—a souvenir tray presented by the father to the mother of the newborn Lorenzo de' Medici (p. 263) in 1449. It symbolizes his parents' Renaissance hope that he will gain fame, the reward of human excellence, as timeless and worldwide as that of the ancients. Image copyright © The Metropolitan Museum of Art/Art Resource, NY

ideals; humanists in other countries looked back to early Christianity, which had developed in the world of ancient Greece and Rome, as a model to which the Christianity of their own time should return. And artists throughout Europe used the lifelike methods of ancient art to give a new reality to the holy events and holy people they depicted. In these ways, humanist ideals helped bring change to Christianity—though they also sometimes acted as a substitute for it.

The Pioneers: Petrarch and Boccaccio

Humanism began in Italy in the fourteenth century—a land where trade, industry, finance, and city life were more highly developed than anywhere else in Europe, but also a land that felt keenly the problems and disasters of the late Middle Ages. The country was torn apart by the conflict between the Holy Roman emperors and the papacy; the popes themselves abandoned Rome, and when they returned, they were challenged by rival popes in France; factional rivalries and class conflicts made city-states almost ungovernable; and a quarter of the population was carried off by the Black Death.

What a difference from the days when the Roman ancestors of the Italians had ruled a vast empire as mighty warriors and self-sacrificing citizens, inspired to virtue and wisdom by splendidly eloquent thinkers, poets, and orators! Of course, Rome had also had plenty of corrupt rulers, class conflicts, epidemic diseases, and civil wars—and it had fallen in the end, as its ruined buildings in countless Italian cities testified. But in this dark time for medieval Italy, the thought of Rome's fall only made Italians more nostalgic for the bright side of the ancient past and more eager to revive its glories.

Petrarch

Francesco Petrarca (Petrarch) **(PEE-trahrk)**, the pioneer of the humanist revival of the past, was born in 1304 in an exiled Florentine family. Urged by his father to study law, he turned instead to a life of reading and writing, and eventually came upon some of Cicero's works. Surely, Petrarch thought, the pagan Cicero, with his eloquence, wisdom, and commitment to public life, was a better guide to human excellence than the Christian thinkers of his time, the schoolmen (p. 235), arguing in the universities over trivial details in pedantic technical Latin. Inspired by his encounter with Cicero, he began a quest to discover the world of ancient Roman authors who had been neglected, ignored, and forgotten, to imitate their Latin eloquence, and to adopt their values.

 **Letter to Posterity: Petrarch Writes His Autobiography** Read Petrarch's account of how he became a humanist.

Petrarch undertook a search for manuscripts in monastic and cathedral libraries all over Italy and in France and Germany as well. He arranged for the works he found to be copied, and built up his own collection of ancient works. His private library, the first of its kind, became a model for humanist scholars and well-to-do people who sympathized with their aims. Later humanists continued his search, so that by 1500 almost all the surviving ancient Roman works had been recovered—and were more widely available than ever before, thanks to printing.

In his own life, too, Petrarch identified with the ancients. Though he was a busy man and spent much of his time in cities and at the courts of aristocrats, he expressed a love of solitude and the peace of nature. But this was a different solitude from that of the hermit; it was closer to the model of the statesman and scholar Cicero. Petrarch spent his private hours not meditating and praying but studying literature; for isolation without books, he declared, was "exile, prison, and torture." And he took the ancient works he studied as models for his own works, writing poems, dialogues, and letters in Latin patterned after the style of Cicero and Virgil.

Yet Petrarch also carried on many traditions of the medieval world in which he lived. When he was growing up, Dante was still writing the *Divine Comedy*, and in some ways, Petrarch continued where Dante left off. He, too, wrote in Italian, most notably his love poems to Laura, a beautiful young married woman whom he idealized in the tradition of medieval courtly love, just as Dante had idealized Beatrice (p. 240). And Petrarch

> **"** *The greatest kings of this age have loved and courted me. They may know why; I certainly do not.* **"**
>
> —Petrarch, from his *Letter to Posterity*

was a devout Catholic, who firmly believed that love of the ancients and Christian faith belonged together. Among his beloved ancient writers was the early Christian thinker Augustine (p. 143)—who Petrarch claimed had been inspired to one of his great statements of Christian faith by reading Cicero. Nearly a thousand years before, another early Christian, Jerome, had believed himself to face a choice between being a Christian and a "Ciceronian." For Petrarch, a Ciceronian was actually the best kind of Christian.

Boccaccio

One of Petrarch's fourteenth-century followers, Giovanni Boccaccio **(boh-KAH-chee-oh)**, the son of a Florentine banker, also wrote Italian works that carried on medieval traditions. In his case, the traditions were the less high-minded kind that originated in fabliaux and Goliard poetry (pp. 237, 239). The characters in *The Decameron*, Boccaccio's best-known work, tell tales borrowed from various countries of Europe and the Islamic world, involving sensual escapades, deceits, and clever revenges.

But Boccaccio was also an earnest humanist scholar, who searched far and wide for ancient manuscripts like Petrarch. Among his prized discoveries was a work of the Roman historian Tacitus (p. 108), which he uncovered in the monastery library at Monte Cassino. When he first saw the neglected condition of the archives there, he burst into tears. And going beyond Petrarch, he also learned ancient Greek—a language only a few western European scholars had studied since Roman times. To be "learned in both languages" (Latin and Greek) remained an unusual accomplishment, but enough humanist scholars followed Boccaccio's example for most surviving ancient Greek works to be available in print by 1500.

Boccaccio also wrote in Latin—most notably, two collections of short biographies intended to provide edifying examples of virtue and vice, *On Famous Men* and *On Famous Women*. Collections of this kind dated back to ancient times, but Boccaccio was the first to write one dealing with women. His collection ran from Eve, through figures of ancient history and myth, to Queen Joan of Naples, a powerful fourteenth-century ruler. In this way, he put important women of his own time on the same level of extraordinary virtue and vice as those of the ancient past—and putting important people of the late Middle Ages on the same level as the ancients was one of humanism's main attractions.

Renaissance Ladies and Gentlemen

Petrarch's and Boccaccio's high valuation of ancient eloquence and virtue won them fame in their own time and soon spread through Italy, evidently because it answered a widely felt need.

By the early fifteenth century, leading Italian humanist scholars were celebrities, greeted by eager devotees of the revived ancient lore as they journeyed from town to town, and rewarded with influential positions as tutors to noble children and professors of rhetoric at universities.

Guarino da Verona and Vittorino da Feltre

One of the most notable humanist academics was Guarino da Verona, who studied Greek in Constantinople and was eventually appointed to the University of Ferrara, not far from Venice. His lectures drew enthusiastic students from all over Italy and the rest of Western Christendom—among them a pioneer of humanist education below the university level, Vittorino da Feltre.

In Mantua, another town near Venice, with the support of the local feudal lord, Vittorino opened a boarding school for boys that was so renowned for its kind treatment of students and its individual attention to their development that it was known as the "Pleasant House." Study of ancient authors and instruction in Latin eloquence were balanced by training in music and athletics. The students came from poor as well as wealthy families, and Vittorino aimed to turn them into young men who were mentally and physically able to live a life of fruitful citizenship inspired by wisdom and virtue, like the revered Roman and Greek ancients. But this ideal was combined with traditional Christian piety: Vittorino's students attended daily prayer services and regularly went to Mass.

> *"Battista and Federico were examples of a powerful new Renaissance ideal—the active, responsible, learned, elegant, and Christian lady and gentleman."*

member of a brotherhood of noble warriors founded by a fourteenth-century king of England and inspired by medieval tales of King Arthur and his knights—as well as a builder of elegant palaces in the latest, Roman-influenced architectural style. And he often stopped by a convent in the town of Urbino to hold uplifting religious discussions with the nuns.

His duchess, Battista Sforza (from the ruling family of Milan, p. 263), also combined eloquence and action. At the age of sixteen, she delivered a public speech in Latin before Pope Pius II, and the pope, who was himself a leading humanist scholar, found her performance "most elegant." And a neighboring lord who was Federico's enemy complained of how good she was at running the dukedom in her husband's absence: "This woman definitely has too much wisdom and foresight—enough to rule the kingdom of France!" Battista and Federico were examples of a powerful new Renaissance ideal—the active, responsible, learned, elegant, and Christian lady and gentleman.

Like all ideals, this one was hard to put into practice. Duke Federico could sometimes be very ungentlemanly—for instance, when he gave underhand support to an abortive plot to murder the ruler of Florence, Lorenzo de' Medici. Not that he had anything personal against Lorenzo, but in the political situation in Italy at the time, the Florentine despot's elimination seemed a sound business move. On a less sinister level, Baldassare Castiglione, a nobleman whose book *The Courtier*, published

Duke Federico and Duchess Battista

Among Vittorino's students was a noble boy, Federico da Montefeltro, who went on to become duke of Urbino, near Florence, from the 1440s to the 1480s (see photo). Duke Federico was a battle-winning condottiere (p. 263) and a splendid Latin orator, a careful administrator of his dukedom and a collector of a huge library of ancient and medieval learning. He was a Knight of the Garter—a

>> **Battista Sforza and Federico da Montefeltro** Renaissance portraits of married couples generally put the husband "first"—on the viewer's left—and the wife "second"—on the right. But in this portrait from about 1470 by the Florentine painter Piero della Francesca, the order is reversed. Otherwise, the right side of Federico's face would be visible, and Piero would have had to falsify the portrait by painting in Federico's missing right eye, poked out by an opponent's lance in a tournament in his youth.
Scala/Ministero per i Beni e le Attivita culturali/Art Resource, NY

in 1528, became the standard work on how to live the gentlemanly and ladylike ideal, found it necessary to warn courtiers who attended banquets not to start food fights. But the ideal's widespread appeal, to middle-class women and men as well as to nobles, guaranteed it a long future.

Humanist Thought: Back to Plato

Now that humanist scholars had direct access to ancient Greek thought, they began to pay attention to other philosophers besides Aristotle—most notably, to Plato (pp. 73–76). Aristotle still ruled in the universities because his methods of logic were so useful to scholastic thinkers. But ever since Petrarch, humanists had despised the schoolmen as quibblers without real wisdom, and besides, Plato had a quality that humanists deeply admired and Aristotle definitely lacked—eloquence. Here was philosophy that was at the same time literature and literature that was philosophy. For the humanists, Plato became the new master.

The New "Academy"

Florence was the leading center for Platonic studies. Cosimo de' Medici, yet another learned Renaissance ruler, founded the Platonic Academy there about 1450. The Academy served as a center for the translation of Plato's writings and discussions of his philosophy. Named after Plato's own circle of disciples, it consisted of only a few select scholars, subsidized by the Medici, and their circle of friends. Yet, the influence of the Academy was widely felt—in art, in literature, in science, and in the Renaissance undertaking of reconciling Christianity with pagan wisdom.

Nicolo Nicoli: A Humanist's Passion for the Classics Read about the humanist Nicolo Nicoli, friend of Cosimo de' Medici.

Marsilio Ficino was the shining light of the Academy (see photo on page 286). Chosen by Cosimo at an early age, he was carefully educated and then installed in a villa in the hills near Florence. From that time until his death, he devoted himself to translating Plato's writings and explaining his doctrines. He presided over polite seminars at the villa and corresponded with notables all over Europe, seeking to demonstrate that Platonic teachings were in agreement with Christianity.

Pico della Mirandola, a disciple of Ficino, went beyond his master and attempted a synthesis (a bringing together) of all learning. This genius of the age knew Arabic and Hebrew as well as Greek and Latin, and he studied Jewish, Babylonian, and Persian writings. He refused to ignore any source of truth merely because it was not labeled "Christian," and he emphasized human freedom and capacity for learning.

> *"For the humanists, Plato became the new master."*

> *"Whatever seeds each man cultivates will grow to maturity and bear in him their own fruit."*
> —Pico della Mirandola from "Oration on the Dignity of Man"

All the same, he believed, like Plato, that humans had become separated from their divine home of pure spirit by some accident of prehistory. Though each soul (spirit) had fallen prisoner to matter (the body), it struggled for liberation and a return to God. This view corresponded to the Christian doctrine of the Fall and the human longing for salvation.

A Renaissance Oration on Human Dignity (Mirandola) Read Mirandola on human nature.

Platonism, Art, and Science

Platonic beliefs also deeply influenced Renaissance art. The feeling for natural beauty, said the Platonists, came from the soul's remembrance of the divine beauty of heaven, and the emotion of physical love was part of a higher urge that moves humans toward the divine source of their being. According to the Florentine intellectuals, art stimulates appreciation of beauty, and love brings the individual closer to the ultimate goal of spiritual reunion with God. Some of the finest Renaissance artists, notably Botticelli and Michelangelo, were absorbed by this idea. And in science, the Platonic notion that the soul may ascend to God by contemplating the visible universe helped inspire the Polish astronomer Nicholas Copernicus to place the sun, which lights the universe, at the center, rather than the earth (p. 358).

Observation and Facts

The manuscripts of ancient writers that Petrarch, Boccaccio, and others collected were the latest of many generations of copies and were liable to contain many generations of copying errors—the results of slips of the pen or of misunderstandings of their meaning. With their deep knowledge of the ancient languages and cultures, humanists were often able to correct these errors and arrive at texts that were closer to what the ancient authors had originally written. This, as well as their rejection of scholasticism, with its system of knowledge based on authority and reason, led them to a more critical attitude toward the written word and greater attention to observed facts. Eventually, many later thinkers came to look for truth by observation, as well as by the related method of experiment (p. 360).

Lorenzo Valla

One of the most notable triumphs of humanist knowledge of ancient languages and cultures was Lorenzo Valla's demonstration in 1440 that the Donation of Constantine was a forgery. This document, according to which the fourth-century Roman emperor Constantine handed over vast powers to Pope Sylvester before leaving Rome to build a new capital at Byzantium, had served for centuries as a basis for papal claims to secular supremacy over the West. Valla showed, however, that the Latin language of the Donation could not have been that of the fourth century but was more likely that of the eighth or ninth century. Furthermore, the document did not square with Valla's humanist knowledge of the period when it was supposed to have been issued. For instance, Constantine declares that the pope shall have supremacy over all "patriarchs," including the one at "Constantinople." How could this be, asked Valla, when at that time, Constantinople was not yet a city and had no patriarch?

Valla had no intention of attacking the religious claims of the popes as rulers of the Church, and Pope Nicholas V—himself a humanist, who founded the Vatican Library as a depository for ancient manuscripts—thought so highly of Valla that he brought him to Rome to translate the ancient Greek historian Thucydides into Latin (p. 71). Still, his exposé stirred a good deal of indignant disagreement. As late as the 1520s, Pope Leo X took the donation as genuine and had his private apartment decorated with a scene of the emperor humbly kneeling before the pope as he made his donation (see photo on page 142). But then Protestants started using Valla's work as ammunition against the papacy, and soon Catholics, too, accepted that it was false.

> *"And for what, after all, do men petition the saints except for foolish things?"*
> —from Erasmus, *In Praise of Folly*

Machiavelli and Leonardo da Vinci

The method of judging the genuineness of a document by the test of known facts had many other applications. Niccolò Machiavelli, basing his view of government and the state on recorded history and personal experience (pp. 265–267), used essentially the same method. So did the painter Leonardo da Vinci, who improved his skill in drawing human and animal bodies by dissecting cadavers and making on-the-spot sketches and comments in notebooks. He found dissection difficult and distasteful, but he insisted that observation was the only means to true knowledge. He also experimented with mechanics and drew up plans for ingenious practical inventions. A man of his times, Leonardo both typified Italian humanism and foreshadowed the age of observation and experiment.

"Universal Leonardo" (http://www.universalleonardo.org/index.php) Discover the wide-ranging interests and investigations of Leonardo.

Humanism and Christian Practice: Erasmus

From 1400 onward, wealthy and educated people in every country of Western Christendom began to take notice of the Italian revival of the ways of thought and life of the ancients.

Scholars journeyed to the Italian centers of learning to learn eloquence and study Greek; leading Italian humanists became internationally famous and were invited to royal courts; Italian diplomats and representatives of banking firms brought word of the "rebirth" to the countries where they were stationed. By 1500, many countries beyond the Alps were home to humanist scholars who rivaled the Italians.

However, scholasticism was still vigorous in many of these countries, and university faculties often looked with disdain upon the humanist reverence for pagan literature and art. Some Oxford masters condemned humanist studies as "dangerous and damnable"—dangerous, that is, to the proper understanding and practice of Christianity. Devout Italian humanists like Petrarch had argued that ancient wisdom and Christian faith were two sides of the same coin. Less devout Italians had delighted too much in the rediscovered ancient lore to bother with its implications for Christianity at all. But humanists outside Italy, who were more likely to be denounced as un-Christian, threw the charge back at their opponents and claimed that it was they who had distorted Christianity.

The most influential of these humanist religious critics was a Dutchman, Erasmus (**uh-RAZ-muhs**) of Rotterdam. Born in 1466, as the out-of-wedlock son of a priest, he went to a school that was supervised by an order of devout laymen, the Brethren of the Common Life. The Brethren offered what seemed to them a purer alternative to traditional practices like devotion to the saints, veneration of their relics, and indulgences (pp. 205–207). These practices had always been open to abuse—by clergy who used them for moneymaking, and by believers who expected from them salvation without real repentance. Instead, the Brethren offered a pious, mystical Christianity, and taught that individual lives should be modeled on the example of Jesus. While subjecting themselves to rigid spiritual discipline, they also emphasized service and love. Erasmus was deeply touched by this early influence, and he adopted the "philosophy of Christ" as his lifetime ideal.

Retrieving Christian Truth

After school, Erasmus entered a monastery, but he soon left and took to the hand-to-mouth life of a wandering scholar. For years, he lived off tutoring jobs and handouts from friends, while he taught himself Greek, studied pagan and Christian ancient authors, and developed a forceful and humorous writing style in Latin—the language of all his books. Finally, he began to make a name for himself as an exceptionally learned humanist, and this gave him the standing to comment on religious and social issues of the time. Thanks to the new technology of printing, his books were bestsellers, and he became famous throughout Europe—deeply admired by some and deeply distrusted by others.

Like Petrarch, Erasmus was sure that true Christianity and pagan wisdom belonged together; in fact, he expressed this idea even more strongly. A character in one of his books invoked the Greek thinker Socrates with the words "Saint Socrates, pray for us!" Earlier Christians had revered Socrates and had even claimed him as a fellow believer because he had been put to death for doubting the pagan gods and goddesses, but no one before Erasmus had ever put an ancient philosopher among the saints. By doing so, Erasmus meant to say that what made a person holy was not by-the-book observance of the traditions and beliefs that had grown up in the Church over the centuries. Instead, it was love of truth and devotion to God—on which baptized Christians did not have a monopoly.

Erasmus did not doubt that the highest truth had been brought by Christ, but he also believed that Christians had forgotten or neglected Christ's message, or hidden it beneath layers of new beliefs and practices—just as the way of living and thinking of the pagan ancients had been forgotten, neglected, or distorted over time. And as with the works of pagan ancients, one way to get back to the original truth of Christianity was to purify its earliest writings of errors that had crept in over the centuries—above all, into the New Testament, which had originally been written in Greek.

Erasmus spent many years preparing a corrected version of the New Testament, which he published in 1516, along with his own Latin translation and commentary. This, he hoped, would lead to a clearer understanding of Christ's message—not only by the learned, but also by the unlearned, who would read or hear the message in translation. "Christ wanted his counsel and his mysteries to be spread around as much as possible," he wrote. "I would like all women to read the gospel . . . and I wish to God it was translated into the languages of all peoples. I wish to God that the plowman would sing a text of scripture at his plow beam, and that with this the weaver at his loom would drive boredom away."

Foolishness in Religion and Society

In addition, Erasmus learned from an ancient writer the use of mockery to drive his message home. He read with delight and translated into Latin the Greek works of Lucian of Samosata (p. 109), who had made a specialty of mocking every kind of pretentiousness and superstition in imperial Rome. Erasmus's most widely read work, *In Praise of Folly* (1509), did the same for the Europe of his own time. He portrayed Folly ironically as an all-powerful goddess, whose worshipers include warriors who think their bloody deeds are glorious, noblemen with nothing to be proud of but their family trees, and believers who pray to the saints to cure their toothaches or find their lost property but never dream of imitating the saints' holy way of life. It is Folly, in fact, who makes the wicked world go round.

 **Pope Julius II Excluded from Heaven (Erasmus)** Read Erasmus's attack on a worldly pope.

Sometimes, Erasmus could be much more explicit, as in an essay inspired by an ancient Roman saying about money-grubbers, "They demand tribute even from the dead":

You can't be baptized . . . without paying for it. . . .
They won't bless your marriage unless you pay;

they only hear your confession because they hope to make money from it. . . . They won't communicate the Body of Christ, except for money. . . . Among the pagans . . . there was at least a place where you could bury your dead without having to pay. Among Christians . . . if you have paid a great deal, you may lie and rot in the church in front of the high altar; if you have given stingily, you can be rained on with the common herd outside.

"They" were greedy clergy whom Erasmus accused of turning the salvation-bringing sacraments of the Church into a cradle-to-grave system for extracting money from the Christian faithful. In a thousand years of denunciation of Church corruption, no one had said anything more powerful.

Erasmus was not the only humanist to criticize both Christian practice and the social order. A few years after *In Praise of Folly*, his English friend Sir Thomas More published *Utopia*, a description of an invented island in the western ocean that revived Plato's tradition of imagining an ideal society where the problems of actual ones were all solved (pp. 73–75). The people of Utopia avoid oppression and class conflict by holding no private property; the men and women are educated alike so that all can develop their human excellence to the fullest; and they avoid religious persecution and war by tolerating all beliefs except atheism.

More's book was not a serious blueprint for social and religious change. Its title was a play on the similar-sounding Greek words for "Good place" and "No place," hinting that his description of a good society was pure fiction. Later on, as a high government official when the Protestant Reformation was getting under way, he supported the burning of heretics, and in the end, he laid down his own life rather than swear loyalty to the king as head of the English Church. Likewise, neither the Church nor society was much changed by Erasmus's sharp words. He wanted a purified Church, not a divided one, and when the Reformation started, he was just as critical of Protestant rage and violence as of Catholic greed and superstition.

All the same, Erasmus and More proclaimed a whole series of inspiring ideals—faith combined with toleration, religion cleansed of superstition, truth shared among all classes of society, peaceful achievement more admired than warlike deeds, society itself structured to avoid conflict and oppression. These were ideals by which future generations would come to judge themselves.

LO² The Renaissance in Art: Ancient Models for Modern Needs

In the visual arts, as in literature and thought, the Renaissance began in fourteenth-century Italy—in this case, in response to religious trends of the time. It was an era when clergy were stressing the human side of Christ and the saints, and Gothic sculptors in France had already made statues of saints that showed their emotions and interactions as they took part in holy events of Christian tradition (p. 231). Now it was the turn of Italian artists to make depictions so life-like that they gave worshipers the feeling of being actual eyewitnesses of holy events, or even participants themselves. And in a land where so many Roman works of art survived, painters and sculptors soon began to turn to the ancient artists for models of lifelike depiction.

"Painting Restored to Life": Giotto

The pioneer of this new trend was the Florentine painter Giotto di Bondone, whose innovations brought him instant success and lasting fame. Prominent citizens, feudal lords, and above all the Franciscan friars, with their urge to involve people deeply in Christian belief and practice (pp. 208–209), ordered his works. Petrarch called Giotto (**JOT-toh**) a "genius," and more than a century later, another humanist scholar, Angelo Poliziano (see photo on page 286), wrote an inscription for his monument in Florence's cathedral: "Lo, I am he by whom dead painting was restored to life, to whose unerring hand all was possible, by whom art became one with nature."

A notable example of Giotto's methods of touching the hearts of worshipers is his *Lamentation* (see photo), one of thirty-seven scenes, mainly from the lives of Christ and the Virgin Mary, that he painted about 1305 on the inside walls of the newly built Arena Chapel in Padua, a town near Venice. The painting shows the Virgin Mary and some of Christ's followers in dramatic attitudes of grief as they mourn over the body of the crucified Savior. They stare into his face as if for a sign of life, touch his hands

> "*Giotto began a practice that generations of Renaissance artists continued—using methods of ancient art to create works that were uniquely their own and belonged to their time.*"

and feet as if they cannot let go of him, and show their grief in other lifelike ways, while the sky above is turbulent with mourning angels. Two of Christ's followers are seen from the back, a favorite device of Giotto's to give the feeling that a scene is really taking place before the viewer's eyes. What also gives this feeling is the clothing of the mourners, which hangs from their bodies in realistic folds, so that they seem solid and weighty although they are painted on a flat surface.

The details of the gestures and the clothing in the *Lamentation* come from Giotto's own imagination. However, he is known to have studied surviving Roman stone coffins with scenes from pagan mythology carved on them, as well as Bible scenes on the walls of churches dating from the time that Rome became Christian. Pagan or Christian, the ancient artists had used dramatic gestures and folds in clothing to depict solid figures expressing real emotions. In this way, Giotto began a practice that generations of Renaissance artists continued—using methods of ancient art to create works that were uniquely their own and belonged to their time.

Surpassing the Ancients: Brunelleschi, Masaccio, Donatello

Early in the fifteenth century, visual artists came under the direct influence of the burgeoning humanist movement—not only in painting, but in architecture and sculpture as well. The highest praise that humanist scholars awarded to a work of literature or art that pleased them was to say that it not only "equaled" but actually "surpassed the ancients." That was what fifteenth-century artists in some ways actually achieved.

Humanist Architecture: Brunelleschi

Among those who did so was a Florentine architect and sculptor, Filippo Brunelleschi (**broon-el-ES-kee**), who revived the building traditions of imperial Rome. In the Santo Spirito (Holy Spirit) Church in Florence (see photo on page 296), the columns and arches do not reach

≪ *"Dead Painting Restored to Life"* In his *Lamentation of Christ,* Giotto uses ancient techniques of arranging figures in groups and creating a three-dimensional appearance so as to create an image of overwhelming sorrow. His work also has roots in the medieval past, however—he has found a way to reproduce in two dimensions the naturalism and human interaction of Gothic sculpture (see photo on page 230).

SIR THOMAS MORE ON POWER POLITICS VERSUS GOOD POLICY

In this excerpt, the explorer of the New World island of Utopia (Greek for "No-place" or "Good-place"), Raphael Hythlodaeus ("Good-at-gabbing"), is speaking to More himself, who makes a brief comment at the end. Raphael contrasts the power politics of France with the good policy of Achoria ("Non-country"), a kingdom near Utopia that has given up foreign conquest.

The lands and cities that Raphael mentions to begin with are places in Italy, the Low Countries, and Spain that the French king wants to dominate. The royal advisers' suggestions include giving pensions (regular payments) to captains of German and "Switzer" (Swiss) mercenary soldiers, as well as to courtiers of foreign rulers. Sir Thomas More was an experienced diplomat himself, and his portrayal of French aims and methods is lifelike.

"Do not you think that if I were about any king, proposing good laws to him, and endeavoring to root out all the cursed seeds of evil that I found in him, I should either be turned out of his court or at least be laughed at for my pains? For instance, what could it signify if I were about the King of France, and were called into his Cabinet Council, where several wise men, in his hearing, were proposing many expedients, as by what arts and practices Milan may be kept, and Naples, that had so oft slipped out of their hands, recovered; how the Venetians, and after them the rest of Italy, may be subdued; and then how Flanders, Brabant, and all Burgundy, and some other kingdoms which he has swallowed already in his designs, may be added to his empire. One proposes a league with the Venetians, to be kept as long as he finds his account in it, and that he ought to communicate councils with them, and give them some share of the spoil, till his success makes him need or fear them less, and then it will be easily taken out of their hands. Another proposes the hiring the Germans, and the securing the Switzers by pensions. Another proposes the gaining the Emperor by money, which is omnipotent with him. Another proposes a peace with the King of Aragon, and, in order to cement it, the yielding up the King of Navarre's pretensions. Another thinks the Prince of Castile is to be wrought on, by the hope of an alliance; and that some of his courtiers are to be gained to the French faction by pensions. The hardest point of all is what to do with England: a treaty of peace is to be set on foot, and if their alliance is not to be depended on, yet it is to be made as firm as possible; and they are to be called friends, but suspected as enemies: therefore the Scots are to be kept in readiness, to be let loose upon England on every occasion:

Nicholas Sapieha/Art Resource, NY

upward to a vault as in medieval churches; instead, they march forward under a flat ceiling, on the model of churches that were built after Rome became Christian (see photo on page 113). And Brunelleschi followed the advice of Roman works on architecture written in pagan times, which stressed that all the dimensions of a building—its overall length, breadth, and height, as well as details such as the height and spacing of columns—must be related to each other in a harmonious system of proportion.

But Brunelleschi did all this for the same purpose as Gothic architects—to make his church reflect the harmony of the universe, and thereby give a glimpse of the mind of the universe's Creator. And in his most famous design, he used the Gothic methods of stone ribs and a pointed shape to raise the great dome of Florence's cathedral far higher than any Roman dome-builder could have imagined possible (see photo).

≪ **A Renaissance Church.** Of several churches that Brunelleschi designed, Santo Spirito is closest to his idea of what a religious building should look like. The church revives both Christian and pagan architectural traditions of ancient Rome and adapts them to the needs of fifteenth-century Florence.

and some banished nobleman is to be supported underhand (for by the league it cannot be done avowedly) who had a pretension to the crown, by which means that suspected prince may be kept in awe.

"Now when things are in so great a fermentation, and so many gallant men are joining councils, how to carry on the war, if so mean a man as I should stand up, and wish them to change all their councils, to let Italy alone, and stay at home, since the Kingdom of France was indeed greater than could be well governed by one man; that therefore he ought not to think of adding others to it: and if after this, I should propose to them the resolutions of the Achorians, a people that lie on the southeast of Utopia, who long ago engaged in war, in order to add to the dominions of their prince another kingdom, to which he had some pretensions by an ancient alliance. This they conquered, but found that the trouble of keeping it was equal to that by which it was gained; that the conquered people were always either in rebellion or exposed to foreign invasions, while they were obliged to be incessantly at war, either for or against them, and consequently could never disband their army; that in the meantime they were oppressed with taxes, their money went out of the kingdom, their blood was spilt for the glory of their King, without procuring the least advantage to the people, who received not the smallest benefit from it even in time of peace; and that their manners being corrupted by a long war, robbery and murders everywhere abounded, and their laws fell into contempt; while their King, distracted with the care of two kingdoms, was the less able to apply his mind to the interests of either.

"When they saw this, and that there would be no end to these evils, they by joint councils made an humble address to their King, desiring him to choose which of the two kingdoms he had the greatest mind to keep, since he could not hold both; for they were too great a people to be governed by a divided king, since no man would willingly have a groom that should be in common between him and another. Upon which the good prince was forced to quit his new kingdom to one of his friends (who was not long after dethroned), and to be contented with his old one. To this I would add that after all those warlike attempts, the vast confusions, and the consumption both of treasure and of people that must follow them; perhaps upon some misfortune, they might be forced to throw up all at last; therefore it seemed much more eligible that the King should improve his ancient kingdom all he could, and make it flourish as much as possible; that he should love his people, and be beloved of them; that he should live among them, govern them gently, and let other kingdoms alone, since that which had fallen to his share was big enough, if not too big for him. Pray how do you think would such a speech as this be heard?"

"I confess," said I, "I think not very well."

EXPLORING THE SOURCE

1. Does More want you to get the impression that cynical power politics is a special feature of France?

2. Why do Raphael and Moore both think that the French king and his advisers wouldn't welcome advice to change to Achoria's policy?

Source: Thomas More, "Dialogue of Counsel," in *Ideal Commonwealths: Comprising More's Utopia, Bacon's New Atlantis, Campanella's City of the Sun, and Harrington's Oceania*, introd. Henry Morley (New York: Colonial Press, 1901), pp. 22–24.

Florence Cathedral Medieval and Renaissance styles combine in a majestic and harmonious group of buildings. A late-thirteenth-century architect, Arnolfo di Cambio, designed the nave exterior in Romanesque style. The interior, and Giotto's fourteenth-century bell tower, are Gothic. The fifteenth-century dome, designed by Filippo Brunelleschi, is 375 feet high including the lantern (the structure on top)—nearly 200 feet higher than its tallest ancient predecessor, Justinian's Hagia Sophia (see photo on page 159).

Vanni Archives/Corbis

Fooling the Eye: Masaccio

That was not the only way in which Brunelleschi improved on ancient models. He also devised an accurate system of **perspective**—of depicting three-dimensional scenes on a flat surface. The new system used exact geometrical rules to determine how the size and shape of objects should change, depending on how far away they are supposed to be from the viewer and on the angle at which the viewer is supposed to be looking at them. Like so many other late medieval inventions, this one was based on knowledge that came from outside Europe—in this case, discoveries by Muslim scientists in the basic geometry of light and vision. The result was that Renaissance artists could give a three-dimensional look to their paintings that was more convincing than ancient artists had ever been able to manage.

One of the first painters to use the new system was Brunelleschi's friend Masaccio **(muh-SAH-chee-oh)**. In 1427, in the Church of Santa Maria Novella (New Saint Mary's) in Florence, he painted the Holy Trinity with the Virgin Mary, Saint John, and the donors of the painting—the wealthy citizens who paid for it (see photo). The subject matter was common enough, but Masaccio followed Brunelleschi's rules to give a "real-life" view of the donors kneeling outside the Roman-style arch and columns, the figures grouped round the crucified Christ and God the Father just inside them, and the high vault fading into the background. As viewers stood back from the wall, they must have gasped at what seemed to be a group of sculptured

Alinari/Art Resource, NY

Surpassing the Ancients Countless late medieval pictures showed scenes like this one, but Masaccio's version (about 1425) is framed by correctly designed ancient columns and an arch like those of Brunelleschi (see photo on page 296). Masaccio has also followed Brunelleschi's rules of perspective to give a "real-life" view of the scene. No ancient artist could create such a convincing illusion of height and distance.

figures placed outside and inside a hollow space in the church's wall.

Humanist Sculpture: Donatello

About the same time as Masaccio painted his three-dimensional scene, another friend of Brunelleschi, the sculptor Donatello, made *The Feast of Herod* as part of the baptismal font (holy-water basin for christenings) of the cathedral in the nearby city of Siena (see photo above). Donatello shows the climax of a Bible story: the Jewish King Herod, at the urging of his stepdaughter Salome, has ordered the beheading of John the Baptist, the forerunner and baptizer of Christ, because John

≪ **The Feast of Herod** Donatello's bronze relief was made about the same time as Masaccio's wall painting (see photo above). Like the painting, it uses perspective to make the scene more lifelike and has a background of Roman arches and columns. In Giotto's tradition, it is a dramatic scene with individual figures expressing similar emotions—in this case, disgust and horror—in different ways. Scala/Art Resource, NY

Gattamelata The Venetian condottiere Erasmo da Narni acquired the nickname "Gattamelata," meaning "Honey-sweet Cat," on account of his combination of a mild manner, sweet talk, and deep cunning, which enabled him to take unwary fellow condottieri by surprise in negotiation and war—activities that often went together. In this statue, Donatello turned the "Honey-sweet Cat" into an updated version of an ancient Roman emperor.
Scala/Art Resource, NY

excellence of an important man by placing a statue of him in a public space. Twenty years after *The Feast of Herod*, Donatello won a commission to make a statue of Gattamelata, a leading condottiere who had recently died in Padua. Donatello's model for Gattamelata's monument was a famous ancient statue of the emperor Marcus Aurelius in Rome, which shows him as a weaponless philosopher-ruler restraining an eager mount (see photo on page 115). But since Marcus's time, the world had changed, and Donatello's statue shows a heavily armed and armored soldier astride a ponderous charger. Donatello revived the Roman sculptors' practice of emphasizing a man's power and dignity by putting him on the back of a horse, but he changed the ancient image of peaceful rule over a vast empire into one of warlike power in a land of competing city-states.

Portraits, Nudes, and Ancient Myths: Botticelli, Leonardo

Later in the fifteenth and in the early sixteenth centuries, humanism opened up to artists a whole range of revived ancient art forms, including portraits of individual people, the naked human body, and scenes of Greek and Roman mythology.

The Female Nude: Modest and Erotic Venuses

Sandro Botticelli (**bot-i-CHEL-ee**), a fifteenth-century Florentine, did much of his work for the Medici rulers and was very much influenced by the Platonism of their Academy. Earthly beauty, said the Platonists, was a reflection of divine beauty, and the human love of beauty came from the longing for the ideal world beyond everyday appearances. In ancient times, poets had sometimes praised the love goddess, Venus, not as an erotic being but as an image of divine beauty, and sculptors had developed a tradition of carving the nude Venus so that her nakedness was divine and noble rather than alluring—a "modest Venus." Renaissance poets had revived this tradition, and Botticelli expressed it in visual form in his most famous work, *The Birth of Venus* (see photo on page 300).

In ancient mythology, Venus was born from the sea foam off the island of Cyprus, and in Botticelli's painting, Zephyrus, god of the West Wind, wafts her toward the land, while a nymph starts to fling a garment about her. The goddess covers her nakedness as best she can, her face suggests deep thought, and she seems to glide above the sea shell that floats her toward the shore. Her beauty is no image of bodily desire, but one of spiritual love that springs from the mind of God.

Once Botticelli had made female nudes respectable, however, artists soon began painting them in ways that were frankly sensual. The Venetian painter Titian is a notable example. In his *Venus of Urbino* (see photo on page 300), which he painted in 1538, he used his supreme mastery of Renaissance artistic techniques to give this painting its sensual power. Perspective makes the

The Nude in the Middle Ages and the Renaissance (http://www.metmuseum.org/toah/hd/numr/hd_numr.htm) View examples of the nude by other Renaissance masters.

has condemned the king's unlawful marriage to Salome's mother. Now Herod and his guests, seated at the banquet table, recoil in horror as Salome shows them the severed head.

The sculpture, carved in clay and then cast in bronze, is a relief—a flat panel with the human figures raised above the surface. The human figures stand out vividly, but Donatello has also created a marvelous illusion of depth. One can look through the rounded arches to Herod's musicians and beyond, through other archways, into the far background. Donatello knew well Giotto's methods of conveying dramatic emotion, he had made a careful study of surviving Roman carvings, and he had mastered Brunelleschi's rules of perspective. All this helped Donatello to create a memorably vivid and terrible scene.

In Donatello's time, a Roman custom was coming back into fashion under humanist influence—commemorating the human

viewer feel the closeness of the naked woman by showing the depth of the room behind her. Her left hand emphasizes rather than covers her nakedness. The arrangement of the figures makes a contrast between the woman boldly gazing at the viewer and her servants who turn away, thereby adding to the intimacy of her glance. This is not the spiritual Venus of Botticelli; in fact, she is probably not meant to be Venus at all. The picture acquired its title long after it was painted, and seems originally to have been a gift to the bride of a sixteenth-century duke of Urbino—a gift that celebrated the erotic side of the marriage bond.

Scala/Art Resource, NY

Modest Venus In Botticelli's *Birth of Venus*, the figure of Venus is inspired by Hellenistic statues depicting her as modest rather than erotic—compare her thoughtful eyes with the bold glance of Titian's *Venus of Urbino* (see photo below).

Representing the Individual: Portrait Painting

Ever since Petrarch had called Giotto a genius, humanists had admired artists for possessing *virtù* that put them on a level with statesmen, warriors, orators, thinkers, and scholars. Leonardo da Vinci became a symbol of this ideal of the artist on the highest level of human excellence. The out-of-wedlock son of a Florentine lawyer and a peasant woman, he apprenticed with a painter (since painting was a business that worked on the guild system, pp. 200–201), made a name for himself as an engineer as well as an artist, and worked for the rulers of Milan and Venice and

then for the pope. He ended his life in France, in a splendid mansion put at his disposal by his close friend, King Francis I.

Leonardo was an exceptionally close observer of anatomy, physiology, and nature. He put all this to use in his painting, and where he reached the limits of what could be observed, he combined lifelike depiction with an element of mystery—most notably in his portrait of the wife of a wealthy Florentine silk merchant, the *Mona Lisa* (see photo opposite).

Portraits of individuals were another revived ancient art form, and Leonardo believed, in accordance with the humanist ideal, that "the good painter has essentially two things to represent: the individual and the state of that individual's mind." It is not certain how much the sitter actually looked like her portrait, since Leonardo worked on it for years after he left Florence. All the same, in the *Mona Lisa*, Leonardo put his advice into practice. His skill of eye and hand gives the illusion of life to the sitter's physical appearance yet also creates a veiled, misty effect. His artistic perception probes her inner nature—including the element of mystery at the core of every human personality. This revealing yet mysterious quality is what has given the portrait its enduring fascination and fame.

Leonardo also painted traditional religious scenes, including *The Last Supper*, completed in 1497 (see photo opposite). He used his skills of accurate observation and lifelike depiction to

Erotic Venus Titian's *Venus of Urbino*, with its memorable depiction of the female nude as an image of desire, was most likely a suggestive wedding gift from a newly married Italian noble to his bride. Scala/Art Resource, NY

Mona Lisa Lisa del Giocondo, known for short as Mona Lisa ("Madam Lisa"), was twenty-four years old in 1503 when Leonardo da Vinci began painting this portrait, which her merchant husband intended as a gift to celebrate the birth of their second son. The couple never took delivery, for Leonardo worked on the picture on and off until he died in 1519. Evidently the commission set him off on a creative quest that took him the rest of his life to complete.

convey the reaction of the disciples when Jesus said, "One of you will betray me." To convey the drama of this moment, he also used the "stagecraft" skills of Giotto and Donatello. He made countless preliminary drawings, "rehearsing" individual disciples in expressions and gestures of protest, astonishment, disbelief—and in the case of Judas, the betrayer (third from left), obstinate defiance. But even with the agitation and tension of the recorded instant, the painting forms a harmonious whole centered on Jesus, whose foreknowledge of betrayal and death leaves him wholly tranquil.

>> "Is It I?" Leonardo's *Last Supper* depicts the disciples reacting to Jesus' announcement that one of them will betray him, and extracts the maximum drama from that moment. For the Milan monks who commissioned this work for their dining hall, it was an unforgettable reminder of the most sacred of all meals. Scala/ Art Resource, NY

The Artistic Climax: Michelangelo

Renaissance artists were often painters, sculptors, and architects all at once, and the mightiest achievements in all three fields were those of Michelangelo Buonarroti. Artists at the time saw his work as the climax of art's "restoration to life" that had begun with Giotto. "Truly," said his pupil Giorgio Vasari, "his coming was . . . an example sent by God to the men of our arts, so that they might learn from his life the nature of noble character, and from his works what true and excellent craftsmen ought to be."

Michelangelo was the son of an official and property owner in Florence. When he showed a talent for painting, he was apprenticed to a leading artist who recommended him to Florence's ruler Lorenzo de' Medici. Lorenzo helped him get a good humanist education, including in Platonic thought. He had a thorny personality, liable to fits of suspicion of colleagues as well as to a sense of sin and rage at life; but he was also a person of enormous energy and persistence as well as exceptional artistic skill. All of this, he poured into his masterpieces of sculpture, painting, and architecture.

The Male Nude: David

Michelangelo's single best-known work of sculpture is in another ancient tradition that had recently been revived by Donatello, the depiction of the naked male body. In 1499, following a political overturn in the Florentine city-state, by way

 A Model for Judas: Leonardo Paints *The Last Supper* Read how Leonardo defended his working method on The Last Supper.

 **Portraiture in Renaissance and Baroque Europe** (http://www .metmuseum.org/ toah/hd/port/hd_port .htm) View examples of portraiture by other Renaissance masters.

Keeping Michelangelo Happy: "We Love You from the Heart" Read a patron's soothing letter to Michelangelo.

of celebration the new rulers commissioned the twenty-six-year-old Michelangelo to carve a larger-than-life-size statue of the ancient Israelite King David, to be placed in Florence's main square. Because of his youthful feat of killing the giant Goliath, David was a traditional symbol of Florence, which prided itself on fighting off such neighboring "Goliaths" as the popes.

The rulers gave Michelangelo an 18-foot-high block of marble, and he set to work first of all with pencil and paper, to figure out, in numerous sketches, exactly how he would depict the Israelite hero. Then he took up his chisel, and with furious energy, he "liberated" an entirely original form from the stone. Statues usually showed David with the head of the defeated Goliath at his feet, but Michelangelo carved him dauntlessly facing the approaching giant. Michelangelo was inspired by serenely balanced poses that he had seen in Roman copies of Hellenistic statues, but this David is not at rest. His balanced pose and his measuring glance are those of a fighter poised to swing into ferocious combat (see photo).

The Soul and Its Maker: The Creation of Adam

Michelangelo's greatest work of painting came about by accident, after he was called to Rome in 1508 by Pope Julius II—himself a Renaissance man of *virtù* who was no saint, but a statesman, general, and patron of the arts. The pope wanted Michelangelo to make him a monumental tomb, but complications arose, and instead, Julius asked Michelangelo to paint the Sistine Chapel, so called after its fifteenth-century builder, Pope Sixtus IV. Its walls had been painted by earlier masters, including Botticelli, but the ceiling remained blank.

Michelangelo much preferred sculpting to painting, but he plunged into the new task with extraordinary vigor. The work took him four years to complete, covered about 10,000 square

David With one statue, Michelangelo tells a whole Bible story. The youthful Israelite hero is naked and unarmored, for the armor of the Israelite King Saul was too heavy for him; and he is armed only with a sling, for "the Lord does not save by sword and spear." He confidently measures with his eye the Philistine warrior-giant Goliath, for he knows that "This very day the Lord will deliver you into my hand."

"Let Us Make Humankind in Our Image" Michelangelo's *Creation of Adam* shows the beginning of the human race, and also its destiny according to Christian belief. Adam, the first man, is stirred to life by the finger of God; Eve, the first woman, and Christ, the redeemer of Adam and Eve's sin, are waiting to fulfill their part in God's plan.

feet, and included more than three hundred figures. It was the largest work ever painted by a single artist.

The main feature of the ceiling is a series of nine panels showing the stories of the Creation and the Flood, among them *The Creation of Adam* (see photo). God, borne by angels on a rushing mighty wind, reaches toward the first man; the mortal body stirs and reaches toward God; and the immortal soul passes from its divine originator to its human recipient. In the crook of God's arm, the still uncreated Eve looks intently toward Adam, the mother of humankind gazing upon its father. Beyond her, God's finger rests on the infant Christ, humankind's future redeemer. Adam's nakedness both follows the Bible story and is in the ancient tradition of celebrating the male body; God and Adam reaching toward each other reflect the Platonic

Vatican Museum's Video and Slide Tour of the Sistine Chapel (http://mv.vatican.va/3_EN/pages/x-Pano/CSN/Visit_CSN_01.html) Tour the Sistine Chapel and see all of Michelangelo's frescoes.

understanding of the divine origin of the soul and the soul's longing for God. In these ways, Michelangelo's depiction gives visual form to a humanist version of Christian beliefs about the human race and its creator.

Outdoing the Ancients: The Dome of Saint Peter's

Later in life, having won fame as a painter and a sculptor, Michelangelo turned to architecture, and here, too, he produced a supreme masterpiece— the dome of Saint Peter's Basilica. In 1503, Pope Julius II decided to tear down the thousand-year-old basilica of the Roman emperor Constantine (p. 142) and replace it with a more splendid building. His chosen architect, Donato Bramante **(bruh-MAHN-tey)**, planned a dome that would dwarf that of another ancient Roman structure, the Pantheon (see photo on page 112), but died before he could carry out the work. In 1547, Michelangelo was put in charge.

The floor plan was for a colossal structure laid out in the form of a Greek (square) cross, with a central dome as the crowning feature. Inspired by Brunelleschi's dome in Florence (see photo on page 297), Michelangelo planned one even steeper and higher—one that would tower over every other building in the Eternal City. Although he died before Saint Peter's was completed and the floor plan was later changed, the dome was finished according to his designs (see photo). Equal in diameter to

"You Are Peter, and on This Rock I Will Build My Church" The saying of Christ to Peter is carved in Latin on the inside of the dome of the rebuilt St. Peter's Basilica, as well as Christ's following words: "I will give you the keys of the kingdom of heaven." Michelangelo's dome, with its solemn splendor and its dizzying height, symbolized the claim of the papacy to supremacy over Christendom at a time when Christendom was for the first time becoming truly worldwide. James Morris/Art Resource, NY

the dome of the Pantheon and 300 feet higher, Michelangelo's dome sets the crown on the most daring of Renaissance undertakings—not just to bring the ancients back to life, but to destroy one of their most revered buildings in order to outdo them.

LO³ Ancient Traditions and Modern Languages: Renaissance Literature and Drama

Humanist scholars believed that their activities benefited the whole human race, and they had always been eager to spread their ideas. Until about 1500, however, their audience was mostly made up of people who could read Latin. In the sixteenth century, as printing made books cheaper and more widely available, humanists took the opportunity to reach a much wider audience—and that meant using the vernacular (native) languages of Europe. They translated ancient works and those of Erasmus and More, and they began writing original works in every language of Western Christendom—works that were then, in turn, translated into every other language. Vernacular literature, one of the great cultural creations of the Middle Ages, now felt the influence of the humanists, and of the ancients whom the humanists had reawakened.

The Liberty-Loving Humorist: Rabelais

In France, the first vernacular author to become widely popular was François Rabelais (**RAB-uh-ley**), an enthusiastic humanist with a talent for satire and parody. Though his books were condemned by religious and civil authorities, they became and remained bestsellers.

Like Erasmus a generation earlier, Rabelais knew the Church and the universities from the inside. From a middle-class family, he had entered a Franciscan monastery in order to become a scholar. But he was a rebel from the beginning; his absorption in ancient literature disturbed his superiors and led to trouble. He switched from one religious order to another, for a time wore the garb of a priest, studied at various universities, and later took up law and medicine. His career, like his writing, followed no visible plan. With a vast appetite for life and learning, he was the personification of a vigorous and spontaneous humanism.

Though Rabelais loved the ancient works and knew them intimately (especially those of Rome), he had no taste for high-minded ideals, and he detested all rules and regulations. One should follow, he insisted, one's own inclinations. Rabelais thus represented a humanism that did not copy ancient models (or any other) but stood as a purely individualistic philosophy. Rejecting the doctrine of original sin (and most other doctrines), he stressed natural goodness; he held that most people, given freedom and proper education (in the lore of the ancients), will live happy and productive lives.

This idea is central to Rabelais's great work, *Gargantua and Pantagruel*. The story, about two imaginary giant-kings, was printed in several volumes beginning in 1538. He wrote the work primarily for amusement, because he believed that laughter (like thought) is a distinctively human function. However, in telling of the heroes' education and adventures, he voiced his opinions on the human traits and institutions of his time. In a tumble of words, learned and playful, he mingled serious ideas with earthy jokes and jibes.

Monasticism was a prime target for Rabelais, as it was for Erasmus. Its stress on self-denial, repression, and regimentation was to him inhumane and hateful. He had Gargantua give funds to a "model" institution that violates monastic practices in every possible way. At this "abbey of Thélème," with its fine libraries and recreational facilities, elegantly dressed men and women are free to do as they please. Monks, hypocrites, lawyers, and peddlers of gloom are barred from the abbey; only handsome, high-spirited people are admitted.

Rabelais disliked pretense and deception and praised the natural instincts and abilities of free persons. Rejecting the ascetic ideal, he expressed humanism in its most robust and optimistic form. In doing so, he also anticipated the modern appetite for unlimited experience and pleasure.

The Skeptical Essayist: Montaigne

Michel de Montaigne (**mon-TEYN**), born a generation after Rabelais, lived through the troubled times of religious struggle between Protestants and Catholics and shared Rabelais's keen interest in the ancients. But his temperament was nearer that of Erasmus. Both men remained loyal to the Catholic Church, and both were dedicated scholars, though Montaigne was more secular-minded and detached than Erasmus.

A Life of Contemplation

The son of a landowning family near Bordeaux in southern France, Montaigne received a superb education. His father held public office, traveled abroad, and believed in a humanistic upbringing for his children. When his father died, Montaigne inherited the family estate and was able to retire at the age of thirty-eight to his library of a thousand books. The ideal humanist way of life was one that combined "action" and "contemplation" (quiet study and thought) like that of Cicero the statesman and thinker. Montaigne, however, chose contemplation, reading and rereading the Latin authors (and some Greeks in translation). As he read, he "attempted," as he put it, to write down briefly and clearly the ideas that came into his mind. The French word for "attempt" is *essai*, and at that time the English word **essay** had the same meaning. It was Montaigne who gave the word its usual modern meaning—a brief and thoughtful discussion of a subject.

Ancient writers like Seneca and Plutarch had written what amounted to essays, and so had Erasmus. But they had written in Latin and Greek, and always on solemn themes, whereas Montaigne wrote in clear and eloquent French on topics ranging from "Freedom of Conscience" and "The Greatness of Rome" to "Drunkenness," "War-horses," and "Not Pretending to Be

Sick." Montaigne's essays usually began with the opinions of traditional authorities, with quotations from their works, and went on to explain his own views. Sometimes he would present opposing answers to a given question and then suggest a compromise solution—or perhaps no solution at all.

Michel de Montaigne on the Fallibility of Human Understanding Read an excerpt from a Montaigne essay.

Montaigne did not try to change the minds of his readers but wrote in large measure for his own satisfaction. And because the essays were based on his own experiences and thoughts, they were also a form of autobiography. As he put it himself, in a note "To the Reader": "I want to be seen in my simple, natural, and ordinary style, without effort or artifice; for it is myself that I paint"—like a Renaissance artist making a self-portrait. That only added to his essays' appeal. Readers enjoyed the feeling of getting to know the ideas and character of an interesting person, and the fact that there was no pressure to share his ideas actually made them more appealing. His more than a hundred "attempts" to express the results of his life of private study and thought were printed beginning in 1580 and had an immense public impact.

The Uncertainty of Judgment

Montaigne wrote often of the limits of reason in efforts to comprehend the universe: neither theology, the wisdom of the ancients, nor science can provide final answers to the "big questions." "Of the Uncertainty of Our Judgment" is the title of one of his essays.

The human mind, observed Montaigne, is erratic; and the senses, which are unreliable, often control the mind. Beliefs, no matter how firmly held, cannot be regarded as constant, for they, too, have their seasons, their birth and death. His **skepticism** (doubting and inquiring attitude, from the Greek word for "inquiry") had a history dating back to ancient Greek thinkers. By reviving this attitude, Montaigne challenged the self-assurance of both Christians and earlier humanists. The uncertain character of knowledge, he thought, ought to teach us that claims to absolute truth are unjustified, and that persecuting people for differing beliefs is wrong. In the midst of frightful struggles between Catholics and Protestants that raged through sixteenth-century France, Montaigne could see that war and homicide are often the outcomes of unwarranted certainty in thought and belief, and pleaded eloquently for skepticism and tolerance.

Like many skeptics, exactly because of his distrust of claims to certainty Montaigne was a conservative, who believed that firm authority was indispensable to peace and order. Though he cherished independence of thought, he did not rebel against established institutions—one of his essays is "On Never Easily Changing a Traditional Law." Instead, he hoped that those

> **"It is impossible to find two opinions exactly alike, not only in different men, but in the same man at different times."**
> —Michel de Montaigne, from his *Essays*

who held power would see the light, ultimately, of moderation and decency. In any event, he stuck to his personal philosophy and remained aloof from other people. In the quiet and security of his library, Montaigne could meditate on one of his favorite sayings: "Rejoice in your present life; all else is beyond you."

skepticism
A doubting and inquiring attitude, from the Greek word for "inquiry."

Globe Theater
A London theater where Shakespeare's plays were performed for paying audiences.

The Master Dramatist: Shakespeare

Along with many other ancient traditions, the humanists revived that of drama—especially Roman drama. Comedies of Plautus and Terence (p. 107), with their complicated plots and happy endings, and tragedies by the Roman thinker Seneca that were full of strong emotions and spectacular bloodshed, were widely read and were sometimes performed at the courts of rulers. In addition, medieval popular drama was still a living art form, and as in so many other fields, the Renaissance combined both ancient and medieval traditions—notably in England, and above all, in the work of William Shakespeare.

The Business of Drama

As Shakespeare's friend (and rival playwright) Ben Jonson said, he knew "small Latin and less Greek." But by Shakespeare's time (around 1600), humanists had translated most of the writings of ancient Greece and Rome, and morality and mystery plays were still being performed. For a generation already, English playwrights had used and expanded on both highbrow ancient themes and lowbrow popular ones, in a vernacular language enriched by borrowings from the eloquence of Greece and Rome. The English drama had universal appeal—from the well-educated rulers Queen Elizabeth I and King James I, who sponsored troops of actors to perform the new plays, to the rowdy audiences in London's newly built theaters.

The new theaters were unlike those of ancient Greece or Rome, which had been religious or public structures with room for tens of thousands of spectators, and with all expenses paid by wealthy citizens (see photos on pages 69 and 104). London's **Globe Theater**, by contrast, held a maximum of three thousand people with considerable overcrowding. Furthermore, it was an admission-charging private business, in which Shakespeare himself owned a one-eighth share, located in a theater and red-light district safely across the River Thames from London itself.

A Virtual Tour from the Official Site of the Globe Theater (http://www.shakespeares-globe.org/virtualtour/) Tour London's Globe Theater.

Circular in outward plan, the theater faced inward on a large courtyard (see photo). The "groundlings," who had paid the cheapest admission, stood or sat in the yard itself, and the quality folk sat in covered galleries. The technical equipment was minimal. Behind the stage were curtains from behind which Polonius could spy on Hamlet, and a balcony where Juliet could be overheard by Romeo; costumes were usually those of the time; and lighting was unnecessary, since this was an open-air theater and performances were given in the afternoon. However, there were occasional special effects that could go badly wrong. In 1613, a cannon that was fired to liven up a battle scene set the roof of the Globe alight, and the theater burned to the ground.

Acting, however, was already a skilled craft. Its aim, according to Shakespeare himself, was "to suit the action to the word, the word to the action," and thereby "to hold the mirror up to nature"—just like Renaissance painting. What distorted the mirror, however, was that women were not supposed to appear on stage, so that female parts were played by boys. But so strong was the desire for lifelike performance that this would soon change. Half a century after Shakespeare's time, women were as prominent on stage as men, even though the feeling persisted that they did not really belong there. Well-known actresses were both idolized for their star quality and condemned for following a disrespectable profession.

"All the World's a Stage"

Like all commercial playwrights, Shakespeare looked for subjects that would excite his audiences, and he generally did not have to invent these for himself. Translated ancient works told of the larger-than-life heroes and villains of Greece and Rome. Patriotic historians narrated the triumphs that England had enjoyed and the disasters it had overcome in the Middle Ages. Sensational storytellers told of the doings of Italians, with their reputation as great lovers and great villains. Geographers described fantastic islands in the western ocean. In addition, Roman comedies and tragedies and

>> **An Elizabethan Playhouse** This sketch of the Swan Theater, of similar construction to the Globe and located in the same London theater district, was made by a visiting Dutchman in 1596. It shows a play under way on the "proscenium" in front of the "actors' building." The lower classes fill the "level space or arena" in front; upper-class spectators climb an "entry" stairway to the "orchestra"; and the middle classes climb higher to the "seating" or the "gallery" directly under the "roof" (top right label).

medieval morality plays provided Shakespeare with models of drama that he could combine at will. "All the world's a stage" says one of Shakespeare's characters—and with his vast range of themes and styles, Shakespeare made those words come true.

The basic plot of his tragedy *Hamlet*, for instance, comes from a medieval Danish tale: Hamlet finds out that his uncle the king, who is also his stepfather, has gained the crown and the queen by secretly murdering his father. Like a character in a medieval morality play (p. 239), Hamlet is faced with a choice, but the choice is one between the Renaissance alternatives of contemplation and action, as he hesitates to take revenge upon his uncle. The result is a series of spectacular deaths, as in Roman tragedies—in this case, eliminating all the main characters, including Hamlet himself. Without these sources and models,

Hamlet would not be *Hamlet*. But it was Shakespeare's deep insight into human nature and the uniquely expressive eloquence of his language that made *Hamlet* and so many of his other plays, as Ben Jonson said, "not of an age but for all time."

Listen to a synopsis of Chapter 16.

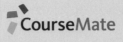

Access to the eBook with additional review material and study tools may be found online at CourseMate for WCIV. Sign in at www.cengagebrain.com.

CHAPTER 17

NEW CHRISTIANITIES: THE REFORMATION, 1500–1700

LEARNING OBJECTIVES

AFTER READING THIS CHAPTER, YOU SHOULD BE ABLE TO DO THE FOLLOWING:

LO¹ Describe the background of the Protestant Reformation.

LO² Trace the evolution of Lutheranism from the Ninety-five Theses to the Religious Peace of Augsburg.

LO³ Discuss the core tenets of Calvinism and its impact on the Reformation.

LO⁴ Outline how the Catholic Church responded to the Protestant challenge.

LO⁵ Explain how the religious wars of the Reformation period led to a new, secular European state system.

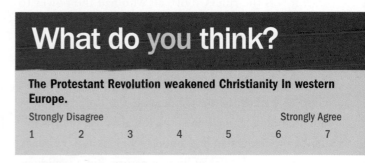

"THE EMERGENCE OF PROTESTANTISM WAS THE GREATEST SINGLE CHANGE IN WESTERN RELIGION SINCE THE END OF ANCIENT PAGANISM."

The **Protestant Reformation** was yet another spectacular change that grew out of the gradual shifts in Western Christendom during the late Middle Ages. In particular, resentment at corruption and abuse among the Catholic clergy that involved the papacy itself began to discredit the religious beliefs and practices on which the power of the clergy and the popes was based. When Martin Luther proclaimed that the Church was leading souls to hell rather than heaven, and must be reformed along lines of Christian freedom and equality, his individual protest soon turned into a mass movement.

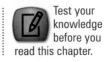 Test your knowledge before you read this chapter.

As Luther's protest spread, however, his followers interpreted his message of reformation in different ways. John Calvin proclaimed a more thoroughgoing break with Catholic tradition, in the name of return to the pure truth of the gospel. Radical groups of reformers claimed that Christian freedom and equality were not just spritual, but applied to society and government as well. These issues seemed to affect the salvation of souls just as much as the disputes between reformers and traditionalists, and the arguments among reformers were just as bitter. Instead of changing the whole Church, the reformers—the Protestants, as they came to be called—split into many different churches, each with its own beliefs and organization.

What do you think?

The Protestant Revolution weakened Christianity In western Europe.

Strongly Disagree						Strongly Agree
1	2	3	4	5	6	7

Meanwhile, by far the largest of the churches was still the Catholic Church. In response to the Protestant challenge, it rallied around its traditional beliefs and practices as the only way to heaven, and around the traditional authority of the papacy as the only guide of Christians. It acted against some of the worst abuses that had brought the clergy into contempt, and regained the trust of many rulers and many believers. And although it lost most of northern Europe to Protestantism, it gained millions of new believers in Latin America.

≪ **The Lord's Supper** A Protestant painter, Lucas Cranach the Elder, shows Jesus and his disciples sharing the Last Supper as friends around a table. The odd man out is Judas, to whom Jesus gives the bread that marks him as the betrayer. The disciple taking a cup of wine—the cup that was so important to Protestants in the Communion service—is Martin Luther, wearing the beard he grew in hiding as an outlawed heretic. For Cranach, Luther is worthy to sit among the original twelve.

Church of St. Marian, Wittenberg, Germany/The Bridgeman Art Library

Most reformers, as well as Catholics, still believed that all Christians should belong to one Church that was allied with the state, so religious disputes also led to persecution and war. These conflicts were further embittered by nonreligious rivalries among rulers and within their countries. About 1650, however, more than a century of religious-political struggles ended in stalemate. Alongside the existing rival Christianities of Catholicism and Orthodoxy, there now existed the third Christianity of Protestantism, itself divided into many different sub-Christianities. The emergence of Protestantism was the greatest single change in Western religion since the end of ancient paganism. It was also one that affected nonreligious areas of civilization, as the Reformation interacted with other changes involved in the remaking of Europe.

The Reformation strengthened both Protestant and Catholic rulers in their partnership with the churches, since it was the rulers above all who had the power to choose and uphold one or other religion. But Calvinists trying to take over kingdoms often championed the rights of subjects against rulers, and radical sects kept alive the belief that Christian freedom and equality applied to this world as well as the next. Likewise, the Reformation at first blighted many ideals of the Renaissance, such as tolerance and understanding among religions and optimism about the possibilities of human nature. But as religious stalemate set in, the idea of toleration revived and was even strengthened by the Protestant belief in freedom of conscience. As the struggles of the churches died down, all these ideas began to get a wider hearing.

LO¹ The Christian Background

For more than a thousand years before the Reformation, the majority of Christians had agreed upon certain basic beliefs about how they would make their way to heaven. They would do so as members of a community founded by Christ himself, the Church, and by taking part in various holy ceremonies that the Church practiced. They accepted that Christ had appointed the clergy as guides and rulers of the Church, and had established its hierarchy of bishops, priests, and lower ranks. They trusted

CHRONOLOGY

1517	Luther's Ninety-five Theses attack the sale of indulgences
1521	Excommunicated by the pope, Luther refuses to recant his beliefs before the Diet of Worms; he translates the Bible into German while under the protection of Frederick of Saxony
1522	Luther returns to Wittenberg; his new version of Christianity gains adherents
1529	Holy Roman Emperor Charles V reaffirms decree prohibiting new religious doctrines in Germany; Lutheran rulers protest and acquire label of "Protestants"
1530s	Armed alliances of Lutherans and Catholics form within the Holy Roman Empire; Augsburg Confession sets out beliefs of new Evangelical Church
1534	Pope Paul III launches Catholic Reformation; England's Parliament passes the Act of Supremacy, breaking ties with the pope
1536	John Calvin's *Institutes of the Christian Religion* is published and widely read; Calvin settles in Geneva, where he establishes a model community
1539	The Society of Jesus (Jesuits) becomes an official Catholic order
1545–1563	Council of Trent meets periodically to initiate Catholic Church reform
1553	Queen Mary launches persecution of English Protestants
1555	Religious Peace of Augsburg allows each ruler within the Holy Roman Empire to choose either Catholicism or Lutheranism for his territory
1562	Beginning of wars between Catholics and Huguenots in France
1588	English defeat Spanish Armada
1598	Edict of Nantes guarantees toleration and military forces for Huguenots
1618–1648	Thirty Years' War devastates Germany, ends with Peace of Westphalia

that monks and nuns, and the saints in heaven, were closer to God than ordinary believers, and could help ordinary believers into heaven by interceding with God for them.

This consensus had not prevented many furious disputes over belief and struggles for power from arising within Christendom, and in the Middle Ages, the Church had already come to be divided between the Catholic West and the Orthodox East (p. 219). Furthermore, in both halves of Christendom there had always been heretics who disagreed with the consensus. Even so, the consensus had survived these challenges, until in the sixteenth-century Catholic West, it broke down.

Many long-standing developments within Western Christendom contributed to this breakdown. In the Middle Ages, changes in religious practices that were intended to ease believers' path to heaven had increased the power of the clergy as gatekeepers on this path—and also increased the temptation for them to exploit this power for political and money-making purposes. The international power of the popes had grown as they rose to become effective rulers of the Catholic Church—and increased power saddled them with increased responsibility for everything that was wrong with the Church. Banking and capitalism made it easier for popes and clergy to exploit the growing wealth of Western Christendom—but also made it easier for landowners, merchants, and rulers of countries to do the same, and to look upon the Church as an unwelcome competitor.

Corruption in the Church, resentment at unworthy clergy, and quarrels between the clergy and other power wielders were nothing new in Western Christendom, and these problems had sometimes provoked zealous mass movements of renewal and reform within the Church. In the fifteenth century, grassroots movements like the Brethren of the Common Life (p. 293) were committed to Catholic piety, and in Spain, Isabella and Fredinand sponsored reform of the clergy. To become truly a mass movement, however, reform had to have the wholehearted backing of the popes. In the fifteenth century, the popes were too busy with power struggles in Italy, and with holding off challenges to their control of the Church by increasingly powerful rulers of countries, to bother much with Church reform.

Instead of provoking renewal and reform, therefore, the problems of the Church began to inspire doubts that it was guiding Christians rightly, and searches began for the true path to salvation. Renaissance humanists contrasted the Church's wealth and corruption with the simple holiness of early Christianity, and insisted that many beliefs that had grown up over the centuries hid the truth that Christ had originally proclaimed (pp. 293–294). Heretic movements grew up that sought to weaken or abolish the clergy's rule, and to change or eliminate many practices and ceremonies (pp. 249–251). By the end of the fifteenth century, furthermore, humanists and heretics had

a new means of spreading their doubts and disagreements to a mass audience, with the advent of printing.

As with many massive and sudden changes in human affairs, no one expected the Reformation until it actually happened. But in many ways, the time was ripe for a religious mass movement that would not be one of reform and renewal within the thousand-year-old consensus, but a revolt against the consensus as such.

LO² The Revolt of Luther

One person who certainly did not expect the Reformation before it happened was the one who began it, Martin Luther. All the same, his own early life was shaped by his search for the true path to salvation, and eventually, he became the leader of a religious revolt motivated by resentment at the clergy and the papacy and by rejection of the traditional beliefs and practices as the way to heaven.

Luther's Search for Salvation

Luther was the son of a well-to-do mine operator in the north German town of Eisleben (see Map 17.1) who wanted him to study law. But he was deeply afraid for his own salvation, and like many pious Catholics who felt that way, he defied his father's wishes and entered a monastery, in the traditional belief that as a monk he would be more pleasing to God than as an ordinary Christian.

> "*As with many massive and sudden changes in human affairs, no one expected the Reformation until it actually happened.*"

For centuries, the Church had taught that praying, fasting, strict obedience to superiors, and abstinence from sex and marriage that made up the ascetic way of life of a monk (p. 144) were "good works"—righteous deeds that were pleasing to God. Together with God's grace, received through the sacraments, they would "justify" Luther (free him from the penalty of sin and admit him to salvation). But no matter how strictly he fasted, prayed, and punished himself, his sense of being unpleasing to God persisted. To give him something else to think about, the head of his monastery sent him to study theology at the nearby University of Wittenberg. After receiving his doctor's degree there in 1512, he stayed on as a professor of theology.

At Wittenberg, Luther began to discover his path to spiritual peace—not in the pronouncements of popes, revered monks, or earlier Christian thinkers, but in humanist fashion, by going back to the words of Christ and the apostles themselves. Above all, he was struck by the words of Paul, in a letter to early believers in Rome: "The one who is righteous will live by faith." Luther took these words to mean, as he later wrote, that "by grace and sheer mercy God justifies us through faith"—an idea that "became to me a gate to heaven." He had been right all along to feel that his "good works" as a monk had not made him pleasing to God. Because of the sinfulness that all humans inherited from Adam and Eve, no one could deserve salvation through his or her

Map 17.1 Catholics and Protestants in 1555

The map shows the religious division of Europe when the Reformation was approaching its height. The Lutheran and Anglican Reformations are dominant in much of northern Europe, and the Calvinist Reformation is gaining in the Netherlands, Scotland, France, and Hungary. But the rest of Western Christendom is still mainly Catholic, and a Catholic religious revival and the support of local rulers will soon bring the spread of Protestantism to an end. © Cengage Learning

Predominant religion in 1555

- Lutheran
- Calvinist (Reformed)
- Church of England
- Roman Catholic
- Orthodox
- Muslim
- ↑ Spread of Calvinism
- ▲ Huguenot center
- ◯ Ottoman Empire, 1566

Interactive Map

0   200   400 Km.
0   200   400 Mi.

ATLANTIC OCEAN

North Sea

Baltic Sea

Black Sea

Mediterranean Sea

Adriatic Sea

IRELAND
Dublin

SCOTLAND 1560
Edinburgh
John Knox, 1505–1572

Penetration of Calvinism to England after 1558

ENGLAND 1536
Oxford
John Wyclif, 1320–1384
London
Plymouth

NORWAY 1536/1607
Bergen

SWEDEN
Stockholm

Helsinki

Riga

LITHUANIA

DENMARK
Copenhagen

Hamburg

BRANDENBURG

PRUSSIA

Warsaw

POLAND

NETHERLANDS
Amsterdam
Antwerp
Brussels
Münster

SAXONY
Wittenberg
Birthplace of Martin Luther,
Eisleben, 1483–1546
Erfurt
Leipzig

Marburg

HOLY ROMAN EMPIRE

Noyon
Birthplace of John Calvin, 1509–1564

Worms
Edict of Worms, 1521

Speyer

Nuremberg
Stuttgart

Augsburg

Prague
Jan Hus, 1369–1415

BOHEMIA

MORAVIA

Munich

Vienna

AUSTRIA

Pest
Buda

HUNGARY

TRANSYLVANIA

MOLDAVIA

BESSARABIA

WALLACHIA
Danube R.

Belgrade
SERBIA

BULGARIA

OTTOMAN EMPIRE

GREECE

Strasbourg

Basel

Zurich
Ulrich Zwingli, 1484–1531

Geneva
John Calvin

Milan

Pavia

Genoa

Council of Trent, 1545–1563
Trent

Venice

Pisa

Florence

Rome
Roman Inquisition established, 1542

ITALY

Naples

Bari

Avignon

Marseilles

FRANCE

Paris

Rennes

Orléans

Nantes
Edict of Nantes, 1598

La Rochelle

Bordeaux

Toulouse

Barcelona

Balearic Is.

Corsica

Sardinia

Sicily

Loyola
Birthplace of Ignatius Loyola, 1491–1556

Madrid

Toledo

SPAIN

Valencia

Granada

Seville

PORTUGAL

Lisbon

MOROCCO

ALGIERS
OTTOMAN EMPIRE

TUNIS

60°N

50°N

40°N

10°W

0°

10°E

20°E

30°E

deeds. Only faith in salvation through Christ and humble trust in God's mercy could "justify" a person—and because of human sinfulness, no one could acquire faith by his or her own efforts, but must receive it as a free gift of God's mercy. We are saved not by works, concluded Luther, but by *faith alone*. If God has given us that faith, we will live as righteously as human sinfulness allows—not because we need to but because we want to.

Luther's Rebellion

The idea of **justification** by faith alone brought Luther immense personal relief, but when he began to apply it to the institution of the Church, he grew troubled. If people received faith as a free gift from God, were not the claims of the clergy to guide people to salvation untrue? If the way of life of monks and nuns was not pleasing to God, what good was it either to themselves or to ordinary believers for whom they were supposed to pray? If the saints themselves had done nothing to deserve God's favor but had simply benefited from his mercy, what was the use of praying to them and making pilgrimages to their shrines? And if these beliefs were deceptive, must not the traditional path to heaven in fact be leading believers to hell?

The Provocation: The Sale of Indulgences

For several years, Luther kept his views to himself, until in 1517 a Dominican friar (p. 209), Johann Tetzel, arrived in Wittenberg on important papal business. Tetzel was a seller of indulgences—grants of time off purgatory issued on the authority of the pope, which believers could obtain both for themselves and also for other people who were already dead (pp. 206–207). People who obtained indulgences were supposed to show sorrow for their sins, but they also had to pay a fee, and popes in need of money would initiate international indulgence-selling campaigns. In this case, the proceeds were to go to the rebuilding of Saint Peter's Basilica in Rome, and Tetzel's catchy sales slogan was allegedly "As soon as the gold in the casket rings, the rescued soul to heaven springs!"

In his indignation, Luther prepared a public statement about indulgences in the form of "**Ninety-five Theses**" (propositions for academic debate). Cautiously but unmistakably, he attacked not just the sale of indulgences but also the whole idea that he believed lay behind them—that the pope could commit God to show mercy in consideration of the merits of deserving persons,

>> **"One Can Be Saved Without an Indulgence from Rome, as Proven by God's Holy Scripture"** In a woodcut from a Lutheran pamphlet of about 1520, a friar holds an indulgence festooned with seals, believers pay up and a cashier rakes in the money, and Christ has departed the Cross, leaving only a crown of thorns. The pope's coat of arms behind the preacher leaves no doubt about who is to blame for this evil, and the slogan at the top drives home the message. © British Library Board, 3906.b.55

when in fact God's mercy was the free gift of his almighty power, which no person could possibly deserve.

Originally, Luther seems to have publicized his theses in the traditional way for professors who wanted to hold debates, by nailing a single handwritten copy to the door of the Wittenberg Castle church. Soon, however, the theses were printed in thousands of copies, and were setting off a chain reaction of dissent and rebellion throughout Germany.

> "*Thus those preachers of indulgences are in error who say that by the indulgences of the Pope a man is freed and saved from all punishment.*"
>
> —No. 21, from the Ninety-five Theses

The Split with Rome

Pope Leo X, an able and cultured Italian despot like many popes at the time, hoped to settle this "squabble among monks," as he called it, by having a reply to Luther published, whereupon Luther published a reply to the reply. That led to yet more publications on both sides, in the course of which Luther stood by the radical consequences of his belief in justification by faith alone and proclaimed them as Christian truth. In addition, he appealed outside

On Aplas von Rom
kan man wol selig werden
durch anzaigung der götlichen
hailigen geschryfft.

Diet of Worms

The assembly of the Holy Roman Empire before which Luther refused to recant his beliefs.

Anabaptists

Radical Protestants who opposed infant baptism and also held various other beliefs that were opposed to beliefs that other Protestants still had in common with Catholics.

sect

In religion, a small group that sees itself as part of a minority of true believers apart from the rest of society.

the ranks of the clergy to secular wielders of power and to Christians in general. In his *Address to the Christian Nobility of the German Nation*, he spoke of the equal "priesthood" of all baptized Christians. In this and other documents, he claimed that not just indulgences, but also an unmarried clergy set apart from and above other believers, as well as monks and nuns, saints and relics and pilgrimages, were all devices of the devil to lead believers away from the true path of salvation. So, too, was the idea of the papacy as the single Christ-appointed guide and ruler of the Church. Instead, Christians should listen to the voice of God himself, speaking to them through the Bible and within them through their own consciences.

Likewise, Luther declared, most of the Church's seven sacraments—the holy ceremonies that helped believers to salvation (pp. 204–205)—were a deception. Using the humanist test of early Christian practice as found in the New Testament, he claimed that Christ had established only two sacraments: baptism and the Eucharist. And he denied the Catholic doctrine of transubstantiation—that in the Eucharist, the priest brings about a miraculous change of bread and wine into the body and blood of Christ. Luther taught, instead, that Christ was present *along with* the bread and wine, and that it is not the priest who makes Christ present, for God is present everywhere and always. Furthermore, it was a wicked violation of Christ's command that only clergy should receive both bread and wine in the Eucharist.

"My Conscience Has Been Taken Captive by the Word of God"

In 1520, Leo finally ordered Luther excommunicated, and Luther responded by burning the document of excommunication before the city gates of Wittenberg. The clergy now called on the Holy Roman emperor Charles V to seize Luther, since it was considered the duty of the civil ruler to punish confirmed heretics, but Luther by now had such widespread support that the emperor hesitated. In particular, the local ruler of Saxony, the elector Frederick (one of the rulers who elected the emperor, p. 267) favored Luther, and insisted that Luther receive a hearing before the Imperial Diet. (The Diet was the assembly of the local rulers and self-governing cities of the empire—in German, *Reichstag* or "imperial day," because it was called for a particular day; the English word *diet* comes from the Latin word for "day.")

"Martin Luther: The Reluctant Revolutionary" (http://www.pbs.org/empires/martinluther/) Learn more about Luther's life and the other major players in his story.

At the **Diet of Worms** (a city in western Germany where the Diet met) in 1521, Luther was given a last chance to recant his heresies. He refused, in words that became the motto for the Reformation appeal against Church tradition to the Bible and individual conscience: "Unless I am convinced by the testimonies of the Holy Scriptures or evident reason (for I believe neither in the Pope nor councils alone, since it has been established that they have often erred and contradicted themselves), I am bound by the Scriptures cited by me, and my conscience has been taken captive by the Word of God, and I am neither able nor willing to recant, since it is neither safe nor right to act against conscience. God help me. Amen."

The Diet then condemned Luther and issued a decree prohibiting all new religious doctrines within the Holy Roman Empire, and the emperor ordered him branded an outlaw. Frederick, however, sent soldiers to "kidnap" Luther as he left Worms and took him secretly to a castle at Wartburg in Saxony, where Luther remained for about a year working on a German translation of the Bible. His "people's" version of Scripture was printed in hundreds of thousands of copies, and helped shape the modern German language as well as Protestant doctrines.

Reforming the Church

When Luther returned to Wittenberg, he found himself the leader of a mass movement that included local rulers, clergy, townspeople, and peasants, and he set about turning this movement into a reformed Christian church. This involved him in a struggle on two fronts—against Catholics who sought to suppress his protest, and against people who wanted to take his protest in directions of which he disapproved.

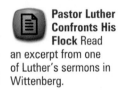

Pastor Luther Confronts His Flock Read an excerpt from one of Luther's sermons in Wittenberg.

The Anabaptist Sects

Many of the second group went under the general name of **Anabaptists** (from the Greek words for "baptize again"). They insisted that baptism was meaningful only after someone old enough to comprehend Christian doctrines had made a voluntary confession of faith. They therefore opposed infant baptism and held that adult Christians who had been baptized as infants must accept the rite again. Baptism of adults had been normal among the earliest Christians; but the earliest Christians had been a tiny minority in a pagan world, mostly made up of people who had in any case converted as adults. The custom of infant baptism had grown up as Christians became numerous and then a majority, and one tradition that Luther still took for granted was the belief that everyone should belong to a single organized Church.

The Anabaptists, by contrast, were not a single organized group but a collection of **sects**—small groups that saw themselves as part of a minority of true believers apart from the rest of society. They varied considerably in their ideas, which often proved troublesome to established society. Some applied New Testament teachings literally to their own times, refused military service, and sought to establish a more egalitarian community. As among the earliest Christians, women were often prominent in their worship, though they were usually the wives of male leaders. Some sects advocated acts of violence against "ungodly" persons and against officials who declined to punish them.

Luther, however, was determined not to let changes in the Church spill over into the rest of society. In 1524, he responded angrily to a peasant revolt that swept through Germany. The serfs were seeking relief from new burdens laid upon them by their feudal lords, especially in eastern Germany, and often used slogans of Christian freedom and equality derived from Luther's protest. But Luther urged the aristocracy to put down the violent uprising without mercy, to slay the rebels as they would "mad dogs." He later admitted that it was he who had commanded the slaughter of the peasants: "All their blood is on my head. But I throw the responsibility on our Lord God, who instructed me to give this order." (Luther also urged harsh measures against Jews, reinforcing the popular anti-Semitism of his times.)

 **Luther Rages Against the "Murdering and Robbing Bands of Peasants"** Read Luther's condemnation of the peasant revolt.

Luther was equally severe with the Anabaptists. He considered them "blasphemers" and believed that they, like persons guilty of rebellion against the state, should be executed. In fact, Lutherans and Catholics alike brutally persecuted the Anabaptists, for they both believed in a Church that included everyone, was integrated with the existing society, and was allied with the state. But would this Church be Catholic or Lutheran? That depended on the wielders of power in the existing society—the local rulers in the Holy Roman Empire, and the emperor Charles V himself.

An Anabaptist Martyr Takes the Stand Read the testimony of an Anabaptist who refused to recant his beliefs.

War and Stalemate

In 1529, Charles and the Catholic members of the Imperial Diet reaffirmed the earlier Worms decree prohibiting all new religious doctrines in Germany. The Lutheran rulers protested this action and acquired the name "Protestant," which in time came to be used for all the rebellious creeds. Meanwhile, in the 1530s, armed alliances of Lutheran and Catholic rulers formed within the empire and eventually went to war.

Which side a particular territory found itself on depended on several factors—Lutheran and Catholic religious leadership, the convictions and interests of its ruler, and its distance from the southern power base of the emperor. Generally, rulers in southern Germany upheld Catholicism in their own territories and were willing to defend it by force. They were less eager to help Charles crush the Lutheran rulers in the north, however, for fear that he would become too powerful and turn his loose imperial authority into real control over them. As a result, several bouts of warfare ended in a truce known as the **Religious Peace of Augsburg** (1555), in which the Diet agreed to leave each ruler free to choose either Catholicism or Lutheranism for his

territory—which in practice meant that the northern territories were mostly Lutheran, while the southern ones remained Catholic. The Catholics had failed to crush the Lutheran revolt, but the Lutherans had failed to reform the Church throughout the empire. It was a foretaste of what would eventually happen between Protestants and Catholics on the scale of Western Christendom as a whole.

The Evangelical Church

Meanwhile, in the Lutheran territories the **Evangelical** (gospel-following) **Church**, as it was usually called, came into being. It was an organized institution like the Catholic Church, though of course with a different set of beliefs that were set out in the **Augsburg Confession** of 1530. Luther did not believe that God had established any particular structure for the Church, except that, like any organized institution, its workings must be orderly. The only people who could guarantee orderliness were rulers, so in each Lutheran territory, the ruler appointed superintendents to oversee the religious establishment—thus subordinating church to state. The formerly Catholic religious buildings and grounds were assigned to the new churches, but the extensive landholdings of bishoprics and monasteries were taken over by the rulers.

The Evangelical Church had neither monks and nuns, nor veneration of saints and relics, and its ministers were expected to marry. Luther himself married a former nun, Katharina von Bora, the daughter of a poverty-stricken nobleman who had handed her over to a convent at the age of five. Soon after the indulgences dispute began, she led a group of nuns in an escape from the convent with Luther's help, and eventually became his wife. As a married woman, in between bearing six children she managed a large property that the Saxon elector had handed over to Luther for religious and charitable purposes. She was among the first of many generations of busy and forceful wives of Protestant clergy—the kinds of wives who were "above rubies," according to the Old Testament proverb (p. 41). She and Luther seem to have made each other happy—though at least once when he annoyed her, she told him: "Before I put up with this, I'd rather go back to the convent and leave you and all our children!" By his acts and teachings, Luther raised the value placed on marriage and upheld the rights of wives to sexual satisfaction; he did not, however, urge any basic changes in the social role of women.

The Evangelical worship service was not much different from the Catholic service, except in two all-important respects. Both ministers and people received bread and wine in the

Religious Peace of Augsburg
An agreement to end religious wars within the Holy Roman Empire by allowing rulers the freedom to determine the faith (Lutheran or Catholic) of their territories.

Evangelical Church
The name given to the church formed by Luther; from *evangelical*, meaning "gospel-following."

Augsburg Confession
A document detailing the beliefs of Luther's Evangelical Church.

THE RELIGIOUS PEACE OF AUGSBURG

In 1555, both Catholics and Lutherans came to the Diet of the Holy Roman Empire (the empire's parliament-like assembly) in the German city of Augsburg, to bring an end to twenty-five years of religious warfare in the empire. Electors (local rulers who chose the emperor), other rulers ranking as princes, high-ranking noblemen, bishops and other leading clergy, and representatives of important cities attended. The Catholic Ferdinand of Habsburg, ruler of the Habsburg territories in central Europe, presided on behalf of his brother the Holy Roman Emperor Charles V. The result of the Diet was an agreement for mutual toleration between opposing versions of Christianity that lasted for more than fifty years.

The various groups at the Diet are referred to here as "estates"; an individual belonging to any one of them is called an "estate." "His Roman Imperial Majesty" is Charles V; "we" and "us" are Ferdinand himself, referring to himself in the plural as was customary for monarchs.

In order that . . . peace, which is especially necessary in view of the divided religions, as is seen from the causes before mentioned, and is demanded by the sad necessity of the Holy Roman Empire of the German nation, may be the better established and made secure and enduring between his Roman Imperial Majesty and us, on the one hand, and the electors, princes, and estates of the Holy Empire of the German nation on the other, therefore his Imperial Majesty, and we, and the electors, princes, and estates of the Holy Empire will not make war upon any estate of the empire on account of the Augsburg Confession and the doctrine, religion, and faith of the same, nor injure nor do violence to those estates that hold it, nor force them, against their conscience, knowledge, and will, to abandon the religion, faith, church usages, ordinances, and ceremonies of the Augsburg Confession, where these have been established, or may hereafter be established, in their principalities, lands, and dominions. Nor shall we, through mandate or in any other way, trouble or disparage them, but shall let them quietly and peacefully enjoy their religion, faith, church usages, ordinances, and ceremonies, as well as their possessions, real and personal property, lands, people, dominions, governments, honors, and rights. . . .

On the other hand, the estates that have accepted the Augsburg Confession shall suffer his Imperial Majesty, us, and the electors, princes, and other estates of the Holy Empire, adhering to the old religion, to abide in like manner by their religion, faith, church usages, ordinances, and ceremonies. They

shall also leave undisturbed their possessions, real and personal property, lands, people, dominions, government, honors, and rights, rents, interest, and tithes. . . .

But all others who are not adherents of either of the above-mentioned religions are not included in this peace, but shall be altogether excluded. . . .

No estate shall urge another estate, or the subjects of the same, to embrace its religion.

But when our subjects and those of the electors, princes, and estates, adhering to the old religion or to the Augsburg Confession, wish, for the sake of their religion, to go with wife and children to another place in the lands, principalities, and cities of the electors, princes, and estates of the Holy Empire, and settle there, such going and coming, and the sale of property and goods, in return for reasonable compensation for serfdom and arrears of taxes, . . . shall be everywhere unhindered, permitted, and granted. . . .

EXPLORING THE SOURCE

1. What are the limits on the religious toleration that this agreement guarantees?

2. What reason is given here for establishing religious toleration?

Source: James Harvey Robinson, ed., *Readings in European History* (Boston: Ginn, 1904), 2:114–116.

Eucharist, in token of the Christian equality between them; and the language was German, so that God could be understood when he spoke to the people. Art and music, and above all the singing of hymns, many composed by Luther himself, added to the impact of the reading and explanation of the Word of God in the Bible.

LO³ The Calvinist Movement

Luther's rebellion soon found sympathizers outside the Holy Roman Empire, but only in Scandinavia—the northern kingdoms of Denmark, Norway, and Sweden—did actual rulers support him and reform the Church on his model. In other regions, there was no way that he could control the rebellion that he had started. Anabaptist sects multiplied across Europe from the Low Countries to Poland and Hungary in spite of persecution. And among reformers who held to the idea of a single Christian Church to which all must belong, leadership passed to a Frenchman with more radical ideas than Luther about the Church's beliefs, practices, and organization—John Calvin.

Calvin: The International Reformer

Younger than Luther by some twenty-five years, Calvin was the son of a well-off lawyer. His father saw to it that he got a good education in Paris, where he gained knowledge of theology, law, and humanist scholarship. To begin with, he was a pious Catholic, but in 1533, as he later put it, "God by a sudden conversion subdued and brought my mind to a teachable frame."

In fear of persecution, he left France and lived in various cities of the Holy Roman Empire that were sympathetic to reform, while he put his early learning and his newfound conviction into writing the *Institutes of* ("Introduction to") *the Christian Religion*. In spite of its title, the book was a detailed and systematic statement of reformed Christian belief as Calvin understood it.

In 1536, the same year that Calvin published the *Institutes*, he settled down in the Swiss city of Geneva (see Map 17.1

The Reformed Temple, Lyon A christening begins at a Calvinist church in the southern French city during the 1560s. In a barn-like structure, well-dressed men and women sit mostly apart, and there are no holy images though the coats of arms of local worthies are displayed. A pulpit takes the place of an altar. A dog gazes faithfully and attentively up at the preacher.
The Granger Collection, New York

predestination
The concept, central to Calvinism, that God chooses who will be saved and who will be lost; a person's ultimate destiny is predetermined by God.

Reformed Church
The name given to the church founded by Calvin.

episcopal
A type of church hierarchy controlled by bishops.

presbyterian
A type of church hierarchy controlled by elected elders—from the Greek word for "elder."

on page 312). Like the rest of Switzerland, Geneva was part of the Holy Roman Empire, and it had just revolted against the local ruler, a bishop. The city was in political and religious turmoil, but Calvin soon achieved dominance in the community and held it until his death in 1564. Reformers all over Europe read the *Institutes* in the original Latin and in translation, and came to Geneva to see how Calvin's version of a reformed Church worked in practice. Calvinism soon became the leading Protestant force across Europe from Scotland to Hungary.

Predestination: The Saved and the Damned

Calvin was very close to Luther in his basic beliefs, but there was a real difference in what they chose to emphasize. For Luther, it was the question of the soul's salvation, which led him to the doctrine of justification through faith alone. For Calvin, it was God's almighty power and human wickedness, which led him to stress the doctrine of **predestination**.

God, declared Calvin, foreknows and determines everything that happens in the universe. It follows that he determines who shall be saved and who shall be forever lost. All people, inheriting hopeless sinfulness from Adam and Eve, would disobey God if left to their own puny powers. But God gives to those he "elects" (chooses) the ability to persevere in his service. The rest, for his own mysterious reasons, he allows to fall. Calvin unflinchingly defined this doctrine in his *Institutes*:

> Predestination we call the eternal decree of God, by which he has determined in himself, what he would have become of every individual of mankind. For they are not all created with a similar destiny; but eternal life is foreordained for some, and eternal damnation for others. Every man, therefore, being created for one or the other of these ends, we say, he is predestinated either to life or to death.

Against the charge that God could not be so unfair as to condemn most of humankind to damnation, Calvin admitted that this was "an awe-inspiring decree." But he insisted that no one actually deserves salvation, and that it is only through God's gracious mercy that some are saved.

> *"Calvinism soon became the leading Protestant force across Europe from Scotland to Hungary."*

Predestination was a traditional Christian belief, which the revered early thinker Augustine had insisted on and which had first been stated by Paul himself (pp. 128, 143). Catholic thinkers mostly accepted that God chose whom to save, but they also believed that he left people free to do good works that would help them into heaven. How God could do both these opposite-seeming things was a divine mystery that human reason could not solve, and which it was best to be cautious about discussing. Luther also accepted predestination, but avoided stressing it for fear of discouraging believers. Calvin, on the other hand, proclaimed predestination as starkly as possible and made it the driving force behind a new and powerful international Protestant movement.

The Reformed Church

Calvin's opponents sometimes argued that predestination destroyed all incentive for following a righteous Christian life, and that it made membership in a Church unnecessary for salvation. Calvin insisted, however, that it was God's will that the elect should be saved through the Church, and that no one knows for certain who is elect and who is "reprobate" (condemned). All people must therefore live righteously as if they enjoyed God's favor, and they must all belong to the Church.

The Presbyterian Hierarchy

Calvin accepted, with Luther, the principle of the "priesthood of all believers." The **Reformed Church**, as it was usually called, gave to its ministers no special powers that set them apart from baptized laypeople. But Calvin also believed, in the humanist tradition, that a God-given model for the workings of the Church was to be found in early Christian churches, with their officials chosen by the congregations (p. 128). Accordingly, the governance and worship of congregations were in the hands of elected elders, with a system of local, regional, and countrywide boards of elders above them. In this way, the Reformed Church held to the Catholic belief in a God-given hierarchy (Church structure), though the actual structure was very different. Whereas the Catholic hierarchy was **episcopal** (controlled by bishops, who at the time were mostly appointed by rulers and confirmed by the pope), the Reformed one was **presbyterian** (controlled by elected elders—from the Greek word for "elder").

Likewise in the humanist tradition, Calvin went behind the worship practices that had grown up over the centuries and insisted that worship be based on what he believed to be the rule of the earliest churches—"that no meeting of the church should take place without the Word, prayers, partaking of the Lord's Supper, and alms-giving." "The Word" meant Bible readings, sermons explaining them, and psalm-singing; the Lord's Supper was the sacrament of the Eucharist. Calvin agreed with Luther that the only sacraments are baptism and the Eucharist, and that all should receive both bread and wine. More radically than Luther, he declared that the presence of Christ in the Eucharist is spiritual, not physical.

The minister wore no splendid robes but a simple black gown—the equivalent of today's business suit. Calvin believed that art and ornamentation had no place in the Church; the awesome Catholic cathedrals, with their stained glass, statues, and splendid altars, he branded as pagan. Instead, Reformed "temples" (named after the Temple in Jerusalem) were modest structures, in which the pulpit often stood in place of the altar (see photo on page 317).

> "Eternal life is foreordained for some, and eternal damnation for others."
>
> —John Calvin

Church and State

However, Calvin did share Catholic ideas on the partnership of Church and state. He believed that the purpose of government was to regulate society according to the will of God, and that the Church was the appointed interpreter of God's will: "Great kings ought not to think it any dishonor to humble themselves before Christ, the King of Kings, nor ought they to be displeased at being judged by the Church. . . . They ought even to wish not to be spared by the pastors, that they may be spared by the Lord." That was similar to what Pope Gelasius had told a Roman emperor about the relationship between "the authority of bishops and the imperial power" more than a thousand years before (p. 147). But the Church authority that Calvin had in mind was that of the pastors (elders charged with teaching and worship), and the partner of the Church that he himself mainly dealt with was the town council of Geneva.

Among the council's duties as upholder of the Church, Calvin believed in traditional fashion, was the suppression of heresy. In 1553, Calvin was the driving force behind the council's trial and execution of a Spaniard, Michael Servetus, who challenged the doctrine of the Trinity (p. 146)—though the council applied the traditional penalty of burning at the stake against Calvin's wishes. In the Reformation, what was heresy and what was orthodoxy often depended on whose side one was on, but Servetus denied a belief that nearly all Christians still upheld. When he was arrested in Geneva, the Reformed town council received a request for his extradition from the Catholic Inquisition (p. 219) in France, which the council denied so that they could burn him themselves.

 **"Calvin 500"** (http://www.calvin500.com/) Learn more about Calvin's life and beliefs.

> "The theater, because of its historical associations with paganism, was closed down in Geneva; art was seen as a distraction from God's word."

"A Godly, Righteous, and Sober Life"

Another function of the Reformed Church, springing from Calvin's belief that all Christians must live according to God's commands, was to ensure that all Christians actually did so. With no sacrament of penance to wash away sin, and no monks, nuns, or saints in heaven to intercede for God's mercy, it was actually more important for the Reformed Church than for the Catholic Church to supervise every detail of its members' behavior.

Calvin criticized any form of decoration lest it lead to vanity and pride—and any form of card playing lest it lead to gambling. The theater, because of its historical associations with paganism, was closed down in Geneva; art was seen as a distraction from God's word. Drinking was condemned as a prelude to intoxication, and dancing was prohibited as a stimulant to desire. The clothing of women had to be plain and ample; the display of personal ornament or the exposure of flesh was a signal to lustfulness. In living such a strictly disciplined life, concluded Calvin, one follows the teachings of the Lord, who "condemned all those pleasures which seduce the heart from chastity and purity."

This strictness was not at all the same as the traditional idea of an ascetic life. Like Luther, Calvin thought that the way of life of the monk or nun, based on the belief that virginity, fasting, and poverty were good works, was a wicked delusion that must lead a person to hell. Instead, God's elect must live what England's Calvinist-influenced *Book of Common Prayer* (p. 325) called "a godly, righteous, and sober life," not an ascetic one. They must eat and drink in moderation, marry and be true to their spouses, accumulate wealth through hard work and thrift, and donate it generously to the relief of the poor. Calvin took for granted (as Luther and Catholic theologians did not) the functions of capital, banking, and large-scale commerce—though, in his day, the biggest merchants and bankers were mostly Catholic, like the Fuggers (p. 255).

To Calvin, a person's conscience was the main guide to living in accordance with God's commands. But if a person could not avoid wrongdoing, Calvin believed, it was up to other Christians to be their "brother's keeper." As chief pastor in Geneva, he used his pulpit to warn and frighten potential sinners. When his sermons failed, he resorted to compulsion. Offenders were hailed before the Consistory, an assembly of elders from the various congregations in Geneva, which might reprimand the accused or impose bread-and-water sentences upon them. Common offenses included profanity, drunken-

 **Religious Law and Order in Calvin's Geneva** Read Calvin's ideas about enforcing religious law and order.

ness, dozing in church, criticizing ministers, and dancing.

In this way, a style of life evolved in Geneva that was imitated by Calvin's followers across Europe. Urged on by the hope of being among the elect and the fear of being among the reprobate, the disciplined, active, and persistent Calvinists became the leaders in the international movement of Protestant reform in the second half of the sixteenth century—at the same time as the Catholics were finally putting their house in order.

LO⁴ Catholic Renewal and Reform

From the 1530s onward, the threatened heretic takeover of the Church galvanized the papacy into wholeheartedly backing reform, while devoted priests founded new religious orders that rallied believers to the Church. The long-delayed Catholic movement of renewal and reform got under way—a movement that today is usually called the **Catholic Reformation**.

The Reforming Popes

By the 1530s, Luther's protest could no longer be seen in Rome as a "squabble among monks," and in 1534, a new pope, Paul III, committed himself seriously to reform. He launched an overhaul of papal administration and ordered a report by a committee of cardinals on abuses among the clergy that was so shocking that he kept it secret. His most decisive measure, however, was to summon a general council of bishops to settle the deep troubles facing the Church.

For the papacy, this was a risky move. The Church had a thousand-year-old tradition of holding general councils to deal with disputes, but councils had often made compromises between opposing beliefs, or they had bowed to the wishes of secular rulers, or they had set themselves up as rival authorities to the popes (pp. 145–146, 248). On the other hand, such a meeting might be able to set the course for a program of Catholic reform and renewal with the papacy at its head. That was what happened on this occasion (see photo).

The Council of Trent

The **Council of Trent** met in the northern Italian city of that name, with lengthy interruptions, over a period of some twenty years (1545–1563). Papal ambassadors presided over the sessions, and the pope had to approve the council's decisions. The growing bitterness of the religious divide meant that Protestants were unwilling to attend and were eventually not permitted to do so. All this enabled the papacy to ensure that the council would do what it wanted.

The council acted vigorously against corruption and wrongdoing within the Church. Bishops were ordered to regain strict discipline over their clergy and to provide better education for the priesthood by establishing seminaries (theological schools). The council passed decrees against simony (the sale of Church positions) and pluralism (the holding of more than one Church office at a time). Simony was already a Church offense, but making pluralism illegal was something new, and from now on, both prohibitions were taken more or less seriously. The council also outlawed the

≪ **Heresy Crushed** A wall painting in a Roman church by a local painter, Pasquale Cati, shows the Council of Trent at work. A panel of cardinals discusses with a bishop, a secretary takes notes, and the Holy Spirit descends to inspire the proceedings. In front, female figures representing Christian virtues—Charity, for instance, nurtures two children—surround a majestic lady representing the Catholic Church, who tramples the demon of Heresy beneath her feet. Santa Maria in Trastevere , Rome/The Bridgeman Art Library

selling of indulgences while affirming that the spiritual grace granted by indulgences was genuine.

On the other hand, the council uncompromisingly upheld traditional beliefs and practices. The special powers of the priesthood, the role of the papacy, the seven sacraments, the doctrine of transubstantiation, the veneration of saints and relics, the belief in purgatory, and above all, the necessity for salvation of good works as well as God's grace—all were specifically confirmed. At the same time, the council condemned the opposing Protestant doctrines. The result was to make orthodoxy clearer than before but also narrower, and to leave Catholic theologians with less freedom of interpretation than in earlier times. In an era of religious struggle, however, that was another sign of the council's success.

The Council of Trent and Catholic Reformation Read a selection from the Council of Trent.

The Jesuits

Like earlier reform movements, this one also needed people who were willing to devote their lives to it, and who would rally ordinary believers to the Church by methods suited to the political, social, and cultural conditions of their time. That was what the Cluniac and Cistercian monks, and later the Franciscan and Dominican friars, had done in the Middle Ages. Now it was the turn of the **Jesuits**.

Ignatius Loyola

Ignatius Loyola, the founder of the Jesuits, grew up in Spain, the one country in Western Christendom where reform had already got under way in the late fifteenth century. Cardinal Ximenes (**hi-MEH-nes**), archbishop of Toledo, had mounted a rigorous campaign to improve the morals and education of the clergy, the Inquisition had ruthlessly enforced orthodoxy against heretics, Jews, and Muslims, and pious rulers from Isabella and Ferdinand onward had overseen these efforts. Like Luther and Calvin, Loyola underwent a profound religious experience as a young man, but it sent him in exactly the opposite direction—to a life of total dedication to the Catholic Church.

Loyola was of noble birth and had an early career as a soldier. But in 1521—the same year that Luther stood before the Diet of Worms—he was fighting in defense of a castle when a cannonball badly wounded him in both legs. In the months of agonizing surgery and tedious convalescence that followed, he turned his warrior instincts of loyalty and courage from the king's service to that of Jesus. He wanted to do some great feat for his new "commander," but he was not sure what it should be. He learned Latin, preached on street corners in cities in Spain, lived for a time as a hermit in a cave, studied theology at the

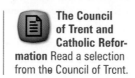

"To attain the truth in all things, we ought always to hold that we believe what seems to us white to be black, if the Hierarchical Church so defines it."

—from Loyola's *Spiritual Exercises*

University of Paris, and thought seriously of moving to the Holy Land and converting the Muslims. Finally, he and a few companions went to Rome, were welcomed by the reforming Pope Paul III, and put themselves at his service for whatever he might order them to do. In 1539, they became an official religious order, the Society of Jesus, with the mission "to employ itself entirely in the defense of the holy Catholic faith."

"Thinking with the Church"

When Loyola died in 1556, the Society of Jesus had grown to about 1,000 members; two centuries later, there were about 20,000 Jesuits. They were carefully selected and rigorously schooled in the same absolute devotion to Jesus that Ignatius himself felt, using methods of prayer and meditation that he explained in his book of *Spiritual Exercises*. ("Exercise," in those days, usually meant "military training.") The *Exercises* included "Rules for Thinking with the Church," among them "Laying aside all private judgment, we ought to keep our minds prepared and ready to obey in all things the true Spouse of Christ our Lord, which is our Holy Mother, the Hierarchical Church." These were very different words from Luther's at the Diet of Worms.

But as purposeful as the Jesuits were in their training and goals, in their methods they were extraordinarily flexible. As revivalist preachers, they stirred crowds of believers with passionate sermons on the torments of hell and the bliss of heaven, the sufferings of Jesus and the miracles of the saints.

Spiritual Exercises: A Manual for Christian Training Read a selection from Loyola's Spiritual Exercises.

As father confessors, they steered the lives of sinners one at a time, using kindly and understanding methods and thereby ensuring that their guidance would be welcomed—including by rulers who could use their power to uphold the Church. As educators, they turned the sons of the middle and upper classes into Renaissance gentlemen with a humanist knowledge of the ancients (pp. 290–292), who also reliably "thought with the Church." As missionaries in China, they dressed and behaved like Chinese gentlemen, and became learned in the literature and thought of that country (pp. 279–280). In ways like these,

"History of the Jesuits" (http://www.historyworld.net/wrldhis/PlainText Histories.asp?historyid=ab30#1577) Learn more about the experiences of the early Jesuit missionaries.

the Jesuits imitated the apostle Paul, who once said that to spread the gospel he had "become all things to all people." That was what enabled them to rally believers to the traditional faith in a changing and expanding Europe.

With popes committed to reform and renewal, a definite course set by the Council of Trent, and the purposeful flexibility of the Jesuits, in the second half of the sixteenth century, the Church moved from stagnation and defensiveness to a bold offensive. Its vigorous response to the Protestant challenge prevented further losses, and the religious divisions of about 1560 (see Map 17.1 on page 312) generally remain today. But it took another century before all sides accepted the divisions as more or less final—a century not just of religious debate, but also of religious repression and religious war.

LO⁵ Religion, Politics, and War

In spite of all the Reformation changes, most of the contending religious groups held to two traditional beliefs. The first was that there must be only one Church, proclaiming one religious truth, to which all people must belong. The second was that rulers and other power wielders must be partners of the Church, helping it to uphold religious truth and guide people to salvation. Now that there was no longer a single religion but several "religions," as they were called, each with its own version of truth, these beliefs in unanimity and partnership actually made for conflict.

In every country, there were also humanists who were in principle against settling religious disputes by force, as well as statesmen who feared that religious repression and war would weaken their countries in nonreligious struggles. But they got a hearing only at times when the rival religious groups had fought each other to a standstill and compromise of some kind seemed inevitable. And even when compromises came about, new religious disputes and nonreligious conflicts supplied new reasons for war.

As a result, wars of religion were fought in three main stages, each inspired by the main religious movements of the time and intertwined with fierce nonreligious conflicts. First came the wars in the Holy Roman Empire arising from the spread of Lutheranism, which ended in the first effort at religious compromise, the Peace of Augsburg of 1555. Then, in the second half of the sixteenth century, the spread of Calvinism resulted in civil and international wars involving the Netherlands and France. Finally, as the Catholic Reformation gathered strength, Catholic efforts to recover lost territory led, in the first half of the seventeenth century, to new struggles in the Holy Roman Empire that reached their height in the Thirty Years' War.

When the Thirty Years' War ended in stalemate, efforts to change the religious balance internationally came to seem so costly and destructive that they were finally seen as clearly harmful to the nonreligious interests of whoever pursued them. As a result, in the second half of the seventeenth century, religion gradually ceased to play a role in international conflicts. In this way, out of the religious wars of the Reformation there grew a new, secular European state system.

Religious Repression

Repression of one kind or another was continually practiced by all sides throughout the era of the Reformation. It took two forms—outright persecution of rival religions using updated methods, and efforts to prevent ideas from spreading by restricting freedom of the press.

≪ **"Force Outbids Reason"** The motto at right gives the message of a cartoon of 1686, when King Louis XIV of France was persecuting Huguenots (French Calvinists). A "Missionary dragoon" (a mounted infantryman—label at bottom left) levels a musket to make a Huguenot sign a drumhead conversion. The dragoon's musket, loaded with a cross, is labeled "Invincible argument"; his sword is labeled "Penetrating argument." The caption at top makes clear that this is happening by order of the king. Bibliotheque Nationale, Paris/Giraudon/The Bridgeman Art Library

THE REFORMATION WAS AN ERA OF WIDESPREAD PERSECUTION, AND OF CIVIL AND INTERNATIONAL WARS OF RELIGION, FOR SEVERAL REASONS:

Attempts to Uphold Different Versions of Religious Truth

- Rulers and churches of dominant religions tried to repress rival religions as part of their duty of upholding religious truth, and to prevent rival believers from taking power and doing the same to them.

- Rulers of countries with different dominant religions made war on each other as part of their duty of upholding religious truth, and to avoid being conquered and persecuted themselves.

- Within countries, believers in out-of-power religions, facing a hostile partnership of Church and state, rebelled and sought help from sympathetic foreign rulers, hoping to become dominant themselves.

Nonreligious Reasons for Conflict

- Rulers continued their endless nonreligious struggles for power, land, and trading opportunities, as well as for personal, dynastic, and national glory.

- Rulers' partnerships with powerful subjects—especially nobles—also continued to be full of frictions.

- Religious disputes did not replace all these conflicts but became entangled with them.

- Religious and nonreligious rivalries reinforced each other, and wars of religion were all the longer and more embittered as a result.

New-Style Persecution

In the Reformation era, medieval methods of persecution mostly went out of style. Only in Spain, Portugal, and Italy did the traditional Inquisition and burnings at the stake continue, but elsewhere, persecution was "modernized" (see photo). Everywhere local clergy were on the watch for religious dissidents, but actual intimidation and punishment became the work of the state. In Catholic countries, troops would be billeted in Protestant districts to live at the people's expense and harass them into conforming; Protestant ministers would be given life sentences as galley slaves; and if all else failed, the Protestants of whole regions would be given the choice between conversion and expulsion. Catholics in Protestant countries were also systematically persecuted. In England, for example, Catholic families could be ruined by huge fines for not attending Protestant services, and priests were sadistically put to death as traitors. In Catholic France and in Habsburg-ruled territories in the Holy Roman Empire, as well as in Protestant England and Scandinavia, these new kinds of persecution drove the rival religions deep underground.

> *"Out of the religious wars of the Reformation there grew a new, secular European state system."*

Religious Censorship

In every country, as the rulers became aware of the power of printed books to spread ideas, they tried to bring the new technology under their control. Printers were licensed by governments or guilds (pp. 200–201), and could lose their licenses and be sent to prison for publishing objectionable books; literature of the wrong religion belonged in this category, along with such material as attacks on rulers, revelations of scandals involving powerful people, and pornography. The most systematic censorship was established in Catholic countries by the Council of Trent. The council authorized an Index (list) of prohibited books, and established the Congregation of the Index to publish the list and keep it current. The Index remained in force until 1965, when it was dropped by order of the Second Vatican Council (p. 556).

But the printing industry was too large and diverse to be easily controlled. Printers could set up underground workshops; books that were prohibited in a country of one religion could be smuggled in from a country of another religion; printers in countries with easygoing censorship, notably Holland, did good business publishing books that were objectionable in countries of every religion. In religion, as in other fields, censorship was no more than a minor drag on the spread of ideas.

The Calvinist Wars: The Netherlands and France

In the late sixteenth century, reformers in many countries rallied to Calvin, and his version of Protestantism often found support from nobles who appreciated the limits he set to the authority of rulers. In Scotland, Calvinist nobles actually overthrew a ruler, Queen Mary; in Hungary, they resisted Habsburg power with the support of the Turks, who occupied much of that country. But the longest conflicts over Calvinism were in the Netherlands and France.

The Revolt of the Netherlands

The Low Countries, or Netherlands, were a center of trade and industry that formed a wealthy part of the Habsburg domains, and the region's powerful cities had a long-standing tradition of self-government. Protestantism first spread there from Germany and then grew rapidly under Calvinist leadership (see Map 17.1 on page 312). At about the same time, the Netherlands came under the rule of the Spanish Habsburgs, following the division of the territories of Charles V (p. 267), and in 1567, King Philip II of Spain responded to the spread of Calvinism with cruel repression. In addition to admitting the Inquisition to the area, he introduced harsh political and economic restrictions. In reaction to this challenge to their self-government, both Catholics and Calvinists rebelled in 1566 under the leadership of a local aristocrat and Habsburg official, William "the Silent," prince of Orange-Nassau.

There followed nearly half a century of wars, in which the Netherlands gradually divided. Spanish armies and growing Catholic mistrust of the Calvinists recovered the southern Netherlands for the old rulers and the old religion. But in the north, the defiant Calvinists, with English help, fought the Habsburg forces on land and sea. In 1581, they declared independence, but it took nearly thirty years before a truce gave them de facto Spanish recognition in 1609. A new country had appeared, the United Provinces of the Netherlands—often known as Holland, the name of its largest province.

Holland's commercial wealth made it a leading contender in European power struggles throughout the seventeenth century, and it became one of the main challengers of Spain and Portugal for control of worldwide trade and empire. It was governed as a loose confederation of provinces, with descendants of William the Silent presiding alongside many other competing power wielders as *stadtholders* (viceroys), the title of the former Spanish governors. There were still many Catholics in Holland, many disagreements among the dominant Calvinists, and many dissident Protestant groups. Persecution would risk renewed civil war in a small country that was still vulnerable to Spanish attack,

and would also be very bad for business. Instead, therefore, Holland became Europe's first country to hold consistently to a policy of religious toleration, though the government stayed under Calvinist control.

Civil War in France

Religion and politics were also mixed in France. Early in the Reformation, persecution by the Catholic rulers had kept Protestantism from spreading, but after the death in 1547 of King Francis I, the country had a series of weak rulers, and noble factions began to spring up that sought either to limit the monarch's power or to bring the government under their control. At about the same time, missionaries from Geneva began to spread their beliefs in France (see Map 17.1 on page 312). Soon, there was a growing **Huguenot (HYOO-guh-noh)** movement (a French slang word for "Swiss"), in which Calvinist ministers supplied religious fervor and powerful nobles provided military force.

The Huguenots never made enough converts or gained enough victories to take over the government, but the rulers were too weak, and had too many independent-minded Catholic nobles to deal with as well, to be able to crush them. The result was a series of civil wars and foreign interventions that continued on and off for most of the second half of the sixteenth century.

The very existence of France as a powerful independent country seemed to be threatened by religious struggles, and a school of thinking grew up, known by the French name *politique* ("political," because it put politics before religion), that sought religious compromise for the sake of national unity. Finally, King Henry IV, legitimate ruler by inheritance but also a Huguenot, brought the wars to an end by following a *politique* strategy. He defeated Catholic forces in battle but himself became a Catholic so as to win the loyalty of the strongest religion. To keep the support of the Huguenots, by the Edict of Nantes (1598) he guaranteed them civil rights, religious tolerance, and even the possession of military forces and strongholds.

 **Henry IV's Edict of Nantes Grants Limited Toleration to the Huguenots** Read a selection from the Edict of Nantes.

In this way, Henry was able to restore both national unity and royal power, but after his death, this second effort to keep religious disputes separate from political struggles broke down. The French rulers became fervent Catholics as the Catholic Reformation took hold, and Cardinal Richelieu (**ree-shuh-LYOO**), the powerful minister of Henry's successor, King Louis XIII, viewed the Huguenots as an obstacle to royal power—a "state within the state." In renewed civil war, he broke the military power of the aristocratic Huguenot faction. For the time being, Huguenots were still tolerated, but they now faced a strong Catholic government that favored those of its own religion. From a powerful faction under noble leadership, the Huguenots became a minority of middle-class townspeople and peasants.

England: A Middle Way?

In sixteenth-century England, shrewd and strong-willed rulers of the Tudor dynasty maintained the powerful monarchy that had emerged from the fifteenth-century Wars of the Roses (p. 262). But England was also caught up in the Reformation, and out of its rulers' efforts to reform the Church while not having their power undermined by religious struggles, there emerged yet another Christianity. **Anglicanism** (from the Latin for "English") borrowed from both Lutheranism and Calvinism but also kept many Catholic features. It was a compelling faith in its own right, which also for a time—but only for a time—saved England from civil war over religion.

"The King's Great Matter"

More than anyone else, it was an actual ruler, King Henry VIII, who opened the door to reform. For most of his long reign, he ruled as a Catholic king in partnership with the Church, and even earned the title "Defender of the Faith" from Pope Leo X for a book that he personally wrote attacking the beliefs of Martin Luther. Then, however, a royal family problem arose that involved the papacy and was also an issue in European power politics—the fact that his only surviving child with his queen, Catherine of Aragon, was a daughter. Powerful noble factions still lurked beneath the surface of the Tudor monarchy, and Henry feared that under a woman's rule, new civil wars would start. He must have a son; the queen was beyond childbearing age and had a young attendant, Anne Boleyn, who had caught his eye; so he needed the pope to annul his marriage so that he could marry Anne.

Popes had done favors of this kind for kings before, but the pope at the time, Clement VII, was under pressure from Catherine's powerful nephew, the Holy Roman emperor Charles V—and in the course of Italian power struggles, Charles had occupied Rome itself. Caught between Charles's wish to have England come under the rule of a relative and Henry's desire for a male heir, the pope decided to do nothing.

For six years, Henry pursued what the English called "the king's great matter" in Rome, until his patience finally ran out. He married Anne Boleyn in 1533, after his newly appointed archbishop, Thomas Cranmer, had declared his marriage to Catherine annulled. Clement promptly excommunicated the king and released Henry's subjects from their obligation of obedience to the crown. In the past, such papal actions had led to vicious power struggles with rulers, but no ruler had challenged the belief that the pope was the Christ-appointed head of the Church. Now, however, in the era of Luther's revolt, Henry "declared independence" from the papacy.

The Royal Supremacy

For this purpose, Henry did what English kings had got into the habit of doing, to rally the support of their subjects behind important measures—he acted with the "advice and consent" of the Parliament (p. 262). In 1534, Parliament passed the Act of Supremacy, which declared that the king was the "only supreme head on earth" of the Church of England. Additional acts forbade communication with and payments to the "bishop of Rome"; gave the crown the right to appoint bishops and abbots; and made refusing to swear to the king's supremacy an act of treason.

The king's break with the papacy encouraged English reformers inspired by Luther and Calvin to expect changes in traditional beliefs and practices as well. In some ways, Henry satisfied them—most radically, by abolishing monasteries and nunneries, confiscating their property, and selling it off to the profit of the crown. But in other ways, he remained a "defender of the faith." In 1539, he had Parliament pass the Act of Six Articles, which ordered penalties up to and including death for denying various traditional beliefs and practices such as transubstantiation and an unmarried clergy.

Meanwhile, Henry's search for a son, his changing love interests, and vicious rivalries at court led him to marry six wives in all, separate from two of them, and behead two others, including Anne Boleyn. When he died in 1547, he left three children, each with a different mother and a different religious upbringing. There were a young boy, Edward, and two adult daughters: Mary, the offspring of Catherine of Aragon; and Anne Boleyn's child, Elizabeth. In eleven years, all these children came to the throne in turn, and with each ruler, England officially changed its religion.

England Between Protestant and Catholic

Edward, as a male heir the first in the line of succession, was related through his mother to powerful noble factions that sympathized with reform. With Edward's uncle as regent (the king's guardian) and Archbishop Cranmer the main influence on questions of belief and practice, in 1549 Parliament passed the reforming Act of Uniformity. This law required that all Church services follow a uniform text, composed in English by Cranmer himself; this was then put into the *Book of Common Prayer*, which is still the basis of Anglican ritual. All subjects of the kingdom were required by the act to attend services regularly, and other forms of public worship were outlawed.

But in 1553 Edward died, and the traditionalist Mary became queen. Parliament repealed (undid) Edward's reforming laws and restored the traditional Latin services, and the pope formally pardoned Mary's subjects for their heresy. Protestant-minded bishops were replaced by Catholics, and several hundred reformers who refused to recant, including Cranmer, were burned at the stake. Furthermore, in hopes of producing a reliably Catholic heir, Mary wed Philip, the Habsburg heir to the Spanish throne.

As England's rulers shifted from one religion to the next, the Parliament, the clergy, and other power wielders mostly followed along. Unsuccessfully opposing the ruler would lead to

> **Anglicanism**
> The faith of the Church of England, with both Protestant and Catholic features.

 Catholicism in Britain Before the Turn to Protestantism (http://www.bbc.co.uk/history/programmes/av/hob/hob_06.ram) Learn about the Catholic faith in England on the eve of Henry VIII's break with the Church.

"Henry VIII and the Reformation" (http://www.bbc.co.uk/history/british/tudors/) Learn more about Henry VIII, one of history's most colorful monarchs.

Elizabethan Settlement
Religious compromise initiated by Queen Elizabeth of England that combined aspects of Lutheranism, Calvinism, and Catholicism in an effort to end religious conflict.

Puritans
English Protestants who wanted the Church of England to meet the standard of the "pure gospel" as Calvin understood it.

terrible punishment, and whatever people's religious beliefs, they mostly also believed that God wanted them to obey the ruler, and that such obedience was the only guarantee of social order and national power. Besides, if they only lay low while the present ruler made unwelcome religious changes, there was always the chance that the next ruler would reverse them.

But Mary was the first ruler to put hundreds of people to death for religion, and by her marriage, she risked her kingdom becoming part of Spain's intercontinental Catholic empire. When she in turn died in 1558 and her reform-minded half-sister Elizabeth took over, the memory of "Bloody Mary" and the Protestant martyrs, as well as fear and envy of Spain, were pushing the kingdom in the Protestant direction.

The Elizabethan Settlement

Once again, Parliament undid its previous actions, reinstating Henry's Act of Supremacy and Edward's Act of Uniformity. Catholic-minded bishops were replaced by Protestants, and under their guidance, the clergy agreed on a new statement of belief, the Thirty-nine Articles. According to the articles, the English Church accepted the authority of the Bible, salvation by faith, only two sacraments, bread and wine for all in the Eucharist, and a married clergy like other Protestant churches. Like the Evangelical Church, it put itself under the authority of the ruler and urged that the belief in predestination not be stressed. Like the Reformed Church, it denied that Christ was bodily present in the Eucharist and particularly warned against sins such as idleness. Like the Catholic Church, it had a hierarchy headed by bishops who claimed authority from Christ himself. And like all three, it proclaimed itself the one and only Church to which all should belong.

This combination—the **Elizabethan Settlement**, as it is usually called today—was one that many believers could live with, but it also dissatisfied wholehearted traditionalists and thoroughgoing reformers alike. Now it was up to the queen, Parliament, and clergy to uphold the settlement against both groups.

The chief upholder of the settlement was the queen herself. Elizabeth was a learned and active Renaissance lady (pp. 290–292), whose reign laid to rest her father's fears about what would happen if a woman should rule. "I know I have the body but of a weak and feeble woman; but I have the heart and stomach of a king,

and of a king of England too," one of her soldiers remembered her as telling them when Spanish invasion threatened in 1588. Scholars debate how reliable his memory was, but the words certainly reflect what she wanted her male subjects to feel about her—protectiveness toward her as a woman, trust in her as a forceful commander, and pride in themselves as belonging to a nation that was at least as great as Spain. She never married, because depending on her bridegroom, that would have committed her to a fully Protestant or a pro-Catholic course, and she preferred to keep foreign rulers and dissidents at home guessing about her ultimate goals. Thereby she gained the aura of a "virgin queen"—married, so to speak, to her subjects. She was also lucky to have a forty-five-year reign, for a long-reigning strong ruler was a guarantee of stability.

For most of Elizabeth's reign, the main threat to the settlement came from the Catholic side. In 1570, after Elizabeth's forces had crushed a Catholic rebellion in the north of England, Pope Pius V declared her deposed, a step that in turn led her to begin systematically persecuting Catholics. About the same time, English merchants and sailors were breaking into Spain's New World empire, English volunteers (and eventually an official English army) fought on the Protestant side in the Netherlands, and Philip II of Spain began to think of conquering England as the key to Catholic victory across Europe.

The Scaffold Speech of a Condemned English Jesuit Read the testimony of a Jesuit accused of treason in Elizabeth's England.

The crisis of Elizabeth's reign came in 1588, when Philip sent an invasion force against England that has gone down in history as the Spanish Armada. His big ships were held off by more maneuverable and better-armed English ones, and many were lost to storms on the way home. Protestants across Europe gave thanks to God, and medals were struck with mottos like "God Blew and They Were Scattered" and "Man Proposes, God Disposes" (see photo). The feeling grew among the English that God had singled them out as a Protestant people, the best hope of reformed Christendom, who would also be a great nation in the new worldwide Europe.

Even so, Elizabeth's religious settlement was not safe. The more England identified with Protestantism, the more influence the thoroughgoing Protestants gained—the **Puritans**, as their opponents called them, from their habit of complaining

"Man Proposes, God Disposes" A medal struck in Holland in 1588 celebrates England's defeat of the Spanish Armada. "Man" in the motto is Philip II of Spain, whose plan to conquer England God has disposed of by sinking his fleet. A Protestant Dutch family gives thanks to God for this deliverance, which means as much to them as to the English themselves. The destruction of the Spanish Armada was a victory for international Protestantism over international Catholicism. Library of Congress, Rare Book Special Collection

that the settlement did not meet the standards of the "pure gospel" as Calvin understood it. In the last years of Elizabeth's reign, she and her officials and bishops spent a great deal of time confiscating pamphlets against government by bishops and dismissing clergy who preached too forthrightly about predestination. In the next century, England would after all face a religious civil war—not between Protestants and Catholics, but among Protestants themselves (pp. 340–341).

The Catholic Counteroffensive: The Thirty Years' War

As Calvinism spread and the Catholic Reformation got under way in the Holy Roman Empire, the Peace of Augsburg began to break down. The Catholic rulers, guided by the Jesuits, stamped out the remnants of Protestant dissent in their territories, but the Lutheran rulers were weakened by bitter squabbles with Calvinist minorities. Sensing danger, some of the Protestant rulers joined together in an armed league in 1608, an action promptly countered by the formation of a Catholic league.

Local Rebellion: The Bohemian Revolt

As each camp eyed the other, revolt exploded in Bohemia, a self-governing kingdom within the Holy Roman Empire. Most of the people of Bohemia were Czechs who were both anti-German and antipapal, and the trouble there had its roots in the Hussite rebellion of the fifteenth century (pp. 250–251). During the sixteenth century, the Protestants of Bohemia had enjoyed toleration under moderate Catholic rulers of the Austrian branch of the Habsburg dynasty. But under a new Habsburg ruler, Ferdinand II, who zealously supported the Catholic Reformation, they feared that their religious and political rights were in jeopardy. Accordingly, in 1618, the Bohemian nobles announced their open defiance of Ferdinand and chose the Calvinist ruler of the Rhineland, a territory in the northwest of the empire, to be their king.

The Catholic league moved swiftly to help Ferdinand crush the poorly organized rebellion, and the support of the Spanish Habsburgs, as well as his election as Holy Roman emperor in 1619, gave him added strength. The imperial armies moved into the Rhineland to attack the possessions of the defeated rival Bohemian king. Ferdinand hoped to overthrow Protestantism throughout the empire and, in the process, to reverse the empire's gradual breakup and turn it into a powerful Catholic state under his own rule. And Catholic victory in the empire, so he and his Spanish relatives as well as the papacy hoped, would be the key to Catholic victory throughout Europe.

European War: The Struggle for the Empire

But what the Habsburgs hoped for, many other rulers—both Protestant and Catholic—feared. Among Protestant rulers, the king of Denmark decided to intervene in Germany to protect Lutheranism and to acquire territory for himself. He was promised help by the English and the Dutch, who also wanted to check the advance of Habsburg (and Spanish) power. Later, Sweden joined the struggle against Ferdinand. Meanwhile, the Catholic local rulers within the empire regularly lost enthusiasm for the struggle whenever it seemed that Ferdinand was too successful and might threaten their independence. Catholic France actually joined the war on the Protestant side. Richelieu wanted to build a powerful Catholic monarchy at home, but he was determined not to let Ferdinand do the same in the Holy Roman Empire.

All of the empire's neighbors became involved at one time or another, but the balance of forces was too even. None of the contenders was able to win a lasting victory, but it took thirty years, from 1618 to 1648, for them finally to give up hope of doing so. Germany was turned into a ghastly battlefield, endlessly fought over by mercenary armies. By the end of the **Thirty Years' War**, fighting, looting, famine, and disease had reduced the population by perhaps as much as one-tenth, and cities, towns, and villages were in ruins (see Map 17.2).

The End of Wars of Religion

The **Peace of Westphalia (west-FEY-lee-uh)**, which concluded the war, is a landmark in European history. In Germany, the terms of the Peace of Augsburg were restored and extended to include Calvinism as well as Lutheranism and Catholicism. The local rulers within the empire won recognition as independent sovereigns, and Switzerland and Holland, which had once been part of the empire, were recognized as independent states. The empire itself continued with the Habsburgs as emperors, but they made no more efforts to turn it into a single state under their rule.

The European State System and International Law

The settlement, whose main provisions lasted until the nineteenth century, marked the emergence of the modern European state system.

Now that there was no longer a common faith and no hope of reimposing one, European countries and rulers more or less deliberately excluded religion from their conflicts. Rulers no longer thought of themselves as belonging to a single Christendom whose harmony was liable to be disturbed by quarrels arising from sinful human nature. Instead, they thought of themselves as sharing a single territory, Europe, whose "balance of power" depended on successful adjustment of mutually competitive interests.

The seventeenth century also saw the emergence of the idea and practice of international law, aimed at regulating relations

Thirty Years' War
A conflict between Catholics and Protestants in the Holy Roman Empire that engaged the major powers of Europe between 1618 and 1648.

Peace of Westphalia
Settlement ending the Thirty Years' War by extending religious freedom in Germany and recognizing the independence of Switzerland and Holland.

Map Labels

NORWAY
SWEDEN
FINLAND
SCOTLAND
Edinburgh
North Sea
ESTONIA
LIVONIA
RUSSIA
IRELAND
Dublin
ENGLAND
London
Copenhagen
DENMARK
Baltic Sea
Vilna
Danzig
PRUSSIA
POLAND-LITHUANIA
Warsaw
UNITED PROVINCES
Amsterdam
Elbe R.
Magdeburg
Berlin
SAXONY
SILESIA
ATLANTIC OCEAN
Antwerp
SPANISH NETHERLANDS
Essen
Cologne
Rhine R.
Prague
BOHEMIA
MORAVIA
Dnieper R.
Paris
Seine R.
Metz
LOWER PALATINATE
UPPER PALATINATE
Nantes
Loire R.
BAVARIA
Augsburg
Vienna
AUSTRIA
STYRIA
Buda
Pest
MOLDAVIA
JEDISAN
FRANCE
FRANCHE-COMTÉ
Zurich
TYROL
Salzburg
CARINTHIA
HUNGARY
TRANSYLVANIA
BESSARABIA
Geneva
SWITZERLAND
Trent
CARNIOLA
SLAVONIA
SAVOY
PIEDMONT
MILAN
Venice
REPUBLIC OF VENICE
CROATIA
Belgrade
WALLACHIA
Black Sea
GENOA
BOSNIA
SERBIA
Danube R.
Ebro R.
Rhône R.
TUSCANY
PAPAL STATES
HERZEGOVINA
MONTENEGRO
BULGARIA
SPAIN
Tagus R.
Rome
Constantinople
OTTOMAN EMPIRE
Corsica (to Genoa)
NAPLES
Naples
Sardinia
Balearic Is.
Adriatic Sea
Aegean Sea
Palermo
Sicily
GREECE
Athens
Mediterranean Sea
Crete (to Rep. Of Venice)

Inset:
North Sea
SWEDEN
JUTLAND
Copenhagen
DENMARK
Baltic Sea
SCHLESWIG
WISMAR
POMERANIA
Lübeck
Hamburg
BREMEN
MECKLENBURG
VERDEN
Elbe R.
BRANDENBURG

Legend:
- Austrian Habsburg lands
- Spanish Habsburg lands
- Other German states
- Swedish lands by 1648
- Ottoman Empire and tributary states
- Boundary of the Holy Roman Empire

0   150   300 Km.
0   150   300 Mi.

Map 17.2 Europe During the Thirty Years' War, 1618–1648

The war began as a religious and political struggle within the Holy Roman Empire, but the empire was a key area in the international conflict of Protestant and Catholic as well as in the dynastic and power struggles of its neighbors. Countries near and far joined in the war at one time or another, from Spain across western and northern Europe to Poland. © Cengage Learning

Interactive Map

among these independent states by mutual agreement. Some rulers, of course, were more careful than others in following the law, but the law at least provided standards that were widely respected. The classic statement of those standards is the *Law of War and Peace* (1625), written by the Dutch lawyer Hugo Grotius partly in response to the atrocities committed early in the Thirty Years' War. Though Grotius recognized war as a "legitimate" state of affairs, he distinguished between just and unjust conflicts and laid down some guidelines for "humane" methods of waging war. Grotius condemned such acts as poisoning wells, mutilating prisoners, and massacring hostages. Drawing on the ancient Roman principles of natural law (p. 111), he also spelled out the rights of neutral states and of civilians in war zones.

Religious wars were still occasionally fought. Late-seventeenth-century struggles between English-backed Protestants and French-backed Catholics in Ireland ended in more than a century of second-class citizenship for the Catholic majority. Repression of out-of-power religions also continued. In France in 1685, King Louis XIV formally revoked the Edict of Nantes, which guaranteed toleration for Huguenots, and tens of thousands of refugees "defected" to Protestant countries (see photo on page 322). But for the most part, religious disputes among Christians ceased to play the leading role in international and civil conflicts that they had played since the sixteenth century.

Continued Church-State Partnership

This did not mean that the traditional parnership between Church and state came to an end. Leading clergy of the dominant religion in each country were still appointed by the ruler, and still set the crown upon the ruler's head. Most Protestant rulers more or less officially controlled the Church, with wide powers of oversight and appointment. Many Catholic rulers held similar powers, and even set new limits on the pope's power, for example, to publish proclamations and decrees without their permission. Popes might protest, but in the now divided Western Christendom, they no longer openly struggled with Catholic rulers.

Meanwhile, with dominant religions by now secure, minority religions gradually came to be tolerated, but their believers were still second-class citizens, excluded from public service and university education. In eighteenth-century England, public officials had to swear that they did not believe in the doctrine of transubstantiation, which no Catholic could do without blasphemy; in Hungary, officials had to take their oath of office in the name of the immaculate (sinless) Virgin Mary (p. 205), which no Protestant could do without idolatry.

Eventually, the newly formed United States actually dissolved the partnership of Church and state, with the First Amendment to its Constitution declaring that "Congress shall make no law respecting an establishment of religion." Few European countries followed this example, but in the nineteenth century, they mostly granted religious minorities, Christian and non-Christian, full toleration and civil equality. Religious freedom and equality became generally accepted Western values, which were violated more often by supporters of new secular ideologies than by religious believers. Such, ironically, was the long-term result of the wars and persecutions of the Reformation era.

 Listen to a synopsis of Chapter 17.

CHAPTER 18

RESTRUCTURING KINGDOMS: ABSOLUTE AND LIMITED MONARCHY,
1600–1700

LEARNING OBJECTIVES

AFTER READING THIS CHAPTER, YOU SHOULD BE
ABLE TO DO THE FOLLOWING:

LO¹ Explain the rise of absolute monarchy during the
seventeenth and eighteenth centuries.

LO² Describe the wars and revolution in the British Isles
during the seventeenth century, and outline the rise of
limited monarchy that resulted from this upheaval.

LO³ Appreciate how artists used Renaissance principles
and techniques to create the Baroque style,
emphasizing dramatic and spectacular effects.

"ABSOLUTE MONARCHY WAS AN IMPORTANT SHIFT IN THE POWER STRUCTURE OF WESTERN CIVILIZATION, BUT NOT A REVOLUTIONARY ONE."

In the fierce seventeenth-century European struggles, rulers came to believe that the only way to uphold government, religion, and social order was for them to gain complete supremacy within their kingdoms by casting off traditional restrictions on their power. They declared that they were not bound by established laws and customs, stopped calling representative assemblies, treated nobles and clergy at best as junior partners, and levied heavier taxes than ever before. They used the money mainly to build up well-equipped standing armies and navies, as well as to foster trade and industry and support science, scholarship, and art, thereby helping forward other Western changes. They often met with opposition as they restructured their kingdoms on this pattern of **absolute monarchy** (unlimited monarchy), but on the whole their subjects accepted them as providers of national security, upholders of religion, and distributors of favors and privileges.

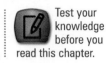

Test your knowledge before you read this chapter.

What do you think?

Governments that violate the rights of individuals should be overthrown.

Strongly Disagree						Strongly Agree
1	2	3	4	5	6	7

Absolute monarchy was an important shift in the power structure of Western civilization, but not a revolutionary one. It continued the growth of royal power that began in some countries in the late Middle Ages (pp. 259–263), and it kept many earlier features of kingship. Absolute monarchs still upheld the long-standing privileges of the nobility and clergy, and they still thought of their power as God-given—in fact, they claimed to be God's actual representatives, entitled to the same total obedience as himself. They were still intent on power and glory for themselves and their dynasties, and they proclaimed their power and glory more splendidly than ever with palaces built and decorated in the dramatic and spectacular style that had developed out of Renaissance art, the Baroque.

≪ Attack and Counterattack A city, ringed by a belt of cannon-resistant walls, has endured a three-month siege. Attackers have demolished a section of walls by digging trenches gradually close enough to tunnel under and explode mines. The city is ready to fall—but a relief army has broken into the besiegers' camp. The picture shows the Turkish siege of Vienna in 1683, but such scenes were normal in every war. The vast scale and expense of new and improved warfare helped drive the seventeenth-century restructuring of government.

Meanwhile, the British Isles were troubled throughout the seventeenth century by intertwined religious, national, and political struggles that reached their height in twenty years of war and revolution during the 1640s and 1650s. The religious conflicts were among Protestants as well as between Protestants and Catholics; the national rivalries involved three peoples of the region, the English, the Scots, and the Irish; and the political disputes pitted kings with absolutist leanings against the English Parliament, which sought a larger share in government.

The outcome of the struggles was yet another restructured kingdom—but on a different pattern from absolute monarchy. England and Scotland joined to form the kingdom of Great Britain, in which they enjoyed a fairly satisfactory partnership and their different forms of Protestantism were secure, while the neighboring, mainly Catholic kingdom of Ireland was ruled as a conquered country. The power of the British rulers diminished and the power of Parliament and the rights of subjects increased, yet under this system of **limited monarchy**, the government was more stable and stronger in both war and peace than before. Reflecting on the British upheavals, John Locke claimed that governments were appointed by societies to enforce the rights of individuals, and that governments that violated these rights could be legitimately resisted or overthrown. Locke's theory helped make the British experience a precedent for later changes in the power structure of many Western lands.

LO¹ Monarchs Supreme in the State: Absolutism

Throughout the Middle Ages, powerful and prosperous kingdoms had been ones where monarchs had the largest share of power in their partnership with nobles and the Church; when rulers lost control, the result was "failed kingdoms," beset by civil war and foreign invasion. Since then, the struggles of the Reformation and conflicts over worldwide trade and empire had greatly increased the stakes for kingdoms in having powerful rulers with armies and navies at the ready. Because of this

1600s	The Austrian Habsburg dynasty consolidates power in central and eastern Europe; Frederick William and his successor Frederick I develop the economic and military might of Prussia
1649	Charles I of England is executed; England becomes a Commonwealth without monarch or House of Lords
1643–1715	Reign of Louis XIV, the "Sun King," in France
1651	Thomas Hobbes describes absolute rule as the alternative to a warring "state of nature" in *Leviathan*
1660	The monarchy is restored in England under Charles II
1670	Jacques Bossuet argues for the divine right of kings in *Politics Drawn from Holy Scripture*
1682–1725	Reign of Tsar Peter "the Great" in Russia
1689	English Bill of Rights makes Parliament an equal partner of the ruler and guarantees many civil liberties
1690	John Locke's *Two Treatises on Government* rejects divine right and defends the right of rebellion
1691	The "Glorious Revolution" is completed in the British Isles, transferring power to the Protestant monarchs William and Mary
1707	England and Scotland become the United Kingdom of Great Britain

drive for military and economic dominance, absolute monarchy became the predominant form of government in seventeenth-century Europe.

Model of Absolutism: Louis XIV

Of all the seventeenth-century absolute monarchies, the most powerful, and for a long time the most successful, was France. The largest and wealthiest of the western European kingdoms, France had moved toward political centralization during the fifteenth century and collapsed into civil war following the Reformation (p. 324). But finally, a winner emerged from the wars—King Henry IV, who founded a new dynasty, the Bourbons (the name of one of their family properties).

MONARCHS GAINED UNLIMITED POWER DURING THE SEVENTEENTH CENTURY FOR SEVERAL REASONS:

The costs of equipping armed forces rose, as innovations in warfare continued from the late Middle Ages

- On land, small firearms (muskets) for foot soldiers became available; engineers devised both cannon-resistant fortifications and new ways of attacking such defenses (see photo on page 330).

- At sea, ships became large enough to carry whole batteries of cannon.

Military spending was necessary even in peacetime

- The long time it took to build ships and train their crews led governments to maintain standing navies.

- Mercenaries had been unreliable during the Thirty Years' War, so governments began to keep standing armies.

- Because of these expenses, rulers needed to tax their countries more heavily. They began to do so at their own discretion, without seeking the approval of representative assemblies.

Nobles and clergy accepted greater royal authority in exchange for favors

- Nobles received lucrative government, military, and Church positions.

- Both nobles and clergy were exempted from taxation.

- Landowners kept wide authority over peasants.

- Religious minorities were discouraged and granted second-class status at best.

Other classes of society also accepted Increased royal power including

- Bankers who lent rulers money.

- Lawyers whom rulers employed as bureaucrats.

- Merchants and manufacturers who supplied rulers with food, clothing, and equipment for their armies.

- Even peasants whom rulers secured against unwelcome changes of religion.

As victors, the Bourbons were in a good position to rebuild royal power. Cardinal Richelieu, the astute minister of Henry's son Louis XIII, crushed the Protestant "state within the state" of the Huguenots, and appointed new regional officials known as *intendants* to see to it that royal orders and policies were carried out across the country. His aim, he declared, was "to make the king supreme in France and France supreme in Europe." Richelieu died in 1642, but his work was continued during the reign of Louis XIV.

> **Richelieu Evaluates the State of the French Monarchy** Read Richelieu's argument for crushing the Huguenots.

The King Supreme in France

Louis came to the throne as a boy in 1643. Boy kings were always a danger to royal power, but his mother, Anne of Austria, and another able minister, Cardinal Mazarin (**MAZ-uh-rin**), held the government together against revolts by noble factions. The rebels were a minority even among the nobles, and they were defeated and so discredited that their revolts were contemptuously called the Fronde—the French word for "sling," since mobs used slings to throw stones at palace windows during the disturbances. By the time Louis personally took over the government in 1661, he was determined that never again would his power be hostage to his subjects. In a reign that lasted more than half a century, he built up a standing army that gave him a monopoly of military force, increased the numbers and powers of intendants, and eliminated the main legal restriction on royal power, the requirement for *parlements* (superior courts in Paris and the provinces) to officially register royal decrees before they went into effect.

> **The Sun King Describes the State of France at the Dawn of His Reign** Read Louis XIV's account of the early days of his reign

In these ways, Louis made himself "supreme in France," but his aim was not just to gain personal power. "I am the state," he is supposed to have said, but he put this differently on his deathbed: "I am going, but the state will remain." He might embody the state, but it was greater and longer-lasting than himself.

Furthermore, Louis never dissolved the traditional royal partnership with the nobles. They remained a privileged elite,

Reunion des Musees Nationaux/Art Resource, NY

king himself. Rulers had always tried to attract leading nobles and win the admiration of their subjects by the splendor of their courts; Louis alone was the "Sun King," the dazzling center round which his court and kingdom revolved (see photo).

Louis also vigorously upheld the traditional royal partnership with the Catholic Church, on terms that put him very much in control. From earlier rulers, he inherited the power to appoint leading clergy, and he encouraged the clergy to think of themselves as a national "Gallican" Church, accepting the pope's authority in matters of belief and worship but otherwise self-governing. He put pressure on the Huguenots, France's large Calvinist minority, to convert, and in the 1680s, he turned to outright persecution. Finally, in 1685, he revoked Henry IV's Edict of Nantes that had guaranteed toleration, and thereby made the Huguenot faith illegal. Most Huguenots became nominal Catholics, but several hundred thousand took their skills as businesspeople and soldiers to Protestant countries.

Royal Power, National Culture, and National Prosperity

In spite of the attack on the Huguenots, Louis's reign was an era of splendid cultural creativity in France, for which some of the credit belonged to the king. His court nourished the architects and artists who built and decorated Versailles (pp. 348–349), and the composers, playwrights, and performers who created entertainments for royal occasions. Louis also favored the French Academy, founded by his father Louis XIII in 1635. Its members had acquired fame in many fields of literature and learning, and it was charged with "giving exact rules to our language, to render it capable of treating the arts and sciences"—so that French would be on a level with the traditional language of the arts and sciences, Latin. The Renaissance belief that creativity and knowledge are among the highest forms of human excellence still held sway (pp. 288–289), and increasingly, the arts and sciences were seen as the key to human power and prosperity as well. It was, therefore, Louis's business as an absolute monarch to foster them for his own splendor and the benefit of his subjects.

The king's splendor, his government bureaucracy, and above all his armed forces were expensive, but he also took measures to increase France's ability to bear the burden. His minister of finance, Jean Baptiste Colbert (kohl-BARE), strengthened the tax system and promoted economic development. Internal trade was aided by

Power and Fashion In Hyacinthe Rigaud's portrait, Louis XIV is a kingly figure with one hand on his hip, the other on his scepter, and his ermine-lined coronation robe cascading around him. The 63-year-old monarch also wears youthful-looking leg-hugging breeches; he personally designed his high-heeled red shoes, which became the correct style for men's foot-wear at court; and he places his feet as recommended by dancing masters. In an aristocratic society, being a leader of fashion was an important part of being an absolute monarch.

and he surrounded himself with men and women of the oldest and wealthiest noble families at his court, which he eventually settled in his newly built palace of Versailles (vehr-SIGH) . At the court, the nobles scrambled for the favor of the king and for the government, army, and Church positions that only he could award—and the wealth and luxury of the courtiers added to the splendor of the

The Official French Government Site for the Palace of Versailles (http://en.chateauversailles.fr/homepage) Tour the Palace of Versailles.

Colbert Promotes "The Advantages of Overseas Trade" Read Colbert's argument for founding colonies in the East Indies.

improved roads and waterways, colonies and trading companies were founded overseas, and French industries were sheltered by protective tariffs and export subsidies.

The purpose of Colbert's program was to increase employment, profits, and state revenues—and above all, to secure for France a favorable **balance of trade** with other countries. According to the prevailing theory of **mercantilism**, a country should sell to other countries goods of greater total value than it bought from them, so that foreigners must pay the balance in gold or silver. The more precious metals flowed into the country, the wealthier it must be, and the better able to bear the burden of royal taxation. Regulation of business was not new in Europe; the towns and guilds had practiced it for centuries (pp. 199–201). But regulation of trade by rulers, based on the belief that a country's wealth consisted in its stock of precious metals, was the first nationwide form of deliberate government intervention in the economy. This policy was well established in seventeenth-century France and other western European trading countries like Spain, Holland, and England.

France Supreme in Europe?

Louis had a passion for territorial expansion and a love of war and glory. His driving desire was to gain and hold France's "natural" frontiers—the Rhine River, the Alps, and the Pyrenees. During his long reign, Louis was able to push France's frontiers farther east and north than ever before, and when the Habsburg rulers of Spain died out, he was able, after many years of war, to win the succession for a branch of his own Bourbon dynasty. Throughout the eighteenth century, the size and strength of France and its alignment with Spain were basic facts of the balance of power (see Map 19.1).

Louis's opponents—above all Britain, Holland, and the Austrian Habsburgs—were able to limit his gains, however. Strong barriers to French expansion remained in the Netherlands and northern Italy. Louis had failed to make France "supreme in Europe," and at his death in 1715, France lay exhausted, its military power spent. Though it recovered and remained the most powerful single country on the mainland of Europe for another hundred years, the power and prestige of its absolute monarchy began a long decline that ended in revolution (pp. 383–387).

The Eastern Monarchies

Absolute monarchy could not prevent kingdoms from losing as well as gaining weight in the European balance of power. In 1600, the Spanish Habsburgs were the mightiest of absolute rulers, but by 1700, Portugal had overthrown their rule, the Protestants were entrenched in the Holy Roman Empire, and western European rivals had taken over much of the trade of the New World. Later, under its eighteenth-century Bourbon rulers, Spain became the junior partner of its former rival, France. Still, absolutism

did seem to guarantee religion, social order, and the survival of kingdoms—so much so that in the Holy Roman Empire, where the emperors failed to impose their absolute power, most local rulers governed their territories as minor absolute monarchs.

In addition, absolute monarchy enabled the rulers of countries farther east in Europe to become far more powerful than before. Since the Middle Ages, these lands had been less wealthy than those of western Europe, many of them were exposed to Turkish invasion, and most of the peasants (the vast majority of the population) were serfs (pp. 251–252, 255–256). In the seventeenth century, the eastern countries were troubled by the same kinds of conflicts as in the western countries—rivalries among rulers, civil wars among noble factions, religious struggles between Catholics and Protestants as well as between Catholics and Orthodox, and campaigns of persecution and massacre against Jews, who now lived in large numbers in the lands between Poland and Russia.

The rulers of Poland, earlier the region's strongest Christian kingdom, could not master the chaos. By the end of the century, they were paralysed by a representative assembly dominated by powerful nobles in which any single member could end a session and nullify any measures passed by calling out "I do not allow it!" But three other dynasties emerged from the turmoil that ruled their lands as absolute monarchies—the Habsburgs of Austria, the Hohenzollerns **(HOH-uhn-zol-ernz)** of Prussia, and the Romanovs of Russia. By exploiting their countries' resources more fully than before, they greatly increased their weight in the balance of power—both against rivals further west, and against the Turks.

Austria

The Austrian Habsburgs had traditionally been junior partners of their Spanish relatives, the Thirty Years' War had left them mere figurehead emperors of the Holy Roman Empire, and in spite of many years of war after the Spanish Habsburgs died out, they finally had to yield Spain to the Bourbons. But they were able to take over some of the Spanish Habsburg possessions in the Netherlands and Italy, they held their own hereditary lands in central and eastern Europe in spite of rebellions by Protestant nobles and peasants, and they gained territory from the Turks in Hungary and the Balkans (see Map. 18.1).

By confiscating the lands of defeated Protestant nobles and selling them cheaply to Catholic followers, the Habsburgs were able to build up a loyal noble class in many of their lands. They did not interfere with the nobles' power over the serfs,

> *"Louis alone was the 'Sun King,' the dazzling center round which his court and kingdom revolved."*

balance of trade
The relationship between a country's imports and exports; in a favorable balance, the value of exports exceeds imports.

mercantilism
An economic theory that measures a country's wealth by its stock of precious metals, accrued through a favorable balance of trade.

Map 18.1 The Balance of Power, 1725

Since 1648 (see Map 17.2 on page 327), a branch of France's Bourbon dynasty has replaced the Habsburgs as rulers of Spain and its empire. The Austrian Habsburgs, however, have reconquered Hungary from the Turks and kept former Spanish Habsburg territories in the Netherlands and Italy. Prussia now stretches from the Rhine to the eastern Baltic, where Russia is pushing westward. England and Scotland have formed the union of Great Britain, which is now the leading worldwide power. © Cengage Learning

Legend:
- French Bourbon lands
- Spanish Bourbon lands
- Austrian Habsburg lands
- Prussian lands
- Great Britain and Ireland
- Boundary of the Holy Roman Empire
- Russian Empire
- Russian gains, by 1725
- Ottoman Empire, 1722

 Interactive Map

ATLANTIC OCEAN

IRELAND — Dublin
SCOTLAND — Edinburgh
GREAT BRITAIN
ENGLAND — London
WALES
Thames R.

North Sea

KINGDOM OF NORWAY — Oslo
KINGDOM OF SWEDEN
KINGDOM OF DENMARK — DENMARK
FINLAND
Baltic Sea
SWEDEN
ESTONIA
LIVONIA — Riga
INGRIA — St. Petersburg

RUSSIAN EMPIRE
Moscow
Smolensk
BELARUS

UNITED NETHERLANDS — Utrecht
HANOVER
BRANDENBURG — Berlin
Elbe R.
SAXONY
PRUSSIA — Königsberg
Gdansk
Vistula R.
Oder R.
SILESIA
LITHUANIA — Minsk
POLAND-LITHUANIA — Warsaw

FRANCE — Paris
Seine R.
Loire R.
LORRAINE
PALATINATE — Strasbourg
Rhine R.
HOLY ROMAN EMPIRE
BOHEMIA
Danube R.
BAVARIA
AUSTRIA — Vienna
HUNGARY — Buda, Pest
CARPATHIAN MTS.
MOLDAVIA
Dniester R.
UKRAINE — Kiev
Dnieper R. — Poltava
COSSACKS
DON COSSACKS
Don R.

SWITZERLAND
ALPS
SAVOY
MILAN
Po R.
GENOA
MODENA
TUSCANY
PAPAL STATES — Rome
REPUBLIC OF VENICE
Adriatic Sea
CROATIA
SLAVONIA
BOSNIA
HERZEGOVINA
SERBIA — Belgrade
MONTENEGRO
ALBANIA
WALLACHIA
Danube R.
TRANSYLVANIA
BULGARIA

Toulouse
Marseilles
Rhône R.
Garonne R.
Ebro R.
CATALONIA
SPAIN — Madrid
Tagus R.
Duero R.
PORTUGAL — Lisbon
GIBRALTAR (Gr. Br.)

Corsica (Genoa)
Sardinia (Austria)
KINGDOM OF NAPLES — Naples
Sicily (Savoy)
Minorca (Gr. Br.)
Balearic Is.

Mediterranean Sea

OTTOMAN EMPIRE
GREECE
Constantinople
ANATOLIA
Aegean Sea
Black Sea
CRIMEA
ARMENIA
KURDISTAN

0 150 300 Km.
0 150 300 Mi.

© Cengage Learning

which the nobles used both in their own interests and as agents of the central government. On these conditions, the nobles were willing to leave government decision making to the rulers and their advisers—who were in any case often leading nobles. Austrian absolute monarchy was less thoroughgoing than in France, but it was strong enough to keep the Habsburgs in the ranks of leading dynasties.

Prussia

The Hohenzollern dynasty rose to power from small beginnings in the Middle Ages, as vassals of the Holy Roman emperors. By the early seventeenth century, they were Protestant rulers of Brandenburg in the northeast of the empire, Prussia beyond the empire's border to the east, and several smaller territories in western Germany; eventually, the name "Prussia" came to be used for all these lands. At the Peace of Westphalia, the elector Frederick William (one of the rulers who elected the emperor, p. 267) gained additional lands.

In the next half-century, Frederick William and then his son Frederick I ruled their holdings as strict and dutiful absolute monarchs. They developed the economy—helped by thousands of Huguenot refugees from France—and raised a large and well-trained standing army. Prussia's noble landowners, like those of Austria, accepted the monarch's authority in return for complete control over their serfs, and supplied the ruler with loyal officials and a hereditary officer class. In 1701, Frederick joined the coalition against Louis XIV, for which the Habsburg emperor awarded him the title of king. By that time, Prussia had become the most efficient of all absolute monarchies, with a weight in the balance of power that was out of all proportion to its size and resources.

Russia

The most spectacular change in eastern Europe was the rise of Russia, which began early in the seventeenth century. In 1613, a new dynasty, the Romanovs, was summoned to power by the nobles in 1613 to end the "Time of Troubles," a period of civil war and foreign invasion like the struggles in France. The earliest Romanov tsars were pious supporters of their country's Orthodox religious traditions and generally ruled in cooperation with the

(above, center) **Tsar Michael Fyodorovich's *Shapka*** This ceremonial headgear, made for the first tsar of the Romanov dynasty in 1627, imitates a Tartar style *shapka* or cap of state given by a fourteenth-century khan to a vassal prince of Moscow (p. 223). The *shapka* was an inheritance from Russia's past as a subject land of an Asian empire; significantly, Peter the Great replaced it with a European-style crown modeled on that of the Holy Roman emperors. Jevgeni German/Russian Picture Service/akg-images

nobles. This brought them stability at home and success in power struggles with their powerful neighbors, Poland, Sweden, and Turkey. These three rivals had other wars to fight in central Europe, the Balkans, and the Middle East, and none of them was Orthodox—the prevailing religion in many of the lands between the Black and Baltic Seas that the Romanovs coveted. The dynasty gradually increased its holdings in this region, while Russian traders and settlers spread across northern Asia to the Pacific Ocean, turning their country into an intercontinental empire (see photo, and Map 15.3 on page 282).

As Russia's power and its western contacts grew, its rulers began to pay attention to the changes under way in western Europe—the cultural innovations, the burgeoning of science and technology, the rulers who wielded absolute power as embodiments of the state. About 1700, Tsar Peter the Great determined to rebuild Russia on the western European model.

Peter's project involved a vast upheaval—one that he pushed forward, even while he fought savage wars against Turkey and Sweden that brought Russia to the actual shorelines of the Black and Baltic Seas (see Map 18.1). He continued to rule through nobles, but treated them as servants of the state rather than as partners with whom he shared power; the ranks and titles of nobles, instead of being hereditary, were determined by their positions in the tsar's service. He replaced Moscow as his capital with the new city of Saint Petersburg on the Baltic Sea, mainly designed by a French architect who had once worked for Louis XIV—but Peter's building project dwarfed even Versailles.

And he pressured the upper classes, who still wore medieval-style tunics and robes, to look like western Europeans—men should shave their beards and wear stylish jackets and pants, and women should have elegant coiffures and low necklines. Dress and hairstyles were no trivial matter. They were a symbol of Peter's determination to make Russia a part of the new civilization that was growing up in western Europe.

Peter was history's first "Westernizer," and like later Westernizers, he only partly changed the society over which he ruled.

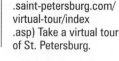

Peter the Great Imposes Western Styles on the Russians Read Peter's decrees on men's clothing and shaving.

A Virtual Tour of St. Petersburg's Monuments (http://www.saint-petersburg.com/virtual-tour/index.asp) Take a virtual tour of St. Petersburg.

He overcame opposition by old-fashioned brutality, he had no thought of ending serfdom, and his changes gave rise to persisting debates: Did Russia's strength lie in imitating western Europe, or in its traditional Orthodox mission as the "Third Rome" (pp. 251–252) and in the unchanging life of its peasants? Still, with

divine right
The idea that the monarch is God's representative on earth and is therefore entitled to total obedience and unlimited power.

its vast size, its modern absolute monarchy, and its enduring traditions, Russia now played a larger part in the power struggles and the cultural life of Europe than ever before.

Absolutist Ideas: Bossuet, Hobbes

In every traditional civilization, the power of monarchs was thought to be linked with divine power. Now that European monarchs were seeking to throw off all restrictions on their power, thinkers added a new twist to the old tradition—the idea of **divine right**.

> "With its vast size, its modern absolute monarchy, and its enduring traditions, Russia now played a larger part in the power struggles and the cultural life of Europe than ever before."

God's Lieutenants

Medieval monarchs had set themselves above their subjects by the religious ceremony of coronation (pp. 167, 173), but they usually accepted that God had set bounds to their authority. Divine right thinkers, however, dropped any notion of limits. The new view was pithily expressed by an actual ruler, King James I of England, early in the seventeenth century. "The state of monarchy," he lectured Parliament, "is the supremest thing on earth, for kings are not only God's lieutenants here below and sit upon God's throne, but even by God himself are called gods." King James did not mean to say that monarchs were actually divine, but he did claim that as God's "lieutenants" (representatives), they wielded the power of God himself and were therefore entitled to the same total obedience.

Later on, a favored bishop at the court of Louis XIV, Jacques Bossuet (baw-SWE), echoed King James's views in *Politics Drawn from Holy Scripture*, a booklet prepared about 1670 for the instruction of Louis's heir. Buttressing his arguments with many quotations from the Bible, he too declared that kings are "ministers of God" and that their power, being that of God himself, has no limits. "Kings should tremble then as they use the power God has granted them," lest they misuse what belongs to him—but "the ruler need render account of his acts to no one" except God. For "the ruler . . . is a public personage, all the state is in him; the will of all the people is included in his. As all perfection and all strength are united in God, so all the power of individuals is united in the person of the prince. What grandeur that a single man should embody so much!"

> "For Hobbes, without the restrictions provided by government, human life would be 'solitary, poor, nasty, brutish, and short.'"

Leviathan

Divine right had wide appeal in an era when monarchs—and most of their subjects—instinctively thought of royal power as God-given. But in the changing Europe of the seventeenth century, thinkers developed new ideas about what it was that upheld the power of rulers. Already in the Renaissance, Machiavelli had described how power was upheld only by the courage and cunning of those who wielded it (pp. 265–267). Now, Thomas Hobbes, a supporter of the Stuart kings in the British wars, developed a whole new theory of absolute power in his book *Leviathan* (le-VYE-uh-thuhn). He derived it not from God's command but from the competing desires and needs of individual human beings.

Drawing on the scientific advances of his time, Hobbes claimed that every human being is a kind of machine, driven by an instinctive need for self-preservation—and this need naturally brings these living machines into conflict with each other. In a "state of nature," with no coercive governing authority, the general human condition is a "war of every man against every man" and human life is "solitary, poor, nasty, brutish, and short." Hobbes did not base this view on any actual society of his own or earlier times; his dismal picture of the "state of nature" arose from his understanding of what drives the human machine.

Hobbes Describes the Natural State of War Read an excerpt from Leviathan.

Fortunately, said Hobbes, humans have a power of reason that enables them to provide an alternative to the anarchy of nature. Because they are selfish egoists, unable to trust one another, they cannot create a cooperative society of equals. What they can do is agree to surrender their individual strength to a higher authority, which alone will have the power to curb individual aggression. Hobbes believed that human society, the state, and civilization itself arose from an imaginary "contract" of each individual with all others: "I authorize and give up my right of governing myself, to this man, or to this assembly of men, on this condition, that thou give up thy right to him, and authorize all his action in like manner. This done, the multitude so united in one person, is called a COMMONWEALTH." The makers of this contract have come together out of pure self-interest. Their need for self-preservation alone is what moves them to form a state and accept total obedience to it.

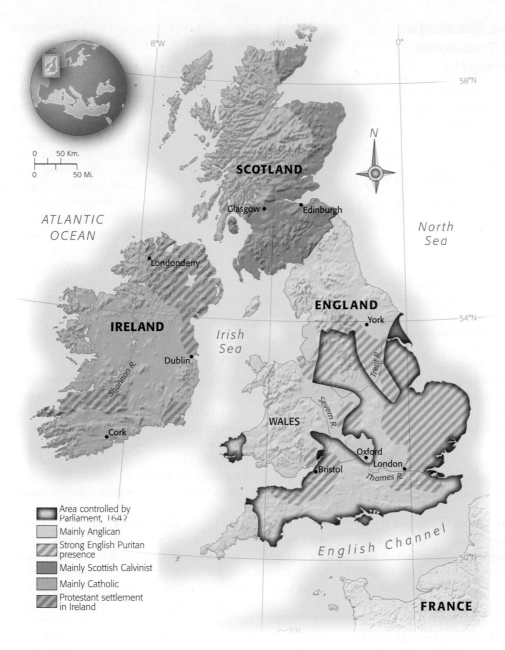

Map 18.2 **The British Isles about 1640**

The Stuart dynasty rules England, Scotland, and Ireland as separate kingdoms. Each is jealous of its independence and has religious and political conflicts both internally and with its partner kingdoms. The three kingdoms are about to enter an era of war and revolution that will end with the fall of the dynasty, the creation of the new kingdom of Britain, and the emergence of a new pattern of government.
© Cengage Learning

 Interactive Map

Map legend:
- Area controlled by Parliament, 1642
- Mainly Anglican
- Strong English Puritan presence
- Mainly Scottish Calvinist
- Mainly Catholic
- Protestant settlement in Ireland

Hobbes's argument did not find favor with supporters of absolute monarchy at the time, for he broke the traditional link between royal and divine power. But by doing so, he turned people's minds to the search for a kind of government authority that would not be based on the direct command of God.

LO² Monarchs and Parliaments: The British Constitution

In the Middle Ages, the British Isles had come to be divided among four countries (see Map 18.2). The island of Britain (or Great Britain, as its inhabitants often proudly called it) was shared between England and its neighbors, Wales on the west and Scotland on the north; and to the west of Britain lay the island of Ireland. The rulers of England, the largest country, often tried to gain power over the other countries, and by 1600 they had united Wales with England and ruled Ireland as a separate kingdom.

Meanwhile, in the sixteenth century the Tudor dynasty of England and the Stuart dynasty of Scotland had intermarried, and in the lottery of marriage and inheritance, it was the Stuarts who won. When the unmarried Queen Elizabeth I died in 1603, her cousin King James VI of Scotland became King James I of England. The British Isles were still divided among three kingdoms, but now they all had the same king—one, furthermore, who believed that "the state of monarchy is the supremest thing on earth."

The Breakdown of Traditional Monarchy

For James actually to rule supreme over his three kingdoms was no easy matter—particularly since the Reformation had added religious conflicts to their continuing national rivalries. Scotland had become fiercely Calvinist and shared Calvin's disapproval of bishops and his belief in the Church's right to pass judgment on kings (p. 319). In Ireland, a fiercely Catholic majority confronted a militant minority of English and Scottish Protestant settlers. In England, the Anglican compromise between Catholicism and Protestantism prevailed but was under attack from Calvinist-influenced Puritans (pp. 326–327), and this religious dispute made it hard for James to win the cooperation of the country's representative assembly, the Parliament.

Traditionally, the Parliament had been a valued but junior partner of the rulers in the government of England. It met for short periods when the rulers decided to summon it—usually when they needed its backing for important measures or money to carry them out, since Parliament had to approve the levying of taxes. Parliament assembled in two houses: nobles and Anglican bishops met in the House of Lords; and elected representatives of country districts and towns who were mostly **gentry** (nonnoble landowners) and wealthy businessmen sat in the House of Commons.

In other countries, the gentry would have counted with the nobles rather than the commoners, but because of the way feudalism had developed in medieval England, actual nobles were a small group of great lords. Neither nobles nor gentry were exempt from royal taxation, so neither of them needed absolute monarchy to help uphold tax privileges. Both groups wielded vast social and economic power, with the gentry usually deferring to the nobles, so that the House of Commons had traditionally followed the lead of the Lords. This system had worked well in the sixteenth century, but under James, it began to break down.

> " *The state of monarchy is the supremest thing on earth.* "
> —King James I

The Road to War

By James's time, the Commons were dominated by Puritans, whereas in the Lords, Puritan nobles were balanced off by Anglican bishops. James, however, who had already defended his royal power against Calvinists in Scotland, was determined to uphold the Anglican Church with its existing worship and bishops, and himself as its "Supreme Governor." Besides this religious disagreement, the Commons were against James's ideas of divine right, they disapproved of the corruption and extravagance of his court, and they distrusted his ability or willingness to uphold Protestantism internationally as the Thirty Years' War broke out on the mainland of Europe. When James asked them for grants to cover government deficits or support military interventions abroad, this led to arguments with Parliament in which the Commons rather than the Lords took the lead.

Under James's son, Charles I, these religious and political tensions built up still further. Charles used harassment and coercion to uphold the Anglican Church against the Puritans, and made the religious conflict worse by marrying a French Catholic princess. From now on, distrust between the Stuart kings and their English and Scottish subjects was heightened by the suspicion that what the rulers really wanted was to revive "popery." Unable to make the English Parliament do his bidding on new taxes, Charles stretched the law in various ways to raise money on his own authority. He brought critics and resisters before courts that ignored the legal safeguards, including jury trial, that had grown up in England since the Magna Carta of 1215 (p. 190).

The Wars of the Three Kingdoms

Charles finally undermined his own position by overreaching in his other two kingdoms. In 1639, the Calvinist Scots rebelled against many years of Stuart efforts to impose Anglican-style worship and bishops on their country. For troops who could be relied on to crush the Scots, Charles began raising an army of Irish Catholics, but in 1640, to pay the expenses of war, he had no choice but to summon the English Parliament. The resentful Parliament, however, proclaimed its sympathy with the Scots and threatened Ireland with invasion—which in turn led to an Irish rebellion against English rule.

Meanwhile, the Parliament tried to make the weakened king bow to its will. It enacted unprecedented restrictions on his power: among other things, rather than calling parliaments when it suited him, the king must call them at least once every three years. In addition, it issued a "Grand Remonstrance" calling for a whole series of changes in government and religion. In the future, the king must respect the traditional liberties of subjects; his ministers and advisers must have the confidence of Parliament; the power of bishops must be curtailed; and "formality and superstition" must be eliminated from worship. Against the king's efforts to enforce Anglicanism and build absolute monarchy, the Parliament—with the Lords now following the Commons—was aiming at supremacy over the king in a Calvinist England. The traditional partnership of ruler and Parliament had broken down.

Parliament Chastises Charles I: The Grand Remonstrance Read an excerpt from Parliament's "Grand Remonstrance."

Finally, in 1642, Charles tried to personally arrest the parliamentary leaders, and finding them gone and the people of London aroused against him, he left the city for the nearby town of Oxford. The king and the Parliament raised opposing armies, and soon England, too, was at war.

The **Wars of the Three Kingdoms**, as they are called today, lasted on and off into the 1650s. In England, the wars pitted Puritans and opponents of arbitrary royal power against Anglicans and believers in obedience to God-given royal authority. In general, outlying northern and western regions were Royalists (supporters of the king), while the country's commercial and agricultural heartland in the south and east was for the Parliament. Of the most influential groups in the country, nobles mostly followed the king, the gentry were divided between the two sides, and businessmen mostly supported the Parliament. The Scots fought to uphold their Calvinist Church, and intervened in England and Ireland to prevent Royalist and Catholic victories there; and for Irish Catholics, the wars were ones of liberation against Protestant oppression.

To start with, the king's opponents did not fight to overthrow him, but to force him to do what they wanted. Gradually, however, the wars changed into a revolution—one that was centered in England. The fighting went badly for the Parliament at first, so it reorganized its forces into the "New Model Army," a force recruited mainly from volunteer **yeomen (YOH-muhn)** (independent small farmers) who were inspired by a Puritan zeal more radical than that of the Parliament itself. Whereas the parliamentary leaders looked to establish an English Calvinist Church in alliance with the monarchy, the soldiers were mostly Independents—believers in self-governing congregations of committed "saints," with no overall Church structure and no alliance with the state. These convictions were shared by the army's commanders—chief among them a middling landowner and novice soldier who in a few years taught himself a great deal about both war and politics, Oliver Cromwell.

The English Revolution

The new English army decisively defeated Charles's forces in 1646, and in 1648 it went on to take power from the Parliament, where the majority of members still hoped for a bargain with the imprisoned king. By that time, Cromwell and his fellow commanders had come to the conclusion that the king would never meet their religious and political demands, and finally they sent a detachment of soldiers to "purge" from the House of Commons all members but those who agreed with the army's views. The military takeover was followed by a truly revolutionary deed, when the surviving "Rump" Commons of some sixty members put the king on trial for treason (see photo).

In 1649, King Charles I, wearing his hat to show his disrespect for a court he did not recognize, faced his judges. No king had been put on trial before, let alone for treason—by seeking "to uphold an unlimited and tyrannical power to rule according to his will, and to overthrow the rights and liberties of the people of England." The sentence was also unprecedented—that Charles "be put to death, by the severing his head from his body." Ten days later, the sentence was carried out.

The "Rump" then declared the monarchy and the House of Lords abolished, and proclaimed England a "Commonwealth" (republic). But the beheaded monarch's family was safe in

exile, and his supporters now recognized his eldest son as King Charles II. Accordingly, brutal warfare continued, mainly with the Scottish Calvinists who hoped for a compromise with their native dynasty, and with the Irish Catholics who looked to the Stuart monarchy to protect them against the Protestants.

By 1654, Cromwell's army had imposed its will on the entire British Isles, and he and his supporters now tried to remodel the region's nations according to their religious and political

A King on Trial Charles confronts a panel of judges selected by a committee headed by Cromwell. Security is tight: armed soldiers watch the public, and the president of the court, John Bradshaw, wears a steel-lined hat. The king will soon be beheaded, but at the Restoration, many of his judges will suffer the far worse penalty of hanging, drawing, and quartering. Bradshaw, having meanwhile died, will be dug up and his skull will dangle on a pole atop this very building.

Bodleian Libraries, University of Oxford, Ashmole 1689, Plate LXX

Restoration
Term applied to the reign of Charles II, in which the monarchy was restored (reinstated) in England.

Glorious Revolution
The regime change in which James II was replaced as monarch by his daughter Mary and her husband William, assuring Protestant rule in Britain.

views. There was no longer a state Church, and Protestants could believe and practice according to their consciences, with the major exception that Anglican worship and Anglican bishops were prohibited. So also was Catholicism, so that in Ireland, the majority lived outside the protection of the law. Taxes were efficiently collected and honestly spent—mainly on the standing army and on a large navy that restored England's standing in European and worldwide power struggles following the end of the Thirty Years' War.

But only a minority actively supported Cromwell's regime, and he found that he could maintain orderly government only through strong personal rule backed by the army. He tried to set up a permanent and legitimate system of rule that would outlast him and, in 1653, took the position of "Lord Protector"—a kind of substitute king. But this was not the kind of government that most of the Puritan and parliamentary opponents of Charles I had wanted, let alone his Anglican and Catholic supporters. In all three kingdoms, power wielders and humble people alike either resentfully obeyed the regime or served it without loyalty, while waiting for it to go away.

 The Oliver Cromwell Website (http://www.olivercromwell.org/index.htm) Learn more about the controversial figure of Oliver Cromwell.

The Growth of a New Order

Following Cromwell's death in 1658, his regime soon collapsed. His son took over as Lord Protector, but the young man was no soldier-politician like his father, and power drifted to Cromwell's military governor of Scotland, General George Monck. The canny general realized that the decision on a new regime must lie mainly with England—specifically with the nobles, gentry, and business interests that traditionally dominated the Parliament. Accordingly, the only way to establish a permanent and legitimate government would be through a Parliament including both Lords and Commons that was free to make its own decisions, and Monck marched his army into England to overawe opponents and make sure that this happened.

The Parliament met in 1660; it received from the would-be King Charles II promises of renewed partnership, pardon for opponents, and religious toleration; and it recognized him as the rightful ruler. He was warmly welcomed home in England, and was accepted also in Scotland and Ireland. The grateful monarch did not forget to make General Monck a duke.

The Restoration

The quarter-century of Charles's reign is known as the era of the Restoration. There was no going back to traditional monarchy, however, for the political, religious, and national rivalries that

had led to revolution were not stilled. Under Charles's rule, there was bitter political strife in England between believers in God-given royal power and supporters of the rights of Parliament and subjects. In spite of the king's promises, the restored Anglican Church harassed English "Dissenters" (as Puritans were now called), bishops were imposed on Calvinist Scotland, and Protestants still had the upper hand over Catholics in Ireland. But Charles astutely maneuvered among the opposing groups in his three kingdoms, took advantage of the widespread fear of civil war and Puritan dictatorship, and avoided risky overreaching. By the end of his reign, he ruled free of parliamentary control and open opposition.

There remained, however, a persistent source of mistrust between the Stuart dynasty and most of its subjects—the specter of "popery." Charles had a Catholic mother and a Catholic queen, and most alarming of all, a Catholic convert brother, James—and since Charles's marriage was childless, James was the heir to the throne. In spite of fierce efforts by opponents of royal power to disinherit him, Charles's brother became king as James II in 1685.

The "Glorious Revolution"

Less cautious than Charles, James appointed Catholics to government, army, and court positions, and declared toleration for both Catholics and Protestant Dissenters. These measures went against acts of Parliament, so he claimed the right to "dispense with" (exempt people from) laws, and pressured power wielders throughout his kingdoms to support his measures. Partly in response to local uprisings but also to overawe peaceful opposition, he also maintained a standing army—the first since Cromwell's time. With these measures, James lost the trust of the Anglican clergy and believers, traditionally the strongest supporters of royal power, without gaining much loyalty from Protestant Dissenters, who were generally "popery's" bitterest foes.

Even so, it seemed best to the king's leading subjects to follow the traditional policy of waiting out an unwelcome reign. The fear of civil war and Puritan dictatorship was still powerful, and besides, James's likely heir was his Protestant daughter, Mary, who was married to William III, the stadtholder (p. 324) of Protestant Holland. In 1688, however, James's queen gave birth to a son who was baptized a Catholic. Faced with the prospect of generations of future Catholic rulers, a small group of influential nobles secretly invited William to land with an army in England. After William arrived, much of James's army deserted, and James quickly sailed for France. Parliament, alleging that James had abdicated (resigned as king), offered the throne to the welcome invader William and the Stuart heiress Mary as joint monarchs.

Soon after, Scotland accepted the English-made regime change—one that rid the Scots, too, of a Catholic king while maintaining a link through Mary with their native dynasty. Only Catholic Ireland stood by James, but he lost a final bout of religious and national warfare there to William, sailed away again, and spent the rest of his days in France. By 1691, the "**Glorious Revolution**," as it had already come to be called, was safe in all three kingdoms.

THE ENGLISH BILL OF RIGHTS

Even at the present day, Britain does not have a constitution consisting of a single document, but is governed under a collection of written laws and unwritten customs that has grown up over the centuries. One of the most important constitutional laws is the English Bill of Rights of 1689, passed by a parliament summoned by William III (mentioned here under one of his titles, the prince of Orange) after the "abdication" of James II. By consenting to this law, William and Mary as joint monarchs legally obliged themselves and their successors to rule in partnership with Parliament and to respect various rights of their subjects.

And whereas the said late King James II having abdicated the government, and the throne being thereby vacant, his Highness the prince of Orange (whom it hath pleased Almighty God to make the glorious instrument of delivering this kingdom from popery and arbitrary power) did (by the advice of the lords spiritual and temporal, and diverse principal persons of the Commons) cause letters to be written to the lords spiritual and temporal, being Protestants, and other letters to the several counties, cities, universities, boroughs, and Cinque Ports [five port towns on the English Channel, having special privileges], for the choosing of such persons to represent them, as were of right to be sent to parliament, to meet and sit at Westminster upon the two and twentieth day of January, in this year 1689, in order to provide such an establishment as that their religion, laws, and liberties might not again be in danger of being subverted; upon which letters elections have been accordingly made.

And thereupon the said lords spiritual and temporal and Commons, pursuant to their respective letters and elections, being now assembled in a full and free representation of this nation, taking into their most serious consideration the best means for attaining the ends aforesaid, do in the first place (as their ancestors in like case have usually done), for the vindication and assertion of their ancient rights and liberties, declare:

1. That the pretended power of suspending laws, or the execution of laws, by regal authority, without consent of parliament is illegal.

2. That the pretended power of dispensing with the laws, or the execution of law by regal authority, as it hath been assumed and exercised of late, is illegal. . . .

4. That levying money for or to the use of the crown by pretense of prerogative, without grant of parliament, for longer time or in other manner than the same is or shall be granted, is illegal.

5. That it is the right of the subjects to petition the king, and all commitments and prosecutions for such petitioning are illegal.

6. That the raising or keeping a standing army within the kingdom in time of peace, unless it be with consent of parliament, is against law.

7. That the subjects which are Protestants may have arms for their defense suitable to their conditions, and as allowed by law.

8. That election of members of parliament ought to be free.

9. That the freedom of speech, and debates or proceedings in parliament, ought not to be impeached or questioned in any court or place out of parliament.

10. That excessive bail ought not to be required, nor excessive fines imposed, nor cruel and unusual punishments inflicted. . . .

13. And that for redress of all grievances, and for the amending, strengthening, and preserving of the laws, parliament ought to be held frequently.

EXPLORING THE SOURCE

1. The bill lists some practices as "illegal," and others as the way government "ought" to be conducted. Why this difference?

2. Which of the bill's clauses would have been most effective in restraining the growth of absolute royal power, and why?

Source: *The Statutes: Revised Edition*, vol. 2 (London: Eyre and Spottiswoode, 1871), pp. 10–12.

The British Constitution

Meanwhile, in 1689, the English Parliament passed the Bill of Rights, which turned the Parliament from a junior partner to an equal partner of the ruler and guaranteed many civil liberties. This historic measure stated that the ruler could suspend laws, raise armies, and levy taxes only with the consent of Parliament; it also provided for frequent meetings of the lawmakers and unlimited debate within their houses. The Bill of Rights also guaranteed every citizen the right to petition the monarch, to keep arms, and to enjoy "due process of law" (trial by jury and freedom from arbitrary arrest and cruel or unusual punishment).

Under the Bill of Rights, the monarch was still the ultimate decider on government, military, and Anglican Church appointments, and was mainly responsible for foreign policy and the conduct of wars. But the monarch's power was explicitly limited by the requirements to cooperate with Parliament and to observe the rights of subjects. From now on, England was legally a limited monarchy, as against the absolute monarchies that prevailed on the mainland of Europe.

In religion, the Anglican Church remained the church of the majority and the monarchs, who in future could neither be Catholics nor marry Catholics. A Toleration Act gave freedom of worship to Protestant Dissenters, but government and army positions as well as university education were closed to them. From challengers of the government and religious order, they became accepted but second-class citizens.

In Scotland, similar measures limited the ruler's power and established toleration among Protestants, though in this case, it was the Calvinist Church that was the official church. The Scots also wanted to continue as a separate kingdom with the right to choose different rulers from England—a notion that horrified leading English politicians. By combining threats to cut off trade with offers of aid to bail the Scots out of a financial crisis, in 1707 they persuaded Scottish representatives to agree to a union of the two kingdoms. The union was deeply unpopular in Scotland, and English public opinion did not welcome it either. But in the new United Kingdom of Great Britain, both nations kept their religious and national identities and their different legal systems while sharing in worldwide trade and empire.

Of the original three kingdoms, the one that had suffered most from the seventeenth-century upheavals was Ireland. The wars there had been at least as devastating as the Thirty Years' War in Germany, and afterward, the country remained a separate kingdom with a long-lasting system of religious oppression. A small Anglican minority owned most of the land and ran the government and the official church; a larger minority of Protestant Dissenters were second-class citizens as in England; and the Catholic majority was mostly landless and rightless. The resulting conflicts and resentments have lasted down to the present day.

Even in Britain, the new order was far from equitable. The House of Lords, consisting of two hundred nobles and bishops, had as much power in the government as the House of Commons. The Commons themselves were elected by a small minority of the male population, who were easily bribed and intimidated by local nobles and gentry. And the monarchs, with the effective government power that they still wielded, could influence parliamentary votes by job offers and other favors.

All the same, the "British Constitution"—the collection of parliamentary acts and unwritten customs under which the government now operated—was felt to guarantee rights to the humble as well as the powerful, and became a focus of widespread patriotic pride. Furthermore, now that Parliament was an equal partner in government, it was far more generous with taxation and far less distrustful of the rulers than before, so that Britain kept its standing army and built a massive navy that gained the country worldwide supremacy. "Rule, Britannia! Britannia rule the waves!" ran a British patriotic song; "Britons never, never, never will be slaves!" In Britain, as in ancient Athens (p. 54), freedom went together with power.

Locke's Justification of Revolution

A byproduct of the British upheaval was John Locke's political theory, which would have a profound influence on future revolutions. Locke, who came from a Puritan family, grew up in the era of war and revolution. In the Restoration era, he joined the king's opponents and spent several years in exile, where he made notable contributions to philosophy (pp. 365–366). After the overthrow of James II he came home, and in 1690 he published *Two Treatises on* ("Studies of") *Government* in defense of the new order. The first treatise rejected the theory of divine right, and the second defended the right of rebellion and became an ideological handbook for revolutionists everywhere.

Like the absolutist thinker Thomas Hobbes, Locke believed that the miserable condition of people in the "state of nature" had given rise to an agreement to establish civil government, but Locke disagreed with Hobbes about the terms of the "social contract." Hobbes had argued that individuals must have turned over their entire "right of governing themselves" to the state as a means of securing order. Locke, on the other hand, believed in specific "natural rights"—a concept that grew out of the ancient belief in natural law (pp. 87, 111), and which he defined as being rights to life, liberty, and property. These rights are "natural" because they are natural features of being human, just as size, shape, and weight are natural features of physical objects, so that there is no way that people can give up any of them. Instead, what they transfer to society is the power to take measures to preserve their rights.

John Locke's Vindication for the Glorious Revolution: The Social Contract Read Locke's critique of absolute monarchy.

A society, said Locke, holds this power as long as the society lasts, but it delegates its power to a government, such as that of a monarch. Should a monarchy or any other type of government use its power to violate natural rights, the society is legally and morally entitled to resist. Who decides whether a government's action is in fact in violation of rights? "The people shall judge,"

Locke replied, and if a government refuses to yield to this judgment, the people have the ultimate right to resort to force—to "appeal to Heaven."

Thus, by building on ancient Greek and Roman ideas of natural rights and natural law, Locke constructed a "universal" political theory. Though it rested neither on scientific facts nor on actual historical events, it served to justify the "Glorious Revolution." In the next two centuries, Locke's ideas were heartily embraced by Thomas Jefferson and by many other revolutionary leaders as "self-evident" truths.

LO³ Art of Faith and Power: The Baroque

In the era of the Reformation and wars of religion, and of the growth of absolute and limited monarchy, Renaissance art evolved into a new style that today is called **Baroque**—a word that originally meant "elaborate" or "excessive." The name is used because painters and sculptors exploited to the limit new Renaissance skills such as accurate perspective (p. 298) for the utmost dramatic effect, while architects stretched the revived ancient rules of design and added an abundance of decorative features to their buildings. But the result was paintings and statues full of movement and excitement and sometimes of awe-inspiring mystery, as well as spectacularly magnificent churches and palaces.

> **"***For he that thinks* absolute Power purifies Mens Bloods, *and corrects the baseness of Humane Nature, need read but the History of this, or any other Age to be convinced of the contrary.* "**
>
> —John Locke

Baroque Painting and Sculpture: Rubens, Gentileschi, Rembrandt, Bernini

Baroque art first reached its full flourishing around 1600 in Catholic countries. The clergy of the Catholic Reformation valued dramatic and emotional presentations of religious scenes; absolute monarchs wanted their triumphant deeds to be spectacularly glorified; and depictions full of movement and drama added excitement to subjects from Greek and Roman mythology. The result was an outpouring of magnificent art, ranging from the mystical to the sensual.

Rubens

The leader of Baroque art was the Flemish painter Peter Paul Rubens (from Flanders, the southern part of the Low Countries, p. 324). As a young man, he studied in Italy, and then worked chiefly in his native Antwerp for international clients including the rulers of Spain, France, and England, for Flemish aristocrats and businesspeople, and for the Church. A man of enormous energy and versatility, he created fine portraits of royalty, nobles, merchants, and his own family; huge wall and ceiling paintings celebrating the owners of royal palaces; altar paintings dramatically depicting the central mysteries of the Catholic faith; and mythological scenes of vigorously cavorting gods and goddesses. So great was the demand for Rubens's work that he set up a well-organized workshop in which he trained specialists to paint certain elements—clothing, animals, or backgrounds. He supervised the production of each picture and himself finished the key features, such as faces and hands. He was blessed by good fortune and a happy disposition, and his paintings are charged with movement and vigor.

In his treatment of a subject from Greek mythology, *The Rape of the Daughters of Leucippus* (see photo on page 346), Rubens depicts Castor and Pollux, horse-riding sons of Zeus, kidnapping Phoebe and Hilaera, the daughters of a mortal king, as brides. The muscular riders reaching down to their struggling naked victims create an image of irresistible male passion overwhelming helpless womanhood. Even the horses, white in the original myth, are a more masculine-looking chestnut and gray. But on the left, and in the middle next to the head of the chestnut horse's rider, are mischievous boy-gods—Cupids. The kidnappers, too, are helpless—mere puppets of Cupid, whose name means "Desire."

Gentileschi

A very different depiction of women in relation to men was the work of an early seventeenth-century Italian painter, Artemisia Gentileschi (**jen-tee-LES-kee**). Her works were commissioned by rulers and admired by colleagues in Italy and abroad: among her clients were King Charles I of England and the Medici ruling family of Florence, where she was the first woman to be admitted to a renowned artistic institution, the Academy of the Arts of Drawing.

Gentileschi's painting *Judith Beheading Holofernes* (**ho-lo-FER-neez**) depicts a Bible story, of the beautiful Israelite widow Judith who made her way to the camp of an invading army, contrived for herself and her serving woman to be alone with the army commander when he was in a drunken stupor, and cut off his head with his own sword. Traditional depictions showed a demure Judith holding the general's head as a trophy; already a renowned Baroque artist, Caravaggio (**Cah-rah-VADZH-yo**) had broken with this tradition and shown the

and avoiding bright colors in favor of browns, dark reds, and golds. The effect is sober but revealing, as in a self-portrait that Rembrandt painted near the end of his life (see photo), in which he goes outside himself and looks inward. He shows himself, like any other sitter, in the dress and with the equipment of his calling. He flatters himself a little with a freehand-painted circle to proclaim his technical skill. But he mainly uses his skill to carry out Leonardo da Vinci's advice (p. 300), to paint "the individual's appearance and the state of his mind"—in this case an aging, weary, but still creative and powerful artist.

Rembrandt used the same methods in religious painting, for example, in his *Supper at Emmaus* (see photo), which shows the Bible story of the risen Christ revealing himself to two loyal followers after walking with them unrecognized to a village tavern near Jerusalem. Catholic artists usually depicted this scene in close-up, with the followers in poses of astonishment. But Rembrandt shows an intimate group in a corner of a shadowy room, with Christ's followers too absorbed by the sight of him to be amazed—perhaps, even, they have quietly and joyfully realized that they knew who he was all along. Rembrandt's deliberate understatement actually makes the unforgettable moment all the more dramatic.

The Rape of the Daughters of Leucippus Rubens depicts with relish the Greek gods Castor and Pollux voluptuously kidnapping their brides . . .

actual deed. But Gentileschi's painting is the most grimly vivid of all Baroque depictions, with the women's faces coldly ruthless, and Judith's pose giving a disturbing sense of the hard work involved in sawing through a man's neck while standing far enough away not to be spattered with blood (see photo). The grimness of the painting probably reflects a traumatic experience of Gentileschi's youth, a rape followed by a lengthy and sordid trial—an experience that creative imagination and artistic skill have turned into a memorably horrific Baroque scene.

Rembrandt

As Rubens was the artistic master of Catholic Flanders, Rembrandt van Rijn (**REM-brant, Rine**) was the master of the northern, Protestant part of the Low Countries—Holland. Like Rubens, though a generation younger, Rembrandt won recognition early in his career. After his beloved and well-to-do wife died in 1642, however, he fell into debt, his popularity vanished, and he turned more and more inward in his thoughts. Yet it was the dark days of tragedy and self-examination that made Rembrandt the most profound of Baroque artists. He made many portraits of Dutch townspeople, shunning dramatic poses

>> *Judith Beheading Holofernes* . . . and Gentileschi coldly observes the Israelite widow Judith and her serving woman hard at work sawing off the head of an Assyrian invader.

Portrait of the Artist Rembrandt made over 80 portraits of himself from youth to old age. His youthful self-portraits were often studies of different facial expressions that sold well and helped to make him well known, but as he grew older they turned into explorations of his own personality, of which this is one of the deepest.

Supper at Emmaus Catholic Baroque artists usually made this scene of Christ being recognized by two travelers into a moment of high drama, but Rembrandt, the sober Protestant, makes it into one of tranquil contemplation.

Bernini

Meanwhile, in Catholic Italy the dominant master was Giovanni Lorenzo Bernini, a sculptor of extraordinary technical skill. In the cold, hard medium of stone, Bernini succeeded in catching the fleeting instant, the throbbing passion, the rhythm of movement.

One such moment of passion that Bernini depicted was the experience of mystical union with God, as described by a sixteenth-century Spanish nun, Saint Teresa of Avila: "The pain was so great that I screamed aloud; but at the same time I wished the pain to last forever. . . . It was the sweetest caressing of the soul by God." In *The Ecstasy of Saint Teresa*, carved for a chapel in a church in Rome, Bernini boldly used theatrical devices to reenact the saint's words. The figures are poised on a cloud with no apparent support, divine rays (and actual light) flood down from above, a smiling angel pierces the saint with the arrow of divine love, and the saint's face echoes the commonest human experience of unbearable pleasure (see photo). The sculpture proves the truth of Bernini's proud claim: "I render marble as supple as wax, and I have united in my works the resources of painting and sculpture."

The Ecstasy of Saint Teresa Bernini's sculpture is set into the end wall of a chapel in a church in Rome belonging to the Carmelite nuns, a religious order of which Teresa had been a member. In theater box-like enclosures on the side walls, statues of members of a Venetian noble family that commissioned the chapel sit observing and discussing the scene of religious drama.

Baroque Architecture: Bernini, Le Brun, Wren

Baroque architects, as well as painters and sculptors, emphasized the spectacular, the magnificent, and the dramatic in their works. The buildings they created spoke of the glory and power of religions, rulers, and nations.

Bernini and Saint Peter's

Bernini was an architect as well as a sculptor, and late in his life, he fashioned Saint Peter's Square, the space in front of Saint Peter's Basilica in Rome. The approach to the church begins with Bernini's vast oval plaza (see photo). The plaza is linked with the basilica by a straight-sided space that widens toward the church's western entrance. The entire area is surrounded by rows of 60-foot-high columns, supporting a roof topped by giant-sized statues of saints. The plaza has an ancient Egyptian obelisk at its center that was brought to the city in the first century A.D. at the command of an emperor; it was moved in front of Saint Peter's and topped with a cross sixteen centuries later on the orders of a pope.

In this way, visitors entering the plaza are embraced, in Bernini's words, by "the maternal arms of Mother Church," and welcomed by many of its most revered men and women through the ages. At the Catholic Church's center, the architecture proclaims that the Church has outlasted Egypt, triumphed over Rome, and spread around the world to embrace the human race.

Le Brun and Versailles

While Bernini was proclaiming the glory of the Catholic Church in Rome, French architects were working in Versailles to do the same for Louis XIV and the French state that he embodied.

The king's new palace was built in the countryside near enough to Paris to allow easy access to the capital and far enough away for the king, his attending officials, clergy, and nobles, and their families and servants to form a self-contained community whose life revolved around the monarch. The palace therefore had to be exceptionally large: the buildings cover 17 acres, and the formal gardens, courts, parade grounds, and surrounding woods stretch over many square miles. The whole complex took the entire half-century of Louis XIV's reign to build, at staggering cost. Even so, the accommodation was basic even for courtiers, let alone for the palace staff, since 10,000 people had to be squeezed into the space.

The royal and public rooms, however, were lavish in the extreme. One of the most dazzling chambers is the Hall of Mirrors (see photo), designed by Charles Le Brun, whose genius for large-scale creations and his shrewdness in gaining and keeping the king's favor made him for many years one of the court's leading artists. The 80-yard-long marbled and mir-

The Church's Embrace Two hundred yards across, 300 yards long, and surrounded by 60-foot-high columns, the space in front of Saint Peter's Basilica designed by Bernini can accommodate a crowd of 300,000 people—a worthy setting for the most festive celebrations of the worldwide Catholic Church. Scala/Art Resource, NY

Erich Lessing/Art Resource, NY

The Hall of Mirrors The symbolic meaning for France's friends and enemies of King Louis XIV's ceremonial chamber has been long-enduring. In this hall in 1871, the invading king of Prussia was proclaimed emperor of Europe's new dominant power, united Germany; and in 1919, France and its allies summoned the Germans back to sign the treaty ending the First World War.

Wren had visited France and Italy and studied the work of architects there, including Bernini, but he had to deal with Anglican clergy, who were conservative in their tastes and eager to avoid any suggestion of "popery." The new Saint Paul's had an awe-inspiring dome like Michelangelo's at Saint Peter's in Rome, as well as many Baroque features of design and decoration like the statues on the roof overlooking the entrance (see photo). But it also had old-fashioned features like the twin towers flanking the entrance as in Gothic cathedrals; and

"Christopher Wren and St. Paul's Cathedral" (http://www .bbc.co.uk/history/british/ civil_war_revolution/ gallery_st_pauls.shtml) Examine Wren's plans for the new St. Paul's Cathedral.

rored chamber was intended for court ceremonies and festivities. The mirrors were themselves a luxury item that spoke of the king's magnificence, while they also multiplied the splendor of all the other decorations that they reflected. For the ceiling, Le Brun made huge paintings of Louis XIV's government achievements and victories over rival rulers, thereby proclaiming "the king supreme in France and France supreme in Europe."

Wren and Saint Paul's

Catholic clergy and absolute monarchs were not the only ones who appreciated the possibilities of Baroque architecture for proclaiming glory and power. In 1666, the Great Fire of London destroyed most of the city's medieval core, including the huge Gothic cathedral that dominated the urban skyline, Saint Paul's. The task of rebuilding the cathedral was given to an Oxford scholar who was mainly noted as an astronomer deeply involved in the burgeoning scientific discoveries of the time, Christopher Wren.

A.F. Kersting/akg-images

>> **Saint Paul's Cathedral** With its stately mixture of Baroque and traditional design, the first cathedral built in England since the Reformation became a national shrine for the new United Kingdom of Britain and an enduring symbol of the nation in good times and bad (see photo on page 505).

genre paintings
Paintings depicting the everyday life of ordinary people.

instead of a huge plaza with an obelisk like Saint Peter's, it had a modest forecourt with a statue of Queen Anne, the British ruler at the time the cathedral was completed in 1710.

Saint Paul's is soberly majestic rather than lavishly spectacular—a restrained version of Baroque that was very suitable for an era when Britain was consolidating Protestant domination, strengthening parliamentary government, and rising to worldwide power. The stately new cathedral became a British shrine where national victories were celebrated and national heroes had their funerals, and Wren became a national hero himself. He is commemorated by a Latin inscription carved into the cathedral's floor: "If you seek a monument, look around you."

Painting Everyday Life: Brueghel

The Renaissance skills of lifelike depiction also opened up to painters new themes that called for realistic treatment, among them the everyday life of ordinary people. This kind of painting has come to be called **genre painting**, from the French *petit genre*, the "small kind" of art depicting scenes of ordinary life, as against the *grand genre*, the "grand kind" of art depicting scenes from religion, mythology, and history. In an era when accurate observation of the world was highly valued (pp. 292–293), "small" subjects came to be admired as well as the traditional "grand" themes.

One of the pioneers of genre painting was Pieter Brueghel (**BROI-guhl**), a sixteenth-century Flemish artist. Among Brueghel's everyday scenes were ones that showed, bluntly and honestly, the ordinary men and women who made up the bulk of European society—the peasants.

Medieval artists had sometimes shown peasants at work, not for their own sake, but to celebrate such themes as orderly government or the seasons of the year. But in his *The Wedding Dance* (see photo), Brueghel shows peasants at play—dancers uproariously flinging themselves about, quietly sociable groups of neighbors, everyone in their Sunday best. He is celebrating peasants themselves, with their spontaneous high spirits, their sense of community, their modest prosperity—and also their social pretensions. Some of the men wear tight-fitting pants complete with suggestively upstanding codpieces, as was the fashion among nobles of the day.

Painters in seventeenth-century Holland, with its well-off townspeople who were willing to spend money on works that

The Wedding Dance As in all traditional civilizations, peasants were the majority of Europe's population until the twentieth century, and not all of them were downtrodden. Brueghel's sixteenth-century depiction shows the well-fed and well-dressed elite of a village enjoying themselves.

Detroit Institute of Arts, USA/ City of Detroit Purchase/ The Bridgeman Art Library

realistically depicted the world they lived in, and its Calvinist Church that frowned on religious art, made a speciality of genre scenes. Dutch painters also specialized in two other newly prominent kinds of painting. One was landscapes—depictions of rural scenery for its own sake, not as background for the doings of saints and heroes. The other was still lifes—depictions of everyday objects in ordinary surroundings such as fruit in a bowl or musical instruments lying on a table. In this way, alongside the splendor of the Baroque, another kind of painting was growing up that foreshadowed Realism and Impressionism

(pp. 449–451)—the nineteenth-century styles that would inaugurate a new age in Western art.

Listen to a synopsis of Chapter 18.

INDEX

God, the one: *See also* Monotheism; Christian (Trinity), 127, 145–146, 319; in Islam, 159, 160, 161; in Judaism, 37, 38–43

Godfrey, duke of Lorraine (c. 1060–1100), 214

Godric of Finchale (c. 1065–1170), 196–197

Gods and goddesses: *See also* Divine kingship; God, the one; Egyptian, 22, 23–25, 27; Germanic, 152–153; Greek, *60–61*, 62–63, 65; Hellenistic, 84; Indo–European, 47; Neolithic, 10; Roman, 93, *94*; Sumerian, 14–15, 16–17, 18, *18*

Gold: in Africa, 271, *271*, 280; in Americas, 284; jewelry, *49, 90*

Golden Ass, The (Apuleius), 119

Golden Mean, 76

Goliardic poets, 237

Gospels, 126, 127, 129, 132. *See also* New Testament

Gothic churches, 227–232

Government and politics: absolute monarchy, 332–339; Bossuet's theory of, 338; Carolingian dynasty, 171; Egyptian, 22; English law and, 189–190; feudal, 184–190; Frankish kingdom, 155; French economy and, 334–335; Greek city-states, 52–53, 73–76; Hobbes' theory of, 338–339; Italian city-states, 263–264; late medieval monarchy, 258–263, 264–267; limited monarchy, 342–344; Locke's theory of, 332, 344–345; Machiavelli's theory of, 265–266, 338; medieval towns, 196, 199–200; in More's *Utopia*, 296–297; papal, 208–211, 247–249, 264; and religious tolerance, in France, 324; rise of Western Europe and, 176; Roman Empire, 136, 137; Roman Republic, 91, 92–93; Spanish colonial, 279; taxation and, 258–259

Gracchi brothers, reforms of, 98–99

Granada, reconquest of, 252, 263

"Grand Remonstrance" (England), 340

Great Britain. *See* Britain

Great lords (barons), 174–177, 184, 187. *See also* Nobles (aristocracy); English kings and, 189, 190; Holy Roman Emperor and, 188, 189

Great Schism, in Western Christendom, 248

Great Sphynx, in Egypt, *23, 26*

Greco-Roman civilization, 3, 103, 180. *See also* Romanization; Egypt and, 119; Islam and, 163; Jews and 118–119, 125

Greco-Roman traditions: humanism and, 289; of natural rights, 111, 345; Renaissance and, 243, 287, 288

Greece: *See also* Hellenistic era; alphabet of, 33, 51, 119; chronology (431–30B.C.), 80; citizenship in, 45, 51–52, 53, 54; city-states of, 51–59 (*See also* Athens; Sparta); colonies of, 50(*map*); crisis of city-states, 80–82; Dark Ages of, 49–50; Egypt and, 29, 51; expansion of, 50 *and map*; geographic knowledge of, 270, 273; government in, 52–53; homeland of, 48(*map*); under Ottoman rule, 251; renewal of, 50–51; Rome and, 89, 91, 97, 118 (*See also* Greco-Roman civilization); Slavs in, 156, 157; wars with Persia, 48(*map*), 56–57, 71, 81

Greek Church. *See* Orthodox (Eastern or Greek) Christianity

Greek language, 49, 51, 83, 84, 290; Christianity and, 127; Roman era, 107, 109, 118

Greek philosophy, 71–77, 87. *See also specific philosophers*; early Christianity and, 132; Islamic thinkers and, 235, 236; in Middle Ages, *224–225, 234,* 235–236; in Renaissance, 292; Romans and, 109–110

Gregory I, the Great (pope 590–604), 154

Gregory VII (pope, 1073–1085), 209–210, 211, 213

Gregory IX (pope), 212

Gregory XI (pope, 1370–1378), 248

Grosseteste, Robert (1175–1253), 236

Grotius, Hugo (1593–1645), 329

Guam, Magellan in, 275

Guide for the Perplexed (Maimonides), 235

Guilds, 200–201, 234, 253

Gundestrup cauldron, *135*

Gunpowder, 256

Guns. *See* Firearms

Gutenberg, Johann (1398–1468), 257

Habsburg dynasty, 282, 323; Austrian branch, 335, 336(*map*), 337; Catholic Church and, 267, 335; Netherlands and, 324; rivalry with Ottomans, 266(*map*); Spanish branch, 335; in Thirty Years' War, 327, 328(*map*)

Hades (Pluto), 62

Hadrian (Rome, 117–138), *112, 119*

Hadrian's Wall, *102–103*

Hagia Sophia, 158, *159*

Hamlet (Shakespeare), 307

Hammurabi (Babylonia, 18th century B.C.), 18–19

Hananiah, letter of, *42*

Han dynasty (China), 116

Hannibal (247–183 B.C.), 95

Hanseatic League, 220

Hatshepsut (Egypt, 1478–1458 B.C.), 23

Hebrew Bible (Old Testament), 37–43, 125, 129–130; men and women in, 41–42; Torah, 42–43

Hegira, 159

Hellenistic era, 78–87; Alexander's conquests in, 82–83; art of, *78–79, 82*; chronology (431 B.C.–30 B.C.), 80; kingdoms of, 83–86 *and map*, 89, 97; Peloponnesian War and, 80–82; rise of Macedonia in, 82; Roman conquest, 89, 97

Helots, in Sparta, 53, 54

Henry II (England, 1154–1189), 188, 189, 190, 238

Henry IV (France, 1589–1610), 324

Henry IV (Holy Roman Empire, 1056–1106), 211

Henry the Lion, Duke of Saxony (1129–1195), 189

Henry the Navigator (1394–1460), 273

Henry V (England, 1413–1422), 259

Henry VII (England, 1485–1509), 262, 275

Henry VIII (England, 1509–1547), 325

Hera, 62; Temple of (Paestum), *64*

Heraclitus of Ephesus (5th century B.C.), 72, 87

Heresy: Albigensian, 187, 212; in early Christianity, 130–132, 145; Hussite, 250; Inquisition and, 204, 209; Protestantism as, 311, 319, *320*

Hermes, 62, 65

Hermes Holding the Infant Dionysos (Praxiteles), *66*

Hermits, in Christianity, 144, 145, 208

Herod (Judaea, 37–4 B.C.), 125

Herodotus (5th century B.C.), 71

Hezekiah (Judah, c. 700 B.C.), 40–41

Hierarchy, in early Christianity, 146

Hieroglyphs, 25, 33, 119

Hildebrand. *See* Gregory VII (pope)

Hipparchia of Maroneia, 85

Hippocrates of Cos (460–377 B.C.), 72

Historia (Herodotus), 71

History (historians): Greek, 71; periodization of, 2–3; Roman era, 94, 108, 109, 120

Hittites, 20, 28, *28*, 32, 51

Hobbes, Thomas (1588–1679), 338–339

Hohenzollern dynasty (Prussia), 335, 337

Holland. *See* Netherlands

Holy Land, Crusades to. *See* Crusades

Holy Roman Empire, 219, 220(*map*), 255, 266(*map*), 336(*map*). *See also* Carolingian ("Roman") Empire; Charlemagne; Frankish kingdom; beginning of, 178; great lords in,

To help you take your reading outside the covers of WCIV, each new text comes with access to the exciting learning environment of a robust eBook.

Working with Your eBook

You can read WCIV wherever and whenever you're online by paging through the eBook on your computer. But you can do more than just read. Your eBook also contains hundreds of live links to

 Primary source documents

 Interactive maps

 Web links for further investigation

 Interactive quizzes

 Audio resources

 Historical simulation activities

 Images

 Field trips

 Video

Each link takes you directly to the source or interactive feature. Your eBook also features easy page navigation, bookmarking, highlighting, note taking, a search engine, and a print function.

You can save your WCIV user name and password for futher reference here:

User Name: _____ Password: _____

Access your eBook and other online tools by going here:

www.cengagebrain.com

Click on the book you are using and enter the Student area of the site. Register using the access code on the card bound into your textbook. Click on the links and have fun exploring!

Add your own favorite websites here:

_____

_____

_____

_____

_____

_____

_____

_____

_____

_____

_____

_____

Key Terms

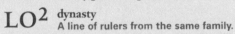

LO¹ prehistory
The period before history was recorded through written documents.

Paleolithic (Old Stone) Age
The earliest and longest period of prehistory, when humans used simple stone tools.

Neolithic (New Stone) Age
The period of human history characterized by advances in stone tool-making and the beginnings of agriculture.

Agricultural Revolution, also called Neolithic Revolution
The shift from hunting and gathering food to a more settled way of life based on farming and herding that occurred gradually between 8000 and 4000 B.C. in much of western Asia, northern Africa, and Europe, and separately in other parts of the world.

polytheism
The belief in many gods and goddesses.

LO² dynasty
A line of rulers from the same family.

city-state
An independent state that consists of a city and its surrounding settlements and countryside.

Bronze Age
The period from around 3000 B.C. to 1000 B.C. in which bronze, a mixture of copper and tin, was widely used for tools and weapons—the first metal to be so used.

cuneiform
A system of writing developed by the Sumerians that consisted of wedge-shaped impressions made by a stylus (a scratching tool made of reed) on clay tablets.

pantheon
The leading gods and goddesses of a people, believed to be a family group.

epic
A long poem or tale telling a story of gods and heroes from earlier times.

ziggurat
A massive stepped tower topped with a temple dedicated to the city's chief god or goddess.

nomads
Groups whose social organization and livelihood are based on raising and herding livestock over large stretches of land.

dowry
Money and goods given by a woman's family to her new household when she marries.

steppes
Vast semiarid grasslands or plains.

CHRONOLOGY

2.5 million before the present (B.P.)	Appearance of first humanlike species
200,000–150,000 B.P.	Scientists have traced our genetic ancestry to a "Scientific Eve" living in Africa at this time
50,000 B.P.	Scientists theorize that humans began migrating out of Africa around this time
8000–4000 B.C.	Agricultural Revolution
3500/3000 B.C.	Rise of first civilizations in Mesopotamia and Egypt
2400 B.C.	Sumer falls to Sargon of Akkad; Sumerian civilization continues under a succession of foreign rulers
1600 B.C.	The Hittites dominate Anatolia
1100 B.C.	End of the New Kingdom in Egypt; Egyptian civilization continues under a succession of foreign rulers

LO¹ Trace the key developments of prehistory, from the emergence of our human ancestors to the beginnings of village life.

Many scientists believe that modern humans emerged in Africa about 200,000 years ago and began to spread out across the globe about 50,000 years ago. The first period in prehistory is called the Paleolithic and refers to the use of rudimentary stone tools for cutting, piercing, and chopping. Throughout the Paleolithic Age, people lived as hunter-gatherers, moving from place to place in search of food. The second period in prehistory, known as the Neolithic, began about 10,000 years ago, with the Agricultural Revolution. This giant step involved the cultivation of plants, the taming of animals, and the appearance of many new skills and technologies to adapt plants and animals to human needs. Farming communities evolved to tend the land, and over many generations, village life came to be regulated by complex systems of belief, tradition, custom, and authority. Trade networks also emerged during the Neolithic period.

LO² Explain why the society that grew up in Sumer is considered one of the first civilizations, and describe later developments in Mesopotamia.

For over one thousand years, the Sumerians controlled the southern parts of Mesopotamia, and for long periods, much of the north as well. They shaped the basic ideas and institutions that would become the models for civilizations throughout Mesopotamia and, later, Europe. Sumer was home to the first true cities in the world, with populations as high as forty thousand. A social hierarchy developed within these large populations, with priests, and, later, military leaders at the top. Farming was not the only livelihood, and many specialized crafts evolved. The Sumerians borrowed technological advances from other peoples but were also innovators—developing one of the first writing systems and also pioneering in the fields of mathematics, science, and engineering. Their polytheistic religion, with a chief god for each city-state, was the source of literary accomplishments such as the Epic of Gilgamesh and architectural wonders such as the ziggurat. Sumerian civilization was absorbed by later conquering peoples such as the Akkadians, the Amorites, the Babylonians, and the Hittites, and also spread through Mesopotamia and beyond by peaceful processes of trade and travel.

LO³ Contrast the ancient civilization of the Nile with that of the Tigris-Euphrates, and discuss the defining features of Egyptian life.

Unlike Mesopotamia, which was subject to war among city-states and invasion by neighboring peoples, Egypt remained a unified, conservative, and rather insulated society for three thousand years. Under the leadership of its pharaohs, who were believed to be the living embodiment of the divine, Egypt enjoyed a continuity and stability that gave its inhabitants a sense of permanence in their way of life. This stability was broken from time to time, so that Egyptian history is divided into "kingdoms" (Old, Middle, New). Egyptian sculpture and architecture—including the pyramids—conveys this sense of stability, permanence, and connection with the gods. The Egyptians also developed a writing system, beginning with hieroglyphs, and were skilled in astronomy and medicine.

Key Terms

LO¹ Iron Age
The period beginning around 1000 B.C. in which iron became the most widely used metal for tools and weapons.

alphabet
A writing system in which each letter represents a basic sound of speech.

LO² empire
A territory larger than a kingdom, including many different peoples, and governed by a single ruler (an emperor or empress) or by a single community such as a city-state.

infantry
Soldiers who fight on foot.

cavalry
Soldiers who fight on horseback.

dualism
The belief in two supremely powerful beings or forces, one good and the other evil, whose conflict shapes the destiny of the world and humans.

CHRONOLOGY

1200–900 B.C.	Invaders from the Mediterranean and others from lands east of Mesopotamia assault the lands between the Indian Ocean and the Mediterranean Sea; Egypt is badly weakened; Hittites and Kassites fall
	Phoenicians develop sea trade; Aramaeans develop overland trade; alphabet spreads
	Beginning of Iron Age
	King David makes Jerusalem his seat of government
900 600 B.C.	Assyrian Empire
587 B.C.	Jerusalem falls to the Chaldeans; Jewish Diaspora intensifies
550–330 B.C.	Persian Empire
	Hebrew Bible evolves

LO¹ Describe how the period from 1200 to 900 B.C. was one of both crisis and innovation in the lands between the Indian Ocean and the Mediterranean Sea.

Around 1200 B.C. a new phase in development began, when the region underwent a massive crisis. It was weakened by internal conflicts; nomadic peoples attacked it from north and south; and established kingdoms were swept away. In the devastated lands of Anatolia, a shortage of the imported tin needed to make bronze led to experiments with iron smelting, ushering in the Iron Age. The city-states of Phoenicia developed seaworthy vessels and established a vast commercial network along the Mediterranean Sea and into the Atlantic. During the same period, the Aramaeans established a network of prosperous city-states that dominated the land trade of the region in the same way that the Phoenicians controlled its sea links to the west. The first alphabet spread throughout the region through these trade and travel networks.

LO² Contrast the Assyrian and Persian methods of conquest and rule, and describe the achievements of these first universal empires.

Both the Assyrians and their successors, the Persians, expanded their empires in stages and depended on extensive road networks to administer their far-flung kingdoms. The Assyrians were fierce warriors who overpowered their enemies on the battlefield with their innovative military organization, tactics, and weaponry. They pursued a policy of deliberate terror to keep their subject peoples in line. The Persians also won land by conquest, but their ruler, Cyrus, sought to win over his opponents through diplomacy and to keep power by rewarding the nobles who administered his lands. Under Persian rule, taxes and military supplies were rigorously collected, but local customs, languages, and religions were left alone.

LO³ monotheism
The belief in a single, all-powerful and all-knowing God.

diaspora
The dispersion of Jews to countries outside of Palestine.

canon
A list of works recognized by the authorities of a monotheistic religion as inspired by God.

synagogue
A Jewish house of worship; the group of people gathered to worship in such a building.

LO³ **Trace the evolution of the Jewish religion as a new kind of faith in one God.**

The monotheism of the Jewish people developed gradually over eight centuries. The early peoples of Palestine worshiped many gods and goddesses, with El as the chief deity. During the time of upheaval and the fall of the Hittite Empire, new groups moved in, and together they formed a distinct people, known as the Israelites. The Israelites believed that they were guided and protected by a mighty god, Yahweh, but they also worshiped other deities, despite the warnings of their prophets. When the Assyrians and then the Chaldeans conquered the kingdoms of Israel and Judah and deported much of their population, exiles from Judah interpreted this as a sign from God. The scattered Jews committed to their faith, and from that commitment evolved the teachings and writings that have come to define Judaism.

Key Terms

LO¹ barbarian
A term used to describe the distinctive way of life based on farming, warfare, and tribal organization that became widespread in Europe beginning around 2500 B.C.

megaliths
Massive rough-cut stones used to construct monuments and tombs.

tribe
A social and political unit consisting of a group of communities held together by common interests, traditions, and real or mythical ties of kinship.

LO² colony
In ancient Greece, a new city-state settled in an oversea territory by a group sponsored by a city-state located elsewhere.

oracle
A priest or priestess who was believed to give answers that were inspired by a god or goddess to questions from worshipers at a temple.

CHRONOLOGY

3500 B.C.	Megalithic structures constructed in Europe
2500 B.C.	Indo-European nomads from the steppes migrate into Europe; European barbarian way of life evolves
2200 B.C.	Minoan civilization takes root in Crete; Greeks arrive in southeastern Europe
1600 B.C.	Greek fortified settlements along the Aegean develop Mycenaean civilization
1400 B.C.	Destruction of Minoan towns
1200 B.C.	Mycenaean civilization falls; beginning of "Dark Ages" of Greek history
800 B.C.	Recovery in the Aegean; Greek city-states form
494–445 B.C.	Persian Wars
460–430 B.C.	Golden Age of Athens

LO¹ Describe the way of life of the barbarian peoples of Europe after the Agricultural Revolution.

By about 4000 B.C., farming and village life had spread throughout Europe, and by 3500 B.C., people in western Europe had organized enough to produce megalithic structures—including Stonehenge—and were perhaps the first to develop the plow. As Indo-European nomads migrated into Europe from the steppes of Asia, they changed the culture of the region. Not only did languages of Indo-European origin come to be spoken throughout the regions but also elements of the warrior culture merged with the agricultural life of the continent. Groups of villages or farmsteads formed tribes, held together by common interests, traditions, and kinship ties. While they were fairly well organized on the local level, the barbarian peoples of Europe had no cities, written records, or fixed structures of government.

LO² Discuss the evolution of early Greek civilization through a series of contacts with other peoples of the lands between the Mediterranean Sea and the Indian Ocean.

The Aegean island of Crete was home to the wealthy Minoan civilization, which arose around the same time that European barbarians were moving into the Greek mainland. By 1600 B.C., Greek chieftains had established fortified settlements along the mainland's southern shore and on some of the islands; from these settlements arose the Mycenaean civilization. The Mycenaeans carried on the warrior traditions of the barbarians, but they also adopted many features of Minoan culture. The Minoans were destroyed around 1400 B.C., and the Mycenaeans fell two hundred years later, ushering in the period known as the "Dark Ages" of Greek history. Greek civilization recovered about 800 B.C., and the new civilization that emerged learned from the neighboring cultures of Egypt and Mesopotamia, while forging a unique identity.

LO³

acropolis
The high fortified citadel and religious center of an ancient Greek town.

hoplite
A heavily armed and armored citizen-soldier of ancient Greece.

phalanx
A unit of several hundred hoplites, who closed ranks by joining shields when approaching the enemy.

monarchy
A state in which supreme power is held by a single, usually hereditary ruler (a monarch).

oligarchy
A state in which supreme power is held by a small group.

triremes
Massive fighting vessels with three banks of oars, used to ram or board enemy ships.

tyranny
Rule by a self-proclaimed dictator (a tyrant).

democracy
In ancient Greece, a form of government in which all adult male citizens were entitled to take part in decision making.

helots
Noncitizens forced to work for landholders in the ancient city-state of Sparta.

aristocrats
Members of prominent and long-established Athenian families.

ostracism
Banishment for ten years by majority vote of the Athenian Assembly.

LO³ Compare the city-states of Sparta and Athens, and describe how the Athenian form of democracy operated.

As Greek civilization recovered from the "Dark Ages," city-states began to form as close-knit communities that relied on their own male citizens in war. Greek armies and navies were able to repel the Persians, but there were also conflicts among the city-states. The most powerful city-states were Sparta and Athens, which had very different forms of government and society. In Sparta, government by oligarchy meant that citizens were expected to obey the decisions of a few powerful men. In addition, male citizens were bound to state service as warriors, although women had more freedom than in other city-states. To protect their rigid way of life, the Spartans tried to avoid contact with outsiders. The Athenians, by contrast, welcomed foreign ideas and visitors and were proud of their free way of life. After periods of rule by monarchy, oligarchy, and tyranny, they developed the first democracy, in which all Athenian-born, free adult males could cast votes in the Assembly and serve on juries. Athenian democracy existed within a traditional society, and women, slaves, and resident aliens were excluded from the community's decision making.

4

New Creations: Greek Religion, Arts, and Ideas, 800–300 B.C.

Chapter in Review

Key Terms

LO¹ mysteries
Secret rites involving death, rebirth, and the promise of everlasting life.

LO² colonnade
A series of regularly spaced columns, usually supporting the upper section of a structure.

LO³ lyric
A shorter form of poetry originally sung to the playing of a lyre.

tragedy
A type of play in which the main character suffers a terrible downfall.

comedy
A type of play characterized by humor and a happy ending.

CHRONOLOGY

ca. late ninth century B.C.	Homer's *Iliad and Odyssey*
sixth century B.C.	Poetry of Sappho; Pre-Socratic philosophers
fifth century B.C.	Parthenon constructed; works of Aeschylus, Sophocles, and Euripides
late fifth to fourth century B.C.	Socrates, Plato, and Aristotle

LO¹ Describe the distinctive features of Greek religious belief and practice and the features that the Greeks shared with other polytheistic peoples.

The gods and goddesses offered the ancient Greeks a way to understand and possibly influence the workings of the universe and human destiny. Because the deities wielded power over human lives, it was vital to win their favor through shows of devotion. Temple ceremonies were central to community life, and people also consulted oracles to learn the will of the gods and participated in mystery rituals in hopes of everlasting life. Some of their gods and goddesses, like Zeus, had come with them as they moved into their new homeland, but others were deities that they had come across in the course of their migrations and international contacts. They shared all these beliefs and practices, including the "borrowing" of foreign deities, with other polytheistic peoples. But they also endowed all of their deities with exceptionally lifelike human personalities and appearance and represented them as more "glorious" than mere mortals.

LO² Explain the evolution of Greek architecture and sculpture.

The supreme achievement of Greek architects is the temple, which evolved from a structure with a rather heavy appearance to the light and graceful ideal embodied in the Parthenon. Sculpture also moved from the rigid forms borrowed from the Egyptians to a more natural yet still idealized representation of the human figure. *The Discus Thrower* represents the classical ideal, a perfectly proportioned body in a dynamic and graceful pose. The Greeks introduced the female nude to art as well. Later Greek art portrayed ordinary people as well as mythical beings and exhibited a fascination with depicting intense emotions.

LO³ Discuss Greek achievements in poetry, drama, and history.

Drama, speechmaking, and history were entirely new forms of the spoken and written word created by the Greeks. They also produced works of poetry that are still read for their insights into the human condition. The earliest type of Greek poetry was the epic, an existing form that the poet Homer brought to new heights with the *Iliad and the Odyssey*. Greek poets also wrote shorter works for public occasions, but the most memorable lyric poems include the personal explorations of Solon and Sappho. Drama began with the Greeks, evolving out of the spring festival to the god Dionysus. Early performances consisted of one to three characters and the members of a chorus. Greek tragedies explored suffering, death, and the moral order, while Greek comedies poked fun at the foibles of politicians and other prominent members of society. Aeschylus, Sophocles, Euripides, and Aristophanes are the most famous Greek playwrights. The Greeks Herodotus and Thucydides were also the first to attempt to analyze the human causes of events and separate fact from fiction in the writing of history.

LO⁴ Pre-Socratic philosophers
The label given to ancient Greek philosophers before Socrates.

Sophists
A group of professional teachers who argued that truth is relative and that it was more important to have a persuasive argument than a sound one.

Socratic method
A form of inquiry involving questions and answers intended to lead from uncertainty to truth.

Golden Mean
Aristotle's concept that there is a place between extremes where perfection lies.

LO⁴ Trace the development of Greek philosophy from the Pre-Socratics through Aristotle.

Greek thinkers began looking beyond the gods and goddesses for explanations about how the universe functioned. The earliest philosophers, now known as the Pre-Socratics, proposed theories about the basic elements that comprised the universe and the human body and debated whether the world was in constant flux or eternal and unchangeable. The Sophists emphasized the powers of persuasion instead of the search for truth, and the philosopher Socrates became their intellectual adversary and a champion for the cause of philosophical inquiry. Through his "Socratic method," Socrates believed that he could recover the truth that lies buried in the mind. Socrates' follower Plato continued this line of reasoning to argue that the imperfect surface of things conceals a perfect and eternal order. Plato also theorized about the ideal society, led by a Guardian class of superior intellects who would devote their lives to the state. Unlike most of his contemporaries, Plato argued that women should share in the responsibilities of citizenship in the Guardian class. Plato's student, Aristotle, developed the rules of logic and argued that a close investigation of reality would reveal the ideal function of things. Aristotle applied his idea that every organ and creature should function according to its design to assess the workings of actual societies.

Key Terms

LO2 **Hellenistic**
Refers to the "international" period of Greek history, when much of the Mediterranean and southwestern Asia was under Greek rule.

metropolis
In ancient times, an exceptionally large city that was both a ruler's seat of government and an international hub.

CHRONOLOGY

431–404 B.C.	Peloponnesian War between the alliances of Sparta and Athens
359 B.C.	King Philip II of Macedonia comes to power; moves to control Greece
338 B.C.	End of democracy in Athens
334 B.C.	Alexander III begins expansion of empire
323 B.C.	Alexander dies; empire is divided; Hellenistic era begins
200 B.C.	Internal rebellions and external invasions begin to weaken Greek rule
30 B.C.	Roman conquest of Egypt; the Hellenistic world lives on under Roman rule

LO1 Trace the crisis of the Greek city-states and the rise of Macedonia.

The rivalry between Athens and Sparta led to the Peloponnesian War (431–404 B.C.), which was triggered when Athens's allies revolted against having to pay tribute money and called on Sparta for support. The Spartans won the lengthy conflict and forced Athens to become their allies under a harshly ruling oligarchy, but Sparta lost a great deal of soldiers and resources; eventually Greece regained its independence. With both rivals weakened, the city-states returned to their traditional pattern of continual struggle. They could not unite in time in the fourth century B.C., when their northern neighbor, Macedonia, moved in to conquer. The Macedonians under Philip II completed their victory over the city-states in 338 B.C., and democracy in Athens ended.

LO2 Explain how Hellenistic-era Greek culture gained international leadership but was also influenced by the peoples the Greeks ruled.

Philip II's son Alexander became one of the greatest conquerors in history, moving beyond the Greek mainland to defeat the Persians and take control of lands from Anatolia and Egypt to the frontiers of India. With the goal of building another "universal" empire, Alexander founded cities in the regions he conquered and sent Greeks or Macedonians to colonize them. After his death in 323 B.C., his empire was divided between three large dynasties and several smaller ones, but in all of them, Greek became the international language of business and politics. Greek rulers built libraries and sponsored research to promote Greek achievements, and the Greek trading network stretched from the coast of Spain to the borders of India. Living side by side, Greeks and their subjects influenced each other. Greek religion absorbed the gods and goddesses of other peoples, and the Greeks developed a version of divine rulership that was built on their own as well as non-Greek beliefs.

LO³ **Epicureanism**

A philosophy based on the teachings of Epicurus, who argued that there is no inherent meaning in life, so we should strive for happiness by becoming fearless and serene.

Stoicism

A Hellenistic philosophy based on the idea that the universe has an inherent meaning and that happiness is achieved by striving for virtue and understanding the natural law.

LO³ **Contrast the Epicurean and Stoic philosophies of the Hellenistic era.**

Epicureanism and Stoicism were very different ways of making sense of the vast and diverse world of the Hellenistic kingdoms. The Epicureans believed that the world operated according to chance and that there was no governing purpose on earth or in the heavens. Epicurus believed that the individual should therefore strive for happiness, not by pursuing sensual pleasures but by cultivating the higher pleasures of literature, recollection and meditation, personal friendship, and the enjoyment of nature. Striving for happiness also involved avoiding pain, especially that caused by fear and ignorance. The Stoics, by contrast, believed that the world is infused with meaning—present in everything orderly and good. Our job is to study philosophy in order to grasp this meaning, accept it by self-discipline, and live in accordance with it by striving for virtue rather than pleasure.

Key Terms

LO¹

patricians
Upper-class citizens who belonged to the oldest and noblest Roman families.

Republic
In reference to ancient Rome, the system of city-state government in which decision-making power was shared between the Senate and assemblies of male citizens.

plebeians
The Roman common people, including workers, small farmers, and wealthy people who were not patricians.

Senate
In ancient Rome, a government assembly appointed by the king, and under the Republic by the consuls; originally all members were patricians, but in time wealthy plebeians were appointed as well.

consuls
In the Roman Republic, two senators who led the government and military for one-year terms and appointed their own successors.

dictator
In the Roman Republic, a single leader with full decision-making powers, appointed for a maximum six-month term during times of emergency.

tribunes
Magistrates elected by the plebeians, who eventually gained the power to initiate and veto laws.

client
A person who provides personal services in return for money and protection from a patron.

patron
A wealthy person who supports others with money and protection in exchange for personal services.

pontiff
In ancient Rome, one of the Republic's leading priests.

paterfamilias
The "family father" in ancient Rome, who had unlimited power over his household.

matron
Title of honor given to a married woman in ancient Rome.

CHRONOLOGY

ninth century B.C.	Etruscans move into Italy
eighth century B.C.	First Greek colonies in southern Italy; settlements near the mouth of the Tiber River join to form the city-state of Rome
seventh century B.C.	Etruscans conquer Latium
500 B.C.	Rome overthrows Etruscan rule
450 B.C.	Twelve Tables, first written Roman legal code
264–146 B.C.	Punic Wars between Rome and Carthage
250 B.C.	All of Italy south of the River Po is in Roman hands; plebeians share political rights with patricians
202 B.C.	Rome wins control of western Mediterranean
first century B.C.	Most non-Romans in Italy win citizen rights; Romans expand into the eastern Mediterranean and then into western Europe
44 B.C.	Julius Caesar becomes dictator for life; members of the Senate assassinate him
31 B.C.	Octavian's forces defeat Antony and Cleopatra; Octavian becomes supreme ruler of Rome

LO¹ Trace the evolution of the Roman Republic and describe its values.

Rome was founded as one of many communities of the Latin people of central Italy who were influenced by the Etruscans and Greeks. The Roman city-state was originally based on the Etruscan model of rule by a king who was advised by a council of elders called the Senate. Rome's republican form of government evolved after the Romans abolished the Etruscan monarchy but retained the Senate, which became a supreme government body, two of whose members served as consuls (chiefs of the government and the army) for a one-year term. The plebeians or commoners were later granted their own assemblies to counter the power of the Senate, and eventually they won admission to the Senate and other rights held by the patricians. The "mixed" system that emerged was a combination of oligarchic and democratic features.

Roman behavior and achievements were influenced by commonly held values. The Romans believed that the community's survival and prosperity depended on deities who were thought to take a particular interest in its destiny. They also believed that it was the right and duty of the men of the community to fight its wars, and hence also to share in its government; at the same time, they wanted their leaders to reject glory and self-seeking and instead embrace the simple country life. They saw the community as a kind of family life on a larger scale, where men wielded fatherly authority for the good of all.

LO² Explain how the Roman Republic was able to expand beyond the Italian peninsula.

Once the Romans successfully defeated the Etruscans, they used their army of farmer-soldiers to expand beyond Latium. Their army was highly effective because it was well trained, had superior weapons and tactics, and was infused with a strong sense of valor and patriotism. Romans usually gave those whom they defeated the status of allies, and they sent colonists into conquered regions to better establish control. Their allies provided additional soldiers and also cavalry, so that the Roman forces increased in strength and striking power in step with their conquests—an important advantage for an expanding empire. With their victories in the Punic Wars, the Romans gained control of the western Mediterranean, and following the wars, they were able to expand into the eastern Mediterranean and northern Europe as well.

LO³ **proletarian**
In ancient Rome, a propertyless but voting citizen.

triumvirate
In ancient Rome, an alliance of three politicians that enabled them to control the Republic's decision making.

LO³ **Describe how the impact of war and conquest led to the overthrow of the Republic.**

The Punic Wars and then the endless further conquests enormously increased the burden of military service on Rome's farmer-soldiers. After serving long terms, soldiers often returned to find their farms spoiled by neglect, and they moved, propertyless, to the city. The Republic included another large and discontented group as well, as the number of slaves grew to make up nearly one-third of the population of Italy. The wealthy became involved in a scramble for the spoils of empire and rejected the efforts of reformers. Soldiers turned to their own commanders to take care of them when they were discharged, and from this situation emerged the dictator Sulla and then Julius Caesar. After Julius Caesar's assassination, his adopted son Octavian Caesar was able to defeat his rivals for power and turn military dictatorship into legitimate and permanent monarchy.

7

Key Terms

LO 1 princeps
"First citizen," a traditional Roman name for prominent leaders who were considered indispensable to the Republic that came to be used by Augustus and other early emperors.

ceasar
The imperial title given to the designated successor of a reigning emperor.

augustus
The imperial title given to a reigning emperor.

Roman Peace (*Pax Romana*)
A term used to refer to the relative stability and prosperity that Roman rule brought to the Mediterranean world and much of Western Europe during the first and second centuries A.D.

CHRONOLOGY

29-19 B.C.	Virgil composes the *Aeneid*
27 B.C.	End of Roman Republic and beginning of rule of Roman emperors
14 A.D.	Augustus dies and Tiberius takes over without challenge
62-70 A.D.	Jewish revolt against Rome
117 A.D.	Under Emperor Trajan, the Roman Empire reaches its greatest extent
126 A.D.	Pantheon built in Rome
212 A.D.	All free inhabitants of the Roman Empire are declared Roman citizens
529 A.D.	Justinian's law code begins to be published, systematizing the laws of Rome

LO 1 Explain how the Augustan settlement led to stable monarchy within the Roman Empire.

While retaining the Senate (though limited to political allies) and other vestiges of the Roman Republic, Augustus Caesar consolidated power and instituted a number of reforms aimed at making his subjects loyal and heading off challenges to his power. He brought the system of government appointments under his control and dismissed incompetent officials. In conquered territories, he showed respect for local institutions and encouraged provincial leaders to fulfill their responsibilities. He shifted the military's focus from conquest to defense and reorganized the army so that he could count on his soldiers' allegiance. He also instituted a permanent monarchy to ensure the peaceful transfer of power.

LO 2 Discuss the themes and concerns of writers and philosophers in the Roman Empire.

Romans writing in Latin produced works based on Greek forms, but they used these forms to express distinctly Roman values and experiences. Roman comedies dealt with the timeless themes of love and money, while nonfiction writers often commented on the current scene in politics and the military. Roman poets such as Virgil, Horace, and Ovid continue to be read today for their emotional power and insights into the human condition. Greek writers within the Roman Empire also produced important histories and analyses of wars, governments, and their leaders' characters. The Greek philosophies of Epicureanism and Stoicism, with their focus on virtuous living, appealed to Roman thinkers and were further developed in the writings of Cicero, Seneca, and Marcus Aurelius.

LO 3 Trace the evolution of Roman law.

Roman law was first recorded in the Twelve Tables to allow for a more equitable administration of justice. As Rome expanded to include noncitizens, two distinct bodies of law grew up. This dual system disappeared when all free inhabitants of the Roman Empire were declared to be citizens, but the volume of law and the body of interpretations continued to expand. Legal scholars observed that the laws of nations had many elements in common and began to argue that the laws of communities should reflect the just and orderly plan of the universe as a whole rather than simply follow the traditions of a particular community. It followed that there was a natural law that should reflect what human reason discovers to be right at all times and in all places.

LO⁴ aqueduct
A channel or tunnel used to convey water across a distance, usually by gravity.

vault
An arch made deep to produce a tunnel-shaped enclosure.

fourm
A public square that served as a civic center in ancient Roman towns.

baslica
A type of building with a wide central aisle (nave), narrower side aisles, and a semicircular chamber (apse) at one or both ends of the nave; originally used for government halls and later for churches.

LO⁵ Greco-Roman
A form of civilization shared by both Greeks and Romans.

Romanization
The process of cultural change in which non-Romans adopted Roman ways.

LO⁴ Describe the distinctive features of Roman architecture and engineering.

The Romans not only exceeded earlier civilizations in the sheer amount of construction, but they also brought architecture to a new level of grandeur, elegance, and display. They employed the arch, vault, and dome to build bridges, aqueducts, and tall structures with vast and uncluttered interiors. While the private residences of the rich were elegant and luxurious, the grandest Roman buildings were public ones. The forum or public square was reconceived as a monument to the emperor's power and the permanence of Rome. The basilica style was used for public meeting halls within the forum, and this style became the basis for church architecture for centuries to come. Recreational structures, such as baths and arenas, were sponsored by the emperors as a way to court favor with the people. Perhaps the most impressive achievement of the Romans was their wide-ranging network of roads, which reached from Rome out to the farthest corners of the empire.

LO⁵ Analyze the social and cultural changes that took place during the Roman Peace.

The vast Roman Empire was home to countless different peoples, but broadly they formed four main groups: Romans, Greeks, non-Greek peoples of the eastern Mediterranean, and the tribal peoples of Europe and northwestern Africa. These people were connected by sea lanes and roads, through which both ideas and goods were exchanged on a new scale. From the increased interactions between Greeks and Romans came an international civilization that historians refer to as "Greco-Roman." Partnership with the Romans meant that imperial rule actually safeguarded Greek dominance in the eastern territories of the empire, and it signaled the end of ancient Egyptian traditions and brought new challenges to the Jewish people. In western Europe, many barbarian tribes adopted Roman ways and experienced Romanization as the conquerors settled in among them. These Roman colonists changed the way they spoke Latin to accommodate what they learned from conquered peoples, and the Latin languages of the present day grew out of these encounters. After Caracalla extended citizenship to all freeborn inhabitants of the empire in A.D. 212, another kind of social distinction emerged—between "worthier" and "humbler" citizens.

Key Terms

LO¹ **Gentiles**
A term for non-Jews; Christians used it to refer to worshipers of the gods and goddesses.

LO² **apostles**
Jesus's followers and messengers of his teachings.

predestination
The doctrine that God determines in advance who will be saved and who will be damned.

clergy
Church ministers—bishops, priests, and deacons—who guide the laity.

laity
Those members of the Church who are not clergy.

orthodoxy
In Christianity, religious practices, customs, and beliefs proclaimed by a Church authority to be righteous or true.

heresy
In Christianity, religious practices, customs, and beliefs proclaimed by a Church authority to be wicked or false.

ascetic
A person who practices a life of self-denial as a way to God.

martyr
A person who is celebrated for accepting death rather than renounce his or her beliefs.

CHRONOLOGY

63 B.C.	Jewish kingdom comes under Roman rule
ca. A.D. 30	Death of Jesus
A.D. 50–60	Paul's letters to Christian communities
A.D. 70	Temple in Jerusalem destroyed by Romans
A.D. 235–284	Series of short-reigning Roman emperors
A.D. 285	Diocletian takes control, begins reforms
A.D. 313	Edict of Milan formally ends persecution of Christians
A.D. 370	Huns enter eastern Europe; barbarians forced from frontier into empire
A.D. 378	Visigoths defeat Romans at the Battle of Adrianople
A.D. 410	Alaric and the Visigoths loot Rome
A.D. 476	Last Western Roman emperor deposed

LO¹ **Describe the effects of Roman rule on the development of Judaism.**

The strong Jewish state that had emerged in the second century B.C. came under Roman dominion in the first century B.C., when the Romans captured Jerusalem. The Jewish kingdom continued under new rulers allied to Rome, but divisions arose among the Jews. Some groups distrusted the new rulers and sought to distance themselves from practices that they viewed as contrary to the Law of God. Others believed that the Messiah would soon come and sweep away the Romans and the rulers allied with them, leaving his loyal followers to live forever in blessedness under his rule. Eventually, the Romans broke up the Jewish kingdom and made Judaea a province of the empire, prompting two revolts. The end result was that the Temple was destroyed and the Jews were forbidden to enter Jerusalem, permanently ending the tradition of Temple worship. A life of prayer, praise, and obedience to the Law completely replaced Temple worship as the heart of Jewish religion. Rabbis attempted to end theological disputes by establishing a canon and became the new leaders of the Jews.

LO² **Trace the development of Christianity during the Roman Peace.**

In its first two hundred years, Christianity acquired many lasting features of belief and practice. Jesus, according to the gospels, was both a Jewish teacher with his own views on the issues facing his people, and the Messiah who would fulfill the Jewish prophecy that the human race would turn to the one God. The apostle Paul, who established communities of believers throughout Asia Minor and Greece, argued that Gentiles did not have to accept Jewish Law in order to be saved; faith in Christ as the savior was of utmost importance. By the end of the first century A.D., the believers in Jesus separated from Jews and began to refer to themselves as Christians. Christians became increasingly aware of belonging to a wider community of their own; they began to think of it as a worldwide or "Catholic" Church that should agree on matters of practice and doctrine. Dissenting ideas about Jesus's nature and the way to salvation were disputed, and Church leaders became defenders of orthodoxy against heresy. A Church hierarchy developed, with bishops, priests, and deacons. As Christianity spread, Roman officials sometimes persecuted it, but persecution did not prevent it from growing and becoming part of Roman society.

LO³ war bands
Groups of leading barbarian warriors who pledged themselves to follow and defend a chieftain in exchange for support and a share of the spoils.

diocese
An administrative unit in the Roman Empire; the term would later refer to the churches under a bishop's charge.

LO⁴ pagans
Worshipers of the gods and goddesses; originally a derogatory Christian term, but today used in a neutral or favorable sense.

hermit
An ascetic who lives alone, removed from ordinary society.

monastery
The residence of an ascetic community.

saint
A holy person believed to reside in heaven and to intervene with God on behalf of the living.

creed
A statement of religious belief.

hierarchy
In Christianity, the clergy with their system of ranks from highest to lowest.

patriarch
In early Christianity, the five leading bishops—those of Rome, Alexandria, Antioch, Constantinople, and Jerusalem.

LO³ Explain the problems facing the Roman Empire beginning in the third century, describe how the emperors responded, and discuss how their efforts failed in the Western half of the empire.

Early in the third century, a period of turmoil for the empire began. The Germanic tribes on the frontier mounted larger and better-organized attacks than ever before, while ordinary citizens were drained by taxes, rising prices, looting by raiders, and supply requisitions by Roman armies. Civil wars and a series of short-reigning emperors destabilized the government. The emperor Diocletian was able to stabilize the empire with a new government structure based on the imperial bureaucracy, the army, and his sacred imperial authority. Power struggles returned when he left office, but Constantine emerged as the founder of a powerful new dynasty, one that favored Christianity and opened the way for it to become the religion of Rome. The empire held off barbarian attacks for most of the fourth century, but during the fifth century its problems became too great for it to mount an effective resistance, and its Western half gradually collapsed.

LO⁴ Discuss how Christianity became the dominant religion of the empire, and describe how the Church became a powerful organized community in partnership and rivalry with the state.

When the emperor Constantine embraced Christianity, it signaled the beginning of a great change both for Christianity and for Rome. Over time, Christianity became the religion of the rulers and the masses, and persecution and discrimination were directed at worshipers of the gods and goddesses instead of at Christians. Monasteries sprang up for those who wished to withdraw from the world or whose families found it best for religious or practical reasons to send them there. Conflicting beliefs about the nature of God and Jesus led to several centuries of struggle, with the Nicene position eventually becoming the dominant one. Bishops controlled massive resources of land and money, and emperors positioned themselves as instruments of God. In the fifth century, as the Western empire collapsed and the Eastern empire was troubled by arguments over belief, the bishop of Rome emerged as the supreme leader of the church in the West and became known as the pope. By A.D. 600, the Church had become a powerful organization in society alongside and linked with the state, though the balance of power between the two partners was liable to be disturbed by rivalries, and also to shift.

Chapter in Review

Key Terms

LO^1 medieval
Refers to the distinctive civilization of the Middle Ages, which developed in Europe after the disintegration of the Roman Empire and before the emergence of the modern West.

noble
A member of the warrior-landowner group that formed the elite of medieval Europe.

Merovingians
The first ruling dynasty of all the Franks, founded by Clovis and named after his family's mythical forefather, Merovech.

mayor of the palace
In the Merovingian kingdom, the head of the royal household who wielded the real power.

LO^2 Byzantium
The present-day name for the changed and shrunken Eastern Roman Empire of Justinian's successors.

CHRONOLOGY

fifth century	Angles and Saxons invade Britain
486	Clovis leads Frankish confederacy against Romans and rival Germanic invaders in Gaul
527–565	Reign of Emperor Justinian in the Eastern empire
542	Plague hits Egypt, then spreads throughout the Mediterranean area and much of western Europe
568	Lombards conquer most of northern Italy
570–632	Life of Muhammad
595	Missionaries sent by the pope begin to convert the pagans of England
711	Muslim invasion of Spain
800	Slavs occupy almost all of eastern Europe

LO^1 Describe the way of life of the Germanic barbarians, and discuss their role in preserving and spreading Roman and Christian civilization.

The Germanic invaders of the West were mostly assimilated by the Roman peoples they conquered, but they changed the way of life of the relatively unmilitary Roman landowners as well; the outcome was a new elite of warrior-landowners. The Anglo-Saxons of England and the Franks of Gaul were able to establish themselves for the long term, and they passed Christian beliefs and practices along to neighboring Germanic peoples. Within the Frankish kingdom, a new decentralized political structure evolved from the constant interplay of monarch, powerful nobles, and leading churchmen.

LO^2 Trace the expansion and contraction of the Eastern empire, and explain how Byzantium served as the main custodian of ancient Greek culture while also sponsoring new art and architecture.

Justinian attempted to restore the Eastern empire to its traditional size, but his endeavor involved years of destructive warfare and only short-lived success. The bubonic plague further weakened the empire, and then, late in the sixth century, new attacks on the empire's overexpanded frontiers put a halt to efforts to reconquer the lands that had once been ruled by Rome. The Slavs took over most of the empire's provinces in southeastern Europe (the Balkans), and the Persian and Muslim invasions further chipped away at the empire. By 650, all that was left of Byzantium was Anatolia, Constantinople and its outskirts, a few other coastal footholds in the Balkans, and its possessions in Italy and Sicily. Nonetheless, Byzantium was still the wealthiest and best organized of European states, and it was a source of cultural inspiration for western Europe. Its archives and libraries held much of the literature of ancient Greece, and its capital city of Constantinople was home to such architectural wonders as the cathedral of Hagia Sophia.

LO³ Discuss the emergence of Islam as a new religion and culture, and explain why the rise of Islam was an important event for European peoples.

Under the leadership of Muhammad, who preached complete submission to the will of Allah as revealed to him, the religion of Islam took root in Arabia. Muhammad's successors continued his path of military expansion, and within a century of his death their empire stretched from Persia to Spain. Muslim civilization built on earlier Greek, Syrian, and Persian traditions to fashion a distinctive new international culture. Muslim rulers commissioned Arabic translations of the Greeks, sponsored great centers of learning at Cairo, Toledo, and Palermo, and created the magnificent city of Córdoba. The Islamization of North Africa and the eastern Mediterranean had the effect, for many centuries, of confining Christianity, and many traditions of Greco-Roman civilization, to the territory of Europe. Yet the Arab world also provided Europeans with a connection to distant lands, from which they gained exotic goods and new ideas.

Key Terms

LO¹ Carolingian
The Frankish dynasty founded by Charles Martel in the eighth century, as successors to the Merovingians.

count
In Charlemagne's time, a local official who represented the crown in a given region (county), presiding over the local court, collecting fines, and, in times of war, calling out the warriors of the county. Later, leading lords would take over these royal offices and convert them to hereditary titles.

duke
A royal official in charge of several counties; came to be a hereditary title.

CHRONOLOGY

732	Charles Martel forces an Arab army to retreat from Frankish kingdom
751	Pope Zachary approves the transfer of royal power from the Merovingian king to Pepin, a Carolingian
756	Donation of Pepin seals the alliance between the Frankish kingdom and the papacy
768–814	Reign of Charlemagne
780	Charlemagne sets up a palace school in Aachen
800	Pope Leo III crowns Charlemagne "Emperor of the Romans"
ca. 800	Charlemagne conquers the barbarian peoples in central Europe; Norsemen begin raids along coastline of western Europe; Byzantium regains control of Greece, begins to push against Slavs and Arabs
843	Treaty of Verdun divides the Frankish kingdom among Charlemagne's three grandsons
871	King Alfred leads the Anglo-Saxons of England against the Danish Viking invaders
911	Last direct descendant of Charlemagne dies in eastern Frankish kingdom
962	Otto I of eastern Frankish kingdom is crowned emperor in Rome; beginning of Holy Roman Empire
987	Hugh Capet replaces last Carolingian in western Frankish kingdom (France)
988	Prince Vladimir of Kiev converts to Christianity
1000	Viking journeys across Atlantic to Iceland, Greenland, and "Vinland" (North America)
1066	Norman conquest of England

LO¹ Trace the rise of the Carolingian dynasty and explain the significance of the Carolingian Renaissance and the coronation of Charlemagne.

By A.D. 700, the kings of the splintered Merovingian dynasty had lost most of their power to the "mayor of the palace." One such mayor, Charles Martel, led a Frankish army to victory against Arab raiders and began reconquering the Frankish kingdom's southern borderlands, and in so doing, he was able to gain the support of Frankish nobles and eventually unite the kingdom under his rule. Charles became ancestor of a new dynasty, the Carolingians, and his son Pepin was able to secure papal approval to take the crown from the Merovingian king. The alliance with the papacy was sealed with the Donation of Pepin, a gift of land across central Italy taken from the Lombards. Pepin's son Charles, known as Charlemagne, was also a successful warrior, and he expanded the boundaries of both Christianity and Frankish power in all directions. Under his rule, the Frankish state became large and strong enough to lay claim to being a restored version of the Roman Empire (and rival to the Eastern Roman Empire), and the pope validated this claim when he crowned Charlemagne emperor on Christmas Day, 800. For his capital at Aachen, Charlemagne sponsored a palace school and art and architectural projects that contributed to a revival of culture known as the "Carolingian Renaissance."

serf
A peasant bound to work for a landowner—a lifelong hereditary status—as a condition for hereditary possession of a small farm.

vassal
A warrior who agreed to serve a greater warrior in exchange for secure possession of land.

lord
The hereditary possessor of lands, revenues, and powers over lesser warriors and peasants.

primogeniture
The custom of passing along the bulk of family property to the eldest son.

tsar
The Slav term for emperor, from the Latin caesar.

LO^2 Describe the collapse of Charlemagne's empire and the rise of western Europe and Byzantine eastern Europe in the ninth and tenth centuries.

Charlemagne's empire was divided by his grandsons in the Treaty of Verdun, a settlement that marked an important early stage in the development of the countries of western Europe. The treaty did not prevent continued fighting among the royal heirs, however, and civil wars erupted. Adding to the violence were outside invaders: Muslim raiders in the Mediterranean, Asiatic nomads on the eastern frontier (the Magyars or Hungarians), and the Norsemen or Vikings of the north, who made their way along the coastline of western Europe and penetrated into the interior.

Out of this violent world emerged an elite of warrior nobles, a larger group of vassals who served the great lords, and a class of unfree peasants known as serfs. At the same time, new forms of royal government appeared to defend whole countries against the invaders. England united against the Danes under King Alfred and his successors; Otto I led the eastern Frankish kingdom against the Hungarians and established the Holy Roman Empire; Hugh Capet laid the groundwork for a strong hereditary monarchy in France. The ninth- and tenth-century invasions ended with the boundaries of Western Christianity greatly expanded.

In Byzantium, as in western Europe, central power grew stronger under the stress of external attack from the seventh century onward as the emperors reorganized their administrative and military system. By about 800, Byzantium had regained control of Greece from the Slavs. During the ninth and tenth centuries, Byzantine emperors and leading churchmen of the Eastern Church were able to bring Christianity and Greek culture to the Slavs outside their direct control, including the Russians.

Key Terms

LO¹ feudalism
A term coined by historians to describe the type of government institutions, as well as the general social and political relationships, that existed among the warrior-landholders in much of Europe during the Middle Ages.

feudal compact
An arrangement between a lord and his vassal involving the exchange of property for personal service.

fief
A grant of land and accompanying government responsibilities and power.

homage
A vassal's act of promising loyalty and obedience to his lord.

baron
A great lord who exercised government authority over vast family territory.

writ
In medieval England, a written royal order to a sheriff.

ordeal
In medieval Europe, a method of judging guilt or innocence by subjecting suspects to tests that were deemed to reveal the "judgment of God."

Magna Carta
The "Great Charter" or agreement between the king of England and the country's barons.

LO² estates
In the Middle Ages, the groups that made up society: often defined as those who pray, those who fight, and those who work.

manor
The principle farming property and social unit of a medieval community, usually belonging to a member of the feudal nobility or to a Church institution.

three-field system
A method of crop rotation designed to maintain the fertility of the soil and to provide for a regular supply of fall and spring crops.

labor service
The work that a serf was required to do as a condition of holding a farm. It included cultivating the lord's crops and performing other tasks such as building roads or clearing forests.

internal colonization
The process of cultivating and settling in formerly wild land in medieval Europe.

CHRONOLOGY

1152–1190	Reign of Holy Roman Emperor Frederick I Barbarossa
1180–1223	Reign of King Philip Augustus of France
1199–1216	Reign of King John of England
1204	France's Philip Augustus seizes Normandy and other French possessions of the English kings
1215	King John of England signs the Magna Carta, granting new rights to barons and subjects in general
1300	Population of Europe hits 100 million

LO¹ Describe how feudalism worked to govern social and political relationships in the Middle Ages.

Feudalism was not a tidy unified system, but it always worked according to two basic principles: (1) warriors of different rank were bound to one another and together stood against enemies; and (2) this elite group controlled land and peasants through special arrangements also designed to protect their interests. By the eleventh century, a feudal contract had evolved in which a lord granted a fief to a vassal, and in exchange, the vassal paid homage to the lord and pledged his services in battle. Church lands were also held as fiefs by clergy who had sworn fealty to counts, dukes, princes, or kings; once clergymen were forbidden to fight, they assigned portions of their properties as fiefs to vassals who pledged to perform the required military services. Feudal relationships also existed between the rulers of countries and the great lords within the countries they ruled, and the balance of power among kings, nobles, and Church leaders constantly shifted. The monarchy of Philip Augustus of France and Frederick I Barbarossa of the Holy Roman Empire serve as examples of rulers who were able to keep their vassals in check, while John of England was forced to make concessions to his barons, as recorded in the Magna Carta.

LO² Discuss the operation of a manor.

A lord's principal farming property was known as the manor. A great fief could consist of hundreds of manors, while a small one could simply include a single manor or even a fraction of one. The manor was worked by peasants: serfs who were bound to their lord for life and owed him labor service and freemen who paid rent to the lord in the form of a share of their crops. Peasants used a three-field system of cultivation, which meant that the manor's plowland was divided into three large, unfenced fields that everyone shared. In a given year, one of these fields would be planted in the fall, another in the spring, and the third would be left unplanted to regain its fertility; the crops would be planted in different fields the following year. This system, and improvements in farm equipment, contributed to higher crop yields. Serfs also cleared the swamps and forests of Europe and increased the amount of productive land that their lords controlled.

charter
A document granting rights and privileges to a person or institution—in particular, a document permitting the establishment of a town and allowing the townspeople to establish their own rules and government in exchange for regular payments of money to the grantor.

guild
An organization of merchants or craftspeople who regulated the activities of their members and set standards and prices.

master
A craftsman who had the right to operate workshops, train others, and vote on guild business.

journeyman
A licensed artisan who had served an apprenticeship and who was employed by a master and paid at a fixed rate per day.

apprentice
A "learner" in the shop of a master.

LO³ Explain how the rural-based civilization of the early Middle Ages became a city-based civilization.

With crop surpluses, church lords and nobles sold some of the produce in the towns in return for cash; or instead of receiving their income in goods and services, they freed their serfs and charged them rents to be paid in money. The lords of the manors and even better-off peasants spent their money on the goods sold in towns, including luxury items brought by traders from afar. Traders also purchased wool and textiles from European producers, and more people became participants in the new trading economy. Towns usually appeared at places where land and water routes converged, and often there were already settlements at these places that welcomed merchants and craftspeople. Protective walls were put up around the towns, and space was at a premium within. Because the whole pattern of life in the towns was different from that of the feudal estate, a new plan for government had to be devised. The townspeople sought charters from the feudal authority over the area and made regular payments of money to the grantor in exchange for freedom from the feudal services and greater self-government. Guilds regulated the work of merchants and craftsmen in the towns.

Key Terms

LO¹ sacrament
In Christian worship, a ceremony meant to grant divine aid to sinners.

grace
In Christian belief, divine aid to sinful men and women without which they cannot be saved.

transubstantiation
In Catholic belief, the process of "transfer of substance" in the Mass, whereby bread and wine are transformed in their inmost nature ("substance") into the body and blood of Christ while keeping their original outward appearance.

purgatory
In Catholic belief, a place where souls that are not hopelessly sinful will be cleansed of sin before entering God's kingdom.

indulgence
A reduction in the time a person must spend in purgatory, issued by the pope.

simony
The selling of Church services or offices—from Simon, reported in the New Testament to have offered money to the apostles for a share of their miraculous powers.

religious order
A group of monasteries following the same way of life.

cardinal
One of the ranking priests of Rome, appointed by the pope and authorized to name his successor.

excommunication
A Church punishment in which an individual is excluded from the Christian community and is not allowed to take the sacraments.

Investitures Dispute
A conflict, originally between Pope Gregory and Emperor Henry IV, over who had the power to select the bishops of the Holy Roman Empire.

Inquisition
A Church tribunal that used complex procedures of investigation and punishment to enforce religious conformity.

LO² Crusades
Holy wars declared by the popes against the enemies of Christendom.

sultan
A Muslim Turkish supreme ruler (from an Arabic word for "ruler").

schism
A division within the Christian Church mainly involving disputes over the powers of Church leaders rather than questions of actual belief.

CHRONOLOGY

910	Monastery of Cluny is founded; beginning of the Cluniac reform
1054	Disputes between the Eastern (Orthodox) and the Western (Catholic) Churches result in mutual excommunications
1095	Pope Urban II launches the First Crusade
1098	Abbey at Cîteaux founded; beginning of the Cistercian order
1099	Crusaders take Jerusalem; Latin Kingdom of Jerusalem established
1122	Investitures Dispute between the pope and emperor is settled in a power-sharing compromise
1170–1221	Life of Dominic, founder of Dominican order
1181–1226	Life of Francis, founder of Franciscan order
1187	Saladin crushes army of Latin Kingdom; regains Jerusalem for Muslims
1204	Constantinople looted by western crusaders; Latin Empire of Constantinople founded
1231	Pope Gregory IX establishes the Inquisition to find and try heretics
1261	Byzantine emperor regains Constantinople

LO¹ Describe the changes in the Church during the Middle Ages, and explain how those changes were related to society and government.

Church worship took on even greater significance in the Middle Ages as a path to divine aid in this world and the afterlife. Western religious thinkers developed a specific theory of how many sacraments there were (seven) and how they worked to confer grace. Images of the crucifixion and the veneration of Mary and other saints became widespread as people sought a deep emotional connection with Christian holy figures. The practice of issuing indulgences was instituted to reduce the amount of time the souls of the dead spent in purgatory. New groups of monks and nuns were founded (the Cluniacs, Cistercians, Franciscans, Poor Clares, and Dominicans)—some to make up for the failings of existing groups that had been spoiled by increasing wealth, and others to adapt to the needs of the growing towns.

All these changes gained approval and backing from the popes, who were striving to bring the whole Church under their central control. Their efforts ran into determined resistance from their partners and rivals, the rulers of the western European feudal states. All the same, the popes acquired such authority that they became, for a time, the most powerful rulers in western Europe. They used their authority to act against heresies and instituted the Inquisition to enforce religious conformity.

LO² Discuss the goals and outcomes of the Crusades.

The largest Crusades were directed against the Muslim Turks who controlled the Holy Land. The First Crusade was called by Pope Urban to free the Holy Land, reopen the roads to pilgrimage, and rescue Byzantium from the Turkish threat. It was successful in preventing the invasion of Constantinople and allowing the crusaders to establish the Latin Kingdom of Jerusalem. Most of the later crusades were undertaken to defend the Christian territories in the Middle East, but the Muslim ruler Saladin was able to win back most of these lands, including Jerusalem. The Fourth Crusade began as another attack on Muslim Turks but evolved into a western attack on the eastern city of Constantinople. While the Latin Empire of Constantinople was short-lived, it weakened Byzantium permanently and deepened the hostility between western and eastern Christendom.

LO³ Describe the challenges facing eastern Europe as western Europe grew stronger.

In spite of their failure, the Crusades were a sign that in government effectiveness and industrial capacity, western Europe was climbing back to the level of ancient Rome. In eastern Europe, the Orthodox world flourished during the thirteenth and fourteenth century under Bulgarian, Serbian, and restored Byzantine rulers. Yet eastern Europe faced social, economic, and political challenges during this period. Its kings were weakened by the accumulated effects of dividing their dominions among numerous heirs rather than passing full control to the eldest as in the West. The rulers of Poland, Hungary, and the eastern territories of the Holy Roman Empire were often unable or unwilling to resist western expansion into their lands. The eastern countries were also exposed to constant attack from nomadic people of the steppes, including the Mongol invasions of 1237 to 1240. The Mongols conquered Russia, but over time, a powerful new Russian state took shape, one that shared in the flourishing religious and cultural life of the Balkans.

Key Terms

LO¹ Romanesque
The "Roman-like" style of church architecture and sculpture in the eleventh and twelfth centuries.

Gothic
A style of architecture and art that evolved in the twelfth century, characterized by spaciousness, height, glowing illumination, and naturalistic images.

cathedral
The head church of a bishopric—from the Greek word for "seat" (of a bishop).

flying buttress
A supporting structure on the outside of a Gothic cathedral that arches over the roof of a side aisle.

LO² schoolmen
The name given to teachers in medieval schools and universities.

scholastic
The term used today to refer to medieval thought.

deductive argument
An argument that relies on reasoning from basic propositions assumed in advance to be true.

LO¹ Describe the Romanesque and Gothic styles.

Western Christendom invested much of its newfound wealth and skills in magnificent religious buildings. The first distinctive style to emerge was the Romanesque, which was based on some features of the Roman basilica but used these features in new ways to serve new purposes. Architects extended the plan to create a cross shape, added a bell tower, and imbued the building with religious symbolism. Sculptors, using as their models the illustrated figures of medieval manuscripts, adorned these buildings with figures that mixed the natural and the supernatural to convey Church teachings. The Gothic style grew out of the Romanesque, with the goal of creating a building that would reflect the true nature of the universe: a vast structure, perfectly harmonious in every detail and glowing with light that flowed from God himself. Through the use of such new features as the pointed arch (from mosques) and the flying buttress, Gothic architects were able to lift roofs to soaring heights and make windows into broad sheets of stained glass. Gothic sculptors filled these spaces with more naturalistic figures, while stained-glass artists created huge and elaborate windows.

LO² Trace the renewal of intellectual life in medieval Europe.

By 1200, it was again normal for nobles and businesspeople to be literate, in addition to the clergy who carried on the tradition of reading and writing after the fall of Rome. Monasteries and cathedrals provided basic education, and for advanced training, young men could attend a new institution—the university—that began in southern Europe (near Muslim and Byzantine sites) and spread northward. The schoolmen who taught within those universities also contributed new ideas about the nature of God and the universe. Scholastic thought was founded on debate, logical arguments, and systematic observation. Among the most important scholastics were Abelard, Aquinas, Albert the Great, Robert Grosseteste, and Roger Bacon.

LO³ **vernacular literature**
Literature written in local languages rather than in Latin; "vernacular" comes from the Latin for "native."

troubadour
A medieval poet-singer, usually of noble origin, who created epics and romances (from the medieval French word for "invent").

fabliaux (fables)
Frank, sensual, and witty works that ridiculed both courtly and priestly life.

passion plays
Dramatizations of Christ's suffering and death.

miracle plays
Dramas with plots involving miraculous happy endings brought about by the Virgin Mary.

morality plays
Dramas in which the characters were torn between noble virtues and tempting vices.

mystery plays
Dramas designed to edify and staged by guilds.

LO³ **Discuss the evolution of medieval literature.**

During the Middle Ages, Latin was the common language for religion, scholarship, and commerce, but it was no longer the language of everyday life. The finest creations in medieval Latin were the prayers and hymns of the Christian worship service. By the thirteenth century, however, vernaculars were the main languages of literature, employed for epics and troubadour songs of romantic love. Two vernacular works of the late Middle Ages, the *Canterbury Tales* of Geoffrey Chaucer and the *Divine Comedy* of Dante, offer vivid portraits of medieval society and its ideals.

Key Terms

LO¹ Jacquerie
A large-scale uprising of French peasants in 1358.

Black Death
A devastating plague that ravaged the Eastern Hemisphere, including Europe, in the mid-fourteenth century.

"Babylonian Captivity"
The period in which the popes resided in Avignon rather than Rome and were thought to be controlled by the French monarchy.

Great Schism
The division of Western Christendom into two competing groups, each with its own pope and college of cardinals.

Ottoman Turks
A Muslim people of nomadic origin who built a powerful empire in the Middle East, North Africa, and southeastern Europe under rulers of the Ottoman dynasty.

LO² capitalism
An economic system that developed as entrepreneurs reinvested their surplus wealth (capital) in order to gain more profits.

Hanseatic League
A commercial league of the port cities of Germany that by the fourteenth century dominated the trade of northern Europe from England to Russia.

"putting-out" or "domestic" system
A system of production in which merchants supply workers with raw materials and pay them by the piece or by measure.

bill of exchange
A paper substitute for gold and silver used for long-distance business transactions.

double-entry bookkeeping
A system of bookkeeping developed in late medieval Europe that involves keeping separate records or "accounts" for the resources and activities of a business, thereby permitting closer control of business operations.

partnership
A type of business organization in which a group of entrepreneurs pool their capital and talent.

second serfdom
The term modern scholars use to characterize the revival of serfdom in eastern Europe after the Black Death.

CHRONOLOGY

1300s	Famines and peasant revolts; changes in feudalism and manorialism; new weaponry begins to change warfare
1309–1377	The "Babylonian Captivity" of the popes in France
1338–1453	Hundred Years' War
1347–1350	The Black Death spreads across Europe
1378–1417	The Great Schism in Western Christendom; John Wiclif and Jan Hus lead movements that challenge the power of the clergy and papacy
1400s	Age of despots in Italy; capitalism and international commerce flourish; banking and merchant partnerships allow for large-scale enterprise; domestic system of production begins; "second serfdom" begins in eastern Europe
1450	Gutenberg develops printing with movable type
1453	Fall of Constantinople to Ottoman Turks
1462	Ivan the Great throws off the "Tartar yoke" in Russia
1492	Ferdinand and Isabella complete the reconquest of Spain
1500s	End of serfdom in England and most of western Europe; rise of national monarchies in Spain, France, and England
1513	Machiavelli writes *The Prince*
1526	Habsburg dynasty reaches greatest extent under Emperor Charles V

LO¹ Detail the crises of the fourteenth century.

The fourteenth century was a time of disasters. An increase in population combined with bad weather and poor harvests led to famines. Peasants' revolts occurred all over Europe, and the Hundred Years' War destroyed many French towns and farms. The cruelest blow of all was the Black Death (bubonic plague), which killed perhaps a quarter of the population of Europe. These catastrophes severely strained the medieval patterns of society.

The fourteenth century was also a time of crisis in the papacy. The French gained a majority at the papal court, and the papacy moved to Avignon from Rome; detractors referred to this as the "Babylonian Captivity." Later, two sets of popes and cardinals—one set in Avignon and the other in Rome—competed for supremacy over the Church. John Wiclif and Jan Hus led movements that attacked Church corruption and challenged Church doctrine. Meanwhile, the Christian peoples of the Balkans became subjects of the Muslim Ottoman Turks, who conquered Constantinople in 1453.

LO² Trace the evolution of capitalism in the late Middle Ages.

In the thirteenth century, Italian merchants pioneered the development of capitalism as they began to reinvest their profits in order to expand into bigger markets. The merchants of Germany formed a commercial league, the Hansa, pooling their resources to build a shipping fleet and win joint trading privileges abroad. Guild control of production was weakened by the "putting-out" or "domestic" system. Banks emerged, as moneylending and using bills of exchange for long-distance commerce became acceptable practices. With the rise of money as a substitute for payment in goods and services, tenants began to take the place of serfs in the countryside. By 1500, serfdom had disappeared from England and had become a rarity in western Europe, although eastern Europe experienced a "second serfdom."

LO³ magnetic compass
An instrument with a rotating magnetized needle that indicates magnetic north.

astrolabe
An instrument used to calculate latitude (a ship's position north or south of the equator) by determining the height of the sun and stars above the horizon.

carrack
The first three-masted sailing ship.

LO⁴ Hundred Years' War
A conflict between France and England over French territory that flared intermittently in the fourteenth and fifteenth centuries.

Estates-General
A French government assembly that represented the three estates (groups that made up society) of France—the clergy, the nobles, and the commoners—and that had the sole power to authorize new taxes.

Parliament
The national representative assembly of England, with two chambers—the House of Lords and the House of Commons—whose approval the monarchy needed to impose new taxes. Its name literally meant "negotiation"—between the king and his subjects.

despot
The term applied today to a self-proclaimed dictator of medieval Italy.

condottieri
Warrior-businessmen of medieval Italy who recruited and trained professional mercenary soldiers.

absolutism
The theory that state power is and should be absolute (unlimited).

elector
One of seven high-ranking vassals of the Holy Roman emperor with the authority to elect the emperor's successor.

LO³ Describe the technical advances that, for the first time, gave Europe worldwide technological leadership.

Europeans adapted the technologies of China and Islam to meet the needs of growing trade. New instruments of navigation and innovations in ship design allowed them to make longer voyages. Innovations in weaponry made it possible for warriors to smash stone castles and town walls. Gutenberg's innovations in printing made possible mass production of books, and with 10 million books in circulation by 1500, the written word had greater power to spread ideas, laws, and standardized paperwork. The mechanical clock was another achievement of the late Middle Ages, ultimately changing the way that people structured their days.

LO⁴ Identify the changes in government and politics that began in the late Middle Ages.

With the rise of trade, banking, and a money-based economy, rulers could employ paid officials and mercenary soldiers rather than relying on the services of vassals. New weapons ended the battlefield superiority of mounted knights, and cannon made noble fortresses vulnerable to attack. Despots restored peace and prosperity to the city-states of Italy, and by the middle of the fifteenth century, the stronger states had absorbed their weaker neighbors. In *The Prince*, Machiavelli argued that Italy should be unified under a single despot, who would be a man of strength and cunning above the rules of Christian conduct. The monarchs of France, England, and Spain were able to consolidate power, and the Habsburgs built a far-flung realm across central and western Europe.

Key Terms

LO¹ The Indies
The medieval European name for the region encompassing eastern and southern Asia.

LO² Treaty of Tordesillas
The 1494 agreement between Portugal and Spain that established the boundary for each country's new territorial claim.

conquistador
Spanish conqueror of the New World.

CHRONOLOGY

1298	Marco Polo dictates his book of travels
1300s	Venice establishes a trading monopoly with Asia
1420s	Portuguese expeditions sponsored by Prince Henry the Navigator begin to chart the West African coastline
1488	Bartolomeu Dias rounds the southern tip of Africa
1492	Christopher Columbus leads an expedition across the Atlantic, reaches the Americas
1494	Treaty of Tordesillas between Portugal and Spain establishes boundary for each country's exploration, trade, and conquest
1497	John Cabot discovers Newfoundland for England
1498	Vasco da Gama reaches India by way of the African coastal route
1519–1522	Magellan's crew circles the globe
1521	Cortés completes the Spanish conquest of the Aztecs
1523	Beginning of trans-Atlantic slave trade
1531	Pizarro completes the Spanish conquest of the Inca
1540	Portuguese trading network extends along the coastline from West Africa to Japan; Jesuit Francis Xavier begins his mission to Asia
1571	Spanish-led Christian alliance defeats Turks at battle of Lepanto, ending Ottoman naval domination of Mediterranean
1600s	English, French, and Dutch begin colonizing North America and establishing trading posts in Asia

LO¹ Explain the developments outside and inside Europe that led to European efforts to find new routes to Asia.

In the thirteenth and fourteenth centuries, Europeans gained new knowledge of Asia and Africa through the tales of Italian merchants such as Marco Polo. Europeans also enjoyed freer access to Asian luxuries and were frustrated when barriers to that access were erected by the rise of the Ottoman Turks and the Venetian trading monopoly. Other European merchants, therefore, were motivated to find freer routes to trade; western rulers also wanted the wealth that increased trade would bring; and western clergy saw an opportunity to expand the reach of Christianity and find allies against Islam.

LO² Discuss the stages of European exploration, from early voyages to overseas empires.

Portugal took the lead in searching for a sea route to the Indies as expeditions sponsored by Prince Henry the Navigator made their way down the western coast of Africa. While Portugal pursued the African coastal route to the East, the Spanish sponsored Columbus's 1492 expedition to find a western route across the Atlantic. Vasco da Gama reached India by the African route in 1498, and over the next fifty years, Portugal built a powerful trading network that controlled major ports from West Africa to Japan. While the Spanish sponsored the first crew to circle the globe, their efforts were largely focused on exploiting the resources of the Americas. The Spanish conquistador Cortés conquered the Aztec Empire, while the conquistador Pizarro conquered the Inca. The Portuguese laid claim to Brazil, and John Cabot claimed Newfoundland for England.

LO³ viceroy
In the Spanish colonies of the
Americas, a high-ranking official who governed as
a "stand-in for the king."

Columbian Exchange
Today's name for the worldwide movement of
plants, animals, diseases, and people between the
New and Old Worlds that began with Columbus's
voyages.

joint-stock company
A type of business partnership in which
individuals pool their capital in exchange for
shares of the venture's profits (and debts).

LO³ Describe the mutual impact between Europe and the rest of the
world from the sixteenth to the eighteenth century.

The impact of Europeans was felt most strongly in the Americas, where indigenous
populations were decimated by Old World diseases and transformed into colonial subjects.
In Asia, Europeans made some inroads in trade and missionary work, but over time, their
activities were strictly controlled by strong Asian governments. In West Africa, the population
was hard hit as the slave trade intensified and Europeans bought Africans to work in New
World plantations and mines. Newly empowered Christian Europeans were also able to halt
the Muslim expansion into eastern Europe.

Key Terms

LO¹ **Renaissance**
From the French word for "rebirth," the term for the period beginning around 1300 when scholars, artists, and writers revived and adapted the traditions of the Greco-Roman past.

humanists
From the Latin *humanitas*, the word Renaissance scholars used to define themselves as seekers of human excellence through the study of Latin and Greek works.

virtù
Human excellence, as conceived by Italian humanists.

CHRONOLOGY

(time spans are life dates)

1266?–1337	Giotto, pioneering artist of the early Renaissance
1304–1374	Petrarch, poet and pioneer of humanist revival
1313–1375	Boccaccio, author of *Decameron* and humanist scholar
1377?–1446	Brunelleschi, architect and sculptor who revived the building traditions of ancient Rome and developed geometrical rules of perspective
1386?–1466	Donatello, pioneering sculptor of *The Feast of Herod* and statue of Gattamelata
1401–1428?	Masaccio, one of the first painters to apply Brunelleschi's rules of perspective
1440	Lorenzo Valla demonstrates that the Donation of Constantine is a forgery
1450	Cosimo de' Medici founds the Platonic Academy in Florence; scholars include Marsilio Ficino and Pico della Mirandola
1445–1510	Botticelli, Platonist and painter of *The Birth of Venus*
1447–1576	Titian, Venetian painter of *Venus of Urbino*
1452–1519	Leonardo, artist, inventor, and symbol of Renaissance ideal
1466?–1536	Erasmus, author of *In Praise of Folly* and corrected version of New Testament
1475–1564	Michelangelo, painter, sculptor, architect of Renaissance masterpieces
1490–1553	Rabelais, popular satirist whose works were condemned by authorities
1533–1592	Montaigne, influential French essayist and skeptic
1564–1616	Shakespeare, English playwright

LO¹ **Describe how Renaissance humanism offered a new set of values based on ancient models.**

Renaissance scholars looked to ancient Latin and Greek literature as a guide to human excellence (*virtù*) and rediscovered the ancient ideal of the fully developed human being whose character was formed by literary study and education. The elite and aspiring elite hoped to imitate the elegance, refinement, and heroic achievements of the ancients. The fourteenth-century Italian scholar Petrarch, who pioneered the humanist revival, valued private hours of study over meditation or prayer, although he also believed that love of the ancients and Christian faith belonged together. Petrarch's student Boccaccio wrote biographies that provided edifying examples of virtue and vice. Fifteenth-century humanist scholars and educators spread the ideal of the active and learned lady and gentleman, and in the sixteenth century, Castiglione's *The Courtier* taught people how to live this ideal. The ancient philosopher Plato became the new master to be emulated for his eloquence and insights into the soul. Humanists rejected scholasticism, with its system of knowledge based on authority and reason, and adopted a critical attitude toward received wisdom. Erasmus and More turned this critical attention to Christian practice and the social order, proclaiming such ideals as toleration and peaceful achievement.

LO² Discuss how humanist ideals and the ancient past shaped the visual arts of the Renaissance.

With the goal of making lifelike depictions of holy events, painters and sculptors of the early Renaissance began to turn to classical art for models. The trend was pioneered by the Florentine painter Giotto, whose moving images of Christ and his followers at the Arena Chapel in Padua brought him lasting fame. Brunelleschi revived the building traditions of imperial Rome but added medieval innovations for an effect that could "surpass the ancients." He also devised an accurate system of perspective that would allow Renaissance painters such as Masaccio to create a convincing illusion of three-dimensional space. Sculptors such as Donatello also merged classical sources and contemporary images. Late in the fifteenth and early in the sixteenth centuries, artists embraced a whole range of revived ancient art forms, including portraits, the nude, and mythological scenes.

LO³ Explain how humanist ideas were spread to a larger audience through vernacular literature.

In the sixteenth century, as printing made books cheaper and more widely available, humanists reached larger audiences by writing in the more accessible vernacular (native) languages. They translated the Latin of ancient works and those of Erasmus and More, and they began writing original works in the native languages of Europe. In France, Rabelais was both condemned and widely read for his satires of hypocritical and corrupt monks. Montaigne pioneered a new genre of personal essays that examined the received wisdom of the day with a skeptical eye. In England, Shakespeare combined both ancient and medieval traditions in drama with an eloquence that ideally represented humanist aspirations.

17

New Christianities: The Reformation, 1500–1700

Chapter in Review

Key Terms

LO¹ Protestant Reformation
A religious mass movement against the Catholic Church that gave rise to Protestant Christianity.

LO² justification
In Christian theology, the process whereby a person is freed from the penalty of sin and admitted to salvation.

Ninety-five Theses
Luther's 1517 argument against the sale of indulgences and the ideas that lay behind the practice.

Diet of Worms
The assembly of the Holy Roman Empire before which Luther refused to recant his beliefs.

Anabaptists
Radical Protestants who opposed infant baptism and also held various other beliefs that were opposed to beliefs that other Protestants still had in common with Catholics.

sect
In religion, a small group that sees itself as part of a minority of true believers apart from the rest of society.

Religious Peace of Augsburg
An agreement to end religious wars within the Holy Roman Empire by allowing rulers the freedom to determine the faith (Lutheran or Catholic) of their territories.

Evangelical Church
The name given to the church formed by Luther; from *evangelical*, meaning "gospel-following."

Augsburg Confession
A document detailing the beliefs of Luther's Evangelical Church.

CHRONOLOGY

1517	Luther's Ninety-five Theses attack the sale of indulgences
1521	Excommunicated by the pope, Luther refuses to recant his beliefs before the Diet of Worms; he translates the Bible into German while under the protection of Frederick of Saxony
1522	Luther returns to Wittenberg; his new version of Christianity gains adherents
1529	Holy Roman Emperor Charles V reaffirms decree prohibiting new religious doctrines in Germany; Lutheran rulers protest and acquire label of "Protestants"
1530s	Armed alliances of Lutherans and Catholics form within the Holy Roman Empire; Augsburg Confession sets out beliefs of new Evangelical Church
1534	Pope Paul III launches Catholic Reformation; England's Parliament passes the Act of Supremacy, breaking ties with the pope
1536	John Calvin's *Institutes of the Christian Religion* is published and widely read; Calvin settles in Geneva, where he establishes a model community
1539	The Society of Jesus (Jesuits) becomes an official Catholic order
1545–1563	Council of Trent meets periodically to initiate Catholic Church reform
1553	Queen Mary launches persecution of English Protestants
1555	Religious Peace of Augsburg allows each ruler within the Holy Roman Empire to choose either Catholicism or Lutheranism for his territory
1562	Beginning of wars between Catholics and Huguenots in France
1588	English defeat Spanish Armada
1598	Edict of Nantes guarantees toleration and military forces for Huguenots
1618–1648	Thirty Years' War devastates Germany, ends with Peace of Westphalia

LO¹ Describe the background of the Protestant Reformation.

Corruption in the Church, resentment at unworthy clergy, and quarrels between the clergy and other power wielders were widespread in the period leading up the Reformation. The popes were too busy with power struggles to attend to Church reform, and the problems of the Church began to inspire doubts about its wisdom and authority. Critics of the Church were able to spread their ideas to a mass audience with the advent of printing.

LO² Trace the evolution of Lutheranism from the Ninety-five Theses to the Religious Peace of Augsburg.

Provoked by the arrival of Johann Tetzel in Wittenberg to sell indulgences, Martin Luther prepared his Ninety-five Theses, which took issue with that practice and the ideas behind it. This public declaration gained a mass audience and ultimately led to Luther's break with the Catholic Church. Luther then established the Evangelical Church, based on the ideas that salvation comes from faith alone, and that the Bible, rather than the pope, offers the true path to salvation. After years of conflict, the Imperial Diet agreed to let each ruler within the empire choose either Catholicism or Lutheranism as the faith of his subjects, and the northern territories became largely Protestant.

LO³ predestination
The concept, central to Calvinism, that God chooses who will be saved and who will be lost; a person's ultimate destiny is predetermined by God.

Reformed Church
The name given to the church founded by Calvin.

episcopal
A type of church hierarchy controlled by bishops.

presbyterian
A type of church hierarchy controlled by elected elders—from the Greek word for "elder."

LO⁴ Catholic Reformation
The Catholic movement of renewal and reform that began in the sixteenth century in response to Protestantism.

Council of Trent
A Catholic council of bishops that upheld traditional doctrine against Protestantism and acted against corruption and wrongdoing within the Church.

Jesuits
The Society of Jesus, a Catholic order founded by Ignatius Loyola with the mission to defend the Catholic faith.

LO⁵ Huguenots
French Calvinists.

politique
A French term for the school of thought that put politics before religion and sought religious compromise for the sake of national unity.

Anglicanism
The faith of the Church of England, with both Protestant and Catholic features.

Elizabethan Settlement
Religious compromise initiated by Queen Elizabeth of England that combined aspects of Lutheranism, Calvinism, and Catholicism in an effort to end religious conflict.

Puritans
English Protestants who wanted the Church of England to meet the standard of the "pure gospel" as Calvin understood it.

Thirty Years' War
A conflict between Catholics and Protestants in the Holy Roman Empire that engaged the major powers of Europe between 1618 and 1648.

Peace of Westphalia
Settlement ending the Thirty Years' War by extending religious freedom in Germany and recognizing the independence of Switzerland and Holland.

LO³ Discuss the core tenets of Calvinism and its impact on the Reformation.

The French-born John Calvin settled in Geneva, where his ideas about a reformed church were embraced by the local government and served as a model for Calvinist governance throughout Europe. Calvinism was based on the idea of predestination—that God alone determined who would be saved (the "elect") and who would be condemned (the "reprobate"). Because no one knew God's plan for each person, all were to live righteously as members of the Calvinist Church. Calvin's idea of a righteous life was one in which card-playing, drinking, dancing, and theater-going were forbidden, and modesty and frugality were expected. The style of life that evolved in Geneva was imitated by Calvin's followers from Scotland to Hungary as they became the leaders in the international movement of Protestant reform in the second half of the sixteenth century.

LO⁴ Outline how the Catholic Church responded to the Protestant challenge.

In the second half of the sixteenth century, the Catholic Church moved from stagnation and defensiveness to a bold offensive against the Protestant challenge. Pope Paul III launched an overhaul of papal administration, ordered a report on abuses among the clergy, and summoned a general council of bishops (the Council of Trent) that acted vigorously against corruption and wrongdoing while also upholding traditional beliefs and practices. The Jesuits rallied ordinary believers to the Church as revivalist preachers, father confessors, educators, and missionaries.

LO⁵ Explain how the religious wars of the Reformation period led to a new, secular European state system.

As different versions of Christianity took root in Europe, the rulers and church leaders of the dominant religion in each region attempted to repress rival religions, acting on the conviction that there must be only one religious truth. As violent religious conflicts played out over the sixteenth and seventeenth centuries, religious compromise began to emerge as an attractive option. When the Thirty Years' War ended in a stalemate, efforts to change the religious balance internationally came to seem too costly. Religion gradually ceased to play a role in international conflicts.

Key Terms

LO¹

absolute monarchy
Rule by a monarch (king or queen) that is not limited by traditional restrictions on power such as established laws, customs, and representative assemblies.

limited monarchy
A monarchy that shares power with a representative assembly and is bound by established laws.

balance of trade
The relationship between a country's imports and exports; in a favorable balance, the value of exports exceeds imports.

mercantilism
An economic theory that measures a country's wealth by its stock of precious metals, accrued through a favorable balance of trade.

divine right
The idea that the monarch is God's representative on earth and is therefore entitled to total obedience and unlimited power.

LO²

gentry
In England, the class of landowners below the nobility.

Wars of the Three Kingdoms
A series of conflicts over royal authority that also involved religious and national rivalries within and among the kingdoms of England, Scotland, and Ireland during the seventeenth century.

yeomen
Independent small farmers, of lower social position than the gentry.

Restoration
Term applied to the reign of Charles II, in which the monarchy was restored (reinstated) in England.

Glorious Revolution
The regime change in which James II was replaced as monarch by his daughter Mary and her husband William, ensuring Protestant rule in Britain.

CHRONOLOGY

1600s	The Austrian Habsburg dynasty consolidates power in central and eastern Europe; Frederick William and his successor Frederick I develop the economic and military might of Prussia
1649	Charles I of England is executed; England becomes a Commonwealth without monarch or House of Lords
1643–1715	Reign of Louis XIV, the "Sun King," in France
1651	Thomas Hobbes describes absolute rule as the alternative to a warring "state of nature" in *Leviathan*
1660	The monarchy is restored in England under Charles II
1670	Jacques Bossuet argues for the divine right of kings in *Politics Drawn from Holy Scripture*
1682–1725	Reign of Tsar Peter "the Great" in Russia
1689	English Bill of Rights makes Parliament an equal partner of the ruler and guarantees many civil liberties
1690	John Locke's *Two Treatises on Government* rejects divine right and defends the right of rebellion
1691	The "Glorious Revolution" is completed in the British Isles, transferring power to the Protestant monarchs William and Mary
1707	England and Scotland become the United Kingdom of Great Britain

LO¹ Explain the rise of absolute monarchy during the seventeenth and eighteenth centuries.

The struggles of the Reformation and conflicts over worldwide trade and empire greatly increased the stakes for kingdoms in having powerful rulers. Furthermore, rulers needed even more control of their kingdoms than before, to be able to mobilize the continually increasing resources needed to fight wars. In France, the Bourbon dynasty rebuilt royal power after decades of civil war, and King Louis XIV exemplified absolute monarchy. He built up a standing army that gave him a monopoly of military force, increased the number and power of regional officials who enforced his orders, eliminated the main legal restrictions on royal power, and created a dazzling persona as the "Sun King" at the center of an impressive court culture. Other leading dynasties of the period were the Austrian Habsburgs, who were able to expand their hereditary lands in central and eastern Europe as the Spanish Habsburgs lost power, and the Hohenzollerns in Prussia, who built one of the strongest economies and best-trained armies in Europe under Frederick William and Frederick I. The most spectacular change in eastern Europe was the rise of Russia, notably under the Romanov tsar Peter the Great, who increased Russian territory while attempting to Westernize Russian society and culture.

LO² Describe the wars and revolution in the British Isles during the seventeenth century, and outline the rise of limited monarchy that resulted from this upheaval.

With the death of Elizabeth I in 1603, her cousin James, king of Scotland, inherited her crown, thus becoming ruler of the three kingdoms of Scotland, England, and Ireland. James I, who held ideas of divine right, faced a hostile House of Commons dominated by Puritans; the situation worsened under his son, Charles I, who inflamed religious antagonisms among Anglicans, Puritans (Calvinist Protestants), and Catholics and stretched the law in various ways to raise money on his own authority. Civil war erupted in the three kingdoms, and the traditional partnership of ruler and Parliament broke down. Gradually, the wars changed into a revolution centered in England, and a radical Puritan army defeated Charles's forces, then took power from Parliament, and gained control of Scotland and Ireland as well. King Charles was beheaded, and Oliver Cromwell ruled as a military dictator over the entire British Isles. After Cromwell's death, the monarchy was restored with Charles II, who promised a renewed partnership with Parliament. His successor, James II, who claimed the right to act against

LO³ **Baroque**
A style of art and architecture that emphasized the spectacular, magnificent, and dramatic, often with the purpose of proclaiming the glory of a state or church power.

genre paintings
Paintings depicting the everyday life of ordinary people.

laws of Parliament, was overthrown in the "Glorious Revolution," and new monarchs, William and Mary, assumed control. In 1689, the English Parliament passed the Bill of Rights, which explicitly limited the monarch's power. A similar measure became law in Scotland, which united with England in 1707 to form the United Kingdom of Great Britain, while Ireland remained a separate kingdom where a Protestant minority dominated the Catholic majority.

LO³ Appreciate how artists used Renaissance principles and techniques to create the Baroque style, emphasizing dramatic and spectacular effects.

Baroque painters, sculptors, and architects emphasized the spectacular, the magnificent, and the dramatic in their works. The leader of Baroque art was the Flemish Catholic painter Peter Paul Rubens, whose large-scale paintings are charged with movement and vigor. More sober and understated, the paintings of the Protestant Rembrandt van Rijn nonetheless have memorable emotional and dramatic impact. In sculpture, Bernini brought extraordinary technical skill to the task of rendering a dramatic moment in marble. His architectural achievement, Saint Peter's Square, speaks of the glory and power of the Catholic Church in Rome, while French architects in Versailles (among them Charles Le Brun) did the same for Louis XIV and the French state that he embodied. The new Saint Paul's cathedral in London, designed by Christopher Wren, offered a restrained and soberly majestic version of Baroque architecture suitable for a country that was consolidating Protestant domination, strengthening parliamentary government, and rising to worldwide power.

Key Terms

LO¹ Scientific Revolution
The general name for the revolutionary discoveries in astronomy and other fields that took place between 1500 and 1700, and above all for the development of new methods that have made the acquisition of scientific knowledge a rapid and continuing process.

Ptolemaic, geocentric
Refers to the earth-centered theory of the universe's movements, argued by the second-century astronomer Ptolemy.

Copernican, heliocentric
Refers to the sun-centered theory of the universe's movements, argued by the sixteenth-century astronomer Nicholas Copernicus.

experiment
Making a natural process take place under conditions that make it measurable, while eliminating effects that might disturb the measurement, in order to answer a question about the process.

deduction
Reasoning from beliefs assumed in advance to be true.

induction
Reasoning from observed facts to the principles and processes that lay behind them.

LO² worldview
A vision of the universe's general purpose and meaning, and of the human condition within it.

philosophes
The name given to eighteenth-century "people of letters" who embraced the Enlightenment worldview.

Enlightenment
The name for the century from 1687 to 1789, when a new "enlightened" view of humanity and God grew out of the new findings of science.

Deism
A religious belief that recognizes a Supreme Being but rejects the idea that such a deity influences nature and human destiny.

agnosticism
A position of uncertainty about the existence of God.

atheism
A position that denies the existence of God.

empiricism
The view that all knowledge comes from experience acquired through the senses, as opposed to being inborn, revealed by God, or derived from self-evident principles.

general will
According to Rousseau, the collective wishes or desires of a society, which must be obeyed as part of the social contract.

CHRONOLOGY

1543	Copernicus argues that the planets orbit the sun
1607	Monteverdi's opera *Orfeo*
1609	Galileo observes the night sky through a telescope
1637	Descartes' *Discourse on Method*
1662	Founding of England's Royal Society for the advancement of science
1687	Newton's *Mathematical Principles of Natural Philosophy*
1690	Locke's *Essay Concerning Human Understanding*
1732–1734	Pope's *Essay on Man*
1740	Frederick II becomes king of Prussia
1741	Handel's *Messiah*
1748	Montesquieu's argument for the separation of powers
1751	First volume of Diderot's *Encyclopedia*
1759	Voltaire's *Candide*
1762	Catherine II becomes empress of Russia
1763	Rousseau's *Social Contract*
1773	Fragonard's *Progress of Love*
1780	Joseph II of Austria embarks on reforms
1792	Virginia State Capitol is constructed
1794	Condorcet's vision of human progress

LO¹ Trace the beginnings of the Scientific Revolution.

The Scientific Revolution started in the field of astronomy, where the prevailing Ptolemaic or geocentric (earth-centered) theory of the universe was challenged by new observations and ideas. Using a telescope for the first time to study the night sky, Galileo gathered evidence to build on the heliocentric (sun-centered) ideas of Copernicus. His support for the Copernican view of planetary movement earned him a lifelong house arrest for suspected heresy, but he continued to dismantle other traditional beliefs about the natural world through imaginative experiments that set a new standard for scientific inquiry. Francis Bacon made the case for induction from careful observation and repeated experiments as the way to expand scientific knowledge. René Descartes argued instead for deduction as a method of arriving at the truth, but rather than starting with traditionally accepted truths, he began by doubting all existing ideas. In physiology, William Harvey made the revolutionary discovery that the same blood circulates throughout the body again and again, rather than being continuously produced and consumed. Using the new methods of observation, experiment, and mathematics, Isaac Newton was able to show the reality of a universe that Ptolemy had deemed absurd. The growth of scientific knowledge began to speed up as distrust of traditional consensus spread; new societies for the advancement of science were established; and the methods of observation, experiment, and mathematics proved fruitful for understanding the universe.

LO² Describe the Enlightenment worldview.

The revolution within science gave educated Westerners a radically new understanding of the workings of the universe, and on this basis, they constructed a new worldview. For many of the philosophes who embraced Enlightenment thinking, God was still viewed as the creator and designer of the universe, but he was no longer thought to be in constant control of its workings. For some, the idea of a universe operating without the hand of God led to agnosticism or atheism. Within this new worldview, the place and powers of humans were dramatically enlarged, and it was believed that through reason, knowledge, and the right social institutions, humans could progress to the point where happiness and virtue would be universal.

LO³ classicism
A cultural fashion in literature of the seventeenth and eighteenth centuries, guided by the attempt to find perfect forms of expression based on ancient models and universal laws.

satire
A type of literature that uses irony, exaggeration, and wit to expose and ridicule human folly.

Rococo
A delicate, ornate, and fanciful style of architecture and painting of the eighteenth century.

neoclassicism
In the visual arts, a style that strictly follows the most admired models of ancient (classical) art, seeking to reproduce their orderliness, proportion, and restraint.

LO⁴ monophonic music
Music made up of a single tune.

homophonic music
Music made of a tune accompanied by harmonizing chords.

polyphonic music
Music made up of two or more independent and overlapping tunes.

opera
A dramatic work combining text (libretto) and musical score, with grand characters, spectacular stage action, and striking musical effects.

oratorio
A religious story set to music with narrators and characters but no stage action.

cantata
A choral composition with musical accompaniment.

chamber music
Music originally intended for performance by small groups at aristocratic courts.

string quartet
A composition for four stringed instruments.

concerto
A composition for an orchestra and one or more solo instruments.

symphony
A lengthy and complex composition for an orchestra.

LO⁵ enlightened despotism
A form of absolute monarchy characterized by reforms intended to better the lives of citizens and strengthen the state.

multinational state
A state in which no single ethnic group forms a majority of the population.

LO³ Appreciate the Enlightenment spirit in literature and art.

In literature, the leading cultural trend was classicism, in which writers aimed to express ideas and emotions in highly structured language. Writers such as Racine, La Fayette, and Pope dealt with moral themes and the place of humanity in the new conception of the universe. The satirist Voltaire expressed disgust with ignorance and prejudice while championing tolerance and freedom of expression. The Rococo style in architecture and painting offered a dazzling stage for court culture, while neoclassicism, the visual equivalent of classicism in literature, proclaimed ideals of ancient Greece and Rome for political as well as aesthetic purposes.

LO⁴ Follow the development of Western music up to the Baroque and classical periods.

Western music has developed over time in step with other features of Western civilization. The ancient Israelites and Greeks revered music's power to express and influence moods and feelings, Greek thinkers explored the relationship between music and number, and music was part of the medieval university curriculum. In ancient and medieval times, too, musical instruments and forms of musical expression became more complex, and the system of writing music down was perfected. By 1600, music possessed the eloquent language of harmony, a broad range of instruments including keyboard and bowed instruments, and an accurate method of notation. Baroque composers from Monteverdi to Handel used these developments to achieve unprecedentedly spectacular and dramatic effects, above all in the new musical form of opera. From 1750, classical composers, notably Haydn and Mozart, created symphonies and other musical forms in which changes of mood and expression were contained within well-proportioned musical structures that gave the feeling of a complete and satisfying whole.

LO⁵ Discuss how the reform efforts of central and eastern European rulers reflected both Enlightenment ideals and power politics.

Operating out of a desire to implement the Enlightenment ideal of human progress in knowledge, happiness, and virtue, and also aware that a reformed state would be more stable, prosperous, and successful in war, the rulers of Prussia, Austria, and Russia initiated changes in society and politics. Frederick II of Prussia described himself as "the state's first servant," promoting religious tolerance and improvements in agriculture while also abolishing torture. Maria Theresa of Austria reined in the nobles who exploited serfs, so that with their higher incomes the serfs could pay more in taxes. Her son Joseph II went even farther in embracing religious toleration, wider access to education, and greater freedom for serfs. In Russia, Elizabeth and then Catherine continued the Westernization program of Peter the Great and sponsored education and the arts on a magnificent scale. None of these despots embraced the Enlightenment ideal of a world without war, however, and all fought to expand their territories.